HISTORY THAT CHANGED THE WORLD

HISTORY THAT CHANGED THE WORLD

From Africa to Outer Space in 300,000 Years

J.C. Peters

Published by Odyssea Publishing
Layout by Merijn de Haen and Daria Lacy
Cover design by Teddi Black
Maps by Dr. Michael Athanson

ISBN: 978-90-825063-5-8

If you have a question about the book, want to read more
from the author, or stay informed about upcoming books by
the author, go to jellepeters.com. The site also features a
challenging history quiz, for those who dare.

For Julien

CONTENTS

TABLE OF MAPS

"What we do in life......echoes in eternity."
Maximus Decimus Meridius, *Gladiator*

INTRODUCTION

The world of today continues to be shaped by the past. Without understanding the pivotal events, movements and revolutions that led us here, it is impossible to understand why we are here or where we are going. Because everything is connected, nothing happens in isolation.

Without the French Revolution, for instance, there would have been no Napoleon, who in turn set the stage for German unification, which then seriously disturbed the balance of power in late 19th century Europe, making the outbreak of the First World War just a matter of time. After the German Empire was subsequently defeated, the Versailles Peace Conference basically created the conditions for the outbreak of World War II. As French Marshal Ferdinand Foch declared at the time: *"This is not peace. It is an Armistice for twenty years."*

And of course World War II brought us the bomb, spurred the decolonization of Africa and Asia, destabilized the Middle East and ignited the cold war, which in turn brought mankind to the brink of nuclear holocaust in October 1962.

It is all connected.

History That Changed The World zooms in on those civilizations, events, movements, inventions and people that have had a deep impact on the course of human history and whose effects continue to echo into our own time.

Because of this filter, many people, places, sometimes even whole civilizations go unmentioned or are reduced to a single footnote, simply because they haven't been able to light much of a torch for the rest of humanity, however great, cultured and sophisticated they may have been.

Of course, to cover everything is to cover nothing. Every history book has to make choices about its focal point, what to include, which viewpoints to support, where to paint with broad strokes and when to sketch a more detailed picture. In the end, no history can ever be complete — or truly objective for that matter.

But although *History That Changed The World* thus does not cover every civilization, every country and every tribe that has ever trod this earth, I promise it will help gain a better understanding of the world of today.

Enjoy the journey.

Part I

In the Beginning

1

THE ARRIVAL OF MODERN MAN

*"I believe I have found the missing link
between animal and civilized man. It is us."*

Konrad Lorenz

Ancestors. We have a lot of them. Hundreds, thousands, tens of thousands even, depending on how far back you want to go — and what your definition of ancestor is. My own grandfather was born in 1913, less than a year after the "unsinkable" ocean steamer Titanic hit an iceberg in the North Atlantic Ocean, sinking her on her maiden voyage, and about a year before the First World War, simply called The Great War at the time because no war like it had ever been fought before.

When my grandfather was five years old, the Spanish flu broke out, one of the deadliest pandemics since the Black Death ravaged Eurasia in the 14th century. Thankfully, he was spared; if he hadn't been, my father would have never existed. He was born 25 years later, in the middle of the Second World War, in German-occupied Holland.

Imagine going back in time for a moment, all the way to when the first modern humans arrived on the scene, some 300,000 years ago (Hublin, "New fossils") .[1] Imagine the many perilous moments these ancestors had to survive to live long enough to bring a new generation into the world, who in turn would have had to survive long enough to bring another new generation into the world and so on and so forth, for 300,000 years, all the way to you. Surviving hunger, long droughts, all kinds of diseases, tribal wars, local wildlife. Granted, humans were much tougher back then, but human life itself was much more fragile.

But we could go even further back, because modern man didn't just happen into existence. His direct ancestor is Homo erectus. This hominid species was not only the first to use fire and complex tools, but also the first hominin to leave Africa (Pringle "Quest for Fire"; Goodman, 240-241). Homo erectus evolved some 1.9 million years ago out of *his* predecessor, Homo habilis, the first member of the genus *Homo*, who evolved around 2.3 million years ago. Homo habilis used tools as well, but simpler ones.

All of this took place during prehistory, the vast expanse of time before the invention of writing enabled humans to create written records of events. Since we only developed writing about 5,000 years ago, the other 2,295,000 years since Homo habilis evolved are considered *pre*historic.

So how do we know all this then? 2.3 million years is a long time ago after all, and if these ancestors didn't write, then how do we know anything about them at all? How do we even know they lived that long ago? The answer lies in our bones. Or more precisely, in theirs.

By digging in the ground, we found bones of early Homo sapiens sapiens, Homo erectus, Homo habilis and even the more apelike ancestors before them.[2] It is said we come from dust and to dust we will return, but in reality it can be very difficult to completely return to dust.[3] Bones do not easily decompose and sometimes fossilize. Through a scientific method called radiometric dating — which measures the decay of radioactive isotopes — the age of rocks and fossilized remains can be measured. This is how we know dinosaurs went extinct around 65 million years ago, long before Homo habilis ever picked up a stick to crack a couple of walnuts.

Because Homo habilis used stone tools, his arrival also marks the beginning of the Stone Age. Other things we know about this ancestor of Homo sapiens is that he walked upright, had a brain that was only slightly larger than that of a chimpanzee, didn't talk, didn't know how to make a fire and made a living as a nomadic scavenger-gatherer, meaning he was always on the move, scrounging for food.

After Homo erectus evolved 1.9 million years ago, it 'only' took him another 1.5 million years or so to figure out how to control fire.[4] Ok, so that wasn't exactly lightning fast, but it was still a monumental achievement. In fact, the mastering of fire is arguably one of the most important inventions in the history of mankind. And while we have our heroic ancestor Homo erectus to thank for it, H. erectus himself had his brain to thank for it, which was about fifty percent larger than that of Homo habilis.

With fire came warmth, protection (against other animals) and the ability to cook meat instead of having to eat it raw.[5] Not a bad price for the occasional burned finger. Because of the development of cooking, Homo erectus also began to eat more meat, which is believed to have led to increased brain growth (Wrangham, "Catching Fire"; Aiello, "Expensive Tissue Hypothesis").

So, by the time Homo sapiens sapiens arrived some 300,000 years ago, hominins had already learned how to control fire and use complex tools such as spears and hand axes. In the 250,000 years that followed, modern man would add to that by developing ever more sophisticated skills, such as language, music and art. During this period, humans (because that is what they were, humans just like us) were still hunter-gatherers, living in caves, but their bigger brains gave them a far greater capacity to think and imagine than earlier species of hominin.

This was a huge step forward. Imagination allows us to create things in our minds —things that do not exist yet in the physical world — and to believe in what may be. It lies at the heart of all hope, ambition and curiosity, those great drivers of human ingenuity.

Without imagination there can be no invention, no art, no religion, no language. Without imagination we would simply do the same things over and over again. Lack of imagination is why so little invention and innovation took place during the time of Homo habilis and Homo erectus, why it took H. erectus 1.5 million years to master fire but modern humans only 300,000 years to develop enough nuclear bombs to destroy the entire planet fourteen times over.

Around 70,000 years ago, humans began to spread outside of Africa, to Europe, Asia and beyond.[6]

There they encountered other hominins, who had evolved from the Homo erectus that had left Africa some 1.5 million years earlier. Neanderthal man was one of them. We don't exactly know what happened next between these sister species, except that there was no more Homo neanderthalensis around 30,000 years ago.[7]

---

1   The term 'modern humans', commonly used to distinguish from earlier hominin

species, refers to a subspecies of Homo sapiens, Homo sapiens sapiens, which emerged some 300,000 years ago (Hublin, "New fossils").

2   The evolutionary paths of humans and apes diverged around four to eight million years ago.

3   *"In the sweat of thy face shalt thou eat bread, till thou return unto the ground; for out of it wast thou taken: for dust thou art, and unto dust shalt thou return."* (The Bible: Authorized King James Version, Gen. 3.19)

4   When early humans exactly discovered the controlled use of fire is part of ongoing academic debate. Some scholars believe the earliest examples date back as far as 1.6 million years, but the evidence for these cases is circumstantial. The earliest evidence for controlled uses of fire for which there is wide scholarly support dates back about 400.000 years.

5   In *How Cooking Made Us Human* (2009), Richard Wrangham, professor of biological anthropology at Harvard, argues that Homo erectus was the first to cook his food.

6   Genetic evidence suggests that the 'Out of Africa' migration of modern humans occurred around 60,000-70,000 years ago, with the exception of the Levant and possibly the Persian Gulf, where tools found at the site of Jebel Faya, in the United Arab Emirates, in 2011, suggest the presence of modern humans some 100,000-125,000 years ago (Armitage, "The Southern Route").

7   Recent study of the human and Neanderthal genome suggests the two species interbred (Green, "Neandertal Genome"; Verno!,"Neandertal Lineages"), meaning we all have a little Neanderthal in us, but it also seems likely Neanderthals were largely replaced through competition. The same fate held for several other sister species.

2

FROM HUNTING AND GATHERING TO FARMING

A society grows great when old men plant trees
whose shade they know they shall never sit in.

Greek Proverb

Around 12,000 years ago humans made another great discovery. Perhaps not as spectacular as the mastering of fire, but one that would nevertheless have far-reaching, fundamental consequences for our way of life.

Since the dawn of Homo erectus some 1.9 million years ago, our ancestors had been living as hunter-gatherers. Because while his predecessor, Homo habilis, is believed to have been more of a scavenger-gatherer, gladly munching on game killed by other animals, Homo erectus did his own killing as a real hunter.[1]

Homo erectus hunted, but he also collected foods such as eggs, nuts and fruits (hence *hunter- gatherer*). He lived in small band societies of between 10 and 50 members, maybe a little bigger when times were good. Together, they migrated over great distances, never calling any place home for long, like backpackers avant la lettre. And for 1.9 million years, their way of life remained the same.

Why?

Because it worked. So well, in fact, that when anatomically modern humans arrived on the scene about 300,000 years ago, they too lived as hunter-gatherers for the first 290,000 years. But 12,000 years ago something started to change, because instead of moving from place to place, hunting and gathering as they had always done, humans began to cultivate crops, work the land and domesticate animals such as dogs, cows, donkeys, llamas and horses.

The Agricultural Revolution (a.k.a Neolithic Revolution) would change our way of life more than anything else had since the invention of the controlled use of fire 400,000 years ago. It wasn't so much the farming itself that was so earth shattering, but everything that came in its wake. Because farming requires modifying one's environment, planting seeds, digging irrigation channels, building fences to keep animals, and — perhaps most important of all — staying in one place. This sedentism would in time lead to the founding of the first cities, after humans and earlier members of the genus *Homo* had roamed the earth as nomadic hunter/scavenger-gatherers for over two million years.

We don't exactly know why humans took to farming after having lived successfully as hunter- gatherers for so long. Some say the reason was the changing climate, which made it much easier to cultivate crops in certain regions, like the Levant. Others suggest that people became increasingly sedentary first, which in turn lead to the growing of crops and the keeping of animals, to ensure a stable food supply. Another explanation is that the development was more or less accidental, like so many of our greatest discoveries have been.[2]

The Agricultural Revolution took place independently in different regions of the world, the so- called 'hearths of domestication', most notably the Fertile Crescent — which extends roughly from Egypt through Israel, Jordan, Lebanon, Syria, the southeastern border region of Turkey, Iraq, Kuwait and western Iran — the Yangtze and Yellow River basins in China and Mesoamerica, a region that includes present-day Mexico, Guatemala, Belize, Honduras, El Salvador, Nicaragua and northern Costa Rica (Barker, 2).[3]

It is no coincidence that the first cities and civilizations were founded about 11,000 years ago. By cultivating crops and keeping animals, a structural surplus of food was created for the first time in history, allowing humans to evolve from living in small, mobile groups to dwelling in much larger, sedentary societies. And while some people concentrated on farming, others concentrated on the construction of homes, manufacturing, or commerce. Because of this labor diversification, societies grew more complex, which in turn called for more regulation and administration.

Life in a permanent settlement of five hundred people is very different from living in a group of fifty people moving from cave to cave. In a hunter-gatherer society of fifty there won't be a lot of stealing, or a lot of possessions for that matter; owning things can be quite a burden if you have to pack them up every time and carry them from place to place. The rules in such a small society would likely be simple and straightforward. There is no room for laziness or complex labor diversification. Painting animals on cave walls is a nice way to pass the time, but there wouldn't be any full-time positions available for cave painting artists.

How different this is in a sedentary society! In such a society possessions *do* make a lot of sense, because one's fortunes are tied to one place. And because many people are no longer needed in food production, those not involved in farming can take on different kinds of jobs, as administrators, craftsmen, merchants, or soldiers.

A different kind of society, a different way of life thus began to take shape in a relatively short time, especially when considering how long humans had been living in band societies. A way of life that offered more food security, more protection and more comfort, but was also more individualistic, more stratified, less equal.

Some kept tilling the ground and eating their bread "in the sweat of thy face" (Gen. 3.19) as they had always done, but others grew rich and powerful through political influence, entrepreneurship, marriage, or through the most common way of all: by way of inheritance. And of course then as now, the successful people wanted to show how wealthy they were. So they hired carpenters to build not just a home, but a palace. They commissioned art from sculptors and painters, instructed tailors to use the finest materials for their clothing and threw lavish parties with more food than anyone could ever eat, embellished with music and other entertainment from full-time artists who literally had no life of their own (a.k.a slaves).

Yes, we were really on our way to civilization now.

---

1   Though most anthropologists and archaeologists now seem to agree that Homo erectus did not rely exclusively on (confrontational) scavenging for his meat

but at the very least also engaged in small game hunting, the hunting- versus-scavenging debate is certainly not over. For an interesting overview of this debate, see Manuel Domínguez- Rodrigo's *Stone Tools and Fossil Bones: Debates in the Archaeology of Human Origins* (117ff.).

2   Graeme Barker discusses the debate about the origins of the Agricultural Revolution at length in chapter 10 of "The Agricultural Revolution". In table 10.1, he also lists a number of causes that have been proposed over the years, ranging from common sense causes like climate change and sedentism to more....exotic ones, like aliens, big men and xenophobia (Barker, 383).

3   The term 'Fertile Crescent' was coined by the Egyptologist James Henry Breasted, who wrote about it in his 1916 book *Ancient Times: A History of he Early World*.

3

FROM STONE TO BRONZE

"The stone age didnt end because
they ran out of stones."

Unknown origin

In 2010, an international team of scientists found fossilized animal bones with stone-tool-inflicted marks on them at Dikika, Ethiopia (McPherron, "Evidence for stone-tool-assisted consumption"). The marks are thought to have been made by an ancestor of Homo habilis, possibly Australopithecus afarensis, a species that also includes the famous 3.2 million year old skeleton remains of 'Lucy' (discovered in Ethiopia in 1974).

The fossils were dated to about 3.4 million years ago and are the oldest evidence of stone tool use so far — 800,000 years earlier than the previous oldest evidence. Since no stone tools were found with the bones, it is not clear if A. afarensis found the tools or made them himself.[1]

The Stone Age is traditionally divided into three main periods, the Paleolithic, the Mesolithic and the Neolithic. Of these, the Paleolithic (or Old Stone Age, derived from the Greek words *palaios*, 'old', and *lithos*, 'stone') covers by far the largest period, starting 2.6 million years ago and running all the way to at least 20,000 years ago, depending on the region.[2]

One widely used stone tool type from the Paleolithic, the Oldowan tool type, a.k.a Mode 1 tool, is also the earliest known stone tool, going back 2.6 million years. Oldowan tools are named after the Olduvai Gorge site in Tanzania, where a great many of these early stone tools were found. The site was occupied by Homo habilis approximately 1.9 million years ago, by Homo erectus 1.2 million years ago and by Homo sapiens some 17,000 years ago.

At first glance, a Mode 1 stone tool doesn't look all that impressive, just a rock with some sharp edges. Sure, it might come in handy for cutting, scraping, chopping or bashing someone's head in, but aren't these kind of rocks just lying around everywhere anyway? As it turns out, they are not. So what Homo habilis did was in fact quite remarkable. He took a useless piece of rock, used another piece of rock to knock off pieces of it and voilà, he had created a sharp-edged rock.

When Homo erectus first arrived on the scene some 700,000 years later, he inherited the Mode 1 tool from Homo habilis. After having used the tool himself a couple of hundred thousand years, he was able to significantly improve upon it, inventing the Mode 2 stone tool about 1.7 million years ago. The Mode 2 is an oval biface hand axe. It fits neatly in a hand and the sharp edge — which is much larger than the one on a Mode 1 — makes cutting flesh very easy. Way to go Homo erectus! The Neanderthals, who lived in Europe and the Near East between 300,000 and 30,000 years ago, further perfected the Mode 2 into a smaller, more knife-like tool (Mode 3).[3] And about 45,000 years ago, the first anatomically modern humans living in Europe developed Mode 4 tools, characterized by long blades, rather than flakes. They also used bone and antler for tools and art.[4] Still later — around the time the Neanderthals became extinct — modern humans invented Mode 5 tools, small, sharp flints, a.k.a Microliths, which they used as tips for hunting weapons, such as spears and (later) arrows.

The Neolithic (New Stone Age) was characterized by the Agricultural Revolution. For the first time in 2.6 million years, the main new stone tool was not a weapon of any kind but something much more useful in a sedentary society: pottery.

The end of the Stone Age is also indubitably connected to humans becoming more grounded to one place. The earliest evidence of copper smelting, a process whereby metal is extracted from its ore by melting it, goes back some 7,000 years, to a place in Serbia, in southeastern Europe.[5] The discovery of the site, in 2010, has challenged the longstanding view that copper smelting spread to Europe from the Fertile Crescent (Radivojevic, "Tainted ores").[6]

It is tempting to speculate as to how copper smelting was invented.

Being a relatively soft metal, copper can easily be cold hammered into shape and small copper artifacts worked this way have been found in various places. Prolonged cold-working can make the metal brittle and eventually cause it to fracture, though. This can be counteracted by heating and then slowly cooling it — a process called annealing — but this too has its limits, as pure copper remains too soft to create large, durable, objects. This is also the reason why the Copper Age (a.k.a Chalcolithic) lasted only briefly. After all, nobody wants a dagger that bends. But by working with copper people must also have realized its potential.

Melting copper — as opposed to heating it a bit — is a whole different ball game though, as its melting point lies at almost 1100 °C (1984 °F). Melting tin and lead had already been discovered, but their melting points lie far below the one for copper and they can be melted in a simple wooden fire, something that could have been easily discovered by accident. But an open fire does not burn hot enough for copper to reach its melting point. It therefore seems likely that the first copper melting was deliberate rather than accidental, taking place in some kind of furnace, with the goal to separate the metal from its ore (smelting).

Whatever the case, copper smelting was discovered and not long after people started mixing it with other elements, in an effort to harden the metal. Tin was an obvious candidate, because it was already known. The resulting alloy, significantly harder than copper, was bronze.[7]

Following the discovery of tin bronze artifacts in Serbia by Miljana Radivojevic et al., the Early Bronze Age can now be said to have begun c. 4650 BCE at the latest, in southeastern Europe (Radivojevic, "Tainted ores").[8] To date, the earliest finds of bronze tools and weapons come from the ancient Near East — roughly spanning the Fertile Crescent, Anatolia and the Caucasus — ancient Greece and the Indus valley, which extends from northeast Afghanistan to Pakistan and northwest India.

It was also in these regions that some of the first great civilizations were born, like the Sumerian, Egyptian, Minoan and Indus Valley Civilization. 5,000 years ago, these civilizations represented the pinnacle of human development. They were among the first to move from hunting-gathering to farming, they founded the first cities and besides bronze also invented things like the wheel, writing, astronomy and mathematics.

It would take more than 3,000 years before the Bronze Age started to give way to the Iron Age.[9]

One of the main reasons for it taking so long was that in its natural form iron is not much harder than bronze, while its melting point of 1538 °C (2800 °F) lies considerably higher than that of copper. In other words, there really wasn't much incentive to switch from bronze to iron. Of course that all changed when it was discovered that combining iron with carbon gives steel, an alloy that *is* considerable harder than bronze. After that, the Golden Age of bronze was over.

---

1   The find at Dikika is also the earliest evidence for meat and marrow consumption in the human lineage.

2   The periodization of the Mesolithic is region-dependent. In the Levant, the Mesolithic ran from about 20,000 BCE to 10,000 BCE, but in Europe it started around 10,000 BCE, lasting until 5,000 BCE. In other parts of the world the Mesolithic began and ended later still, but a few hundred years BCE most regions had switched from hunting and gathering to farming, marking the beginning of the Neolithic.

3   Making good Mode 3 tools requires quite some skill and ingenuity. They were made using the Levallois technique, which involved chipping off flakes from a central core, to create a so-called tortoise core. The worked core was then struck from the side, to (hopefully) chip off a large flake, with sharp edges all around from the earlier trimming.

4   The oldest figurative art works, the Venus of Hohle Fels and the Löwenmensch figurine — both discovered in South Germany — are made from mammoth ivory and go back about 40,000 years.

5   The site was discovered by the archaeological team headed by Miljana Radivojevic and described in a 2010 article in the *Journal of Archaeological Science* ("On the origins of extractive metallurgy").

6   In the Americas copper smelting was also independently invented, though apparently not before at least 200 CE.

7   Bronze can also be produced by alloying copper with other elements, such as arsenic, aluminimum, silicon and phosphorus, but the most common alloying agent is tin.

8   It is possible, even likely, that evidence of at least similarly aged copper

smelting will be unearthed in the ancient Near East in the years to come, as the region is home to some of the world's oldest civilizations (and bronze objects). Radivojevic's discovery has, however, definitively extended the periodization of the Bronze Age by about 1500 years.

9   The Iron Age began around 1300 BCE in the ancient Near East and parts of Europe and India.

4

THE FIRST CITIES

*"This city is what it is, because our
citizens are what they are"*

Plato

In 2009, more than half of the world's population lived in urban
areas for the first time in history ("World Urbanization Prospects").
In our time, big cities are crowded epicenters of life in the fast lane,
full of lights, colors, sounds, stores, bars, billboards, sandwich shops,
restaurants and small eateries lining streets buzzing with cars, buses,
scooters, bicycles and armies of pedestrians. But what was life like in
the first cities? And when and where were they founded?

Ironically, the first cities were established as a result of the
Agricultural Revolution, because working the land, cultivating crops
and domesticating animals required a more sedentary lifestyle. Of
course it didn't happen overnight. People only gradually lengthened
their stay in the place where they had started farming, until the yield
was sufficient enough to provide food year-round. Settlements started
to form. Not every permanent settlement can be called a city, though.
Exactly how large a settlement had to be for it to be deserving the
moniker 'city' is still subject to debate, but most scholars agree that it
had to have been home to at least a couple of hundred people. To get
more clarity on what constituted a city in ancient times, the Australian
archaeologist V. Gordon Childe formulated ten general metrics that
define a historic city, among them the payment of taxes to a deity or
king, trade and import of raw materials, the existence of monumental
public buildings and differentiation of the population, meaning that not
all residents grow their own food (Childe, "The Urban Revolution").

In other words, a city is more than just a place where a lot of people
are living together. For a settlement to be rightly called a city, it had

to have an organized government, professional administrators, certain regulations, a system of record keeping and enough of a surplus of raw materials to support trade, craftsmen, tax collectors. A way of life that was certainly a lot more complex than going from cave to cave, throwing spears at rabbits, gathering nuts and fruits and try to get a fire going. No wonder Childe called it 'the urban revolution' (Childe, "The Urban Revolution").

Was there also a First City? A city that was founded before all others, standing tall, proud and singular as man's first attempt to create a lasting haven to live, work and worship? There are a couple of candidates.

Same as when buying a home, the three most important things to consider when founding a city are location, location, location. There weren't that many places on earth, though, where the climatic and environmental conditions were optimal for an easy transition from hunting and gathering to farming. With the aid of modern technology humans can survive and thrive just about anywhere on the planet — perhaps one day even on other planets. But in ancient times, without any technology and having just barely mastered the first rudimentary principles of agriculture, only those places that were ideally suited for permanent habitation had a chance of becoming the birthplace of the first city.

10,000 to 12,000 years ago, these places were located in regions like the Caucasus, the Balkans, the Indus Valley and the Fertile Crescent. It is within or close to the latter that we find our most promising candidates for the title of first city, namely Eridu, Çatalhöyük and Jericho. Let's take a closer look at each of them.

Eridu was an ancient Sumerian city founded c. 5000 BCE in southern Mesopotamia, present-day Iraq. According to an ancient stone tablet called the *Sumerian King List* — listing the kings of Sumer — it was the first city in the world (Leick, 3). Of course the Sumerians might have been a bit biased when naming one of their own cities as the first city in the world, but the Sumerian Civilization is certainly one of the world's oldest.

Located close to the Persian Gulf, near the mouth of the Euphrates River, Eridu was a port city and its citizens lived off fishing, sheep and goat herding and the cultivating of crops through irrigation agriculture.

According to the Sumerians, the city belonged to the god Enki, who was not only the keeper of the gifts of civilization but also the god of water, intelligence and creation. Enki was believed to live in the Abzu (*ab* meaning 'water' and *zu* 'deep'), the ocean underneath the earth which the Sumerians believed lakes, rivers, wells, etc, drew their water from. Enki had his own temple in Eridu, called E- abzu, meaning 'house of the abzu'.

Temples were very important in Eridu, indeed throughout Mesopotamia, because they were built not just by the Sumerians but also by the Babylonians, Akkadians, Elamites and Assyrians. Called ziggurats, they were shaped in a particular, rectangular form, like a terraced step pyramid. The oldest religious structure of Eridu, a primitive chapel no larger than three square meters (32 sq. ft), is estimated to have been constructed c. 4900 BCE (Leick, 5-6).

Eridu was a great city, but over time the center of power in Mesopotamia moved from South to North, spelling slow but certain decline for Eridu. The city was finally abandoned and left to fall into ruin in the 6th century BCE. A sad end for a once great city.

On to the next candidate. In 1958 an ancient city called Çatalhöyük was discovered in southern Anatolia, present-day Turkey.[1] It was subsequently excavated between 1961-65 and again from 1993.[2] Excavation is still going on as of 2017 and you can even visit the site if you want to see for yourself how the Çatalhöyükians lived c. 9,500 years ago.

Because the city is so well preserved we know a good deal about how its inhabitants lived, which in many ways was very different from how we do. For instance, there were no streets in Çatalhöyük. Houses were built side by side in a honeycomb-like maze. So how did people get into their houses? Through a hole in the roof. The hole doubled as ventilation — which explains why the oven was next to the ladder people used to get in and out of their homes — while the rooftops doubled as streets and squares. Imagine lying in your bed at night, listening to the villagers walking home over your ceiling.

Don't think of the combined rooftops as the kind of smooth surface that could be used for a soccer match, though. Aside from all the holes, some homes also stood higher than others. Not because they were more important — there is no evidence of any class differences in Çatalhöyük — but because over time new homes would be built on top of the rubble of old ones (Hodder, 15). All in all, excavators have uncovered eighteen levels of settlement.

But rubble was not the only foundation for the new homes; the people of Çatalhöyük also had the habit of burying their dead under their houses, in pits beneath the floors, hearths, even under their beds.[3] In some cases, the heads were removed from the skeleton and put elsewhere. Some of those heads have even been plastered and painted, to recreate faces.

No public buildings have been found in Çatalhöyük, nor any temples, at least not yet (Hodder, 13). That doesn't mean the inhabitants of Çatalhöyük weren't religious — in fact, discovered murals and figurines suggest they most certainly were — but perhaps they didn't believe their gods needed earthly places where people could go and worship together (Hodder, 2-3).

At the height of its existence, up to 10,000 people may have lived in the honeycomb-maze of Çatalhöyük, but around 5700 BCE the city was abandoned.[4] We don't know why exactly. It has been suggested that the growing attraction of Mesopotamia caused people to move away from southern Anatolia. A change of climate might also have contributed to the decline of this remarkable city. Whatever the reason, though, after almost two millennia of continuous habitation, it was over and done for Çatalhöyük.

The last candidate for First City of the World is also the only one of the three that is still inhabited today. In fact, Tell es-Sultan, the ancient city of Jericho, located in the West Bank, Palestinian Territories, has been almost continuously inhabited since 9600 BCE.

It was founded around a perennial spring by the Natufians, an ancient culture that was sedentary (or at least semi-sedentary) even before the introduction of agriculture.[5] One possible reason for this was that the area where they lived, the Levant, offered abundant resources due to a favorable climate.[6] Today the Levant is dry and barren, but 11,000 years ago the soil was fertile and rains were frequent.[7] Life must have been good there, with a pleasant climate and lots of hunting and gathering of eggs, fruits, nuts and wild cereals.

The first dwellings of Jericho were circular ones, measuring about five meters (16 ft) across, built of clay and straw bricks that were dried in the sun and then plastered together with mud mortar (Mithen, 58). There was something else, though, that made this early town very special: a wall. A massive stone wall, standing more than three meters high and almost two meters wide. Inside the wall, a tower was erected with an internal staircase, counting 22 stone steps (Akkermans, 57).

That first wall — there would be several over the next millennia — was built around 8000 BCE (Kenyon, "Excavations at Jericho", 6), making Jericho the first walled town in the world, which seems only natural, considering Jericho's long history of violence, occupation, conflict, destruction and reconstruction,

Because over the next 10,000 years, Jericho would subsequently (but not exclusively) be occupied by the Egyptians, the Israelites, the Babylonians, the Persians, the Israelites again, Alexander the Great, the Maccabees, the Romans, the Arabs, the Ottomans, the British, the Jordanians, Israel again and, from 1994, the Palestinian Authority. A rich history indeed.

Excavators have unearthed the remains of more than twenty successive settlements at Jericho, so whatever else, people apparently really liked living in Jericho. It has never grown into a really big city, though. Today it is home to some 20,000 inhabitants.

One of Jericho's most famous periods lies in the Middle Bronze Age, when the city was conquered for the first time by the Israelites, who were returning from bondage in Egypt. According to the narrative in the Bible, the mighty walls of Jericho fell after the Israelites had marched around the city once a day for six straight days, while blowing on their horns, and seven times on the seventh day (Joshua 6: 3-20). There is evidence that the walls of Jericho were indeed destroyed, but whether this feat was achieved by marching and blowing on horns cannot be verified.[8]

In the 8th century BCE it was the Assyrians who conquered the city, followed by the Babylonians (apparently without any horn blowing). After Persian King Cyrus the Great conquered Babylon in 539 BCE, he allowed the Jewish exiles living in Babylon to return to the Land of Israel. In 332 BCE Alexander the Great bursted onto the scene and kicked the Persians out again, while the Maccabees — a Jewish rebel army — in turn wrested control of the city a couple of centuries later from the Seleucid Empire, a Hellenistic state founded by one of Alexander's generals after his death.

At one point Jericho even served as a romantic gift, when Roman general Mark Anthony gave it to his sweetheart Cleopatra, the last Pharaoh of ancient Egypt. In the second half of the first millennium CE, Jericho came under Arab rule, through the Umayyad and the Abbasid Caliphate, respectively, followed by the Seljuk Turks. Next came the Crusaders, who were convinced that the best way to serve God was by conquering the Holy Land and killing as many heathens as possible. After a while the Crusaders were expelled by legendary Muslim conquerer Saladin (Ṣalāḥ al-Dīn),

founder of the Ayyubid dynasty.[9] Then came the Mamluks, followed by the Ottomans for a couple of hundred years, followed by the British, who took over from the Ottoman empire after it had collapsed at the end of World War I. Thirty years later, just after World War II, it was the British empire that did the collapsing and the Kingdom of Jordan jumped in to occupy the ancient city. But in 1967, Jordan, Egypt and Syria were decisively defeated by tiny Israel during the Six-Day War, putting the 'Israelites' in charge of Jericho once again, until in 1994 Jericho became the first city Israel handed over to the Palestinian Authority, in accordance with the Oslo accords.

Jericho's history is indeed one of violence, occupation, conflict and destruction, but it is also one of reconstruction, hope and new beginnings. Being an optimist, I would like to believe that after

10,000 years of turmoil Jericho will perhaps soon be awarded some peace and quiet. Until then, it will have to make do with the award of being the very First City in the World.

---

1   The site was first discovered by British archaeologist James Mellaart.

2   The 1961-65 excavations were led by James Mellaart, who wrote a report for each year the excavations took place, the first of which was published in 1962 (Mellaart).

3   In 'Religion at Work', Ian Hodder, project director of the excavations at Çatalhöyük, notes that many of those buried in the foundation of several of

the buildings were newborns, which may suggest the inhabitants believed they gave vitality to the house (242, 342).

4   The East Mound of the city was first settled around 7500 BCE and finally abandoned sometime between 6200 and 5900 BCE. Radiocarbon dating of samples taken from a building on the West Mound indicated the building had been occupied between 6030 and 5700 BCE. Because the building stood on archaeological deposits roughly five meters (16 ft) deep, the West Mound was probably founded some two to three hundred years earlier (Balter, 334-335).

5   The spring, called Ain es-Sultan, still exists today.

6   The climate in the Levant was less favorable during the so-called Younger Dryas Cold Event, a climate event that occurred between ca. 12,900-11,600 years ago. The cold and drought this event caused in the Levant may have moved the Natufians to adopt agriculture as one of the first people in the world. When the Younger Dryas came to an end, climatic conditions approved once more, helping Jericho evolve into a more permanent settlement.

7   The ancient Levant includes present-day Syria, Lebanon, the Palestinian territories, Israel, Jordan and the island of Cyprus.

8   British archeologist Kathleen Kenyon, who excavated at Jericho between 1952-58, contended that Jericho was destroyed c. 1580 BCE and that it was deserted around 1400 BCE, the biblical date for Joshua's conquest ("Digging Up Jericho", 229). This has since been accepted by most scholars, although creationist archaeologists — notably the biblical archaeologist Bryant G. Wood — have attempted to refute Kenyon's evidence.

9   Saladin captured Jerusalem from the Crusaders in 1187, ending the first Kingdom of Jerusalem and the Crusader presence in Jericho.

5

THE BEGINNING OF HISTORY

"Set thine heart on being a scribe, that
thou mayest direct the whole earth"
From: *Do Not Be a Charioteer*, Papyrus
Anastasi III, c. 1200 BCE.[1]

History, we say, begins with the invention of writing, almost 5,500 years ago, in the Early Bronze Age. That is not to say nothing of significance happened before that, just that there is a big difference between circumstantial evidence — which is what unrecorded history really amounts to — and written record keeping.

But what, exactly, counts as writing?

In 2003, archaeologists unearthed 8,500 year old turtle shells with markings inscribed on them at an Early Neolithic mass-burial site at Jiahu, Henan Province, China (Li, "Earliest writing?"). Some archaeologists have since argued that the markings represent *"some form of sign use or early writing"* (Harbottle, qtd. in Pilcher, "Earliest handwriting found?") and that they show resemblance with the currently accepted earliest evidence of Chinese writing, dated more than 5,000 years later. Others disagree. They point to the fact that so far only isolated instances of these early markings have been found, whereas a real writing system is expected to be much more widely used. Also, there seems to be no *"meaningful order of repetition"* (Boltz, 35) between the markings, or evidence that they represent words used to form sentences (Qiu, 29-30, 39).

In other words, just scribbling a couple of pictograms on a turtle shell (or any other animal bone for that matter) doesn't make it writing. A writing system can consist entirely of pictograms — like the Egyptian hieroglyphs, for instance — but it has to represent a spoken language.

Such a system is likely not invented overnight but rather the result of centuries of development. Take the Sumerian cuneiform script, in use from approximately 3200 BCE to the 2nd century CE and believed to be the oldest script in the world, older even than the Egyptian hieroglyphic script. It evolved out of a system of physical tokens used to count agricultural and manufactured goods, which had been in use for millennia (Houston, 73).[2] Later these tokens were placed in hollow clay containers, which were then sealed and marked on the outside with impressions of their contents (Houston, 74).

At the ancient Sumerian city of Uruk (present-day Southeast Iraq), devices were also found with both numerical notations and a few graphic symbols, which cuneiform expert Robert K. Englund has called *"the missing link between numerical notations ... and the mixed notations of numerical signs and ideograms which mark the inception of proto-cuneiform"* (qtd. in Houston, 74). By 3200 BCE the system had evolved into one that used hundreds of signs (Houston, 75). These signs were first traced on pillow-shaped tablets of moist clay with a sharp reed stylus, but later a blunt stylus was instead impressed upon the clay to form the symbols, which was easier and faster; it also stimulated the development of more abstract symbols (Mieroop, 10).[3]

Interestingly, tracing the development of Sumerian cuneiform also helps to answer the question *why* writing was developed.

By the time of the 3rd millennium BCE, several civilizations had far outgrown the simple hunting and gathering mentality that had served modern humans so well in the first 190,000 years of their existence. Between 10,000 BCE and 3,000 BCE our ancestors went from living in nomadic groups of fifty people to living in empires that in some cases numbered hundreds of thousands of citizens — at least in some regions, like the ancient Near East.[4] They had developed agriculture, built cities and temples, introduced taxes and invented organized warfare, hacking away at enemies with bronze swords and daggers instead of stone axes.

In ancient times the vanquished were usually killed or sold into slavery, while the victors grew their empire with the spoils of war. It was good to be the king, yes, but also increasingly complex when managing an expanding empire. Imagine how difficult it must have been to convey orders to administrators in other cities, to levy taxes, to keep track of public building projects, food supplies, the royal treasury, all without written record keeping.

Such was the problem of the Mesopotamian kings and Egyptian pharaohs and why writing was likely developed; because it was necessary. And when the Sumerians figured out the solution before everybody else did, other civilizations in the neighborhood — the Assyrians, the Babylonians, the Elamites, the Hittites, the Egyptians — were quick to adopt it (whether they wrote the Sumerians a thank-you note is unknown).

The cuneiform script remained in use for more than 3,000 years before it was gradually replaced by the Phoenician alphabet. By the 2nd century CE it had become entirely extinct, together with the knowledge of how to read the script. It would take until 1857 before it was deciphered again.[5]

Other writing systems suffered the same fate as the cuneiform script as a result of the development of the Phoenician alphabet, the ancestor of most writing systems in use today, including the Latin, Arabic, Cyrillic, Coptic and Brahmi alphabet.[6] How did the Phoenicians pull that off?

For one, it was much simpler than other writing systems. Whereas cuneiform and the Egyptian hieroglyphic script were chiefly logophonetic, containing hundreds of complex characters, the Phoenician alphabet was the first fully phonemic script, with one sound representing one symbol. Because it was so simple, it could be fairly easily adapted to other languages.

Another reason for the widespread adaptation of the Phoenician alphabet was the nature and geographic location of the Phoenician Civilization. Hailing from the coastal part of the Levant (present-day Lebanon, Israel, Syria) the Phoenicians were an enterprising, seafaring people, whose culture spread across the Mediterranean between c.1200-300 BCE. From Anatolia to Crete, from Cyprus to Carthage, from Tingis (present-day Tangier) to Sardinia and beyond, if you were living on the Mediterranean and needed something the Phoenicians were the go to guys. If they couldn't get it, it didn't exist.

It made sense for the Phoenicians to develop an easy to use writing system. As entrepreneurial mariners they would have had a great need for record keeping but not a lot of time to do so, as opposed to the well educated scribes working for the royal and religious elite of Egypt and Mesopotamia.

In other words it needed to be quick and easy, which is also what made it so attractive to other cultures. To the Greeks, for instance, who adopted it to form the Greek alphabet, around the middle of the eighth century BCE (Daniels, 271).[7] And because the Greek alphabet is the father of the Latin, Cyrillic and Coptic alphabet, the Phoenician alphabet is sort of their grandfather. And let's not forget the Aramaic alphabet, which was also adapted from the Phoenician alphabet and served as the *lingua franca* in both the Neo-Assyrian and Achaemenid Empire and on which almost all present-day writing systems in the Middle East are based (Hebrew being a notable exception). With the widespread adaptation of the Phoenician alphabet, reading and writing also became more mainstream, whereas up to then it had remained mostly confined to a very small elite (Fisher, 68-69). This in turn would have a profound effect on the development and social structures of many of the civilizations using the new writing system.

It is tempting to compare the differences between the ancient Phoenician alphabet and Sumerian cuneiform with those between modern English and Chinese. The Chinese script is one of the oldest continuously used writing systems in the world, dating back to at least 1200 BCE. It is also one of the most difficult writing systems to master, however, requiring knowledge of thousands of characters for even moderate comprehension, while English, which uses the Latin script, is relatively easy to learn.

It must have been unimaginable for the Sumerians to think that their beautiful writing system would one day go extinct, after having been used for over 3,000 years. But it did.

---

1   Papyrus Anastasi, iii. 6. 2ff (qtd. in Erman, 195). With special thanks to Tom Standage for setting me on the path to this quote by citing it in his article 'Writing is the Greatest Invention' (2012).

2   Until the 1970s, most scholars believed that the invention of writing was not so much the result of a slowly progressing evolution but rather of a sudden revolution. The influential Dutch archaeologist Henri Frankfort, for example,

wrote in his 1951 work *The Birth of Civilization in the Near East*, that "*The script appears from the first as a system of conventional signs - partly arbitrary tokens, partly pictograms - such as might well have been introduced all at once.*" (qtd. in Bahrani, xiii). Today, it is widely accepted that the invention of writing was an evolutionary process, although some scholars still endeavor to "*restore the revolutionary character of that moment*" (Bahrani, xiv). Among them is the French cuneiform specialist Jean-Jacques Glassner, whose position is aptly described by the translators of his work *The Invention of Cuneiform: Writing in Sumer* (Bahrani, xi-xvii).

3   The wedge-shaped signs left by the blunt stylus also gave cuneiform its name, which is a combination of the Latin words for 'wedge', *cuneus*, and 'shape', *forma*.

4   Following the method of multiplying the total area settled by a constant figure of persons per hectare — which for Mesopotamia is estimated at 100 to 200 people — Susan Pollock arrives at a maximum of 200,000 people during the Early Dynastic III period, 2600-2300 BCE (Pollock, 64-65)

5   By Dr. Edward Hincks, Sir Henry Rawlinson and Henry Fox Talbot.

6   Some — mostly Indian — scholars have theorized that the Brahmi script might have been developed autonomously or is descended from the (indigenous) Indus script, though this script is as of yet still undeciphered and its status as a true writing system remains subject to debate.

7   For a clear comparison of the Phoenician consonantal signs and the letters of the Greek alphabet, see Daniels, 262.

Part II

Antiquity

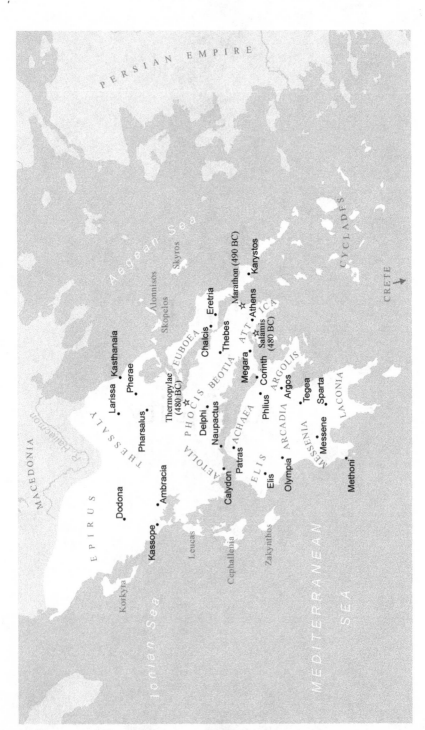

Map 1: Ancient Greece

6

ANCIENT GREECE

*"If the sharp-sightedness of the Greeks had kept
pace with their intelligence, then maybe even the
Industrial Revolution had begun one thousand
years before Columbus. And so, in our era, we
would not just try to visit the Moon, but we would
already have arrived on other close planets."*

Sir Arthur C. Clarke

Looking at Greece today, it is hard to imagine how powerful and far ahead of the rest of the world it once was. How adventurous, tough, curious, creative and artistic the Ancient Greeks were, establishing colonies from Libya to Russia and Turkey to Spain. At the height of its power, Ancient Greece was the envy of the world, economically, militarily, artistically and scientifically. Oh, how the mighty have fallen.

No other civilization has had such a deep, long-lasting and all-encompassing impact on the world as Ancient Greece. Aside from the wealth of colonies the Greeks founded in the Mediterranean and Black Sea region and the spread of Hellenistic culture throughout Alexander the Great's vast territories in the Ancient Near East and South Asia, Ancient Greek culture is also the foundation of Western culture and — through the later Byzantine Empire — had a profound influence on Slavic and Islamic culture (Thomas, 1-5).[1]

Take the Latin alphabet, for instance, by far the most widely used writing system in the world. It is based on the Greek alphabet, sometimes considered to be the first true alphabet because it has vowels.[2] The Greeks also practically invented literature and drama, through epic poems like *The Iliad* and *The Odyssey* and the plays of Aeschylus, Sophocles and Euripides. How about

philosophy? Greek. Democracy? Greek. Those classical columns used at Capitol Hill and the White House? Greek. The Hippocratic oath? Greek. The Pythagorean theorem? Greek. The first person to calculate the circumference of the Earth? A man named Eratosthenes, who was — you guessed it — a Greek.

So what made the Greeks have such a lasting impact on the rest of the world? In part it was luck, plain and simple. First, the greatest conquerer mankind has ever seen, Alexander the Great, was born and raised in Ancient Greece. In just eleven years, Alexander would conquer his way to an empire covering some 2 million square miles (5.2 million sq. kilometers). After his untimely death, a war of succession broke out among his generals, eventually leading to the formation of four large 'successor states', which ensured the continuance of Hellenistic dominance in large parts of Alexander's territories for another 200-300 years.

Second, in the 2nd century BCE Greece itself was conquered by one of the greatest, longest lasting empires in the history of the world, the Roman Empire. The Romans loved everything that came out of Hellas, a point eloquently captured by the Roman poet Horace, who wrote that *"Conquered Greece took captive her savage conquerer and brought her arts into rustic Latium"*.[3] Through the Romans, Ancient Greece would subsequently also exert a profound influence on the civilization that conquered and dominated most of the world from the 15th century on: Western Civilization.

The rise of Ancient Greece was preceded by the collapse of an earlier Greek culture, the Mycenaean Civilization, around 1200 BCE. How it collapsed is still unclear. Most historians think it was the result of an invasion by the Dorians — a people that presumably originated from northwest Greece — but the (archaeological) evidence leaves room for debate about its periodization and suggested alternative theories, such as that there might have been multiple invasions or that the invasion might not have been an invasion at all but rather a revolution of already-present Dorians against their Mycenaean masters.[4]

Whatever the case, after the collapse of the Mycenaean Civilization the population of Greece dropped dramatically and almost all the major settlements were abandoned, with the exception of Athens. Writing ceased, trade with other cultures diminished and high level public organization disappeared. This period is known as the Greek Dark Ages.[5]

Things started to change in the 8th century BCE, when Greece was being influenced by several Ancient Near East civilizations such as the Egyptians, the Assyrians and the Phoenicians. The latter introduced their alphabet to the Greeks around this time.[6] This easy and elegant writing system would prove indispensable for both the (re)construction of Ancient Greek civilization and its longevity.

Emerging from their darker ages, the Greeks began to organize themselves in city states. The formation of these *poleis* was in no small part the result of Greece's geography, because with so many islands and mountain ranges it was virtually impossible to successfully control a large territory. Not that this prevented the Greeks from fighting each other, or others for that matter — on the contrary. Between 800-337 BCE, when the Greek city states (except Sparta) were unified in the League of Corinth by Philip II of Macedon — Alexander the Great's father — the Greeks fought numerous conflicts within their own city states, with each other's city states and with the mighty Persian Empire.

Several city-states were doing very well. They traded extensively with the East and through newly settled colonies in Southern Italy, Sicily, Northeastern Spain and Southern France, where they founded Marseille, the oldest French city. The establishment of these colonies was also partly driven by a sharp increase in the population of 8th century Greece, after centuries of very slow growth (Pomeroy, 71-72). Since arable land was limited, emigration was the only viable option for some.

The inequality between the landowning aristocracy — who also held all political and judicial power — and the rest of the people, ranging from the dirt poor to well-to-do farmers and merchants, was a destabilizing factor (Pomeroy, 97-98). From time to time a tyrant would rise to power, supported by the people but vehemently opposed by the aristocracy — and with reason, because although these tyrants were members of the aristocracy themselves, they garnered support from the masses by promising to end the injustices' suffered by the people (Pomeroy, 105-107).

One such tyrant, Peisistratos, took control of Athens around 560 BCE and introduced an early form of socialism, confiscating land belonging to the aristocracy and giving it to the poor. He also funded all kinds of artistic and religious programs and launched several public building projects, which provided jobs for the unemployed and beautified the city (Pomeroy, 170-171).

After Peisistratos' death in 527 his son Hippias ruled, but when his brother was assassinated in 514, Hippias became a cruel and bitter ruler, losing the support of the people. With the help of Sparta, the nobleman Cleisthenes — a member of the powerful Alcmaeonid family — drove Hippias from power in 510. A new power struggle soon erupted, though, this time between Cleisthenes and fellow nobleman Isagoras, who not only secured the support of the aristocracy by proposing to revoke the citizenship of those whose ancestors had first received it under the tyrants Solon and Peisistratos, but who also had the backing of Spartan King Cleomenes I (Pomeroy, 174).

Cleisthenes was exiled, but Isagoras proved to be such a bad leader that the people drove him — and King Cleomenes I and his Spartan troops — from the soil of Attica, the triangular peninsula that includes Athens. Cleisthenes was recalled and in 508/7 reformed the Athenian government so that all free citizens would share in the political power, regardless of their status, a new and revolutionary system of government dubbed 'democracy'.[7] A big success with the Athenians, it was also quickly adopted by other city states. (Cleisthenes is often referred to as 'the father of democracy' in recognition of his efforts,).

Meanwhile, far away from Athens (though evidently not far enough) a great empire had been founded and was now setting its sights on Greece, after having conquered everything else in its path. No, not the Roman Empire — at least not yet— but the Persian Empire of Cyrus the Great. On paper, the outcome of a war between this mighty empire and the Greek city states seemed a done deal. No self-respecting bookmaker would have hesitated to give odds of at least 100 to 1 against the Greeks annexing the Persian Empire, instead of the other way around. But whatever the odds, 162 years after the first Persian invasion of Greece it would be Alexander the Great and the League of Corinth who crushed the Persian Empire, with Alexander entering its ceremonial capital Persepolis a conquering hero in 330 BCE.

During the first Persian invasion, in 492, Persian general Mardonius conquered both Thrace and Macedon before a big storm destroyed his entire fleet. According to Herodotus, Mardonius lost 300 ships and 20,000 men, forcing him to retreat ("Histories", 6.44).

Two years later, king Darius I sent a large force to punish Athens and another city-state, Eretria, for capturing and burning the Persian city of Sardis, located in present-day Turkey (Holland, 160). The Persians landed at the bay of Marathon, roughly 25 miles (40 km) from Athens, but found themselves blocked from exiting the plain of Marathon by the Athenian army. The Athenians are estimated to have been about 10,000 men strong, while estimates for the Persian army are put at a minimum of 25,000 infantry, plus 1,000 cavalry (Davis, 11).

The ensuing battle ended in crushing defeat for the Persians, who according to Herodotus lost more than 6,400 men, against 192 Athenian lives ("Histories", 6.117). Most Persians were able to retreat to their ships though, which subsequently set course for Athens, to attack the city directly. While the Persian fleet sailed around Cape Sounion, the Athenians hurried back to the city as well. Fortunately for them it was a much shorter trip over land than over sea, and they made it back in time to prevent Darius' soldiers from landing (Herodotus, 6.115-116). The Persians then reluctantly decided to retreat and live to fight another day.

That day came ten years later, in 480 BCE. This time, the plan was to conquer Greece completely. Darius I had died a couple of years before, but his son Xerxes I was determined to see his father's plans through. He amassed a massive army and set out to subdue the Greek city states, marching into the Greek heartland through Macedon and Thrace. Herodotus estimated the number of fighting men in the Persian army at 2.6 million souls, plus an equal amount of service men, concluding that *"the number, then, of those whom Xerxes son of Darius led as far as the Sepiad headland and Thermopylae was five million, two hundred and eighty-three thousand, two hundred and twenty"* ("Histories", 7.186). Modern historians generally put the number somewhere between 150,000 and 300,000, though, mostly based on estimates about the logistic capabilities of the Persian army and the characteristics of the region the army was traversing (Bury, 269).[8]

In the summer of 480 Xerxes' invasion force arrived at Thermopylae, where the allied Greek army had taken up a defensive position. With an army of only about 7,000 strong, the Greeks were vastly outnumbered by the mighty Xerxes, but they had chosen their terrain well (Bury, 272). Thermopylae, located in eastern central Greece, was a narrow pass on the only land route from North to South. Flanked by mountains to the West and the Malian Gulf in the East, it was only about 110 yards (100 m) wide at its narrowest point. And that is exactly where the Greeks were.

But however solid the Greek position, if Xerxes wanted to march south to subdue Thebes, Athens, Corinth, Sparta and the rest of the city states he really had no choice but to send his army through the pass and attack the Greeks.

And so, after the Hoplites — primarily free citizens who had received basic military training and were able to afford their own military gear — had easily deflected a barrage of arrows with their bronze shields, helmets and armor suits, Xerxes ordered a full frontal assault to overrun the Greeks. But the phalanx formation — a dense, defensive position in which shields are locked together and long spears protrude out from the sides of the shields — soon proved impossible to break for the lighter armed Persian troops fighting on the narrow plain.

For two days Xerxes sent in wave after wave, only to find that his advantage in numbers meant nothing because the pass was so narrow that the Greeks could even afford to rotate their troops to prevent fatigue among their numbers. Flabbergasted by this turn of events, Xerxes was going over his options at the end of the second day when a local Greek called Ephialtes — hoping for a rich reward — told him he knew a mountain path around Thermopylae, which the Persians could use to get troops behind the Greek lines.

Wasting no time, Xerxes sent Hydarnes and the Immortals — his elite force — to outflank the Greeks via the mountain path (Bury, 275). In the early morning of the third day of battle, the Greek commander, Spartan king Leonidas I, learned from the troops guarding the path that the Persians were coming. Faced with the impossible decision of allowing his army to be enveloped and massacred if it stood its ground or cut down by the Persian cavalry if it retreated in haste, Leonidas decided to send most of the Greek troops away and guard their retreat with 300 Spartans, 700 Thespians, 400 Thebans and perhaps 300 Helots (Holland, 397). After heavy fighting the Thebans decided to surrender but the Spartans and Thespians fought to the last man — including Leonidas himself — thus buying the rest of the Greek army valuable time to retreat.

After Persian soldiers had recovered the body of Leonidas, Xerxes angrily ordered it to be decapitated and then crucified.[9] Today, on the hill on which the last of the Spartans died, an engraved epitaph on a commemorative stone reads: *"Stranger, go tell the Spartans that we lie here obedient to their commands."* (Herodotus, 7.228).

After their hard-fought victory at Thermopylae, the Persians marched on and captured an evacuated Athens. Eager for a decisive battle with the now all but defeated Greeks, Xerxes was lured into a large naval engagement at the island of Salamis, about 10 miles (16 km) from Athens. With its estimated 1,200 ships the Persian fleet outnumbered the Greek fleet four to one, but the field of battle would once again prove to be heavily in favor of the Greeks (Herodotus, 7.89, Aeschylus, 340-345).[10] In the narrow straits between Salamis and the mainland, Xerxes' numerical advantage turned into a major liability, allowing the Greeks to sink more than 200 Persian ships, while losing only 40 themselves (Strauss, 204). It must have been a spectacular sight, and no one had a better view of the Persian defeat than Xerxes himself, who was watching the battle from a hastily erected throne at Mount Egaleo (Holland, 318). After the battle Xerxes retreated to Asia with the remainder of his fleet, never to return.

It has been argued that the Greek victories at Marathon and Salamis are among the most significant battles in human history, since a Persian victory might very well have hampered (or even ended) the development of Ancient Greece, which had only just entered its Golden Age. Socrates, arguably one of the greatest philosophers of all time, hadn't even been born yet in 480 BCE. Would he have been allowed to flourish and teach his philosophies under Persian rule? And what about the future of democracy? Having only just taken its first baby steps, it would have been immediately abolished by Xerxes. Also, with Persian hegemony firmly established, Roman conquest of Greece — and with it the spread of Greek culture in the West — would have been far from sure. In other words, a Persian victory at Marathon or Salamis might very well have had a profound influence on the development of Western civilization and thus on the world as it is today.[11]

In any case, thanks to the Greek victory at Salamis, Socrates was born in a free Athens, c. 470 BCE. He lived a long life and asked a lot of questions, but unfortunately did not leave any writings behind (at least none that we know of). This is why we don't know anything about Socrates through Socrates himself, only through the writings of others, his students and contemporaries (a conundrum known as the Socratic problem). Socrates being Socrates — that is to say, if what his students wrote about him is true — he probably would have loved it that studying his teachings still begins and ends with a question: 'Are these the thoughts of Socrates, or of the author of the text?' Socrates is mostly known for asking questions, meant to stimulate critical thinking and the discovery of new ideas about the topic of discussion. Known as the Socratic method, it is still being used to examine ideas and thoughts. But however useful the Socratic method can be, one can imagine how Socrates must have also driven people to sheer madness with his eternal questions, without ever answering any of them himself. Some undoubtedly found him a nuisance, always questioning everything they liked, loved and believed. Whether this also played a role in the decision to put the 71-year-old philosopher on trial for his life — for failing to acknowledge the gods and corrupting the Athenian youth with his politico-philosophic questions — is unclear. Socrates was subsequently found guilty and sentenced to death by drinking a mixture containing poison hemlock, which he promptly did.

He was never forgotten, though. The famous Roman orator Marcus Tullius Cicero later wrote that Socrates was *"the first who brought down philosophy from the heavens, placed it in cities, introduced it into families, and obliged it to examine into life and morals, good and evil."* ("Tusculan Disputations", 5.4).

Socrates' place in history and lasting influence on Western philosophy was secured through his legendary students —and the students of his students. His most famous student, Plato, who was undoubtedly greatly influenced by him, wrote a lot about his teachings, while Plato's own most famous student, Aristotle (who also taught Alexander the Great) was so influential during the Middle Ages that the great medieval thinker Thomas Aquinas simply called him 'The Philosopher' ("Summa Theologica", Q.1 Art. 3, Q.2 Art.1, Q.5 Art 1, Art 3, etc).

Influential schools of philosophy like Cynicism, Stoicism and Epicureanism all have roots in the teachings of Socrates, his students and his students' students, effectively making Socrates the 'Pater Familias' of philosophy.

The Classical period, Ancient Greece's Golden Age, roughly runs from the birth of Socrates until the death of Alexander the Great (470-323 BCE). At its beginning, the Persians had just been definitively repelled and the democratic experiment had proven itself a hit with the city states. In the decades that followed, philosophy, art and the sciences flourished. The Greeks were all powerful, it was their time, their moment to shine.

It wouldn't last very long though. Instead of building an empire of their own, the city states spent much of the Golden Age fighting each other, often by forming leagues with other city states. The Athenian league against the Spartans and their Peloponnesian league, the Boeotian League against the Athenians, the Macedonians against the Phocians, the Athenians and the Thebans, the Ancient Greeks never seemed to run out of Ancient Greek enemies. But unlike the Romans, who would slowly but certainly conquer the whole Italian peninsula (and then some), no Greek city-state was ever able to dominate Greece for long.

And so Ancient Greece was finally conquered and annexed by the Romans, in 146 BCE, ending Greek independence for the next 2,000 years, until the Greeks were finally able to wrestle themselves free from the Ottoman Empire, in 1830.

But at the beginning of the 21st century Greece has lost its sovereignty once again. In 2010, after years of political infighting, corruption and financial mismanagement had brought the country to the brink of bankruptcy, it was forced to plead for massive financial aid from other European Union member states and the International Monetary Fund. This time it wasn't the Romans or the Ottomans calling the shots but the Germans, dictating strict re-financing terms and closely monitoring progress on the necessary fiscal and economic reforms.[12] It is a new invasion. And this kind of invasion will not be stopped at Marathon, Thermopylae or Salamis.

---

1   Ancient Greek influence on Slavic culture was transferred through the Byzantine Empire (a.k.a. the Eastern Roman Empire) where many aspects of Ancient Greek culture and knowledge survived throughout the Middle Ages, albeit it within ever shrinking borders (Thomas, 47-48). The Muslims first came into contact with Hellenistic culture in the seventh century, through the conquest of the Byzantine Levant. Ancient Greek influence on Islamic culture was mostly confined to the fields of mathematics, the sciences and philosophy though, as the Muslims were not interested in humanistic values. (Thomas, 2-3, 76).

2   The Greek alphabet is itself based on the Phoenician alphabet, but this has no vowels, which is why some consider the Greek alphabet the first true alphabet. However, since the development of *matres lectionis* — consonants used in such a way they indicate a vowel — in Phoenician has become better understood, the view of the Greek alphabet as being a revolutionary, radical break from the Phoenician alphabet has lost some of its strength (Coulmas, 118).

3   *Graecia capta ferum victorem cepit et artes intulit agresti Latio* (Horace, epistle I, 156-157).

4   Irene Lemos gives a condensed, but well-sourced overview of the Dorian Invasion theory and alternative explanations for the destruction of the Mycenaean civilization (*Protogeometric Aegean*, 191-193). The Athenian historian Thucydides (460-395 BCE) seems to suggest that the "Hellenes" of ancient times might have destroyed themselves, writing: *"For in ancient times both Hellenes and Barbarians, as well the inhabitants of the coast as of the islands, when they began to find their way to one another by sea had recourse to piracy. They were commanded by powerful chiefs, who took this means of increasing their wealth and providing for their poor followers. They would fall upon the unwalled and straggling towns, or rather villages, which they plundered, and maintained themselves by the plunder of them"* (*History of the Peloponnesian War*, 1.1.5).

5   It has been argued that the rather pejorative term for this period — the Greek Dark Ages — is mostly based on the fact that we know relatively little about it and that it conveniently begins with the end of the use of Linear B — a writing script used by Mycenaean Greece — and ends with the introduction of the

Greek alphabet, in the 8th century (Fagan, 253-255).

6 In *A History of the Archaic Greek World*, Prof. Jonathan M. Hall writes that the earliest evidence of Ancient Greek has been found on painted pottery dating back to the eighth century, concluding dryly that though "it is entirely possible that the Greeks [also] wrote on perishable materials, it is perhaps less likely that they studiously avoided scratching graffiti on ceramic vessels until the eighth century" (Hall, "A history", 57,58).

7 The word democracy combines the Greek words *dêmos* ('people') and *krátos* ('force', or 'power').

8 Davis and Holland both list several modern estimates in their respective works "100 Decisive Battles" and "Persian Fire", which for the most part lie between 150,000 and 300,00 (Davis, 14, Holland, 394).

9 Forty years after the battle, Leonidas' bones were belatedly returned to Sparta, where he was buried with full funeral honors (Pausanias, 3.14).

10 The famous playwright Aeschylus, who wrote about the Persian invasion of Greece, actually fought in the Battle of Salamis himself.

11 Then again, the Persians were highly advanced and civilized themselves, so even if Persian conquest of Greece might indeed have had a deep impact on Western history, it would not necessarily have meant the end of Greek culture.

12 Technically the EU and the IMF are responsible for this, but Germany, as the largest and richest EU member state, has been the most powerful advocate for Greek economic reform.

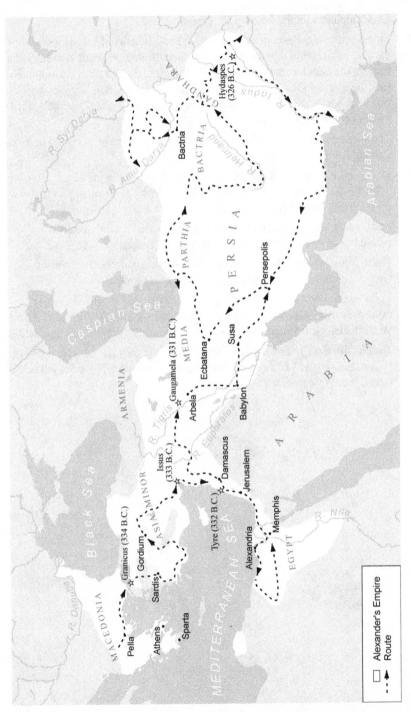

Map 2: Conquests of Alexander the Great

7

WHY ALEXANDER WAS SO GREAT

*"I have something to say; It's better
to burn out than to fade away!"[1]*

The Kurgan, *Highlander*, 1986

The Temple of Artemis — one of the Seven Wonders of the Ancient World — burned down on the day he was born.[2] When he was 10, he tamed the wild horse that would carry him through his later conquests. When he was 14, the great philosopher Aristotle became his teacher and when he was 16 he founded his first city. He was proclaimed King of Macedon at 20, Pharaoh of Egypt at 24, King of Kings of the Persian Empire at 26 and dead at 32. He was Alexander the Great.

Alexander III of Macedon was many things. Ambitious, confident, brave, a natural born leader, a gifted military tactician and a successful commander. But most of all, he was restless. Between 334 and 323 BCE, the year of his death, he conquered his way through present-day Turkey, Syria, Lebanon, Israel, Egypt, Libya, Iraq, Iran, Afghanistan, Pakistan, India, Nepal, Tajikistan, Uzbekistan and Turkmenistan, covering a distance of some 22,000 miles (Wood, 9).

Why? Was it blind ambition, a belief in divine predestination to rule the world? Was he doing it all to make his father proud, who had had plans of his own to invade Persia before he was assassinated? What kept him going, year after year, country after country, kingdom after kingdom?

We don't really know. Perhaps Alexander was the kind of young man who always wants to see what comes next; the next city, the next valley, the next country, the other end of the river, the other end of the desert, behind the next hill, the next mountain range. Perhaps what kept him going was the same primal fire raging in the bellies of the great explorers. That, and a massive army of hardened, experienced soldiers carrying 20 feet long spears.

His father, King Philip II of Macedon, had been the same kind of man. He had inherited his kingdom while it was under siege from multiple sides — Illyrians, Paionians, Thracians, Athenians, rival pretenders to the throne — but had quickly put his house in order using diplomacy, bribery, deceit and, when necessary, ruthless violence (Worthington, 29-30). In the 23 years of his reign, Philip would slowly but certainly submit all of Greece to his will, with the exception of the Spartans. He did send them a threatening message once, after having secured control over all the other important city states. It read: *"If once I enter into your territories, I will destroy ye all, never to rise again."* (Plutarch, "Morals", *On Talkativeness*, 17). The Spartans replied with one word: *"If"*. Philip decided not to invade Sparta.

When Alexander was 16, Philip deemed him ready for more serious business and left him in charge as regent and heir apparent, while he went off to wage war against the city of Byzantium (Worthington, 97).[3] Philip had barely left when young Alexander received his baptism of fire, having to put down a Maedian revolt, which he quickly did. To prevent any future surprises from the Maedians, he subsequently founded a city, Alexandropolis — the first in a long line of cities Alexander would name after himself — and populated it with Greeks, Macedonians and Thracians (Worthington, 97). In the years that followed, Philip and Alexander would often campaign together, with the elder teaching the younger the art of practical warfare, diplomacy and how to be king. On one of those campaigns Alexander even saved his father's life (Aikin, 152).

Relations between father and son soured, though, when Philip married a young woman called Cleopatra Eurydice. Unlike Alexander's mother Olympias, Eurydice was Macedonian, meaning that any son she would bare by Philip would be a full-blood Macedonian heir, while Alexander himself was only half-Macedonian, a fact pointed out not so subtly at Eurydice's wedding by her uncle, General Attalus, when he implored the gods for a lawful successor to the kingdom, i.e., one provided by his niece (Plutarch, "Alexander", 9.4). When Alexander took offense, Philip took Attalus' side, drew his sword and drunkenly tried to attack his son. Fortunately for one of the greatest stories in history, Philip slipped and the attack came to nothing. Humiliated, Alexander said mockingly: *"Look now, men! here is one who was preparing to cross from Europe into Asia; and he is upset trying to cross from couch to couch."* (Plutarch, "Alexander", 9.5). After this, Alexander went into exile with his mother. Six months later, after some mediation, he returned.

Some time after that, in 336, Philip was assassinated by the captain of his bodyguard, Pausanias. The assassin was subsequently killed himself by Philip's bodyguards while trying to escape. Alexander was proclaimed king by the nobles and the army the same day. Some historians have suggested Pausanias killed Philip because they had been lovers until Philip had chosen another and because Philip did not come to his aid when General Attalus humiliated him (Diodorus, "Library of History", Vol. VIII, 16.93-94). Others say that Alexander and his mother — being the chief beneficiaries of Philip's death — might have had a hand in the assassination themselves.(Justin, 9.7).

What is the first thing a young king does after rising to power? Today it is probably going on a public relations tour, but back in the day the name of the game was killing your rivals, and Alexander was no exception. He killed a cousin, some princes, and his half-brother Caranus and half-sister Europa, by Philip's aforementioned young Macedonian wife Cleopatra Eurydice (Green, 141-142). Next, he had to deal with revolting city states, who thought now was the time to regain their freedom. Unfortunately for them, they were up against the Mozart of warfare, so they really didn't stand a chance. And so, like his father had done before him, Alexander quickly put his house in order upon inheriting his kingdom.

After that it was time to conquer the world. In 334, two years after becoming king, Alexander crossed the Hellespont with 43,000 infantry and 6,000 cavalry, intent on conquering the whole of Asia (Green, 157). He would never return home again. Nor would most of his men.

At the Granicus River (present-day Biga River, Turkey) he was met by a Persian army made up of forces from various satraps (governors) from the western Persian Empire, intent on stopping him. They almost succeeded.

While engaged in the thick of battle with his cavalry, two Persian commanders attacked Alexander at the same time. Avoiding the first, Alexander clashed with the second, breaking his spear upon his breastplate. He immediately drew his sword, but at that moment the first attacker prepared to strike Alexander down with a blow from his battle-axe. Just when the Persian raised his arm for the deadly stroke, Cleitus the Black, one of Alexander's generals, came to the rescue and ran the attacker through with his spear, while Alexander struck down the other Persian with his sword (Plutarch, "Alexander", 16.5-6).

Saving a king's life usually greatly improves the prospects of the lucky hero, but for poor Cleitus things would ultimately not end well. During a drunken quarrel some years after the battle at Granicus, he accused Alexander of having forgotten the Macedonian way of life, with his newfound Persian customs and clothing, after which the young Macedonian king, drunk and offended, angrily threw a spear at Cleitus, killing him (Plutarch, "Alexander", 51).

A year after Granicus, Alexander faced the king of the Persian Empire himself for the first time. Darius III was not a great leader by design, nor did he have any leadership experience or had he shown any ambition to rule before he became king. In fact, he had been installed as a puppet king by the powerful but treacherous chiliarch Bagoas, who had the previous ruler and all of his sons killed (Diodorus, "Library of History", Vol. VIII, 17.3).[4] When it turned out that Darius could not be controlled Bagoas tried to poison him too, but Darius was warned and forced the regicide to drink his own poison (Diodorus, "Library of History", Vol. VIII, 17.3). That was about his most commanding act during his six-year reign.

The first battle between Alexander and Darius III took place in November 333, close to the ancient town of Issus (present-day southern Turkey, near the Gulf of Iskenderun). Persian forces, numbering about 100,000 and led by Darius himself, took position on one side of the small river Pinarus, while the 40,000 strong Macedonian army took position on the other (Worthington, 165-66).[5] The battlefield was relatively small though, wedged in between the gulf of Issus and a nearby mountain range, meaning Darius could not really take advantage of his superiority in numbers.

With the Persians lined up in a defensive position, Alexander had his troops advance slowly, trying to entice Darius to attack. Unsurprisingly, the Persian king was not the least bit interested in giving up his strong position, though he did suddenly strengthen his right wing, dispatching crack cavalry squadrons to be deployed opposite Parmenio's troops, making the Macedonian left wing alarmingly vulnerable (Green, 229). After sending reinforcements to Parmenio, Alexander decided any further delay might lose him the initiative. It was late afternoon already, time for a decisive victory was running out. Concentrating on the Persian left wing, which was made up of archers and light-armed infantry, Alexander quickly led the Companions —his elite cavalry — across the riverbed for a full-blown assault (Green, 230). Stunned and defenseless against the Macedonian horse, the Persian archers and infantry were overrun in a matter of minutes.

As soon as the Persian left flank was broken, Alexander swung his cavalry against the Persian rear and the Royal Bodyguard, for a direct assault against Darius III himself (Green, 231). But the Persian king of kings, seeing Alexander coming, quickly fled the battlefield. Alexander wanted to give pursuit and capture him, but right at that moment he received an urgent appeal to come to the aide of his phalanx, which was fighting — and losing — at the center, while Parmenio, barely holding the Macedonian left, was in danger of being overrun by the Persian heavy cavalry (Green, 232). Frustrated but decisively, Alexander crashed his entire right wing into the flank of the Persian center, crushing the Greek mercenaries who were pressuring his phalanx.

When the Persian heavy cavalry saw the center crumble and found out Darius III had already fled the field, they too lost heart. Suddenly, the entire Persian Imperial Army was on the run. Greek mercenaries, Persian infantry, archers, everybody was trying to save their skin. Many were killed by Alexander's archers or ridden down by their own cavalry (Green, 232).

Because he had had to save his center and left flank Alexander was not able to catch the fleeing Darius, but it was nevertheless an impressive victory. To commemorate it, he founded a city close to the battlefield, Alexandretta. It still stands today, as Iskenderun.

After the battle Darius III wrote to Alexander, offering him half the kingdom, a huge ransom for captured family members and the hand of his eldest daughter in marriage. When Alexander told his generals, Parmenio said *"If I were Alexander, I would accept these terms."* Alexander responded: *"And so indeed would I, were I Parmenio."* But to Darius, he wrote: *"Come to me, and thou shalt receive every courtesy; but otherwise I shall march at once against thee."* (Plutarch, "Alexander", 29.4).

This Darius did not do, and so, two years later, in October 331, a second battle was fought, at Gaugamela. The exact location of the battlefield is unknown, but most historians think it was likely east of Mosul, in present-day northern Iraq.

With the Persian king fielding an estimated 100,000 men against Alexander's 50,000, Darius III outnumbered his nemesis two to one again, and this time the battlefield was an open plain with plenty of space, ensuring Darius III could take advantage of his superior numbers (Green, 283, 288; Worthington, 189).

After the Greeks had made camp, Alexander's generals suggested to mount a surprise attack during the night, to offset Darius' numerical advantage (Plutarch, "Alexander", 31.6). But Alexander famously replied *"I will not steal my victory"* and went to bed for a good night's sleep (Plutarch, "Alexander", 31.7). Meanwhile, Darius — fearing a surprise attack under the cover of darkness — kept his troops awake and alert the entire night, while the Macedonians slept, giving them a considerable advantage the next day (Plutarch, "Alexander", 31.4). Was Alexander's decision mere boyish hubris or the premeditated move of an accomplished chess player, foreseeing his opponents' every move? Perhaps you need a little of both to become one of the most successful military commanders in history.

When the battle commenced next morning, Alexander rode in front of his Companions again. Both armies inched forward and sideways, neither side wanting to initiate the first attack (Green, 292). This made sense, especially for Alexander. Because his army was vastly outnumbered, his best chance to win the day would be a hard and fast counter-attack, and for that he needed Darius to strike first. The key was to lure Darius' cavalry — which outnumbered his own five to one — into launching an attack on his flanks (Green, 289-90). Alexander had therefore made sure his flanks looked much weaker than they actually were, though this could not have been all that hard, considering both his flanks were outflanked by the massive Persian army from the beginning.

As they progressed, the sideways movement of both armies brought them close to the end of the terrain the Persians had cleared for their chariots and heavy armored cavalry (Green, 292). Deciding that the only way to prevent his army from having to fight on the rough terrain was to halt the Macedonian advance, Darius reluctantly ordered his cavalry to attack (Green, 292).

After the Persian cavalry had made contact with the seemingly weak flanks, Alexander started reinforcing them with crack troops from the rear, so as to draw in more and more cavalry, until most of the Persian horse was committed and Darius' center was — if only for a short moment — seriously weakened (Green, 292-93). This was the moment Alexander had been waiting for.

With both of his flanks being heavily pressured and only minutes away from collapsing, Alexander, riding in front of the Companions, charged head-on into the weakened Persian center. Had he gone sooner the center would not have been weak enough to be shattered by his charge, had he waited just a few moments longer his own defeat might have already been imminent. Timing was everything.

Darius, stationed in the center as was the Persian tradition, saw Alexander coming again, just as at the battle of Issus, and fled the field again, just as at the battle of Issus. The Persian center crumbled, exposing the flanks of the Persian attack to Alexander's Companions and the remaining forces coming in behind them, which included the Guards Brigade, several phalanx battalions and light-armed troops (Green, 293-94).

Bessus, the commander of the Persian left wing — which was heavily engaged on Alexander's right — feared that after opening up the center, Alexander might swing his forces around and attack the Persian left from the rear, a very real possibility, leaving him no choice but to sound the retreat (Green, 293-94).

With the Persian center and left flank now on the run, Alexander prepared to set out in pursuit of Darius and end the war right then and there, but at that moment he received an alarming message from Parmenio that the left flank could not be held much longer and was in danger of collapsing (Green, 294). Faced once again with the choice of saving his army or catching Darius, Alexander reluctantly decided to relieve his embattled left flank. And so, as at Issus, the battle was won but Darius had escaped.

There would not be a third battle between the two kings, though. Less than a year after Gaugamela Darius was murdered by Bessus, who subsequently crowned himself as the new King of Kings of Persia (Diodorus, "Library of History", Vol. VIII, 17.73-74). Unfortunately for Bessus he did not live long to enjoy it, though, because Alexander pursued, captured and executed him not two years later (Arrian, "History", IV.7).[6]

Having conquered the Persian Empire, Alexander set out to merge the two great cultures. By allowing the Persians to keep many of their customs and traditions while simultaneously introducing Greek customs and education, Alexander hoped the people he had conquered would work with him instead of against him. The young Macedonian warrior king thus proved himself a benevolent and generous ruler, who did not seek to oppress or exploit the people he conquered but instead respected them and wanted to include them into his kingdom.

To set the example, Alexander started wearing Persian clothing himself and adopted several Persian customs regulating behavior at court (Arrian, "History", IV.9).[7] His own men strongly disapproved of this behavior, though. Even Alexander's closest friends decried his infatuation with everything Persian and said they did not want to mix 'barbarian' ways with their own. Alexander subsequently retracted some of the adopted customs.

Another difference between Alexander and his friends was that they were perfectly content with the days of conquest being over. The Persian Empire had been annexed — together with its great riches — and his men were taking full advantage of it, basking themselves in a lavishly luxurious lifestyle. According to Plutarch, one of Alexander's friends wore silver nails in his shoes, while another had camels bring him dust from Egypt just for his gymnastic exercises ("Alexander",

40.1). Several used only the best oils for bathing instead of plain olive oil and had servants follow them everywhere they went (Plutarch, "Alexander", 40.1). In other words, they had grown soft.

Alexander's own hunger for conquest was nowhere near satisfied, though, so in 327 he marched his army east again and invaded the Indian subcontinent, fighting and defeating several chieftains and kings in a region comprising present-day Pakistan and northern India.

One of the greatest battles Alexander fought there was against King Porus of Paurava, in May 326 BCE, at the river Hydaspes (in the Punjab region, present-day Pakistan). According to Plutarch, Porus was an exceptionally tall and big man, whose *size and majesty of his body made his elephant seem as fitting a mount for him as a horse for a horseman* ("Alexander", 60.6). He was a noble and brave warrior, not to mention a formidable enemy who outnumbered Alexander more than three to one and had maybe 200 war elephants at his disposal.[8]

The river Hydaspes posed another challenge. With Porus ensconced on its opposite bank, Alexander needed to find a way across that did not involve a full frontal assault — which would surely end in defeat, given his inferiority in numbers. Leaving most of his army at the command of general Craterus and charging him with keeping Porus busy, Alexander himself therefore secretly crossed the river further upstream with the remainder of his troops, under the cover of darkness and bad weather (Arrian, "History", V.11-12). When Porus found out about it, Alexander had already crossed the river. Now threatened from two sides, Porus decided to meet Alexander with the largest part of his army, leaving the remainder to fend off Craterus' forces on the opposite bank (Arrian, "History", V.15).

When Alexander saw the Indian forces draw up in battle formation and position most of their elephants at the center, he quickly decided on a two-pronged attack to annihilate the Indian left wing (Arrian, "History", V.16). The first part was an all-out charge on Porus' left wing cavalry by the Companions, led by Alexander himself (Arrian, "History", V.16). Reasoning correctly that Porus would dispatch his right wing cavalry to aid the pressured left, Alexander ordered general Coenus, one of his most able and faithful commanders, to ride around the Indian right flank with his cavalry contingent and follow the

Indian right wing cavalry as it rode to relieve the left wing (Arrian, "History", V.16). When the Indian cavalry was thus fully engaged, Coenus deployed the second part of the strategy, smashing into the already battered Indian left flank from the rear, causing it to collapse (Arrian, "History", V.16).

Meanwhile, the Macedonian center had to hold at all cost against the enemy infantry and a frightening horde of war elephants. Initially, the Macedonian phalanx had great difficulty defending against the elephants, but when they eventually succeeded in repelling the colossal animals with their long spikes, the trumpeting elephants ran over much of the Indian infantry in their flight to safety and the day was won (Diodorus, "Library of History", Vol. VIII, 17.88).

After the battle Alexander asked the defeated King Porus — who had fought bravely and in a manner a king becoming — how he expected to be treated. Porus answered *"Like a king"* (Plutarch, "Alexander", 60.8). This Alexander did, allowing him to continue to govern his kingdom as a satrap and even adding territory to it from the various tribes he had conquered before.

After this great victory Alexander wanted to press on and cross the river Ganges to conquer the rest of India, but when his men heard about this they revolted. Because not only had they been told that the Ganges was very deep and broad, they had also heard that the kingdoms on the other side of the Ganges commanded some 200,000 soldiers, 80,000 horses, 8,000 chariots and 6,000 fighting elephants (Plutarch, "Alexander", 62.2). Having just encountered 200 war elephants they had no taste for fighting any more of them, especially not to conquer kingdoms that were even further away from home than they already were.

Unable to persuade them, Alexander shut himself up in his tent and sulked for days. After a while his friends were able to convince him to turn back. The return trip would not be any less hazardous than fighting ferocious war elephants, though, because Alexander decided to take the southern route home, through the Gedrosian desert (present-day Balochistan, in southern Pakistan and Iran). It was a mistake. On the 60-day march through the desert Alexander lost almost all of the livestock, most of his baggage train and a considerable number of men (Arrian, "History", VI.25).

Why did he elect to cross the desert instead of taking the coastal route? Perhaps it was just curiosity after a region of which little was known. Or perhaps it was simply the natural choice for a young man who had always pushed on where others had hesitated or turned back. The 2nd-century Greek historian Arrian suggests it was to imitate and surpass Cyrus the Great, whom Alexander greatly admired and who had crossed the desert at great cost to his army, with only himself and seven others surviving ("History", VI.24). Whatever the reason, the decision to needlessly cross the unforgiving desert is considered Alexander's largest blunder.

Shortly after returning to Babylon, on June 10 or 11, 323 BCE, Alexander died, just 32 years old.[9]

At the time of his death, his empire was the largest and most powerful state in the world, covering more than two million square miles. The Roman Republic, which was only about six thousand square miles at that point, would need centuries to accomplish what Alexander had achieved in just eleven years.

And he had had plans for many more conquests and the founding of many more cities, as became clear from written instructions he had given not long before his death. They talked of circumnavigating Arabia and Africa and the construction of thousands of ships, to make war on the Carthaginians and others living on the Mediterranean coastline (Plutarch, "Alexander", 68.1-3; Diodorus, "Library of History",Vol. IX, 18.4.4).[10] Alexander also envisioned *"to transplant populations from Asia to Europe and in the opposite direction from Europe to Asia, in order to bring the largest continents to common unity and to friendly kinship by means of intermarriages and family ties."* (Diodorus, "Library of History", Vol. IX, 18.4.4).

Unfortunately, with Alexander not having named a successor other than that it should be *"the strongest"*, there would not be much *"common unity and friendly kinship"* in his empire in the immediate aftermath of his death; civil war for control of the empire broke out almost immediately between some of his generals (Justin, 12.15).[11] Following years of unrest a number of stable kingdoms emerged, the so-called successor states, the biggest of which being the Seleucid empire, which would survive until 63 BCE, when the last part of it was conquered by the Roman general Pompey.

The fall of the Ptolemaic Kingdom, the last remaining successor state, in 31 BCE, marked the definitive end of the Hellenistic period, during which Greek culture had spread throughout Europe and Asia. In philosophy, political organization, science, the arts, literature, architecture and mathematics, Greece had shown the way in a vast part of the known world.

It is said that what makes Alexander great is the fact that he was never defeated in battle. But while that certainly makes him a great general, it does not necessarily make him a great man. More than a great general, though, more even than a great conquerer, Alexander was a great ruler, improving the lives of the people he conquered by introducing them to the rich Greek culture while at the same time respecting their own ways. *That* is what made him great.

---

1   The line *"it's better to burn out than to fade away"* is originally from a 1978 song from Neil Young, *Hey Hey, My My (into the Black)*. The line became infamous after Nirvana lead singer Curt Cobain quoted it in his suicide note, in 1994.

2   Plutarch makes mention of this in his 'Life of Alexander', but it is possible Alexander's birth date has been moved somewhat to facilitate the coincidence (*Alexander*, 3.3).

3   Byzantium was founded as a Greek colony in the 7th century BCE. It was rebuilt by Roman Emperor Constantine I, who in 324 CE designated it as the new capital of the Roman Empire. The city was renamed Constantinople. Today it is known as Istanbul.

4   Chiliarch is the Greek title for one of the chief offices of state in Archaemenid Persia, comparable to the later office of vizier. It is presumably translated from the Old Persian word hazārapati (Yarshater, 423-424).

5   Worthington notes that ancient writers such as Arrian, Plutarch, Diodorus and Justin came up with far higher numbers for the Persian army, but contends that these are exaggerations, meant to make the Macedonian victory even more impressive ("By the Spear", 166). Green agrees and even suggests that Darius' army was not larger — or perhaps even smaller — than Alexander's ("Alexander", 226).

6   According to Diodorus, Bessus was seized by his own generals and handed over to Alexander in return for a reward. Alexander subsequently turned Bessus over to Darius' brother and other relatives, who executed him (Diodorus, "Library of History", Vol. VIII, 17.83).

7   Among these was the custom of proskynesis, the traditional Persian act of bowing, kneeling or even fully laying oneself flat on the ground face downward, in full submission and/or reverence. To the Greeks, such submission was reserved for the gods only; they found it barbaric, not to mention ridiculous, to humble oneself so deeply for another mortal. See James Romm's *Alexander the Great* for a more in-depth explanation of the so-called "proskynesis crisis" (103ff.)

8   Arrian writes that Porus had 4,000 cavalry at his disposal, 300 chariots, 200 elephants and almost 30,000 infantry, while Alexander had 6,000 infantry and 5,000 cavalry ("History", V.14-15). According to Diodorus, Porus had 50,000 infantry, 3,000 horses, more than 1,000 chariots and 130 elephants ("Library of History", Vol. VIII, 17.87).

9   Alexander may have been poisoned, though it was never proven. His death struggle of twelve days seems to argue against poison, though poison experts from New Zealand in 2014 published a theory in the medical journal *Clinical Toxicology* about a specific, slow-acting poison that might have been used in Alexander's case (Schep, "Death of Alexander").

10   The Romans shared Alexander's vision of dominating the Mediterranean and would succeed in conquering the entire Mediterranean coastline some 400 years after his death.

11   Diodorus writes that Alexander said *"To the best man; for I foresee that a great combat of my friends will be my funeral games."* ("Library of History", Vol. IX, 18.1.4). Plutarch, on the contrary, writes Alexander was speechless in the final days of his life ("Alexander", 76.3-4). Arrian agrees with Plutarch that Alexander had lost his speech shortly before his death, but also mentions other authors having the dying king reply *"To the strongest"*, to the question *"to whom he would bequeath his empire"* (Arrian, "History", VII.26).

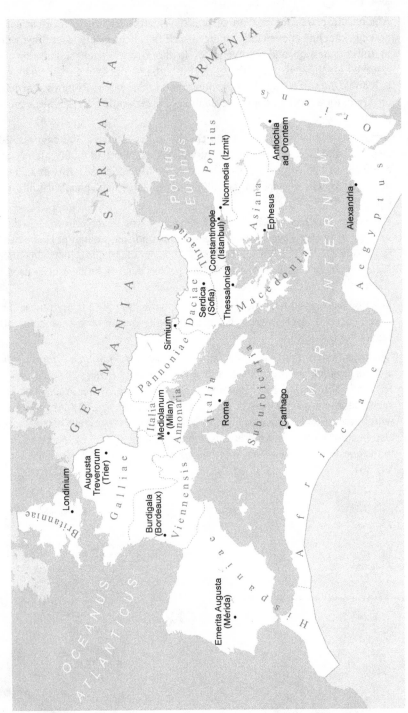

Map 3: The Roman Empire at its Zenith (117 CE.)

8

The Longest Lasting Empire in History

"All right, but apart from the sanitation, the medicine, education, wine, public order, irrigation, roads, the fresh water system, and public health.... what have the Romans ever done for us!?"

"Brought peace!"

"Oh, shut up!"

Life of Brian, 1979

Looking at today's Romans, fashion, good food, wine and the pope seem to be among the things most important to them. But it wasn't always so. 2,500 years ago, long before they fell in love with beauty, food, art and Catholicism, the Romans were tough, ruthless, disciplined, organized, independent and above all ambitious. Characteristics that would serve them well while patiently building one of the largest empires the world had ever seen and presiding over a period of unprecedented peace and prosperity.

Legend has it that the city of Rome was founded on April 21, 753 BCE, by twin brothers Romulus and Remus. The date was calculated in the 1st century BCE by the Roman scholar Marcus Terentius Varro and was declared the official founding year under Emperor Augustus, but since the calculation is partly based on assumption it remains a myth.[1] The same goes for the story of Romulus and Remus. According to the story, the two brothers quarreled about where to found the city. It must have been some quarrel, because at one point Romulus even killed Remus, after which he not only got to decide on the exact location of the city, but also on its name (Livy, 1.7). Had Remus won, we would have perhaps been talking about the city of Reme and the great Remian empire.

Of course Rome didn't start out as a great empire. In fact, it was a rather insignificant settlement the first few centuries, made up of mostly farmers. Moreover, being located close to the older and more established Etruscan civilization, the city wasn't completely independent either. Several of the seven kings who ruled Rome before it became a Republic came from an Etruscan family, including the last one, Tarquin the Proud.

In 509 BCE, the unpopular Tarquin was deposed through a revolt led by Lucius Junius Brutus, who used the rape of a family member by the king's son to get rid of the absolute monarchy and subsequently established a system of government whereby citizens would elect people to hold public office for a limited period of time, in other words a Republic.[2-3]

. At this point Rome was already the largest city-state in the Latium region, dominating the so-called Latin league, a defensive alliance of Latium cities against invasions by people from central and southern Italy. Over the next decades, the young Republic would also bring a centuries old war with the Etruscan city-state Veii to a decisive end, finally capturing the city after a siege that had lasted 10 years. With the annexation of Veii, the Roman Republic gained considerable territory and manpower.

The Roman path to world domination was not without hiccups, though. In 390 BCE, for instance, an invading Gaulish war band defeated the Romans at the banks of the Allia river, 10 miles north of Rome, leaving the city unprotected (Livy, 5.38). As the Gauls approached, many citizens fled the city in panic. The ones who were able to fight stayed behind, making their final stand at Capitoline Hill.

After they sacked the city, the Gauls laid siege to Capitoline Hill and waited for the remaining Romans to surrender, but they held firm, at one point even repelling a nightly surprise attack (Livy, 5.47). Meanwhile, the Gauls suffered more from laying siege than the Romans did from being besieged and, according to Livy, *"died off like sheep*" from hunger, disease and the unforgiving heat (5.48). The Roman historian goes on to write that the Gauls "*soon grew weary of burying their dead singly, so they piled the bodies into heaps and burned them indiscriminately*" (5.48).

Though the Gauls did not want give up their siege, they knew they could not keep it in place indefinitely either. Negotiations were therefore opened and both parties agreed to a settlement of 1,000 pounds of gold, "*the ransom of a people, who were soon after to be the rulers of the world*", as Livy remarked, not entirely without a sense of drama (5.48).

Just when the Romans noticed that the Gauls were using false weights, the Roman commander Marcus Furius Camillus — who had been appointed Dictator temporarily — arrived with fresh troops from nearby Veii. He immediately declared the settlement deal invalid and told the Gauls to get ready for battle, because Romans "*deliver their city with iron and not with gold*" (Plutarch, *Camillus*, 29.2). In the subsequent battle the Gauls were utterly defeated. Camillus, hero of the day, was declared "'*A Romulus*', '*The Father of his country*', '*The Second Founder of the City*'" (Livy, 5.49).

Meanwhile, the neighboring Etrurians, Volsci and Aequi, sensed an opportunity and formed a hostile alliance to attack Rome. But Camillus quickly defeated all three of them as well, further establishing his own legend and Rome's dominance of the region (Livy, 6.2-4).

Now the genie was out of the bottle, and in the century that followed Rome succeeded in subduing the entire Italian peninsula, aided by the enlargement and successful reorganization of the army, between 315-300 BCE, which saw the abandonment of the traditional phalanx formation — a dense, rectangular military formation — in favor of the more flexible manipular system (from *manipulus*, meaning 'a handful').[4] The system was most likely copied from the Samnites — another Italian people — after the Romans had suffered several serious defeats against their much more flexible army in the rugged terrain of central Italy.[5]

Between 390 and 264 BCE, Rome thus fought the Gauls, the Etrurians, the Volsci, several Latin city-states, the Samnites, the Hernici, the Aequi, the Paeligni, the Marrucini, the Frentani, the

Lucanians, the Bruttians, the Epirotes, the Umbrians, the Picentes, the Sallentini and the Messapii. The Samnites proved to be a particularly tough opponent; the Republic had to fight three wars before finally forcing them into an alliance on Rome's terms.

In 264 BCE the whole Italian peninsula was finally completely under Roman control. Time for some peace and quiet you might say, but apparently world domination could not wait, because that same year consul Appius Claudius Caudex led a Roman expedition to Sicily, which was partly occupied by mighty Carthage, thus triggering the first Punic War.

At that point, the Roman army was still made up exclusively of free, property-owning citizens, not professional soldiers.They had to pay for their own equipment and generally served in specific (usually annual) campaigns. The foundation of the military was in essence still defensive, its goal to protect Rome and its citizens, its ranks filled with those who had something to lose.

This made a lot of sense in the early days of the Republic, when life on the Italian Peninsula was hard and danger could (and did) come from all sides and over long distances. In those days, the Romans had to fight to survive, kill or be killed, conquer or be conquered. At some point, though, what used to be waging war to ensure survival just became part of life, engrained in Roman culture and upbringing. But even if its survival was no longer at stake, Rome's ever growing power and territory ensured that potential enemies were never too far away, paving the way for a host of preemptive defensive wars (a.k.a offensive wars).

Of course with greater conquest also came greater loss of life, and the epic clash between the Roman Republic and the Carthaginian Empire and their long struggle for dominance of the Western Mediterranean, known as the Punic Wars (264-146 BCE), eventually forced the Republic to abandon its longstanding principle of all soldiers having to be property-owning citizens.[6]

The Republic would fight three wars with Carthage, ending with the utter destruction of the once proud and powerful North African civilization.

The First Punic War lasted 23 years (from 264 to 241 BCE) and was mostly fought at sea and in Sicily. The eventual Roman victory is all the more remarkable, because at the start of the conflict the Romans had virtually no experience in naval warfare, while Carthage was one of the dominant naval powers in the Mediterranean. On top of that, the Romans lost two fleets in a storm, the most devastating of which caused the loss of 270 ships and 100,000 souls. But they refused to give up even then, instead securing donations from wealthy citizens to build one last fleet (crowd funding avant-la-lettre, so to speak). Tellingly, when the Carthaginians were faced with a similar problem somewhat later, they were unable to build another fleet and subsequently had to cede naval control to the Republic.

Thus forced to sue for peace, Carthage had to relinquish Sicily and pay a huge war indemnity of 5,000 talents of silver (Polybius, 15.8.7).[7] This in turn compelled the Carthaginians to look for additional revenue, which they found in the rich silver mines of southern Spain.

For a while Rome and Carthage kept the peace — though mostly the cold war kind — but when Carthaginian general Hannibal Barca in 219 BCE attacked the prosperous, strategically located city-state Saguntum, a Roman ally in eastern Spain, it became clear that a new conflict between the two Mediterranean powers loomed on the horizon.[8]

Saguntum fell after a siege of eight months, after which Hannibal marched his army north, along the Spanish coast, towards the Pyrenees, with 90,000 infantry, 12,000 cavalry and 37 war elephants (Polybius, 3.35.1, 42.11).[9] After having crossed the river Ebro in northern Spain and subduing several tribes in the area — at considerable losses — Hannibal left 10,000 infantry and 1,000 cavalry with his nephew Hanno, placing him in charge of the region he had just conquered, and sent an equal number of troops home (Polybius, 3.35.2-7). With the remainder of his army, about 50,000 infantry and 9,000 cavalry, he then crossed the Pyrenees (Polybius, 3.35.7).

In October 218 BCE, five months after the start of the march, Hannibal crossed the Alps, emerging on the Italian side of the mountain range fifteen gruesome days later with 20,000 hardened soldiers and 6,000 cavalry (Polybius, 3.56.4).[10] The ambitious young Carthaginian general was now in the backyard of the Republic.

Hannibal's riveting opening act in this Second Punic War (218-201 BCE) foretold that this would be a war of heroes, of the boldness of attack, the shrewdness of retreat and of historic battles that would keep being reenacted in the Colosseum for centuries to come.

After some early Carthaginian victories had established Hannibal's reputation as a brilliant commander, the Roman Senate appointed former consul and general Quintis Fabius Maximus Verrucosus as temporary Dictator, to deal with the Carthaginian threat.[11] Fabius decided not to give Hannibal open battle anymore, but rather slow him down through skirmishes and the disruption of supply lines (Polybius, 3.89-90).[12]

But although the strategy was a success, it was still deeply unpopular with the Romans, who considered it cowardice. The Senate did therefore not renew Fabius' dictatorial powers at the end of his six-month term. Soon after, consuls Gaius Terentius Varro and Lucius Aemilius Paulus finally gave Hannibal the battle he had sought for so long, at Cannae.

The Romans had never before fielded such a large army. It easily outnumbered Hannibal's, which, at about 40,000 infantry and 10,000 cavalry, was massive in its own right (Polybius, 3.114). Some 80,000 Roman and allied infantry and 6,000 Roman and allied cavalry entered the battlefield near Cannae on August 2, 216 BCE (Polybius, 3.107.9-12). More than 75,000 of them would never leave it again.[13] Hannibal lost far less, about 5,500 infantry and 200 cavalry (Polybius, 3.117).

It remains the second biggest defeat in the long history of Rome, prolonging the Second Punic War by a decade. Military strategists still regard the *double envelopment* maneuver that Hannibal executed at the Battle of Cannae as one of the greatest battlefield maneuvers in history; it continues to be studied at military academies around the world.[14]

In the immediate aftermath of the battle Rome was in complete disarray. In less than two years, the Republic had lost a fifth of the total male population over seventeen years of age in battles against Hannibal (Cottrell, 148). Seeking to benefit from his strong position while also realizing he could not sustain himself on the Italian peninsula indefinitely, Hannibal sent the captured soldiers of Rome's allies home and allowed the captured Roman soldiers to ransom themselves at vary reasonable terms (Livy, 22.58). He sent ten Roman soldiers to the Senate after they had given their word they would return and had them accompanied by a Carthaginian nobleman, who could offer terms if the Romans were inclined to make peace (Livy, 22.58). Any other nation would have graciously accepted Hannibal's proposal and be more than a little relieved that the Carthaginian general favored making peace over waging more war, but not the Republic.

As Polybius wrote in his version of the events: *"they* [the Romans] *were so far from acceding to this request, that they did not allow their pity for their kinsmen, or the consideration of the service the men would render them, to prevail, but defeated Hannibal's calculation and the hopes he had based on them by refusing to ransom the men, and at the same time imposed by law on their own troops the duty of either conquering or dying in the field, as there was no hope of safety for them if defeated."* (Polybius, 6.58).

When the senate refused to pay the ransom for the 10,000 Roman prisoners, Hannibal instead sold them into slavery. According to Livy, 1,200 of them were bought and liberated by the Greeks in 194 BCE at the request of Titus Quinctius Flamininus, the Roman general responsible for establishing Roman hegemony over Greece (34.50).

Meanwhile, instead of licking its wounds and trying to come to an understanding, the Republic redoubled its efforts in search for total victory. It was characteristic for the Romans at the time, long before they would get fat, soft and complacent from the glut, peace and religion spread by the later emperors. In the days of the Republic, Romans did not give up, did not back down. The harder you hit them, the harder they came back. And so, instead of negotiating with their Carthaginian nemesis, the Senate declared full mobilization, conscripting every male capable of holding a sword, even slaves and criminals (Healy, 86).

Several new armies were forged from these new conscripts, to continue the fight against Hannibal in Italy and his brother Hasdrubal in Spain. The war in Spain was important, because the Senate realized only too well that the Carthaginians could not be allowed to control the Iberian Peninsula unopposed, as this would allow Hasdrubal to easily send troops, money and supplies to Hannibal (Polybius, 3.97).

The Spanish forces were commanded by the brothers Publius Cornelius Scipio and Gnaeus Cornelius Scipio. Between 218-211 BCE, the brothers succeeded in gaining a foothold in Spain and fighting Hasdrubal to a stalemate, but in 211 both brothers were killed in two separate battles,

fought only a few days apart (Livy, 25.34-36). Their job would be finished by Publius' son, also named Publius Cornelius Scipio and soon to become the most famous member of the family.

Two years after his father's death, Scipio captured the Carthaginian stronghold New Carthage, on the eastern coast of Spain (present-day Cartagena), and three years after that, in 206 BCE, he decisively defeated a large Carthaginian army at Ilipa, in southern Spain (about 10 miles from Seville), expelling the Carthaginians from the Iberian Peninsula altogether.

Next, he brought the battle to Africa, to confront the Carthaginians on their home turf, as Hannibal had been doing in Italy for over a decade. After Scipio had destroyed a large army of Carthaginian and allied Numidian forces, Hannibal was recalled to Africa, where he was subsequently defeated by Scipio himself, at the Battle of Zama (October 19, 202 BCE). In recognition of his monumental victory over Carthage, Scipio received the cognomen 'Africanus' upon his return to Rome — the first commander in chief to be honored with the name of the people he had conquered, according to Livy (30.45.6-7).

Carthage had lost for the second time and was crippled with a war indemnity of 10,000 talents, payable in fifty years, an even bigger sum than after the first war (Polybius, 15.8.7). The Carthaginians also had to surrender their entire fleet with the exception of ten triremes, all their elephants, all their prisoners of war and all the deserters that had fallen into their hands (Polybius, 15.8.3-4).[15] Finally — and almost certain a future casus belli — they were forbidden to make war on any nation outside Africa, and had to get Roman consent for any war inside Africa (Polybius, 15.18.4).

When it disobeyed this last condition some 50 years later by going to war with Numidia, Rome sent an army commanded by Scipio Aemilianus to Carthage, to teach the Carthaginians a third and final lesson.[16] In 146 BCE, after a three year siege, Scipio successfully assaulted the city of Ancient Carthage. The Greek historian Appian gives a hair-raising description of the final days of the proud 700-year-old city:

"Then came new scenes of horror. As the fire spread and carried everything down, the soldiers did not wait to destroy the buildings little by little, but all in a heap. So the crashing grew louder, and many corpses fell with the stones into the midst. Others were seen still living, especially old men, women, and young children who had hidden in the inmost nooks of the houses, some of them wounded, some more or less burned, and uttering piteous cries. Still others, thrust out and falling from such a height with the stones, timbers, and fire, were torn asunder in all shapes of horror, crushed and mangled." (Appian, "Punic Wars", 19.129).

Out of a city that once counted hundreds of thousands only 50,000 survived, who were sold into slavery while their city was burned to the ground (Appian, "Punic Wars", 19.130).[17] Thus the once great Carthaginian threat was forever nullified.

To the East, the Republic picked off the successor states that had taken over Alexander the Great's empire one by one. Macedonia, the Greek city-states, the Ptolemaic Kingdom (based in Egypt), even the Seleucid empire — which at the beginning of the 3rd century BCE had spanned more than 1.5 million square miles (3.9 million square kilometers) — were all put to Rome's heel.[18]

In the second half of the 2nd century BCE Rome had thus become the dominant civilization of the mediterranean. It was good to be a Roman citizen. More accurately, it was good to be a *rich* Roman citizen. Many people living within the Roman Republic lacked one or both of these characteristics, though. All those conquests in far away kingdoms and empires had brought treasure, slaves and new lands, greatly increasing the possessions of the Roman elite. But small farmers and workers suffered, because the slaves reduced the availability of paid work and the development of large farms in the conquered provinces made it hard for small-scale farmers to compete. This caused the wealth gap between the Plebeians — lower class citizens such as small farmers, shopkeepers, skilled and unskilled workers — and the Patricians — the Roman aristocracy — to grow.

And then there were the allied states on the Italian Peninsula, some of which had fought side by side with the Romans for centuries but whose people still did not have full citizenship.[19] Tensions were growing. Between rich and poor, plebeian and patrician, Rome and the allied states, even within the Senate, where the *Populares* pressed for land reforms and the expansion of citizenship to communities outside of Rome, while the *Optimates* wanted to keep things as they were.

In 133 BCE plebeian tribune Tiberius Gracchus was murdered, shortly after having succeeded in passing a law that enabled the redistribution of public land amongst tenant farmers.[20] It was the start of almost a century of social unrest and civil wars that would ultimately lead to the end of the Roman Republic and the beginning of the Roman Empire.

In 91 BCE, the so-called Social War broke out between Rome and the allied Italian states, over the thorny question of citizenship rights (Dillon, 481). The war lasted three years and was eventually won by the Republic, partly because it decided to grant citizenship to all the Italian states that had not revolted. According to the Roman historian Velleius Paterculus, the war cost the lives of 300,000 "*of the youth of Italy*" ("Roman History", II.15.3).

But a new conflict was already brewing, another civil war, this time between two Roman generals. The immediate cause was the appointment of Roman general Lucius Cornelius Sulla — a hero of the Social War who had recently been elected consul — as commander of the army that would fight King Mithridates VI of Pontus in Asia Minor, a position that had also been coveted by another powerful Roman general, Gaius Marius (Appian, "Civil Wars", I.55).

At 69, Marius was an old man, a fact apparently not just reflected by his physique but also by his hesitant actions on the battlefield during the Social War (Plutarch, "Marius", 33.1). But whatever his capabilities, his ambitions were as virile as ever, as was his power and influence. He was, after all, a giant of the Republic, who had successfully reformed the military and defeated several invading Germanic tribes, for which he had even been hailed as the Third

Founder of Rome (Plutarch, "Marius", 27.5). He had also served as consul an unprecedented six times.

After Sulla had already been given the command, Marius nevertheless persuaded a tribune of the Plebeian Council, Sulpicius, to propose a law that would offer the command in the Mithridatic war to him (Appian, "Civil Wars", I.55). When the two consuls (one of whom was Sulla) subsequently decreed a suspension of all public business to prevent voting on the law, Sulpicius — who according to Plutarch was *"second to none in prime villainies"* — sprang into action and sent armed men to the forum to force the consuls to annul the suspension, or otherwise kill them (Plutarch, "Sulla", 8.1-2).[21]

Both consuls initially fled the scene, but Sulla was captured and forced to rescind the suspension, after which Sulpicius succeeded in passing the law and Marius was chosen as commander in the war against Mithridates in place of Sulla (Appian, "Civil Wars", I.56).[22] After this, Sulla managed to flee the city and reach Nola, where his legions were encamped. When the 35,000 soldiers heard of the recent events they were outraged and eager to follow their general on a march back to the city (Plutarch, "Marius", 35.4, "Sulla", 9.3).[23]

Now it was Marius and his supporters who were forced to flee. Marius eventually ended up in North Africa, while Sulla — after enacting a series of constitutional reforms that strengthened the Roman aristocracy and the Senate — left for Asia Minor to fight Mithridatus (Appian, "Civil Wars" I.59, 64).[24]

With Sulla out of Rome and engaged in the East, Marius sensed an opportunity for a comeback. He raised an army, returned to the Italian Peninsula and marched his legions on Rome just as Sulla had done. Upon entering the city he immediately started exacting his revenge on Sulla's supporters, killing many (Appian, "Civil Wars", I.71-74). The Senate then appointed Marius consul for the seventh time and commander of the army in the East. But just seventeen days later, on January 13, 86 BCE, Marius, by then a confused, delusional man, died in his bed, aged 70 (Plutarch, "Marius", 45.5-7).

When Mithridates was defeated a few years later Sulla returned to Italy, landing at Brundisium in 83 BCE with five veteran legions and some other troops from Greece, about 40,000 men in total (Appian,

"Civil Wars", I.79). He was joined by the young commander Gnaeus Pompeius, who had brought three legions of his own with him.[25]

Several battles were fought between the Marian and the Sullan faction during the campaign season of 82, all won by Sulla (Appian, "Civil Wars", I.85-94). Finally, in November of that same year, a decisive confrontation between the two factions took place at Rome's Colline Gate. Starting late in the afternoon and continuing through the night, it was a bitter, chaotic battle that, according to Appian, cost the lives of 50,000 men ("Civil Wars", I.93). In the end it was Sulla who prevailed. Next, Sulla ordered the Senate to appoint a dictator *until such time as he should firmly re-establish the city and Italy and the government generally, shattered as it was by factions and wars,"* in other words for as long as that dictator would see fit (Appian, "Civil Wars", I.99). Unsurprisingly, the dictator the Senate subsequently elected was Sulla himself.

To further strengthen his position, Sulla then ordered the execution of thousands of Marians and many others whose only crime it was that they were the enemies of Sulla's supporters (Plutarch, "Sulla", 31-32). Among those on the hit lists was also one young Gaius Julius Caesar. After intervention from his relatives — many of whom were Sulla supporters — the dictator grudgingly agreed to spare sixteen-year-old Julius, but not before acidly remarking: *"Have your way and take him; only bear in mind that the man you are so eager to save will one day deal the death blow to the cause of the aristocracy, which you have joined with me in upholding; for in this Caesar there is more than one Marius."*(qtd. in Suetonius, "Julius Caesar", 1.3).

Sulla, who died in 78 BCE, aged 60, would turn out to be quite right about young Julius, but there would be plenty of unrest in the Republic in the years leading up to Caesar's legendary rise to power, with the Sertorian War (80-72 BCE), the Lepidus rebellion of 77 and the Catiline Conspiracy of 63.[26]

The Catiline Conspiracy was a plot designed by Senator Catiline to overthrow the Republic. Catiline was a member of one of the oldest patrician families of Rome, albeit one in decline. He enlisted the support of a number of other disaffected aristocrats of senatorial and equestrian rank, while at the same time finding favor with the

poor and unfortunate by promising the cancellation of all debts —
which he himself had collected a lot of — once he would come to
power (Sallust, 21.2). The conspiracy was exposed by then consul
Marcus Tullius Cicero, who forced Catiline to flee and had several
other leading conspirators put to death. Appian relates the story of
the Catiline Conspiracy at the beginning of book II of *The Civil Wars*
(II.2-7).

Caesar was also implicated in the Catiline Conspiracy (Sallust,
49). One reason for suspicion was that he was the only senator who
had passionately argued for mere imprisonment of Catiline's co-
conspirators, instead of putting them to death right away as many
other senators wanted (Plutarch, "Caesar", 7-8). In addition, Caesar
had fallen greatly into debt, giving him a motive for joining Catiline
(Sallust, 49).Two informers, both of whom were involved in the
conspiracy themselves, offered further proof for Caesar's involvement,
but Cicero still deemed it insufficient to arrest him (Suetonius, *Julius
Caesar*, 17.1).[27]

That same year Caesar was elected Pontifex Maximus and three
years after that he was elected consul for the year 59 BCE with the
help of two powerful men, Marcus Licinius Crassus and Gnaeus
Pompeius, the former the richest man in the Republic, the latter one
of its most famous generals.[28] Crassus and Pompey had shared the
consulship for the year 70 BCE — when Pompey had been just 35
years old — but they were also great rivals, accusing each other of
taking credit for things the other had accomplished.

Politically they shared many interests, though, something Caesar
handily used in bringing the three of them together in the unofficial
politico-military alliance known as the First Triumvirate (Appian,
"Civil Wars", II.9; Suetonius, "Julius Caesar", 19.2).[29] Aside from its
obvious primary goal of advancing the interests of its three members,
the Triumvirate pursued a Popularist political agenda, including
agrarian law reform that aimed to distribute public lands to the poor
and Pompey's veterans, which pitted it against a majority of the
Senate (Appian, "Civil Wars", II.10). Caesar's co- consul Marcus
Bibulus vehemently opposed the agrarian law reform, but after he
was violently driven from the forum by armed Caesarians he confined
himself to his house for the remainder of his term (Plutarch, "Caesar",

14.9). This caused the pundits of the day to mockingly speak of the consulship of "*Julius and Caesar*" (qtd. in Suetonius, "Julius Caesar", 20.2).

Caesar used his consulship to further increase his popularity. Aside from catering to the needs of the plebeians, he also released the equites — an aristocratic class below the patricians — from certain obligations to the state, which gained him powerful allies (Appian, "Civil Wars", II.13). Meanwhile, to further strengthen his alliance with Pompey, Caesar betrothed his daughter Julia to him, breaking of her engagement with another (Plutarch, "Caesar", 14.7).

After his consulship ended, Caesar was appointed governor of Illyricum and Cisalpine and Transalpine Gaul with the help of Crassus and Pompey, for a period of five years and with the command of four legions (Plutarch, "Caesar", 14.10; Appian, "Civil Wars", II.13).[30] And when, in 55 BCE, Pompey and Crassus served together as consuls again, they saw to it that Caesar's term as governor was extended by another five years (Suetonius, "Julius Caesar", 24.1).

Why did Caesar want Gaul? Because if he ever wanted to become the most powerful man in the Republic — and he most certainly did — he would need two things: money and glory. Crassus had the first, Pompey had both, he had neither.[31] But Gaul could get him both.

Much of Gaul was ruled by native Gallic tribes, but by seizing upon every opportunity for war — and if necessary creating one — Caesar conquered the whole of Gaul (roughly present-day France and Belgium) and even ventured into Britain during his nine years as governor there, firmly establishing his reputation as one of the greatest commanders in the history of the Republic (Suetonius, "Julius Caesar", 24-25).

Plutarch writes that Caesar, during his years in Gaul, "*took by storm more than eight hundred cities, subdued three hundred nations, and fought pitched battles at different times with three million men, of whom he slew one million in hand to hand fighting and took as many more prisoners*" ("Caesar", 15.5) and that as a soldier and commander he surpassed great men such as Fabius, Scipio, Sulla, Marius, "*even Pompey himself*" ("Caesar", 15.3-4). Suetonius, too, was clearly impressed with Caesar's conquest of Gaul, adding that he was able to exact a tribute of 40,000,000 sesterces on the newly acquired territories (Suetonius, "Julius Caesar", 25.1).

Meanwhile, though, dark clouds were gathering over the alliance between the three most powerful men of the Republic. In 54 BCE, Julia, Caesar's daughter and Pompey's wife, died in child birth, the baby surviving its mother only a few days (Plutarch, "Caesar", 23.5-6). With this, the only real bond between Pompey and Caesar was broken, and that at a time when Pompey was beginning to see more of a rival than an ally in the popular conquerer of Gaul. And when Crassus died a year later while campaigning in the East against the Parthian Empire, the Triumvirate was dead in more ways than one.

Caesar tried to restore the bond with Pompey by offering him his niece Octavia in marriage — even though she was already married — but Pompey declined and married someone else.[32] Not long after, Rome was in uproar after the murder of the famous popularist tribune Publius Clodius. To restore order, the Senate decided to elect only one consul for the year 52 BCE, Pompey (Suetonius, "Julius Caesar", 26.1).

One of the first laws Pompey passed — supposedly to end public disorder — allowed each citizen to bring charges of corruption against anyone who had held public office in the past twenty years (Appian, "Civil Wars", 23). This would make Caesar vulnerable to prosecution as soon as he was a private citizen again — and he had many enemies in the Senate. Realizing this only too well, Caesar tried to get an extension on the term of his governorship of Gaul, but the new consul, an *Optimate* and staunch supporter of Pompey, refused (Appian, "Civil Wars", 25).

The next year (50 BCE), Caesar's term as governor was ending, but by now he did not want to give up his legions — which were attached to his governorship — unless Pompey would do the same. The vast majority of the Senate opposed this, though, and instead moved to declare Caesar a public enemy if he did not lay down his arms by a fixed date (Plutarch, "Caesar", 30.4-6).

In a last attempt to stave off civil war between two of the greatest generals Rome had ever known, Cicero tried to reconcile both parties by letting Caesar keep his governorship and a few thousand soldiers until he stood for his second consulship (Plutarch, "Caesar", 31). Pompey was ready to accept this, but one of the consuls for the year 49 BCE, Lucius Lentulus — another opponent of Caesar — blocked it (Plutarch, "Caesar", 31). The Senate instead issued a final decree (*Senatus consultum ultimum*), which put the Republic in a state of martial law and handed limitless — if temporary — power to the consuls (Caesar, "Civil Wars", I.5).

The time for negotiating was over. A few days later, Caesar arrived at the Rubicon river, the southeastern border between his province Cisalpine Gaul and Italy proper (about 60 miles southeast of Bologna and 200 miles north of Rome). Beyond it, his *imperium*, his right to command, ceased, and leading soldiers without proper imperium was forbidden on pain of death, for the defiant general as well as his men. The river thus constituted a clear point of no return. Beyond it lay years of civil war, before it......

Caesar hesitated. Was there anything left to save from *this* side of the river? Did he still have options besides the highly uncertain gamble of civil war? Options that would not mean the end of his political career, land him in prison, or worse, if they didn't work out? But he knew there weren't. Too many in the Senate smelled blood in the water and would settle for nothing less than his destruction. They had hated the alliance between Crassus, Pompey and himself and were only too glad that Crassus was dead and Pompey had proved susceptible to the Optimates' cause — if only out of fear of being upstaged by the conquerer of Gaul. And now they had Caesar exactly where they wanted him: out of options. Well then, he would not disappoint them.[33]

And so, on January 10, 49 BCE, after speaking the famous words "*Alea iacta est*" ('the die is cast'), Caesar led a single legion — the Thirteenth — across the Rubicon (Plutarch, "Caesar", 32.8; Suetonius, "Julius Caesar", 32).[34]

Four years and several battles later Caesar stood victorious. He had already been proclaimed dictator for ten consecutive years, but in 44 BCE all pretense of temporality was done away with and Caesar had himself appointed dictator for life (Plutarch, "Caesar", 57.1; Suetonius, "Julius Caesar", 76.1).[35] He would not be allowed to enjoy it for long though, because on March 15, 44 BCE, Caesar was assassinated on the Senate floor by some 60 Senators, led by Marcus Junius Brutus, who together stabbed him 23 times (Suetonius, "Julius Caesar", 80.4, 82; Plutarch, "Caesar", 66.6-14).

Soon after Caesar's assassination, his friend Marc Antony, who had served him as general during the Gallic Wars and had been elected consul beside him for the year 44, took steps to inherit his political power as well as his property. This brought Antony in conflict with Caesar's eighteen-year- old nephew Octavian, whom Caesar had appointed as his heir not long before his death (Dio, 44.53.1-5).

Antony also came in conflict with the Senate, when it refused to award him the governorship of Cisalpine Gaul after the end of his term as consul, giving him Macedonia instead, from where it would be much more difficult to exercise control over the political affairs in Italy (Appian, "Civil Wars", III.27). Refusing to take no for an answer, Antony subsequently marched with an army to besiege Mutina (modern Modena, northern Italy), where the appointed governor of Cisalpine Gaul, Decimus Brutus, one of Caesar's murderers, had confined himself (Appian, "Civil Wars", III.49). When Antony would not relent, the Senate declared him a public enemy and sent the two new consuls and Octavian — whose popularity was on the rise — to deal with the renegade (Appian, "Civil Wars", III.63; Dio, 29.4-6).

In the subsequent Battle of Mutina (April 43 BCE), the Republican forces defeated Marc Antony, but not decisively enough to neutralize him as a threat. With both consuls slain in battle, Octavian hoped the Senate would now appoint him consul, but the Senate instead ceased upon the moment to try and further weaken the Caesarian faction and outmaneuver Octavian (Dio, 46.40.1-4).

But this Caesar had inherited more than just name and property from his famous great-uncle, because in addition to possessing political acumen, Octavian, though still a teenager, also quickly proved himself an inspiring military commander, capable of rallying soldiers to his cause in much the same fashion as his adopted father had done before him, as became evident when he marched his eight legions to Rome in the Summer of 43 BCE to show the Senate who was boss (Appian, "Civil Wars", III.88).[36] When he arrived at the Quirinal hill northeast of the city, many citizens came out to greet him and the three Republican legions that were supposed to defend the city defected to him (Appian, "Civil Wars", III.92). Soon after, Octavian was elected consul, together with another, whom he had preferred as his colleague (Appian, "Civil Wars", III.94).

Now in control of Rome, Octavian made overtures towards Antony and Marcus Aemilius Lepidus — the governor of Hispania and Narbonese Gaul, who had already aligned himself with Antony — to form an alliance against Marcus Junius Brutus and Gaius Cassius Longinus.[37] Brutus and Cassius, two of the leading conspirators against Julius Caesar, controlled Rome's eastern territories and had a force of some twenty legions (Appian, "Civil Wars", IV.1-2).

Octavian, Antony and Lepidus agreed to give Antony the whole of Gaul except Narbonese Gaul, which, together with Spain, was given to Lepidus, while Octavian received Africa (Appian, "Civil Wars", IV.2). Italy proper was ruled collectively.

The first order of business for this Second Triumvirate was to fill the empty Treasury, the second to defeat Brutus and Cassius. To deal with the first, the triumvirs took a leaf from Sulla's book, who had proscribed thousands of citizens in 82 BCE, thus not only killing many enemies but also having their property fall to the state. According to Appian, the three triumvirs had about 300 senators sentenced to death and some 2,000 equites, with all of their property confiscated by the state ("Civil Wars", IV.5).[38]

Next, they marched for Brutus and Cassius, who, with an army of nineteen legions, had taken up position close to the ancient city of Philippi, in eastern Macedonia, on two hills on either side of the Via Egnatia (Appian "Civil Wars", IV.88).[39] There, on October 3, 42 BCE, the forces of Antony clashed with those of Cassius, while Octavian's army engaged that of Brutus. Antony succeeded in routing the forces of Cassius, who, believing Brutus had also lost against Octavian, then ordered his shield-bearer to kill him (Appian "Civil Wars", IV.113). Had he waited just a while longer, he would have found out that Brutus had not been beaten but on the contrary had routed Octavian's forces, making the battle a draw.

Both sides regrouped. Brutus held on to his excellent defensive position on the hill and was well- stocked for a prolonged siege, but Antony and Octavian's forces were by now desperately in need of supplies (Appian, "Civil Wars", IV.123). Well aware of this, Brutus had no intention of giving battle, but his soldiers, who still had the taste of victory in their mouth from defeating Octavian's forces and plundering his camp, were eager to attack. When the officers joined in and also urged Brutus to attack as long as the men were still hungry for battle, he finally yielded, lamenting *"I seem likely to carry on war like Pompey the Great, not so much commanding now as commanded."* (Appian, "Civil Wars", IV.124). His fate would also be much the same as Pompey's. Brutus lost the battle and subsequently fled to the mountains with four legions. When the officers of the remaining legions told him they would no longer follow him in battle, Brutus committed suicide (Appian, "Civil Wars", IV.131).

Although victorious, the Second Triumvirate, like the first one, would not last long. Following their victory, Antony and Octavian divided all the provinces amongst themselves, taking those of Lepidus as well, on some trumped-up charge from Octavian that Lepidus had betrayed the affairs of the triumvirate to Sextus Pompey (son of Pompey Magnus), the last of the opposition, who was in control of Sicily (Appian, "Civil Wars", V.3).

Having divided the spoils, relations between Antony and Octavian quickly deteriorated as well, though, and two years later open hostilities broke out between them at the port city of Brundisium, in southern Italy. But neither side was looking forward to a prolonged war with an equally matched enemy and when Antony's wife Fulvia unexpectedly died, the two rivals used it as an excuse to come to terms (Dio, 48.28.2-3).

They agreed for Antony to have control over the East and Octavian over the West, while Lepidus was allowed control over the African territories (Appian, "Civil Wars", V.65). Another few years later Octavian managed to push out Lepidus entirely, and then there were only two.

Meanwhile, the enmity between Octavian and Marc Antony continued to grow. Though now married to Octavian's sister Octavia, with whom he also had two daughters, Antony struck up an affair with Cleopatra, the Queen of Egypt (and Julius Caesar's former lover) as well, siring three children with her.

When Octavian gained access to Antony's will and found out that Antony left his children by Cleopatra large bequests and requested to be buried in Alexandria, he used this to convince the Senate to declare war on Cleopatra, in 32 BCE (Dio, 50.3-4).

It would not be a long war. After a naval battle at Actium (northwestern Greece) that went spectacularly bad for Antony and an equally disastrous land battle at Alexandria, Antony withdrew into the city with Cleopatra (Dio, 50.32-35, 51.10.1-5). Realizing all was lost, Antony committed suicide by falling on his sword, after good Roman tradition (Dio, 51.10.7). Cleopatra killed herself a couple of days later, when she realized — after first having fruitlessly tried to beguile Octavian as she had Julius Caesar and Antony — that this Caesar was only interested in parading her at his triumph back in Rome (Dio, 51.13).

Thus ended the final war of the Roman Republic and, within a few years, also the Republic itself. In 27 BCE, the Senate gave Octavian the titles of *Augustus* ('venerable'), and *Princeps* ('first citizen'). In the years that followed he consolidated his position as de facto emperor, though he remained mindful of the existing constitutional principles.

Augustus proved himself a great emperor, the 40 years of his long rule marking the beginning of the so-called *Pax Romana*, a period of relative peace and prosperity throughout the empire that would last more than 200 years. Augustus also greatly increased Rome's territories —annexing Egypt and several other regions, completing the conquest of Hispania and moving into Germania — made peace with the Parthian empire and established a standing army that consisted exclusively of professional soldiers, thus increasing the stability of the military.[40]

In 117 CE, during the reign of Trajan — another great emperor — the empire would reach its zenith in terms of size.[41] Around that time, an estimated 70 million people lived and died under Roman reign, a huge population for that time (Scheidel, "Roman Empire").

Yes, Augustus and Trajan were great emperors. The problem with emperors and other absolute rulers, though, is that they are almost never like Augustus or Trajan. In fact, most of them are barely suited to run the local pet store, let alone an empire. And those aren't even the worst ones, the certifiably crazy ones — the psychopaths, the megalomaniacs, the borderliners.

Like emperor Nero, who burned Rome to clear land for his grand palatial complex (Dio, 62.16.1-2). Or emperor Commodus, who once rounded up all the men in the city who had lost their feet, fastened some dragon-like extremities about their knees, gave them sponges to throw instead of stones and then clubbed them all to death, pretending they were giants (Dio, 73.20.3). Putting the average megalomaniac to shame, Commodus also ordered the city of Rome to be renamed *Commodiana* and the legions *Commodian* (Dio, 73.15.2). And if you think *that's* cruel and crazy, how about emperor Caligula, who once even went so far as ordering his guards to throw people from the crowd in the arena to the wild beasts, because there weren't enough condemned criminals to feed them (Dio, 59,10.3).

Caligula was also the first emperor who was assassinated, though he certainly wouldn't be the last. In fact, of the 118 Roman emperors who ruled between 14 and 797 CE — some of them only in either the Western or Eastern Empire — 27 were assassinated, 11 were deposed and executed, 9 were killed in battle, 6 committed suicide, 4 were poisoned, 3 were captured and executed, another 3 were mutilated and 1 was stoned to death by a Roman mob. A staggering 54 percent! Clearly Roman emperor was not a very safe profession.

During the 3rd century, the Roman empire faced a crisis not unlike the last 100 years of the Republic. It was marked by civil unrest, the temporary splitting up of the empire into three competing states, a parade of unremarkable emperors reigning for only a short period of time, invasions from foreign tribes and economic depression. But the 44th Emperor, Aurelian — another great emperor — reunited the empire during his short reign and beat back all the foreign tribes, before being assassinated in 275. All was well again. Until the late 4th century.

Constantine the Great (272-337) had been the first emperor to convert to Christianity himself (on his deathbed) but it was Emperor

Theodosius I who in 380 made Christianity the state religion. It has been contended — perhaps most notably by the English historian Edward Gibbon — that the real death sentence for the Roman Empire was Christianity, as it made the Romans less warlike and more peace loving.[42] It certainly made them less tolerant of pagan practices as well, though, thereby increasing tensions within the empire.

Around the same time, Gothic tribes were pushed westward by the invading Huns. In 376, a large group of Goths, many of them warriors, arrived on the Danube River in the eastern Balkans and requested asylum in the Roman Empire. Emperor Valens, thinking he could certainly use more warriors in his war against the Sasanian Empire (a.k.a. Neo-Persian Empire) graciously granted the request.[43]

The new arrivals were temporarily settled along the south bank of the Danube River, in the Roman province of Moesia. Providing food for all those new immigrants proved difficult, though, and before long the Goths revolted (Heather, 163).

At the subsequent Battle of Adrianople, in 378, the Romans were decisively defeated and Emperor Valens was killed. The defeat showed the Roman Empire had weakened so much that it could no longer defend its territory even against barbarians within its own borders. It would prove to be the beginning of the end, even though Valens' successor Gratian, together with Theodosius I, eventually managed to make peace with the Goths four years later.

In the decades that followed, the Western Empire would be plagued by many more barbarian invasions, until in 476, Romulus Augustus, the last Roman emperor of the Western Empire, was deposed by the German military leader Odoacer.

Though the Eastern Empire would continue to exist for almost 1,000 years, it would never again rival the greatness of the Roman Empire of the first centuries, instead growing weaker and weaker, smaller and smaller, year after year, century after century, until on May 29, 1453, its capital Constantinople finally fell.

The Roman Empire was gone.

---

[1] [1] The work in which Varro laid out the year-by-year chronology of Roman history up to his own time, his 'Chronicles' (*Annales*), has not survived. The

correctness of his chronology has been disputed but is nevertheless still widely in use. For an explanation of the Varronian chronology and its errors, see *The Cambridge Ancient History* (348-350).

2 Almost 500 years later, a descendent of Lucius Brutus, Marcus Brutus, would be the most famous of Julius Caesar's assassins. Caesar had had himself proclaimed *Dictator perpetuo* ('dictator in perpetuity') in 44 BCE — thus effectively ending the Republic founded by the elder Brutus — but was killed only weeks later by a group of senators that included Marcus Brutus.

3 The word republic is derived from *Res Publica,* meaning 'public matter', to signify that the government of the city was a matter for all citizens.

4 The Roman manipular system organized the infantry into three lines, the *hastati* (120 each), the *principes* (120 each) and the *triarii* (60 each). The hastati, made up of young, inexperienced soldiers, were put in front. Behind them were the more seasoned principes, men in the prime of their life. And finally the triarii, made up of veteran soldiers. The triarii acted as a last resort, a function captured by the saying *"ad triarios redisse"* ("it has come to the triarii").

5 The Samnite Wars were fought between 343-290 BCE.

6 The Romans called the Carthaginians *Punici,* a derivative from *Phoenici,* which referred to the Carthaginians' Phoenician ancestry, hence 'Punic wars'.

7 The Talent was an ancient unit of mass. A Roman talent weighed 71 pounds (32 kilograms), so 5,000 talents of silver would come to 355,000 pounds of silver, or 160,000 kilograms.

8 Interestingly, Hannibal was the son of Hamilcar Barca, who had been commander of the Sicilian forces during the First Punic War.

9 Polybius does not actually specify with how many elephants Hannibal crossed the Pyrenees, but does mention (at 3.42.11) how Hannibal had difficulty crossing the French river Rhone with his elephants, *"thirty-seven in number".*

10 Polybius writes that Hannibal himself had inscribed the total number of troops with which he entered Italy on a column at Lacinium (3.56.4).

11 The Roman Senate traditionally resorted to the measure of appointing an all-powerful dictator for a short period of time in case of an extreme situation.

12 The strategy would come to be known as the Fabian Strategy and far outlive its namesake. For instance, some 2,000 years after Fabius' dealings with Hannibal, the Russians would use the exact same strategy against another great general, Napoleon Bonaparte, thereby forcing him to abandon his plan of conquering Russia for the French Empire.

13 Polybius writes that of the infantry about 10,000 were captured while 70,000 died on the battlefield; of the cavalry, less than 500 of the 6,000 cavalry managed to escape the carnage (3.117).

14 The *double envelopment* is a tactical maneuver that draws in the opposing army to the center, while simultaneous flanking movements push the opponent's

flanks to the center as well. If both flanks are able to link up in the opponent's rear, the enemy is encircled. The maneuver is considered risky even when operating with superiority in numbers. When outnumbered — as Hannibal was — it requires exceptional commanding skills to execute successfully.

15 Livy writes that all the deserters belonging to the Latin contingents were beheaded, while the Roman deserters were crucified (30.43.13).

16 Scipio Aemilianus was the younger son of Lucius Aemilius Paulus Macedonicus, the conquerer of Macedon, whose father was the consul who had been defeated and killed in the Battle of Cannae. Scipio Aemilianus was also the adopted son of Publius Cornelius Scipio, the eldest son of Scipio Africanus, which is why he is also known als Sciptio Africanus the Younger.

17 Ancient sources estimated Carthage's population at 700,000, but most modern historians consider this an exaggeration and arrive at estimations between 125,000-250,000 (Walbank, 502).

18 The Seleucid Empire (312-63 BCE), the largest successor state, was founded by Seleucus I Nicator, who had served as an infantry general under Alexander the Great. At one point, the empire included most of the eastern part of Alexander the Great's empire, but when Seleucid Emperor Antiochus III tried to establish a foothold in Greece in 192 BCE he found the Romans on his path. One hundred and thirty years later the Roman commander Pompey made the once vast empire into a Roman province.

19 Because the allied states did not have full citizenship rights, they had little autonomy in governing their local affairs, even though they contributed significant numbers of soldiers to the Roman army.

20 The main goal of the *Lex Sempronia Agraria* was to end the practice of large landowners owning large swaths of public land, worked on by slaves, while a growing group of landless citizens was declining into poverty little by little (Appian, "Civil Wars", 1.1.9). The new law caused great unrest among the rich, whose fortunes were tied to their large landholdings. It was not passed without controversy, though. During the procedure to pass the law in the Plebeian Council, one tribune, Marcus Octavius, remained resolutely against the new law and continued to veto it, as was his right (Appian, "Civil Wars", 1.1.12). Gracchus then had him voted out of office by the other tribunes, though this was unconstitutional under Roman law (Appian, "Civil Wars", 1.1.12). Another person was subsquently elected tribune in Marcus Octavius' place, after which the law was passed without further problems ((Appian, "Civil Wars", 1.1.12), 1.1.13).

21 Plutarch further writes about Sulpicius that "*he maintained three thousand swordsmen, and had about him a body of young men of the equestrian order who were ready for everything, and whom he called his anti-senate. Further, though he got a law passed that no senator should incur a debt of more than two thousand drachmas, he himself left behind him after death a debt of three millions.*" ("Sulla", 8.2).

22 Plutarch states that the other consul, Quintus Pompeius Rufus, managed to escape unnoticed, but that Sulla was pursued into the house of Marius and was forced to come out and rescind the decree ("Sulla", 8.3). Appian makes no mention of this.

23 Sulla was the first Roman general to cross the city limits with his army, an act strongly forbidden and considered highly unethical. He would not be the last.

24 Among Sulla's most important reforms were the restoration of *patrum auctoritas* ("authority of the fathers") and of the Servian organization of the Centuriate Assembly. *Patrum auctoritas* required approval of the Senate for any law passed by one of the legislative assemblies — be it the Centuriate Assembly, the Tribal Assembly or the Plebeian Council — while the return to the Servian organization of the Centuriate Assembly restored the power of the wealthier Centuries in the Assembly. Appian writes that both measures were aimed at having the voting controlled "*by the well-to-do and sober-minded rather than by the pauper and reckless classes*" (Appian, I.59).

25 This was the same Gnaeus Pompeius (a.k.a. Pompey) who would later enter into the military-political alliance known as the First Triumvirate with Marcus Licinius Crassus and Gaius Julius Caesar. After the death of Crassus in 53 BCE ended the First Triumvirate, Pompey and Caesar fought a civil war over control of Rome, which effectively ended with Pompey's decisive defeat at the Battle of Pharsalus, on August 9, 48 BCE. Pompey then fled to Egypt, where he was assassinated less than two months later.

26 There is discussion on the exact years the Sertorian War — a conflict fought in Spain between supporters and opponents of Sulla — took place, see *Lucullus: A Life* (Keaveney, 275ff.). The Lepidus rebellion revolved around consul Marcus Aemilius Lepidus (120 BC-77 BC), who after the death of Sulla tried to reverse the Sullan constitution with measures favored by the *Populares*. He was defeated in battle by his rival, the other consul, Quintus Catulus (Appian, "Civil Wars", I.107).

27 Both Appian and Plutarch suggest that Cicero refrained from acting against Caesar because of the latter's popularity (Appian, "Civil Wars", II.6; Plutarch, "Caesar", 8.4-5). Plutarch adds that Cicero was later blamed for not having removed Caesar when he had the chance ("Caesar", 8.4).

28 Pompey had helped Sulla win his second civil war, successfully fought Marian supporter Quintus Sertorius in Spain and conquered the Kingdom of Pontus in the third and final Mithridatic War.

29 The alliance was not called Triumvirate at the time, but, according to Appian, Varro did write a book about the alliance entitled *Tricaranus*, i.e., the three-headed-monster ("Civil Wars", II.9).

30 Illyricum was a Roman province in southeastern Europe, partly located in present-day Albania. Cisalpine Gaul was a province in northern Italy, Transalpine Gaul lay in southern France.

31 In fact, Caesar was still heavily indebted after his consulship. According to Plutarch, Caesar spent vast amounts of money to curry favor with people and increase his changes of being awarded with public offices ("Caesar", 5). Suetonius writes that Caesar was very good to both his officers and the gentry of the provinces he ruled, but also gives examples of Caesar's sheer profligacy ("Julius Caesar", 46-48).

32 Octavia's brother, Octavian, would later become the first Roman Emperor, Augustus.

33 Both Plutarch and Suetonius mention Caesar contemplated his situation before actually crossing the Rubicon (Plutarch, "Caesar", 32.5-7, Suetonius, "Julius Caesar", 31-32). Caesar himself does not mention it in his *Civil Wars*.

34 Interestingly, Caesar himself does not mention crossing the Rubicon in his work *Civil Wars*. But he does mention being in Ravenna, addressing the soldiers of the Thirteenth Legion and then setting out for and reaching Ariminum, modern Rimini ("Civil Wars", I.5-8). Since the only way to travel from Ravenna to Ariminum was by crossing the Rubicon, there is no doubt Caesar did in fact cross it.

35 Caesar had first been made dictator by the Senate in 49, but after only eleven days he had laid down the office and appointed himself consul instead, together with another (Appian, *Civil Wars*, II.48.1). He was again named dictator by the Senate for the year 47 - the first time a dictatorship was granted for a full year instead of the traditional six months (Plutarch, *Caesar*, 51.1) - and the following year for ten consecutive years (Dio, 43.14.4)

36 Octavian assumed his great-uncle's name upon his posthumous adoption by Gaius Julius Caesar, but for the sake of clarity I keep referring to him as Octavian. Contemporary historians did refer to him as 'Caesar', though.

37 This Marcus Aemilius Lepidus — an ally of Julius Caesar — was the son of the Marcus Aemilius Lepidus who had been consul in 78 and led a rebellion in 77, trying to undo much of the Sulla's measures. Interestingly, Lepidus' fellow rebel, Marcus Junius Brutus the Elder, was the father of the Marcus Junius Brutus who had conspired against Caesar and would lead the main opposition against the Second Triumvirate of Octavian, Antony and Lepidus the Younger.

38 Contrary to Appian, Cassius Dio does not mention an exact number, but from his description of the events it is clear there must have been many victims (Dio, 47.3-13). Dio does say that the proscriptions were chiefly committed by Lepidus and Antony, because, "*as they had been holding offices and governorships for a long time they had many enemies*" (47.7). One of the most prominent victims of the proscription of the Second Triumvirate was Marcus Tullius Cicero.

39 The Via Egnatia was the main road from the Roman province of Illyricum (present-day Albania) to the city of Byzantium, the later Constantinople (present-day Istanbul).

40 Augustus was also the one who set up the famous Praetorian Guard, charged

with protecting the emperor.

41 1.93 million square miles, or 5 million square kilometers (Turchin, "Historical Empires", table 1).

42 In his *History of the Decline and Fall of the Roman Empire*, Edward Gibbon writes: "*As the happiness of a future life is the great object of religion, we may hear without surprise or scandal, that the introduction or at least the abuse, of Christianity had some influence on the decline and fall of the Roman empire. The clergy successfully preached the doctrines of patience and pusillanimity: the active virtues of society were discouraged; and the last remains of military spirit were buried in the cloister*" (Gibbon, 507).

43 Not all historians agree that Emperor Valens was happy with the arrival of the Goths. Late Antiquity historian Peter Heather, for instance, argues that given the fact that the Roman army in the region was too small to be militarily in control of the new situation — most troops were being deployed in the war against the Persians in the East — Valens could not have been too happy with the arrival of a band of unruly barbarians to his rear, though he probably still hoped to use them to his advantage and enlist the Gothic warriors to fight the Persian nemesis (Heather, 161).

9

WHEN IN ROME

"I've stood upon Achilles' tomb, And heard
Troy doubted: time will doubt of Rome"[1]
Lord Byron (1788-1824)

Most people tend to think civilization will be much more advanced a thousand years from now. That posterity will criticize us for putting criminals in jail, polluting the environment and allowing poverty to exist in a world of plenty. But what if it will be the other way around?

What if, a thousand years from now, posterity will discover books filled with advanced knowledge and ancient wisdom that had long been forgotten, marvel at the uncovered ruins of vast cities connected by a dense network of roads made of some kind of super smooth stone, and gawk at the remains of an impressive structure called 'The Pentagon', a building that apparently served as some sort of defense center.

Think that's impossible? Then consider for a moment what the world would look like a thousand years from now if nuclear war broke out within the next hundred years or so.

When the Europeans rediscovered Classical antiquity in the 14th century, they realized that although ancient Rome was a civilization that had disappeared from Western Europe almost a thousand years ago, it was still far more advanced than their own respective societies.[2]

The city of Rome, for instance, had reached a population of more than a million people during the 1st century CE, a city size that would not be seen again until the 1800s, when London finally reached the same milestone (Modelski, 49-50). Most citizens lived in one of the 40,000 *insulae*, apartment blocks that could be several stories tall. Only the most wealthy citizens of Rome were able to afford a *domus* on the Palatine Hill, complete with marble-floored pool, beautiful frescos, elegant columns, colored mosaics, expensive paintings, inspiring statues and a small army of slaves to make sure everything went smoothly for the masters.[3]

To keep the plebeians happy (and prevent them from raiding Palatine Hill) the state provided lots of games and festivities. Rome's *Circus Maximus* for instance, a massive entertainment venue and racing stadium whose origins date back to the 6th century BCE, when Rome was still a kingdom, could house 150,000 spectators by the time of the late Republic — more than the entire population of early 13th century Paris (Humphrey, 126). The *Colosseum*, Rome's amphitheater, could accommodate ca. 50,000 (Welch, 131). It is still there. Visit it on a quiet hour, listen closely and hear the war cries of gladiators in the fight of their lives, their swords clashing, their shields catching blows as the crowd roars and cheers, waiting for their favorite fighter to deal the deathly blow to his unfortunate opponent.

Opposite all this blood and gore stood the beauty and sophistication of Greek culture, which had slowly but certainly been making its way into Roman life since even before the dawn of the Republic, by first influencing the Etruscans, who in turn had influenced the Romans and many of the other tribes on the Italian Peninsula that Rome would come to dominate.[4]

In many ways, the Greeks were everything the Romans were not: artistic, literate, philosophical, sophisticated and susceptible to all the pleasures life had to offer, while the early Romans were little more than stubborn, hardworking farmers who lived a sober life. They scorned Greek softness, but at the same time were also drawn to it.

After the Roman conquest of Greece in the 2nd century BCE, Greek influence on Roman culture further increased, with Greek teachers, artists, architects and scientists coming to Rome and enriching Roman culture with philosophy, science, poetry, plays, architecture, sculptures and, last but not least, manners. Soon, the spread of Greco-Roman culture, with its love for fine food, sophistication, art and soft manners, was unstoppable, criticism on Greek decadence by some Roman conservatives notwithstanding.[5]

Another part of Roman civilization that would remain unrivaled until the 1800s was its infrastructure. Stone-paved roads — twenty-nine of which started in the city of Rome itself — connected all the important parts of the empire. Covered with a layer of concrete — a material that would not be used in Europe after the disappearance of the Roman Empire for almost a thousand years — the roads provided the legions with a smooth means of transportation. In all, Roman public highways ran for more than 50,000 miles and were so reliable and strong that they were used until the 18th century.[6] The same goes for the many stone and concrete bridges the Romans built, the first bridges that lasted beyond a couple of decades.

The public highways were paid for by the state, and with good reason, because the Romans quickly discovered that to expand — and defend — their territory, they needed a mobile army and efficient supply lines. And while simple dirt roads might be sufficient for trade routes in far away provinces, they would not be for thousands of marching soldiers and their baggage train, not to mention the continuous supplies all those soldiers needed. They needed roads that would last.

And last they did. In fact, part of the Via Appia, one of Rome's oldest roads — started by censor Appius Claudius Caecus in 312 BCE, to help supply the Roman army in its war with the Samnites — is still being used today, the only difference being that buses, cars and tourists have supplanted the chariots, carts and marching legions (Gabriel, 228).[7]

The roads were not just for the military, civilians could use them too, though not entirely free of charge; toll gates were often present at city gates and important bridges (Tilburg, 87). Other public services and works were completely free, such as public baths, fountains, flush toilets and running water (After the collapse of the Roman Empire it would take until the Industrial Revolution before Europeans would hear a toilet flush again).

It was in no small measure thanks to a strong, centralized state, that all these major public works were possible. Just imagine what an organization it must have been to construct the nine aqueducts — measuring around 260 miles (420 km) in total — that provided the city of Rome with roughly 569,000 Cubic meter (150 million US liquid gallon) of water each day by the first century CE.[8] Or how about the aqueducts that delivered water to Constantinople, the capital of the Eastern Empire; they ran for 220 miles (335 km) and started 74 miles (120 km) away from the city.

Being located in a violent region that was home to many competing tribes and cities, Rome had needed a strong state from the beginning. In the early days, many Roman citizens were both farmers and soldiers, paying for their own military equipment and serving on several campaigns during their lifetime. Every able-bodied man needed to pitch in to help Rome survive, by making it stronger and better. With its territory expanding decade after decade, century after century, its roads kept growing too, as did the number of active legions, the number of military outposts that needed to be connected to the highway system and the number of city dwellers that needed to be fed and entertained. A strong, centralized state was therefore essential not only for the Republic's expansion but also for its consolidation in later centuries.

Every male citizen of Rome could play a part in its government, by voting or standing for public office, though some positions (and initially all of them) were reserved for the patricians, the Roman aristocracy, whose members were descendants of the first 100 senators of Rome (Livy, I.8). The vote of a patrician also weighed more than that of a plebeian. Then again, just being able to vote at all was already considered a privilege; it would take centuries before people from outside Rome would be granted citizenship rights that allowed them to vote.[9]

Roman society was divided into several classes, some of which overlapped. There was the division between patricians and plebeians of course, but it didn't stop there. Citizens were also divided by property; the more property, the more rights and privileges. During the first centuries of the Republic, for instance, a minimum amount of property was needed to qualify for the military, something which improved one's social status. These property qualifications were gradually reduced, as Rome needed more and more soldiers to fight its wars and secure its rapidly growing borders. Finally, in 107 BCE, Consul Gaius Marius abolished the qualifications altogether.[10]

Below the citizens of Rome were those of the allied states, who did not have the right to vote — at least not until the Social War of 91-88 BCE led to Roman citizenship for those who had not taken up arms against Rome — but who did enjoy some other privileges (and duties). Then came freed men, and finally, all the way at the bottom, the slaves, who were considered property and therefore had no rights at all. Women could be citizens, but did not have the right to vote, nor were they allowed to stand for public office.

Even clothing was dependent on class. Poor plebeians wore tunics from rough, dark cloth, while patricians wore ones made of linen or white wool. A senator could be recognized by the purple stripe on his tunic, while military tunics were somewhat shorter than the civilian ones. The toga, a heavy, bulky garment, draped around the body and over the shoulder, was worn over the tunic. Made of wool, it was usually white, but depending on one's social status and public function, there were also purple-striped and solid purple variants. The toga was thus much more than a — rather uncomfortable — piece of clothing; it was a statement, a uniform, depicting the wearer's position in life, the office he held. Some togas were reserved for a specific occasion, such as the *toga picta*, which was purple with gold embroidery and only worn by a general on his triumph (Edmondson, 219).

Women wore a long tunic called a *stola*, a garment that was usually brightly colored because Romans loved lively, active colors. In colder weather, a thick woolen mantle called a *palla* was worn over the stola. And of course there were all kinds of accessories to further improve appearances and accentuate social status, such as brooches, armlets, anklets, necklaces and breast chains.

Food and drink were more related to money than to class, though the two often went hand in hand. The staple foods of the lower classes were porridge and bread, with the occasional fish, some meat, olives and fruit. Rich Romans had much more elaborate dinners, with different kinds of fish and meat. Both rich and poor Romans ate with their fingers, while women and children ate separately from the men until the later centuries of the Empire. The usual drink for Romans rich and poor was wine, but always mixed with water. Roman men probably drank about one liter of wine per day, women half a liter. And although drinking pure wine was viewed as a sure sign of alcoholism, that didn't stop famous alcoholics like Mark Antony, Cato the Younger and emperor Tiberius Claudius Nero from being regularly inebriated (Plutarch, "Antony", 9; "Cato", 6). The latter was even nicknamed *Biberius Caldius Mero,* a play on his name expressing his love for wine, by his troops (Suetonius, "Tiberius", 42).[11]

Though food did not play a very important role in the life of poorer Romans, religion certainly did. Every family had its own little shrine where members of the household prayed, performed rituals and sacrificed. Romans prayed to many gods and there was always room for more. They easily adopted and incorporated other people's religions — with the exception of Judaism and Christianity, because these monotheistic religions could not be merged with Rome's polytheism.

Christians were often persecuted in the first centuries, because their refusal to swear loyalty to the emperor and offer sacrifices to him was viewed as both sacrilegious and treasonous. They also made great scapegoats. Emperor Nero (37-68) was the first to use Christians for this purpose, accusing them of starting the great fire of Rome in 64 — which he had likely started himself, possibly to make room for a grand palace.[12]

But in 312 emperor Constantine the Great converted to Christianity (or at the very least acquired a more favorable opinion of it), after having a vision he took as a sign from the Christian God on the eve of an important battle.[13] Fought in northern Rome in front of the Milvian Bridge (*Ponte Milvio* — which still stands today — the battle was the decisive clash between Constantine and his rival Maxentius for control of Rome and the Western Empire. It was won by Constantine (Maxentius drowned in the Tiber during the battle). The following year Constantine issued the Edict of Milan, which established religious tolerance, granted Christianity legal status and ordered all property confiscated from Christians to be returned.[14] Less than 70 years later, in 380, emperor Theodosius I declared the Catholic Church the only legitimate Imperial religion.

By then Roman civilization had long since peaked both culturally and militarily, though, and after the fall of the Western Empire, in 476, Europeans would forget how to do as the Romans do for almost

1,000 years. But when they finally remembered, they fell in love with Roman ways all over again. It is a love affair that continues to this day.

1   Byron, canto IV, CI.

2   Of course the Eastern Roman Empire was still there — it would end with the fall of Constantinople, in 1453 — but the Byzantine Empire, as it was also called, had been mostly confined to Anatolia and Greece for the last couple of centuries. It was still referred to as the Roman Empire by its inhabitants, though.

3   The word 'palace' is derived from the Latin *Collis Palatinus*, Palatine Hill.

4   Greek influence on Etruscan culture has been significant, though the Etruscans adapted Greek mythology, architecture and art to their own preferences. An interesting description of Etruscan adaption of Greek mythology is given in *Etruscan Myth, Sacred History, and Legend*, by Nancy Thomson de Grummond (12-15).

5   One such conservative, the famous Roman statesman Cato the Elder (234-149 BCE), said in one of his writings, *Praecepta ad Filium,* a sort of manual for his son: "*Concerning those Greeks, son Marcus, I will speak to you more at length on the befitting occasion. I will show you the results of my own experience at Athens, and that, while it is a good plan to dip into their literature, it is not worth while to make a thorough acquaintance with it. They are a most iniquitous and intractable race, and you may take my word as the word of a prophet, when I tell you, that whenever that nation shall bestow its literature upon Rome it will mar everything.*" (qtd. in Pliny, 29.6-7).

6   The Romans constructed a total of some 250,000 miles of roads, 50,000 miles of which were stone-paved (Gabriel, 9). This compares to a U.S. interstate highway system of 44,000 miles of paved roads (Gabriel, 228).

7   The second war with the Samnites (326-304 BCE) was won partly thanks to the new road, because it helped solve the supply problem that had cost the Romans victory in the first Samnite war.

8   This is an estimate, as the Romans themselves did not measure the volume capacity of the aqueducts. They did however measure the delivery capacity of the pipe system in the city. For this they used the *quinaria*, a standard area unit. One quinaria pipe measured 0.91 inches (2.31 centimeters) in diameter. According to Water Commissioner Frontinus (40-103 CE) the nine aqueducts of the city of Rome at the time had a total delivery capacity of 14,018 quinaria. (Frontinus, II.62). In 1916, the Italian engineer Claudio Di Fenizio put the capacity of one quinaria at a minimum of 0,47 liter per second, or 40.6 m^3/24 hours (Frontinus, Rodgers, 342-345). Following these numbers, we arrive at an estimate of 569,000 m^3 liters per day. In Appendix C of Frontinus' *De Aquaeductu Urbis Romae*, H.W. Rodgers discusses Fenizio's methods and calculations in detail (Frontinus, Rodgers, 342-345).

9   The *Lex Julia de Civitate Latinis Danda* (90 BCE) offered Roman citizenship to the citizens of allied states who had not taken up arms against Rome in the Social War of 91-88 BCE. The law was introduced by consul Lucius Julius Caesar (who was from a different branch of the Julii than the most famous Caesar), hence the moniker Lex Julia.

10 Known as the Marian Reforms, the sweeping changes also included the creation of a professional standing army, providing even the poorest of men a career path and a chance at respectability. After twenty years of service, soldiers were given a pension and a plot of land in a conquered region so they could retire.

11 Tiberius (42 BCE-37 CE), Emperor Augustus' stepson, was a highly unpopular emperor. After he died, people shouted *"To the Tiber with Tiberius!"* in the streets. His ashes were spared this cruel fate, though, and were instead interred in the Mausoleum of Augustus (Suetonius, "Tiberius", 75).

12 Suetonius leaves no doubt about the fire being purposefully ignited, writing *""For under cover of displeasure at the ugliness of the old buildings and the narrow, crooked streets, he* [Nero] *set fire to the city."* ("Nero", 38.1). Tacitus is less certain about the cause of the fire ("The Annals", XV.38) but does mention Nero had a grand palace built on *"the ruins of his fatherland"*, consisting of *"fields and lakes and the air of solitude given by wooded ground alternating with clear tracts and open landscapes"* ("The Annals", XV.42).

13 Constantine's long path to full conversion to Christianity, which is said to have begun in 312 with his vision on the eve of the Battle of the Milvian Bridge, arguably only ended on his deathbed, in 337, with his actual baptism.

14 Constantine issued the Edict of Milan together with Licinius, the emperor of the Eastern Empire, whom he would later defeat — and subsequently execute — in a civil war for sole reign of the Roman Empire.

10

THE LAST GREAT EMPEROR

"The precepts of the law are these: to live honestly,
to injure no one, and to give everyone else his due."
The Institutes of Justinian, I.3

People can achieve greatness in many ways. They can be great fighters, like Achilles, who so outclassed even the fiercest of his opponents that he went from being a man of flesh and blood to being the stuff of myth and legend. They can be great thinkers, like Socrates, who didn't even have to write down his teachings to be remembered as one of the greatest philosophers who ever lived. Or great leaders, like Alexander, who conquered half the world in just eleven years.

There are also those who are great because of just one act, one thing they did. Like Justinian I, emperor of the Eastern Roman Empire in the 6th century. Actually, Justinian didn't even do the thing that made him great himself, he only ordered someone else to do it. But the work he ordered was done so well and would have an influence of such magnitude on later civilizations, that simply ordering someone else to do it was enough to make Justinian himself Great.

When he became emperor in 527 Justinian already had great plans.[1] He wanted to restore the Empire to its former glory and reconquer the western half of the Roman empire, something that sounds so logical one would almost forget it meant conquering an area of roughly two million square kilometers (772,200 square miles). As fate would have it, though, Justinian would not only be blessed with a long reign — he died at 82 — but also with one of the greatest generals in history, Flavius Belisarius, the last general who was ever granted a Roman Triumph, after recovering north Africa from the Vandals.

Impressively, Justinian — or more accurately Belisarius — indeed succeeded in reconquering substantial parts of the former Western

Empire, including Italy, Sicily, parts of northern Africa and southern Spain, but it is still not what would make him great.

Of course it is impossible to know whether one will go down in history as Great. History can judge harshly, or worse, not at all, and being on the losing side of history — something one has very limited control over, really — never helps either. After all, you can win all the battles and wars you fight, but what about the battles and wars fought by others after you are long gone?

For instance, if Charles Martel had not stopped the Islamic conquest of Europe by defeating Abdul Rahman Al Ghafiqi at the battle of Tours in 732, Christianity might have been marginalized, Arabic could have become the lingua franca instead of Latin and Sharia could have become the law of the land in Europe. Such an outcome would have significantly diminished the impact of the one great thing Justininian I did and thus likely also cost him the epithet "Great". In other words, even though he had already been dead for over 150 years when Martel stopped the advancement of the Umayyad empire at Tours, the Roman emperor still had a dog in that fight.

Okay so what was this great thing he ordered, who did all the actual work, and why isn't he the one called "Great"? The short answer: *Corpus Iuris Civilis*, Tribonian, because he wasn't the emperor.

The slightly longer answer then.

In 528 Justinian appointed a commission of ten, including Tribonian, to prepare a new collection of imperial constitutions, to bring more unity to the legal system (Jolowicz, 479).[2] Tribonian and his legal team subsequently set out to produce three compilations. The first, the *Codex* (Code), was a compilation of the laws, imperial decrees, statutes and constitutions of the emperors. The second, the *Digesta* (Digest), was a collection of legal opinions and commentaries of the most famous Roman jurists. The third compilation was a student textbook called the *Institutiones* (Institutes), basically a training manual for jurists. Together, they formed the *Corpus Iuris Civilis*.[3]

The Digest is by far the largest book and also considered the most valuable, as it contains a thousand years of legal thought from 38 of the most brilliant Roman jurists, taken from 207 treatises and 1,544 books (Roby, xxiv).[4]

After Justinian had reconquered parts of the former Western Empire the *Corpus Iuris Civilis* (CIC) was distributed there as well. Shortly after Justinian's death all those territories would be lost again, though, and the relatively primitive European societies that remained had no great need for complicated legal texts; at least not during the first couple of centuries.

But in the late 11th century the work was rediscovered in Europe, probably by Catholic researchers, who used it to improve church law (canon law). It soon became clear what a huge treasure trove of legal knowledge the *Corpus Iuris Civilis* — in particular the *Digesta* — was, and a significant effort was made to study the texts. The University of Bologna, for instance, the world's oldest university in continuous operation, was established in 1088 in large part to study the *Digesta*. As a result, the first important commentators (called glossators) of the CIC were all students from the University of Bologna.

From the late Middle Ages on, the education of legal students throughout continental Europe was based on the *Corpus Iuris Civilis*. In cases were no local law seemed applicable — or the outcome of the interpretation of applicable law was unsatisfactory — the CIC was often used to come up with a better answer. Thus the legal reasoning and logic of Roman jurists who hadn't drawn breath for over a millennium continued to exert massive influence on the great legal minds of the Middle Ages, the Renaissance and beyond.

In 1800 Justinian caught another lucky break, when the young and ambitious First Consul of France, Napoleon Bonaparte, formed a commission to reform French civil law, and the eminent jurists whom Napoleon appointed to the commission subsequently decided to base the new French *Code Civil* on the CIC.

Of course, aside from having a passion for the law, Napoleon also turned out to be a fervent collector of countries, city states, kingdoms, princedoms and fiefdoms, which helped spread the Napoleonic Code throughout continental Europe and many of its colonies. And after *L'Empereur* had finally been safely tucked away on the island of St. Helena, the countries and territories he had conquered — such as Italy, the Netherlands, Belgium, Spain, Portugal, Poland and parts of

Germany — based their new civil law codes on the Napoleonic Code.

Justinian himself likely thought that it was his reconquest of large parts of the former Western Empire that would secure his place in history. Little did he know that just three years after his death Italy was lost again, conquered by a Germanic tribe called the Lombards. And the other reconquered territories in the West would follow not long after, with southern Spain going to the Visigoths and northern Africa to the Umayyad Caliphate, this time forever lost to the Empire.

But the seeds of what would become the reason for Justinian's greatness had already been planted in many of those territories with the *Corpus Iuris Civilis*, this great legal collection filled with the wisdom of great jurists, compiled and structured by Tribonian and his team, studied for centuries to come by more great legal minds and finally injected into the modern civil law codes of Europe with the help of the short, fellow conquerer from Corsica.

In short, Justinian was made great by many who came before, during and after him.

---

1   Justinian was born in Tauresium, present-day Macedonia, just 125 mi. (200 km.) from the birthplace of Alexander the Great.

2   The first edition of the Codex was actually headed by John the Cappadocian, but soon after the completion of the Digest and the Institutes by Tribonian, the Codex was found obsolete and a new edition had to be made.

3   Later a fourth part was added to the *Corpus Iuris Civilis*, called the *Novellae Constitutiones* (New Laws).

4   In his *Introduction to the Study of Justinian's Digest*, H.J. Roby describes the selection methods Justinian and Tribonian used in compiling the Digest (xxiii-xxviii).

Part III

Middle Ages

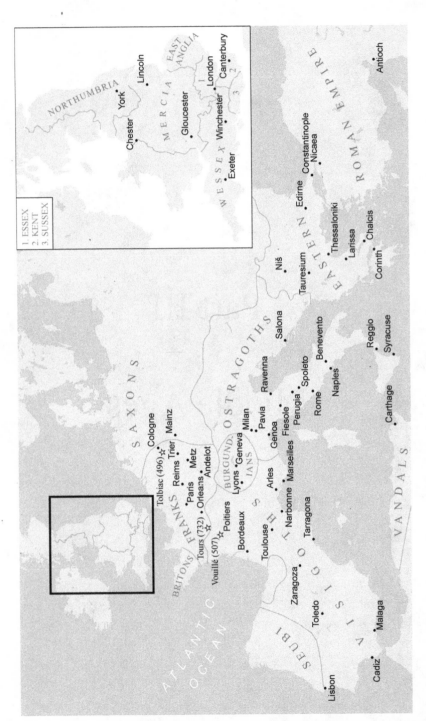

Map 4: Map of Europe 500-800 CE.

11

THE TIME OF MANY KINGDOMS

*"Amidst the errors there shone forth men of
genius, no less keen were their eyes, although they
were surrounded by darkness and dense gloom."1*

Francesco Petrarch, 1304 – 1374, on the
period after the Roman Empire

If the United States would dissolve into 50 sovereign states today,
chances are you would hear about it within a couple of hours,
minutes even. A giant tsunami of news, comments and opinions would
roll over the globe, shocking and roiling every nation in its wake.
Speculation on the new geopolitical reality would begin immediately.
With the U.S. gone from the world stage, which country would jump
in the power vacuum? Would strong states like California, New York
and Texas isolate themselves or seek alliances with other states?
What would be the chances of independent survival for some of the
poorer states and what would be the ramifications for Europe, Russia,
China and the Middle East, particularly Israel? What would be the
consequences for the global economy and stability?

Within 24 hours our heads would spin from all the historic profiles
about the United States, the speculations and analyses about threats,
opportunities, consequences. The world would never be the same
again.

On September 4, 476, the last Emperor of the Western Roman Empire,
Romulus Augustus, was deposed by Odoacer, a Germanic chieftain.
By then, the Western Empire was no more than a shadow of its former
glorious self. Still, the deposition of the emperor himself, right in the
heart of the empire, signified the end of an era. It must have sent a
shockwave through Europe and the Eastern Empire, even if compared
to modern times it was a very slow shockwave, taking weeks instead

of minutes to deliver the once-in-a-millennium kind of news that the Western Roman Empire was no more.

The Roman state had always provided a lot of public services, like stone roads, aqueducts, public baths, all kinds of entertainment, and garrisons to protect against raiders and invaders. But the level of complexity and sophistication required to run an advanced metropolis like Rome proved to be too much for the Germanic tribes that had forced the empire to its knees. And so the city went from 500,000 inhabitants in the early 5th century to 80,000 in the early 6th century and 50,000 by the end of the 7th (Lancon, 14; Tellier, 185). The same pattern — people leaving the cities and returning to a more rural way of life —was seen throughout the rest of the former Western empire between the 5th and 8th century.[2]

Monasteries were the only part of society where some level of sophistication remained. Not only did they have a profound effect on religious life in Western Europe, converting people to Christianity region by region, community by community, they also served as the main centers of education and literacy. Many of the few books written in the Early Middle Ages (6th — 10th century) were authored by monks. They also copied many of the surviving Roman works, thus saving them for later generations, which would rediscover and study them from the beginning of the Renaissance (14th — 17th century).

Of course just as Rome wasn't built in a day, it didn't really fall in a day either. The Western Empire had been on a path of steady decline for more than two centuries before it officially ended, suffering from a string of weak emperors, economic crises and loss of territory to invading barbarians. There is still much debate over what exactly caused the decline of this empire that was once so omnipotent. Likely, it was a combination of factors that made it increasingly difficult to keep the garden of Rome pristine amidst a world of weeds.

Fact is that Barbarian invasions — both peacefully and not so peacefully — had been going on for a long time before the actual fall of the Western Empire. After 1000 BCE, Germanic tribes from present-day Scandinavia, Denmark and north Germany began to slowly migrate southward and eastward. In the 1st century BCE their advance was temporarily halted at the Rhine and the Danube by the

Roman legions, but from the 2nd century CE they would eventually invade and settle within the borders of the empire.

There were the Franks — a major player in post-Roman society — who, after being defeated by Emperor Julian in 358, were allowed to settle peacefully in Gaul as Roman allies (Dawson, 83). The Vandals and the Goths, who entered the empire on the run from the Huns — a nomadic people from Central Asia that conquered a huge territory under the command of their leader Attila.[3] The Lombards, the Saxons and the Suebi, who invaded Roman lands and later carved out kingdoms of their own. And many others.

After deposing Romulus Augustus, the military commander Odoacer made himself the first King of Italy. His reign would not be the start of a dynasty, though, because thirteen years later, Theodoric the Great, leader of the Ostrogoths, a branch of the Goths, invaded Italy and took the Italian peninsula by storm. Odoacer had to take refuge in the well-defended city of Ravenna. After a siege of more than two years, Theodoric and Odoacer agreed to a treaty proposed by the bishop of Ravenna, to occupy Ravenna together and jointly rule Italy. Theodoric was thus able to enter Ravenna without bloodshed (Wolfram, 283). Ten days later, at a banquet, Theodoric drew his sword and killed Odoacer with a single stroke, becoming the unchallenged master of Italy until his death in 526, thirty-three years later (Wolfram, 283).

In 540, Belisarius, the brilliant general under the command of Eastern Emperor Justinian I, captured the Ostrogoth capital of Ravenna and ended the Italian kingdom of the Ostrogoths. The actions of his general allowed Justinian to dream the dream of a restored Western Empire. But in 568, just three years after Justinian's death, the Lombards invaded Italy and took the Mediterranean boot away from the Roman Empire once more — this time for good. Following their successful invasion of Italy, the Lombards — who had originally migrated from present-day southern Scandinavia to northwestern Germany and from there to Austria — established a kingdom there that would last 200 years.[4]

Another branch of the Goths, the Visigoths, had been allowed to settle within the empire after having decisively defeated a Roman army at the Battle of Adrianople, in 378.[5] With the Roman Empire unable to hold on to Gaul and Hispania, the Visigoths eventually established an independent kingdom in the southwest of present-day France in the second part of the 5th century, with Toulouse as its capital. During the decades that followed they expanded into the Iberian peninsula at the expense of the Suebi and the Vandals, two other Germanic tribes. The Suebi managed to hold on to their kingdom in present-day northern Portugal for some time, until they were decisively defeated by the Visigoths in 585.

The Visigoths ruled the Iberian Peninsula until 711, when they in turn were defeated by the Muslims, who had conquered their way from Mecca to the shores of Spain in less than 100 years.[6]

The Umayyad Caliphate even pushed into the southwest of France, until it was decisively defeated by Frankish leader Charles Martel at the Battle of Tours (732).[7] Martel's victory halted the Islamic advance in Western Europe and pushed the Caliphate out of France, but the Iberian Peninsula would remain occupied by the Muslims for centuries to come.

Meanwhile, the Saxons, a Germanic tribe from present-day northern Germany and the northeastern part of the Netherlands who had harassed the coastal Roman settlements of Britannia for centuries, emigrated en masse to the British island in the 5th century (in the wake of the Roman empire's retreat from it) and created the Kingdoms of Essex, Sussex and Wessex.

In the centuries that followed the Saxons mixed with the Angles, another Germanic tribe from northern Germany that had risked the perilous journey crossing the North Sea to Britannia and had settled three kingdoms of their own, *Nord Angelnen* (Northumbria), *Ost Angelnen* (East Anglia) and *Mittlere Angelnen* (Mercia). Together, they would become known as the Anglo-Saxons.

The native Britons were either driven from their lands or subsumed into the new, dominant Anglo- Saxon culture, although they managed to hold onto the kingdom of Rheged in the northwest of England until the early 7th century and the kingdom of Dumnonia in the southwest until the late 9th century.

The Britons didn't keep all their eggs in one basket, though. Seeking refuge from the Anglo-Saxon invaders, they emigrated to a region in northwestern France — still known today as *Bretagne,* Brittany — in the 5th and 6th centuries. There they established several small kingdoms and remained independent until Bretagne was unified with France in 1532.

While we're in France, let's swing back to the Franks, who would come to play such a pivotal role in the development of Europe. The Franks had been living in Gaul (roughly present-day France, Belgium, and parts of the southern Netherlands, western Germany and northern Italy) since the 4th century. Initially as *foederati* (allies) of the Roman Empire, supplying soldiers to Rome in exchange for autonomy.

There were several Frankish tribes, but eventually they would all be united under Clovis I, who succeeded his father Childeric I as king of the Salian Franks in 481, at the age of fifteen. His father had served as an ally of the Romans but Clovis would break with that tradition and instead wage war with the last Roman ruler in Gaul, Syagrius, whom he decisively defeated at the Battle of Soissons in 486, thus ending the last Western Roman presence outside of Italy.[8] In the years that followed he also dealt with several other Frankish kings, mostly by killing them.

In 496, after defeating the Alemanni — a confederation of Germanic tribes, still recognizable in the French (*Allemagne*) and Spanish (*Alemania*) name for Germany— at the battle of Tolbiac, Clovis converted to Catholicism.[9] This ignited the construction of a network of monasteries to Christianize his entire realm, something that would come to have a far-reaching effect on the rest of Europe as well.

Conversion did not quench Clovis' thirst for conquest, though. In 500 he saw his attempts to subdue the Kingdom of Burgundy thwarted, but a couple of years later he did succeed in expelling the Visigoths from Gaul, after defeating them decisively at the Battle of Vouillé in 507, a victory that saw the region of Aquitaine, in the southwest of France, added to his domain (Tours, II.32-33, 37). By then, Clovis' Frankish kingdom, with its capital in Paris, already largely resembled modern-day France.

Upon his death in 511, Clovis' kingdom was divided among his four sons, leading to the creation of four kingdoms. The unification of Frankish Gaul that Clovis had achieved was thus undone again. But the seeds of unity had been sown and some 250 years later another great king, Charlemagne, would bring them to fruition again.

1 Quoted by Theodore Mommsen in "Petrarch's Conception of the 'Dark Ages'" (227).

2 In *Urban World History*, Luc-Normand Tellier writes that the urbanization of Western Europe dropped from 8–15 percent to 5–8 percent when looking at cities with a population over 2,000, and that while around 5 percent of the people in Roman Europe lived in cities with a population over 10,000 in the first century CE, by the year 1000 only four towns in Europe still exceeded the 10,000 mark (185).

3 After Attila's death in 453, the Hunnic empire quickly dissolved.

4 The Lombard Kingdom would come to an end in 774, when Charlemagne defeated the Lombards and captured their capital Pavia. The Lombard Duchy of Benevento in the Southern Italy managed to stay largely independent, though, until the Norman conquest of Southern Italy in the 11th century finally ended Lombard rule there as well.

5 Eastern Roman Emperor Valens was killed in this battle. The Battle of Adrianople is often considered the beginning of the end for the Western Roman Empire.

6 The Muslim conquests started in the 620s under Muhammad. In the decades that followed, Western Asia and Northern Africa were added to the rapidly expanding Islamic empire. Spain was invaded in 711 and by 718 most of the Iberian Peninsula had come under Muslim control.

7 The Battle of Tours is also known as the Battle of Poitiers. The commander of the Umayyad forces, Abdul Rahman Al Ghafiqi, was killed in the battle.

8 In July 1918, more than 1,400 years after Clovis had defeated Syagrius at Soissons, French-American forces launched a successful counter-offensive at Soissons to stop the last major German offensive of World War I.

9 In his *History of the Franks*, the 6th century Gallo-Roman historian Gregory of Tours describes how Clovis converted to Christianity after having beseeched Jesus Christ — *"whom Clotilda [Clovis' wife] asserts to be the son of the living God"* — during the battle with the Alemanni, to grant him victory in exchange for his conversion (II.30). There is scholarly debate about the year when Clovis was baptized, ranging from 496 to 506, possibly even 508 (Lynch, "Christianizing Kinship", 39; Shanzer, "Dating the baptism of Clovis"). For a summary of this debate, see W.M. Daly's article "Clovis: How Barbaric, How Pagan?", specifically his note on p. 620.

12

LIFE IN THE MIDDLE AGES

"Those darling by-gone times, Mr Carker,'
said Cleopatra, 'with their delicious fortresses,
and their dear old dungeons, and their delightful
places of torture, and their romantic vengeances,
and their picturesque assaults and sieges, and
everything that makes life truly charming!
How dreadfully we have degenerated!" [1]

Charles Dickens, Dombey and Son

In 1442, the Italian humanist Leonardo Bruni published *The History of the Florentine People*, the first book that divided history into the three distinct periods Antiquity, Middle Ages and Modern. Bruni, like Francesco Petrarca before him, viewed the period following the fall of the Roman Empire as dark and in decline compared to the culturally rich Antiquity, but he also argued that in the second half of the thirteenth century Florence had emerged from the Middle Ages as a modern city-state, ruled by elected officials rather than being controlled by the Holy Roman Empire (Bruni, xviii). [2]

Ironically, according to many modern historians, Bruni himself was still living in the Middle Ages when he first published his *Historiarum Florentini populi*. Like Bruni, most modern scholars have the Middle Ages start with the fall of the Western Roman Empire, in 476, but its end is often marked with the fall of Constantinople, in 1453 — which set off European exploration — or 1492, when Columbus discovered America. [3] Johannes Gutenberg's invention of the printing press, around 1440, could also be seen as the start of a new era. It was this invention, after all, that would prove instrumental in spreading exactly that which had been so utterly absent in the Early Middle Ages: knowledge and culture.

The people of the early Renaissance loved Antiquity almost as much as they loathed the Middle Ages. Like teenagers developing opinions and theories of their own for the first time, denouncing everything their parents had taught them as out of touch and antiquated, so too did the people of the Renaissance denounce the Middle Ages. Nothing good had come out of it (except, of course, the Renaissance). Petrarch (1304–1774) for instance, denounced the whole period between the fall of the Western Roman Empire and his own time as an age of "darkness", writing "What else, then, is all history, if not the praise of Rome?" (qtd. in Mommsen, 237).

The concept of a "Dark Age", to justify sweeping everything coming out of the Middle Ages under the rug of oblivion, would prove popular and long-lasting, at one point encompassing almost a thousand years, from the 5th until the 15th century.[4]

But a thousand years is a long time to be entirely without progress. And if there really was no progress, how did the Renaissance come to happen in the first place? Did people just suddenly realize they needed universities to study classical texts, that they wanted more art, more philosophy, a different approach to science? Of course not. Viewpoints and interests changed, yes, but these changes did not happen overnight. They were made possible by developments in those very Middle Ages that Renaissance man so derisively dismissed.

The truth is that much of the period the people of the Renaissance referred to as the Dark Ages was actually pretty well-lit, with the exception perhaps of the Early Middle Ages, the 300 years between the fall of the Western Roman Empire and the reign of Charlemagne when nobody could read or write — let alone produce literary or scholarly works — except for the clergy, when there was no higher education, no artistic development, no scientific innovation.

The Early Middle Ages were a rough time for Europe. Large cities emptied and the rate of urbanization declined to below 10 percent.[5] Most Europeans returned to the country and peasant life, working on lands owned by a local lord. They were given a strip of land to cultivate in exchange for a share of the produce, but were bound to that land in servitude. Serfs also had to work on the demesne, land attached to the manor that the lord retained for his own use (Bishop, 111).

The serf was all the way at the bottom of a new social system called feudalism, in which each man served a superior in exchange for land and protection. That is, each man except the king of course, who sat comfortably at the top of the feudal pyramid. In the absence of an administrative bureaucracy — which required literacy, a skill too few possessed — the feudal system was the only way for a king to exert some control over a vast area. He would give lands (called 'fiefs') in tenure to vassals, in exchange for their allegiance and service. The vassals divided their lands into fiefs as well, giving them in tenure to *their* vassals, who might divide their fief among their vassals (if it was large enough), who then made sure the serfs on the land worked hard enough.

When the English philosopher Thomas Hobbes described the state of anarchy in his famous book *Leviathan* (1651), he wrote that life in such a state was *"solitary, poor, nasty, brutish, and short"*.[6]

Since then, this phrase has often been used to describe the Middle Ages. Though it goes too far to summarize the entire 1,000 year period with it, peasant life in the Early Middle Ages seems to have come pretty close to it.

Life expectancy was only about 30 years, partly because of a brutally high infant mortality rate, estimated to have been between perhaps more than 30 percent among children up until the age of five (Scott, "Miracle Cures", 9-10).[7] Many children died at birth — as did many of the mothers — others suffocated in their cradle or died from one of the many diseases floating around, like influenza, respiratory diseases, measles, smallpox, tuberculosis and of course the bubonic plague. Most children who did make it past the age of five did not have to worry about having to go to school every day, because apart from a limited number of monastic and cathedral schools and nunneries there were no schools, at least not until the later Middle Ages. In fact, there was no special time allotted for childhood whatsoever; children were expected to contribute with chores or other work, like helping out their parents in the field, a common occurrence since peasants made up about 90 percent of the population.

The number one crop of the time was barley, the staple food source of the poor (i.e., mostly everyone). Though not as tasty as wheat, barley is easier to grow because it requires less rain. People ate barley porridge, barley bread, put barley in their soup, made barley beer and used barley stalks to weave sleeping mats, shoes and baskets.

The rich ate a lot better — though not necessary healthier. Their diet contained lots of meat, fruit and bread made out of wheat. They also used salt, which was very expensive and scarce at the time. Still, most peasants were likely more occupied with getting enough food in their bellies than with spicing it up. Many people didn't have enough to eat on a regular basis and suffered from malnutrition (Adamson, 172-174). Land parcels were often too small to provide a farmer with enough yield to feed his family and townspeople often had to spend a large portion of their disposable income on food. And that was in normal years. Storms, early frost, long droughts or excessive rain meant going from malnutrition to starvation. Famines were not uncommon. Malnutrition also made people easier targets for all kinds of diseases, which roamed freely (Adamson, 172).

Meanwhile, medieval towns and villages were a real paradise for infectious diseases. People simply threw their waste in ditches and rivers. Floors were often covered with rushes, which were only occasionally renewed. A receptacle for food scraps, spilled beer and the occasional urinal leaking of cats and dogs, the rushes offered a warm and cosy welcome to all kinds of bacteria, not to mention rats.

On the other hand, the personal hygiene of people in the Middle Ages was better than it is often portrayed. People loved to bathe and many towns had public bath houses (Newman, 153-154). Most people washed their face daily and their hands before dinner. Soap was readily available, both for personal hygiene and cleaning clothes and bed linens (Newman, 155-156). Dental hygiene was also considered important, which is not hard to believe considering that the only remedy against a bad tooth ache was to pull the thing out, without any form of anesthetic. After a meal many people would pick their teeth and — if they followed contemporary health manuals — rinse out their mouths with water, wine or vinegar and rub their teeth with a cloth (Newman, 155).

Compared to the peasants, the nobility had it a lot better. They did not suffer from malnutrition and their children did not have to work in the fields, in fact no member of the nobility did, that's what they had the serfs for. The nobleman ruled the lands and peasants under his control, served the lord that had given him his fief and provided the king with military support when called upon. As for the noblewoman, her main job was to have children — the more the better — run the household and be pious and pretty. Noblewomen tried to stave off old age for as long as possible, dyeing their hair and applying make-up to achieve a pale complexion, which was considered very desirable. Sometimes women even bled themselves to look more pale.[8]

Following the fall of the Carolingian Empire in the late 9th century, local lords started building stone castles, not for aesthetic reasons but to protect themselves against raids from rivals, robber bands, rebellions, Vikings, Muslims or Magyars, depending on the region. The stone castles also had a destabilizing effect on the realm. Kings already had difficulty enough actively controlling all their fiefdoms. Now they had to deal with a growing number of unruly vassals too, who — safely behind their thick castle walls — increasingly treated their fiefs as their own little kingdoms (Coulson, 20-21).

And while the king lorded over the nobles (or tried to at least), the nobles lorded over the peasants and the peasants lorded over, well, the barley, the clergy lorded over spiritual life and education. The importance of the latter is hard to overestimate, because during the Early Middle Ages the monasteries were the only centers of education and thus effectively responsible for guarding the knowledge of classical Western civilization for later generations.

From the sixth century on, the monks collected and painstakingly copied classical manuscripts, saving many works that would have very likely been lost otherwise. Recognizing the great importance of this work, Frankish ruler Charlemagne later helped the monasteries boost their output through extensive support and educational reforms during his reign (768—814).

Education in medieval Europe made a new leap forward in 1088 — eight years before the start of the first Crusade — with the founding of the first university in Bologna, Italy (it still exists).[9] One of the reasons for its founding was to study the recently rediscovered, 500 year old *Code of Justinian* (a.k.a. *Corpus Iuris Civilis*), the body of laws and legal opinions from the Roman Empire, collected by Tribonian, senior legal advisor to Eastern Emperor Justinian I. In the two centuries that followed, universities were also founded in Paris, Oxford, Cambridge, Padua, Naples and Toulouse, among others. Hardly the stuff of Dark Ages.

The universities made higher education available to a growing number of people, which in turn stimulated new works in theology, law, medicine, philosophy and the seven liberal arts, arithmetic, geometry, astronomy, music theory, grammar, logic and rhetoric. Almost all the early universities were founded with the help of the Catholic Church, but they were nevertheless autonomous centers of education and would gradually end the centuries old educational monopoly of the church.

God — more precisely the Catholic Church, one of the few institutions that had survived the Western Roman Empire — was everywhere in Medieval Europe. Helped by the conquests of Charlemagne, the Catholic Church was able to gradually convert even those stubborn Germanic tribes Rome had never been able to subdue. After Charlemagne, Christianity pretty much reigned supreme in Europe, except on the Iberian peninsula, where Islam would hold on to an ever shrinking domain until 1492, when the Emirate of Granada, the last Muslim vestige there, was finally defeated by the joint forces of Castile and Aragon.

The Church had its own lands, imposed taxes and received gifts from people rich and poor who wanted to remain — or return — in the good graces of the various priests and bishops. People feared and respected the clerics, who were seen as God's representatives on Earth, with the power to condemn and forgive, to ruin or bless one's afterlife.

The Bible was taken quite literally and people firmly believed in the existence of Hell and Purgatory. Not that they had any choice in the matter, because there was no room whatsoever for any personal interpretation of the Bible.[10] Anything deviating from the teachings of the Catholic Church was considered heresy. Early reformers like John Wycliffe and Jan Hus were therefore burned as heretics.[11]

Other religions, like Judaism, Islam, any form of Paganism or —

God forbid —Atheism, were met with the same vigor and intolerance. Jews living in European cities were regularly persecuted and killed when something bad happened, like a storm destroying the harvest or the outbreak of a disease.

In 1095, Pope Urban II called for the first of several Crusades to the Holy Land, to recapture the holy city of Jerusalem and kill as many Muslims as possible.[12] People going on a Crusade were promised forgiveness for all sins, making it an especially attractive proposition for the worst kind of people.

During the time of the Crusades, Europe experienced a period of increased prosperity. The climate improved, resulting in longer, more productive growing seasons, more land was cleared for agriculture and better farming techniques further increased harvests. And with the winding down of Viking, Magyar and Arab raids, political stability also improved. Between 1000 and 1300, the European population thus grew from an estimated 35 million to 80 million (Crouzet, 12).[13] Things were definitely looking up.

Then the 14th century arrived.

First, between 1315–17, excessive rains caused a Great Famine in Europe. Localized famines were rather common, but this one was particularly severe, long lasting and spread all over Europe. Contemporary writers tell of parents leaving their children behind in the forest and elderly people voluntarily starving themselves to save their grandchildren. People ate horses, pets, tree bark, even each other — or so the rumors went (Jordan, 148-149; Childs, 121). Another story tells of how even King Edward II of England had trouble buying bread for himself and his household when he visited St. Albans between 10–12 August, 1315 (Trokelowe, Annales).

Five to ten percent percent of city and town populations are estimated to have perished during the Great Famine of 1315–1317 (Jordan, 147-148). Even after the weather returned to normal patterns it would take a decade before the food supply was fully restored, because much of the seed stock had been eaten and so many people had died.

Those who were lucky enough to survive the Great Famine might have lived to see the start of the Hundred Years' War between France and England twenty years later, in 1337. With the throne of France as its ultimate prize, the French and English would fight 58 major battles over a period of 116 years. Ultimately, the war would end in a victory for France, but at a high price for both sides.

But the greatest survival challenge of the 14th century would not be the Hundred Years' War or even the Great Famine, but the Black Death, the plague, returning to Europe in 1348 stronger and deadlier than ever before after a centuries long absence, killing an estimated 60 percent of the entire European population in just two horrible years (Benedictow, 382-83).

For those that survived, things changed. The plague had killed so many that the very foundations of medieval society were shaken. Poor people who had been serfs all their lives suddenly found themselves in greater demand than ever before, with more land available than they could possibly work. As a result of these mathematics of survival, serfdom would disappear from Western Europe in the decades following the Black Death (Benedictow, 391). Skilled laborers could negotiate better wages, thus improving their station in life. Laws against rising wages and the introduction of higher taxes to compensate for lower tax income led to popular uprisings in several European countries. Meanwhile, the position of the nobles and clergy weakened. The income of the nobles was based on their landholdings, but the now more expensive workers drove their cost up, while the plague had simultaneously diminished demand for their produce. To raise money, the nobles sold freedom to their serfs and all kinds of rights to the towns and villages under their control, but in time this would only further erode their power base.

The clergy, for their part, had lost some of their authority for not being able to prevent, cure or pray away the Black Death. To compensate for diminished income from their own landholdings they resorted to selling church offices and stepping up their sales of indulgences, thus further undermining the respect people had for the Catholic Church and ultimately leading to the Protestant Reformation of the early 16th century.

Yes, change was in the air. And although it would not come as rapidly, or be as radically upending as the later revolutions of the 18th and 19th centuries, the seeds that were sown in the 14th century would fundamentally change the way people viewed themselves, their church and the world around them — not to mention pave the way for those later revolutions. The final victim of the Black Death may therefore well have been the Middle Ages.

---

1   Dickens, 243.

2   Petrarca (1304—1374) — anglicized name Petrarch — was an Italian poet and scholar who collected and extensively studied Greek and Roman manuscripts at the beginning of the Italian Renaissance. He has been called the 'Father of Humanism' for refocusing attention on man himself, on his artistic, creative and philosophical abilities, instead of only on religion and the sciences.

3   The Hundred Years' war between France and England also ended in 1453.

4   The *American Cyclopedia* of 1873, for example read : *"The Dark Ages is a term applied in its widest sense to that period of intellectual depression in the history of Europe from the establishment of the barbarian supremacy in the fifth century to the revival of learning about the beginning of the fifteenth, thus nearly corresponding in extent with the Middle Ages."* (qtd. in Mommsen, 226)

5   Luc-Normand Tellier has estimated that the rate of urbanization in Europe, based on cities with a population over 2,000, dropped from 8—15 percent to 5—8 percent after the fall of Rome. And while in the first century about 5 percent of Roman Europe lived in cities larger than 10,000, that rate had dropped to almost zero percent in the year 1000, when there were only four towns left with a population of over 10,000 ("Urban World History", 185-186).

6   *"In such condition there is no place for industry, because the fruit thereof is uncertain: and consequently no culture of the earth; no navigation, nor use of the commodities that may be imported by sea; no commodious building; no instruments of moving, and removing such things as require much force; no knowledge of the face of the earth; no account of time; no arts; no letters; no society; and which is worst of all, continuall feare, and danger of violent death; and the life of man, solitary, poore, nasty, brutish, and short."* (Hobbes, 89).

7   There are no accurate figures available on infant mortality rates during the early middle ages and estimates are the result of varied methods, such as gathering cemetery evidence or assessing disease mortality rates. In *Miracle Cures: Saints, Pilgrimage, and the Healing Powers of Belief*, Robert Scott mentions a variety of sources in an accompanying note (note 38, page 184), one of which estimates as much as half of all newborns died before the age of five.

8   In *Dresses and Decorations of the Middle Ages*, Henry Shaw quotes part of a poem by 12th century scholar Alexander Neckam, which talks about women

"perforating their ears in order to hang them with jewels, of fasting and bleeding themselves in order to look pale, of tightening their waists and breasts in order to mend their shape, and of colouring their hair to give it a yellow tint." (Shaw, Introduction, iv).

9   There had been other, earlier places of higher education, the Academy founded by Plato ca. 387 BCE in Athens for instance, or the Lyceum founded by Aristotle ca. 335 BCE, also in Athens, but the educational institute at Bologna was the first to use the term *universitas* in the context of describing a community of teachers and scholars (*universitas magistrorum et scholarium*), specifically organized for the purpose of higher learning.

10   Since most people couldn't read anyway, this did not pose much of problem for the Catholic church, until Martin Luther finished his translation of the Bible into German, in 1534, and made it widely available with the help of the printing press.

11   The burning of John Wycliffe (1320—1384) took place 44 years after his death, when Pope Martin V ordered his posthumous execution, after which his remains were exhumed and burned. Jan Hus (1369–1415) was not so lucky, he was executed while still alive.

12   *"I, or rather the Lord, beseech you (..) to carry aid promptly to those Christians and to destroy that vile race from the lands of our friends"*. Fulcher of Chartres' version of Pope Urban II's speech at the Council of Clermont (qtd in Allen, 34-35).

13   The figures mentioned include Russia; without, the estimates are 30 million ca. 1000 and 70 million ca. 1300 (Crouzet, 11, table 1.1).

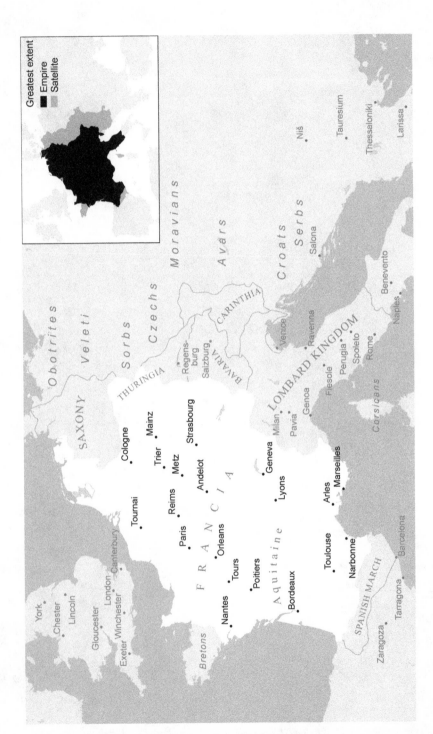

Map 5: The Empire of Charlemagne

13

CHARLEMAGNE

"If your zeal were imitated by others,
we might see a new Athens rising up in
Francia, more splendid than the old..."

Alcuin of York, in a letter to Charlemagne[1]

In May 1000, nineteen-year-old Holy Roman Emperor Otto III had Charlemagne's tomb opened and went inside. One of the courtiers who accompanied Otto later wrote that the dead emperor sat on his throne as if he were still alive, instead of lying in a casket.[2] He was wearing a golden crown andheld a scepter in his gloved hands. The courtier wrote that Charlemagne's fingernails had penetrated his gloves and that his body had been remarkably well preserved (Bethmann, Scriptores, vol.21, III. 32). Only the tip of his nose was gone — which Otto replaced with gold. He also took a tooth out of Charles's mouth, to serve as a relic.

In January 1002 Otto suddenly developed a high fever while on his way to Rome and died. His body was carried back to Aachen, where he was buried in the Cathedral, alongside the body of the man who's tooth he had taken not two years before.

In 1165, Emperor Frederick Barbarossa also had the vault opened and Charlemagne's remains placed in a beautifully sculptured, marble sarcophagus. 50 years later, Frederick Barbarossa's grandchild, Frederick II, then took the bones out of the sarcophagus and put them in an even more precious casket of silver and gold. In 1349 Holy Roman Emperor Charles IV had some of Charlemagne's bones removed to serve as relics, thereby apparently setting an example for French king Louis XI, who commissioned an arm reliquary in 1481, which was to hold the actual ulna and radius from Charlemagne's right arm.[3]

In 1861 Charlemagne's remains were exhumed by scientists to

verify historical accounts that he had been an unusually tall man. In 1988, Charlemagne's remains were again asked for a scientific contribution, this time to determine once and for all if the remains really belonged to the legendary Frankish king. Twenty-six years later, on january 28, 2014, exactly 1200 years after his death, one of the researchers said that *"with great likelihood"* the remains indeed belonged to Charlemagne.[4]

So, quite an eventful afterlife, to be sure. But why this fascination with a man who died so long ago? What has he done to deserve it? Turns out, quite a lot.

Charlemagne was born in 742, most likely in Herstal, present-day Belgium, where his family had its main residence. He came from famous stock. His grandfather, Charles Martel — who had died less than a year earlier — had been the victor of the Battle of Tours (732), where he had stopped the Muslim advance in Western Europe, while his father, Pepin the Short, had considerably expanded the Frankish kingdom during his reign as the first Carolingian king. Large shoes to fill, a task made even more challenging by the fact that his father's kingdom would be divided among his sons, as was the Frankish custom.

When Pepin died in 768, his kingdom was indeed divided equally between Charles and his brother Carloman, who was nine years his junior. This created such an uneasy and tense situation between the brothers that before long they only communicated with each other through their mother.

But three years later Carloman died, just 20 years old. The timing couldn't have been better, because Charles was close to going to war with both his brother and the Lombard King Desiderius. The latter had just been gravely insulted by Charles because he had nullified the marriage with his daughter, Desiderata, after less than a year of marriage.

Carloman is said to have died of natural causes, with a contemporary report suggesting he suffered some sort of hemorrhage (Bachrach, 181-182). Whether that hemorrhage was caused by the sharp end of a sword will likely remain a mystery. Fact is that Charles benefitted greatly from Carloman's death, annexing his brother's territories shortly after his demise, even though the inheritance should have gone to his nephews.

Now the sole ruler of the Franks, an ambitious Charles set out to expand his kingdom and unite all the Germanic tribes under his rule. Few things are more potent than an absolute ruler with a mission and the necessary skills to complete it.[5] A talented military strategist and administrator,

Charlemagne would wage war almost his entire life to accomplish his goals, fighting more than 50 battles and leading most of them in person.

During his long reign of 47 years, Charlemagne conquered the Lombard kingdom and Thuringa (774), finished his father's war in Aquitaine (778), conquered Bavaria and neighboring Carinthia (788), pushed into present-day northern Spain, capturing Barcelona (797), and finally even subdued those ornery, unruly Saxons, in 804.

Charlemagne wanted to do more than just conquering, though, he wanted to Christianize the Germanic people. Deeply religious himself — like his father and grandfather before him — he felt it his task to spread the faith. Of course this would make him Best-Friends-Forever with the Catholic Church, which found a more powerful and ideologically better aligned ally in Charlemagne than it had ever had in the Byzantine Emperors.

But however religious he was, Charlemagne certainly was no saint. Aside from wartime brutalities, there were also several Catholic no-no's in his family life. The fact that he had a marriage nullified, for instance, or that he kept several mistresses and that some of his eighteen children were illegitimate. He also forbade his daughters to marry and kept them at his court — one explanation for this being that he loved them too much to let them go (Einhard, book 19). He did allow them to have extramarital relationships, which in turn resulted in several illegitimate grandchildren (McKitterick, 91-92).

Charlemagne showed more uncompromising religious zeal in his political endeavors. One of the first things he did when he came to power, for instance, was to help Pope Adrian I get back some of the papal cities the Lombards had captured. The cities had been part of a gift of Charlemagne's father Pepin to the Catholic Church, known as the *Donation of Pepin*. The donation ensured the independence of the papacy — a great gift indeed — for which a grateful Pope had anointed Pepin as well as his sons.[6] When the Lombards recaptured the cities in 772, Charlemagne crossed the Alps with his army and laid siege to Pavia, where the Lombard king Desiderius had fled to (Einhard, book 6). After a couple of months the Lombards surrendered in exchange for their lives. Desiderius was sent to the abbey of Corbie, where he lived out the remainder of his days.

If the subjugation of the Lombards was a piece of cake for Charlemagne, the Saxons were an entirely different story. Charles defeated this tough Germanic tribe (located in present-day northwest Germany and the northeast Netherlands) several times, but they kept resisting his rule. As soon as he had left with his army after yet another successful expedition to bring them to heel, the Saxons would start raiding Frankish territories again and continue with their pagan rituals.

Their paganism was a thorn in Charlemagne's side. He could not, would not let it slide. In a protracted war of over 30 years (772–804), he returned to Saxony again and again, crushing whatever fresh rebellion the Saxons had mounted, forcing them to convert and imprisoning those that refused. Once he even ordered the beheading of 4,500 Saxons, after Saxon leader Widukind had annihilated a division of the Frankish army that included four counts and some twenty other distinguished nobles (Scholz, 60-61). The so-called *Massacre of Verden* would be the biggest stain on Charles' reputation.

Three years later, in 785, in an effort to put an end to Saxon Paganism once and for all,

Charlemagne instituted a legal code that, among other things, made paganism an offense punishable by death.[7] The English scholar Alcuin of York — one of Charlemagne's closest advisors — urged him to be more lenient towards the heathens, arguing in a letter in 796 that "*an ignorant race, at the beginning of the faith*" should not be subjected to the same strictness as those "*born and brought up and taught in the Catholic faith*", and that the Saxons should not be forced to be baptized, "*lest the ablution of sacred baptism of the body profit nothing.*"(qtd. in Browne, 287-288). Perhaps it helped, because a year later Charlemagne abolished the death penalty for Paganism again.

Alcuin was part of a group of scholars Charlemagne had gathered around him to educate his family and himself and to help spread education and culture throughout his kingdom. This emphasis on education, culture and the arts sparked a light in the Dark Ages known as the Carolingian Renaissance. For the first time since the fall of the Western Roman Empire, the classical texts were studied and taught again in Europe.

Regional language differences initially presented both students and scholars with a problem, though, as the original Latin had diverged into regional dialects since the fall of the Western Empire 300 years ago.[8] Charlemagne quickly realized the importance of having one common language throughout his growing realm, not just so that scholars could easier communicate with each other and their students, but also to make it easier for his administration to communicate with all the different regions throughout his growing empire.

He could have chosen his own native language — *Althochdeutsch* (Old High German) — and force all his subjects to learn to speak it, but instead he decided on a standardized form of Latin as the lingua franca. (If only the European leaders of today would have the same insight and resolve Charlemagne had 1,200 years ago).

Charlemagne also stimulated the development of a common calligraphic standard known as the *Caroline miniscule,* to ensure that the literate class could recognize the letters and words from one region to another. Perhaps not the most spectacular reform but extremely important nevertheless. After all, if you can't recognize the letters you won't be able to understand the words either, even if you share a common language.

Book production was also stimulated, libraries were financed and the number of monastic schools and *scriptoria,* the centers of book copying, was drastically increased during Charlemagne's reign. And to great effect, because many of the earliest available copies of classical texts are still from the Carolingian Renaissance. Some historians — perhaps most notably Kenneth Clark — argue that Western civilization might not have survived if all those classical texts had not been copied and preserved by the Carolingian scribes.[9] The Carolingian Renaissance also saw an increase in the creation of new works of architecture, literature and other art, though these artistic endeavors remained mostly confined to a small group of scholars and the clergy.

Charlemagne himself kept studying as well, mostly focusing on the fields of dialectic, astronomy and arithmetic. In later life he also tried to learn to write, but of this effort his biographer Einhard wrote: "*as he did not begin his efforts in due season, but late in life, they met with ill success.*" (Einhard, book 25).

As a ruler Charlemagne was very successful, though. Conquering an empire is one thing, uniting it — with all those different regions and their different traditions, faiths and languages — quite another. Throughout his entire reign, Charlemagne worked to bring the people of Europe closer together. One king, one faith, one language, one law.

And he didn't stop there. To stimulate commerce, he abolished the gold standard and adopted a standardized currency based on silver. One important reason for this was the shortage of gold, which seriously inhibited the production of new coins, thus hampering economic growth. Weight, measures and customs dues were also standardized, further improving commerce and trade throughout Europe.

For the first time since the days of the Roman Empire, much of Western Europe was united, secure, stable and culturally flourishing again. It seemed only natural to elevate the status of the man who had made it all happen to one more befitting the impressive reach of his realm. And so, on Christmas Day 800, the pope crowned Charles as Emperor of the Romans in the Saint Peter's Basilica in Rome.[10]

Einhard wrote that the king was not aware of the Pope's intentions to crown him Emperor and that he "*would not have set foot in the Church*" had he known (Einhard, book 28). Some historians dispute the likelihood of this, but fact is that Charlemagne's new title increased tensions with the Eastern Roman Empire — which saw itself as the only rightful heir to the Roman Empire — that could not have been very welcome to Charlemagne. On the other hand, the coronation also solidified the position of the Carolingian dynasty and strengthened the bond between Charlemagne's Empire and the Catholic Church.[11]

Being crowned Emperor was in many ways the highlight of Charlemagne's reign. He would live another fourteen years to enjoy it, most of them in good health. Charles the Great died on January

28, 814, at the age of 72. He was buried that same day at Aachen Cathedral, in the same tomb Emperor Otto III would find him almost 200 years later.

One could say that where Clovis united the Franks, Charlemagne united the Europeans. He has even been called the father of Europe, and with good reason. He was the first ruler in more than 300 years to unify Western Europe, introduced a common language, a common currency and a common faith. He greatly stimulated culture and education and saved the classical texts of the Roman Empire that would come to play such an important role in the Europe of the second millennium. Unfortunately he also made a fatal error, one that might have prevented countless wars had he not made it, between the European nations that would emerge in later centuries because of it — the same nations that are still struggling today to unite the way they were united under Charlemagne. That fatal error was to not change the Frankish inheritance law so as to prevent the kingdom from ever being divided among multiple sons.

Charles himself was 'lucky' enough to have only one surviving (legitimate) son — Louis the Pious — but when he died in 840, civil war broke out among Louis' three surviving sons. Three years later the *Treaty of Verdun* was signed, dividing the Carolingian Empire into three separate kingdoms. One kingdom would be the basis of France, one the basis of the Low Countries and one the basis of Germany.

In 1916, one of the most infamous and deadliest battles of World War I would be fought at the same place where the treaty dividing the Carolingian Empire had been signed, by the same countries that had been united under Charlemagne.

---

1   Qtd. in Sergeant, 278.

2   The account of the courier, Count Otto of Lomello, was reported in the Chronicle of Novalesia (ca. 1026) and later published in the *Monumenta Germaniae Historica, Scriptores rerum Germanicarum*, vol. 21, III.32 (Bethmann). There are two other early eleventh-century sources that tell the story of Otto's visit to Charlemagne's tomb. Thietmar of Merseburg's *Chronicon* was the first to mention the event. Adémar of Chabannes' *Chronique* was written around 1030. For differences between their accounts, see Garrison, 63-64.

3   The arm reliquary is still on display in the Treasury of the Aachen Cathedral.

4   According to Professor Frank Rühli of the University of Zurich, who was among the scientists involved in the study of the remains (Griffiths, "Charlemagne's bones identified").

5   But woe to the subjects of the absolute ruler who has a mission but lacks the skills to complete it.

6   The anointing of Pepin and his sons by Pope Stephen II took place at the church of Saint-Denis in Paris on July 28, 754, a ceremony that would be remembered in the coronation rites of the French kings for a thousand years.

7   Several of the 34 original laws of the "Capitulary for the Saxon Regions" (*Capitulatio de Partibus Saxoniae*) are directed against pagan practices, notably law 8, which states: "*If any one of the race of the Saxons hereafter, concealed among them, shall have wished to hide himself unbaptized, and shall have scorned to come to baptism, and shall have wished to remain a pagan, let him be punished by death.*" (qtd. in Ogg, 121)

8   These regional dialects would eventually evolve into Romance languages such as French, Italian, Spanish and Portuguese.

9   Art historian Kenneth Clark gained fame through the 1969 BBC series *Civilisation: A Personal View by Kenneth Clark.* He also published a book by the same title.

10   The Old St. Peter's Basilica— constructed on the orders of Emperor Constantine I in the 4th century — would be torn down in the early 16th century on the orders of Pope Julius II, because it was falling into ruin. The new St. Peter's Basilica was built on the same spot.

11   Of course by giving himself the power to decide which temporal leader was to be emperor, the pope also greatly increased his *own* power and significance.

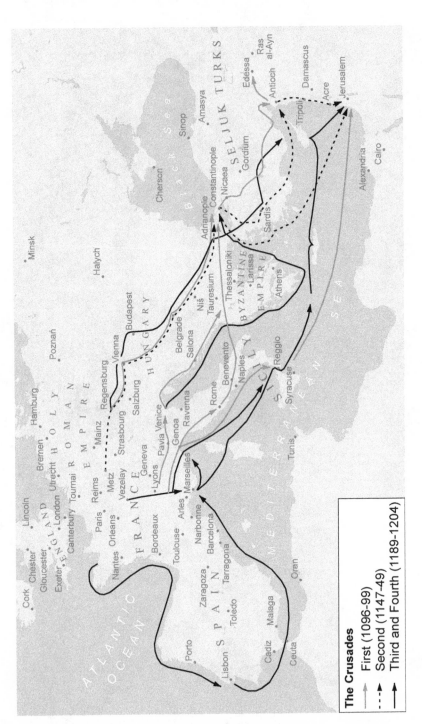

Map 6: The Crusades

The Crusades

First (1096-99)

Second (1147-49)

Third and Fourth (1189-1204)

14

GOD WILLS IT!

"Let this be your war-cry in combats, because this word is given to you by God. When an armed attack is made upon the enemy, let this one cry be raised by all the soldiers of God: It is the will of God! It is the will of God!"[1]

Pope Urban II, Council of Clermont, 1095

The presumed will of God has had an outsize influence on human history from the moment people started presuming to know it. In the Middle Ages, many believed His will was to kill the non-believers and take their lands. Some still do.

In the early days of Islam, when Muslims were actively persecuted, its founder Muhammad formulated the principle of *Jihad* (meaning 'struggle'), giving his followers the right to resist those who oppressed them. But soon after Muhammad's death, in 632, the interpretation of Jihad was widened to include the idea of holy war; not just to defend the Islamic state, but to expand it.

And expand it did. The Arabs took their holy war across North Africa, to the Iberian Peninsula, over the Pyrenees and into the South of France, until they were finally stopped by the Franks at the Battle of Tours, exactly 100 years after Muhammad's death. The Islamic conquests were far from over, though.

More than 350 years later, on November 27, 1095, pope Urban II delivered a passionate, powerful speech to a group of some 300 clerics and French nobles in Clermont, France, in which he reproached the nobles for fighting amongst themselves and neglecting their job of administering justice, which in turn had led to an increase in violence and crime. He demanded the nobles keep the peace in their provinces.

They solemnly promised they would.

Urban II then moved to another pressing matter, saying Byzantine Emperor Alexios I Komnenos had recently asked him for help in his struggle against the Seljuk Turks, who had already taken nearly all of Asia Minor from the Byzantines. According to Urban II, churches and holy places were being destroyed by the Turks and many Christians had already been killed. That the Byzantine Emperor had asked the pope for help at all was proof enough of the seriousness of the situation, seeing as the relationship between the Eastern and Western branches of the Christian church had been tense for decades.

Originally there had been only one Roman Catholic Church, but after the fall of the Western Roman Empire in 476, the memory of a common foundation had slowly faded. About 30 years before Urban's speech at the Council of Clermont, the Pope and the Patriarch — the leader of the Eastern Orthodox Church — had even excommunicated each other for not recognizing the other as the true head of the whole church, an event that would later be viewed as the official break between the two churches (also known as the East-West Schism).

But now, in his speech, Urban II called the Eastern Orthodox Christians their *"brethren"*, who must be aided in their struggle against the infidels, and urged all true Christians to travel to the East and drive the Seljuk Turks, a *"despised and base race, which worships demons"*, *"from the lands of our friends"*(Allen, "The Crusades", 34).[2] Urban concluded his speech threatening those willingly staying on the sideline with the wrath of God, while promising forgiveness of all sins for those who died on the journey or in battle against the Pagans (Allen, "The Crusades", 34).

The crowd ate it up, zealously shouting *"Deus Vult! Deus Vult!"*, God wills it! God wills it! (Peters, 22). After the first noble, Adhemar of Le Puy, put a purple cross on his clothes as a sign of his commitment to the cause, many nobles followed.

Those who answered Urban's call to arms were known as *fideles Sancti Petri* (the faithful of St. Peter) or *milites Christi* (knights of Christ). The term 'Crusader' came into use much later.[3] The Muslims simply called them Franks, because the vast majority of the first Crusaders were Franks.

In the months that followed the pope traveled all over France to gather support for the holy war. The response was overwhelming, especially among the peasants. Tens of thousands of people took up the cross, committing themselves to a perilous journey of thousands of miles to fight against a people they knew nothing of, the Seljuk Turks, in support of another people they knew nothing of, the Byzantines.

And so, the following year, in 1096, an army of 35,000 men embarked on the long journey to Constantinople, the capital of the Byzantine Empire (Nicolle, "First Crusade", 32). When they finally arrived there, Byzantine Emperor Alexios I Komnenos, not too keen on having the French nobles and their vast army encamped outside his beautiful city for too long — especially after an earlier group of peasant Crusaders had attacked Constantinople and pillaged the surrounding country side — arranged for their swift transport across the Bosporus, into Asia Minor. (That the Crusaders could indeed pose a real threat to the Byzantines would become clear a century later, when they captured and sacked Constantinople during the Fourth Crusade).

On July 15, 1099, three and half years after Pope Urban's speech, Jerusalem fell to the Crusaders. Following their holy victory, the "faithful of St. Peter" promptly slaughtered the Muslims and Jews who had defended the city, a massacre that has since gained notoriety among Christians and Muslims alike, although killing the inhabitants of a captured city that had persisted in its refusal to surrender was hardly uncommon at the time. But this war being a holy war — and Jerusalem being Jerusalem — the massacre has lived on in infamy.

There has also been debate among historians over how extensive the killing really was. Contemporary reports speak of a slaughter so great *"that our men waded in blood up to their ankles"* (Krey, 256). But this was likely also meant as a reference to the book of Revelation 14:20 (Madden, 34).[4] There is no doubt that many Jewish and Muslim citizens of Jerusalem were indeed killed by the Crusaders, but at the same time some eyewitnesses likely exaggerated the killings as a result of their zealous jubilation, as a description of the events by Raymond D'Aguilers, a clergyman and eyewitness, illustrates: *"So let it suffice to say this much, at least, that in the Temple and porch of Solomon, men rode in blood up to their knees and bridle reins. Indeed, it was a just and splendid judgment of God that this place should be filled with the blood of the unbelievers, since it had suffered so long from their blasphemies. The city was filled with corpses and blood."* (qtd. in Krey, 261).

Fact is that there was no massacre at all when Muslim leader Saladin recaptured Jerusalem 88 years later (although pope Urban III literally died of a heart attack upon hearing the news that the Holy City had fallen to the Muslims). Saladin also set a very low ransom for the Christians in the city — letting many people go who could not even afford that — and allowed the Jews to resettle in Jerusalem. It was one of several lessons in chivalry the great Muslim leader would give to the Crusaders.

For the Europeans the First Crusade was a great success. Jerusalem was under Christian rule again for the first time in 461 years, as were several other cities in the Holy Land, allowing for the establishment of four Crusader States, of which the Kingdom of Jerusalem would be the most important one.

For the Byzantine Empire, the "help" from the Crusaders turned out to be a mixed bag at best. Yes, they had successfully stopped the Muslim advance, giving the empire some much needed breathing room. But the Crusaders did not give any of the conquered territory back to the Byzantines and would even sack Constantinople during the Fourth Crusade. Not the best allies to have. Ultimately, the Crusades would therefore hurt and weaken the Eastern Roman Empire more than help it.

There would be eight other Crusades to the Middle East, but they were much less successful — some even disastrous — and within 200 years the Europeans would lose their last stronghold in the Levant. They did not return until 1799, when Napoleon tried to conquer the Holy Land for France — exactly 700 years after the Crusaders had captured Jerusalem — but saw his plans frustrated when he failed to take the strategic city of Acre. Finally, in 1917, the British defeated the Ottomans at the Battle of Jerusalem, ending more than 700 years of near continuous Islamic rule of the city (apart from two brief spells of Christian rule between 1229-1244).

Apart from the nine Crusades to the Levant there were also crusades on the Iberian Peninsula and in Eastern Europe. The so-called *Reconquista* (722-1492) of present-day Spain and Portugal by Christian forces began as a simple war of conquest in the Early Middle Ages, but gradually shifted to a holy war against the Muslims. Several popes called on Europeans to go and fight for Christianity in Iberia, promising all their sins would be forgiven. Many went.

But why? What made people sign up for the Crusades, especially the commoners? Was it out of a sense of adventure, hope for a better life, the wish to wash away one's sins, a genuine belief in the cause, or just plain and simple greed? We don't really know.

Looking back in time through a 21st century filter, most people in the West are probably tempted to assume that the chief reasons must have been material instead of spiritual. For many of us it is difficult to imagine and appreciate how important religion was to people in the Middle Ages, how wholeheartedly they believed that living a sinful life would lead to an extended stay in purgatory for purification by fire or even a one-way ticket to hell, where they would suffer an eternity of agonising, never ending torment. With that in mind, who wouldn't be tempted to become a Crusader and kill infidels in return for a fast ticket to paradise?

Of course the higher up the food chain, the bigger also the earthly rewards for going on a Crusade. Land, titles, wealth, prestige, for the nobles who brought knights and soldiers with them the potential rewards could be great. This was especially true for second, third and later sons of a nobleman, because they could not inherit their father's title.

The pope, too, had much to gain from the Crusades, aside from helping the Christians in the East. For one, waging a holy war made the Christian faith — and therefore the church — more important to both nobles and commoners. At the same time, finding the nobles a common enemy also helped decrease the wars they fought against each other, thus improving stability in Europe. And last but not least, by helping to save the Byzantine Empire the pope hoped to reunite the Roman Catholic Church and the Eastern Orthodox Church again — under his own divinely inspired leadership of course.

In all, the Christian Crusader presence in the Holy Land lasted less then 200 years. And although the capture of Jerusalem certainly spoke to the imagination of the faithful, in terms of religious conquest the *Reconquista* would prove much more successful in the long run, expelling the Muslims from the Iberian Peninsula altogether in 1492.

Having said that, the Crusades to the Holy Land did bring Europe other long-term benefits, which would help propel it to world domination in the centuries to come, such as better organized secular governments, access to Arabian knowledge — notably in the fields of astronomy, algebra and medicine — renewed access to ancient Greek knowledge and increased trading throughout Europe. Before the Crusades, the Muslims of the Levant and the Iberian Peninsula were much more advanced than the Europeans, who were still a long way away from the level of civilization they had reached during the days of the Western Roman Empire. But by venturing into the Eastern Empire and coming into contact with the Muslims, the Crusaders were introduced to a wealth of new knowledge.

Knowledge of ancient Greek had been lost in Europe since the fall of the Western Roman Empire, but now many ancient Greek texts were transmitted back to Europe in Arabic and subsequently translated into Latin, including the works of great thinkers like Homer, Plato and Aristotle. The latter proved particularly inspiring to many Western philosophers, among them Thomas Aquinas, one of the most important philosophers of the Middle Ages.[5]

Then there was the significantly increased trade throughout Europe because of all those Crusaders making their way East. They needed equipment, supplies, transport. The Italian city states located en route to the Holy Land benefitted handsomely from all those visitors from all over Europe (as they still do). And of course there was also increased trading between East and West. New trade routes were opened and new products — spices, gunpowder, coffee, mirrors, carpets, ships compasses, writing paper, wheelbarrows — started making their way into Europe via trade conduits such as Venice, Florence, Genoa and Pisa.[6] It was in these Italian city states that the Renaissance would first see the light of day in the late 14th century.

Another important side effect of the Crusades in the Levant was that it postponed the Islamic advance in the East for several centuries, buying Europe some much needed time. The Ottoman Turks would still come to Europe, but their advance would eventually be stopped at the battle of Vienna, in 1683.

After the Ottoman Empire was finally pushed out of most of Europe in the 18th century, the concept of holy war took a backseat to more secular reasons for going to war, until making a comeback in the latter part of the 20th and early 21st century with radical islamists, who decided to stretch the concept of *Jihad* to the point of it authorizing the killing of anyone who does not subscribe to their interpretation of Islam. They say God wills it.

---

1   Quoted in Peters, 28-29.The quote comes from Robert the Monk's version of the speech of Urban, written down in his chronicle *Historia Hierosolymitana.* It is unclear whether Robert was present at the Council of Clermont to hear Pope Urban II's fiery speech himself. He used the Gesta Francorum version of the speech as a source.

2   I used the Fulcher of Chartres version of Urban's speech.

3   In the late 16th century the French word *croisade* came into fashion for describing the earlier Christian military endeavors against the Muslims. The word *croisade* has its roots in *croisée,* meaning 'being marked with the cross', which is itself based on the Latin word *crux,* 'cross', and the Spanish *cruzado.*

4   The quote is from a translated version of the Gesta Francorum, one of the most important eyewitness accounts of the First Crusade, used extensively by August Krey in his work *The First Crusade: The Accounts of Eye-Witnesses and Participants.* In an attempt to verify contemporary accounts that Muslim blood was indeed running through the streets of Jerusalem ankle-deep or worse from all the killing, Thomas Madden does some interesting calculations in his article "Rivers of Blood: An Analysis of One Aspect of the Crusader Conquest of Jerusalem". Madden concludes it would have been impossible for even the floor space of 'Solomon's Temple and Portico' (i.e., the al-Aqsa mosque) — let alone the streets of Jerusalem — to have been filled with enough blood to reach ankle height, much less reach *"up to the bridle of the horses"*, as Raymond D'Aguilers, another eyewitness, described (Madden 34-37).

5   Aquinas considered Aristotle so important he referred to him simply as 'The Philosopher' in his influential work 'Summa Theologica'. See for instance ST part I, Question 14, Article 11. Also, I: Q25, A3, and I:Q34, A1.

6   After the fall of Constantinople, in 1453, Europeans were cut off from important trade routes with the East by the Ottomans, forcing them to look for new trade routes. During this Age of Exploration (15th-17th century) mercantile power would shift from the Italian city states to Western European countries like Portugal, Spain, the Netherlands, England and France.

MAGNA CARTA

*"No freeman shall be taken, or imprisoned,
or disseised, or outlawed, or exiled, or in
any way harmed — nor will we go upon or
send upon him — save by lawful judgment
of his peers, or by the law of the land."* [1]

Magna Carta, clause 39, 1215

The first King of England was the Anglo-Saxon Athelstan, who ruled from 927 to 939. Back in those days, kings exercised near absolute power over their realm. There were feudal customs and traditions they mostly abided by, but nothing was written in stone. Kings declared war on their own, gave lands to vassals as fiefs — and sometimes took them back again — levied as much taxes as they saw fit, charged payments for certain valuable offices and demanded military support and services from their vassals. In short, it was good to be the king. This went on for several centuries, until the reign of King John of England (1199-1216).

But first there was Richard, John's older brother. Richard was a hero. "Richard the Lionheart" people called him, because he was such a courageous warrior and great military leader, something he had proven while still a teenager, campaigning in France for his father, Henry II.

After Richard had been crowned King of England on September 3, 1189, he immediately started preparing for a Crusade to the Holy Land to recapture Jerusalem, which had fallen to Saladin two years earlier. To pay for his Crusade, Richard plundered the treasury, raised taxes, sold official positions and forced those who already had such a position to pay a hefty sum to keep it. He also sold rights, privileges and pieces of land. Six months after his coronation he left for the Holy Land, having appointed two nobles as justiciar to rule in his absence, none of them being his younger brother John.[2]

Even worse for John was that Richard had named their three-year-old nephew Arthur of Brittany (the son of their deceased brother Geoffrey, who was older than John but younger than Richard) as heir to the throne. In other words, should Richard die on the long and dangerous journey to Jerusalem or while fighting against Salah ad-Din — a definite possibility — the throne of England would go to Arthur the toddler instead of John Lackland, as he was called, not to his amusement.[3]

Recognizing his younger brother's frustration and ambition — a powerful and dangerous combination — Richard gave John valuable lands all over England, including the counties of Cornwall, Somerset and Nottingham, to prevent him from trying to grab power in his absence (Warren, 40). In return, John promised not to visit England for three years (Warren, 40). It was a promise he would not keep, because as soon as Richard was gone John started scheming with whomever could help him to the throne, including the King of France, and before long John was king in everything but name.

Legend has it that a certain Robin Hood and his merry men fought against the misrule of John Lackland. Fact is that they were not the only ones, and when organized fighting broke out between John's mercenaries and forces loyal to Richard, John backed down and agreed to a truce. When Richard returned somewhat later, John surrendered and begged forgiveness, which he received (Warren, 46).

When Richard died in 1199 John was at last crowned King of England for real. He did face some resistance from his now twelve-year-old nephew Arthur of Brittany, but John's forces captured the young duke two years later. He was imprisoned in Rouen and disappeared a couple of months later, never to be seen again. One persistent rumor went that John had killed his nephew with his own hands, tied a heavy stone around his body and thrown him into the Seine (McLynn, 306). Meanwhile, John was also entangled in a war with King Philip II of France, with many of his French possessions at stake.[4] He had raised an expensive mercenary army to ward off Philip's attempts to cease his French lands, but John was not nearly as brilliant a military commander as his brother Richard had been and by 1204 had lost all his possessions in France except the Duchy of Aquitaine.

In desperate need of funds to pay for new campaigns in France, John started raising money any way he could think of. Apart from levying new and higher taxes, the justice system in particular proved to be an excellent cash cow. Thinking creatively, John found he could sell almost anything having to do with justice; the right to be heard by the royal courts, to a more speedy trial, the delay of a trial, freedom instead of incarceration, they all became privileges bringing in extra revenue for the king. And if people did not have enough money to pay for those privileges they could always borrow money from the crown — at huge interest rates of course. Yes, it was still good to be the king.

The war with France did not go well, though, and on July 27, 1214, King John lost the decisive Battle of Bouvines, costing him almost all of his possessions in France, including Normandy, Brittany, Anjou, Maine and the Touraine, which meant loss of fiefs and income for the barons as well.

It was the final straw. After a decade of seeing new taxes introduced without being consulted, of justice based on favoritism and the financial needs of the crown, of failed campaigns and costly defeats, the barons decided they had had enough and revolted.

John tried to stall for time so he could raise an army of mercenaries to deal with them, but after a couple of months the barons had enough of John's procrastination and rode to London armed and ready. On June 10, 1215, the city opened its gates — revealing where the people's sympathies lay in the matter — and the barons rode to Westminster, catching the king off guard.

Five days later, on June 15, 1215, King John was brought to a meadow in Runnymede, some 20 miles west of London, where he was forced to sign a document limiting his powers and recognizing certain rights of freemen, after which the barons renewed their oath of fealty to him.[5] It was the first time a king was forced to recognize he was not above the law, that he could not rule arbitrarily, punishing whoever he disliked or could not pay up, while forgiving the crimes of those he favored or had deep pockets. The document would later come to be known as *Magna Carta*, Great Charter.[6]

Among the more important clauses of the Magna Carta were number 12, stating that taxes can only be levied and assessed by the common counsel of the realm, number 20, stating that fines should be proportionate to the offense, number 24, stating that crown officials must not try a crime in place of a judge, number 38, stating that no one can be put on trial based solely on the unsupported word of one official and number 40, which forbids justice to be sold, denied or delayed.[7]

The most famous clause is number 39, which says: *"No freeman shall be taken, or imprisoned, or disseised, or outlawed, or exiled, or in any way harmed — nor will we go upon or send upon him — save by lawful judgment of his peers, or by the law of the land."*

Clause 39 established the right to be brought before a court, which would then determine the legality under which a person was taken or imprisoned by the government. It is one of the most important protections against arbitrary state action, known as *habeas corpus*. Clause 39 is one of three clauses from the Magna Carta that are still law today in Great Britain. It has been adopted by many other constitutions throughout the civilized world, including the U.S. Constitution (Art. I, Sec 9).

Other parts of the U.S. Constitution that can be traced back to the Magna Carta are the Fifth Amendment (right to trial, due process), Sixth Amendment (right to speedy trial) Seventh Amendment (right to trial, adherence to the law of the land) Eight Amendment (proportionality of fines) and Fourteenth Amendment (due process obligation of the states). Given this influence on the Constitution, it comes as no surprise that the US Supreme Court still regularly refers to Magna Carta in its Decisions.[8]

Another, quite revolutionary clause in the Magna Carta was number 61. It stated that the barons would choose twenty-five barons from among themselves who would monitor if the King adhered to the charter, and who — if he did not — could seek redress by seizing the king's *"castles, lands and possessions, and in every other way that they can, until amends shall have been made according to their judgement. Saving the persons of ourselves, our queen and our children."* The clause effectively created a parliament, not just a council the king could consult whenever he felt like it, but a legal entity that limited the power of the executive branch, in this case the king. Clause 61 was a bridge too far. It basically dethroned the king and gave supremacy to a council of barons. Sure enough, open warfare broke out between the barons and the king within three months after the signing at Runnymede (the First Barons' War). But when King John died a year later, the main reason for the war died with him. The barons placed his nine-year-old son Henry III on the throne and forced him to sign a new version of the Magna Carta, this one without Clause 61.

The concept of a parliament survived, though, and within a century the Parliament of England would be institutionalized, its members coming from the clergy, aristocracy and commoners. One of its core powers was the right to grant or deny new taxes to the king. Of course effective governing is impossible without levying taxes and Parliament increasingly used its influence on the king's public finances to influence him in other affairs as well.

Over the next centuries, English monarchs continued to wrestle with Parliament and the Great Charter, which to them felt like nothing but an annoying straitjacket, limiting their God-given power. But the genie did not let itself be put back in the bottle and in 1642 it came to a head between Parliament and the King. Parliament won, King Charles I lost — both the war and his head. From then on, supremacy in England lay with Parliament.

More than a century later and on the other side of the Atlantic, American colonists revolted against King George III. One of the main reasons for their rebellion was that they were taxed without being represented in Parliament, hence the slogan "No Taxation Without Representation", which had come into fashion in the colonies in the 1760s, a decade before the start of the American Revolution. The colonists argued that since it was forbidden to impose taxes without the consent of Parliament and they were not represented in Parliament, the taxes violated their constitutional rights such as they were stipulated in Magna Carta and the Bill of Rights of 1689.[9]

Even if the original Magna Carta only meant to protect the interests of the barons against the king, its symbolic meaning has had a far greater impact. Over time, Magna Carta came to signify a social contract existing between the government and the governed. A social contract based on the rule of law, stating what the government can and cannot do, and giving the people the right to resist if and when their government does not hold up its end of the bargain.

A powerful, revolutionary principle, and one the noble barons no doubt never meant to establish. All they wanted was to protect themselves against King John's absolutism. They probably couldn't care less about the commoners and their rights. Ironically, though, it would be the commoners who ultimately benefited the most from Magna Carta, using its legal concepts to end tyranny — and in some cases the nobles.

---

1   Quote taken from *Medieval Worlds: A Sourcebook* (Anderson), which publishes the entire text of the 1215 version of the Magna Carta on pages 152-160.

2   The justiciar was the chief political and legal officer and thus very powerful. He presided over the King's court and also deputized for the King in his absence. The office existed in practice from the reign of William the Conquerer (1066-1087) until that of Henry III, when the last justiciar was removed from office, in 1232. Appointing two justiciars would prove to be a poor decision on Richard the Lionheart's part, because the two nobles soon found themselves in a power struggle with each other.

3   Because John was the youngest of the five sons of King Henry II and Eleanor of Aquitaine, there were no lands available for him to inherit, earning him the nickname "Lackland" at an early age.

4   The war was started by Philip II when John refused to appear at the French court in his capacity as the Count of Poitou, though feudal custom demanded this of him, given that he had a dispute with one of the Poitou nobles. In the subsequent Normandy Campaigns (1200-1204) John lost Normandy, Anjou and Poitou.

5   The term "freeman" (*liber homo*) was most likely meant as synonymous with "freeholder", meaning a feudal tenant, thus excluding the ordinary peasantry and villagers. In later centuries however, the "freeman" of the Magna Carta came to mean all Englishmen (McKechnie, 114-115).

6   The document that was signed on June 15 is known as the *Articles of the Barons*. It was modified in the days following the signing at Runnymede, leading to a formal version issued on June 19. It was this second version that came to be known as the *Magna Carta* (Warren 236).

7   The 1215 version was not yet numbered or divided in clauses. This was done by the English jurist Sir William Blackstone, in 1759.

8   Magna Carta has been cited more than a hundred times in US Supreme Court cases (Turner, 218).

9   The Bill of Rights of 1689, not be confused with the United States Bill of
    Rights of 1789 (ratified 1791), limits the power of the Crown and lays out the
    rights of Parliament as well as certain basic rights for all Englishmen. It is still
    in effect.

16

LET THERE BE GUNPOWDER

*"For such is the shock of artillery
that there is no wall so strong that in a
few days it will not batter down."*

Niccolò Machiavelli, Discourses, II.XVII, 1517

On August 2, 1939, less than a month before the start of WW II, Albert Einstein sent a letter to President Franklin D. Roosevelt, warning him of the possibility that *"extremely powerful bombs of a new type"* may be constructed, because of recent scientific breakthroughs in generating nuclear chain reactions in a large mass of uranium (Einstein, "Letter to Roosevelt"). To illustrate the point, the letter mentioned the example of such a bomb being detonated in a port, which *"might very well destroy the whole port together with some of the surrounding territory"* (Einstein, "Letter to Roosevelt"). Einstein used a lot of possibles, mights and may be's, but the message was clear: a scientific breakthrough had been made that could lead to the development of a very, very big bomb.

About a thousand years earlier, we were only just beginning to figure out the idea of a bomb. Most historians agree that it was probably Chinese alchemists searching for the elixir of life (oh, irony) who in the ninth century discovered that mixing saltpeter, sulfur and charcoal together could cause a powerful incendiary reaction.[1] Believing the mixture was perhaps the key to immortality, they called it 'fire drug' (Kelly, "Gunpowder", 2-3). It was the earliest form of gunpowder.

The Chinese already knew that saltpeter — gunpowder's key ingredient — burned with a purple flame, thus providing a way to distinguish it from other inorganic salts and also making it possible to evaluate and compare purification techniques (Chase, 31). At first the Chinese were primarily interested in using saltpeter for medicinal mixtures, but that changed when they discovered the incendiary propensity of saltpeter mixed with sulfur and charcoal.

When the Arabs first referred to saltpeter, in the 13th century, they called it Chinese snow, suggesting they had acquired it through Chinese sources, either directly or indirectly, perhaps through India (Kelly, "Gunpowder", 22). The Syrian chemist Hasan al-Rammah wrote about how to purify saltpeter in his book *al-Furusiyya wa al-Manasib al-Harbiyya* (The Book of Military Horsemanship and Ingenious War Devices, c. 1280). He also mentioned several incendiary mixtures involving saltpeter, sulfur and charcoal, but none of them were powerful enough to create an explosion; they were more suited as rocket propellant or for use in fireworks (Partington, 202-203). The Europeans acquired knowledge of gunpowder around the same time, possibly from the Arabs, or perhaps more likely from the Mongols, who had invaded Eastern Europe and reportedly used Chinese gunpowder weapons at the Battle of Mohi, in present-day Hungary, in 1241 (Chase, 58). It has also been suggested that the Arabs and the Europeans might have discovered gunpowder independently, but since the Chinese had already discovered it some 400 years earlier this doesn't seem very likely.

Then again, if the Chinese really were the first to discover gunpowder, as the evidence suggests, why aren't we all speaking Mandarin? After all we are talking about gunpowder here — the most significant military invention since the pointy stick — and the Chinese apparently had it some 400 years before everybody else. So why didn't the Chinese use their invention to conquer the world? Were they pacifists, satisfied with what they had, at peace with everybody? Far from it.

In reality gunpowder was not so much a discovery as it was a development, though. It was not just a matter of mixing saltpeter, sulfur and charcoal together, the trick was mixing them together in the right proportions. And finding that right formula was a process of trial and error that took centuries. The earliest mention of a mixture containing the three key ingredients was in 808 (Lorge, 32), but more than two hundred years later the Chinese still did not have a mixture that was powerful enough to create an explosion. Other ingredients like garlic and honey were wrongfully mixed with the three key ingredients and none of the tried formulas held enough saltpeter, because the underlying chemical process of gunpowder was not yet fully understood. During this time gunpowder does not seem to have played much of a role on the battlefield. In fact, the first confirmed use of a gunpowder-based weapon, the Chinese "fire lance", a flamethrower of sorts, used at the siege of De'an in 1132, came more than 300 years after the early form of gunpowder had been discovered (Lorge, 33-34; Chase, 31).[2]

Considering that (real) gunpowder and warfare are like two peas in a pod, there is a case to be made for arguing that as long as it wasn't used on the battlefield, it wasn't really gunpowder yet, just a promising mixture of saltpeter, charcoal and sulfur.[3] What is certain is that at the end of the 13th century, the Chinese, Europeans, Arabs, Turks and Indians had all acquired the knowledge of battlefield-grade gunpowder. The next challenge — how to put it to good use — took considerably less time. Again it was the Chinese who took the first steps, because together with improvements in the gunpowder formula, the aforementioned fire lance soon gave rise to the cannon.

Early Chinese and European cannon were both made of cast bronze, but the Chinese also used cast iron from 1356, while early European iron cannon were made from wrought iron staves, hammer- welded together and strengthened by hoops (Turnbull, 19). In the mid-1500s iron cast cannon were also introduced in Europe, thanks to the blast furnace (Chase,144). Manufacturing iron cast cannon was cheaper and faster, but if the iron was impure and the casting not skillfully done the cannon could explode. A cast bronze cannon tended to split or rapture instead, which, while inconvenient, was obviously less lethal for the gun crew. Over time the cast iron cannon nevertheless prevailed.

In those early days cannon were probably almost as dangerous to those who used them as to their enemy. Just loading a cannon required considerable skill and bravery. Not only could the gunpowder accidentally explode if not properly handled, there was also the danger of the cannon barrel bursting when fired, turning it into one big, deadly grenade, shredding everyone standing around it. One prominent victim of exploding cannon was King James II of Scotland (1430-1460), an ardent artillery enthusiast. As the Scottish chronicler Robert Lindsay of Pitscottie wrote in his *History of Scotland: "But while this Prince, more curious than became him, or the Majesty of a King, did stand nearhand the Gunners, when the Artillery was discharged, his Thigh-Bone was dung in two with a Piece of misframed Gun, that brake in shooting; by the which he was stricken to the Ground, and died hastily."* (64).

Their potential was undeniable, though, so everybody soldiered on. It was the first time in history that military technology was so actively and widely developed and improved upon. Before the advent of gunpowder, the basic weapons of war — spear, sword, shield, bow and arrow, horse — had remained largely unchanged for hundreds, even thousands of years. A Roman Republican army from the 3rd century BCE, for instance, was equipped with the same kind of weapons as a 12th century French Crusader army. But gunpowder was a game changer and everybody knew it.

And so chemists kept tweaking the gunpowder formula, because the better the formula, the bigger the bang. Metallurgy, mathematics and engineering also became more important with the arrival of gunpowder artillery, especially in Europe, where numerous kingdoms and city states were constantly at war with each other.

In the early 15th century Europeans also found a way to improve the production process of gunpowder, which was about time, because making gunpowder was even more dangerous than operating a cannon (Hall, xxvii).[4] The mixing process was improved upon by adding liquid, which greatly diminished the chance of an accidental explosion. The resulting paste was then pressed into grains, after it had been discovered that gunpowder grains ignited faster, making them ballistically stronger than uncorned, so-called "serpentine" gunpowder (Hall, xxvii). One important effect of this corned powder was the introduction of the first shoulder firearms, such as the arquebus, for which the stronger gunpowder was perfect (Hall, xxvii). Because corned powder was so much more powerful, it also spurred widespread innovation in artillery, reducing the risk of the cannon barrel exploding while at the same time delivering greater range (Hall, xxvii-xxviii).

The nature of warfare fundamentally changed with the introduction

HISTORY THAT CHANGED THE WORLD - 149

of gunpowder. An arms race ensued between the offensive power of gunpowder weapons and the defensive capabilities of stone walls and personal armor plating. It would go on for several centuries, but the eventual outcome was clear from the start.

Walls were made thicker and angulated, towers were made round instead of rectangular, to deflect cannon balls. But as gunpowder became more effective and cannon cheaper and better casted, the cost of building huge walls at one point just stopped weighing up against the extra time it bought the defenders. At the siege and subsequent fall of Constantinople, for instance, in 1453, the Ottomans used a cannon that was 27ft long (8.2 m), with a barrel of 32 inches (81 cm) in diameter, a monster that could fire a stone cannonball of 1200 lbs (544 kg) and had a range of up to 1 mile (Runciman, 78). How big of a stone wall would one have to build to defend against such a cannon? Plate armor also thickened between the 15th and 17th century, to keep up with the increasing firepower of the arquebus, and, later, the musket. Introduced on the battlefield in the mid-16th century, the musket was a heavier and more powerful firearm than the arquebus, capable of piercing existing plate armor at longer range. As the musket improved and became more widely used, both the infantry and cavalry gradually shed their heavy plating in exchange for increased maneuverability.[5]

The huge impact gunpowder came to have throughout the world was based on one simple truth: gunpowder made it easier to kill. In movies, sword fighting always seems easy enough, just pick up a blade and start dealing blows to the enemy, usually an equally skillful and relentless fighter. Using a bow and arrow seems even simpler; grab a bow, nock the arrow, draw, aim, and release. Of course the reality was quite different. Learning to fight effectively with a sword or becoming a skillful archer took years and it certainly wasn't for everybody. Strong men were required for the job and they had to be extensively trained.

How different this was for riflemen. Almost every peasant could be turned into a reasonably effective musketeer in a matter of weeks, easily outmatching a sword yielding knight who had had years of training. The knights looked down on the use of gunpowder weapons and considered them honorless, but what good is honor when you are being shot from 50 feet away while bravely charging on horseback?

With a professional warrior class no longer necessary, the position of the nobility grew weaker over time. No longer did a king have to depend on well-trained knights for the defense of his realm, he could simply conscript young peasants, mold them into disciplined soldiers and teach them how to shoot guns and cannon, all in a matter of weeks. As a result, armies grew considerably in size. Of course bigger armies also meant (many) more casualties, but such losses were relatively easily replenished.

To enlist sufficient soldiers, commoners were at times drafted, tempted with signing bonuses or inspired to volunteer (for instance by appealing to religious or nationalistic fervor). Because the new armies were not only bigger but also more expensive, taxation also increased, leading to the increased importance of the commercial classes and a better organized, centralized government. The nobles still played an important role in the military as officers, but never again as independent lords with their own fiefdoms and soldiers. Thus feudal society gave way to the modern nation state.

The increased power of the commoners led to increased tensions with the aristocracy, which held on to its privileged positions from the old days even though their military power base had pretty much disappeared. Over time, kings too would find out that trading in a few powerful nobles for a multitude of commoners did not necessarily improve their own power base.

Because gunpowder weapons were so much more powerful than 'classic' weapons like the sword, spear and bow, those who had them could dominate those who did not, something European nations were quick to discover — and exploit. From the 1500s to the mid-1900s, military superior countries such as Spain, Portugal, Britain, France and the Netherlands conquered many ancient civilizations in Asia, Africa and the Americas, establishing large colonial empires that lasted for centuries. It was really a question of bringing guns to a knife fight. One telling example is the Battle of Rorke's Drift, in 1879, during the Anglo-Zulu War, when 150 British troops armed with Martini- Henry breech-loading rifles successfully defended a garrison against 4,000 experienced Zulu warriors mostly armed with a short stabbing spear and cow-hide shield.[6] An estimated 350 Zulus were killed and 500 wounded, against 17 British deaths and 15 wounded.

In an effort to create a gunpowder that was more stable and produced less smoke —which gave away the positions of snipers and obscured the view from the battlefield, sometimes making it all but impossible to communicate effectively with the troops during battle — a new propellant was sought, and found, in the late 19th century. Using gaseous combustion ingredients instead of solid ones, smokeless powder quickly replaced 'traditional' gunpowder, finally ending its 1,000-year- reign (Kelly, 231-233).[7]

Black powder is still used as a propellant in fireworks and by hunters, battle re-enactors and competitive black powder shooters. More than a few sports fans even make their own black powder. Why use the riskier, noisier and smokier black powder instead of smokeless powder? Well, as one audiophile answered when asked why he still roamed the internet in search for those scratchable, breakable and unwieldy LP records: *"Because they sound better"*. Now how can you argue with that?

---

1 The first written evidence of a mixture containing saltpeter, sulfur and charcoal is found in the work *Taishang Guaizu Danjing Mijue* (c. 808), by the Taoist priest Qing Xuzi (Lorge, 32).

2 Both Lorge and Chase point out that the fire-lance was certainly much older, on account of it being depicted on a mid- tenth century Buddhist wall painting at Dunhuang. There was no other mention of it, though, until the siege of De'an.

3 For those who plan to take a time machine and travel back to the Middle Ages, be sure to etch the following formula in your brain, so you'll have something valuable to offer to the medieval powers that be: 75 percent Saltpeter, 15 percent Charcoal, 10 percent Sulfur.

4 Whether corned gunpowder was indeed a European invention is not beyond dispute, but both Kenneth Chase, in his work *Firearms: A Global History to 1700*, and Bert Hall in his introduction to Partington's *A History of Greek Fire and Gunpowder*, give some evidence suggesting the technique originated in Europe rather than China (Chase, 144; Hall, xxviii).

5 Initially, the musket was used as a specialist, armor-piercing weapon, alongside the arquebus and the pike. But as the musket became lighter and more portable, the arquebus was gradually edged out, while the addition of the bayonet replaced the pike.

6   Some Zulus were equipped with old muskets, but their marksmanship training was poor, as was the quality and supply of their powder and shot (Knight, 33).

7   After it was replaced by smokeless powder, traditional gunpowder composed of saltpeter, charcoal and sulfur came to be known as black powder.

17

THE BLACK DEATH

"And so they died. And none could be found to
bury the dead for money or friendship. Members of
a household brought their dead to a ditch as best
they could, without priest, without divine offices.
Nor did the death bell sound. And in many places
in Siena great pits were dug and piled deep with the
multitude of dead. And they died by the hundreds
both day and night, and all were thrown in those
ditches and covered over with earth. And as soon
as those ditches were filled more were dug. And
I, Agnolo di Tura, called the Fat, buried my five
children with my own hands.....And so many died
that all believed that it was the end of the world."[1]

The Plague in Siena: An Italian Chronicle,
Agnolo di Tura del Grasso.

In the spring of 2003 the world was gripped by fear of a mysterious infectious disease. The outbreak had started in November 2002, in China's Guangdong province, but had been kept under wraps for months by the Chinese government, until an American succumbed to the disease in a Hong Kong hospital. By then, the World Health Organization (WHO) had already put out a global alert about a new infectious disease of unknown origin in both Vietnam and Hong Kong. It was called Severe Acute Respiratory Syndrome, SARS.

News, rumors and disinformation about the SARS outbreak quickly spread over the internet, igniting fear and panic around the globe. Surgical masks were quickly sold out, more than a few people started hoarding food, and business in Hong Kong came almost to a standstill, same for New York's Chinatown, even after Mayor

Bloomberg said there were only ten confirmed cases of SARS in New York (Murphy, "SARS Epidemic").

Even if worldwide only a couple of thousand people had been infected up to that point, people were afraid. Because we know what viruses and bacterial diseases are capable of, we know how fast epidemics can go from a few thousand infected to hundreds of thousands, millions. We know, because it is seared into our collective memory. Influenza, tuberculosis, cholera, tetanus, smallpox, and of course the bubonic plague. We know.

Ultimately, SARS did not become a pandemic. According to the WHO, a total of 8,096 cases worldwide resulted in 774 deaths (WHO, "SARS cases"). SARS had a fatality rate of 9,6 percent, but it turned out to be not nearly as contagious or deadly as a true global killer like the Black Death, the worst pandemic in history, which killed upwards of 75 million people between 1346-1353.[2]

The plague. Just imagine the sense of panic that must have gripped the people living in mid- fourteenth century Europe when the first cases began to appear. One moment everything was fine, the next people were dying by the thousands. Friends, neighbors, family members, fathers, mothers, sons, daughters, whole towns depopulated in a matter of weeks.

Fever, vomiting and diarrhea were the first symptoms, followed by a swelling of the lymph glands (called buboes, hence the name bubonic plaque) in the armpits, neck and groin. Not long after, black spots would appear as a final notice that death was approaching. Because of those spots the plaque would later be called the "Black Death", but at the time the disease was simply called the

"Great Pestilence" or the "Great Mortality".[3] Of those infected with the bubonic plague, between 40 and 70 percent died within a week. People infected with the rarer pneumonic or septicemic form of the plague had less than one percent chance of survival.

The plague was not a new disease, but the last major outbreak had been 600 years earlier.[4] The Justinian plague, named after Byzantine Emperor Justinian I, had first wreaked havoc on the Byzantine and Sasanian Empire in 541-542, but resurfaced several times until the first half of the 8th century. The Byzantine historian Procopius of

Caesarea wrote that at the height of that first outbreak, the Justinian plague killed more than 10,000 people a day in Constantinople ("History", II.23). The plague of 541-542 might have wiped out up to 50 percent of the Byzantine Empire's population, as it later would in Europe.

After having disappeared for centuries, the plague resurfaced again in China in the 1330s. In the fifteen years before arriving in Europe, it killed an estimated 25 million people in China, India and the rest of Asia (Kohn, 31). Traveling along the silk road — an ancient merchant route that connected Asia with the Middle East and Europe — the plague reached Constantinople in 1347. Another route through which the plague may have entered Europe led over water, from the Crimean port city of Caffa (present-day Feodosiya, Crimea) to Italy. The Mongols besieged Caffa in 1346, and when their army was struck with the plague they reportedly catapulted infected corpses over the city walls, in an early form of biological warfare (Wheelis, "Siege of Caffa").[5] Genoese traders fleeing the city by ship then took the plague to Sicily, Genoa and Venice. From there, it spread through the rest of Europe.

The Black Death moved fast, arriving in England in June 1348, only a couple of months after having been introduced to Italy. Nobody knew what it was or how it was caused, let alone how to treat it. The medical faculty of Paris tried to explain the outbreak with the help of philosophy and astronomy, stating that one of the causes of the pestilence was the *"configuration of the havens"*, dating back to 1345, when *"at one hour after noon on 20 March, there was a major conjunction of three planets in Aquarius. This conjunction, along with other earlier conjunctions and eclipses, by causing a deadly corruption of the air around us, signifies mortality and famine - and also other things about which we will not speak here because they are not relevant."* (qtd. in Horrox, 159).

Of course they were just making stuff up. They had no idea what caused the plague. Nobody did, and nobody would for the next 500 years. Not until 1894, when, during the last major plague pandemic, the culprit was finally found: a bacterium, named *Yersinia pestis,* after the bacteriologist who discovered it, Alexandre Yersin. *Yersinia pestis* was transmitted to humans by infected rats and fleas, after which humans infected each other.

But in 1348, the "bad air" theory of the Paris' medical faculty was the most widely accepted explanation. Some people also thought the plague was a punishment from God. Believing salvation and protection lay in self-punishment, they marched in procession from city to city, flagellating themselves until they bled, thereby no doubt carrying the disease from one city to the next (Byrne, 204-205). Then there was the theory that the plague had been caused by the Jews, who had presumably poisoned the wells. And so, in Strasbourg, Erfurt, Mainz, Cologne, Frankfurt, Basel and many other European cities, Jews did not even get the chance to die of the Black Death.[6] Whole Jewish communities were completely exterminated. It was not the first time, nor would it be the last.

There is no excuse for it of course, but people were very scared and very desperate. No one knew what to do. A lot was advised and tried. Some of it helped, most of it did not. Scented materials were believed to keep the sickness away, frequent bathing was advised by some physicians while discouraged by others. Many doctors practiced bloodletting (thus further weakening the patient), others punctured the boils or put frogs on them, to "rebalance the juices of the body". In Milan, doctors advised the authorities to wall up the houses of the sick, even with healthy family members inside (Benedictow, 95). An extreme measure, but it worked, because while Milan was largely spared, some other Italian cities — notably Florence — lost up to 80 percent of their population. Some people fled the city in panic, leaving behind fathers, mothers, brothers, sisters, spouses, children.[7] Some people tried to survive by living soberly, secluding themselves from the infected and banning all talk and news about the epidemic raging all around them. Others concluded they were likely doomed anyway and decided to party until the sun went down, drinking, laughing, dancing and doing whatever else they wanted. Still others resigned to the inevitability of their fate and tried to live as they had always done, save maybe praying a little more than usual and buying some scented herbs, until they too were taken by the disease.

When a society loses half of its population, things change. The survivors had lost friends, husbands, wives, family members, children (the latter having been hit especially hard by the plague). Death was never far away in the Middle Ages, but losing so many in such a short time had a profound impact on those who survived. Some became even more pious than they had been before, many others decided to focus more on the here and now and enjoy life for as long as it lasted.

The social order of society was also deeply effected. Many houses, farms and land parcels were left abandoned, giving surviving have-nots a unique opportunity to improve their station in life. And with landlords and entrepreneurs suddenly having trouble finding enough skilled laborers, the negotiating position of workers who had survived the plague improved significantly (Herlihy, 48). Farmers, millers and laborers who used to be more or less owned by dukes, counts and barons, realized that the tables had turned. Many nobles were suddenly more than willing to free their remaining laborers if only they stayed, worked the land and tended the animals. Landowners even tried to poach workers from each other, offering higher wages and better living conditions, thus further emancipating the workers. Meanwhile, with labor so expensive, achieving higher productivity also became much more important, giving a boost to innovation and the acquisition of better tools and machines (Herlihy, 49).

To protect the landowners, laws were enacted against higher wages and leaving one's post, but many workers didn't obey them.[8] Over the next decades, uprisings would break out in France (the Jacquerie, 1358), Italy (the Ciompi Revolt, 1378) and England (the Peasants Revolt, 1381), pitting the working class against the nobility. And although the authorities were able to put these rebellions down, they were a telling sign of things to come in later centuries, when the common people would rise up again, only this time with a different result.

The position of the Catholic Church also weakened. The priests, bishops and cardinals had not been able to prevent or cure the plague, on the contrary, they had died just as easily as everybody else. For many of the survivors, religion would never play as big a role in their lives again as it had before the Black Death. Others became more open to different interpretations of the Bible, thus paving the way for 14th century reformers like Jan Hus and John Wycliffe and the champions of the 16th century Protestant Reformation, John Calvin and Martin Luther.

The medieval period was coming to an end. In the decades following the Black Death, the Renaissance would spread its wings and take off from the very region where the plague had also begun its lethal European journey: Italy. And though it is too simple to say that the Black Death caused the Renaissance, it no doubt contributed to this new focus on culture, education and science. Unfortunately people had not seen the last of the plague. It would return regularly in the 14th and subsequent centuries, killing large parts of the population, until the cause of the disease was finally found by Alexandre Yersin in the late 19th century.

And even though the plague is under control today, it still exists. Each year, a couple of thousand of human cases are reported worldwide. Unlike smallpox, the plague can never be eradicated, because it lives in millions of rodents who carry the disease without being killed by it themselves. In other words, should we ever return to the sanitary conditions of the Middle Ages and lose the knowledge of how to treat the plague, our old nemesis would no doubt return among us.

Then again, perhaps we won't need to return to the Middle Ages for that to happen. During the Second World War, for instance, the Japanese dropped plague-infested fleas over the Chinese cities of Ningbo and Changde (Barenblatt, 220-221).[9] And both the United States and Soviet Russia researched weaponizing aerosolized pneumonic plague during the Cold War (Inglesby, "Biological Weapon", 2282). It is unclear whether they succeeded.

---

1   Quoted in Bowsky, 13.

2   Due to poor and in many cases non-existent record keeping, it is impossible to give hard numbers about the total number of people that died of the Black Death. For Europe, estimates were traditionally put at about 30 percent of the total population, but since most of the used sources are tax registers and manorial registers — the majority of which only recorded householders who paid the taxes — they tend to focus on the better-off adult men. Taking this into account, more recent research arrives at a mortality rate closer to 50 percent. With the European population an estimated 80 million at the time, that would mean some 40 million people perished from the Black Death in Europe alone.

3   In his 1908 work *The Black Death of 1348 and 1349*, the English abbot and

historian Francis Gasquet suggested it might have been the Dutch-Danish historian J.I. Pontanus who, in his work *Rerum Danicarum Historia* (1631) first used the term '*atra mors*' (black death) to describe the great mortality (Gasquet, 38). However, it was not before 1823 that the name Black Death was first used in English, by Elizabeth Penrose in her work *A History of England from the First Invasion by the Romans to the End of the Reign of George III*.

4   The oldest written records of the existence of the plague are the ones from the Justinian plague, in the 6th and 7th century, but an international study after the origins of the plague concluded in 2010 that the disease first appeared in China, more than 2,600 years ago (Morelli, "Yersinia pestis").

5   In his article "Biological Warfare at the 1346 Siege of Caffa", Wheelis argues it is plausible that the plaque indeed entered Caffa through the biological warfare attack of the Mongols described by the 14th-century Genoese Gabriele de' Mussi, part of whose narrative he quotes.

6   In *The Black Death*, Rosemary Horrox gives various translated contemporary evidence of Jews being tortured and burned for their supposed poisoning of the wells. To quote the contemporary account of Franciscan friar Herman Gigas: "*And many Jews confessed as much under torture: that they had bred spiders and toads in pots and pans, and had obtained poison from overseas; and that not every Jew knew about this wickedness, only the more powerful ones, so that it would not be betrayed. (..) God, the lord of vengeance, has not suffered the malice of the Jews to go unpunished. Throughout Germany, in all but a few places, they were burnt. This action was taken against the Jews in 1349, and it still continues unabated, for in a number of regions many people, noble and humble alike, have laid plans against them and their defenders which they will never abandon until the whole Jewish race has been destroyed.*" (qtd. in Horrox, 207).

7   The narrative of Giovanni Boccaccio's (1313-1375) famous 14th century literary work *Decamerone* centers around seven young women and three young men who flee Florence during the Black Death, finding shelter in a deserted villa in the countryside, where they tell each other stories ranging from erotic to tragic.

8   Such as The Ordinance of Labourers 1349, issued by King Edward III of England on June 18, 1349, which stated that "*every man or woman in our realm of England, whether free or unfree, who is physically fit and below the age of sixty, not living by trade or by exercising a particular craft, and not having private means or land of their own upon which they need work, and not working for someone else, shall, if offered employment consonent with their status, be obliged to accept the employment offered, and they should be paid only the fees, liveries, payements or salaries which were usually paid in the part of the country where they are working the twentieth year of our reign [1346] or in some other appropriate year five or six years ago.*" (qtd. in Horrox, 288).

9   Barenblatt quotes part of the courtroom examination of Major General Kiyashi

Kawashima, who had served in Unit 731, the covert unit of the Imperial Japanese Army that was responsible, among other things, for biological and chemical warfare experimentation and deployment. After the war, the United States granted immunity to physicians and leaders of Unit 731 in exchange for providing only the U.S. their data on biological warfare (Gold, 109-113).

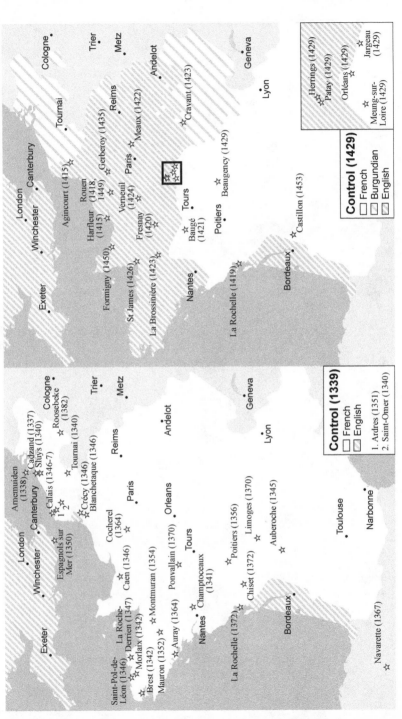

Map 7: The Hundred Years' War

18

THE HUNDRED YEARS' WAR

*"Of the love or hate God may bear the English,
and what he does with their souls, I know nothing;
but I know that they will be put forth out of France,
with the exception of such as shall perish in it."[1]*

Joan of Arc, trial records, March 15, 1431

In January 1066, King Edward the Confessor, on his deathbed, named the English earl Harold Godwinson as his successor. However, the duke of Normandy, one William II, claimed the king had promised him the throne years ago and that earl Harold had sworn to support his claim. When Harold was nevertheless crowned king, William built a large fleet, sailed across the English channel and invaded England. On October 14, 1066, at the Battle of Hastings, William decisively defeated Harold by killing him and was subsequently crowned king himself before the year was out, on Christmas Day. From then on he would be known as William the Conquerer.

Now, William had been born and raised in France, and after ruling England for 20 years he would also die in France. His descendants continued to rule as king of England and duke of Normandy. In 1154, after King Henry II of England married Eleanor of Aquitaine, the duchy of Aquitaine was added to the already considerable English possessions on French soil.[2]

Naturally the French kings weren't particularly happy with all this and tried to reclaim English territory in France at every chance they got. During the reign of King John (1199-1216) the French succeeded in wresting Normandy, Anjou and Poitou from English control, leaving the Duchy of Aquitaine as the sole English possession on the continent, but French King Philip II could only do this after John gave him cause, because the English kings were in fact the rightful rulers of the French lands under their control.

In the case of King John, cause — or excuse, depending on the viewpoint — was found when he refused to appear before Philip II of France to solve a dispute John had with one of his French vassals. It might seem odd that the King of England would be obligated to appear before the King of France, but when it came to his French possessions John of England was not the highest authority, the king of France was. So, king or no king, when John was summoned to the French court as count of the Poitou, feudal tradition demanded he go. When he nevertheless refused, Philip II confiscated his lands. John tried to take them back but he proved a weak military commander and failed.

Things would go rather different for the French some 130 years later, though, when Philip VI tried the same tactic against King Edward III of England. Because when, in 1337, Edward III also refused to appear in person at the French court — as the duke of Aquitaine — and the French king decided to strip him of his duchy, Edward responded by claiming the throne of France — to which he had a pretty strong claim by the way — thus stripping Philip VI of his kingdom and igniting the Hundred Years' War.[3]

Lasting a total of 116 years, The Hundred Years' War would be a war of great kings and terrible kings — even an insane one — of legendary battles and brilliant military commanders, a war fought with both trusted old weapons and revolutionary new ones, a war of valor versus shrewdness, of intrigue and betrayal, of sacrifice and sainthood, a war in which fortunes would reverse more than once, until a seventeen-year-old farm girl finally tipped the scales in favor of the ultimate victor. Many lives would be lost along the way.

The first casualties were made at sea, when Edward III — determined to assert his right to the French throne — crossed the channel with a fleet filled with archers and men-at-arms, on June 22, 1340. Meanwhile, the French, aware of Edward's plans, had assembled a large fleet in the port of Sluys (off the coast of present-day southwestern Netherlands), to prevent the English from landing an army in Flanders. On June 24, the English fleet arrived at the entrance of the tidal inlet leading to Sluys and moved in on the French. The French fleet had taken up a three line defensive formation, the ships anchored and connected through boarding lines so that soldiers could easily move from ship to ship to counter enemy boarding parties (Sumption, 324-325). Of course being shackled together also deprived the ships of any maneuverability. Realizing this, Edward sent his ships to the French left flank and started picking the French ships off one by one.

Several English ships armed with archers and men-at-arms would come alongside a French one, and after the longbowmen had decimated the crew with a shower of arches, the men-at-arms boarded the ship and finished the job. The English longbow proved especially effective for this tactic, not least because the French and Genoese crossbowmen could only span and shoot twice a minute, whereas a longbowman could shoot up to 20 aimed arrows in the same time (Curry 1994, 162). When the battle of Sluys was over the French fleet was so utterly annihilated that England would rule the waves for the next thirty years. Fortunately for France, though, lack of funds prevented Edward to immediately follow up with an all-out French campaign. For the next few years, the conflict concentrated mostly around a succession war in the Duchy of Brittany, in which Edward backed one contender and Philip another.

But in July 1346 Edward III sailed across the Channel again, this time landing an invasion force in Normandy, not far from the site where another invasion force would land almost 600 years later. Edward took the city of Caen in a day, sacked it and killed 3,000 of its citizens.[4]

After leaving Caen, Edward pillaged his way north, more bent on looting than on asserting territorial claims, a tactic the English would often resort to throughout the war. For weeks the French tried to force the English to give battle, but Edward continued to outmaneuver Philip, until — heavy from wagonloads of loot — he couldn't anymore. With the French army closing in on him fast, the only thing Edward could do was carefully select the ground where he would make his last stand, a hill on flat farmland near Crécy, in northern France.

There the English made their defensive preparations, digging ditches to prevent the French cavalry from storming the hill, placing the wagons of loot behind them and strategically positioning the archers. After that all they could do was wait for the French, who arrived the next day. The French infantry and Genoese crossbowmen were tired from days of marching, but the nobles — who had been carried by their horses — were all riled up and ready to fight for honor and glory.

Of course there was no rush whatsoever for the French. With their army of at least 20,000-25,000 strong against Edward's 10,000-15,000, they were outnumbering their enemy roughly two to one.[5]

Moreover, the English were cornered on a hill and on foreign soil. The French didn't have to attack, they could simply wait until the English ran out of food and drink and would be forced to surrender, which would be before long; after all, this was not a castle, with its own well and a vast food supply, this was an army trapped on a hill with wagons that held more silver and gold than bread and water.

But starving an enemy was not the noble thing to do. Effective yes, but how could there be glory in waiting? *Non, absolument non!* So the French nobles did what they always did and would continue to do for most of the war, until they were almost wiped out: they attacked right away. They didn't even rest until the next day.

King Philip VI opened the attack by sending in the tired Genoese crossbowmen, even though the crossbows could match neither the range nor the firing rate of the already reputable English longbow. To make matters worse for the crossbowmen, a brief but heavy rainstorm just before the attack had drenched their bowstrings, thus greatly reducing their range. The English longbowmen had simply unstrung their bows during the rain and covered them up, but a crossbow could not be unstrung without special tools. After the first — failed — crossbow volley, the longbowmen quickly restrung their bows and hit back with deadly accuracy (Chateaubriand, 132). When the Genoese suffered massive casualties and retreated, Philip had them hacked down by his own cavalry, which then proceeded right away with a full frontal assault.

A full frontal assault, the favorite French strategy at the time, is more often than not a terrible strategy, especially when you have to approach over flat ground without cover and then climb a hill where your enemy has ensconced himself. The English even had a couple of cannons at their disposal.[6] But let nobody say the French nobleman wasn't brave. Charge after charge they attacked, each time met by a shower of arrows, mercilessly striking men and horse. Each charge also more difficult than the last one, because of all the dead and wounded already lying on the battlefield. Charge, after charge, after charge; it was a legendary example of both valor and stupidity.[7]

The Battle of Crécy (Aug. 26, 1346) was an enormous victory for king Edward III, who had shown himself to be a skilled military tactician once again. His 16-year-old son Edward of Woodstock — later called the Black Prince, possibly because of his black armor — had also proved to have the makings of an outstanding soldier, by successfully commanding one of the three main divisions of the English forces.[8]

One long-lasting result of the English victory at Crécy was the capture of the strategically important port city of Calais after a costly year-long siege, made possible by a surge of English public support for the war after Crécy and a severely weakened French army (Sumption, 538-539). For the rest of the war, England would use Calais as a supply station and venture point for its campaigns. The city would remain under English control until 1558, more than a century after the end of the Hundred Years' War.

Around the same time the French and English were fighting each other at Crécy, the Mongols were catapulting plague-ridden corpses over the walls of Caffa. A few months later, the plague arrived in Italy and not long after that France and England were also affected. With so many being killed by the Black Death there was not much point in killing each other with swords and arrows, so hostilities were suspended.

But in 1355 the English were back. The Black Prince, who had fought so formidably as a teenager at Crécy, began a scorched earth campaign, burning and pillaging his way from Aquitaine, located in the southwest of France, to the Languedoc. This kind of military raid — known as a *chevauchée* — was a brutal, yet common tactic in the Middle Ages, aimed at breaking the morale of enemy peasants and decreasing the productivity and income of a region, thus forcing its rulers to the negotiating table.[9]

In 1356 the Black Prince went on a second *chevauchée*, this time raiding and looting his way to the middle of France, burning the suburbs of Bourges and capturing a couple of smaller towns, before being forced to retreat by the advancing army of King Jean II of France — who had succeeded his father Philip VI in 1350. At Poitiers, Jean II caught up with the Black Prince.

Finding himself on the defensive against a much larger army, the Prince of Wales took a page from his father's playbook and entrenched himself on a hill near Poitiers, enclosed by hedges and thickets of thorn (Michelet, 437). Behind the English position was the dense forest of Nouaillé and to the west the forest of Saint-Pierre, flanked by the river Miausson. It was a good position, to be sure, but of course the French would not have to attack to win; a siege of a few days would be enough to capture the English crown prince and John Chandos, one of England's most brilliant military strategists, together with a flock of English and Gascon nobles and all the loot the English had collected on their *chevauchée*. But simply waiting the English out would also mean the French nobles had dressed up for nothing...

The Cardinal of Périgord tried to negotiate a peaceful solution but John II told him that *"never in all our life will we make peace unless we get into our keeping the castles and all the land that he has wasted and ravaged, wrongfully and sinfully, since he came from England, and are also quit of the quarrel for which the war is renewed."* (qtd. in Chandos Herald, 767). To this Edward could not agree. He did offer to surrender all his loot and prisoners and not to carry arms against France for seven years, but this in turn King John II refused (Michelet, 437). With no peace agreement in sight both sides thus readied for battle.

When the French nobles saw movement in the English camp the next morning, they immediately charged the English line (Chandos Herald, 1121). As at Crécy, the French greatly outnumbered the English, but, also like Crécy, there was one thing the English had plenty of: arrows.[10]

When the English archers noticed the arrows didn't do enough damage because of the heavy French armor, they moved to the sides of the cavalry and shot the horses in the flanks, stopping the cavalry charge dead in its tracks (Baker, "Chronicle", 127). Many knights were unhorsed, while wounded, panicked horses ran through the

French infantry line, trampling whoever was in their path (Baker, "Chronicle", 127).

It was a bad start for the French, but they could still win the day, because the forces of King Jean II still significantly outnumbered those of the Black Prince. The remaining three divisions — the first led by the Dauphin (the title for the French crown prince), Charles, the second by the Duke of Orleans and the third by King Jean II himself — The French main thrust began on foot, after the horses proved particularly vulnerable to the English archers.

Advancing in this fashion — with the first division in front of the second and the second in front of the third — the French could not benefit from their advantage in numbers. During the advance, the Dauphin's division was constantly harassed by showers of arrows. When they were close to the English position Edward's cavalry attacked, forcing the Dauphin to hastily retreat and causing his division to collude with the 2nd division, behind them (Curry, "Armies and Fortifications", 12-13). Engulfed in chaos, both divisions now fell back on the King's division, which continued to advance. Meanwhile, the Black Prince, realizing he had the initiative, prepared for an all-out cavalry assault, and when the French were once again nearing his position, Edward charged their center hard, while the Gascon commander Captal de Buch undertook a flanking movement with his cavalry and drove into the French ranks from the right (Curry, "Armies and Fortifications", 13).[11] The English archers also joined in, leaving their longbows behind and unsheathing their daggers.

Seeing that things were taking a turn for the worse, King Jean II sent his sons away with an escort of 800 lances — an understandable precaution, though not exactly a boost to his troops' morale (Michelet, 437). Only his youngest son Philip, just fourteen years old, stayed behind and continued to fight side by side with his father, warning him of each new assault "Father, guard your right, guard your left" — until the very end (qtd. in Michelet, 437). Both were captured, as were many other important French nobles. And so, what had started out as a day with bleak prospects for the English unexpectedly ended in an enormous victory for the Black Prince.

With its king captured, France fell into disarray and the people of Paris and many peasants revolted against the French nobility. Meanwhile, king Edward III of England marched an army to Reims, this time not to raid and pillage but to be crowned as king of France (the coronation of French kings traditionally took place at the Notre-Dame of Reims). The citizens of Reims didn't want Edward as their king, though, and closed the city gates. Edward laid siege for a few weeks but then broke for Paris — only to find that the Parisians resisted him as well.

It seemed Edward III had awakened — perhaps even created — the spirit of patriotism in France's hour of need. A spirit that was clearly dead set against an Englishman on the French throne, even if his mother was French and his forefather, William the Conquerer, hailed from Normandy. With Edward's plans to capture the French throne thus thwarted and the French more than fed up with English armies burning and pillaging their way through their beautiful country for the last two decades, both sides sought to end the war. On May 8, 1360, they signed the Treaty of Brétigny.

The treaty increased Edward's holdings in France considerably, with the French conceding, among the more important territories, Poitou, Limousin, Rouergue and Saintonge in the south and Calais, Guînes and Ponthieu in the north (Ogg, 441-442, note 1). Article 7 of the treaty recognized the English king's full sovereignty over his French territories, i.e., free of feudal responsibilities to the crown of France, which had basically been the source of the conflict in the first place (Ogg, 442). Furthermore, article 13 of the treaty stipulated that France would pay a huge ransom of three million gold crowns for the release of King Jean II. In return, Edward gave up his claim to the throne of France.

And they all lived happily ever after.

Well, no. The peace lasted from 1360 to 1369, then war broke out again. This time because several nobles in Aquitaine objected to a new tax instituted by the Black Prince. They asked the new French king, Charles V, to intervene, and he gladly stepped in.[12] He summoned the Prince of Wales to Paris, who of course refused, after which Charles stripped king Edward III of all his French possessions, who then renewed his claim to the throne of France (Wagner, 117). Sounds familiar, does it not? It was like 1337 all over again.

The next decade was not an English one. In the space of one year both the Black Prince and King Edward III died, the son in 1376, the father in 1377. Both had been highly skilled military commanders, unlike most of the French royals. Edward's grandson Richard II was hastily put on the throne of England, but he was still a child. Meanwhile, for the first time in a long time, the French had a very wise king in Charles V.

One of the wise things he did was appointing the gifted military commander Bertrand du Guesclin as Constable of France, the highest military position, traditionally reserved for someone of high nobility, which du Guesclin most certainly was not.[13] Contrary to his predecessors, Du Guesclin avoided large-scale pitched battles against the English whenever he could, knowing the perfected English longbow tactics would have him at a disadvantage in such battles. Instead he preferred smart and sneaky Fabian strategies like ambushes, hit and run raids and nightly attacks.[14] In his ten years as Constable of France, Du Guesclin kept pushing the English back further and further. By the time he died, in 1380, he had recovered most of the territory France had lost with the Treaty of Brétigny (Rogers, "Medieval Warfare", 227). King Charles V died the same year, just a few months after Du Guesclin.

Not much happened between 1389 and 1415, but then the English made an impressive comeback. Their new king, Henry V, had an aptitude for military strategy that was reminiscent of his great-grandfather, Edward III. During his short reign — from 1413 to 1422 — Henry would deal several crushing blows to the French and come within an inch of the French throne.

In August 1415, he crossed the English channel with a force of 12,000 men and laid siege to the port city of Harfleur, capturing it after a couple of weeks. He then embarked on a campaign of burning and pillaging the countryside — in keeping with the time-honored tradition established by his forefathers — since it was too late in the season to march his army to Paris.

Of course the French tried to stop him, and on October 24, 1415, they caught up with Henry at Agincourt, in northern France, about 50 miles from Calais. The English were outnumbered, tired from weeks of hard marching, suffering from sickness and low on supplies.[15] Henry constructed a defensive position on a terrain of about 1,000 yards wide, flanked by forest on both sides. He organized his troops in three battle groups and placed his archers on the sides, behind thick wooden stakes with sharpened points aimed in the direction of the French cavalry.[16] Then he waited. A couple of hours went by before Henry realized the French would not be so easily tempted to attack, and the longer he waited, the more French troops would arrive (Rogers in Villalon, 41).

Stuck between a rock and a hard case, Henry decided to move his line forward and bring his longbowmen in range (Rogers in Villalon, 41). The catch was that by breaking up and rebuilding his defenses, his troops would be exposed. It was a risky move, but certainly preferable to simply waiting until the French attack begun.

Had the French paid better attention, their cavalry could have crushed the English while they were rebuilding their defenses. But for whatever reason, the French waited until the English attacked *them*. In other words, if at Crécy and Poitiers the French cavalry had been too eager to attack, at Agincourt they were too hesitant.

Apart from the forests on either side of the battlefield, the muddy terrain also worked to the advantage of the English, because it made it difficult for the heavily armored French knights to move. And while the French cavalry was struggling in the mud, the English longbowmen shot their horses from underneath them, not just stopping the charge but also creating chaos on the field, just like they had done at Crécy and Poitiers (Rogers in Villalon, 41). The subsequent French main infantry assault suffered equally heavy casualties from the unrelenting hail of arrows.

After the battered French vanguard had come into contact with the English men-at-arms and the second French line moved in to support the first, the longbowmen put down their bows and attacked the French flanks and rear in hand-to-hand combat (Rogers in Villalon, 41). When the French first and second line were thus overwhelmed, news reached Henry that the baggage train in the rear was being attacked. Due to this new threat, together with the danger that scattered parts of the French first and second line would regroup, Henry gave the order that all the prisoners should be killed.[17]

Seeing this, the mounted French third line, which had seemed prepared to attack, withdrew (Rogers in Villalon, 41-42).

When it was all over, the English had maybe suffered a few hundred dead, while the French had lost at least 5,000.[18] It was a great blow to the French nobility.

During the next couple of years, Henry V retook much of Normandy, reclaiming it for the first time since John Lackland had lost it two centuries before. Even more important was the alliance Henry was able to forge with Philip the Good, the powerful Duke of Burgundy, in 1420. Philip's father had been assassinated by the Dauphin the year before, and naturally he wanted to prevent the murderer of his father from becoming king of France.

Together, England and Burgundy now controlled more than half of France, including Paris and Reims, the city where the French kings were traditionally crowned. On May 21, 1420, Henry V and Philip the Good forced King Charles VI of France — known as Charles the Mad, because he suffered from periods of mental illness — to sign the Treaty of Troyes. This arranged for the marriage between Henry V and Charles VI's daughter, Catherine of Valois. Article 6 of the treaty also named Henry and his future sons regent and heir to the throne of France, disinheriting King Charles VI's own son, the Dauphin (Ogg, 443).

Henry was now just one heartbeat away from the throne of France. Unfortunately for him, his own heart would not wait around for much longer. On August 31, 1422, Henry V, aged 35, died of dysentery in the Château de Vincennes, just a few miles from Paris. Charles the Mad followed him six weeks later. Henry V and Catherine of Valois had one child together, a nine-month-old son also called Henry. This Henry VI would turn out to be more of a Valois than a Lancaster, though, inheriting the mental instability of his maternal grandfather but none of the leadership qualities of his father.

The final turning point in the Hundred Years' War came a few years later, in 1428, when the English laid siege to the strategically important city of Orléans, about 80 miles south of Paris. Things looked dire for the French. If the city fell, there would be nothing to stop the English from marching on the city of Bourges — located in the center of France, about 70 miles south of Orléans— where Charles

VII had his court (because all the other important French cities where already under control of England and Burgundy). The French were disorganized and suffered from low morale, until a seventeen-year-old peasant girl arrived on the scene who somehow convinced the Dauphin she could lift the siege of Orléans.[19]

Only in the Middle Ages, with its steadfast belief in God and satan, heaven and hell, miracles and curses, angels and demons, witches and wizards, was it conceivable that an illiterate farm girl, without any experience or education, be given the command of an army on the brink of defeat, because she said God had told her so. Most people living in the 21st century would probably suggest the girl visit a psychiatrist, but back in the 14th century people put far more stock in religion and were less critical about its perceived truths and powers, so if a teenage girl said God had told her to save France, it had to be true. Also, the situation of the French was pretty desperate at the moment, so the Dauphin may have simply reasoned he did not have a lot to lose.

In any case, Joan of Arc traveled to Orléans with the Dauphin's blessing, lifted the siege and proceeded to lead the French to a number of victories, including the capture of Reims, thus finally enabling the Dauphin to be crowned King Charles VII of France.

Not long after, Joan of Arc was captured by the Burgundians. They ransomed her, but Charles VII refused to buy her freedom, something that would not reflect too well on his sense of honor. Eventually, the English bought her, tried her for heresy and burned her at the stake on May 30, 1431. She had accomplished what she had set out to do, though. The French were more organized and their morale had been revived, Orléans was safe and Charles VII had been crowned in Reims. He would prove to be an able leader, ruling for more than 30 years.

Over the next two decades, the English were gradually pushed back. One important change Charles VII made was replacing the feudal system of having to demand military support from his vassals, with a professional, state-run army — the first in Western Europe — which made for a much better organized fighting force and reduced Charles' dependence on feudal lords, who so often caused trouble with their intrigues, insubordination and continuous infighting (Wagner, 91-92). The last battle of the Hundred Years' War was fought near Castillon-la-Bataille, in Aquitaine, on July 17, 1453. It was a decisive French victory and meant the end of all English landholdings in France, except for Calais and the Channel Islands. Calais would remain English for another century, the Channel Islands remain under British control to this day.

The Hundred Years' War was not the first time French and English kings fought against each other, but it was the first time the French and English people fought for their country as well as their king. This was particularly true for the French, who increasingly viewed the conflict as being about repelling a foreign invader.

Another important consequence of the Hundred Years' War was the fatal blow it dealt to feudalism.

At the beginning of the war the French army had been considered much more powerful than the English army because it boasted so many knights, but the English longbows slaughtered those knights again and again, at Crécy, Poitiers, Agincourt, diminishing their value. The war thus marked the beginning of the end for the knight as a fighting force, reducing the king's dependence on the nobles and paving the way for the end of feudalism and the rise of the modern, centralized nation state.

In England, the high cost of the war and the repatriation of the English forces from France after its conclusion, contributed to the outbreak of civil war between the ruling House of Lancaster and the powerful House of York, in 1455. Known as the Wars of the Roses, it would eventually establish the House of Tudor, after Henry of Tudor killed the Yorkist king Richard III at the Battle of Bosworth Field, in 1485.[20]

Over the course of the next centuries, France and England continued to wage war against each other, in Europe but increasingly also in other parts of the world, as a result of their vast colonial empires. The Napoleonic Wars between 1792-1815 marked the last armed conflict between England and France, and towards the end of the 19th century the rise of a new kid on the European block would even unite the old foes in a military alliance.

Had the English won the Hundred Years' War, the balance of power in Europe — and the rest of the world — would have been fundamentally different. Would the American colonists still have been able to successfully fight the British without the support of the French? Would there still have been a French revolution, an emperor Napoleon Bonaparte? Or would Europe perhaps have evolved into the United States of England, preventing the rise of an independent Germany, of the outbreak of the First and Second World War? And if so, would the colonies in Africa and Asia still have been able to gain their independence in the second half of the 20th century? Perhaps not.

But whatever would have happened, the French would still be the French.

---

1   Quoted in Michelet, 142.

2   Eleanor had previously also been married to Louis VII, King of France, but had sought annulment of her marriage. After first rejecting it, the pope granted annulment when Louis and Eleanor's second child was another girl. The official reason for the annulment was consanguinity within the fourth degree. Eleanor married Henry eight weeks after her annulment.

3   Edward III's mother, Isabella of France, was the sister of the late King Charles IV of France. When Charles IV died, in 1328, the French nobles decided that Philip of Valois — son of the late king's uncle — should be king, even though Edward was closer in line to the throne than Philip. But, unlike Edward, Philip descended from a male line and French tradition favored the male line, a point the French barons — balking at the prospect of an English king on the throne of France — were of course happy to drive home.

4   On July 9, 1944, Caen was liberated by British I Corps after a British and Canadian bombardment that destroyed 70 percent of the town and killed 2,000 citizens. William the Conquerer's final resting place — Edward III's forefather — is also in Caen, in the Abbey of Saint-Etienne. Over the centuries his grave has been disturbed several times, most notably during the French Wars of Religion (1562-1598), when his bones were scattered and lost, except for one thigh bone.

5   Historians' estimates on the size of the forces at Crécy vary. The contemporary Flemish chronicler Jean Le Bel mentions the division of the English forces into three battlegroups and arrives at a total of 4,000 men-at-arms, 3,000 Welshmen and 11,000 archers (Rogers, "Wars of Edward III", 133-134). The British medieval historian Jonathan Sumption puts the total number lower, between 7,000 and 10,000, and estimates the French forces between 20,000-25,000

(Sumption, 497, 526). Estimates of the size of the French forces are less certain because administrative records are lost, but there is strong consensus that the French significantly outnumbered the English. Jules Michelet writes how the English, reviewing the field after the battle, found "*amongst the slain, eleven princes, eighty lords-banneret, twelve hundred knights and thirty thousand common men.*" ("History of France", 426). Interesting is also King Edwards III's own estimate, which he conveys in a letter to a Northern baron, writing that the enemy "*had more than 12,000 men-at-arms*", to which 6,000 Genoese crossbowmen would have to be added and an unknown number of common men (qtd. in Rogers, "Wars of Edward III", 130; Sumption, 526).

6   The battle of Crécy is one of the first battles in Europe that saw the use of cannon.

7   In his seminal work, *History of France*, 19th century French historian Jules Michelet can scarcely hide his admiration for the "*great barons of France*" and their brave galloping and seems to have an even harder time grasping the impudence of the "*Welsh and Cornish dagsmen*", who "*flung themselves on the unhorsed knights, and slew them with their knives without mercy, no matter how highly born.*" ("History of France", 426).

8   During his lifetime, the Black Prince was known as Edward of Woodstock, after his place of birth. It is only 150 years later that the nickname 'Black Prince' started to be used. Why he was called the Black Prince remains uncertain. Some sources attribute the nickname to Edward having worn black armor, but there are also — mainly French — sources who suggest the name comes from Edward having been brutal of reputation, especially against the French in Aquitaine.

9   Though the term *chevauchée* might conjure up images of chivalrous and civilized behavior, the *chevauchée* was actually closely related to the modern concept of 'total war', making no distinction between combatants and non-combatants and viewing almost every action as being part of the war effort.

10 According to Michelet, the Prince of Wales had 2,000 cavalry, 4,000 archers and 2,000 light troops at Poitiers, while King Jean II had a total of 50,000 men at his disposal ("History of France", 436). Chateaubriand estimates the French forces even stronger at more than 60,000, while giving largely the same numbers as Michelet for the English forces and not failing to mention that of the roughly 8,000 troops of the Prince of Wales scarcely 3,000 were English, the rest being either French or Gascon ("Oeuvres", 150-151).

11 Captal de Buch was a feudal title in Gascony, but when the title is used in relation to the Hundred Years' War, it is generally referring to the most famous Captal de Buch: Jean III de Grailly.

12 Jean II had died in captivitiy in London in 1364. He had been released in 1360 after the signing of the Treaty of Brétigny, under the condition that several other nobles take his place until the ransom was paid, among them Jean's second son Louis, Duke of Anjou. When it turned out that payment of the full ransom

would take much longer than expected, Louis escaped. His father, dismayed by this unchivalrous behavior, voluntarily returned to captivity in London, where he died a few months later.

13   Du Guesclin (1320-1380) was in fact of minor Breton nobility.

14   The Fabian strategy gets its name from the Roman general Quintus Fabius (280 BCE-203 BCE), who was the first to use this guerilla-style warfare strategy, against the Carthaginian general Hannibal Barca.

15   As often with medieval battles, it is impossible to give a definitive, accurate estimate of the strength of the opposing armies. In the case of Agincourt, all modern historians agree that the French outnumbered the English, but whereas British medieval historian Anne Curry arrives at 12,000 French and 9,000 English troops in her book *Agincourt: A New History* (187, 192, 233, 248), most other estimates range from the French outnumbering the English two to one to up to six to one. Juliet Barker, for instance, writes in *Agincourt: The King, the Campaign, the Battle,* that only about half of Henry's original invasion force of 12,000 men walked on the field at Agincourt, facing a French army that *"outnumbered them by at least four to one and possibly as much as six to one."* (preface, i). And in "The Battle of Agincourt." Clifford Rogers names several sources that estimate the strength of the French at 24,000, mentioning that this would give a ratio of French to English combatants of four to one (in "The Hundred Years War", Villalon, 57).

16   For an interesting elaboration about the wooden stakes of the archers, what they looked like, how they were likely set up and how far apart they stood, see Clifford Rogers' analysis in *The Hundred Years War (part II): Different Vistas,* edited by Villalon and Kagay (53-56).

17   In *The Battle of Agincourt: Sources and Interpretations,* Anny Curry cites one contemporary and two eye-witness accounts confirming the English killed many French prisoners during the battle (163-164).

18   Anne Curry presents a list of 15th century chroniclers and their estimates of English and French dead ("Agincourt: Sources and Interpretations", 12). Clifford Rogers writes in Villalon's *The Hundred Years War (part II): Different Vistas,* that the death rate of the 10,000 French men-at-arms alone *"seems to have been at least 45%, and quite possibly 60%"* (Villalon, 104). Though it is impossible to accurately assess the number of casualties, historians agree French casualties vastly outweighed the English ones.

19   Because Charles VII had not been crowned king yet and controlled neither Paris nor Reims, he was still called the Dauphin, or sometimes, more derisively, 'King of Bourges', for having to keep court there.

20   Richard III was the only English king whose last resting place was unknown, until in August 2012 his remains were found under a car park in Leicester, in central England. In February 2013, scientists from the University of Leicester were able to confirm beyond reasonable doubt that the remains indeed belonged to Richard III. On March 26, 2015, He was reburied in Leicester Cathedral.

Part IV

Europe Rises

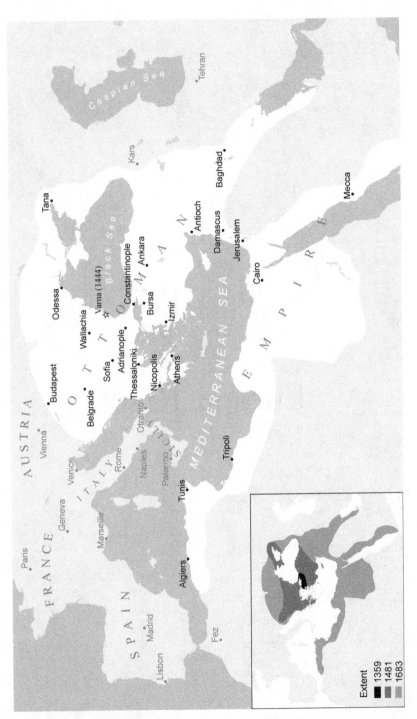

Map 8: The Ottoman Empire

19

From Constantinople to Vienna (and back)

"Venimus, Vidimus, Deus vicit" — We
came, We saw, God conquered
John III Sobieski, after defeating the Ottomans
at Vienna, September 12, 1683

Whether or not Turkey should be allowed to join the European Union has been debated since the 1960s. Most Europeans are against it, citing human rights issues, cultural and religious differences as their main reasons. Most Turks also don't feel European, which is understandable, given the fact that only a tiny part of Turkey is actually located in Europe. That part, Eastern Thrace — sometimes referred to as European Turkey — accounts for about 3 percent of Turkey. The other 97 percent is located in Asia.

Officially Turkey is a secular republic, but since the Islamist Recep Tayyip Erdogan and his Islamist AK Party came to power in 2003, state-sponsored Islamism has slowly but certainly crept back into the republic, something that does not sit well with a great majority of the Europeans — nor with a significant number of Turks.

The rule of law has also come increasingly under pressure, especially after a failed military coup in July 2016, which Erdogan immediately accused his former-ally-turned-arch-enemy Fethullah Gülen of masterminding — though without offering any proof. In the nine months after the coup, more than 110,000 people were detained by Turkish authorities, nearly 50,000 of them arrested on charges linking them to the coup, including almost 11,000 police officers, 2,500 judges and prosecutors and 100 journalists; more than 2,500 journalists were dismissed, 179 news outlets were shut down (Vonberg, "Turkey's post-coup crackdown").

In April 2017, president Erdogan organized a constitutional referendum to transform Turkey from a parliamentary into a presidential republic with far-reaching powers for the president. According to the Turkish High Electoral Board (HEB), Erdogan narrowly won the referendum, with about 51 percent of the electorate voting "yes". The results were disputed by the secular Republican People's Party (CHP) — in particular the controversial decision by the HEB to allow voting ballot papers without official stamps to be counted — but the electoral board did not change its ruling (Fraser, "Electoral Board"). International election monitors delivered a scathing verdict on the Turkish referendum, concluding that *"The legal framework remained inadequate for the holding of a genuinely democratic referendum"* (qtd. in Masters, "International monitors").

Turkey's ambivalence towards Europe — and vice versa — runs through the entire long and rich history of its predecessor state, the Ottoman Empire (which Mr. Erdogan and his AK Party have consistently professed their admiration for). For though founded in Asia, it first became an empire in Europe.

Let's go back.

So before Turkey became the republic it is today, it was an empire. Before that, it was a kingdom and before that it was the Sultanate of Rûm, a Muslim state established by the Seljuk Turks, which existed from 1077 until 1307.[1] It was the Sultanate of Rûm — threatening to overrun the Byzantine Empire — that awakened the religious zest for crusades in the Europeans of the late 11th century. Although the Crusaders were ultimately unable to hold on to their conquests in the Holy Land, they did slow the Seljuks down, buying Europe some much needed respite from Muslim conquest.

The Sultanate prospered in the 12th and early 13th century, annexing other Turkish states in Anatolia and capturing important Byzantine cities such as the Mediterranean harbor city of Attilia (present-day Antalya) and the Black Sea port Sinop. But while the Seljuks successfully repelled the Crusaders and pushed the Byzantians ever further West, a formidable threat was drawing nearer from the East.

That threat — the Mongol Empire — was advancing from Central into Western Asia during the first half of the 13th century and caused many Muslims from these regions to migrate westward. One of them was a man from northeastern Iran called Süleyman Şah, who was the leader of the Kayi tribe of Turkomans. Though Süleyman died during the journey (he drowned while crossing the Euphrates into Syria) and two of his sons subsequently led most of the family back East again to enter into Mongol service, a third son, Ertuğrul, decided to push on and succeeded in leading part of the tribe into Anatolia (Shaw, "Ottoman Empire", 13).[2]

There, Ertuğrul offered his services to the Rûm Sultanate and was given a small *beylik* (a principality) in the western part of the Sultanate, which he could further expand at the expense of the Byzantine Empire. Ertuğrul would continue to pledge allegiance to the Sultan throughout his reign, but his son Osman declared his principality independent and himself Sultan in 1299.

Apart from being a gifted military commander and leader, Osman's quest to expand his territory was helped by a continuous influx of Muslim warriors — who were on the run from the Mongols — and a weak neighbor to the west. But while militarily weak, the Byzantine Empire was also highly civilized, boasting a great infrastructure and a well-educated population, making it an irresistible target for every Anatolian ruler with a serious taste for empire. During his 45-year-long rule, Osman I succeeded in significantly enlarging his initially small principality, laying the foundations for the later Ottoman Empire, named after him ('Osman' is the Turkish version of the Arabic name 'Othman').

Just before Osman's death in 1326, the Ottomans captured the strategically important Byzantine city of Bursa, after a siege that had lasted nine years.[3] It was made the capital of the kingdom and established the Ottomans as the undisputed major power of Asia minor. During the next century, Osman's successors would conquer the rest of northwestern Anatolia and most of the Balkans. The Christians mounted several attempts to stop the Turkish advancement into Europe but were defeated again and again.

In September 1396, an allied Crusader army of French, Burgundian, German, Hungarian, Bulgarian and Wallachian forces laid siege to the

Ottoman-occupied Bulgarian city of Nicopolis. The Christians settled in for a prolonged siege, but within two weeks Sultan Bayezid I and his army arrived to drive the Crusaders from the field.

The commander of the allied forces, King Sigismund of Hungary, had drawn up a battle plan that would put Wallachian foot soldiers in the vanguard of the first attack, on account of their experience fighting the Turks and also because the Ottomans habitually sent in their weakest troops first. But the French knights insisted on riding first, since it would be dishonorable to follow footmen in battle (Tuchman, 558).

Sigismund supposedly remarked that the honor and glory in battle did not lie in the first blows but in the last, which decided the victory, but Philip of Artois — Count of Eu and Constable of France\ — would have none of it and indignantly replied that French knights had not come all the way to follow a miserable peasant militia into battle (Tuchman, 558). *"To take up the rear is to dishonor us and expose us to the contempt of all,"* the count said angrily (qtd. in Tuchman, 558).[4]

A few hours later, Sigismund received word that the troops of Bayezid were within six hours march of Nicopolis (Tuchman 558-559). It was only the Turkish vanguard that had been sighted, though, and Sigismund asked the French not to go on the offensive before the scouts had returned with more information on the strength and whereabouts of the main Turkish force (Tuchman 558-559). Several of the highest French nobles agreed to wait, but the Count of Eu, who sensed an excellent opportunity to earn even more glory, immediately made it clear he did not wish to wait, exclaiming *"Forward, in the name of God and St. George, you shall see me today a valorous knight!"* (qtd. in Tuchman, 559).

And so the brave French knights rode out alone to meet the Turks, only to be unhorsed by a hail of arrows and stakes piercing the stomachs of their horses (Tuchman, 559-561). But still they fought on, furiously slashing their heavy swords left and right, as if writing their own glorious history with each cut they made, until they were finally enveloped and utterly defeated (Tuchman, 559-561).

The battle of Nicopolis was a crushing defeat for the Christians. It solidified the position of the Ottomans in the Balkans and increased their threat to Central Europe, while also keeping the pressure on

Constantinople. Sigismund — who went on to become Holy Roman Emperor — would later say *"We lost the day by the pride and vanity of these French. If they believed my advice, we had enough men to fight our enemies."* (qtd. in Tuchman, 561).

Some 50 years later, on November 10, 1444, at the Battle of Varna, Sultan Murad II defeated another coalition of Christian forces, this one consisting of Poles, Hungarians, Moldavians, Bosnians, Croatians, Teutonic Knights, and others (no French this time). The Christian force of 20,000 had intended to set sail for Constantinople from the Black Sea port of Varna (in present-day Bulgaria) but was soundly defeated by Murad II and his 60,000 strong army.

Murad II had actually already retired as Sultan when the Christians were en route to Varna, but Grand Vizier Çandarlı Halil Pasha had asked him to come out of retirement because the new Sultan — Murad's twelve-year-old son Mehmed II — could not yet be counted on to effectively organize and lead the army against the Crusaders (Shaw, "Ottoman Empire", 52-53). So Murad II returned, led the army and won the battle of Varna. After this he was hoping to return back to his retired life of contemplation in southwestern Anatolia again, but when an uprising of the Janissaries (an elite infantry corps) broke out, Çandarlı Halil Pasha convinced Murad to stay on as emperor until Mehmed was more experienced (Shaw, "Ottoman Empire", 52-53).

In 1451, Mehmed II, then 19 years old, returned to power. Almost immediately he turned his attention to Constantinople, determined to remove the transcontinental Christian thorn in his side once and for all.

When Mehmed arrived at the city with his army, on April 1, 1453, Constantinople had been the capital of the Byzantine Empire for over a thousand years. One of the greatest European cities — and certainly the best defended one — it was also of great strategic value, as it controlled both the land route from Europe to Asia and the seaway between the Mediterranean and the Black Sea.

In the months leading up to the inevitable siege, Byzantine Emperor Constantine XI had beseeched Pope Nicholas V for help, but there was not much the pope could do, since many of Europe's kingdoms and principalities were engrossed in their own affairs. France and England were both weakened from the Hundred Years' War, Spain was in the final stages of the *Reconquista* (the almost 800-year-long struggle to end Muslim rule on the Iberian peninsula) German principalities were busy fighting amongst themselves and Poland and Hungary were still recovering from their defeat at the Battle of Varna. A couple of hundred men had arrived from Genoa on their own, but however welcome they were it was not nearly enough to organize a sufficient defense against the estimated 80,000-120,000 Turks (Runciman, 76, 83-84).[5] Emperor Constantine's forces were less than 7,000 (Runciman, 85).

And then there were Mehmed's guns, 68 of them. The largest — 27-ft (8.2 m), a bronze barrel 8 inches thick and with a diameter of 30 inches — was capable of firing stone balls of more than 1,200 lb (544 kg) over a distance of a mile (Runciman, 78). It was a monster of a gun and could fire only seven times a day, but that was enough to inflict enormous damage (Runciman, 97).

But however numerous their forces and impressive their guns, after seven weeks of bombarding, tunneling (in an effort to undermine the walls) and counter-tunneling (by the Byzantines, in an effort to undermine the underminers), the Ottomans still had not broken through Constantinople's defenses. Mehmed realized that the only way to force the city to its knees would be a no holds barred, get-rich-or-die-trying all-out assault, and on May 29, 1453, shortly after midnight, he gave the order for just that.

What followed was a battle for the ages, filling the air with the sounds of swords clashing, arrows whooshing, raw battle cries and ear-piercing death screams. The Byzantines fought to save their empire, the Ottomans to expand their empire. But this was not just a battle of Turks against Byzantines, it was a battle of Muslims against Christians, Asians against Europeans, East against West.

After hours of hard fighting by both sides and at several gates, the Ottomans finally managed to capture one of the smaller gates, the Kerkoporta. When the defenders saw the Turkish flags flying above the gate, they cried "*the city is taken*" and panic spread through the city (Runciman, 139). The defense collapsed and the day was lost (or won, depending on the viewpoint).

To reward his soldiers for their unflinching bravery and historic victory, Mehmed II allowed them three days of looting, a longstanding Muslim tradition for dealing with conquered Christian cities that had refused to surrender (Runciman, 199). But on the third day the sultan ordered his troops to stop looting and return to their camps outside the city walls.[6] Mehmed declared that citizens who had been in hiding could come out, that no questions would be asked and that they could continue to live their lives as they had done before.

The most important church — the Hagia Sophia — was converted into a mosque and would remain in use until 1931.[7] The second most important church was left untouched; it is still a Greek Orthodox church today. Greek Orthodox Christians, Roman Catholics and Jews were all allowed to practice their faith and live under the rules of their own religion. Under the so-called *Millet* system, all people in the Ottoman Empire were governed by their own religion, as long as they remained loyal to the empire. Whenever there was a dispute among citizens, the law of the injured party would apply, except when it involved a Muslim, in which case Islamic law (*sharia*) would always apply.

The fall of Constantinople — less than two months before the last battle of the Hundred Years' War was fought, at Castillon, in the southwest of France — was a watershed moment, sometimes viewed as the end of the Middle Ages. With it, the final curtain also fell for the Byzantine Empire, though some Peloponnesian remnants of the empire would survive until 1460. Many Greek scholars, writers and artists fled the city and emigrated to Italy, contributing to the acceleration of the Renaissance there. The fall of Constantinople also brought trade between Europe and Asia completely under control of the Ottoman Empire, to the great benefit of its economy. This in turn contributed to the Europeans taking to the seas in search for another route to Asia, bringing about the Age of Exploration.

Mehmed II moved the Ottoman capital to Constantinople (no surprise there) and a few years later ordered the construction of the great Topkapi Palace, making it the residence of the Ottoman Sultans for the next 400 years. The young sultan also claimed the title 'Caesar of Rome' — on account of Constantinople having been the seat of the Roman Empire — but his claim was never recognized by the Patriarch of Constantinople, nor by Christian Europe. Still, conquering the

Byzantine Empire did rightfully turn the Ottoman Kingdom into the Ottoman *Empire*.

In the following decades, Mehmed the Conquerer pushed further into Europe, conquering Serbia, Bosnia and most of the kingdom of Hungary. Moldavia and Wallachia (which together form present-day Romania) were also subjugated, but only after suffering heavy losses at the hands of the Wallachian ruler Prince Vlad III Dracula, nicknamed *Vlad the Impaler*, who was responsible for the death of tens of thousands of Turks, impaling many of them on wooden stakes.[8]

Towards the end of his reign, Mehmed II set out to conquer the Italian peninsula as well, possibly with the goal of capturing Rome in mind, which would make him the first 'Caesar' in a millennium to rule over a united Eastern and Western Empire.

An invasion fleet was sent to capture the port city of Brindisi, but strong Adriatic winds forced the fleet to the south, and on July 28, 1480, it arrived near the Neapolitan city of Otranto instead. The city itself fell in a day, but the citizens quickly retreated to the citadel and continued to offer fierce resistance from there for two more weeks before Ottoman admiral Gedik Ahmed Pasha and his troops finally captured the citadel. The Ottoman admiral reportedly then had some 800 male citizens of Otranto executed, after having offered them a chance to save their lives by converting to Islam, which they collectively refused (Byfield, 131).[9]

During the two weeks of Otrantan resistance, the king of Naples had time to organize his defenses, aided by other Italian city-states, who answered the crusader call of Pope Sixtus IV to protect Rome from falling in the hands of the Muslims. Meeting more resistance than expected, Gedik Ahmed Pasha returned to Constantinople in October that same year without having achieved much, with the intention of returning to Italy next summer. But the sudden death of Mehmed II on May 3, 1481, and the subsequent quarrels about his succession put everything on hold, and Italy was saved. Otranto was liberated the same month Mehmed II died.

Some 50 years later, In 1529, Suleiman the Magnificent — the longest reigning sultan of the Ottoman Empire — laid siege to Vienna. A sound strategic choice, because if captured, it would not only solidify

Ottoman hegemony in Central Europe but also provide a perfect staging point for the invasion of Western Europe. The city was defended by an allied Christian force of approximately 22,000 soldiers and 2,000 horse from the Holy Roman Empire, Bohemia and Spain, while the Ottoman army was likely at least 125,000 strong (Pratt, 144; Duffy, 201).[10] Heavy rains had forced Suleiman to leave his heavy artillery behind en route to Vienna, meaning he only had light artillery at his disposal, which proved insufficient to breach the walls (Pratt, 145). After several unsuccessful attacks, including a fierce final assault, the Ottomans retreated in defeat, having lost over 15,000 men (Pratt, 147).

Three years later Suleiman led another campaign against Vienna. This time his army was stalled at Kőszeg, a town in Hungary, bordering on Austria. There, 800 Croatian defenders held a small border fort without cannon for almost a month against 120,000 Turks, suffering continuous bombardments and fighting off nineteen all-out assaults (Wheatcroft, 59). When the August rains set in, Suleiman returned without having taken the fort, let alone Vienna.

151 years later, in 1683, the Muslims tried to take Vienna one last time, laying siege to the city in the summer. Two months later, on September 11, a relief force from various Christian nations arrived, led by Jan III Sobieski, the King of Poland. The next day, the 100,000 strong Ottoman army faced off against the Christian coalition force of about 70,000 men in an epic battle that would change the course of history (Rosner, 185-186).

The coalition had positioned its forces along a six mile ridge running alongside the Danube, stretching southwestward from the Kahlenberg to the Rosskopf (Wheatcroft, 172). Most of the infantry was placed on the left, commanded by Charles V, Duke of Lorraine, while most of the cavalry was on the right, with Jan Sobieski himself commanding the Polish cavalry on the outer right flank (Wheatcroft, 173). The center was made up of Franconian and Bavarian infantry under the command of Count Waldeck. The plan was to descend the hill in one huge arc, stretching from the Danube to beyond the Wien River, attacking the entire Western side of the vast Ottoman camp that encircled the city.

But when huge armies are in such close proximity to each other, small incidents can easily escalate into much larger hostilities, rendering even the most carefully thought-out battle plan obsolete before the battle has even begun, which is exactly what happened when around 5:00 a.m. a group of Turkish skirmishers fired their muskets at Austrian forces positioned on the left flank of the Kahlenberg (Wheatcroft, 177).

The Austrians shot back but their lighter muskets did not carry as far as the Ottoman ones. Forced to think on their feet, the Austrian troops quickly formed into two lines and began advancing downhill to get within range (Wheatcroft, 177-178). It worked and the skirmishers were easily overwhelmed. Meanwhile, though, the Saxons, seeing the Austrians on the move, had also begun to descend from the hill (Wheatcroft, 177-178).

The Duke of Lorraine, alarmed when seeing that part of his left wing had already started to descend — thus opening itself up to Ottoman flanking movements — quickly dispatched a series of gallopers ordering the Austrian infantry to slow their advance (Wheatcroft, 178). Around 10:00 a.m. the advance indeed slowed down, but by now the Turks had fully engaged in battle and furious fighting had broken out along the left front.

Around 1:00 p.m. King Jan III Sobieski began leading the Polish cavalry slowly downhill (Wheatcroft, 181). Given the rough terrain, he had expected it would take one or even two days before he could secure a position on good, flat ground from where to launch his attack, but things progressed much more advantageously and by about 4:00 pm the cavalry was already in a position to strike (Wheatcroft, 181).

Meanwhile, the Duke of Lorraine and his infantry had also progressed faster than anticipated, thus presenting both commanders with the same vital dilemma that so often means the difference between victory and defeat: push on and go for gold or wait and regroup (Wheatcroft, 182). Independently of each other both men decided they would move in for the kill and not risk the Turks slipping away after nightfall.

Around 6:00 p.m., Sobieski gave his cavalry the order to prepare for the final attack. But ahead of them, the Turks, confronted with 3,000 bristling horses carrying 3,000 heavily armored Polish hussars (*husaria*) and another 3,000 cavalry in the second line behind them

— lost heart and started to flee (Wheatcroft, 184-187). Realizing the charge would be more about cutting down retreating troops than forcing their way into an orderly line of well-armed, disciplined infantry, the husaria quickly exchanged their lances for sabers and stormed forward (Wheatcroft, 186).

Many Muslims had likely dreamed of a different ending to their glorious march on Vienna than being ridden down by Polish cavalry while running for their lives, but that is nevertheless how it ended for many of them. By 7:00 p.m. it was all over and the Christians had won the day. Vienna was saved from the Muslims once again, this time for good.[11]

The Battle of Vienna would prove to be the turning point for the Ottoman Empire. Within twenty years the Ottomans were forced to sign the Treaty of Karlowitz (1699), after having suffered several additional defeats. The treaty meant the loss of most of the Turkish territories in Central Europe, many of them permanently.

During the 18th and 19th century the Ottoman Empire continued to decline, slowly but certainly losing almost all of its territories in Europe, Africa and the Middle East. After Albania declared its independence from the Ottoman Empire in 1912, Ottoman possessions in Europe were reduced to just Eastern Thrace, the same area that makes up the only European part of present-day Turkey.

So where did it go wrong? What caused the powerful Muslim war machine to collapse and turn the Ottoman Empire from the scourge of Christian Europe into the "sick man of Europe" — as Tsar Nicholas I of Russia famously said in the mid-nineteenth century?

For one, the rising importance of nationalism. Outside of Turkey, the Ottoman Empire was made up of several different peoples (as empires tend to be). In the nineteenth century, the growing realization that one was Bulgarian, Greek, Macedonian, or Albanian, rather than the inhabitant of some fiefdom of a Muslim empire, fueled several independence movements, especially in regions where Christians made up the majority of the population, as they were being treated as lesser subjects than the Muslims.

The all-powerful place of Islam in society also hampered education and reform in the Ottoman Empire. A lot of educational resources went into learning Arabic and the studying of the Koran, for instance, time the "infidels" of Western Europe could spend studying science. And then there was the printing press, a game-changing invention the Ottomans had known about since the late 15th century, but which religious authorities had forbidden for works in Turkish and Arabic until 1727, more than 270 years after Gutenberg had invented it.[12] Reforming the military after Western example was also held back by Islamic clerics for religious reasons.

The rise of Russia and the Western powers posed another problem for the Ottoman Empire. More technologically advanced than the Turks from the 18th century on, they were looking for ways to expand their own empires and frequently did so at the cost of the Ottomans. And if that wasn't enough, the empire also suffered from structural economic problems — high unemployment, an uncompetitive economy — and a string of weak Sultans (one of the classic dangers in an absolutist system). Of course, in the end, every empire has to meet its maker.

After having fought on the losing side during WW I, its victors carved up the Ottoman Empire into several nations, most of which came under the influence of the victorious British and French. Constantinople — so proudly conquered by Mehmed II in 1453 — was occupied by Western forces. But in 1923, after the Turkish War of Independence, Constantinople was given back to Turkey under the Treaty of Lausanne and renamed Istanbul. That same year the Republic of Turkey was declared and on March 3, 1924, the Ottoman Caliphate — the Islamic state — was formally declared abolished. Turkey became a secular Republic.

Officially, it still is today.

---

1   The Seljuk Turks used the term Rûm to refer to the Eastern Roman Empire (a.k.a the Byzantine Empire). Their use of the designation Rûm was not meant to imply the Sultanate was the successor state of the Roman Empire, though, merely that their lands were located on territory which had long been held by the Romans (Peacock, 79-81).

2   Reliable information about the early Ottoman history being scarce, the veracity of this story remains uncertain.

3   Whether Osman was still alive when the city fell is unclear. According to historian Cathal Nolan he was not, while Donald Pitcher writes that the city

was taken by Osman's son and successor Orhan just before his death (Nolan, 100-101; Pitcher, 37).

4   The Count of Eu was captured during the battle and died in captivity less than a year later.

5   Based on Turkish sources, Runciman arrives at a total of 80,000 regular troops, plus maybe 20,000 irregular troops and several thousand non-combatant camp-followers. Venetian and Greek estimates came in much higher, at 150,000 and 300,000-400,000, respectively (Runciman, 76).

6   On that same day, June 1, 1453, Mehmed II also had Çandarlı Halil Pasha — who had twice showed so little confidence in him when he was younger — executed and his property confiscated.

7   Since 1935 it has been a museum.

8   Prince Vlad III Dracula also served as inspiration for the character of Count Dracula in Bram Stoker's classic novel *Dracula*.

9   On May 12, 2013, Pope Francis canonized all 813 victims as martyrs.

10 Fletcher Pratt writes that the Ottomans were "*nearly 350,000*" strong, while Christopher Duffy gives the more conservative estimate of 125,000 (Pratt, 144; Duffy, 201). Albert Lybyer settles for an estimate of 300,000 in his *Government of the Ottoman Empire in the Time of Suleiman the Magnificent*, while also listing a number of contemporary estimates that range from 170,000 to a cool million in an accompanying note, though many of these estimates make a distinction between fighting men and other persons (107, note 1).

11 Later that year, on Christmas day, the battle at Vienna demanded one final casualty. Ottoman commander Kara Mustafa Pasha was executed in Belgrade at the order of sultan Mehmed IV for losing the battle.

12 The first printing presses in the Ottoman Empire had been set up in the late 15th century by Spanish Jews, but censorship laws forbade printing in Turkish and Arabic, while allowing it in Spanish, Hebrew, Greek, and Latin. In other words, throughout the Ottoman Empire, the ones benefitting from this vital new technology were mostly non- Muslims (Agoston, 130).

20

RENAISSANCE

*"What a piece of work is a man, how noble
in reason, how infinite in faculties, in form and
moving how express and admirable, in action how
like an angel, in apprehension how like a god!"1*
William Shakespeare, Hamlet, Act II, Scene 2

How will history look back on us and our time? Most people in the West probably consider their respective societies pretty advanced. We have democracy, civil rights, a (mostly) humane prison system, the highest life expectancy in the history of mankind and access to an abundance of food, water, entertainment and technology (or at least most of us do).

In fact, looking back at earlier times, right up until the end of the Second World War, it is almost hard not to feel sorry for our ancestors, who had to work eighteen hours a day in a factory, serve as cannon fodder on numerous battlefields and were often so poor they were literally starving to death. Yes, we've certainly come a long way. But will those coming after us agree, or will they see more similarities between us and those from a century ago than we do?

In the 14th century, Italian scholars and artists rediscovered classical antiquity and proclaimed that the light of civilization — which they felt had been extinguished ever since the fall of Rome — was finally shining again. Florentine historian Leonardo Bruni even called it a new age. In his book *History of the Florentine People* — sometimes called the first modern history book — Bruni proudly distinguished three periods of history: Antiquity, Middle Ages and Modern.

The 19th century French historian Jean Michelet was the first to view the Renaissance as a distinct period in European history that touched upon all aspects of life and was radically different from the

Middle Ages. He devoted an entire volume to the Renaissance in his magnum opus *Histoire de France*.[2] It was through this work that the word Renaissance stuck, even though he was not the first to use the term rebirth to describe the rediscovery of Antiquity. That honor goes to Giorgio Vasari, who had already used the term *la rinascita* (Italian for rebirth) three hundred years earlier, in his 1550 work *Vite de'più eccellenti architetti, pittori, et scultori Italiani* — Lives of the most eminent Italian painters, sculptors, and architects (Morillo, 106, note 12).

In our time, the traditional view on the Renaissance has come under pressure. Modern historians agree that significant developments took place during the Renaissance which had a profound impact on the arts, politics, literature, science and religion, but there is no consensus about the periodization, about it being a true break from the Middle Ages or even about it being a true historical period.

It is also argued that the Renaissance would not have been possible without certain events and developments during the Middle Ages, such as the copying of classical texts by monasteries, the Crusades that brought Europe into contact with the Byzantines and the founding of the first universities to study classical sources. Instead of being a clear-cut break from the "Dark Ages" — as the Italian writer Francesco Petrarch (1304-1374) so contemptuously called the period between the fall of Rome and his own time — the Renaissance owes so much to the Middle Ages that it is in many ways its child, its heir. As art historian Erwin Panofsky wrote: "*the Renaissance* [is] *connected with the Middle Ages by a thousand ties.*" (Panofsky, 201-202).

Meant to express a rebirth of classical antiquity, a period revered by artists and scholars of the 13th and 14th century alike, the term "Renaissance" indubitably wears a hint of arrogance on its educated face, showing off its cultural sophistication and emphasis on classical antiquity the way a popular girl might parade her mother's jewelry on prom night.

Suddenly, everything from the classical period was cool. Scholars like Poggio Bracciolini and Petrarch enthusiastically searched through monastic libraries — delighted with every old, crumbled, half forgotten manuscript they could get their hands on — artists tried to imitate the elegant classicist style, people even changed their name to make them look more Roman.[3] The famous Dutch humanist Erasmus, for instance, who was from the city of Rotterdam, called himself "Desiderius Erasmus Roterodamus", Francesco Petracco latinized his name to Petrarca and the Flemish anatomist Andries van Wezel — the father of modern human anatomy — changed his name to Andreas Vesalius.[4]

In many ways Renaissance scholars and artists were like teenagers, free at last, discovering themselves and their place in the world, learning all kinds of new things, looking up to popular teachers and mentors (albeit dead ones) and above all: denouncing everything the Middle Ages had taught them as being outdated and meaningless.

Traditionally, the Renaissance is dated between the 14th and 17th century, but even before that time there were unmistakable signs of an increasing fascination with classical antiquity and an emerging shift in artistic focus and style. One early example is the pulpit for the baptistery of Pisa by the Italian sculptor Nicola Pisano (1220-1285), which shows clear classical Roman influences. Another example is the famous fresco for the Scrovegni Chapel in Padua, by Italian painter Giotto (1266-1337). The works of the great Italian writers Dante Alighieri (1265-1321), Francesco Petrarca (1304-1374) and Giovanni Boccaccio (1313-1375) are also considered part of this 'proto- renaissance', renaissance in the making so to speak.[5]

If when the Renaissance started is subject to debate, *where* it started is not: Northern Italy, particularly in the Tuscan city of Florence.[6] Some of the most famous Renaissance artists hailed from this equally famous city, among them Michelangelo, Leonardo da Vinci, Botticelli, Filippo Brunelleschi, Giotto, Donatello and Dante Alighieri, to name a few.[7] There, merchants and bankers had money to burn, having grown rich in the late 13th, early 14th century from the woolen cloth trade and handling all banking activities for the papacy, including tax collecting for the Holy See throughout Latin Christendom, a highly lucrative job (Brucker, 53-55). The Florentine merchants and bankers became great patrons of the arts, commissioning painters, sculptors and architects to create beautiful works of art, often donating them to the church in the hopes it would shave of time in purgatory.[8]

But there was more going on. During the 13th century, artists and scholars increasingly looked to classical antiquity for knowledge and inspiration. The rediscovery of classical texts in monastic libraries, together with the influx of Greek scholars and artists who were relocating to Italy from the ever shrinking Byzantine Empire — thanks to the Ottoman Turks — brought many long forgotten works back into the limelight. And with the fall of Constantinople in 1453, the number of Greek artists and scholars fleeing the Turks rose even further, leading some to favor this exact year as the 'real' start of the Renaissance.

Though the end of the Eastern Roman Empire seems a plausible enough moment for the end of one era and the beginning of another, what lies at the heart of the Renaissance is something too big to have started in any one year, perhaps even in any one century. Rediscovering the classical texts was important, yes, as was the influx of Greek artists and scholars, but at its core the Renaissance was not about great works of art being commissioned by rich merchants and bankers, the development of new artistic skills and styles or even renewed interest in the classical era, it was about placing man in the center of the universe. Man, instead of God.

In the Renaissance the individual became the new focal point. His life on earth, his thoughts, his reasoning, his emotions, his body (and hers as well of course). No longer was life just about God, the afterlife and doing penance for past sins. Not that the Renaissance man was not religious — because he most certainly was — he just rediscovered himself and the world around him with renewed passion and awe. People simply wanted to see things for what they really are, by observing and studying them.

So when Florentine architect Filippo Brunelleschi developed linear perspective in the early 1400s, the technique quickly spread throughout Europe, opening a realm of possibilities for Spanish, French and Netherlandish painters.[9] Wanting to paint and sculpt an object as realistically as possible, artists studied anatomy to learn more about movements, muscles, tissue and bone structure. Leonardo da Vinci even dissected several human corpses himself — in addition to a host of cows, birds, bears, monkeys and frogs.

But it wasn't just the visual arts that were rocked by the new way of thinking. Literature, nature, science, philosophy, politics, even religion, everything was reexamined, reevaluated, questioned and discussed.

Giovanni Boccacio's *Decamerone,* for instance — a collection of 100 tales, told by ten young people who have fled plague-ridden Florence to a villa in the country side — is filled with racy, witty and edgy stories, some very critical of religion, the Catholic Church and the behavior of its priests. The Florentine writer, politician and historian Niccolò Machiavelli wrote a book about the realities of politics and the means by which a ruler could gain and retain his power. Describing all manner of devious methods to subjugate the people, *Il Principe* (The Prince, first published in 1532) thus broke with the tradition of political idealism. The Catholic Church banned the book in 1559. And then there was the Polish mathematician and astronomer Nicolaus Copernicus, who reasoned that the Sun, not the Earth, was at the center of the universe. Because this theory conflicted with some parts of the Bible, his book *De Revolutionibus Orbium Coelestium* (On the Revolutions of the Celestial Spheres, first published in 1543) was also forbidden by the Catholic Church, in 1616.[10]

But why then and why there? Why did the Renaissance ignite in Northern Italy in the 14th century? Why not in Constantinople in the 11th century, or in Spain, or London, or Paris? It seems there are a number of factors that, together, created the necessary environment for the new paradigm — man himself as the focal point — to flourish in Florence and other Italian city states first.

Money certainly played its part. The economic prowess of the Italian city states and the system of patronage — through which wealthy citizens hired all manner of artists — allowed for a larger part of society to make a living as an artist, writer or scholar, who in turn not only created many wonderful works of art but also fueled new artistic movements and scientific development.

The (past) greatness of Rome was also more visible in Italy than elsewhere in Europe. Roman villas, theaters, roads, bridges, columns and arches surrounded the Italians of the late Middle Ages and kept the memory of the beauty that was ancient Rome alive, making it easy to covet and imitate.

The 14th century was also a very tough century, bringing hardship and death to many. There was the Great Famine of 1315-1317, the Black Death of 1346-1353, the start of the Hundred Years' War between England and France in 1337, several other plague epidemics in the second half of the 14th century and several other wars. The city of Florence likely lost more than half of its population to the plague in 1348, deeply affecting its economy — cheaper land, cheaper housing, more expensive labor — and social order (Kohn, 126).

The many disasters that ravaged the 14th century also weakened the power of the church, because it had not been able to prevent the famine nor cure the plague. The Bible was filled with stories about miraculous savings, feedings and healings but those who had survived the Black Death wondered why the priests and the bishops had not been able to stave off the terrible ordeal with God's help. Fact was that priests and bishops had died like flies same as everybody else, making it clear that prayer alone could not save a person from sickness and suffering. With life being this short and fragile, many survivors reasoned it was best to simply enjoy it while it lasted.

Meanwhile the Papal Schism — a split within the Catholic Church between 1378-1417 — hardly helped in rebuilding confidence in the clergy of the Mother Church. During this period there were two popes, one in Rome and one in Avignon; at one point, there were even three popes![11] There were also numerous examples of priests, bishops, cardinals and even popes who drank, partied and fornicated like there was no tomorrow. Pope Alexander VI, for instance (born Rodrigo de Borja and in office from 1492 until his death in 1503) had many mistresses and sired several illegitimate children. Besides adultery, he was also accused of corruption, torture and murder.

In the 16th century, the tainted reputation of the Catholic Church would bring about a religious Renaissance of sorts, although the Church of Rome would not see it like that. Reformers like Martin Luther, John Calvin and Huldrych Zwingli objected to the abusive behavior of many clerics, the devotion to saints and the selling of indulgences, which granted full or partial remission of the punishment of sin.

On October 31, 1517, Luther nailed a document to the door of the *Schloßkirche* (Castle Church) in Wittenberg which contained ninety-five scholarly objections and challenges to several church practices he

considered at odds with core values of Christianity.[12] The document —
later known as the Ninety-Five Theses — caused a religious storm in
Europe that would rage for centuries, inciting rebellions, revolutions
and (civil) wars that divided age-old nations and empires and created
new ones, killing millions of people in the process.

Luther's questioning and reexamining of values and doctrines
that had been commonly accepted for centuries fitted perfectly with
the *zeitgeist* of the Renaissance. For Luther, the individual relation
between man and God lay at the heart of Christianity. No cleric was
needed to talk to God, no indulgence was needed to shorten the time
in purgatory, no saint was needed for protection; God alone was
enough. To this end, Luther set himself to translating the entire Bible
from Latin to German (finishing the work in 1534), so that ordinary
citizens could read the holy book for themselves. The printing press
— invented less than a century before — would help spread his
translation quickly and in great numbers.

The Renaissance awakened the belief in human exceptionalism and
put man firmly in the center of attention. This paradigm shift in focus
would not remain limited to artists or scholars. Helped by the increased
usage of everyday language in both literary and scholarly works, an
increase in literacy and the widespread distribution of books through
the printing press, ordinary people also got access to new, radical
ideas that emphasized the importance of the individual.

The Renaissance thus paved the way for Reformation and
Revolution, shaking things up for centuries to come, including our
own. Because looking at the world of today, it is clear that in many
ways we are still being reborn.

---

1   Shakespeare, 163.

2   Michelet (1798-1874) worked for more than 30 years on his masterpiece,
     publishing separate volumes of the work between 1833-1867.

3   In 1345, Petrarch discovered copies from Marcus Tullius Cicero's letters to Titus
     Pomponius Atticus, in the Bibliotheca Capitolare at Verona. This discovery
     has often been viewed as a foundational moment for the Italian Renaissance.
     Among the great number of classical Latin manuscripts Bracciolini recovered
     was Lucretius' *De rerum natura* (on the nature of things), a poem of 7,400 lines
     explaining Epicurean philosophy, the only known copy of the work to have
     survived.

4   The birth name of Erasmus is thought to have been Geert Geerts or Gerhard Gerhards, but there is no definitive proof for this.

5   Dante Alighieri is best known for the *Divina Comedia* (The Divine Comedy), while Boccaccio is renowned for his *Decamerone* (Decameron).

6   Other periods are now also sometimes classified as being a "Renaissance", like the Carolingian Renaissance, the Ottonian Renaissance and the Renaissance of the 12th century, but when discussing the Renaissance in this chapter, I simply refer to what is traditionally regarded as *The* Renaissance.

7   Micheleangelo and Leonardo da Vinci were not born in the city of Florence itself but in small towns that were part of the Republic of Florence, Michelangelo in Caprese and Leonardo da Vinci in....you guessed it, Vinci. Michelangelo's family returned to Florence when he was just a couple of months old, Leonardo left the country village of his childhood for Florence during his early teenage years, to become an apprentice of the Florentine painter Andrea del Verrocchio.

8   According to Roman Catholic doctrine, purgatory is a very unpleasant waiting room between heaven and hell, where sinners — meaning everybody — have to suffer for their sins before they can go to heaven. Thankfully, though, time in Purgatory can be shortened by almsgiving, indulgences and works of penance ("Compendium of the Catechism of the Catholic Church", questions 210-211).

9   Brunelleschi (1377-1446) is also the architect of the famous dome of the Florence cathedral, the Santa Maria del Fiore.

10   As Martin Luther said in 1539: "*People gave ear to an upstart astrologer who strove to show that the earth revolves, not the heavens or the firmament, the sun and the moon ... This fool wishes to reverse the entire science of astronomy; but sacred Scripture tells us* [Joshua 10:13] *that Joshua commanded the sun to stand still, and not the earth.*" (qtd. in Kuhn, 191). De Revolutionibus Orbium Coelestium was forbidden by a decree of the Holy Congregation in charge of the Index Librorum Prohibitorum (Index of Forbidden Books) on March 5, 1616. The Holy Congregation did not completely forbid Copernicus' book but suspended its publication until corrected — meaning until the offending passages about the universe being heliocentric instead of geocentric had been removed.

11   The third pope had been elected by a church council in Pisa in 1409. The council also deposed the other two popes, but they ignored the council's decision.

12   Whether Luther actually nailed the Ninety-Five Theses to the church door is a matter of some dispute, as real evidence for it is scarce (Marshall, 42; Hendrix, 20-21). It was, however, common practice at the time to post academic theses on a door for public discussion, so for Martin Luther, a theology professor at the newly founded University of Wittenberg (1502), nailing his theological theses to a church door would have been less of a theatrical act than one might think at first. Luther's most strenuous objections were directed against the sale of indulgences, which he argued went against Christ's original intention of sins being forgiven through confession and genuine penance.

21

THE GREATEST INVENTION
OF THE MILLENNIUM

*"Before printing was discovered, a century
was equal to a thousand years."[1]*

Henry David Thoreau

In 1908, the Italian archaeologist Luigi Pernier discovered a mysterious clay disc in an ancient Minoan palace at Phaistos, on the South Coast of Crete. Dated between 1850-1550 BCE, the disk measured about 6 inches (15 cm) in diameter and was covered in symbols — 241 in total, with 45 unique signs — running in a spiral pattern on both sides. The mysterious part was that the matching symbols were completely identical, suggesting they were stamped in the soft clay rather than manually inscribed.[2] If true, that would make the Phaistos Disc the earliest known example of the use of movable type printing.

More than 2,500 years later, around 1040 CE, a man named Pi Sheng invented movable type in China, using clay.[3] After first cutting out the characters in the soft clay, he baked them in a fire to harden them (Needham, Vol. V:1, 201). To print a page, Pi Sheng arranged the different types together on an iron plate that had been previously prepared with a paste of pine resin, wax and paper ashes (Needham, Vol. V:1, 201). He then placed the iron plate near a fire to warm it. When the paste was slightly melted, he took a smooth board and pressed it over the surface, to even out the block of type (Needham, Vol. V:1, 201). Time consuming, yes, and hardly suitable for printing just a couple of pages, but very fast when printing hundreds or thousands.

The Koreans were the first to make movable type out of metal instead of wood or clay, in the 13th century. But the Korean emperor forbade all non-official printing activities and kept a monopoly on the use of metal movable type, so that it served only the nobility (Sohn, 103). Depending on the viewpoint, it was either one of the dumbest or one of the smartest decisions ever made.

But although movable type printing was discovered centuries earlier in Asia than in Europe (aside from the possible implications of the Cretan Phaistos Disc), it did not revolutionize the East as it would the West. One possible reason for this is that Asian languages are character-based. Chinese, for instance, consists of tens of thousands of different characters, demanding a sizable investment from anyone wanting to set up his own print shop .[4] Woodblock printing — carving out a whole page on a single block, which is faster than manual writing for large volumes but not nearly as fast as movable type printing — therefore remained popular throughout Asia up until the 19th century, long after the printing press had revolutionized knowledge distribution in Europe.

The first to mechanize printing was the German Johannes Gutenberg, around 1440.[5] He used a wine press — something that had been around since the time of the Roman Empire — to apply pressure to a blank page lying on the surface of an inked type. Gutenberg was the first to develop an oil- based ink, which did not soak the paper the way water-based inks did. He also devised a special lead-based alloy for the type — which proved very durable — and a mold to mass produce the letters; the fact that he was a goldsmith by profession must have come in handy there.

Operated by two pressmen, Gutenberg's printing press could turn out a stunning 250 sheets per hour, printed on one side (Moran, 32). Taking into account that the hourly capacity likely dropped toward the end of the twelve-hour workday, a daily capacity of 2,500 sheets per printing press seems reasonable. Put differently: a book that for thousands of years had taken the average scribe a year to copy, could suddenly be produced in little over an hour.

The first major book produced with the printing press was the Gutenberg Bible, in 1456. Some 200 copies were made and quickly sold out. The price of one copy was 30 florins, which at the time was about three years' wages for a common clerk. As more printers set up shop all over Europe the price of subsequent books quickly dropped, except for those first edition Gutenberg Bibles...[6]

The printing press was a huge hit and went viral with unprecedented speed for the time. In 1480, less than 25 years after the introduction of the Gutenberg Bible, printing presses were already active in more than 110 European cities (Febvre, 182). By 1500, 20 million book copies had been produced with the printing press in Europe; in 1550 alone, the total output of the Western European printing industry was over three million books — more than the total number of manuscripts produced during the entire 14th century — and in 1790 more than 20 million copies were churned out (Febvre, 248; Buringh 2009).[7] Something that had always been reserved for a small group of scholars, clergymen and nobles thus became ubiquitous rather quickly, especially considering the normal pace of transmission at the time.

Several factors contributed to the success of the printing press. The availability of paper, for instance, which had greatly increased with the introduction of water-powered paper mills and was much cheaper than the parchment and vellum that had been in use for most of the Middle Ages. The first German paper mill was set up in 1320, in Mainz, the same city where Gutenberg would later set up his printing press. About a quarter of the first edition of the Gutenberg Bible was still printed on vellum, but in later years paper would push out parchment and vellum altogether.

Another major factor contributing to the success of the printing press was the Renaissance, which saw an increased focus on education, produced new ideas that were put in writing and widely discussed, and awakened the love for the works of long dead writers from classical antiquity. The printing press therefore found a ready and hungry market for its products from the start.

For the study of Latin — the lingua franca of both church and university — the *Disticha* (a.k.a the Cato, after its author, Dionysius Cato), a collection of moral advice in two-liners, was a popular work; by 1500, it could boast 69 printed editions in Latin, 36 in German and Latin and 9 in Italian and Latin (Febvre, 254). The fables of the Ancient Greek storyteller Aesop were also very popular, with more than 80 Latin editions alone before 1500 (Febvre, 254).[8]

For the first time, students could also possess their very own copy of Plato's *The Republic* and *The Letters of Cicero* — which had so inspired Petrarch in the 14th century. These days, with its easy accessibility to near limitless information, it is hard to imagine what a big deal it must have been for a law student in the late 14th century to actually own his own copy of the *Digesta* and study it at length, without having to worry about library hours or being dependent on what part of the *Digesta* his law professor would touch upon.[9]

It also became much easier for scholars to publish works of their own. Before the printing press, the distribution of a new book was so expensive and time consuming it rarely happened. This greatly hampered academic comparison and discussion of different viewpoints and made it difficult to build upon each other's intellectual work. Academics working in the same field exchanged views through written correspondence, but their letters were not publicly available, so whatever scholar A wrote to scholar B could not be commented on by scholar C, unless scholar A copied his letters and sent them to both or asked scholar B to pass his letter on. The invention of the printing press changed all this. Scholars started publishing their views and comments on the views of others, leading to the publishing of rebuttals and challenges and all those other things that keep scholars so wonderfully busy.

That the printing press could also be used as a very powerful weapon of change was first made clear by the speed with which the ideas of the Reformation spread through Europe. On October 31, 1517, Martin Luther supposedly nailed his Ninety-Five Theses on the door of the Castle Church of Wittenberg.[10] In January 1518 they were translated into German and immediately distributed in great numbers. Between 1517 and 1520 Luther also wrote some 30 tracts, of which a total of 300,000 copies were distributed (Ozment, 199). In the six years following the publication of the Ninety-Five Theses, the publication of books in Germany increased sevenfold (Ozment, 199). That must have drawn a fair number of Hallelujahs from German printers.

A later example of the power of the printing press is Thomas Paine's revolutionary seventy-seven page pamphlet *Common Sense*, which played such an important role in stirring up support for the American Revolution and of which an estimated 100,000 copies were sold in 1776 alone (Paine, "Political Writings", x). One paper, the *Connecticut Courant*, even printed the whole pamphlet in its February 19th issue (Aldridge, 45).

For some, the potential threat to the status quo outweighed the benefits of cheap and easy access to knowledge. The religious and ruling elite of the Ottoman Empire, for instance, decided against the printing press — In 1483, Sultan Bayezid II prohibited printing in Arabic script on pain of death — thereby undoubtedly contributing to the decline of the empire from the 17th century on. In 1727, the printing of non-religious books in Turkish was finally permitted, but it would take until 1803 before the ban on the printing of religious works was also lifted (Agoston, 130). At first, the Ottoman state had a monopoly on printing. When private printing shops were finally allowed, heavy censorship was introduced which remained in effect until 'the sick man of Europe' finally drew his last breath, following the defeat in World War I (Agoston, 130).

To what extent the printing press contributed to the dissemination of powerful, radical ideas such as the Protestant Reformation and the revolutions in the Netherlands (16th century), England (17th century), France and the United States (18th century), remains a hotly debated issue to this day. Literacy certainly increased as a result of the invention of the printing press, but until universal education systems were introduced in the 19th century, the literacy rate remained far below 50 percent in most countries (Buringh 2009, table 9).[11]

It has also been pointed out that the printing press did not just produce great works of knowledge and literature but also low-quality work *"popularizing long-cherished beliefs, strengthening traditional prejudices and giving authority to seductive fallacies"* (Febvre, 278).

Of course the same has been said about the influence of radio, television and, more recently, the internet. And it's true. Print media, radio stations, television networks and the internet do indeed produce a lot of low-quality work, filled with unsubstantiated, prejudicial, unnecessary, unhelpful information. Readers / listeners / viewers have to espouse a critical mindset lest they unwittingly fill their heads with nonsense. Then again, before the printing press, the same held true for listening to village storytellers or priests whose teachings were based on a book most people did not have access to and which in any case was written in a language they did not understand (not that they could read).

In any case, the printing press gave a growing number of people access to a multitude of knowledge. It seems neither surprising nor coincidental that in the centuries following its invention all kinds of new ideas, theories and philosophies were dreamed up and distributed that would radically change the world.

---

1   Thoreau, 68.

2   The symbols have yet to be deciphered, although many attempts have been undertaken since the disc was first discovered. Most linguists think decipherment of the disc is unlikely until more examples of the script are found. The fact that this has not happened yet is all the more remarkable since the stamping of the symbols on the disc implies mass-production capability.

3   There is only one record of this, in the book *Meng-ch'i pi-t'an* (Dream Pool Essays) from the Chinese polymath scientist Shen Kua (1031-1095). Shen Kua describes how Pi Sheng *"a man of unofficial position, made moveable type"* (qtd. in Needham, Vol. V:1, 201).

4   In *Chinese History: A Manual*, Endymion Wilkinson mentions a number of Chinese dictionaries, one of which, the *Hanyu da zidian*, lists 54,678 characters (Wilkinson, 76).

5   The earliest information about Gutenberg as the inventor of the printing press comes through the record of a lawsuit that was brought against him in 1439. To finance work on his printing press he had taken on three partners. When one of these partners died, his brothers wanted to inherit the partnership, knowing Gutenberg was working on something special (Hook, 39-40). They had also found pieces of equipment in their brother's house — cutting instruments, forms and a press (Hook, 39-40).

6   The last time a complete Gutenberg Bible was sold, in 1978, it fetched $2,2 million. In 2008, the potential value of a complete Gutenberg Bible was estimated at $25 to $35 million, with single pages being worth around $25,000, according to Kenneth Gloss, rare book appraiser and owner of the antiquarian book shop Brattle Book Shop, in Boston, MA

7   From 500 to 700, the average European production rate of manuscripts was a very modest 120 copies per year, which goes a long way to explaining why this period continues to be referred to as "The Dark Ages" (Buringh 2009).

8   Books from classical writers were always in high demand, but religion was by far the most popular category in the early days of printing. According to French historian Lucien Febvre, 45 percent of all books printed before 1500 were

religious in nature, from complete bibles — predominantly in Latin — to parts of the bible and other Catholic religious texts such as breviaries and missals (Febvre, 249-250). Classical, medieval and contemporary literature accounted for a little over 30 percent, law books a little over 10 percent and science books also around 10 percent (Febvre, 249-250).

9   The *Digesta* is part of the *Corpus Juris Civilis*, a collection of juristic writings dating back to the first centuries of the Roman Republic.

10   This is a matter of some debate. See note 12 of chapter 20 for more explanation.

11   Notably exceptions were Great Britain, with 53 percent literacy, and the Netherlands, which was far ahead of the curve with its 85 percent literacy rate (Buringh 2009, table 9).

Map 9: Waldseemüller map or *Universalis Cosmographia*,
by Martin Waldseemüller (1507),
courtesy of the Library of Congress

22

AGE OF EXPLORATION

"We grant you [King Alfonso V of Portugal]
by these present documents, with our Apostolic
Authority, full and free permission to invade,
search out, capture, and subjugate the Saracens
and pagans and any other unbelievers and
enemies of Christ wherever they may be, as
well as their kingdoms, duchies, counties,
principalities, and other property [...] and to
reduce their persons into perpetual slavery."1

Papal bull Dum Diversas, issued by Pope
Nicholas V on June 18, 1452

On May 31, 2012, Dutch non-profit foundation *Mars One*
announced its plan for a manned Mars mission in 2022, with
the goal of establishing a permanent human colony on Mars in 2023
("Mars One").[2] The plan is to send four people on the first mission
and four new people every two years after that. All are one-way trips,
no one is coming back, but that hasn't deterred people from wanting
to go. In the first two weeks alone, 78,000 people applied on the *Mars
One* website to become a Mars Conquistador (Prigg, "Mars").

In February 2013, American non-profit foundation *Inspiration
Mars* announced plans for a Mars flyby mission in January 2018 — or
2021 if the first deadline was missed ("Inspiration Mars"). The goal
is to fly to Mars and back in 501 days, an unusually short time, made
possible by a planetary alignment that happens only twice every 15
years. Though the astronauts would not actually land on Mars, they
would come within 100 miles of it. It would be the farthest humans
have ever traveled.

In other words: the race for the Red Planet is on.

600 years ago, a similar kind of race was on: the race for the rest of the world. For centuries, Europe had traded with Asia and the Middle East, mostly through (maritime) Italian city states like Venice, Florence and Genoa, making them fabulously rich (and voted "most likely to start the Renaissance"). But after the fall of Constantinople in 1453, the important Mediterranean and Black Sea routes that for so long had linked Europe to the East were cut off by the Ottomans, prompting several European nations to find a new route East.

During the 13th and first half of the 14th century Europeans had also used the famous Silk Road, a mostly land based route that ran through the territory of the vast Mongol Empire, connecting Eastern Europe with the Middle East and Asia.[3] The so-called *Pax Mongolica* enabled safe traveling and trading between Europe and China, with Caravans full of goods like silk, nutmeg, pepper and cinnamon finding their way West, while European traders in turn traveled to Asia with silver, linen, fine cloth and other goods.[4]

But in the second half of the 14th century, the Mongol Empire — and with it the Silk Road — collapsed, due to internal, mostly religious strife and the Black Death, which killed tens of millions in Asia during the 1330s and 1340s.

When the maritime routes to the East were also cut off, Europeans had to find a different route to Asia if they wanted to continue enjoying their silk, nutmeg, pepper and cinnamon. And since safe traveling over land through West Asia, Asia Minor and the Middle East was ruled out, that new route had to be over sea, giving strong seafaring nations an unbeatable edge.

First to the scene were the Portuguese. They had already done some maritime exploration in the early 14th century, after ending their *Reconquista* — the reconquering of their lands from the Muslims — but the main driving force behind the Portuguese maritime efforts would be Prince Henry the Navigator (1394-1460), a younger son of King John I of Portugal. Henry was fascinated with the exploration of the African coast, map making and finding the source of the West African gold trade.

To make exploration of the West African coast and the Atlantic Ocean possible, Prince Henry sponsored the development of a lighter, faster and highly maneuverable ship, the Caravel, which, thanks to its lateen sails, could sail much closer to the wind than square-rigged vessels, making it more suitable for the open seas.

Henry also encouraged exploration beyond the much feared *Cape Bojador* ('bulging cape'), on the African West Coast, of which the 15th century Portuguese chronicler Gomes Eanes de Zurara said that, according to the mariners, *"this much is clear, that beyond this Cape there is no race of men nor place of inhabitants; nor is the land less sandy than the deserts of Libya, where there is no water, no tree, no green herb — and the sea is so shallow that a whole league from land it is only a fathom deep, while the currents are so terrible that no ship having once passed the Cape, will ever be able to return."* (Zurara, 31).

But Henry was determined, obsessed even, with rounding the feared cape. For twelve years he kept sending his ships, and in 1434, on the fifteenth expedition, Gil Eanes, one of his navigators, finally succeeded where others had failed, becoming the first to sail beyond Cape Bojador, thus opening up Africa to exploration by the Portuguese (Diffie, 68). It also opened up the African slave trade to the Portuguese, and the first slaves arrived in Portugal that same year (Diffie, 76,77).

In 1488, Portuguese explorer Bartolomeu Dias became the first to round the southernmost tip of Africa. It was later named Cape of Good Hope by King John II of Portugal, because its very existence gave reason for optimism about the East being indeed accessible through this route, disproving the theory following from Ptolemy's famous work *Geography* (2nd century CE) that the Indian Ocean was landlocked and could thus not be reached from Europe by sea (Suarez, 86). Theories about the Indian Ocean being an open sea had been around for centuries, but penning a theory about it and getting in a boat to actually prove it are two very different things (Suarez, 87). In other words, even though Bartolomeu Dias and his men might have suspected that there would be an eventual end to the seemingly endless African continent, they did not know for sure. They just sailed and sailed and sailed, moving ever further from Portugal without knowing what lay beyond. Talk about bravery. (however brave the first astronauts traveling to Mars will be, at least they know the Red

214 - J.C. PETERS

Planet is actually there!)

Ten years later, Vasco Da Gama was the first to sail all the way from Portugal to India. Departing from Lisbon on July 8, 1497 in his caravel (thank you Henry the Navigator), traveling past Cape Bojador (thank you Gil Eanes) and rounding the Cape of Good Hope (thank you Bartolomeu Dias), the Portuguese fleet arrived at Kappad — a beach close to the city of Calicut, in southern India — on May 20, 1498. Now the Portuguese had their very own sea route to Asia. The French, English and Dutch would follow soon enough, though, establishing a centuries-long European domination over India, Indonesia, the Philippines and many other Asian countries in the process.

Though the most logical way to sail from Europe to the East seemed to be, well, to sail east, a certain explorer from Genoa nevertheless wanted to sail *west* into the Atlantic, instead of south along the African coast, and then just keep sailing until reaching the Orient. In 1485, three years before Bartolomeu Dias would first round Cape of Good Hope, he presented this rather fantastic idea to King John II of Portugal.

The king asked his experts to review the proposal of this Christoforo Colombo, but they rejected it, arguing that his estimate of the distance from the Canary Islands to Japan was far too low — which, at 2,400 nautical miles, it was indeed (Mancall, 207). In 1488 Columbus tried again, but this time the news of Bartolomeu Dias rounding the southernmost tip of Africa put a spoke in Columbus' wheel, as Bartolomeu's achievement made the search for a Western route superfluous, at least for the Portuguese.

At the Spanish court Columbus found a more willing ear, albeit after two years of lobbying. In 1492, just after the Spanish had recaptured Granada — finally completing the *Reconquista* of the Iberian Peninsula, after almost 800 years — Spanish King Ferdinand and his Queen Isabella received Columbus, giving him a chance to convince them of his quest. Isabella rejected it, but Ferdinand found the prospect of an exclusively Spanish route to the East too hard to resist and granted the Italian explorer half of his necessary funding, effectively green-lighting the voyage, since Columbus had already lined up enough private investors for the other half.

Rationally speaking, the experts of the king of Portugal had been right in rejecting Columbus' proposal. His estimate of the distance from Europe to Asia when traveling westward was indeed far too low. Columbus' calculations were way off because he *over*estimated the size of the Eurasian landmass and *under*estimated the size of the Earth (even though the latter had already been correctly calculated by the Greek Eratosthenes in 240 BCE and his calculations were widely known in Columbus' day).[5]

The real distance from the Canary Islands to Japan when traveling westward is 10,600 nautical miles, not the 2,400 nautical miles that Columbus estimated (McIlwraith, 34).[6] Given that the existence of the Americas was not yet known, most navigators thought the western sea route to Asia would therefore entail a voyage of a whopping 10,000 nautical miles through open ocean, very difficult to navigate and too long a journey considering how much food and water ships could carry at the time.

So what essentially happened was that Columbus set sail for India based on his own faulty and potentially deadly calculations, but bumped into the Americas on his way there, saving him and his men from dying of starvation on the open sea. Setting sail on August 3, 1492, Columbus landed on the Bahamas on October 12, 1492, a day still celebrated throughout many countries in the Americas — including the United States — though the Italian explorer never actually set foot on U.S. soil. Thus Columbus unwittingly discovered the New World, an entire continent unknown to the rest of the world, though he himself did not realize it at the time. Columbus thought he had indeed landed in India, which is why he called the primitive inhabitants he encountered 'Indians'.

The Florentine navigator Amerigo Vespucci, who sailed west to "Asia" (i.e., the new world) several times shortly after Columbus, was the first to call his fellow explorer's discovery for what it really was: a New World. Early 1503, Vespucci wrote about this *Mundus Novus* in a letter to his friend Lorenzo di Pierfrancesco de' Medici (a cousin of Lorenzo 'Il Magnifico' de' Medici, the legendary ruler of the Florentine Republic), claiming enthusiastically that "*My last voyage has proved it, for I have found a continent in that southern part; more populous and more full of animals than our Europe, or Asia, or Africa.*"(Vespucci, 42). Vespucci's letter was published and became an instant and raving success; twenty-three editions appeared between 1504 and 1506 alone (Fernández- Armesto, 131). When the German cartographer Martin Waldseemüller published a new map of the world not long after, he called the new landmass America, in honor of the person who had first recognized the discovered land for a New World.[7]

With Spain now fully in the game thanks to Columbus, the two seafaring nations on the Iberian Peninsula worked out a treaty dividing the world between them. In the Treaty of Tordesillas (1494), they agreed upon a line of demarcation about halfway between the Portuguese Cape Verde Islands (on the African West coast) and the Bahamas, recently discovered by Columbus. Spain got roughly everything to the West of the line and Portugal everything to the East of it.

The Portuguese explorer Pedro Álvares Cabral's sort of accidental discovery of Brazil a few years later, in 1500, happened to be just on the Portuguese side of the line.[8] At the time, Cabral thought he had discovered a large island, but when it turned out to be part of the South American continent, the Spanish did not object to the Portuguese exploration and colonization of Brazil across the Meridian line that formed the border of the treaty.

The early 1500s were heavy with new discoveries and achievements by men hunger for gold and glory, men who did not take no for an answer and who sailed and soldiered on with a mix of stubbornness, bravery and stupidity where lesser men would perhaps have turned back. Following the Treaty of Tordesillas, the Portuguese concentrated their efforts mainly on further exploring the Indian Ocean, while the Spanish busied themselves with digging around in the New World and trying to find a westward route to Asia.

In 1513, Spanish conquistador Vasco Núñez de Balboa fought, canoed and jungled his way through the Isthmus of Panama, thus becoming the first European to reach the Pacific Ocean from the New World and adding credibility to the idea of a sailable westward route to Asia. In 1514, the Portuguese explorer Jorge Alvares arrived at the Chinese island of Nei Lingding, in the Pearl River estuary in the southeastern province of Guangdong, becoming the first European in modern times to reach China by sea (Zhang, 35; Twitchett, 336).[9] The following year, another Portuguese explorer, Rafael Perestrello — a cousin of Christopher Columbus' wife — also visited the island in the Pearl River estuary and reportedly made a hefty profit of twenty to one trading with the Chinese merchants there (Zhang, 34, 38).

In August 1519, Ferdinand Magellan (Fernão de Magalhães), a Portuguese nobleman in Spanish service, set sail for the New World from Seville, Spain, with five ships and a crew of 270, with the objective of reaching the Pacific, more specifically the Spice Islands (now known as the Banda Islands, part of the Indonesian province of Maluku), by sailing around the southernmost tip of the South American continent.[10]

Magellan and his men found a passage through the southern tip in October 1520. Four ships entered the passage (one ship had already been lost in a previous mutiny), but on November 28, after a tough 373 miles, only three came out in the Pacific, the fourth having deserted and returned to Spain.[11] In March 1521 Magellan landed at the Homonhon Island (part of present-day Philippines), roughly 950 nautical miles from the Spice Islands and its nutmeg, mace and cloves.

Though the mission was already a success, Magellan himself would not live to see the Spice Islands or complete the circumnavigation of the globe for which he is now so famous.[12] On April 27, 1521, a few weeks after landing at the Philippines, Magellan died in the Battle of Mactan, fighting the forces of Cilapulapu, a local chieftain who had refused to recognize the King of Spain as his sovereign (Pigafetta, 56-57). The remaining crew reached the Spice Islands without their expedition leader, becoming the second Europeans — after the Portuguese — to trade with the locals. After many more setbacks and adventures, eighteen survivors out of the original 270 eventually returned to Seville on September 6, 1522, on the last remaining ship, named, somewhat ironically, *Victoria*.[13]

Of course other European nations did not recognize the Spanish-Portuguese Treaty of Tordesillas and before long started sending their own expeditions to the New World. In 1497, the Italian Zuan Caboto (John Cabot) was commissioned by King Henry VII of England to lead an expedition in search of a Northwest passage to the East. When Cabot instead found land on the North American coast, King Henry VII referred to it as "New Found Launde" (Newfoundland, present-day Canada).[14] The French also sent an Italian explorer on a voyage to the new world, Giovanni da Verrazzano.[15] He made landfall at or near Cape Fear, on the coast of North Carolina on March 1, 1524 (Baker, "Explorers", 566).

The English and the Dutch — not yet knowing of the Portuguese southward route — also tried to find a Northeast passage to Asia, through the Arctic, along the northern coast of the Eurasian landmass. In 1553, the English explorer Hugh Willoughby made an attempt at it, until heavy storms forced him to winter in a bay east of Murmansk. The frozen crew was found next spring by Russian fishermen; none had survived (Gordon, "The Fate of Sir Hugh Willoughby").

Dutch explorer Willem Barentsz made three voyages between 1594-96 to find a Northeast passage. The first time he had to turn back because of large icebergs, the second time because the Kara Sea (part of the Arctic Ocean) was frozen. The third time the ship became stuck within the many icebergs and the crew was forced to winter on the ice of Novaya Zemlya (Russian for new land). They used wood from the ship to build a cabin they called *Het Behouden Huys* (The Saved House) and hunted arctic foxes and polar bears to stay alive (Veer, 105ff.).[16] Barentsz survived the winter but died in June 1597, trying to reach northwestern Russia in an open boat with the remaining survivors.

Somewhat later, in 1609, while still fighting their independence war against Spain, the Dutch hired English explorer Henry Hudson to find a Northeast passage to Asia. Like the explorers before him, the unforgiving conditions of the Arctic forced Hudson to turn back, after which he decided to explore a possible Northwest passage. Somehow he ended up exploring part of the East Coast of North America, which the Dutch subsequently mapped and colonized in the decades that followed. The Dutch called their American colony New Netherland and its main city New Amsterdam (present-day New York City).

Meanwhile the Dutch had also discovered the Portuguese route East, around the Cape of Good Hope, and organized their first expeditions to the East Indies, which would prove to be the beginning of the end of Portugal's dominance of Southeast Asia.

A few years after these first expeditions, in March 1606, the Dutch explorer Willem Janszoon, sailing from Bantam, Java, discovered Australia, and in 1642, Abel Tasman, another Dutch explorer, discovered New-Zealand (Grimbly, 108-109).[17] Two years later, Tasman also explored a considerable portion of Australia's West Coast, calling the territory New Holland, a name that would remain in use well into the 19th century. In the decades that followed Tasman's explorations, the Dutch gradually pushed out the Spanish and Portuguese to establish their dominance over the Dutch East Indies, present-day Indonesia.

The Age of Exploration would have a profound impact on peoples and civilizations around the world through trade, colonization and exploitation. In what historian Alfred W. Crosby has named the "Columbian Exchange", a wide variety of plants, animals, human populations — including slaves, mostly from Africa — and diseases were exchanged between cultures who had never before been in contact with each other.

Potatoes, tomatoes and maize were introduced in Europe from the New World, while the European (re)introduction of horses in America had a huge impact on the Native American culture of the Great Plains, who shifted to a nomadic existence, hunting bison on horseback. Portuguese traders introduced Cassava and maize into Africa from Brazil in the 16th century (Nweke, "Cassava Transformation"). Today, about half the world production of Cassava comes from 40 African countries, while maize is the most important African food crop (Nweke, "Cassava Transformation").

Coffee from Africa and sugar cane from Asia were introduced to South America with great success, chili peppers were introduced from South America to India, while chocolate, also from South America, was introduced to Europe by the Spaniards, who also introduced oranges to Florida. In fact, Christopher Columbus himself had already taken seeds of oranges, lemons and citrons to Haiti and the Caribbean on his second voyage, in 1493. And these are just a few examples of all the fruits, vegetables, animals and human populations that were introduced back and forth, changing the diet, agriculture and ethnic composition of civilizations all over the world.

Unwittingly, Europeans also introduced all kinds of diseases to the Americas, like smallpox, measles, tuberculosis, typhus and influenza (Francis, 296ff.). They would wreak havoc among the native populations of the New World, who had never developed natural immunity against them. According to historian and demographer Nobel David Cook, these "new" diseases may have killed more than 80 percent of the native populations in the first 100-150 years after their introduction (Cook, 5).

In the centuries following their first explorations, the Spanish, Portuguese, English, French and Dutch would divide most of the world between them. Ancient civilizations in the Americas, Africa and Asia were conquered, its peoples subdued, while vast colonial empires were established and many Europeans emigrated to the New World. One wonders if things would have gone differently had the native Americans, Africans and Asians discovered Europe first.

---

1   Curran, 67.

2   In December 2016, the date for the landing of the first crew on Mars was moved up to 2032.

3   At its zenith, the Mongol Empire was the largest contiguous land empire in history, measuring an astonishing 24 million square miles (Turchin 2006, table 1). For comparison, the Roman Empire at its height measured 5 million square miles.

4   One of the merchants traveling the Silk Road was the Venetian Marco Polo (1254-1324). When, at one point, he was imprisoned in Genoa — Venice and Genoa were at war at the time and Polo had been captured by the Genoese navy at the Battle of Curzola or possibly at the Battle of Laiazzo — he told stories of his wondrous travels to the Far East to fellow inmate Rustichello da Pisa, who made a book of them (Ross, ix-x; Cliff, "Introduction", note 1). *The Travels of Marco Polo* (original title *Livre des merveilles du monde*) was a huge success, a rare feat at the time, considering the printing press had not yet been invented. The book introduced many Europeans for the first time to Central Asia and mysterious China. It also inspired many later European travelers, notably Christopher Columbus, who brought a copy of Marco Polo's book with him on his travels to the New World.

5   According to Thomas McIlwraith and Edward Muller, Colombus mistakenly valued a degree of longitude at the equator at about 45 nautical miles in length

while the actual length was 60 nautical miles, causing him to underestimate the earth's size by 25 percent (McIlwraith, 34).

6   Another reason for Columbus' overly low estimate of the distance between the Canary Islands and Japan was that he placed Japan much further eastward than its actual position.

7   The map, called *Universalis Cosmographia* (a.k.a Waldseemüller map) was first published on April 25, 1507. A single copy of the map survives and is preserved in the Library of Congress in Washington, D.C.

8   Whether Cabral's discovery was really accidental has long been debated among historians. It has been pointed out that Cabral did not need to have sailed so far West to steer clear of the doldrums of the African coast. Also, the demarcation line of the Treaty of Tordesillas agreed to six years earlier conveniently put the South American bulge where Cabral landed just inside Portugal's sphere of influence (Crow, 136-137).

9   Nei Lingding Island is also known as Lintin or Lintun Island and Tunmen or Tun-Men (island).

10 Magellan was obsessed with finding a westward route to the Spice Islands, something Portuguese King Manuel I was obviously not very interested in, since Portugal had already discovered the eastward route. Magellan therefore offered his services to Spanish King Charles I (who also reigned as Holy Roman Emperor Charles V), something the Portuguese did not look kindly upon, to say the least.

11 The passage is nowadays known as the Strait of Magellan.

12 It had never been Magellan's intention to circumnavigate the globe, he had just wanted to find a westward route to the Spice Islands.

13 Antonio Pigafetta, who wrote the first hand account *The First Voyage Around The World, 1519 - 1522: An Account Of Magellan's Expedition,* was among those eighteen survivors, as was Juan Sebastián Elcano, who had taken over command of the *Victoria* after the remaining members of the expedition had reached the Spice Islands.

14 The island of Newfoundland had already been discovered some 500 years earlier by Norse Vikings, led by Leif Erikson. They had established a settlement at the northernmost tip of Newfoundland, at L'Anse aux Meadows, around 1000 CE (Ingstad, iv-v).

15 Though as with the voyage of John Cabot, the objective was not so much the New World, but finding a western passage to Asia (McIlwraith, 39).

16 Gerrit de Veer was a Dutch officer on the third voyage. He kept a diary of the unfortunate events that transpired.

17 Tasman initially named New Zealand 'Staten-Landt', presumably because he thought it was part of an earlier discovered island off the coast of South America. It was later renamed Nova Zeelandia, New Zealand, after the Dutch province Zeeland (Johnston, 137).

23

"And yet it moves"

I would say here something that was heard from
an ecclesiastic of the most eminent degree: "That
the intention of the Holy Ghost is to teach us how
one goes to heaven, not how heaven goes."1

Galileo Galilei, letter to the Grand Duchess Christina, 1615

In May 2012, fifteen-year-old Jack Andraka was awarded the grand prize of the *Intel International Science and Engineering Fair,* for developing a faster, cheaper and more sensitive method to detect pancreatic, ovarian and lung cancer (Burris 2012). The idea came to him while secretly reading about carbon nanotubes during a biology class at North County High School that happened to be about antibodies. He combined the two topics in his head and used Google Search and free online scientific journals to learn more about nanotubes and cancer biochemistry.

Andraka then contacted about 200 professors to get laboratory help. All rejected his request, except Dr. Anirban Maitra of Johns Hopkins School of Medicine. In an interview with the Baltimore Sun, Professor Maitra later said that *"this kid is the Edison of our times. There are going to be a lot of light bulbs coming from him"* (qtd. in Burris 2012).

But however remarkable the story of Jack Andraka, these days there are many more brilliant teenage scientists like him.[2] Truth is, our time will probably produce many more Edisons than ever before, because, thanks to the internet, never before was so much information so easily and freely available to so many people. Therefore, if history repeats itself (and it always does), we are on the cusp of a new scientific revolution, similar to the one that took place in Europe between the 16th and 18th century.

Back then, the printing press was the great catalyst, allowing for cheap and widespread access (at least much more widespread than ever before) to all kinds of knowledge. Rediscovered knowledge from the ancient Greeks and Romans, knowledge from contemporary European scientists — which before the invention of the printing press had been limited to a small circle of people around those scientists themselves — even knowledge from Arabian and Chinese scientists, which had previously been only sparsely available in Europe.

Another factor in the scientific revolution that would spawn such eminent scientists as Nicolaus Copernicus, Galileo Galilei, Johannes Kepler and Sir Isaac Newton, was the Renaissance, which transformed the way people looked at the world and themselves. For the first time, man and the world he lived in were placed firmly in the center of attention, replacing God and the afterlife as the most important focal point. A hungry interest in the works of artists, writers and scientists from classical antiquity emerged and the importance of education increased.

All over Europe universities were opened to cater to eager young minds, who, for the first time, were ready to question pretty much everything and wanted to study the treasure trove of rediscovered classical works, from Emperor Justinian's *Corpus Iuris Civilis* to the books from intellectual giants such as Aristotle, Plato, Cicero, Herodotus and Virgil.

The astonishing discoveries of explorers like Bartolomeu Dias, Christopher Columbus, Vasco Da Gama, Ferdinand Magellan, Henry Hudson and Abel Tasman further reinforced the notion that the world was a much bigger place than previously thought and that nothing could be taken for granted. In short, everything was in place for a scientific confrontation between long accepted, dust-covered dogmas and doctrines, and sparkling, crisp new theories about the universe, the world and everything in it.

In 1543, one such theory was published by the Polish scientist Nicolaus Copernicus. His book, *De Revolutionibus Orbium Coelestium* (On the Revolutions of the Heavenly Spheres), which he only published just before his death and at the urging of others, was the result of 30 years work. *De Revolutionibus* is often mentioned as the start of the Scientific Revolution, because it goes directly against the Ptolemaic system and its geocentric model, which had been assumed to be the correct model of the cosmos since the 2nd century CE and was long since accepted religious doctrine (DeWitt, 123).[3] *De Revolutionibus* makes the case for the concept of heliocentrism, in other words, Copernicus argued that the Earth revolved around the Sun instead of the other way around, and that the reason for the apparent daily motion of the Sun and the stars was that the Earth rotated daily around its own axis.

It was a theory considered at odds with several parts of the Bible and therefore vehemently opposed by both the nascent Protestant movement and the Catholic Church. Martin Luther called Copernicus a *"fool"* [who] *wishes to reverse the entire science of astronomy; but sacred Scripture tells us that Joshua commanded the Sun to stand still, and not the Earth"*(Joshua 10:13, qtd. in Kuhn, 191). Philipp Melanchthon, the intellectual leader of the Lutheran Reformation, suggested that severe measures be taken against the impiety of Copernicans (Kuhn, 192). Unfortunately for Melanchthon Copernicus was already dead, so severe measures could no longer be taken against the primary culprit.

On March 5, 1616, more than 70 years after its initial publication, the Holy Congregation of the Most Illustrious Lord Cardinals placed *De Revolutionibus* on the Index of Forbidden Books *"until corrected"* (qtd. in Finocchiaro, 149). About a week earlier, the Holy Office had already determined in a special Consultants' Report on Copernicanism, that the proposition that the Sun was the center of the world and was itself completely devoid of local motion, was *"foolish and absurd in philosophy, and formally heretical since it explicitly contradicts in many places the sense of Holy Scripture, according to the literal meaning of the words and according to the common interpretation and understanding of the Holy Fathers and the doctors of theology."*[4]

For the Church, geocentrism clearly was a line in the sand. For centuries it had supported, spread and stimulated knowledge and education. The Carolingian monasteries of the 8th century had played an important part in saving many of the surviving manuscripts from classical antiquity that were later rediscovered during the Renaissance, some of the most prominent medieval philosophers and scientists had been men of the cloth and the Church had also played an active role in the founding and funding of the first European universities. That science could ever go against established church doctrine was unthinkable — and it never had. Until now. And this was only the beginning. It would get worse. Much worse.

In 1608, three Dutch spectacle makers independently and simultaneously invented the telescope. When Italian scientist Galileo Galilei heard about it the following year, he build one himself, increasing the magnification in subsequent versions from 3x to 30x (Allen 1943). Pointing it to the heavens, he soon discovered three of Jupiter's four moons (first thinking they were stars) and observed they were orbiting the planet (Drake, 150-152). This went against the Ptolemaic system, in which all celestial bodies orbited around the Earth. Late 1610 Galilei also observed all the phases of the planet Venus, proving it evolved around the Sun instead of the Earth (Drake, 164).[5]

Although his observations went against the accepted doctrine of geocentrism, Galilei was long protected from persecution by the Inquisition because of his good standing with Pope Urban VIII. This changed in 1632, with the publication of his *Dialogue sopra i due massimi sistemi del mondo* (Dialogue Concerning the Two Chief World Systems). In it, a Copernican scientist named Salviati has a discussion with an Aristotelian scientist who goes by the name Simplicio. The latter puts forward arguments in support of geocentrism, but nevertheless finds himself on the losing side of the discussion (no surprise there). The book was a great success but also sealed Galilei's fate. A few months after publication of the book, Galileo was ordered to stand trial and found *"vehemently suspect of heresy"* by the Inquisition (qtd. in Finocchiaro, 291).[6] The *Dialogue* was banned and Galileo was ordered to *"abjure, curse, and detest"* his opinions on heliocentrism and to *"recite the seven penitential Psalms once a week for the next three years."* (qtd. in Finocchiaro, 291). He was also placed under house arrest in what would amount to the rest of his life.

On June 22, 1633, Galileo complied and abjured, cursed and detested his "errors and heresies", but popular legend has it that he whispered *"Eppur si muove"* (and yet it moves) after doing so. True or not, the utterance brings to the fore the foundation of the Scientific Revolution: like it or not, these are the facts, this is the truth.

Ultimately, the Church would lose its battle with science, although it would take the Catholic Church until 1835 before silently admitting defeat and take Copernicus' *De Revolutionibus Orbium Coelestium* off its Index of of Forbidden Books, long after Sir Isaac Newton's (1642-1727) *Philosophiæ Naturalis Principia Mathematica* (1687) had removed any possible doubt about the validity of the heliocentric model.[7]

Meanwhile, progress was being made not just in astronomy and mathematics but also in biology, physics, law, medicine and philosophy. So fundamental were some of theses advances, that many of today's modern sciences, among them human anatomy, microbiology and chemistry, to name a few, are considered to have been founded during the Scientific Revolution.

Many famous inventions also saw first light of day between the 16th and 18th century, such as the barometer, the pendulum clock and the pocket watch, the microscope, the fire extinguisher, the thermometer, the sextant, James Watt's steam engine (which would be so essential for the Industrial Revolution), Benjamin Franklin's eyeglasses, the Montgolfier brothers' hot air balloon, and of course champagne.

Obviously, the benefits of more widespread education and information availability were not limited to the exact sciences. Philosophers like Baruch Spinoza, John Locke, Jean-Jacques Rousseau and Montesquieu formulated revolutionary theories — in the true sense of the word — about religious tolerance, the supremacy of the rule of law, the separation of powers and the importance of the will of the people. Theories that would find an ever growing audience and rock the world, beginning in Europe and the Americas, but later also spreading to other parts of the world and still going strong at the beginning of the 21st century.

Still, the most important contributions of the Scientific Revolution were not the many inventions, the scientific breakthroughs or even the revolutionary theories, it was the establishment of the supremacy of science over religion in matters of the truth. Science would henceforth adhere to reason, logic, observation and falsification — in short, the scientific method — before anything else. The Scientific Revolution thus solidified the separation of church and science, recognizing that without doing so, real science would be impossible.

1 Galilei, "Discoveries", 186.

2 Eighteen-year-old Eesha Khare for instance, who won one of two *Intel Foundation Young Scientist Awards* in May 2013 for inventing a super capacitor that can charge a cell phone in less than 30 seconds ("Recharge"). Or seventeen-year-old Henry Lin, who won the other award for simulating thousands of galaxies, providing scientists with new data to better understand the mysteries of astrophysics ("Recharge"). And nineteen-year-old Romanian Ionut Budisteanu, winner of the 2013 edition of the *Intel International Science and Engineering Fair,* for creating a viable model for a low-cost, self-driving car, using artificial intelligence ("Recharge").

3 Developed by the Alexandrian scientist Claudius Ptolemy (c. 90 CE-168) and published in his work *Almagest* (c.150 CE), the Ptolemaic system held that the Earth itself was stationary and located at the center of a spherical cosmos. Each of the planets moved along its own small sphere, called an epicycle, which itself moved along the larger sphere, thus revolving around the Earth.

4 Consultants' Report on Copernicanism, 24 February 1616 (qtd. in Finocchiaro, 146-147).

5 The phases of Venus are variations of lighting seen on the planet's surface, similar to the phases of the Moon. In the geocentric Ptolemaic system they would not all be visible, because for Venus to be fully lit from Earth's perspective it would have to be on the far side of the Sun, which is impossible in the Ptolemaic system since it requires Venus' orbit to be between the Earth and the Sun.

6 The inquisition, after examination, trial and confession stated that *"We say, pronounce, sentence, and declare that you, the above-mentioned Galileo, because of the things deduced in the trial and confessed by you as above, have rendered yourself according to this Holy Office vehemently suspected of heresy, namely of having held and believed a doctine which is false and contrary to the divine and Holy Scripture: that the sun is the center of the world and does not move from east to west, and the earth moves and is not the center of the world, and that one may hold and defend as probable an opinion after it has been declared and defined contrary to Holy Scripture."* (qtd. in Galilei, "Essential", 292).

7 The Catholic Church formally admitted that Galileo's heliocentric view was correct in 1992.

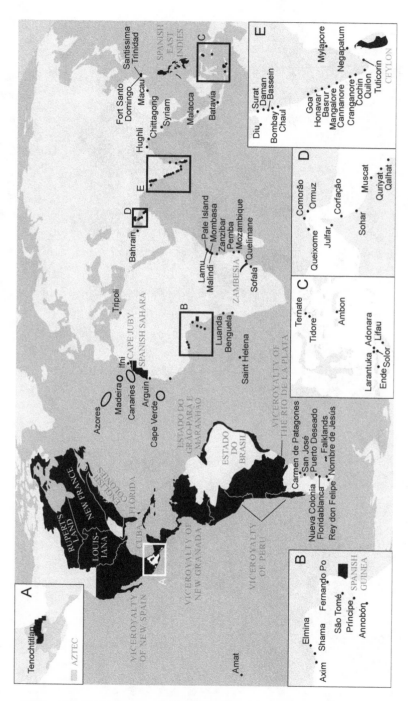

Map 10: European Colonization of the New World and
Asia (16th-17th century)

Inset A: Tenochtitlán · AZTEC

Inset B: Elmina · Axim · Shama · São Tomé · Príncipe · Fernando Po · Annobón · Amat · SPANISH GUINEA

Inset C: Ternate · Tidore · Ambon · Larantuka · Ende Solor · Adonara · Lifau · Solor

Inset D: Comorão · Ormuz · Queixome · Julfar · Corfação · Sohar · Muscat · Quriyat · Qalhat

Inset E: Diu · Surat · Daman · Bassein · Bombay · Chaul · Goa · Honavar · Basrur · Mangalore · Cannanore · Cranganore · Cochin · Quilon · Tuticorin · Negapatum · Mylapore · CEYLON

Main map labels:

Santíssima Trinidad · Macau · Fort Santo Domingo · Chittagong · Syriam · Malacca · Batavia · SPANISH EAST INDIES · Hughli

Azores · Madeira · Canaries · Ifni · CAPE JUBY · SPANISH SAHARA · Arguin · Cape Verde · Tripoli

Bahrain · Lamu · Malindi · Pate Island · Mombasa · Zanzibar · Pemba · Mozambique · Quelimane · Sofala · ZAMBESIA · Luanda · Benguela · Saint Helena

ENGLISH COLONIES · RUPERT'S LAND · NEW FRANCE · LOUISIANA · FLORIDA · CUBA · VICEROYALTY OF NEW SPAIN · VICEROYALTY OF NEW GRANADA · VICEROYALTY OF PERU · ESTADO DO GRÃO-PARÁ E MARANHÃO · ESTADO DO BRASIL · VICEROYALTY OF THE RIO DE LA PLATA

Carmen de Patagones · San José · Puerto Deseado · Falklands · Nombre de Jesús · Nueva Colonia · Floridablanca · Rey don Felipe

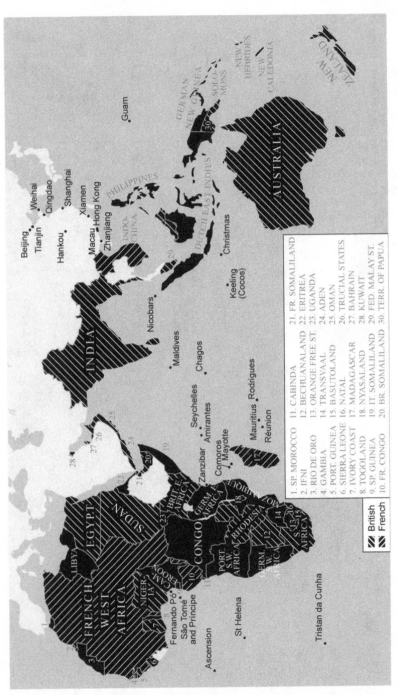

Map 11: European Colonization of Africa and Asia
(19th century)

British
French

1. SP. MOROCCO
2. IFNI
3. RIO DE ORO
4. GAMBIA
5. PORT. GUINEA
6. SIERRA LEONE
7. IVORY COAST
8. TOGOLAND
9. SP. GUINEA
10. FR. CONGO
11. CABINDA
12. BECHUANALAND
13. ORANGE FREE ST.
14. TRANSVAAL
15. BASUTOLAND
16. NATAL
17. MADAGASCAR
18. NYASALAND
19. IT. SOMALILAND
20. BR. SOMALILAND
21. FR. SOMALILAND
22. ERITREA
23. UGANDA
24. ADEN
25. OMAN
26. TRUCIAL STATES
27. BAHRAIN
28. KUWAIT
29. FED. MALAY ST.
30. TERR. OF PAPUA

EUROPE RULES THE WORLD

"With great power comes great responsibility."
Stan Lee

Deep in the Amazon basin of Brazil, 20,000 laborers are building the world's third largest hydroelectric dam. Conceived in 1979 and originally projected to be ready in the year 2000, the *Belo Monte Dam* will have a massive maximum capacity of 11,233 MW per year when finished in 2019, or rather *if* finished, because the project has been mired in difficulty due to protests from both the environmental movement and Brazil's indigenous population.[1]

These are different times. Before the 1960s, if some company wanted to build a dam or mine a sought-after commodity like gold, oil or gas — things Brazil has plenty of — it was a lot easier to flood the lands and bulldoze the homes of indigenous Brazilians. But after a 1967 report revealed that Brazilian Indians had been poisoned, tortured, enslaved, even bombed in the 1940s, 50s and 60s, things started to change, and their rights were written into the new Brazilian Constitution of 1988 (Watts, "Brazil's 'lost report'").[2]

Still, forcibly displacing native populations whenever their lands are needed for, say, a new dam reservoir, has remained relatively easy. And Brazil has a lot of dams, illustrated by the fact that 83 percent of its electricity is generated by hydroelectric power plants ("World Energy Outlook", 479). In the 21st century protests of indigenous people and environmentalist groups have grown more effective, though, putting mounting pressure on the state. The Brazilian government seems more sympathetic than ever to the complaints of the approximately 500,000 Amerindians, but at the same time also has to meet the needs of 207 million other Brazilians (2017 estimate), who want electricity, clean air and jobs, things hydroelectric power plants like the Belo Monte can provide. And so, 20,000 Juruna and Arara Indians will still be displaced to make room for the world's third largest hydroelectric dam. Because even in the 21st century, protecting the rights of indigenous people is easier pledged than enforced.

Of course the Portuguese who discovered Brazil in 1500 had no such qualms. As far as they were concerned, the natives were nothing more than stone-age heathens, barely dressed and speaking a funny language. They simply had to convert to Christianity, learn Portuguese and work the land for their new Portuguese masters. The only sensitive issue the Portuguese recognized in relation to Brazil concerned the Spanish, because according to the Treaty of Tordesillas of 1494 — in which Portugal and Spain had divided the world amongst themselves — only a small part of Brazil lay in the Portuguese zone. Fortunately, the Spanish raised no objections to Portuguese exploration beyond their zone, as they already had quite enough New World territory on their hands to explore, conquer and settle.

At first, the Portuguese weren't even all that interested in their newly discovered American territory, with Vasco Da Gama having just returned from his first voyage to India with spices worth their weight in gold, the start of an eastern trading empire that went unchallenged for more than a century (McAlister, 76, 251-252).[3] But when competition with other European powers mounted in the Orient, Portugal started paying more attention to its colony in the New World. During the 16th and 17th century both the French and the Dutch nibbled away at Portuguese-controlled Brazil, occupying coastal areas including Rio de Janeiro and Salvador, but eventually the Portuguese got rid of them.

By then, Brazil was yielding handsome profits for the colonial motherland through its gold mines, wood and sugar export. The heavy lifting in those gold mines and on the sugar plantations was done by African slaves, who were being imported in large numbers after the indigenous people proved uncooperative and vulnerable to diseases the Europeans had brought with them.[4]

The natives had no natural defense against diseases like smallpox, flu, tuberculosis, pneumonia, or even the common cold, and many of the estimated more than 2.5 million Brazilian indigenous people died because of them.[5] It was the same for other native American populations; up to 80 percent are believed to have perished from infectious diseases in the first century and a half after the arrival of the Europeans (Cook, 5).

Brazil's 21st century demographics still bear testimony of the fate of the indigenous population. In 2010, about 48 percent of the Brazilian population was of direct European descent. Around 43 percent identified as '*pardo*' — a racial mix between black, European and Amerindian — and 8 percent identified as black ("Population Census", table 1.3.1). Only a very small part of the population — roughly 800,000 out of Brazilian's population of 190 million (in 2010 census) — identified as indigenous ("Population Census", table 1.3.1).

The rest of South America and much of Central and North America was colonized by Spain — without any opposition from Portugal, in accordance with the Treaty of Tordesillas. Over time, Central and North America would become part of New Spain, while most of South America would be brought under what was called the Viceroyalty of Peru.

The foundation for New Spain was laid by the conquest of the Aztec Empire in Central America by Spanish conquistador Hernán Cortés, between 1519-1521. At its height, New Spain included present-day Mexico, Central America (except Panama), most of the United States west of the Mississippi River and the Floridas.[6]

A decade after Cortés' conquest of the Aztec Empire, another Spanish conquistador, Francisco Pizarro, marched into Inca territory, located in western South America, having received permission from the Queen of Spain to conquer a region the Spanish called Peru.[7] The Inca Empire was the largest empire in pre-Columbian America, measuring close to 800,000 square miles at its zenith (roughly 40 percent of the Roman Empire at its height). The Inca had a sophisticated, centralized administration and system of government, as well as knowledge of advanced architecture, mathematics and astronomy. Pizarro entered this vast empire — bent on conquering it — with 62 horsemen, 106 foot-soldiers, and four cannon (Hemming, "Conquest", 27; MacQuarrie, 70).

But apart from having cojones the size of melons and what must have been a sizable dose of brazen stupidity and unchecked arrogance, Pizarro also had Lady Luck on his side, because the Inca had been considerably weakened by the wave of European diseases and a bloody three-year civil war between Inca emperor Huáscar and his brother Atahualpa, which had just ended in a victory for the latter. Feeling boisterous from the victory against his brother, Atahualpa agreed to meet with Pizarro in the largely deserted town of Cajamarca (located in the northern highlands of Peru), with the intention of learning as much as he could from the strange foreigners — before disposing of them.

On November 16, 1532, Atahualpa entered Cajamarca with with five or six thousand men, lightly armed with small battle axes and slings and pouches filled with stones, hidden under their tunics (Hemming, "Conquest", 39). The rest of Atahualpa's 80,000 strong army of experienced, professional soldiers was camped half a mile outside the city (Hemming, "Conquest", 36).

Atahualpa had styled his arrival in the town as a full-blown victory parade, with all his men wearing gold and silver disks like crowns on their heads and a squadron in the front — dressed in a livery of checkered colors — sweeping the roadway, to make sure it was properly cleaned for their emperor (Hemming, "Conquest", 38). Atahualpa himself, richly dressed and with his crown on his head, was transported on a very fine litter, ornamented with colorful parrot feathers and plates of gold and silver, and carried by eighty lords dressed in blue livery (Hemming, "Conquest", 39).

Meanwhile the Spanish had concealed themselves in the buildings around the plaza. The only ones to meet Atahualpa and his impressive procession in the town square were the Dominican friar Vicente de Valverde and his interpreter. Atahualpa was surprised no one else had come out to greet him, but suspected it was because they simply feared his great army (Hemming, "Conquest", 40). Valverde, clutching a cross and a missal, stepped forward, introduced himself and told the Inca emperor what his function was and that he had been sent by the Spanish King Charles V to spread the word of God, which, he said, was further explained in the book he had brought with him. Atahualpa asked to see the missal and leafed through it for a moment, before angrily throwing it on the ground (Hemming, "Conquest", 41).

Valverde's interpreter quickly fetched the book and returned it to the friar, but the meeting was clearly over. Valverde hastily returned to Pizarro, while shouting, according to one eyewitness account: *"Come out! Come out, Christians! Come at these enemy dogs who reject the things of God. That chief has thrown my book of holy law to the ground!"* (qtd. in Hemming, "Conquest", 41).[8]

In the ensuing battle, the Inca showed great bravery trying to protect their emperor. Still, they were no match for the fearless Spanish soldiers with their guns, horses, steel swords, helmets and armor - all of which were unknown to the Inca. And so, in just two hours, 168 Spanish conquistadors slaughtered some 6,000 Inca braves. Not a single Spanish soldier was killed.

Atahualpa was captured by Pizarro himself. In the months that followed, the imprisoned emperor promised a large room filled once with gold and twice with silver in exchange for his freedom, but Pizarro nevertheless ordered his execution. The Inca emperor was sentenced to die by burning on July 25, 1533, but when, already tied to the stake — in the same Cajamarcan square he had rode into on a richly dressed litter at the head of 6,000 men less than nine months earlier — he requested baptism, friar Valverde immediately obliged him (Hemming, "Conquest", 78).[9] After Valverde had christened him Francisco (after Francisco Pizarro), the emperor-formerly-known-as-Atahualpa was promptly garroted by a piece of rope tied around his neck, instead of burned to death (Hemming, "Conquest", 78). Thus, Atahualpa was at least spared the terrible idea of his soul not being able to go to the afterlife, which the Inca believed would be impossible if the body was burned. He was given a Christian burial.

Of course capturing and killing Atahualpa was not the end of the Inca Empire. The war between the Spanish and the Inca would go on for the better part of the 16th century. The final curtain only fell in 1572, with the capture and execution of Túpac Amaru, the last Inca Emperor.

To administer control from afar over its vast South American territories, the Spanish Crown instituted the *encomienda* system (from *encomendar*, to entrust), which granted conquistadors and a selected few local notables a certain number of natives to extract tribute from, in exchange for protecting and educating them in the Christian faith. In practice the *encomienda* system was not much different from slavery, with the conquistadors doing pretty much as they pleased with the natives entrusted to them. When this ran into objections from part of the clergy, King Charles V issued a body of New Laws, in 1542, so as to better protect the rights of the indigenous people.[10]

Viceroy of Peru Blasco Núñez Vela was charged with enforcing the New Laws, but the *encomenderos* (the grantees of the *encomienda*) were so vehemently opposed to this upending of the status quo that a rebellion broke out, led by Francisco Pizarro's half brother, Gonzalo Pizarro. The armies of Pizarro and Núñez Vela met at Añaquito, just outside the ancient city of Quito, the present-day capital of Ecuador, on January 18, 1546. Though Núñez Vela was badly outnumbered, he valiantly decided to stay and fight anyway, saying *"We have come to fight, not to parley; and we must do our duty like good and loyal cavaliers. I will do mine."* (qtd. in Prescott, "History", Vol. 2, 197). He did indeed, but after he was mortally wounded in battle his head was cut off and put on a pike, to show his soldiers that the conquistadors had won the battle (Prescott, "History", Vol. 2, 199-200).

Charles V, fearing he would lose control over Peru and its rich gold and silver mines, subsequently sent the skilled diplomat Pedro de la Gasca to Peru to restore the peace. Arriving without an army or money, Gasca nevertheless succeeded in appeasing most of the rebels, announcing that the king no longer insisted on suppressing the *encomiendas* and offering pardons to many of the rebels (Francis, 235). Pizarro himself kept resisting, but most of his men deserted him on the eve of the decisive Battle of Jaquijahuana (April 9, 1548). Pizarro was defeated, captured and beheaded the day after the battle. The New Laws were never implemented.

While the Portuguese were busy building their trading empire in the East and colonizing Brazil and the Spanish explored and conquered their way through the rest of South America, Central America and North America, vanquishing ancient empires left and right, the French and English were still cautiously exploring the North American East Coast and the Dutch were trying to find a Northeast passage to Asia.

The French had founded New France as early as 1534, to administer their American colonies, but it would take until 1608 before the first serious French colony, Quebec City (in present-day Canada), was even established. At its peak, in the early 18th century, New France encompassed more than three million square miles in the eastern part of North America. But the French colonization efforts in North America were never a great success, and in the aftermath of the Seven Years' War (1756-1763), France ceded all of its North American mainland territories to the British, except for Louisiana, which it ceded to Spain. The French were thus completely out of mainland North America by the time the Thirteen Colonies declared independence from Great Britain, in 1776. The Dutch had founded their North American colony, New Netherland, in 1614. Located on the

East Coast of North America and with New Amsterdam (present-day New York City) as its capital, it included parts of present-day U.S. states New York, New Jersey, Delaware and Connecticut. Unlike the English and the French, the Dutch were more interested in trading opportunities than in large-scale colonization. During the 1650s, the importance of New Amsterdam as a trading hub between North America, Europe and the Caribbean rapidly grew, but in the 1660s the British forced the Dutch out. Their cultural influence on New York would prove longer-lasting, though. The Dutch Republic was a progressive, culturally diverse, egalitarian, open society and its American colony was based on those same values. They had been woven into the cultural fabric of New Amsterdam and would continue to make the city unique in the United States long after its name change (Shorto, 6). Civil liberties, religious freedom, tolerance and republicanism were all part of the baggage Dutch colonists — citizens of a young nation that had only just won its independence from the Spanish — had taken with them to the New World. As John Adams, one of the founding fathers and second President of the United States, would later say: *"The origins of the two republics are so much alike that the history of one seems but a transcript from that of the other"* (qtd. in Staloff, 200).

The British would be very successful in North America, eventually rivaling the Spanish territories there. At its peak, in 1763 — after the British had just won the Seven Years' War — British America included the Thirteen British Colonies on the East Coast, East Florida and West

Florida, Quebec and Newfoundland, as well as several islands in the Caribbean Sea and the Atlantic Ocean, including Jamaica, the Cayman Islands, the Bahamas and Grenada.

Things went somewhat differently in Asia. Here, the Portuguese were first, thanks to the southward route to the Indian Ocean they had discovered, around Cape of Good Hope. The Portuguese deployed a strategy of capturing key positions, aimed at controlling important entrances to the Indian Ocean. After winning several sea battles against the Turks and Egyptians, the Portuguese were able to establish naval dominance in the region.

Armed trading posts in places such as Calicut (India), Ceylon (Sri Lanka), Macau (China) and Malacca (Malaysia), created a trading network that not only provided Europe with Asian products such as black pepper, cinnamon, cloves and nutmeg, but also served countries bordering the Indian Ocean.[11] A particularly profitable trading connection for the Portuguese was acting as trading intermediary between Japan and China, from 1557 — the year Portugal established a permanent trading base at Macau — until 1638 — when the Portuguese were expelled from Japan — because the Chinese emperor had forbidden Chinese merchants to trade with Japan, as punishment for Japanese piracy (Souza, 48).

In the early 17th century other European powers joined the party, soon spoiling things for Portugal. The Dutch in particular made it hard on the Portuguese, after they learned of the Portuguese route to the Orient, having acquired detailed sailing directions from a Dutch merchant who had sailed to India in Portuguese service.[12] During the Dutch-Portuguese War (1602-1663), the young republic and the old kingdom fought each other all over the world. The war ended with the Portuguese retreating from the East, while the Dutch ceded their Brazilian territories — most of which they had conquered during the war — back to Portugal.

During the 17th century the Dutch Republic became the world's dominant naval power. Never much interested in settling colonies to build a new world — like the English and the French — or in converting native populations to Christianity — like the Spanish and the Portuguese — the Dutch were mainly focused on international trade. Their colonies on the East Coast of North and South America and in Southeast Asia had only one goal: to make money.[13]

After they had gotten rid of the Portuguese in the Indian Ocean, the Dutch took over the lucrative trade with Japan, and for the next 200 years the Dutch were the only European power allowed to trade with Nippon. Japan's period of self-chosen isolation — the so-called *Sakoku* — only ended in 1853, when Commodore Matthew C. Perry of the U.S. Navy anchored in front of Tokyo Bay (then Edo Bay) with four warships and demanded Japan open trade negotiations with the United States. Throughout the 16th and 17th century, the English followed a similar strategy as the Portuguese and Dutch in Asia, setting up armed trading posts and establishing a trading network for commercial activities both within Asia and between Asia and Europe.

While still fighting with the Portuguese, the Dutch also engaged in naval warfare with the English for global naval dominance. The First Anglo-Dutch War (1652-1654) was won by the English, but the Second and Third Anglo-Dutch War confirmed the Dutch Republic's position as the leading naval power of the 17th century.[14] Hostilities between the two European powers ceased when Dutch Prince William of Orange ascended the English throne as William III of England, following the Glorious Revolution of 1688. A deal was made which granted the more valuable spice trade to the Republic and the Indian textile industry to England. It seemed a good deal for the Dutch at the time, but during the 18th century the textile trade would become more profitable than the spice trade, causing the British to overtake the Dutch in sales by 1720 (Ferguson, 19-20).

The French arrived relatively late on the scene in Asia. The French East India Company was not established until 1664 — six decades after the British and Dutch East India Companies — and the first French factory in Asia was only set up in 1668, in Surat, India (Malleson, 15).

France was all the more active during the so called Scramble for Africa (1880s-1914) though, when European powers rushed to colonize Africa after a wave of American independence wars between 1770-1825 had ended European dominance of the New World. One by one, American colonies had declared their independence: The Thirteen Colonies (1776), Ecuador (1809), Colombia (1810), Mexico (1810),

Venezuela (1811), Chile (1818), Peru (1821), Brazil (1822), Bolivia (1825), they all went their own way.[15]

This second European colonial wave saw the arrival of two new European colonial powers, and one old one trying to making a comeback. Belgium and Germany — both new nations, established in 1830, 1871 respectively — saw the Scramble for Africa as a chance to build a little empire of their own, while Italy tried to regain some of its former glory as an ancient colonial powerhouse, with the attempted colonization of the North-African nation of Ethiopia.

In May 1889, Italy had signed the Treaty of Wuchale with Menelik of Shewa, soon to be emperor Menelik II of Ethiopia, which ceded territories that together formed present-day Eritrea to Italy, in exchange for financial aid and military supplies. But not long after a conflict arose over the precise wording of the treaty, due to a translation error. According to Menelik, the treaty said that he *could* ask the Italian authorities to assist him in communicating with other powers, whereas, according to Italy, the treaty said he *should* do so. A tiny difference in wording, but one with enormous political ramifications, as the Italian point of view effectively turned the whole of Ethiopia into a client state. When Menelik did not acquiesce, Italy invaded Ethiopia from Eritrea. A short war followed (1895-96), in which the Italians were surprisingly but soundly defeated by the Ethiopians, who were supported by Russia.

In the 1930s, Italy tried its hand at conquering once more, this time instigated by fascist dictator Benito Mussolini. But even though Ethiopia possessed only a handful of armored vehicles and just three operational aircraft, it still took Italy more than six months to bring Ethiopia to its knees — hardly the stuff of Roman Empire legend (Nicolle, "Italian Invasion", 24).[16]

Still, even though the Italians colonized Eritrea, the Belgians established Belgian Congo in Central Africa (present-day Republic of Congo), and Germany grabbed territories in East Africa (Rwanda, Burundi, Tanzania) South West Africa (Namibia) and West Africa (Cameroon, Togo), the 19th century colonization of Africa was predominantly a French / British matter, with the French concentrating on North-West Africa and the British on North-East and South Africa.

In Asia, the Dutch concentrated on the colonization of the Dutch East Indies, while the British brought most of India, Pakistan and Bangladesh under its control. The British also colonized Australia, Hong Kong, Singapore, Burma (Myanmar), Ceylon (Sri Lanka) and part of the Middle East, while the French established themselves in French Indochina (present-day Laos, Cambodia and Vietnam.)

To regulate all that imperial competition and prevent the outbreak of full-scale war between the colonial powers simply because of unclarity about who owned what, a conference was organized in Berlin to set some ground rules (1884-1885). The parties involved agreed that effective occupation would be the criterion used to determine the validity of territorial claims; in other words, countries needed to have a significant military presence in their colonies for them to be recognized as such.[17]

Considering this, it will come as no surprise that European military strength in Africa grew considerably between 1885-1914 (the start of World War I) as a result of the Berlin conference. The conference was a success, in that it gave the colonial powers room to breathe and diffused latent hostilities among them, but under the surface, the growing militarization, colonization and nationalism — empowered by the Industrial Revolution and a flurry of inventions and innovations in the late 19th and early 20th century — continued to brew a cocktail of tension and resentment that would turn the might of the European powers against each other in a way such as the world had never seen.

The Great War of 1914-1918 caused unprecedented devastation and 37.5 million casualties, of which 8.5 million dead.[18] It considerably weakened the European empires, but not enough to force them to give up their colonies — or to never want to fight each other again.[19]

Twenty years after signing the Treaty of Versailles a newly militarized Germany invaded Poland, triggering the start of the Second World War. Six years and 50 million dead later that war was over too and again the British, French, Dutch and Belgians tried carrying on with their colonial empires as if nothing had changed — but this time things were different.[20]

Many African and Asian colonies ceased the momentum and rose up in rebellion against their weakened colonial overlords, others simply requested and received independence. Between 1945-1975, a host of new and independent nations came into being: Indonesia (1945), India and Pakistan (1947), Burma (1948), Libya (1951), Morocco and Tunisia (1956), Senegal, Togo, Mali, Madagascar, Congo, Somalia, Benin, Niger, Ivory Coast, Gabon (all in 1960) — and many others. The retreat of the European colonial powers caused growing instability in several regions and in some cases laid the foundations for later wars. The British partition of the Indian subcontinent into India and Pakistan, for instance, created an enduring tension between the two countries — both nuclear powers — while the British retreat from Palestine and the subsequent creation of the state of Israel, in 1948, laid the foundation for a volatile territorial conflict that continues to this day.

The French, for their part, had trouble letting go of Vietnam and Algeria, igniting bloody wars in both colonies. When the Viet Minh launched a rebellion to achieve Vietnamese independence, shortly after the end of WW II, the French responded by sending in troops. Nine years of war followed. The French Union and its local allies, Laos, Cambodia and the State of Vietnam, suffered more than 172,000 casualties, of which 94,000 dead, the Viet Minh lost maybe three times that number (Tucker, 535). An estimated 250,000 civilians also perished before the French finally pulled out, following the Geneva Conference of 1954 (Tucker, 535).[21]

Unfortunately for the Vietnamese it would not be the end of armed conflict in Vietnam, though, as another Western power soon would soon step in to fill the vacuum left by France and try to prevent the communist takeover of South Vietnam: the United States.

The 450 years of European colonization — from the colonization of the Americas, Asia, and Africa to the decolonization after WW II — have had a profound and lasting impact on countless people on all continents except Antarctica. Millions of English, French, Spanish, Portuguese and Dutch citizens emigrated to the Americas and elsewhere to settle new societies and help build giant trading empires for their respective countries. Through them, European languages, religion, culture, philosophy, political thought and technological advances found their way to the New World, as did an array of infectious diseases, millions of African slaves and a generally self-righteous and demeaning attitude towards indigenous people, who had been living their way of life for thousands of years. In Asia and Africa the Europeans did less settling and more trading, but there as well they had a profound impact on the development of the indigenous populations. The debate about the pros and cons of European colonization has been ongoing for centuries. Some focus on the fact that the Europeans had no right to conquer and dominate other peoples simply because they could — though, in all fairness, throughout most of history and for most civilizations, this was all that was needed. Others focus on the more positive aspects of colonization, such as the cultural diffusion that followed in its wake — though it also destroyed ancient traditions and religions people had sometimes been practicing undisturbed for hundreds, even thousands of years. Suffice it to say that it is all too easy to pass judgment on the past based on the moral laws of the present.

Deep in the vast Brazilian Amazon rainforest, an estimated 80 so far uncontacted tribes still live the way they always have.[22] Aerial pictures and videos have been made of some of them. They show stone-age level people, mostly naked, frightfully pointing at the plane in the sky from which the footage is shot. They have escaped European colonization.

---

1   Critics argue that the Belo Monte Dam will be very inefficient compared to other hydroelectric power plants and will operate at only 40 percent of its maximum capacity. According to the engineers who designed the dam, this is because the Belo Monte Dam uses a relatively small reservoir — about half that of Brazil's biggest hydroplant, at Itaipu — to limit the area that will be flooded (Watts, "Belo Monte"). An official of Norte Energia, the dam operator, called it "*the price we pay to preserve the environment. We cannot save the forest and live in the dark without TV. There is a conflict of interest here. We need balance. I think Belo Monte is a compromise.*" (qtd. in Watts, "Belo Monte").

2   Constitution of the Federative Republic of Brazil. Chapter VII, Article 231 ("Brazil: 1988 Constitution").

3   The Dutch were the second European power to arrive land at the Indian subcontinent, in 1605, the British followed in 1619.

4   According to the Trans-Atlantic Slave Trade Database, some 4.9 million slaves were shipped to Brazil, more than any other country in the Americas. Rio alone received 1.8 million African slaves, more than any other city in the Americas

and roughly 21 percent of all slaves who were transported to the New World (Romero, "Slave Past").

5 Historian John Hemming estimates that by the middle of the 18th century, there were between 1 million and 1.5 million Brazilian Indians, from 2.5 million around the arrival of the Portuguese in 1500 (Hemming, "Amazon Frontier", 5).

6 Spanish Florida included the state of Florida, southern Georgia, southern Alabama, southern Mississippi and southeastern Louisiana.

7 American historian and Hispanist W.H. Prescott writes in *The Conquest of Peru* that according to the Spanish-Incan historian Garcilasso de la Vega, the name "Peru" comes from *Pelu*, the Indian name for "river", which was said by one of the natives in answer to a question from the Spanish, who erroneously took it for the name of the entire country (Prescott, "Conquest", Vol. I, 43).

8 Hemming mentions three eyewitness sources, Mena, Xerez and Hernando Pizarro. The quote used here is from Mena's account.

9 Hemming uses Pizarro secretary Pedro Sancho's account of the execution.

10 One of the main defenders of the rights of the natives was Bartolomé de las Casas (1484-1566), a historian and Dominican friar. He was also the first officially appointed 'Protector of the Indians'.

11 Macau remained a Portuguese colony until 1999, when it was handed over to China, per the Sino-Portuguese Treaty of Peking of 1885.

12 The Dutch merchant and explorer Jan Huyghen van Linschoten, who had sailed to the Portuguese colony Goa (India) in service of the newly appointed Portuguese Archbishop there, wrote a book containing numerous detailed sailing directions from Portugal to the East Indies colonies after he returned to Lisbon. The book, titled *Reys-gheschrift van de navigatien der Portugaloysers in Orienten* (Travel Accounts of Portuguese Navigation in the Orient) was first published in Dutch in 1595, but English, German and Latin editions soon followed.

13 One (in)famous example of the Dutch entrepreneurial spirit is that they continued selling guns to the Spanish while fighting their war of independence against...the Spanish (Jong, 172-174).

14 The Second and Third Anglo-Dutch War were fought between 1665-1667 and 1672-1674, respectively. The Raid on Medway, in June 1667, was in many ways emblematic for the Dutch naval domination of the British at the time. During the raid, Dutch Admiral Michiel de Ruyter sailed up the River Thames to the English naval base of Chatham and burned several ships there, before towing the British flagship Royal Charles back to the Republic. The audacious attack shocked England to its core. When, not long after, new reports surfaced of Dutch fleet threatening Portsmouth, Plymouth and Dartmouth, Sir William Batten, naval officer and MP, reportedly cried out: "*By God, I think the Devil shits Dutchmen.*" (qtd. in Pepys, 345). The raid is still considered one of the

worst defeats in the history of the Royal Navy.

15 One notable exception is Canada, which would not adopt its own constitution until 1867 and even then did not become fully independent. Only with the Constitution Act of 1982 did Canada gain full sovereignty, though the British Monarch continues to serve as the formal head of state of Canada.

16 The Italian occupation of Ethiopia ended five years later, with the defeat of Italian forces in East Africa by British-led Allied forces, in the East African Campaign of World War II.

17 As article 35 of the General Act of the Conference of Berlin states: *"The Signatory Powers of the present Act recognize the obligation to insure the establishment of authority in the regions occupied by them on the coasts of the African continent sufficient to protect existing rights, and, as the case may be, freedom of trade and of transit under the conditions agreed upon."* (qtd. in Botchway, 78)

18 As reported by the U.S. War Department, February 1924. U.S. casualties amended by the Statistical Services Center, Office of the Secretary of Defense, November 7, 1957 (see also table in Hosch, 219).

19 A few colonies did manage to gain independence shortly after WW I, among them Afghanistan (1919), Egypt (1922) and Iraq (1932).

20 World War II casualty estimates mostly range between 40-75 million, but as Matthew White points out in his excellent work *The 100 Deadliest Episodes in Human History*, a majority of historians — including John Haywood, John Keegan, Charles Messenger and J.M Roberts — arrive at a total of 50 million military and civilian deaths (White, 605). The high number of civilian deaths is also the reason there is so much variation between the different estimates.

21 Using figures from French general / historian Yves Gras (who served in Indochine), the American journalist Arthur J. Dommen wrote there were 400,000 civilian casualties, *"of which an estimated 100,000 to 150,000 had been assassinated by the Viet Minh."* (Dommen, 252).

22 Estimate from the Brazilian National Indian Foundation (FUNAI).

Inverness

Aberdeen

Seacroft Moor (1643) ☆
Leeds (1643) ☆
Heptonstall (1643)
☆
Adwalton Manor (1643)
Wakefield (1643) ☆

Stirling
Iverkeithing (1651) ☆ Dunbar (1650) ☆
Edinburgh
Hieton (1650) ☆
Ayr

NORTH

SEA

Newburn (1640) ☆ Newcastle ☆
Boldon Hill (1644)

Penrith

Lancaster Marston Moor
(1644) ☆ York
Preston (1648) ☆ ☆☆ Selby (1644) ☆
Ormskirk (1644) ☆ ☆☆
Warrington Bridge (1651) ☆ Wigan Lane (1651)
Gainsborough (1643)
Chester ☆ Lincoln Winceby (1643)
Middlewich (1643) ☆ Nantwich (1644)
Rowton Heath (1645) Newark (1644) ☆
Hopton Heath (1643) ☆ ☆ Burton Bridge (1643) Norwich
Tipton Green (1644) ☆ Camp Hill (1643)
Stourbridge Heath (1644) ☆ ☆
Kings Norton (1642) Edgehill ☆ Naseby (1645)
Worcester (1651) ☆ (1642)
Powick Bridge (1642) ☆ ☆ Olney Bridge (1643)
Upton (1651) ☆ ☆ Cropredy Bridge (1644)
Ripple Field (1643) Colchester
Gloucester ☆ Stow-on-the- ☆ Aylesbury (1642)
Wold (1646) Oxford
Aldbourne ☆ Chalgrove Field (1643)
St Fagans (1648) ☆ Chase (1643) Brentford (1642) ☆☆ London
Lansdowne (1643) ☆ ☆ ☆ Turnham Green (1642)
Bristol (1643) ☆ Roundaway ☆ Newbury (1643, 1644)
Down (1643) Alton (1643) Maidstone Canterbury
Torrington (1646) ☆ ☆ (1648)
Stratton (1643) Langport (1645) Winchester ☆
☆ Sourton Down (1643) Cheriton (1644)
Braddock Southampton
Down Exeter
(1643) ☆☆
Lostwithiel (1644)

English Channel

Map 12: English Civil Wars (1642-1651)

25

FROM CIVIL WAR TO GLORIOUS REVOLUTION (AND BEYOND)

*"but I must tell you that their liberty and
freedom consists in having government.... It is
not their having a share in the government; that
is nothing appertaining unto them. A subject
and a sovereign are clean different things!"*[1]

Charles I of England, January 30, 1649,
last speech before his beheading

When King Henry VIII of England wanted to marry Anne Boleyn, in 1527, there was only one problem: he was already married to Catherine of Aragon. Henry tried to get Pope Clement VII to annul the marriage, but when it became clear that the pope would not consent, while Anne — young, beautiful, smart, anything but submissive Anne (what more could an absolute ruler wish for?) — had already made it clear she was not interested in merely becoming the king's mistress, Henry opted for door number three, which was to dispense with the Catholic Church altogether. So he convened Parliament and had it pass several acts transferring ecclesiastical power in England from the pope to the king.[2]

Meanwhile, Henry and Anne had already married in secret. Anne soon became pregnant and a public wedding service followed on January 25, 1533. Newly appointed Archbishop of Canterbury Thomas Cranmer was entrusted with the task of declaring their marriage valid and that of Henry and Catherine null and void, which he promptly did. The pope excommunicated Henry soon after, but who cares about being excommunicated when they are on top of the world and married to wonderful young upstart Anne Boleyn? Clearly, Henry did not.

The royal love story would not have a happy ending, though. Having failed to provide Henry with a male heir and progressively irritating him with the same intellectual, well-informed and independent attitude that had so enamored him while he was pursuing her, Anne was arrested, tried and convicted for treasonous adultery and incest (Warnicke, 1, 204). She was executed on May 19, 1536.

But however short-lived the immediate reason for England's breakaway from the Catholic Church, the religious reforms themselves would long outlast both Henry VIII and the reign of the House of Tudor he was part of, playing a significant role in England's turbulent 17th century, when three civil wars and one Glorious Revolution would decide once and for all whether the king had the right to decide the fate and faith of his people.[3]

In 1603, Queen Elizabeth I of England, Henry VIII and Anne Boleyn's only child and the last of the five Tudor monarchs, died, after a long reign of 44 years. Having no children of her own, she was succeeded by her cousin James VI, King of Scotland.[4] Thus, for the first time, the crowns of Scotland, Ireland and England were united under one king — though Scotland and England remained separate countries.

James based his rule on the Divine Right of Kings doctrine, which held that the king was beholden to no earthly authority and derived his right to rule not from the people, parliament, nobility or even any ecclesiastical authority, but directly from God. He even wrote a book about it, *The True Law of Free Monarchies* (published 1598). At its core, the Divine Right of Kings meant that the king was untouchable and could never be deposed, even if he was a terrible king.

Unsurprisingly, James' attitude towards Parliament was less than forthcoming, viewing it as nothing more than part of his court, with no real authority whatsoever. *"Hold no Parliaments, but for the necesitie of new Lawes, which would be but seldome"*, he wrote in the *Basilikon Doron* (1599), another book by his hand, meant as a sort of practical guide to kingship for his oldest son Henry, who was five years old at the time (James, 20).

Henry Frederick grew up a pious, promising and very popular young heir, but unfortunately died of typhoid fever when he was only eighteen years old, leaving his younger brother Charles as heir apparent. When James himself died in 1625, 24-year-old Charles succeeded his father as Charles I, King of England, Ireland and Scotland.

Charles I immediately started off on the wrong foot with many of his subjects, though, when he married devout Catholic Henrietta Maria of France, shortly after his accession to the throne.[5] A sister of king Louis XIII of France, Henrietta Maria was very open about her Catholic faith, which put Charles in a difficult position. Even worse in the eyes of Protestant England was the prospect of any future royal children possibly being baptized as Catholics, something that would set the nation on the path to a Catholic monarch again, an unbearable idea to many.

People also feared Charles I would perhaps relax religious restrictions because of his marriage to Henrietta Maria, who was soon called 'Queen Mary' by the English people, an allusion to Charles' Catholic grandmother Mary, Queen of Scots and Catholic Queen Mary I of England, a.k.a. Bloody Mary, the daughter of Henry III and Catherine of Aragon (Purkiss, 35).[6] And although Charles promised Parliament he would do no such thing, he had in fact indeed promised Louis XIII in a secret agreement to make extensive concessions to English Papists (Hill, 59).

Charles had also promised French regent Cardinal Richelieu to send ships to help suppress the Protestant Huguenots at La Rochelle, in return for French help against the Spanish, news of which led to great outrage in England and even mutiny among the crew of the promised ships (Hill, 59).

One year into his reign, Charles I came into conflict with Parliament, which had started a procedure of impeachment against the unpopular George Villiers, 1st Duke of Buckingham, for various offenses.[7] But Buckingham was a great favorite of Charles, and when Parliament refused to desist the king dissolved it.[8] This strengthened the belief that, like his father, Charles I would disregard Parliament whenever he saw fit.

At the time, Parliament had very little power to begin with. It could not convene by itself but had to be called upon by the king, who could also dissolve it at any time. Parliament could not pass any laws either, let alone judge the king. There was one thing, however, for which the king did need Parliament. Money. Because ever since Magna Carta

— the document first signed by King John I of England, back in 1215 — new taxes had to be approved by Parliament.[9]

And as it happened, Charles needed a lot of money, to finance England's involvement in the Thirty Years' war (1618-1648), a bloody, largely religious conflict on the European continent between Protestants and Catholics. When Parliament did not acquiesce to his demands, Charles decided to raise the money he needed through a "forced loan" — basically a tax for which no Parliamentary consent was given — and imprison anyone who refused to pay up (Cust, 65-67).

More than a hundred wealthy landowners were subsequently jailed without any form of trial (Cust, 65). They were not charged with anything, simply held *"by command of the King"* (Hill, 53; Cust, 67). When five of them argued in front of the court that this was in violation of the habeas corpus principle, because they hadn't done anything unlawful, the court ruled in favor of Charles I, stating that common law had no authority over royal prerogatives.[10]

Confronted with an increasingly restive population as well as unruly, unpaid soldiers, quartered in private homes while waiting to be shipped overseas, Charles proclaimed martial law for large parts of the country, essentially revoking the rule of law altogether in those parts and leaving law and order in the hands of local military commanders (Hill, 53).

An increasing number of people nevertheless continued to resist, and in 1628, his funds dwindling, Charles was forced to call yet another Parliament. This Parliament was even less sympathetic to the king's demands than the last one and drew up a *Petition of Right* that Charles was asked to accept before Parliament would approve any new taxes. The petition listed specific liberties the king would henceforth be obliged to respect, among them that no freeman could be forced to pay any tax or loan unless in accordance with an act of Parliament, that no freeman could be imprisoned contrary to the rule of law, that no freeman could be held without due process of law, and that soldiers could not be billeted on private persons (Hill, 53).

Together with the Magna Carta (1215) and the later Bill of Rights (1689), the Petition of Right of 1628 is considered one of the most important constitutional documents of the United Kingdom (Adams, 294-295).[11] It has also influenced the Constitution of the United States.[12] The Petition's main author, Member of Parliament Sir Edward Coke, considered the greatest jurist of his time, has also had a profound influence on both British and U.S. common law.[13]

After some back and forth, Charles finally accepted the Petition of Right on June 7, 1628. Church bells rang throughout the country and for a short while it seemed that Parliament and the king would live happily ever after. But when Parliament reconvened a couple of months later, conflict quickly broke out again between Charles and Parliament, this time over the tonnage and poundage tax. Parliament had only granted Charles the right to levy this tax for a year — contrary to custom, which was to grant it to a new king for life — and had not renewed it, but the king had nevertheless confiscated goods of those who refused to pay it (Hill, 49).

Charles dissolved Parliament again, but could not prevent Members of Parliament (MP) holding Speaker John Finch in his chair long enough to read out and adopt all kinds of resolutions against Catholicism and poundage and tonnage (Hill, 54; Cust, 118).[14] Deeply distressed over so much insolence, Charles had nine MPs arrested over the matter (Cust, 118).

In the months that followed, Charles made peace with France and Spain, correctly reasoning that as long as he was not at war with anyone, he would not need Parliament for any new taxes either. Continuing on this path, Charles subsequently ruled alone from 1629 to 1640.

A couple of years into this so-called Personal Rule — also known as the slightly less flattering "Eleven Years' Tyranny" — Charles started taking steps to unite the Church of England and the Church of Scotland, an old dream of his father. The Scots were of a different mind however, and when Charles introduced a new — High Anglican — version of the English Book of Common Prayer in 1637, Scottish presbyterians adopted a National Covenant against "*superstitious and papistical rites*" and swore an oath to maintain the reformed religion.[15]

Charles responded by sending an army to Scotland, but the Covenanters had also assembled a fighting force, which was well-trained and very determined. The First Bishops' War (1639) — so-called because Charles wanted an episcopal church government (i.e., with bishops), while the presbyterian Covenanters most emphatically did not — ended undecided, because neither side really wanted to fight. A treaty to cease hostilities was signed and an uneasy truce followed. Desperately in need of funds for a second military campaign against the contumacious Scots, Charles called a Parliament for the first time in eleven years. Happy to be finally needed again, the new Parliament took the opportunity to immediately voice a veritable buffet of grievances, to which

Charles responded by immediately dissolving it, hence its nickname, "The Short Parliament" (April 13-May 5, 1640).

Sensing an opportunity in Charles' failure to come to some sort of understanding with his Parliament, the Covenanters invaded Northumberland and advanced towards the northeastern town of Newcastle, vital at the time for London's coal supply. At Newburn, some six miles from Newcastle, the Scots were met by an English Royalist army. The English were heavily outnumbered, badly trained, lacked the proper weapons and suffered from low morale — on account of not having been properly (Fissel, 52). Unfortunately for them, though, this time the Scots *did* want to fight. And although history knows many famous battles that were won by heavily outnumbered, outgunned and unskilled soldiers, the battle of Newburn is not one of them. The English forces were decisively defeated, after which the Covenanters went on to occupy Newcastle. Now Charles really had a problem. He had no choice but to sign a humiliating truce that forced him to pay for the daily expenses of the Scottish army that occupied Newcastle — fixed at £850 a day in the Treaty of Ripon — even though he could not even maintain an army of his own (Borough, xxxiii).

Wedged into an impossible position, Charles called a new Parliament. This one proved even more rebellious than the last one, though it would last considerably longer, hence its nickname, "The Long Parliament". It soon passed the Triennial Act, which required Parliament to be convened at least once every three years and for a minimum session of fifty days, with or without the king's consent (Triennial Act 1641, article II, VI). It also passed other laws constraining the power of the king and increasing that of Parliament.

In January 1642 things went from bad to worse, when Charles marched into Parliament with an army of 400 men in an attempt to arrest five Members of Parliament for treason. His plan failed (the five weren't there) and Parliament, shocked by Charles' invasion of the House of Commons — the first English monarch to do so — responded by passing a number of resolutions that effectively gave it control over the city of London (Cust, 326). This, together with several massive demonstrations in support of Parliament, showed Charles he was no longer in control of the situation. A few days later, he took his family and fled to Hampton Court (Cust, 326).

During the summer months negotiations between Charles and Parliament continued, but no progress was being made. And while the sun was shining, the dark clouds of civil war began gathering over the nation, with cities and counties declaring for or against the king.

On September 23, 1642, Royalist and Parliamentarian cavalry fought the first major skirmish of the civil war, at Powick Bridge, not far from Worcester, in the West Midlands of England, the same location where the final battle of the third and last civil war would also be fought, nine years later, on September 3, 1651.

The Royalist cavalry, led by young, energetic Prince Rupert, nephew of King Charles I, succeeded in routing the Parliamentarian cavalry. A nice morale boost for Rupert and his horsemen, to be sure, though no strategic advantage was gained.

Although the main Parliamentarian army, led by the Earl of Essex, was camped at Worcester, and Charles was looking for a quick victory, the king nevertheless decided to advance towards London, because, as the Earl of Clarendon, a moderate Royalist and advisor to the king would later remark, this made it *"morally sure, that the earl of Essex would put himself in their way"* (Clarendon, vol. 3, 251).

On October 23, the two armies indeed met, near Edgehill and Kineton, in southern Warwickshire, West Midlands. Occupying the high ground around Edgehill, the Royalists first waited for the Parliamentarians to attack, but when they proved unwilling to leave their defensive position around the lower area of Kineton, Charles'

254 - J.C. PETERS

forces descended from the hill to give battle in the open field. Despite their eagerness to fight and decide the war then and there, the Royalists were nevertheless incapable of taking the field, nor were the Parliamentarians for that matter. The first battle of the civil war thus ended undecided (though because of Essex' withdrawal to Warwick castle after the battle — leaving the road to London under Royalist control — it could also be viewed as a tactical victory for Charles I).

With Essex withdrawn to the North, Prince Rupert urged the king to exploit the advantage and allow his cavalry to press for London immediately, but Charles decided to advance more cautiously, with his army intact, via Banbury and Oxford, thus giving Essex the opportunity to reach London before him, which he did (Cust, 366-367).

On the urging of many of his officers the king opened negotiations and a peace treaty seemed within reach, but then Charles decided to advance on London to improve his negotiating position. On the night of November 11, he ordered Prince Rupert to take the town of Brentford (today part of the Greater London area), where Essex had some troops stationed. But Rupert, boisterous, cavalier and always prepared to go above and beyond the call of duty, did not just defeat the Parliamentarian forces the following day, he also thoroughly sacked the town (Gardiner, vol.1, 56-57).

Hearing of the fate of Brentford, many Londoners sided with the Parliamentarian cause and took up arms to defend their city (Gardiner, vol. 1, 57). The next day, Essex — whose numbers had swelled to 24,000 armed Londoners — advanced towards Turnham Green, closing in on the Royalist army, which had about half his numbers. Realizing he would not be able to take the city under these conditions, Charles retreated, returning to Oxford for the winter (Gardiner, vol. 1, 58, 63).

Early 1643 the Royalists had the upper hand, winning several battles and pushing Essex in the defensive. The majority of Parliamentarians began to favor peace, even under unfavorable terms (Gardiner, vol. 1, 74-81). But for Charles, who wholeheartedly believed "*it most unreasonable, to be pressed to diminish his own just rights himself, because others had violated and usurped them*", nothing short of total victory would do (qtd. in Clarendon, vol. 4, 11). To this, however, the Parliamentarians could not agree and mid April 1643 negotiations were broken off again.

In the second half of 1643, Royalist initiative was checked through a series of Parliamentarian victories, among them the lifting of the siege of Gloucester and decisive victories at the battles of Newbury and Winceby.[16]

A few days after the failed siege of Gloucester, Charles forged a truce with the Irish, who had also been in rebellion. Faced with the prospect of an army of Irish "papists" coming to Charles' aid, the Parliamentarians quickly entered into an agreement with the Scottish Covenanters only days later, the Solemn League and Covenant, in which both sides agreed to work towards a civil and religious (i.e., presbyterian) union between England, Scotland and Ireland, and the utter destruction of "popery" and prelacy in all three kingdoms.

The third year of the war brought a mixed bag for both sides. First the Parliamentarians, together with the Scots, won the important battle of Marston Moor (July 2, 1644), in North East England, which brought Northern England under their control.

But then, just one month later, they suffered a major setback in South West England, at the Battle of Lostwithiel, after the Earl of Essex had invaded the Royalist stronghold of Cornwall, only to be trapped by a much larger Royalist army led by King Charles I himself. Essex managed to escape in a fishing boat, but his army was forced to surrender and his military career was effectively over.

The real turning point of the war came in 1645, after the Parliamentarians had created the New Model Army, an army made up of full-time, professional soldiers who were not tied to any one region and could therefore be deployed everywhere — as opposed to the local, part-time militia most of the Parliamentarian army had consisted of up until then. Most of the soldiers of the New Model Army were Puritans, devout Protestants who felt the English Reformation had not gone far enough and were therefore fanatically opposed to Charles and his Catholic sympathies.

Officers of the New Model Army were prohibited from holding a seat in Parliament, so as to separate military leadership from political affiliations.[17] One of the men involved in the creation of the New Model Army was Oliver Cromwell, a Member of Parliament and Lieutenant-General of the horse, who had distinguished himself at the Battle of Marston Moor. Cromwell, made second-in- command of the New Model Army, would come to play a major part both throughout and after the English Civil Wars.[18]

The important battles of Naseby (June 14, 1645) and Longport (July 10, 1645) were both won by the New Model Army and proved decisive for the outcome of the First Civil War.[19] Charles tried to regroup, but, left with limited resources, decided to give himself up to the Scots a couple of months later.

After haggling with Parliament for a few months, the Scots agreed to hand over Charles for a total sum of £400,000, delivering him to the Parliamentary Commissioners after payment of the first installment of £100,000 (Gardiner, vol. 3, 188; Hume, 123). On February 3, 1647, the Commissioners escorted Charles from Newcastle to Holmby House, which was closer to London. Charles was placed under house arrest and negotiations with Parliament began. At this point, nobody wanted to get rid of the king — or at least it wasn't on the table. Most Parliamentarians merely wanted to carve out a serious, independent role for Parliament and the unequivocal recognition, by the king, of the liberties and protections voiced in the Petition of Right. Charles stalled for time, meanwhile cutting a secret deal with the Scottish Covenanters, who agreed to invade England and restore Charles to the throne in exchange for the establishment of Presbyterianism in England for three years.[20]

Early 1648, Royalist and Presbyterian uprisings broke out in several parts of England. None of these proved too difficult to put down, though, and when the Scottish 'Engagers' (Scots in favor of the secret deal with Charles) were crushed by Oliver Cromwell's forces at the Battle of Preston in August 1648, the Second Civil War was over and done with before it had very well begun.[21]

Charles returned to the negotiating table again and offered terms to Parliament, more or less accepting the reform proposals Parliament had put forward before the First Civil War had broken out. On December 5 the House of Commons voted 129 votes to 83 that Charles' responses were "*sufficient grounds to proceed upon for the settlement of the peace of the kingdom*", but the more radical Independent party and the New Model Army were done with Charles (qtd. in Robertson, 118).[22]

Faced with the prospect of being ruled once more by a king who could not be trusted and was far too accommodating to Catholicism, the Army intervened. On the following morning, December 6, in what is arguably the only *coup d'état* in the history of England, Colonel Thomas Pride marched a troop detachment to Westminster Hall and took up position at the entrance to the House of Commons (Robertson, 118). Personally checking every Member of Parliament entering the building, he arrested some 41 MPs who had voted in favor of negotiations.[23] All in all, 143 supporters of further negotiations with the king were prevented from entering the House of Commons during "Pride's Purge", while many more stayed away voluntarily (Gardiner, vol. 4, 273). The remaining members formed what came to be known as the "Rump Parliament". One of its first orders of business was setting up a High Court of Justice to try Charles I for treason. At the beginning of his trial, on January 20, 1649, Charles posed the only question relevant at such an occasion to someone who believed he ruled by Divine Right: "*I would know by what power I am called hither. (...) I would know by what authority, I mean lawful*" (qtd. in Robertson, 155-156).

Of course there was none. Then again, ultimately all authority is derived from the capability of successfully asserting, solidifying and defending it. The law then simply enshrines that authority. In this case, Parliament — or rather the New Model Army — constituted a new beginning, a new authority, asserting its dominance over others, including the king.

The trial lasted a week and ended with Charles being convicted and sentenced to death. He was executed on Tuesday, January 30, 1649. Charles put his head on the block, said a prayer, signaled the executioner he was ready by extending his arms and was beheaded with one clean stroke (Hume, 139). His severed and bleeding head was then held up and shown to the public by the executioner, as he said, "*Behold the head of a traitor!*" (Gardiner, vol. 4, 323).[24] The next day the royal head was sewn back on, the body embalmed and placed in a leaden coffin (Gregg, 445). A few days later he was buried in St. George's Chapel at Windsor Castle, in the choir, where Henry VIII is also interred (Gregg, 445).

Things wouldn't quiet down just yet, though. During the next eleven years, England would try out both a republic, ruled by Parliament (the Commonwealth of England, 1649-1653) and a military dictatorship, ruled by Oliver Cromwell (the Protectorate, 1653-1659). Cromwell was made Lord Protector for life and invested with the power of the *"Supreme Legislative Authority of the Commonwealth of England, Scotland, and Ireland "* and *"the chief magistracy and the administration of government"*.[25]

In 1657, Parliament even offered Cromwell the crown, but after thinking about it long and hard he decided against it, saying *"I would not seek to set up that which Providence hath destroyed and laid in the dust, and I would not build Jericho again!"* (Lomas, vol. 3, 71).

Cromwell died in 1658. His son Richard succeeded him as Lord Protector but this would not work out, because Richard had no power base in either Parliament or the Army, nor had he any military credentials or was he able to act as a bridge between Army and Parliament, causing rising suspicion among the officers that Parliament wanted to reduce the military. Richard was pushed out of power by the Army within the year (Hill, 117).

A few months of chaos followed, in which different sides tried to fill the power vacuum without success. Early 1660, George Monck, the Governor of Scotland, marched his army into London and allowed the return to Parliament of the members who had been excluded since Pride's Purge (Hill, 118). The Long Parliament finally dissolved itself after having prepared a general election for a new parliament. Presbyterian-Royalist in composition, this Convention Parliament met for the first time on April 25 (Hill, 118).

Meanwhile, Charles I's oldest son, Charles II, who had been living in exile in France, the Dutch Republic and the Spanish Netherlands, had issued a Declaration from Breda on April 4, 1660, promising a general pardon for political crimes committed during the civil wars and the interregnum to all who recognized him as their lawful king (Hill, 118). On May 8, the Convention Parliament subsequently proclaimed Charles II to have been king since the *"Death of his most Royal Father"* and invited him to *"make his speedy Return to his Parliament, and to the Exercise of his Kingly Office"*, thus paving the way for the Restoration (House of Commons, May 8, 1660).

Charles II did indeed show far more mercy than was customary at the time after he was crowned king, though with some exceptions, notably with regards to the Commissioners who had sat in judgement at his father's trial. Of the 78 Commissioners, 59 had signed the king's death warrant, 31 of which were still alive at the time of the Restoration (Kirby, 25). Eight of them were hanged, drawn and quartered (a rather unpleasant way to go), fourteen spent the remainder of their lives in prison, twelve fled, two died before their execution, one was too sick for trial and one was pardoned.

In some cases, punishment was even inflicted posthumously. The corpse of Oliver Cromwell, for instance, was exhumed, hanged by the neck and then beheaded, after which the head was stuck on a pole outside Westminster Hall (Knoppers, 182). Several others were also posthumously executed. The body of Thomas Pride was ordered to undergo the same fate, but this sentence was not carried out because they couldn't find his body (Bradshaw, 379).

The civil wars were over, but it would take another major event to definitively reduce the near- absolute power of the king and prevent Catholicism from ever re-entering the center of English government again. This event, the Glorious Revolution of 1688, was in many ways a repetition of the issues that had led to the civil wars, only this time, instead of raising an army of their own, Parliamentarians would call upon a foreign power to intervene.

When Charles II died, in 1685, he was succeeded by James II, Charles I's second surviving son. Like his father before him, James tried to rule alone and was married to a Catholic woman. Even worse, he was a Catholic himself. But what really brought things to a boil was the birth of a son (when James was already 55), which changed the existing line of succession and displaced his daughter Mary — who was a Protestant and married to Protestant William III of Orange — thus opening the path to a Catholic royal dynasty.[26] Faced with this unbearable prospect, the Parliamentarians asked *stadtholder* William

III of Orange to invade England and dethrone James II.[27]

After a summer of secret messages with English politicians and forming a defensive alliance with Holy Roman Emperor Leopold I against the French, William sailed for England from the Dutch harbor Hellevoetsluis on November 1, 1688, with a fleet numbering close to 500 ships, roughly four times the Spanish Armada of 1588 (Troost, 237-238; Israel, 106). Four days later he landed at Brixham, South West England, with an army of approximately 21,000 men and 5,000 horses (Israel, 106).

James II didn't put up much of a fight, though, but instead tried to flee the country, while anti- Catholic riots broke out in several towns. He was captured, but later allowed to leave the country and join his wife and son, who had already fled to France, thus avoiding the delicate question of what to do with him.

William and Mary were crowned King and Queen of England a few months later, on April 11, 1689. At the start of their reign they both signed a Bill of Rights, limiting the power of the king and laying out certain basic rights for all Englishmen. It also barred Roman Catholics from ever inheriting the crown of England again, stating that "*it hath been found by experience that it is inconsistent with the safety and welfare of this Protestant kingdom to be governed by a popish prince, or by any king or queen marrying a papist.*" (Bill of Rights, 1689).

While the English Civil Wars laid the foundation for the supremacy of Parliament and guaranteed civil liberties, it was the Glorious Revolution of 1688 that made the end of royal absolutism irrevocable and introduced the constitutional monarchy as the English form of government. The impact of this half century of turbulent events in English history and the political concepts and convictions it inspired would reverberate far beyond 17th century England, though, both in time and in place.

On the other side of the Atlantic, for instance, the Founding Fathers of the American Revolution of 1776 would benefit greatly from the lessons of the Glorious Revolution and borrow heavily from both the Petition of Right and the English Bill of Rights when writing their own constitutional documents.[28]

Some of the most influential political philosophers of the 17th and

18th century were also deeply influenced by the events of the English civil war and the Glorious Revolution. John Locke (1632-1704), who has been referred to as "The Philosopher of the American Revolution", experienced the civil war from up close and personal as a young boy, because his father served as a captain of the horse on the Parliamentary side (Dworetz, 5-6). Locke later wrote the highly influential work *Two Treatises of Government* (first published 1689), in which he argued against absolute monarchy. Locke believed all people are born equal — something by no means deemed self-evident at the time — and formulated the theory of natural rights, being that *"no one ought to harm another in his life, health, liberty or possessions..."*, which later served as inspiration to Thomas Jefferson for the famous second sentence of the American Declaration of Independence (Locke, "Two Treatises", 191).[29]

Locke also held that people went into a social contract with government to establish a civil society, which would resolve conflicts in a civil way. If government did not hold up its end of the contract, people had the right — in some cases even the obligation — to resist. This theory strongly resonated with Founding Fathers like Alexander Hamilton, James Madison (often referred to as the

'Father of the Constitution') and Thomas Jefferson. The latter would later call Locke one of the *"three greatest men that have ever lived"*.[30]

The French political philosopher Montesquieu (1689-1755) was also influenced by the events of the Glorious Revolution and referred to it repeatedly in his work. The idea of separate powers in government — articulated by Montesquieu and later enshrined in all Western democracies— had its constitutional birth in the English Bill of Rights, which gave the sole power to tax to Parliament and declared that judges should be independent.

Still in effect today, the English Bill of Rights has been used throughout the British colonies and is considered a predecessor to the U.S. Bill of Rights of 1789 (the 2nd, 3rd, 4th, 5th and 8th amendment are based on the English Bill of Rights), the French Declaration of the Rights of Man and of the Citizen of 1789 (*Déclaration des Droits de l'Homme et du Citoyen*), the Universal Declaration of Human Rights of 1948 and the European Convention of Human Rights of 1950.

Just imagine the world of today if Anne Boleyn had not told Henry to put a ring on her finger first.

1   Qtd. in Gardiner, Vol. IV, 322.

2   Among the acts the so-called Reformation Parliament passed between 1529 and 1536 were the Statute in Restraint of Appeals of 1533, which made the king the final authority in all religious matters in his realm instead of the pope, the Act of Supremacy of 1534, making the king the *"onely supreme hede in erthe of the Churche of England"*, and the Oath of Supremacy of 1535, requiring people taking public or church office to swear allegiance to the king as the supreme head of the Church of England.

3   Interestingly, it was Henry VIII and Anne Boleyn's only child, Elizabeth, who would reinstate the reforms during her reign, after her half-sister Mary (daughter of Henry VIII and Catherine of Aragon) had reinstated Papal authority during her own short time on the throne.

4   James VI of Scotland would rule England and Ireland as James I. James VI's great-grandmother was Margaret Tudor, elder sister of king Henry VIII, Elizabeth's father.

5   The U.S. State of Maryland is named after Henrietta Maria. Charles I choose the name himself, giving the new colony the name *"Terra Mariae, anglicize, Maryland"*.

6   During her short, five-year reign, Mary I of England, a devout Catholic who had never agreed with her father's break away from Rome, relentlessly persecuted and had executed hundreds of protestants, later gaining her the nickname 'Bloody Mary'.

7   George Villiers had been the lover of James I, who had appointed him Earl of Buckingham in 1617 (Stewart, 271, 280-282). Various contemporary sources hint at the relationship between James I and Buckingham, including a preserved letter from 1624 from James I himself, in which he writes to Villiers: *"God bless you, my sweet child and wife, and grant that ye may ever be a comfort to your dear dad and husband."* (qtd. in Bergeron, 175).

8   Buckingham would not enjoy his victory over Parliament for long. On August 23, 1628, he was stabbed to death in a pub by a disgruntled army officer (Lockyer, 453-458).

9   The principle of the king needing the consent of Parliament for any new taxes remained disputed by the Crown, though, and had not been accepted by Charles I's father, James I of England (Cust, 65). The matter would finally be resolved once and for all with the Glorious Revolution of 1688.

10   The case, known as the Five Knight's case (a.k.a. Darnell's Case, 1627) provoked a national outcry, because it unhinged the fundamental principle of protection against unlawful detention.

11   The significance of the Petition of Right as a constitutional document lies not

so much in its clear-cut legal terminology, defining what the state can and cannot do, but in the constitutional precedent it created, that Parliament could force the king to acknowledge the supremacy of the law (Adams, 294-295; Halliday, 224; Flemion, 196).

12 Third Amendment — quartering soldiers — Fifth Amendment — due process clause — Sixth Amendment — criminal trial clauses — and Seventh Amendment — civil jury trial clause (Bachmann, 275-279).

13 Coke's greatest work, *Institutes of the Lawes of England*, is viewed as a foundational document for common law. As John Marshall Gest wrote in "The Writings of Sir Edward Coke": *"There are few principles of the common law that can be studied without an examination of Coke's* Institutes *and* Reports." (Gest, 505).

14 One resolution went so far as to brand anyone who paid the tonnage and poundage levy *"a capital enemy to the kingdom and commonwealth."* (qtd. in Cust, 118).

15 This covenant, signed on February 28, 1638, was based on an earlier covenant from 1581, which denounced the pope and the doctrines of the Roman Catholic Church.

16 The city of Gloucester was strategically located between Oxford — Charles' wartime capital — Wales and West England. The Royalists besieged the city in the summer of 1643 but were unable to take it, despite taking heavy casualties. A few weeks later, at the first Battle of Newbury, the Royalists failed to stop Essex' main army from retreating to London, even though their cavalry was better trained and superior in number. The defeat at the Battle of Winceby less than a month after that was another blow to the Royalist cause, costing them the county of Lincolnshire, in the East of England.

17 This was the result of the Self-denying Ordinance, passed by the Long Parliament on April 3, 1645.

18 Interestingly, Cromwell was the only exception to the Self-Denying Ordinance, being allowed to hold on to his seat in Parliament as well as his military commission (Thoyras, 169).

19 At the Battle of Naseby, Charles I's main army was decisively defeated. His army suffered around 1,000 casualties, while 5,000 — out of a total of around 8,000 — were captured. The king's personal correspondance was also captured, and was published soon after under the title *The King's Cabinet Opened*. Clearly showing the king's Catholic sympathies, the publication proved a boost for the Parliamentarian cause (Evans, 86). Less than a month after Naseby, the last Royalist army was destroyed at the Battle of Longport.

20 Known as The Engagement (signed December 26, 1647), Charles I's secret deal with the Covenanters was not supported by all of them, but after the opposition, the Kirk Party, was defeated in a small skirmish at Mauchline, the deal was nevertheless pushed through, though resistance against the agreement remained.

21   The Battle of Preston was an impressive victory for Oliver Cromwell. While his army suffered fewer than 100 casualties, the Scottish / Royalist force counted 2,000 dead and about 9,000 captured out of a total force of 14,000-17,000 (Bull, 100, 37).

22   Parliament had become divided into two factions, the Presbyterians — who wanted the church ruled by elders and a strict doctrine — and the Independents, who wanted a localized, decentralized organization of the church and who were more tolerant towards non-conformist congregations. The Independents were closely aligned with the interests of the New Model Army (Lindley, 26).

23   In subsequent days a few more MPs were arrested, making their total 45 (Gardiner, vol. 4, 270, 273).

24   According to Hume, the head was not held up by the executioner but by *"another, in a like disguise"* (Hume, 139).

25   The quotes are parts of the Instrument of Government, article I, II, respectively. For the complete Instrument of Government, see *Acts and Ordinances of the Interregnum, 1642-1660* , Vol. II (Firth, 813-822).

26   William and Mary were cousins, as both were grandchildren of Charles I, William through his mother's side — Mary Princess Royal, Charles I's eldest daughter — and Mary through her father, James II.

27   The *stadtholder* had evolved from a steward who governed one or more disctricts in the Burgundian and later the Habsburg Netherlands in service of the lord who owned the lands, to the highest executive official in the Dutch Republic (founded after seven Dutch provinces had seceded from the Spanish Empire), albeit one who was officially appointed by the states of each province. The office of *stadtholder* was retained in part because the successful Dutch Revolt against the Spanish had been led by William I of Orange, a.k.a. William the Silent, who was the *stadtholder* of several Dutch provinces. William III of Orange was a direct descendant of William the Silent. He was the *stadtholder* of all but two of the seven Dutch provinces of the Republic.

28   See also *Our First Revolution: The Remarkable British Upheaval that Inspired America's Founding Fathers* (Michael Barone, 2007), for a history of the Glorious Revolution of 1688 and how it led to the American Revolution.

29   Locke also coined the phrase "pursuit of happiness", in his *Essay Concerning Human Understanding* (171). Taken together with his phrase that *"no one ought to harm another in his life, health, liberty or possessions"*, it becomes clear how much Jefferson leaned on Locke's ideas when writing *"We hold these truths to be self-evident, that all men are created equal, that they are endowed by their Creator with certain unalienable Rights, that among these are Life, Liberty and the pursuit of Happiness."* (Declaration of Independence).

30   In a letter to Edward Bancroft on Jan. 26, 1789, Jefferson writes: *"Bacon, Locke and Newton, whose pictures I will trouble you to have copied for me: and as I consider them as the three greatest men that have ever lived, without any*

exception, and as having laid the foundation of those superstructures which have been raised in the Physical & Moral sciences (..)" (qtd. in Holmes, 107).

26

ILLUMINATION

*"If we are asked, "Do we now live in an
enlightened age?" the answer is, "No," but we
do live in an age of enlightenment. As things now
stand, much is lacking which prevents men from
being, or easily becoming, capable of correctly
using their own reason in religious matters with
assurance and free from outside direction. But
on the other hand, we have clear indications that
the field has now been opened wherein men may
freely deal with these things and that the obstacles
to general enlightenment or the release from self-
imposed tutelage are gradually being reduced."*[1]

Immanuel Kant, "What is Enlightenment?", 1784

On December 17, 2010, street vendor Mohamed Bouazizi set
himself on fire in Sidi Bouzid, Tunisia, to protest police corruption
and ill treatment, after the local police had harassed and humiliated
him and illegally confiscated his wares (Fahim, "Tunesia"). His
desperate action ignited angry and violent protests throughout the
country, forcing dictator Zine El Abidine Ben Ali from power within
a month.

The success of the Tunisian Revolution ignited a revolutionary
wave throughout the Arab world and Non-Arab countries in the region
also ruled by authoritarian regimes, causing regime change in Tunisia,
Libya, Egypt and Yemen, civil war in Syria (still ongoing as of May
2017) and civil unrest in Morocco, Algeria, Yemen, Iran and Turkey,
among other countries.

In the West it was hoped that the Arab Spring would supplant
dictatorships and establish liberal democracies, but it soon became

clear that in many of the North African and Middle Eastern nations where the revolutionary juices were suddenly flowing (again), the will of the people was not all that homogenous and certainly not predominantly secular, let alone liberal. In Tunisia and Egypt, for instance, Islamist parties won the free elections that followed successful revolution, while Syrian President Bashar al-Assad's most formidable enemy in the civil war is the Islamic State of Iraq and Syria (ISIS), which wants to establish a caliphate modeled on early Islam, when mosque and state were inseparable.[2]

In Europe, work on the road to religious freedom and separation of Church and State began in earnest after the end of the Thirty Years' War (1618-1648), the last and also bloodiest pan-European religious war. Most historians estimate the number of casualties as a result of this war at around seven or eight million, caused by fighting, famine, destruction and war related diseases.[3] The war — largely fought along Catholic and Protestant battle lines — destroyed large parts of Germany and divided it into many different territories, seriously and permanently weakening the Holy Roman Empire. Catholic Spain also lost and was forced to recognize the independence of the Dutch Republic (which had been fighting for religious freedom and independence since 1568).

Meanwhile, England fought three civil wars and one Glorious Revolution during the 17th century to make sure no *popish prince* would ever ascend the English throne again.[4]

At the same time, remarkable progress was being made in the scientific world, uprooting long established ideas and beliefs using observation, reason, experimentation and an open mind. Think of Nicolaus Copernicus and his astronomical model — placing the Sun at the center of the universe instead of the Earth — Galileo Galilei, who discovered four moons orbiting the planet Jupiter with his self-improved telescope, and Antonie van Leeuwenhoek, who discovered a whole new world of microorganisms with his microscope. The success of this Scientific Revolution amid a time of so much social, political and religious conflict, prompted several 17th century intellectuals to advocate the scientific method as a means to reform society itself as well.

In our own time, a critical attitude towards society, religion and the state may be second nature (or at least in the West it is), but back in 1650, questioning the contents of the Bible or the right of a king to rule was considered radical. Philosophers like Descartes, Hobbes, Spinoza, Locke, Rousseau, Voltaire and Montesquieu nevertheless wanted to apply reason and logic to every problem — political or otherwise — believing it was the best way to arrive at a satisfactory solution.

The guiding axiom of the Age of Enlightenment was much the same as that of the Renaissance: a willingness, a longing even, to reexamine fundamental beliefs and age-old traditions. And while the Renaissance had led to Reformation, Enlightenment would lead to Revolution.[5]

No single subject matter was excluded from reexamination, safe perhaps the existence of God himself, which was still a bridge too far for most at the time. The primary focus was no longer on religion anyway, though, but on social and political reform.[6]

Of course truly unrestrained philosophical reasoning can lead to radical outcomes. Just take a look at the following questions, some of which would have been quite unsettling to even the most radical 17th century intellectuals: Why do people have to be ruled by a monarch? Are people bound to obey their government at all time? What is the legal justification for the institute of slavery? If women are just as smart as men, why aren't they allowed an equal role in society? If the existence of God cannot be proven scientifically, how can we know He exists? Why would we believe in anything that cannot be proven to exist? Does this generation have the right to legally bind the next generation? Why should anyone be forced to pay taxes? Should we have direct government by the people if it were technologically possible?

Most were not looking to go all the way down the rabbit hole, though. They wanted to use reason to reform existing systems of authority from within, not break them. Noting this difference among philosophers of the Enlightenment, historian Jonathan Israel identifies two basic schools, *radical enlightenment* and *moderate enlightenment* (Israel, "Revolution", 15ff.).

Radical enlightenment, according to Israel, "*is a set of basic principles that can be summed up as: "democracy, racial and sexual equality, individual liberty of lifestyle, full freedom of thought, expression, and the press, eradication of religious authority from the legislative process and education; and full separation of church and state"* (Israel, "Revolution", vii-viii). An example of someone from the school of radical enlightenment would be the Dutch philosopher Baruch Spinoza, who challenged even some of the most fundamental concepts of religion — including the existence of an immortal soul — tradition and morality (Israel, "Radical", 159).[7] A prominent example from the school of moderate enlightenment would be John Locke, who wrote against absolute monarchy but did not necessarily want to do away with the king altogether.

When it comes to dissemination of these new ideas, the Reformation, Scientific Revolution and Enlightenment were all equally indebted to the printing press. Had it not been invented mid 15th century, it is doubtful that all these new ideas, scientific discoveries and inventions would have made it passed the inner circle of the philosophers, scientists and inventors who came up with them. At the very least they would have spread much, much slower (meaning Europe would be somewhere in the middle of the Reformation around this time).

Take Thomas Paine's revolutionary 77 page pamphlet *Common Sense*, of which an estimated 100,000 copies were sold in 1776 alone; try copying that by hand in the same time (Paine, "Political Writings", x).[8] One paper, the *Connecticut Courant*, even printed the whole pamphlet in its February 19th issue (Aldridge, 45). The printing press thus helped Paine to reach almost everyone of the 2.5 million colonists within a year, and *Common Sense* to serve as a (if not *the*) major inspiration for the American Revolution.

A growing population, increasing urbanization and the introduction of coffee houses — a novelty in 17th century Europe that came over from the Ottoman Empire— also helped to spread the revolutionary ideas of democracy, the justness of revolt against an unjust king and the natural right to life, liberty and the pursuit of happiness.[9]

Coffee houses became popular meeting places and political hotspots, where intellectual debates entertained, informed and challenged a wide variety of coffee-sipping customers. The second coffee house in Paris, Café Procope (established in 1686 and still open today), counted Voltaire, Rousseau and Denis Diderot — who created a great Encyclopedia, together with Jean le Rond D'Alembert — among its customers.[10] Voltaire, Rousseau, Montesquieu and other famous French intellectuals all contributed to Diderot and D'Alembert's *Encyclopédie*, which Diderot wanted to embody all the world's knowledge. Published between 1751-1772, the *Encyclopédie* is famous for emphasizing political theories of the Enlightenment and criticizing religion, especially the Catholic Church. It played an important role in providing French citizens intellectual ammunition for their coming revolution.

The 17th and 18th centuries were a period of great changes in many areas. The discovery of the Americas and the exploration of Asia and the Indian Ocean had made the world much bigger and more diverse. Advances in the sciences had put many long-held beliefs out to pasture and provided explanations for things that had been a mystery for as long as man had walked the Earth. Even religion was no longer the unwavering bulwark it had always been. People themselves were changing too. Literacy rates were going up and common people were getting better informed through newspapers and affordable books. All in all pretty fertile ground for radical new ideas such as government with "*consent of the governed*", the right to religious freedom and the importance of an independent judiciary.[11]

For those who wanted radical change, the young Dutch Republic (founded 1581) served as an excellent example of how self-governing could lead to great success. In the sixteenth century, the Habsburg Netherlands had belonged to Spain, which ruled it mostly from afar. When conflict broke out with the seven northern provinces over religion and taxation, few thought that the Dutch could hold out very long against mighty Spain. But they did.[12] And not only that, they prospered, growing into a powerful new nation and attracting religiously persecuted people from all over Europe because of its religious tolerance.

In some regions reforms were also carried out by absolute rulers themselves. Enlightened despots like Russian Tsar Peter I (1672-1725), Prussian King Frederick II (1712-1786) and Tsarina Catherine

272 - J.C. PETERS

II (1729-1796) increased religious tolerance, stimulated the sciences and patronized the arts. They did not go so far as to introduce something as crazy as democracy of course, but they did help modernize and strengthen their country and increase the happiness of their people, thus in many ways keeping up their end of the social contract as theorized by John Locke — even if the people could not actually give their consent to any of their policies.

In England, France and the American colonies the Age of Enlightenment would lead to full-blown wars and revolutions, though. And whereas the English Civil Wars and Glorious Revolution had still been largely aimed at reforming the monarchy, the American colonists and the French *peuple* — like the Dutch before them — would get rid of the monarchy altogether and establish a new system of government: a republic, ruled by the people instead of the nobility.

The French Revolution (1789-1799) had initially followed the same path as the Glorious Revolution — that is, forcing the king to listen to the National Constituent Assembly and subscribe to the Declaration of the Rights of Man and Citizen — but took a much more radical and violent turn between 1793-1794. Some 16,000 people were executed by guillotine during this so-called Reign of Terror, among them King Louis XVI and his wife Marie Antoinette (Greer, 38).[13] Another 20,000-25,000 were summarily executed or died in prison (Greer, 37).[14] But however high the cost in human lives of ending the French monarchy turned out to be, the newly established republic would soon be abolished itself by Napoleon Bonaparte, who, in 1804, crowned himself Emperor of the French, thus sending France back to square one again — at least temporarily.

Unfortunately, it seems the same holds true for most of the countries that were touched by the Arab Spring.[15]

---

1   Qtd. in Appleby, 109.

2   On July 3, 2013, the democratically elected Egyptian President Mohamed Morsi was ousted by the military, following massive demonstrations against his efforts to force through an islamist-slanted constitution and increased crackdowns on free speech and independent journalism (Kingsley, "Protesters"). On May 16, 2015, Morsi was senteced to death by an Egyptian court, but in November 2016 that sentence was overturned. As of June 2017, Mr. Morsi is still imprisoned.

3   In *Europe A History*, Norman Davies estimates the population in Germany declined from 21 million to 13 million (568). At 3-4 million, Geoffrey Parker's estimate for the decline in population of the Holy Roman Empire is considerably lower (*The Thirty Years' War,* 188). Tryntje Helfferich follows the most used estimate of 7-8 million in her work *The Thirty Years War: A Documentary History*, while emphasizing that countless other "lives or minds were shattered" because of the long war (164).

4   Quote is from the English Bill of Rights (1689).

5   Put differently, the Renaissance had resulted in religious revolution, while Enlightenment led to political revolution.

6   An interesting exception was the rising popularity of Deism, the belief that reason and the natural world presented proof enough for the existence of God and that miracles, superstitions and church authority were not necessary, even detrimental, to acquire knowledge about God. Apart from Agnosticism and Atheism, Deism was the most radical way to try and reconcile religion with reason. Two prominent advocates of Deism were Thomas Jefferson and Thomas Paine, the writer of the political pamphlet *Common Sense.* Jefferson even rewrote the entire Bible, cutting out everything pertaining to miracles and superstition. The Jefferson Bible was first published in 1895, 69 years after Jefferson's death. From 1904 until the 1950s, a copy of the Jefferson Bible was given to new members of Congress each year by the United States Government Printing Office.

7   According to Israel, no other philosopher between 1650-1750 came even close to Spinoza in notoriety "*as the chief challenger of the fundamentals of revealed religion, received ideas, tradition, morality, and (...) divinely constituted political authority.*" (Israel, "Radical", 159).

8   Paine donated all the profits from his remarkable success to George Washington's Continental Army, to be used for mittens (Nelson, 90).

9   The first coffee house in Europe opened in Venice, in 1645; from there the phenomenon spread to the rest of Europe.

10 It has also been said that Diderot and D'Alembert first hit upon the idea for the *Encyclopédie, ou dictionnaire raisonné des sciences, des arts et des métiers* (Encyclopaedia, or a Systematic Dictionary of the Sciences, Arts, and Crafts) at café Procope, but this is most likely folklore.

11 The quote "*consent of the governed*" comes from the Declaration of Independence. "*We hold these truths to be self- evident, that all men are created equal, that they are endowed by their Creator with certain unalienable Rights, that among these are Life, Liberty and the pursuit of Happiness.--That to secure these rights, Governments are instituted among Men, deriving their just powers from the consent of the governed (..)*". The concept of government with consent of the governed was first put forward by the English philosopher John Locke, who, in his seminal work *Two Treatises of Government*, wrote: "*every man being, as has been shewed* [should], *naturally free, and nothing being able to*

put him into subjection to any earthly power, but only his own consent" (291, par. 119).

12 The Dutch War of Independence (a.k.a. the Eighty Years' War) lasted from 1568 until 1648.

13 The guillotine was named after Dr. Joseph-Ignace Guillotin. Contrary to popular fiction, though, Dr. Guillotin neither invented the guillotine nor was he put to death by it. He was, however, the one who proposed carrying out the death penalty with a device that would ensure a clean, quick death for every convict, regardless of class. Dr. Guillotin died in 1814 of natural causes.

14 In *The Incidence of Terror during the French Revolution: a statistical interpretation*, Donald Greer writes that there were 16,594 official death sentences carried out during the Reign of Terror, but that the total death toll was likely between 35,000-40,000, if those who died in prison or were summarily executed are included (Greer, 37-38). Greer put the total number of political prisoners during the Terror at perhaps 500,000 (Greer, 29). Given the conditions in French prisons at the time, his total number of deaths from imprisonment and execution without trial seems on the conservative side. For a discussion of death toll estimates in different French regions, see Greer 25-37.

15 A notable exception is Tunesia, which, after the overthrow of Zine El Abidine Ben Ali, managed to transform itself into a representative democracatic republic.

Map 13: Russia during Peter the Great

27

PETER THE GREAT

*"It is my great desire to reform my
subjects, and yet I am ashamed to confess
that I am unable to reform myself."[1]*

Peter the Great

Vladimir Vladimirovich Putin has ruled Russia since 2000. He did serve as prime minister under his protégé Dmitry Medvedev between 2008-2012, but that was only because the Russian Constitution prohibits serving more than two consecutive terms in office. Neither man ever forgot who was the real president, though — nor did anyone else.[2]

Putin has steered Russia back to the Soviet era in many ways, except for the Soviet part. Recognizing that the U.S.S.R. lost the Cold War in large part because communism could not compete with capitalism economically, Putin has for the most part pursued a business friendly, growth stimulating economic policy, reorganizing the tax system and lowering the overall tax burden, while at the same time stimulating the creation of so-called "National Champions" — large, vertically integrated companies in strategically important sectors — to stimulate growth and investment in these sectors (Goldman, 98ff.). And with some success, because from 1999 to 2013, Russia's Gross Domestic Product (GDP) grew from $195.5 billion to $2,231 billion.[3]

At the same time, Russian military spending has also dramatically increased again under Putin, from around $20 billion in 2000 to more than $90 billion in 2016.[4] Russia's political and military clout have been growing concurrently and the country is increasingly flexing its military muscle, as evidenced by its annexation of Crimea in 2014 and the military intervention in the Donbass region in Eastern Ukraine (2014-present) and in the Syrian Civil War since late 2015.

Critics also point to serious setbacks in Putin's Russia regarding nascent democratic freedoms and the adherence of the state to the rule of law, not to mention the growing suppression of human rights — which is somewhat ironic when considering that Putin has a degree in International Law from Leningrad State University.[5] Then again, the rights of the individual never were that popular in Russia — at least not among its absolute rulers, of whom Russia has had many.

Russia has always been shaped by strong leaders, who swayed the fate of the nation with immense energy and vitality. In the 14th century, it was Prince Dmitry Donskoy of Moscow, the first to challenge Mongol authority in Russia, defeating them in the great Battle of Kulikovo in 1380. A century later Ivan the Great definitively ended the dominance of the Mongols over the Rus region, and in the 16th century another Ivan — this one nicknamed the Terrible, also the first to rule as "Tsar of all Russia" — doubled the already sizable Russian territory, turning a medieval state into a medieval empire.

Of course by then the Middle Ages had already ended in Europe. Reformation, exploration, colonization and scientific experimentation were changing the way Europeans viewed themselves and the world around them, influencing their way of life, how they did business, how they behaved, viewed their government, even how they worshipped. But not Russia. Though extremely large and unified under a single Tsar, Russia was still a decentralized state with a largely feudal economy. It lacked higher education institutions, a strong army and a navy.

But one man would change all that.

Pyotr Alekseyevich Romanov was born in 1672 as the oldest son from Tsar Alexis I's second marriage. Since Alexis I also had 13 children with his first wife, it wasn't very likely that young Pyotr would ever rise to the top of the Romanov pyramid.[6] But when Alexis I died in 1676 and the new Tsar, Pyotr's oldest half-brother, Feodor, followed his father just six years later, a power struggle broke out between the families of the two widows of late Tsar Alexis I, the Milosalvskys and the Naryshkins.

The tsarist candidate of the Milosalvskys, Ivan, was the oldest, but he was also half-blind and mentally challenged, while the candidate of the Naryshkins, young Pyotr (Peter), was healthy and bright (Moss,

171). The Patriarch and an assembly of nobles elected Peter as the new Tsar and his mother as regent until his coming of age, but soon after, the *streltsy* — an elite military corps — rebelled (Moss, 171).

The *streltsy* had several grievances and felt the political unstable climate was an excellent opportunity to increase their influence in Moscow. Rumors that the Naryshkins had murdered Feodor and Ivan and that Peter's mother Natalya — the new regent — favored Western practices and religious heresies also helped fuel the *streltsy* rebellion (Moss, 171).

Whether the rumors were initially spread by the Miloslavskys and to what extent the *streltsy* rebellion was controlled by Ivan's energetic and politically capable sister Sophia remains unclear, but what is certain is that after some back and forth it was agreed that Peter and Ivan would be proclaimed joint Tzars, with Sophia as regent until Peter had come of age (Moss, 172).

For the next seven years Sophia ruled as an autocrat, but in 1689, Peter, now seventeen, demanded Sophia step down as regent. She refused (no surprise there) and tried to secure the support of the *Streltsy* again, but this time most of them demurred, leaving Sophia with few options. She decided to surrender to Peter, who forced her to enter the Novodevichy Convent in Moscow.[7] After Peter's mother died in 1694 and poor Ivan in 1696, Peter finally ruled supreme and alone.

More than anything else, Peter wanted to emulate Western nation states and modernize his empire, with a modern army and navy, universities, a centralized system of government that was less dependent on the aristocracy, more industry and urbanization, fewer peasants and fewer monks. One of the first things Peter did was create a navy. Ever since he was a boy, he had been fascinated with boats and sailing, no doubt dreaming about historic sea battles that had decided the fate of nations and empires, and about the great European explorers who were sailing for Asia and the New World. Now he could finally put those dreams into action.

That Russia really needed a navy became apparent in 1695, when Peter failed to capture the strategically important Ottoman fortress of Azov over land.[8] The Ottomans had built the fortress more than

200 years earlier and used it ever since to block Russian access to the Azov Sea and the Black Sea. Fully recognizing the importance of the fortress, Peter immediately ordered the construction of a fleet of warships and returned to Azov within a year, this time with 27 ships and a large army (Philips 39-42).[9] The Ottoman fleet engaged the Russian fleet on the river Don, but withdrew after losing two warships and nine smaller vessels in a subsequent skirmish (Philips, 43). After a subsequent intense Russian bombardment from both land and sea, the Ottomans surrendered the fortress.

The war against the Ottoman Empire (1686-1700) was one of two defining wars for Peter the Great, the other being the Great Northern War (1700-1721) against the Swedish Empire, for control over the Baltic Sea region. Many of Peter's military, social and tax reforms would be connected to these wars, which not only cost a lot of money but also required a well-organized, well-equipped modern army and navy.

To increase revenue Peter introduced all sorts of taxes, the most sweeping one a head tax that came in lieu of the existing land tax, which had only taxed landowners. The head tax meant that male peasants and serfs suddenly had to pay an individual tax of 74 kopeks (Moss, 242; Hughes, 139). This came on top of taxes for wearing a beard — which Peter wanted to discourage because he deemed it unwestern — for bathing, beekeeping, and other things (Moss, 242; Ziegler, 37). Needless to say he did not make many friends among the common people with all these taxes, but they must have loved him at the Treasury, because state income increased almost sixfold between 1680 and 1724 (Riasanovsky, 234).

Another thing that made him deeply unpopular with the lowest rung of society was his effort to increase the subjugation of the serf to the landowner. Peter firmly believed in the class system (especially with him at the top) and held that the place of the serf was with his master. One of his decrees stated that a serf could only leave his master's estate with written permission from the master (Moss, 242-243). He did abolish what remained of slavery in 1723, but only so he could turn household slaves into taxpaying serfs (Moss, 242-243). And since the material difference between serfs and slaves had been gradually reduced to the point of non-existent, not much changed for these lowest ranked members of Russian society — except that they now had to pay taxes too.

But the Russian nobles would not escape Peter's reforms either. In 1722, he introduced the so-called

Table of Ranks, meant to curb the power of the nobility. The Table of Ranks was a list of positions in the military, government and at court, divided into fourteen different ranks. Rising through these ranks was determined by an individual's ability and performance, rather than his birth or seniority. The Table thus decreased the power of the nobility, while gradually improving upward social mobility and the level of education and service of those working for the state.[10]

In 1697, following his victory over the Ottomans at Azov, Peter traveled incognito to several Western European nations to try and enlist their support for a war against the Turks. While his mission was largely unsuccessful, his travels did teach him a lot about life in Western Europe and the political situation there.

He also gained a lot of firsthand knowledge about shipbuilding, working at the shipyard of the Dutch East India Company in Amsterdam for four months, during which time he lived as "carpenter Peter" in the small wooden house of the master rope maker with several of his comrades, cooking his own meals and enthusiastically learning everything there was to learn about Dutch shipbuilding (Massie, 186). So enamored was Peter with Amsterdam, the greatest port of Europe and the wealthiest city in the world, that he used its architecture as inspiration for the construction of his own great city, Saint Petersburg.

Not long after his return, the Great Northern War (1700-1721) began, a long struggle for control of Northern, Central and Eastern Europe between a Russia-led coalition and the Swedish Empire.[11]

For Russia, one of the most important goals of the war was to regain access to the Baltic sea, which had been lost after the last Russian-Swedish war.[12]

Initially, the war did not go well for the alliance. All members suffered crushing defeats against the young, inexperienced Swedish King Charles XII, who proved himself a talented military commander. By 1706, with Russia's allies all soundly defeated, Charles began directing his full attention to Russia.

282 - J.C. PETERS

On January 1, 1708, Charles XII invaded Russia with 44,000 men, 24,000 of them cavalry (Tucker, 704). Avoiding battle with the experienced Swedish soldiers, Peter instead deployed a scorched earth strategy, dispersing the live stock, hiding the grain and burning unharvested crops along the marching route of the advancing Swedish army. A very effective — if peasant unfriendly — strategy (Tucker, 704).[13]

The Swedish invasion force was also hit hard by the Great Frost of 1709, the coldest European winter in 500 years (Luterbacher 2004). In the spring of 1709, the remaining Swedish troops — about half of the original invasion force — suffered a total defeat at the Battle of Poltava, forcing Charles XII to flee to the south and seek the protection of the Ottoman Empire. It would prove to be the turning point of the Great Northern War (Tucker, 710). During the next decade, Sweden was pushed back on all fronts and eventually forced into disadvantageous peace treaties with Russia, Prussia and Denmark. The war marked the end of the Swedish Empire and the ascension of Russia as a new European power.

In anticipation of this new status, Peter had founded a new city on conquered Swedish land a few years earlier (1703), naming it after his patron saint, the apostle Peter (which conveniently happened to be his own first name too). Saint Petersburg started as a fortress at the head of the Gulf of Finland, on the Baltic Sea, but by 1704 Peter had already designated it to become the new capital.[14]

In 1724, a year before his death, Peter also established the first university of Russia in Saint Petersburg, the *Saint Petersburg Academy of Sciences*, predecessor of Saint Petersburg State University — known as Leningrad State University during the Soviet period, when Vladimir Putin studied there.

The Emperor of All Russia died on February 8, 1725. He was 52 years old.

Peter the Great was no saint. He was an autocratic ruler who crushed several rebellions against him, weakened the — already abominable — position of the serfs even further and taxed his people even more than modern French socialist presidents dare to do (quite an achievement in and of itself).

But, he also brought Russia out of the Middle Ages, reorganized the state administration, modernized and professionalized the army, created the navy, secured Russian access to the Baltic Sea and the Black Sea, increased social mobility, stimulated education, founded what is arguably the most beautiful Russian city and established the first university.

He was, in every way, an enlightened despot, who strengthened his rule, his country and his people, thereby creating a new European power that would come to play a vital role in the great pivotal wars — both hot and cold — of the 19th and 20th century.

And in the best of times and the worst of times, it is the way Russia is still ruled today.

1   Quoted in Abbott, 318.

2   The Russian Constitution does not limit the number of terms someone may serve as president, only that a person has to sit out one complete term before being eligible for office again. Following the 2008 amendments to the constitution, the presidential term was extended from four to six years.

3   Falling oil prices between mid-2014 and early 2016, as well as the negative consequences resulting from Russia's military intervention in Ukraine in 2014 — chiefly international sanctions and capital flight — caused a significant economic contraction between 2014-15, resulting in a 2015 GDP of $1,331 billion. The IMF projects Russian GDP will grow to $1,560 billion in 2017.

4   At $55 billion (mid-2017 exchange rate), the official Russian defense budget figures for 2016 are lower than the north of $90 billion estimate given here, but information services company IHS Markit, the International Institute of Strategic Studies (IISS) and the Stockholm International Peace Research Institute (SIPRI) all arrive at higher estimates (Gady, "Russia's Military Spending"). According to the SIPRI Military Expenditure Database, Russian military spending increased from around $20 billion in 2000 to $90 billion in 2012 (2012 US dollars), while IHS notes that Russian military spending was set to increase from $68 billion in 2013 to $98 billion in 2016 ("Global Defence Budgets").

5   After the dissolution of the Soviet Union in 1991, Leningrad State University was renamed back to Saint Petersburg State University. The university is the successor of the first Russian institute of higher education, the Saint Petersburg Academy of Sciences, established in 1724 by a decree of Peter the Great.

6   Of the thirteen children Tsar Alexis I's first wife had bore him, five were sons. Two of them had died before the age of five, though, and another at the age of

sixteen. The remaining two, Feodor and Ivan, survived their father, as did the one son he had by his second marriage, Pyotr.

7 She did not have to become a nun as well, but nine years later, after an unsuccessful attempt by the *Streltsy* to put Sophia on the throne, she was forced to take the veil after all.

8 The Azov fortress is located at the mouth of the river Don, in the Northern Caucasus (to the East of Ukraine), today part of the Southern Federal District of Russia.

9 Peter's fleet consisted of 23 galleys and 4 fire ships. The ships were produced in a massive effort during the winter of 1695/96. Even Peter himself had worked on the construction of one of the ships (Philips, 39-42).

10 The system would remain in effect until the communist revolution of 1917.

11 Prussia, Saxony, Hanover, Denmark-Norway, Poland-Lithuania, Moldavia and Great Britain were at one point part of this alliance against the Swedish Empire.

12 This war (1610-1617) was a disaster for Russia. It had ended with the Treaty of Stolbovo, which brought the Baltic regions of Ingria, Estonia and Livonia under uncontested Swedish control, thus depriving Russia of direct access to the Baltic Sea.

13 The Russians would successfully redeploy this same strategy against Napoleon's *Grande Armée* in 1812, and again in 1941, against Hitler's four million strong invasion force.

14 Except for a brief period between 1728-1732, Saint Petersburg would remain the Russian capital from 1712 until the end of the House of Romanov — also the end of tsarist rule in Russia — in 1917.

Part V

Revolution!

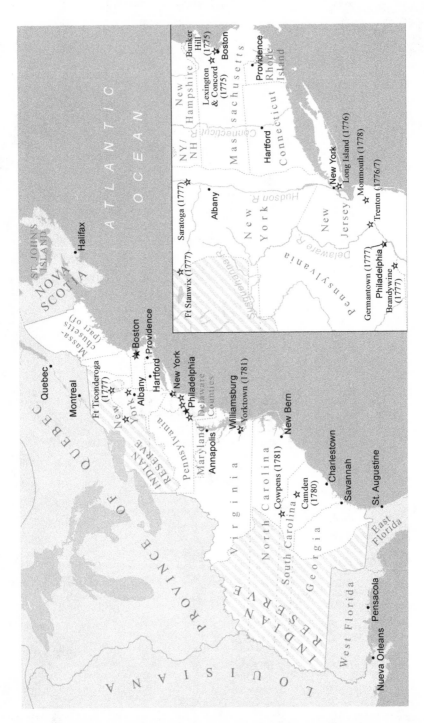

Map 14: Britain's Thirteen Colonies, c. 1775

28

WE THE PEOPLE

*"Yesterday the greatest question was decided
which ever was debated in America; and a greater
perhaps never was, nor will be, decided among
men. A resolution was passed without one dissenting
colony, that these United Colonies are, and of right
ought to be, free and independent States..."*

John Adams, July 3, 1776, letter to Abigail Adams

On November 9, 2012, an online petition was created on the 'We the People' section of the White House website, asking to grant Texas the right to secede from the Union and form its own, independent nation.[1] In a short time, more than 125,000 people signed the petition, well above the bar of 25,000 the White House had set for a petition to qualify for an official response.

That response was a 522 words long, polite, eloquent but nevertheless resounding 'no'. Apart from the inescapable reflection on the (supposed) will of the founding fathers, the response also harked back to the Civil War of 1861-65, in which more than 600,000 Americans had died and which, according to the response, *"vindicated the principle that the Constitution establishes a permanent union between the States"* (Carson, "Our States").[2]

There is no doubt Texas could survive on its own — as a country it would have the 12th largest economy in the world — nor would it be the first time for the Lone Star State to be called a country, since it had also been a nation in its own right after winning its independence from Mexico in the Texan Revolution of 1835-36.[3] But back then, the freshly minted Republic of Texas soon asked to be annexed by the United States and in 1845 was admitted as the 28th State, formally relinquishing its sovereignty on February 19, 1846, just shy of ten years after having been founded (Stephens, 108). A short fifteen years later, in a remarkable twist, Texas decided its future lay outside the Union after all and seceded, only to be forced to rejoin after losing the Civil War.

In 1868, the U.S. Supreme Court ruled that individual states did not have a right to secede.[4] No doubt King George III of England (1738-1820) would have agreed, though he would have probably preferred to avoid the word 'states' when talking about his colonies on the Atlantic coast of North America, a.k.a. the Thirteen Colonies.

Not only was secession of the 'Colonies and Plantations in North America' wholly unthinkable to King George III, it almost seemed he felt personally wronged by those *"dangerous and ill designing men"* in open rebellion, when he stated in the Proclamation of Rebellion, issued on August 23, 1775, that they were *"forgetting the allegiance which they owe to the power that has protected and supported them"* (qtd. in MacDonald, 189-90).

The proclamation came after numerous petitions from the colonists asking King George III to intervene in Parliament on their behalf, as they felt wronged by several laws they had had no part in drafting but that were nevertheless relentlessly enforced by the king's ministers. As late as July 1775, the Continental Congress had sent a petition to the king, humbly beseeching *"your majesty, that your royal authority and influence may be graciously interposed to procure us relief from our afflicting fears and jealousies, occasioned by the system before mentioned* [i.e., the king's ministers]*"* (qtd. in Morse, 187).

In the same petition, the colonists also sought to assure the king that they remained *"Attached to your majesty's person, family, and government with all devotion that principle and affection can inspire, connected with Great Britain by the strongest ties that can unite societies, and deploring every event that tends in any degree to weaken them, we solemnly assure your majesty, that we not only most ardently desire the former harmony between her and these colonies may be restored, but that a concord may be established between them upon so firm a basis as to perpetuate its blessings (..)"* (qtd. in Morse, 186) .

King George III never formally received the petition, but

his Proclamation of Rebellion, issued shortly after the colonial representatives had delivered their petition in person to Lord Dartmouth, Secretary of State for the Colonies, could be considered as a reply of sorts (Brown, 31-32).[5]

The seeds of conflict had been sown long before though, nurtured by a fundamental difference of interest between the colonies and the mother country. The latter thought it should first and foremost benefit from the colonies, not be burdened by it. In other words, the colonies should turn a profit, plain and simple. Otherwise, why would a country go through all the trouble of settling a colony in the first place? For the colonists, meanwhile, that which at first had perhaps been nothing more than a place to make a living, a refuge from religious persecution, a second chance, had over time become their home.

Friction between England and its American colonies went back to the 17th century, when British mercantilist policies forbade all trade outside the empire, blocking the American colonists from trading with Dutch, French and Spanish merchants.[6]

From 1651, the British government enacted a series of laws known as the Navigation Acts, designed to protect English merchants against foreign rivals, especially the Dutch, who, after the conclusion of their Eighty Years' War with Spain in 1648 were quickly becoming the world's dominant trading nation. The 80 laws that were imposed on American colonial trade between 1650-1750 required an ever growing number of goods to be shipped by English and American ships, via English ports (Nester, 76). Mercantilism protected English merchants and enriched the state, but it hampered economic growth in the colonies and forced high-priced, inferior products on the colonists.

An example was the Molasses Act of 1733, which imposed a high tax on molasses imports from non-British colonies, to protect the sugar trade from the British West Indies against competition with sugar from the French West indies. The policy threatened to destroy New England rum production — the region's largest and most prosperous industry — but the Crown was more concerned about the French West Indies growing at the expense of the British West Indies than it was about the livelihood of the American colonists.

The only way the New England colonists could save their

businesses was by resorting to smuggling molasses, which they did in great numbers. For a while the English government tried to enforce the act, without much success (Miller, "Origins", 99). The failure of the Molasses Act was an early sign that the American colonies were not going to accept any and all new taxes without putting up a fight.

Things heated up after the end of the Seven Years' War, in 1763.[7] Fought between several European powers in Europe, North America, South America and India, its result was a complex reshuffling of colonial possessions, most notably in North America, where New France was divided between

Great Britain and Spain. All French lands east of the Mississippi River — including Canada, Acadia and part of Louisiana — went to Great Britain, while the larger part of Louisiana went to Spain.[8]

Though the war had gone well for Great Britain, it had also been pretty much bankrupted by it. To pay for the war and the continued presence of British troops in North America after its conclusion, several new taxes were imposed on the colonies, which in turn invoked growing irritation among the colonists.

There was the Sugar Act of 1764, reintroducing a tax on the import of non-British molasses. The

Currency Act, also of 1764, prohibiting the colonies from issuing paper money as legal tender for public or private debts, thus protecting British merchants from being paid in colonial currency but also creating a money shortage throughout the colonies, hampering economic growth (Allen, 98). The Quartering Act of 1765, ordering local governments of American colonies to provide accommodations for British soldiers, together with *"fire, candles, vinegar, and salt, bedding, utensils for dressing their victuals, and small beer or cyder, not exceeding five pints, or half a pint of rum mixed with a quart of water, to each man, without paying any thing for the same (…)"*.[9] And of course the Stamp Act of 1765, requiring that printed materials such as legal documents, newspapers and magazines were produced on special paper from London that carried an embossed revenue stamp.

The Stamp Act particularly infuriated the colonists, because it was a tax based entirely on activities within the colonies, a so-called 'internal tax', as opposed to an 'external tax', which was more trade related, such as tariffs.[10]

The Act led to violent street protests in several colonies. In Massachusetts, the house of Lieutenant Governor Thomas Hutchinson was vandalized by an angry mob. In Rhode Island, the houses of stamp distributors suffered a similar fate and in New York posters were put up warning people not to distribute or use stamped paper if they valued their house, person and possessions. Many colonists also took to systematically boycotting British goods out of anger over the new taxes (Northrup, 53).

In October 1765, nine of the thirteen colonies sent representatives to New York City to participate in the Stamp Act Congress. It was the first time elected representatives from several colonies came together to discuss a joint reaction to the British Parliament. The resulting Resolutions of the Stamp Act Congress (a.k.a the Declaration of Rights and Grievances) asserted that there should be no taxation without representation, and that since the colonies were not represented in Parliament, Parliament did not have the right to tax the colonists, only the colonial assemblies had that right.[11]

It was the same fundamental question that had plagued England a century earlier: who has the right to tax the people? Back then, the dispute had been between the king, who claimed absolute rule based on the divine right of kings, and Parliament, which claimed that only the representatives of the people could pass new taxes. It had led to civil war, chaos, revolution, the beheading of one king and the ousting of another, before Parliament had finally been victorious in the Glorious Revolution of 1688.

Of course this time around, in dealing with the grievances of the colonists, Parliament was on the other side of the argument. Enlightenment called for government with consent of the governed, for democracy and the rule of law, principles Parliament had based its own resistance on during the civil wars and the Glorious Revolution but which now served as legal foundation for the American colonists and *their* resistance.

The colonists argued that since they were not represented in Parliament, they should not be affected by its laws, least of all be taxed by it. That would be a breach of their rights as Englishmen.[12]

Parliament, on the other hand, held that the colonists were 'virtually represented', because members of Parliament had the right to speak for all British subjects, not just for those districts that had elected them. (Of course in reality this virtual representation existed in name only, since politicians rarely cater to those who cannot vote for them). Because the colonists had no representation in Parliament, they had zero control over new legislation and felt wholly at the mercy of this small group of people more than 3,000 miles away. Samuel Adams (1722-1803), a politician in colonial Massachusetts and one of the leaders of the early revolutionary movement, perhaps best formulated that fundamental fear of the colonists with regards to British tax policy in the Americas in a statement drafted in May 1764, writing: *"For if our Trade may be taxed why not our Lands? Why not the Produce of our Lands and every thing we possess or make use of? This we apprehend annihilates our Charter Right to govern and tax ourselves – It strikes our British Privileges, which as we have never forfeited them, we hold in common with our Fellow Subjects who are Natives of Britain: If Taxes are laid upon us in any shape without our having a legal Representation where they are laid, are we not reduced from the Character of free Subjects to the miserable State of tributary Slaves."* (qtd. in Cushing, 5).[13]

Both the Sugar Act and the Stamp Act were repealed in 1766 — mostly because boycotts were hurting British trade — but at the same time Parliament explicitly asserted its right to tax the colonies by passing the Declaratory Act (on the same day it repealed the Stamp Act), which stated that Parliament *"had, hath, and of right ought to have, full power and authority to make laws and statutes of sufficient force and validity to bind the colonies and people of America, subjects of Great Britain, in all cases whatsoever."* (qtd. in MacDonald, 140).

At this point, the colonists were still not seeking independence from Great Britain, merely a greater freedom to govern themselves. Of course the more freedom a colonial people are allowed in governing themselves the less colonial they become, begging the question whether the colonists would have been satisfied even if Parliament had granted them the right to tax themselves. Then again, perhaps the colonists were still a bit like teenagers during those 1760s and early 1770s, longing to be free of their parents but not quite ready yet to move out of the house.

So far, both sides were unhappy with the other but neither one was willing to bring it to the next level. The colonists grumbled and sent petitions, while Parliament repealed some of its most provocative laws but at the same time reaffirmed its right to legislate and tax the colonies.

Then, in 1767, Parliament passed the Townshend Acts — named after Charles Townshend, the chancellor of the exchequer — a series of laws that, among other things, slapped tariffs on a number of goods imported by the colonies, such as paper, paint, lead, glass and tea, all items the colonists were only allowed to buy from Great Britain (MacDonald, 144).[14] Needless to say the Townshend Acts became very unpopular among the colonists.

In Boston, Massachusetts, British troops had to be stationed to protect the officials charged with enforcing the hated laws.[15] The presence of British soldiers only increased the tensions in Boston though and on March 5, 1770, things got badly out of hand when an angry mob threatened a group of nine soldiers, some of whom lost their nerve at one point and fired into the crowd without orders. Three people were killed instantly, eight others were wounded, two of whom later died of their wounds. Following an official inquiry, the soldiers were tried in a court of law.[16] Six of them were acquitted, two were convicted of manslaughter but received only a branding on their thumb after John Adams successfully invoked an exception enabling leniency (Allison, 50).[17] Captain Thomas Preston was tried separately and acquitted, because the jury did not believe he had ordered his troops to fire (Allison, 39-40).

The Boston Massacre brought the civil unrest to a new level and the subsequent occupation of the city by British troops convinced some early revolutionaries that full independence was now the only solution. Memory of the massacre was kept alive by annual commemorations and fiery pamphlets, thus preparing the ground for more incidents, such as the attack on the British customs schooner HMS Gaspée, two years later.

The HMS Gaspée was attacked, looted and set ablaze in June 1772 after it had run aground in Warwick, Rhode Island.[18] It was not the first time a British customs vessel had been attacked by the colonials, but it was the first time the Crown decided to try the raiders for high

294 - J.C. PETERS

treason (Bartlett, 51-52).[19] Ultimately no one was tried though, because the Royal Commission of Inquiry could not obtain sufficient evidence against any individual colonist.

A year later, a group of angry Bostonians boarded three ships full of taxed tea from Britain and dumped the entire cargo of tea in the Boston Harbor.[20] Known as the Boston Tea Party (December 16, 1773) it in turn elicited a harsh response from Parliament in the form of the Coercive Acts — a.k.a the Intolerable Acts — meant to punish Massachusetts and especially Boston for its resistance. The Acts severely restricted Massachusetts' self-governing rights, closed Boston Harbor until Britain had been compensated for all the tea the Bostonians had dumped in the harbor, ordered British soldiers to be tried in Britain instead of the colonies and allowed governors to house British soldiers in the homes of citizens without their consent.[21]

The colonies responded by forming the First Continental Congress, meeting in Carpenters' Hall in Philadelphia between September 5-October 26, 1774. Twelve of the thirteen colonies (Georgia being the exception) sent a total of 56 members from their colonial legislatures. On October 14, the members adopted a Declaration of Rights and Grievances, outlining their grievances and their objections against the Coercive Acts and their intent to enter into a *"Non-Importation, Non- Consumption, and Non-Exportation Agreement or Association"* (i.e., a boycott), until their grievances were addressed and resolved ("Journals of the Continental Congress", 19-22). The Congress also agreed to prepare a *"loyal address to his majesty"*, and to meet again the following year if the grievances had not been attended to ("Journals of the Continental Congress", 22).

When the Second Continental Congress indeed convened in Philadelphia the following year, on May 10, 1775, the American Revolutionary War had already begun. Three weeks earlier, on April 19, British Army regulars seeking to capture and destroy the militia's military supplies, had clashed with the Massachusetts militia at Lexington and Concord.[22] The first shots were fired at North Bridge, close to the town of Concord, an event the poet Ralph Waldo Emerson later epitomized as "the *shot heard 'round the world*".[23] The result of the battles was a surprising colonial victory.

But even though the war was already underway, the outcome of the

Second Continental Congress was not a done deal. In fact, several members still wanted to try and come to reconciliation with the Crown. So, on july 8, 1775, the Olive Branch Petition was sent to the king, in a final attempt to mend the already severely broken fence.

But King George III's 'answer' in the form of the Proclamation of Rebellion made it clear to all that there was no more turning back, and in the months that followed Congress slowly but surely moved toward the only logical outcome in the face of a war that was already being waged.[24] On July 2, 1776, the Second Continental Congress finally approved a resolution of independence and on the 4th of July it adopted the Declaration of Independence.[25]

But although the Thirteen Colonies now officially considered themselves a new nation, independence would not be given, it had to be won.

The early stage of the war did not go very well for the Americans. The invasion of the province of Quebec for instance, which had begun in August 1775 with the dual aim of preventing the British to invade from the North and convincing the French-speaking Canadians to join the revolution, ended in disaster. And while the Continentals did succeed in chasing the British from Boston in March 1776, the opposite happened a few months later in New York, when the Continental Army under General George Washington was badly defeated at the Battle of Long Island, on August 27, less than two months after the United States had officially declared its independence.[26]

After the battle, Washington managed to retreat from Brooklyn Heights to Manhattan, but another two lost battles later — at White Plains and Fort Washington — he decided to withdraw from New York altogether. The Continentals were subsequently chased across New Jersey by General Lord Cornwallis until they crossed the Delaware river and retreated into Pennsylvania, in December 1776 (Stedman, 223).[27]

Following the American retreat the British retired for the winter, but in a surprise move Washington then crossed the Delaware again, in the night of December 25th, and defeated the British-hired Hessian forces at Trenton, New Jersey. A few days later Washington crossed the river a third time, this time defeating British reinforcements under

Cornwallis. The victories gave the colonials a much needed morale boost.

The real turning point of the war came in the fall of 1777, when General John Burgoyne's invasion army was decisively defeated at Saratoga, New York, by the Continental Army under General Gates, resulting in the surrender of some 6,000 men, the capture of 73 guns and thousands of muskets, as well as powder and cannon balls (Luzader, 339-40).[28] The victory convinced the French to actively join the war, after they had already supported the revolutionaries with loans, donations, technical assistance, gunpowder and ammunition (Luzader, x-xi). The Spanish and the Dutch later also joined as active contributors to the American war effort, further hampering the British (Luzader, x-xi).

More than anything else, the British strategy depended on the might of its navy and colonial support from the loyalists. The latter factor ultimately proved to be small and ineffective though, while British naval power was eventually checked by the French at the Battle of the Chesapeake (a.k.a. Battle of the Capes, September 5, 1781), a decisive French victory of great strategic value, as it prevented both reinforcement and evacuation of General Cornwallis' army in Yorktown, Virginia, where it was besieged by a joined American and French Army.

Two weeks before the Battle of the Chesapeake, General Washington and Comte de Rochambeau, the commander of the French Army, had marched from Newport, Rhode Island. Washington had gone to great lengths to make the British believe the American-French army was headed for British occupied New York City — including fictitious correspondence and summoning provisions, boats etc., for a drive against New York — but the real goal was Yorktown (Greene, 18).

On September 14, 1781, Washington arrived in Williamsburg, about fifteen miles from Yorktown. Somewhat later additional troops arrived and on September 28 Washington had Yorktown surrounded with a force of 18,000 men, made up of French and American regulars plus militia (Greene, 79).[29] Cornwallis and his 9,000 strong army were trapped (Greene, 79, 33).[30]

With the British cornered, the Americans and French started bringing their artillery in position, further weakening British morale with the promise of a forthcoming brutal bombardment, which on October 9 indeed began (Washington himself fired the first cannon). After a few days of relentless shelling, the British organized a desperate, if valiant, attack on the allied cannons, but after spiking six of them they were pushed back to Yorktown.

On October 17, Lord Cornwallis resigned in the hopelessness of his situation and asked for terms. Two days later the British officially surrendered, though Cornwallis himself was not present at the ceremony of surrender, delegating the duty of surrendering his sword to Brigadier General Charles O'Hara (Lengel, 343). Apart from its strategic importance and the surrender of 8,000 British soldiers, the victory at Yorktown also came with considerable spoils, including 244 pieces of artillery, a number of transport ships, almost 3,000 muskets, 80,000 musket cartridges and an abundance of food supplies (Lengel, 308-09).

The Battle of Yorktown was the last major engagement of the American Revolutionary War, though several smaller battles would follow. Four months after Yorktown, on February 27, 1782, the British House of Commons voted to end the war in America. Negotiations began soon after and a preliminary Treaty of Paris was signed that same year, on November 30.[31]

The United States of America had secured its independence as a new nation, but exactly what kind of nation it would be remained a struggle for decades. Initially, the idea was for the United States to be a confederation of sovereign states. Consequently, its first constitution, the Articles of Confederation of 1777 (adopted March 1, 1781) gave almost no power to the federal government, except where foreign policy and defense were concerned. The Articles did not even call the United States a nation, speaking instead of a *"firm league of friendship"* ("Articles", art. III). Recognizing the dangers of an overly weak central government, nationalists such as Alexander Hamilton, James Madison and John Jay pushed for more power at the federal level. The result was the U.S. Constitution of 1789, with the first ten amendments (a.k.a the Bill of Rights) attached to it, to assuage fears for an overbearing federal government. But the friction between those favoring states' rights and those advocating a strong federal government remained.

And so, within a century after the adoption of the Declaration of Independence, Americans from the states of Virginia, North Carolina, South Carolina, Arkansas, Tennessee, Missouri, Kentucky, Mississippi, Florida, Alabama, Georgia, Louisiana and Texas would fight for their independence once again. Only this time they lost, thus vindicating the principle *"that the Constitution establishes a permanent union between the States"*.

1 The petition was titled *"Peacefully grant the State of Texas to withdraw from the United States of America and create its own NEW government."*

2 Of course, invariably, vindication is the privilege of the victorious.

3 According to the U.S. Bureau of Economic Analysis, the Gross state product of Texas was $1.532 trillion in 2013, which would make it the world's 12th economy, ranking just below Canada (BEA, "Texas"; IMF, "Report").

4 In Texas v. White - 74 U.S. 700 (1868), Chief Justice Salmon P. Chase wrote that *"The Constitution, in all its provisions, looks to an indestructible Union composed of indestructible States"* (725).

5 The position of the British might have further hardened in the weeks that followed by the publication of an intercepted letter from John Adams to James Warren, written on July 24, 1775 — i.e., a few weeks *after* the Olive Branch Petition had been sent to England — and published in *Lloyd's Evening Post* and *British Chronicle*, 18-20 September (Taylor, 89-93). In the letter Adams advocated that the colonists should first prepare for war and independence and only then negotiate for peace and reconciliation, thus clearly contradicting the conciliatory tone of the official public statements of the Continental Congress (Brown, 29-30; Taylor, 89-93).

6 The Crown's first mercantilist act for the colonies goes back as far as 1621, when it ordered Virginia to export its tobacco only to English ports (Nester, 76).

7 The North American part of the Seven Years' War is known as the French and Indian War.

8 Spain returned Louisiana to France in 1800, but three years later Napoleon sold the territory to the United States (known in the U.S. as the Louisiana Purchase), thus permanently ending French colonial rule on the North American mainland.

9 Quartering Act of 1765. Art. VI, VII.

10 The relevance of any distinction between 'internal' and 'external' tax was debated both in England and in the colonies. The English doubted American opposition to the Stamp Act was really based on it being an 'internal' tax, but by using this as a chief argument — as Benjamin Franklin did, among others — repeal of the act was perhaps made more palpable for Parliament (Morgan, 283-87).

11 Resolutions of the Stamp Act Congress, articles 3,4,5. October 19, 1765

(MacDonald, 136-39).

12 Resolution two of the Resolutions of the Stamp Act Congress emphasized the colonials' rights as Englishmen by stating that *"his majesty's liege subjects in these colonies, are entitled to all the inherent rights and liberties of his natural born subjects, within the kingdom of Great-Britain"* (qtd. in MacDonald, 137).

13 Part of a set of written instructions for the Representatives of the Massachusetts House, following the Boston Town Meeting in May 1764. The complete text can be found in: *The Writings of Samuel Adams*, IV Volumes, 1:1-7, edited by Harry A Cushing.

14 The idea behind the Revenue Act of June 29, 1767 (7 Geo. III c. 46) was that the Crown still needed to replenish its coffers from the expensive Seven Years' War and that the repeal of the Stamp Act and the reduction of the land tax simply required another source of revenue. Townshend thought that by framing the Revenue Act as an external tax the colonies would not object to it, but this proved to be a fallacy, since the tax was still imposed on the colonists without consulting them (MacDonald, 143).

15 Two regiments, elements of a third and accompanying artillery arrived on October 1, 1768. Two more regiments began arriving in November. Samuel Adams later said that the arrival of these troops had convinced him that America must become independent (Alexander, 65).

16 The soldiers were defended by John Adams, who would later become one of the Founding Fathers of the United States and its second president. Adams was a lawyer by trade.

17 The exception, *benefit of clergy*, went back to medieval times. The branding of the thumb was to ensure a convict would only invoke the exception once (Allison, 50).

18 For a detailed description of the event by eyewitness Aaron Briggs, see: *A History of the Destruction of His Britannic Majesty's Schooner Gaspee in Narragansett Bay, on the 10th June, 1772* (Bartlett, 84-87).

19 Source contains a portion of a letter from Secretary of State for the Colonies Lord Dartmouth to the Governor of Rhode Island, Joseph Wanton, informing the latter of the intent of the Crown to consider the act as *"high treason, viz.: levying war against he King."* (qtd. in Bartlett, 51).

20 In several other colonies, protesters had succeeded in forcing the tea consignees to resign and return the tea ships to England, their cargo still on board, but in Boston, Thomas Hutchinson — Governor of the Province of Massachusetts Bay and a staunch Loyalist — had refused to let the tea ships return to England with their cargo.

21 The Coercive Acts were four separate punitive measures, the Boston Port Act, the Massachusetts Government Act, the Administration of Justice Act and the Quartering Act (MacDonald, 150-62).

22 The militia had been warned of the approaching British by Bostonian silversmith

Paul Revere. The Battles of Lexington and Concord were fought in Middlesex County, Province of Massachusetts Bay, not far from Boston.

23 As the first verse of Emerson's "Concord Hymn" goes: *By the rude bridge that arched the flood | Their flag to April's breeze unfurled | Here once the embattled farmers stood | And fired the shot heard round the world.* The phrase would later also be used for the assassination of Austrian Archduke Franz Ferdinand by Serbian nationalist Gavrilo Princip, in Sarajevo, June 1914, which ignited World War I.

24 That King George III had already decided not to try to resolve things with the colonists through negotiation, becomes clear from his correspondence with British Prime Minister Lord North. In September 1774 — while the First Continental Congress was in session — he wrote that " *the die is now cast, the colonies must either submit or triumph*" (qtd. in Black, 215). And two months later, in another letter to North: "*The New England governments are in a state of rebellion....blows must decide whether they are to be subject to this country or independent.*" (qtd. in Black, 215).

25 The original document is actually titled *The unanimous Declaration of the thirteen united States of America.* The term 'Declaration of Independence' is not mentioned in the text.

26 Washington's army suffered 1,000 casualties during the battle, while another 1,000 were captured.

27 Charles Stedman served under Generals Sir William Howe and Marquis Charles Cornwallis during the American Revolutionary war.

28 General Burgoyne's army had also suffered about 1,000 casualties in the two battles of Saratoga.

29 According to Greene, the nominal strength of the French Army was 8,600, that of the Continental Army 8,280 and that of the militia 5,535 (Greene, 77-79). But he also estimates that some 1,500 Continentals and 600 French regulars "*were absent due to sickness or other reasons at any given time*", and that the effective strength of the militia was not more than 3,500, which is how he arrives at an estimated 18,000 strong American-French army (Greene, 77-79).

30 Greene states that mid-September 1781 the nominal strength of Cornwallis' army was 9,700 — including 840 seamen who were part of the British ships anchored at Yorktown — but in the months leading up to the siege, Cornwallis himself reported that the effective strength fluctuated between 5,000-5,500, though this excluded the 840 seaman and the Hessian mercenaries (Greene, 33).

31 The formal Treaty of Paris was signed on September 3, 1783, and ratified by both sides early 1784.

29

FROM A FIRM LEAGUE OF FRIENDSHIP TO A MORE PERFECT UNION

"Let Americans disdain to be the instruments of European greatness! Let the thirteen States, bound together in a strict and indissoluble Union, concur in erecting one great American system, superior to the control of all transatlantic force or influence, and able to dictate the terms of the connection between the old and the new world!"

Alexander Hamilton, The Federalist
Papers, No.11, November 24, 1787

In April 2010, the fate of Eurozone member state Greece hangs in the balance. Its sovereign debt rating has just been slashed to junk bond status, following the admission by the Greek government that Greece's financial situation is much worse than previously reported. After performing its own analysis, Eurostat, the European Union's statistical bureau, finds that the Greek budget deficit is not five but a staggering fifteen percent, while the Greek national debt is also revised upward, from 113 to 130 percent.

The junk bond status sends the already high interest rate on Greek government bonds into the stratosphere, effectively shutting Greece out of the bond markets. No longer able to issue new government bonds, the country is in danger of default. Desperate for a lifeline and out of options, Greece turns to Brussels and asks for a loan.

The other Eurozone countries are not too keen to help profligate Greece. Fiscally conservative countries like Germany, the Netherlands,

Austria and Finland are especially loath to help a country that over-borrowed and overspent for years while they themselves took pains to run a fiscally responsible budget.

Time is quickly running out though, because in the weeks that follow, the Greek crisis threatens to spread to other financially vulnerable Eurozone countries, like Portugal, Ireland, possibly even Spain and Italy — the latter two the world's 12th and 8th largest economy, respectively.[1] And with many financial institutions so heavily invested in European government bonds, another systemic crisis — like the one that occurred after the collapse of Lehman Brothers in September 2008 — suddenly seems perilously close.

On May 2, 2010, Germany is the last country to cave and agree to a €110 billion bailout package for debt-stricken Greece, albeit under strict conditions. Greece has to implement tough austerity measures, privatize €50 billion worth of government assets and implement a host of (long overdue) structural economic reforms. The Greeks grumble, protest, strike and sigh, but it is clear they have no choice. They simply cannot afford sovereignty anymore.

In the late 18th century, several American states faced the same problem. The American Revolutionary War — though won — had left the U.S. federal government with a debt of $39 million and the individual states with a total debt of $21 million, an enormous amount of money for the time (Dewey, 56). Some states, like Virginia, had relatively small debts, but others owed a boatload and were nowhere near repayment. Massachusetts and South Carolina, for instance, each had debts of over $4 million (Miller, "Alexander Hamilton", 242). Massachusetts was particularly mired in economic problems. Part of its economy was agriculture- based, while the area around Massachusetts Bay was merchant-based. After the war had ended, European traders began to demand payment in hard currency from Massachusetts merchants, who in turn started to demand payment in hard currency from their local customers, many of them farmers (Szatmary, 19-20). As there was a shortage of such currency, many farmers and small businesses simply could no longer buy anything.

In a country just refreshed by revolution the first task of any new government is to prevent another. The risk is very real, because in the immediate aftermath of a rebellion the state is still weak. There could be a counter-revolution — perhaps supported by a neighboring state ceasing upon the opportunity to increase its influence — or a new rebellion, fueled by even more radical revolutionaries or disgruntled veteran revolutionaries.

The latter is what happened in Massachusetts in August 1786, when a violent uprising broke out as a result of the ongoing economic depression of Massachusetts and the harsh fiscal policies of a state government desperately trying to pay off its huge debt (Richards, 87-88).[2] In the months that followed, Shays' rebellion — named after one of the rebel leaders, Revolutionary War veteran Daniel Shays — threatened to topple the Massachusetts government, greatly alarming the governments and legislatures of the other states as well.[3]

In September of that same summer of 1786, delegates of five of the thirteen states met in Annapolis, Maryland, to discuss how to improve the constitution of the United States, the Articles of Confederation.[4] At the Convention, Alexander Hamilton, representative from New York and a long- time proponent of a much stronger federal government, drafted a resolution proposing the individual states appoint Commissioners *"to meet at Philadelphia on the second Monday in May next, to take into consideration the situation of the United States, to devise such further provisions as shall appear to them necessary to render the constitution of the Federal Government adequate to the exigencies of the Union"*, in other words to work out the deficiencies of the Articles of Confederation ("Proceedings of Commissioners", Sept. 14). The resolution was passed unanimously by the 12 attending delegates.

To be sure, the Articles of Confederation had been created only ten years earlier, between June and early July 1776, during the same weeks the Declaration of Independence had been drafted.[5] The war had already begun and the last thing most members of Congress wanted was to exchange a strong, tyrannical government on the other side of the Atlantic for a strong, tyrannical government on *this* side of the Atlantic. The Articles of Confederation therefore focused on individual states' rights and limiting the powers of the federal government.

The states wanted to work together where they felt they had to, such as in defending their borders, establishing and maintaining diplomatic relations, negotiating commercial agreements with foreign powers and deciding disputes between states, but retain sovereignty in everything else.

Strictly speaking, the United States of America was not even a country according to the Articles of Confederation. It was a confederacy, meant to provide a *"firm league of friendship"* between individual states.[6] In dividing power and responsibilities between the federal government and the individual states, the Articles left no doubt about who was to have the upper hand. Article II of the Articles stipulated that *"each state retains its sovereignty, freedom, and independence, and every power, jurisdiction, and right, which is not by this Confederation expressly delegated to the United States, in Congress assembled."*

Under the Articles, the United States did not have a president, king, emperor or any other head of state, no executive agencies, no judiciary and no tax base. The federal government could not even collect customs duties after a bill to this effect was vetoed by Rhode Island in 1782 (Risjord, 198). Vetoes like this effectively crippled the Congress of the Confederation, because most of the legislation it proposed needed unanimous approval from all thirteen states.

Since Congress was not able to collect taxes, it could only *request* money from the states, not demand it. But the states were much more concerned with paying down their own debts and rarely paid up.[7] Congress did have the right to print money, but because it lacked ways to raise actual revenue, these 'Continental Dollars' quickly depreciated in value. As early as 1779, General Washington lamented in a letter to the President of Congress that *"A wagon-load of money will scarcely purchase a wagon-load of provisions"* (letter qtd. in Sparks, 227-29). No wonder the phrase 'not worth a continental' made its way into everyday vocabulary as denoting something utterly worthless.

Though the Confederation Congress was charged with declaring war and maintaining the peace — one of its few powers — it had no money to maintain an army. After the war had ended the Continental Army was largely disbanded, and from June 1784 only 80 enlisted men and a few officers remained (Waddell, 23). Additionally, Congress called on the states to provide 700 soldiers from their respective militias for one year service on the frontier (Bennett, 3). The weakness of the post-war Continental Army caused the British to linger longer in the frontier forts than the Treaty of Paris allowed for.[8]

Complaints about the ineffectiveness of the federal government had been growing since the early 1780s, as had momentum to amend the Articles of Confederation to strengthen the federal government and curb the power of the individual states. Support for a stronger federal government was voiced by the so-called federalists, with Alexander Hamilton, James Madison, John Jay, George Washington, John Adams and Benjamin Franklin among them.[9]

The federalists contended that Congress should decide by majority instead of unanimity and have the right to tax, that the federal government should have an executive branch, led by a chief executive, and that there should be a federal bank, which would assume the national debt, including the debt incurred by the individual states during the Revolutionary War.[10]

Anti-Federalists, like Samuel Adams, the revolutionary from Boston, Patrick Henry, the Virginian who had led opposition against the Stamp Act of 1765 and is still famous for the phrase "*Give me Liberty, or give me Death*", and James Monroe, also from Virginia and later the fifth President of the United States, were dead set against a strong central government. They feared the 'chief executive' would evolve into a king of sorts and that states' and citizens' rights would be increasingly trampled by an overbearing, omnipotent federal government.

But although strong opposition to the federalist viewpoint remained, a Constitutional Convention nevertheless convened in Philadelphia on the 'second Monday in May', 1787, as had been agreed to at the Annapolis Convention the previous year.[11]

A majority of the delegates agreed that the current state of affairs demanded fundamental changes. Providing a fearsome real-life example of what could happen if the states kept insisting on going at it alone, the events of Shays' rebellion — though largely suppressed by the time the Constitutional Convention began — must have surely contributed to this feeling.

306 - J.C. PETERS

George Washington for instance, reacting to Shays' Rebellion in a letter to Henry Lee on October 31, 1786, wrote: *"You talk, my good Sir, of employing influence to appease the present tumults in Massachusetts. I know not where that influence is to be found; and if attainable, that it would be a proper remedy for the disorders. Influence is no Government. Let us have one by which our lives, liberties and properties will be secured; or let us know the worst at once."* (letter qtd. in Fitzpatrick, 33-35).[12]

Though the task of the Constitutional Convention had originally been to *"render the constitution of the Federal Government adequate to the exigencies of the Union"*, the final version of the document the delegates of the Constitutional Convention agreed to on September 17, 1787 was not an improvement of the existing constitution but an entirely new constitution.[13]

Moreover, rather than following the procedure for constitutional revision as laid out in the Articles of Confederation — requiring all thirteen states for ratification — the new constitution stated in article VII that *"The Ratification of the Convention of nine States, shall be sufficient for the Establishment of this Constitution between the States so ratifying the Same."* ("Constitution"). Strictly speaking, the Constitutional Convention was of course out of order bypassing the ratification procedure of the Articles of Confederation like this, but what choice did it have?[14] No amendment to strengthen the federal government had ever been agreed to by all thirteen states, and here an entirely new constitution was proposed whose chief aim it was to increase the power of the federal government at the cost of states' rights. It would have had no chance of passing unanimously, even though most Americans recognized the need for change.

Defending the Convention's choice to supersede the Articles' strictures, James Madison, one of the principal Framers of the new constitution, argued in The Federalist No. 40 *"that in all great changes of established governments, forms ought to give way to substance; that a rigid adherence in such cases to the former, would render nominal and nugatory the transcendent and precious right of the people to "abolish or alter their governments as to them shall seem most likely to effect their safety and happiness""*.[15]

To legitimize the proposed ratification process, the Framers asked the Confederation Congress in a separate resolution to forward the proposed constitution to the state legislatures and that the state legislatures in turn call special elections for their ratifying conventions. This way, the decision of ratification would lie with the people rather than with the state legislatures, contrary to the ratification procedure that had been followed with the Articles of Confederation. It was an important distinction, because, as Madison had explained at the Convention: *"the difference between a system founded on the Legislatures only, and one founded on the people,* [is] *the true difference between a league or treaty, and a Constitution."* (qtd. in Elliot, 398).[16]

Congress debated whether or not it should simply forward the constitution to the states without commenting on it, or instead debate it clause by clause and perhaps send a plan of its own to the states as well, alongside the constitution as proposed by the Convention (Maier, 53-59). But in the end Congress unanimously decided to grant the request of the Convention and forward the document unamended and uncommented to the individual states.

In the months that followed, the pros and cons of the new constitution were debated in public meetings, newspaper articles and pamphlets, with anti-federalists arguing that the document was illegal — on account of its supersedence of the ratification rules of the Articles of Confederation — and lacked guarantees of citizens' rights, while the federalists contended that the failure to adopt the constitution would surely lead to (more) anarchy and rebellion.[17]

But the anti-federalists were at a definite disadvantage, having to defend something that clearly was not working according to the vast majority of the people. Perhaps most people therefore ultimately decided in favor of the new constitution on the same grounds as Benjamin Franklin, who, at the end of the Convention, had said: *"There are several parts of this Constitution which I do not at present approve, but I am not sure I shall never approve them." (...) "Thus I consent, Sir, to this Constitution because I expect no better, and because I am not sure, that it is not the best. The opinions I have had of its errors, I sacrifice to the public good."* (qtd. in Elliot, 617-18).[18]

Ten months later, the first nine states had approved the Constitution, after which the key states of Virginia and New York both narrowly voted in favor of the Constitution as numbers ten and eleven. North Carolina ratified the Constitution in November 1789, after a Bill of Rights had been proposed in Congress. Finally, Rhode Island, the last holdout, having already rejected the Constitution, called a convention in 1790 and ratified it on May 29 of that same year by the narrowest of margins, 34 against 32.

But although the federalists had won the battle for the founding principles of the 'more perfect union' with the adoption of the Constitution, they had not won the war. Over the next two centuries, the federalists and anti-federalists would continue to come into conflict over states' rights vs. supremacy of the federal government, most notably and devastatingly during the American Civil War of 1861-65.[19]

The question whether to be a less influential part of something larger or a more independent part of something smaller has continued to play a significant role throughout the existence of the United States — indeed from its earliest beginnings. To many Americans it may have seemed (seem) as though they were (are) drawn into that 'something larger' against their will. Having to join the 'more perfect union' following the Constitutional Convention of 1787, being forced to rejoin that union after the Civil War and being sucked into two — largely European — wars in 1917 and 1941. The world of today — and the outcome of both World Wars — would have likely looked very different though, had a Confederate United States retained its Articles of Confederation.

Over the last few decades, the same question has also become increasingly important in the European Union, where individual states continue to jealously guard their sovereignty, even though most of them realize further integration is a necessity if the bloc is to remain a serious global player in an ever more globalized world.

Think historians will one day write about how the problems of debt-laden Eurozone member states like Greece, Portugal and Ireland contributed to a Constitutional Convention in Brussels that led to the United States of Europe?

Neither did most Americans in the 1780s.

1   In 2010, according to IMF data.

2   In *Shays' Rebellion: The American Revolution's Final Battle*, Leonard Richards
    writes that the taxes levied by the in 1785 elected Governor James Bowdoin
    *"were now much more oppressive - indeed, many times more oppressive - than
    those that had been levied by the British on the eve of the American Revolution."*
    (88).

3   The rebellion was largely put down in February 1787, with very few casualties
    on either side. Most of the rebels were pardoned. Two rebel leaders were
    hanged, but Daniel Shays himself was pardoned. Though Shays' rebellion
    convinced many prominent revolutionaries that a stronger central government
    was needed, Thomas Jefferson, apparently undisturbed by the rebellion, wrote
    in a letter to a friend on September 13, 1787: *"We have had 13 states independent
    11 years. There has been one rebellion. That comes to one rebellion in a century
    and a half for each state. What country before ever existed a century and a
    half without a rebellion?"* (qtd. in Ford, 362). Jefferson goes on to argue that a
    rebellion warns rulers *"that their people preserve the spirit of resistance"* and
    that *"The tree of liberty must be refreshed from time to time with the blood of
    patriots and tyrants. It is its natural manure"* (qtd. in Ford, 362).

4   Though known as the Annapolis Convention, the meeting was formally titled
    'Meeting of Commissioners to Remedy Defects of the Federal Government'.

5   The June-July 1776 version of the Articles of Confederation was the first draft.
    The final draft was prepared in the summer of 1777 and sent to the individual
    states for ratification by the Second Continental Congress in November 1777.
    The Articles were ratified five years later, on February 2, 1781 (ceremonial
    ratification on March 1, 1781).

6   Article III of The Articles of Confederation and Perpetual Union: *"The said
    States hereby severally enter into a firm league of friendship with each other,
    for their common defense, the security of their liberties, and their mutual
    and general welfare, binding themselves to assist each other, against all force
    offered to, or attacks made upon them, or any of them, on account of religion,
    sovereignty, trade, or any other pretense whatever."*

7   In fact, the main reason Rhode Island vetoed the impost amendment that would
    have given Congress the power to collect customs duties, was that its *own* tax
    system subsisted mainly on impost duties on imported goods, part of which it
    used to pay off its debts (Risjord, 198).

8   Apart from the inability and/or unwillingness of raising a proper national
    army, the individual states also showed a lack of coordination in foreign policy,
    making it impossible to retaliate effectively against British mercantilist policies.

9   Hamilton, Madison and Jay were also the authors of a series of articles called
    'The Federalist' (1787-88), later known as The Federalist Papers, which
    promoted the ratification of the (new) U.S. Constitution. Though the effect
    of The Federalist Papers on the ratification debates in the individual states —
    particularly in the state of New York, where the articles were initially published

— is hard to discern, its impact on the U.S. judicial system has been notable, with 291 quoted mentions in the Supreme Court by the year 2000 (Chernow, 260). The political influence of the three authors is also hard to overestimate. Hamilton went on to become the first U.S. Secretary of the Treasury, Madison the fourth President of the United States and Jay the first Chief Justice of the United States.

10   After Alexander Hamilton became the first Secretary of the Treasury on September 11, 1789, he proposed that the federal government assume all state debts incurred during the Revolutionary War. Apart from giving the federal government more power, this would also increase the creditworthiness of the United States and free the individual states of a burden some were unable to shake off. States that had already paid most of their debts, most notably Virginia, objected, but a complex compromise ensured the narrow passage of Hamilton's plan on July 26, 1790. Part of that compromise was Hamilton's support for moving the national capital to the banks of the Potomac River, the border between Virginia and Maryland (Miller, "Alexander Hamilton", 250-51).

11   Very few delegates actually made it on time though and it took until May 25 before a full quorum of seven states was reached.

12   Henry "Light-Horse Harry" Lee had served as a cavalry officer in the Continental Army during the American Revolution. He was also the father of Robert E. Lee, the later general and commander of the Army of Northern Virginia during the American Civil War.

13   Quote is from the Annapolis Convention Resolution, September 14, 1786 ("Proceedings of Commissioners").

14   Article XIII of the Articles of the Confederation stated that "*the Articles of this Confederation shall be inviolably observed by every State, and the Union shall be perpetual; nor shall any alteration at any time hereafter be made in any of them; unless such alteration be agreed to in a Congress of the United States, and be afterwards confirmed by the legislatures of every State.*"

15   *The Federalist No. 40. On the Powers of the Convention to Form a Mixed Government Examined and Sustained.* James Madison. New York Packet. January 18, 1788. The quote Madison uses is from the Declaration of Independence.

16   Debates in the Federal Convention, Monday July 23, 1787.

17   Though the Federalists were against a Bill of Rights, arguing that the inclusion of specific citizens' rights was unnecessary since the constitution did not ask the people to give up any rights, they nevertheless agreed to include a Bill of Rights as soon as the constitution was ratified.

18   Debates in the Federal Convention, Tuesday September 17, 1787.

19   Another example is the resistance of several southern states to racial integration in schools during the 1950s and 60s, even after the Supreme Court in 1954 ruled

in favor of such integration in Brown v. Board of Education. More recently, conservative groups have mounted resistance against the Affordable Care Act of 2010 (a.k.a. 'Obamacare'), calling the comprehensive healthcare reform legislation unconstitutional on several points, most notably its requirements that states participate in the expansion of Medicaid or risk losing Medicaid funding and that citizens secure medical insurance or face a penalty (the so-called individual mandate), which conservatives argued exceeded Congress's taxing power. In its 2012 ruling in *National Federation of Independent Business v. Sebelius*, the Supreme Court upheld the constitutionality of most of the ACA's provisions, including the individual mandate, but did strike down the provision that forced states to participate in the expansion of Medicaid.

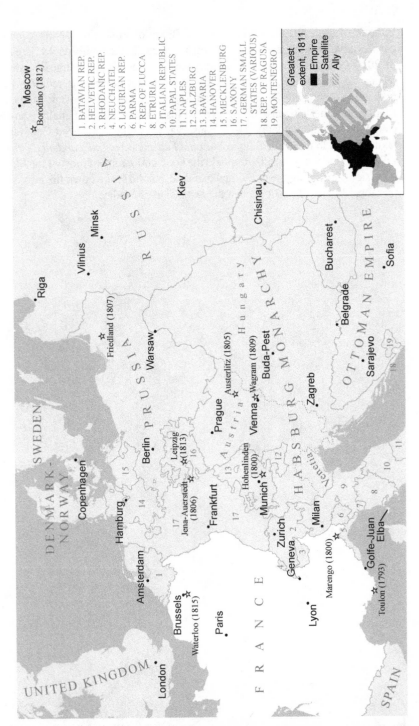

Map 15: The French Empire in Europe, c. 1803

Legend:

Greatest extent, 1811
- Empire
- Satellite
- Ally

1. BATAVIAN REP.
2. HELVETIC REP.
3. RHODANIC REP.
4. NEUCHATEL
5. LIGURIAN REP.
6. PARMA
7. REP. OF LUCCA
8. ETRURIA
9. ITALIAN REPUBLIC
10. PAPAL STATES
11. NAPLES
12. SALZBURG
13. BAVARIA
14. HANOVER
15. MECKLENBURG
16. SAXONY
17. GERMAN SMALL STATES (VARIOUS)
18. REP. OF RAGUSA
19. MONTENEGRO

Labels on map:

Moscow
Borodino (1812)
RUSSIA
Kiev
Minsk
Vilnius
Riga
PRUSSIA
Warsaw
Friedland (1807)
Berlin
Leipzig (1813)
Jena-Auerstedt (1806)
Hamburg
Copenhagen
DENMARK-NORWAY
SWEDEN
Amsterdam
Frankfurt
Prague
Austria
Hohenlinden (1800)
Munich
Zurich
Geneva
Marengo (1800)
Lyon
Paris
Brussels
Waterloo (1815)
UNITED KINGDOM
London
FRANCE
SPAIN
Austerlitz (1805)
Wagram (1809)
Vienna
Hungary
Buda-Pest
HABSBURG MONARCHY
Zagreb
Venetia
Milan
Golfe-Juan
Elba
Toulon (1793)
Chisinau
Bucharest
Sofia
Belgrade
Sarajevo
OTTOMAN EMPIRE

30

THE LITTLE CORPORAL

*"Henceforth, until the enemies have been driven
from the territory of the Republic, the French people
are in permanent requisition for army service. The
young men shall go to battle; the married men shall
forge arms and transport provisions; the women
shall make tents and clothes, and shall serve in
the hospitals; the children shall turn old linen into
lint; the old men shall repair to the public places,
to stimulate the courage of the warriors and preach
the unity of the Republic and hatred of kings."[1]*

Convention Nationale, August 23, 1793

What do the Battle of Trafalgar, a burning Moscow and the islands of Elba and Saint Helena have in common? They would all feature in a new theme park dubbed "Napoleonland" (Schofield, "Napoleon"). Plans for the park include reenactments of the taking of the Bastille — the event that ignited the French Revolution and would later enable Napoleon to shine — the naval Battle of Trafalgar and the crossing of the Berezina River during Napoleon's disastrous retreat from Russia, complete with frozen corpses of soldiers and horses lying on the side of the road, or so is the plan (Schofield, "Napoleon"). Other ideas for attractions in the park are computerized exhibits of Napoleon's many achievements, high-tech simulations of his most important battles and reconstructions of sites that played an important part in Napoleon's life, such as the Pyramids and the Gates of Moscow (Schofield, "Napoleon").

The plan is to build Napoleonland at the site of the Battle of Montereau, 55 miles southeast of Paris, where the French Emperor achieved one of his last victories. Initiator Yves Jego, deputy mayor of

Montereau: *"Napoleon is the best-known French figure in the world. He's someone who in 15 years changed the history of the world. In two centuries, 80,000 books have been written about him. Yet we don't have a dedicated museum to him in France."* (qtd. in Chrisafis, "Vive la révolution").

That is because the French are rather ambivalent towards Napoleon, and not entirely without reason. On the one hand, the fiery Corsican brought France stability after it had been ravished by the Reign of Terror following the French Revolution.[2] He also enacted many reforms that solidified the ideas of Enlightenment that had been at the heart of the revolution, such as opening education to everyone, creating a code of clear and accessible laws that made everyone equal under the law, institutionalizing religious freedom, establishing the French central bank, reforming the bureaucratic system and ending feudalism.

But, on the other hand, an estimated 1,000,000 Frenchmen lost their lives in the Napoleonic Wars, through battle, disease and the Russian winter (Bodart, 131-33). Napoleon also reinstated slavery in France's overseas colonies and opined that women should simply marry and have children, nothing else.[3] And although most French people did not have much of a problem with slavery or sexism 200 years ago, they do now. And of course in the end Napoleon also lost, making the British Empire — France's perennial foe — the undisputed dominant world power of the nineteenth century, a period known as the Pax Britannica.

Still, to put all the French casualties of the Napoleonic Wars on Bonaparte's tab would be all too easy, as they were in many ways a continuation of the French Revolutionary Wars, instigated against the newborn French Republic by several European monarchs who feared French revolutionary ideas could become a threat to their own power base.

Things had started heating up in August 1791, when Holy Roman Emperor Leopold II and Frederick William II of Prussia — having followed the developments in France with a wary eye and spurred on by the French émigrés who had packed their bags in time — called upon all European nations to unite against the French Republic and restore Louis XVI fully to the throne.[4-5]

The French Republican government took the joint declaration as an imminent declaration of war — not altogether far-fetched, though in reality it was not — and decided to act first. On April 20, 1792, France declared war on Austria, which had just entered into a formal alliance with Prussia two months earlier. When the French further aggravated the situation by executing Louis XVI, on January 21, 1793 — his wife Marie Antoinette would follow him a few months later, on October 16 — Portugal, Spain, Great Britain, several Italian city states and the Dutch Republic joined the Holy Roman Empire and Prussia in their coalition against the French Republic. France was surrounded on all sides, or, to be more precise, the French Revolution was.

Desperate to survive, the French revolutionary government came up with the idea of total war, which, at the time, was at least as revolutionary in warfare as the idea of democracy was in (French) politics. Later conceptualized by military strategist Von Clausewitz and German World War I general Erich Ludendorff, it meant the conscription of the entire population and all its available resources to achieve victory.[6] In order to mobilize as many soldiers as possible, France introduced the so-called *levée en masse* (general conscription), the first modern nation state to do so. When Napoleon came to power a few years later, he simply inherited this greatly expanded army.

Due to France's massive efforts, it was victorious in the Revolutionary Wars fought between 1792-1802 and was even able to expand its territory. By then, Napoleon had already proven himself to be an exceptionally brilliant military commander and seized power as First Consul in a classic *coup d'etat,* in 1799. But when the wars started, he had just been a captain in the French revolutionary army.

Being from minor nobility — his father had been the Corsican Representative at the court of Louis XVI — Napoleon had been given a few chances early in life not open to everyone in the *Ancien Régime,* such as attending the elite *École Militaire* in Paris. But in the years after the revolution young Napoleon advanced himself through talent, ambition and hard work and would in that respect epitomize the love child of Enlightenment and Revolution.[7]

The first time history took note of his military talent was in 1793, during the siege of Toulon, an important naval port city in southern France that had revolted against the Republican government and had turned itself over to the British. Napoleon had just been promoted artillery commander of the besieging republican forces there, thanks to some connections.[8] After evaluating the situation, he conceived a plan to capture a hill from where the British ships in the harbor could be bombarded by his artillery, which would force the British to leave (Englund, 63-64). Napoleon's plan was executed and indeed led to the capture of the city. As a reward, the 24 year old artillery commander was promoted to the rank of Brigadier General and put in charge of the artillery of France's Army of Italy (McLynn, 76-77).

Two years later, in October 1795, royalists rose in rebellion against the National Convention to protest the new Constitution.[9] Paul Barras, general of the Army of the Interior and future member of the *Directoire,* appointed Napoleon to command the ad hoc defense forces at the Tuileries Palace — where the Convention was seated — based on the young general's achievement at Toulon.[10] True to his field of expertise, Napoleon used artillery against the royalist rebels in the streets of Paris, killing 1400 of them. Rebellion over (McLynn, 94-96).[11]

A grateful *Directoire* rewarded Napoleon with the command of the Army of Italy. Wasting no time, Bonaparte invaded Italy in 1796, decisively defeated the Austrian forces there and subsequently invaded Austria itself, forcing the Austrians to sue for peace. The resulting Treaty of Leoben gave France control of most of Northern Italy and the Austrian Netherlands (present-day Belgium).

In August 1797, Napoleon proposed a military expedition to the Levant to conquer Egypt, arguing this would enable the Republic to better protect its trade interests in the Indies, while simultaneously frustrating the British ones.[12]

The expedition started auspiciously enough, with Napoleon and his army disembarking in Alexandria, Egypt, on July 1, 1798, and quickly taking the city. But on the march for Cairo his army was met by a large force of Mamluks, the military caste that ruled Egypt semi-autonomously (Egypt was officially a province of the Ottoman Empire at the time).

Because the Mamluk cavalry greatly outnumbered the French

cavalry, the French could do little more than maintain a strict defensive position. To that effect, Napoleon devised a defensive tactic whereby his soldiers would form large hollow squares, with cavalry and supplies in the center and artillery at the corners (Herold, 98). At the Battle of Shubra Khit, and a few days later at the Battle of the Pyramids, the Mamluks tried to penetrate the French defenses with large-scale cavalry charges, but were repelled each time, suffering massive casualties in the process. At the Battle of the Pyramids alone, the Mamluks suffered 10,000 dead, against only twenty-nine Frenchmen (McLynn, 178-79).

Napoleon achieved several other decisive victories in both Egypt and Syria, but an outbreak of the bubonic plague severely reduced his army. Worse, or at least equally bad, was the defeat of the French fleet by the British Royal Navy at the Battle of the Nile (August 1-3, 1798), cutting off resupplies and the way home — or at least for the troops it did, not for Napoleon himself.

With a now weakened army preventing him to achieve further greatness in Egypt and alarmed by rising political instability at home, Napoleon decided to return home, even though he had not received orders to do so. Leaving command of the Oriental army in the hands of general Kléber, Napoleon departed from Cairo on August 22, 1799, on the French frigate Muiron.[13]

That same year, on November 9, Bonaparte led a *coup d'etat* overthrowing the *Directoire* and securing his own election as First Consul (i.e., dictator), thus becoming the most powerful man in France just before the turn of the century.

Soon after becoming First Consul, Napoleon defeated the Austrians in the Battle of Marengo (June 14, 1800), in northwestern Italy, leading the Habsburg Empire to quit Italy altogether.[14] The victory also strengthened Napoleon's political position at home. A few months later, General Moreau (a rival of Napoleon who would later be exiled) won the Battle of Hohenlinden, another decisive French victory over the Austrians, and Bavarians, which effectively ended the War of the Second Coalition.

On March 27, 1802, the British signed a peace treaty with the French as well, though it was destined to be short-lived, even if the parties to the Treaty of Amiens faithfully promised to "*carefully avoid every thing which might herafter affect the union happily re-established*", as article one stated (qtd. in "Official papers", 56). Signed by Napoleon's older brother Joseph Bonaparte and Lord Cornwallis — the same who had surrendered to the American and French forces at Yorktown in 1781 — it would last only a year and was to be the only peace time between England and France in the period 1793-1815.

During that period, a grand total of seven coalitions would march against revolutionary France and Napoleon. At first mainly to restore the French monarchy, later to stop Napoleon from taking over Europe. The British were the main driver behind these coalitions, which is hardly surprising considering the two countries' long history of animosity and rivalry, going back centuries, all the way to the Hundred Years' War of 1337-1453, perhaps even to Norman nobleman William the Conquerer's conquest of England in 1066. Though Britain maintained a relatively small army during the Napoleonic Wars, it ruled the waves with its formidable Royal Navy and also heavily subsidized other coalition powers who fielded armies against "Boney", as the English liked to call Napoleon (Hall, 22, 113).[15]

Of the seven wars the various coalitions fought against France, the first five ended with a French victory. The wars of the first two coalitions had started before Napoleon had seized power, but he was still largely responsible for ending them favorably for France.

The War of the Third Coalition was kicked off with Britain declaring war on France, in May 1803 (thus 'un-establishing' the happy union again). During the next two years the British heavily lobbied several other European countries to join them, which — helped along by various French political blunders and provocative actions — Sweden, Russia and Austria finally did mid-1805.[16]

It would be a short war though, because at the Battle of Austerlitz (December 2, 1805), Napoleon, who had crowned himself Emperor of the French exactly one year earlier, defeated a numerical superior Russo-Austrian army in such a total way that it ended the Third Coalition right then and there.

The battle was a tactical masterpiece, in which Napoleon deliberately weakened his right flank to entice the allied forces to attack it, while holding his main force out of sight. When the allies took the bait,

Napoleon's main force recaptured strategic higher ground on the right flank and from there attacked the allied center, now weakened from its attack on the French flank. After breaking the allied center, Napoleon's forces encircled it from the rear and mopped it up (Fremont-Barnes, 19). Russian and Austrian casualties numbered around 27,000, of which 15,000 dead, out of a combined army of 73,000, while the French had close to 9,000 casualties, including 1,300 dead, out of an army of 67,000 (Chandler, 432).

The Fourth Coalition was decisively defeated through victories at the Battles of Jena (1806) and Friedland (1807), the Fifth Coalition ended with the Austrian defeat at the Battle of Wagram (1809). Napoleon was master of Europe, occupying and/or controlling Spain, the Dutch Republic, Italy, a slew of German kingdoms, duchies, principalities and towns, Denmark, Austria, Switzerland, and a large part of present-day Poland. The wars that the European powers had brought to the French Republic to restore the monarchy had thus turned around and bit them in their *derrières,* so to speak. The general conscription that revolutionary France had introduced to survive the first two coalitions against it, had grown into an army of over 2,500,000 men and given a highly intelligent, ambitious, energetic, charismatic military commander the chance to rise to the occasion and do what he did best: wage war.

Napoleon's military genius lay not so much in revolutionizing warfare but in its innovation, notably through improved tactical organization, flexibility and mobility. One such innovation was grouping divisions into multiple smaller army corps, comprised of infantry, artillery and cavalry, capable of functioning as miniature armies and operating independently. The movements of these different army corps could be highly deceptive to the enemy, while their logistical burden was obviously lighter than that of a bigger army. As a rule, Napoleon dispersed his corps while on the march, so that they could help each other when an advantageous position to give battle emerged.

In Napoleon's own words: "*Here is the principle of war - a corps of 25,000-30,000 men can be left on its own. Well handled, it can fight or alternatively avoid action, and maneuver according to circumstances without any harm coming to it, because an opponent cannot force it to accept an engagement but if it chooses to do so it can fight alone for a long time.*" (qtd. in Chandler, 154).

In addition to his aptitude for (military) innovation and command, Napoleon was also highly energetic — habitually working eighteen to twenty hours a day — and gifted with a photographic memory. One anecdote goes that while on campaign in 1805, one of his subordinates could not locate his unit. While his aides were searching through maps and papers, the emperor effortlessly cited the unit's current location to the officer, as well as where it would be for the next three nights, what its strength was and what the embarrassed officer's military record was. And this out of an army of 200,000 men, with all the units on the move (Dean, "Napoleon").

But there were also mistakes. Like the Peninsular War (1807-14), in which Napoleon fought the Spanish, Portuguese and British for control of the Iberian Peninsula. It evolved into a costly guerrilla war, draining French resources while achieving little. As Napoleon would later lament in his memoirs: "*All the circumstances of my disasters are connected with that fatal knot: it destroyed my moral power in Europe, rendered my embarrassments more complicated, and opened a school for the English soldiers. It was I who trained the English army in the Peninsula.*" (qtd. in Las Cases, 135).[17]

And then there was the disastrous invasion of Russia in 1812, aimed at forcing that vast country to the East to commit to the Continental System, a large-scale embargo against Great Britain.

As Napoleon's *Grande Armée* advanced through Western Russia in the summer of 1812, the Russians deployed a combination of Fabian and scorched earth strategy, continuously retreating while simultaneously burning, dispersing and destroying all the resources, luring the French further and further into the Russian Empire.[18]

On September 7, 1812, the Russians finally engaged the French, at the Battle of Borodino. Though Napoleon won the battle, he did not succeed in destroying the Russian army — a failure that may have lost him the war. Losses were heavy on both sides, but of course unlike the Russians, the French could not replenish their forces.

A week later Napoleon entered an empty Moscow. Its citizens had evacuated, food stores had been destroyed or plundered. To make matters worse, the governor of the city had left behind a police detachment whom he had charged with burning the city to the ground, as the French learned after catching a Russian police officer (Caulaincourt, 121). [19]

A month later, with no victory in sight and worried about the political stability at home, Napoleon began his retreat through the winter wonder landscape of a hostile Russia. But what began as the disappointing retreat of an undefeated army quickly morphed into a death march, claiming hundreds of thousands of lives through hunger, disease, drowning (while crossing the Berezina river), incessant attacks on the rearguard and of course the cold. Eventually, only 112,000 returned to France at the end of 1812, out of the 680,00 strong army (including 68,000 non-combatants) that had begun the Russian campaign. [20]

With the French army now severely weakened and Napoleon's reputation of invincibility seriously damaged, the other European powers smelled blood in the water and formed a Sixth Coalition. On October 16, 1813, a coalition of Russian, Prussian, Austrian and Swedish forces met Napoleon's hastily rebuilt army — which was about half the size of the coalition army — at Leipzig. The subsequent Battle of Leipzig (a.k.a the Battle of the Nations), the largest battle in Europe before World War I, involved 600,000 soldiers and lasted for three days. It ended in a decisive French defeat, forcing Napoleon to abdicate as Emperor of the French not long after, on april 11, 1814. [21]

The victors subsequently exiled their nemesis to the island of Elba, about 15 miles off the Tuscan coast and also not far from Liguria, where his ancestors had been from. [22] Napoleon was given sovereignty over the island and allowed to retain his title of emperor. [23] The first few months he really tried to make something of his rule of Elba, but what was a small island to a man accustomed to play with kingdoms and empires? So, less than a year after his arrival, the Emperor of Elba escaped and sailed for France. And while the nations of Europe were still deliberating the new borders of Europe at the Congress of Vienna, Napoleon landed at the Golfe-Juan, on the Côte d'Azur, on March 1, 1815.

On the road to Paris, he was stopped by the 5th Infantry Regiment, sent to intercept and arrest him. For a moment, it seemed the comeback of the defeated, deposed and banished Corsican was over before it had begun, but then he demonstrated why he was Napoleon.

"*Here I am. Kill your Emperor, if you wish.*", he said to the soldiers pointing their muskets at him (McLynn, 605). But instead of firing or taking him into custody, they shouted "*Vive L'Empereur!*" and marched to Paris with him (McLynn, 605).

The greatest talent of the man affectionately called '*le petit caporal*' (the little corporal) by his men, was not his sheer limitless energy, impressive intelligence, photographic memory, organizational skill or even his strategic instinct. It was his charismatic personality, creating the kind of loyalty that has men follow their leader to the ends of the world and back, capable of suffering defeat, dead comrades, frozen body parts, starvation and lost honor without wavering in their willingness to pledge their lives to this man on a horse who had fled captivity and was now on his way back to Paris.

With Bonaparte approaching, Louis XVIII, brother of the executed Louis XVI and the new king of France, quickly fled the country. Napoleon was master of the castle once again. But this time, his reign would last only 100 days.

On June 18, 1815, at Waterloo (present-day Belgium), Napoleon fought and lost his last battle against the allied forces of the Seventh Coalition, mainly comprised of soldiers from Great Britain, Prussia and the Netherlands. Talking to British Member of Parliament Thomas Creevey in Brussels just after the battle, the Duke of Wellington, the British commander of the allied forces, called it "*the nearest run thing your ever saw in your life*", but Napoleon had nevertheless lost decisively (Creevey, 236). He was captured within a month and this time exiled to Saint Helena island, in the Atlantic Ocean, far away from any coast, where he died six years later, on May 5, 1821, aged 51.

Napoleon's reign, however short, controversial and full of conflict, has had a profound and lasting influence on France, Europe and many other parts of the world, during as well as long after the fifteen years he ruled, fought and reformed.

His battles and military innovations would be studied at length by all the great commanders of the 19th and 20th century. Even the

Duke of Wellington, the hero of Waterloo, when asked by John Le Couteur, Aide-de-camp to Queen Victoria, whom he considered to be the greatest soldier of his age, answered: "*In this age, in past ages, in any age, Napoleon.*" (Roberts, "Waterloo", 272).[24]

At the U.S. military academy of West Point, cadets who would later fight as generals during the American Civil War — such as Robert E. Lee, John F. Reynolds and George B. McClellan — all received their military strategy training from professor Dennis Hart Mahan, an American military theorist who was deeply influenced by Napoleon and used the translated writings of Antoine-Henri Jomini — one of Napoleon's former generals, who had sought to systemize Napoleonic warfare — as the main textbooks on military strategy (Chambers, 558).

Napoleon was also largely responsible for the pan-Continental European adoption of the metric system, just as his *Code Napoléon* — the French civil law code — was adopted in many countries occupied by the French during the Napoleonic Wars, including Italy, Spain, Portugal, the Netherlands, Belgium and a large part of Germany. And through colonial ties, Napoleon's Civil Code also influenced the legal systems of several Latin American and African nations, the Canadian province of Quebec and the U.S. state of Louisiana.[25]

With a single stroke of the pen Napoleon also managed to have a lasting effect on the United States, when, in 1803 — after deciding to abandon the idea of rebuilding France's New World Empire and instead concentrate on Europe — he sold the entire French claim in North America to the young country that had won its independence from France's archenemy only twenty years earlier. The Louisiana Purchase was by far the largest territorial gain in U.S. history and doubled the size of the country, encompassing (part of) fifteen present-day U.S. states.[26]

As for South America, Napoleon's invasion and subsequent occupation of Spain in 1808 brought *de facto* autonomy to the Spanish colonies there, igniting a spark that would lead to a host of revolutionary wars between 1808-33, through which Argentine, Chile, Peru, Bolivia, Ecuador, Colombia, Venezuela and Mexico all won their independence.

In Europe the old order of things had also been shaken up, most notably in the German and Italian region, where Napoleon had reorganized numerous kingdoms, duchies and principalities into larger entities, thus laying the foundation for a later wave of nationalism from which two new nations would ultimately emerge, one of whom would have a particularly strong influence on some of the most deadly and disturbing events of the turbulent 20th century.

But that's something for another theme park.

---

1 Translated from French and quoted in Stewart, *A Documentary Survey of the French Revolution* (473).

2 In *The Incidence of Terror during the French Revolution: a statistical interpretation*, Donald Greer writes there were 16,594 official death sentences carried out during the Reign of Terror, between September 1793 and July 1794, but that the total death toll would likely rise to 35,000-40,000 if those who died in prison or were summarily executed are included (Greer, 37-38). Greer put the total number of political prisoners during the Reign of Terror at perhaps 500,000 (Greer, 29). Given the conditions in French prisons at the time, his total number of deaths from imprisonment and execution without trial seems on the conservative side. For a discussion of death toll estimates in different French regions, see Greer 25-37.

3 The Law of 20 May 1802 revoked an earlier law that had abolished slavery in all French colonies.

4 The so-called Declaration of Pillnitz, named after Pillnitz Castle, where Frederick William II and Leopold II issued their united call to arms.

5 In the period following the storming of the Bastille on July 14, 1789, Louis XVI had already been largely stripped of his powers, remaining king in name only. He subsequently sealed his fate with a botched escape attempt to Austria — his wife Marie-Antoinette's home country — in June 1791. Louis XVI was officially deposed on September 21, 1792, but by then he had already been arrested and sent to the Temple, a medieval fortress in Paris.

6 *Vom Kriege* (On War), Carl von Clausewitz, 1832. *Der Totale Krieg* (The Total War), Erich Friedrich Wilhelm Ludendorff, 1935.

7 Napoleon graduated from the *École Militaire* in 1785, after one year instead of the customary two. Just turned sixteen, he was one of the youngest officers in France and the only Corsican lieutenant of artillery (Englund, 23).

8 One key connection was fellow Corsican Antoine Saliceti, representative at the National Convention and former Corsican proconsul. Saliceti also introduced Napoleon to Augustin Robespierre, brother of Maximilien Robespierre, the leader of the Jacobin faction, which controlled the Republican government during the Reign of Terror of 1793-94 (Englund, 63, 67).

9 The rebellion is known as *13 Vendémiaire*, named after the first month in the

French Republican calendar. The date corresponds with October 5, 1795 in the Gregorian calendar.

10 The *Directoire* would be the French government from November 1795 until November 1799.

11 The Scottish historian Thomas Carlyle would later say that Napoleon had quelled the rebellion with a "*whiff of grapeshot*" (Carlyle, 892). The phrase is sometimes (incorrectly) attributed to Napoleon himself.

12 The idea was to send an army from the Egyptian city of Suez to link up with the forces of Tipu Sultan, the ruler of Mysore, a kingdom in southern India (Roberts, "Long Duel", 18-19). As Napoleon had noted a decade earlier: "*Through Egypt we shall invade India, we shall reestablish the old route through Suez, and cause the route by the Cape of Good Hope to be abandoned.*" (qtd. in Roberts, "Long Duel", 18-19).

13 Though the French occupied Egypt for only three years, it would have a considerable impact on the country. Apart from his soldiers, Napoleon had also brought a small army of scientists with him — mathematicians, historians, archeologists, naturalists, chemists — who not only learned a lot about Egypt's rich history but also infused the Middle Eastern region with knowledge from the modern world.

14 Around 1800, the Habsburg Empire was a composite monarchy, made up of several countries and provinces located mostly in Central and Eastern Europe, ruled by the same monarch, the Holy Roman Emperor, from the House of Habsburg. The Habsburg Empire would be replaced by the Austrian Empire in 1806, in the aftermath of the disastrous defeat at the Battle of Austerlitz (1805), after which Napoleon reorganized most of the Habsburg Empire's German possessions into the Confederation of the Rhine, a collection of French client states.

15 One of the coalition powers that received millions of pounds in British subsidies was Russia, which, between 1812-15 was paid a grand total of more than £6.8 million (Hartley, 77).

16 One such blunder was the execution of Louis Antoine de Bourbon, Duke of Enghien, on March 21, 1804, after he had been falsely implemented in a royalist conspiracy. Being a member of the House of Bourbon and a royalist who had fought against the French Republic, Napoleon considered the Duke a potential danger to the stability of his government (Burke, 158-61). The young Duke's death shocked the European aristocracy. Sweden cut off diplomatic relations with France after the incident. Another provocative move by Napoleon was letting himself be crowned king of Italy in May 1805, which ticked off the Austrians, who considered Northern Italy within their traditional sphere of influence.

17 "*Spanish ulcer*" was another, not so flattering moniker Napoleon used for the Peninsular War (Rose, 173).

326 - J.C. PETERS

18 The Fabian strategy is named after Roman dictator Fabius Maximus, who, against Hannibal Barca and his Carthaginian army, which invaded the Italian peninsula in 218 BCE, deployed a strategy of avoiding large, pitched battles while constantly harassing the enemy through small skirmishes.

19 Armand de Gaulaincourt was a general in Napoleon's army who accompanied him on his Russian campaign as Officer of Horse, meaning he was in charge of the horses of Napoleon and his guard. Gaulaincourt was still working on his memoirs when he died. The work was lost but eventually rediscovered after World War I and published for the first time in 1935.

20 Of the 612,000 combatants, 100,000 were killed in battle, 200,000 died of hunger, exhaustion, cold, or disease, 100,000 were captured, 50,000 ended up in hospitals and another 50,000 deserted. Of the 68,000 non-combatants, about half perished while the other half deserted (Bodart, 127).

21 The French suffered 73,000 casualties and the allies 54,000 at Leipzig (Chandler, 1120). The Germans dubbed the battle *Die Völkerschlacht,* which somehow sounds more honest than the English 'Battle of the Nations'; perhaps because the German word 'Schlacht' can mean battle as well as slaughter.

22 The Buonapartes had emigrated to Corsica in the 16th century.

23 Article III of the Treaty of Fontainebleau (April 11, 1814): "*The Isle of Elba, adopted by his majesty the Emperor Napoleon as the place of his residence, shall form, during his life, a separate principality, which shall be possessed by him in all sovereignty and property.*" (qtd. in Kelly, 752).

24 Of course, since Wellington was the one who eventually defeated Napoleon, praising Napoleon for being the greatest soldier ever to have walked the face of the earth made him the soldier who had bested the greatest soldier who had ever walked the face of the earth....

25 As Napoleon correctly predicted to Charles Montholon, one of his former generals who had accompanied him to Saint Helena and stayed with him until the end: "*My true glory is not to have won forty battles....Waterloo will erase the memory of so many victories....But what nothing will destroy, what will live forever, is my Civil Code.*" ("Ma gloire n'est pas d'avoir gagné quarante batailles....Waterloo effacera le souvenir de tant de victoires....Mais ce que rien ne'effacera, ce qui vivra éternellement, c'est mon code civil.") (qtd. in Montholon, 401).

26 The Louisiana Purchase Treaty was signed in Paris on April 30, 1803. Formal ownership was transferred to the United States on March 10, 1804.

31

THE INDUSTRIAL REVOLUTION

*"We have not made the Revolution,
the Revolution has made us."*
Georg Büchner (1813-1837), *Dantons Tod*, Act II. 1835.

On May 5, 2013, open-source organization Defense Distributed made files for the world's first fully 3D printable gun publicly available. The gun, a .380 single shot pistol aptly named the *Liberator*, was entirely made out of plastic except for the firing pin, and thus undetectable by metal detectors.[1]

The design for the Liberator was downloaded more than 100,000 times in the first two days (Ernesto, "Pirate Bay"). On May 9, the United States Department of State requested Defense Distributed to remove the download links from its site. The organization complied, but by then the files were already available through a host of other online sources, including the notoriously libertarian torrent site The Pirate Bay, which refused to take links to the files down, stating: *"TPB* [The Pirate Bay] *has close to 10 years been operating without taking down one single torrent due to pressure from the outside. And it will never start doing that."* (qtd. in Ernesto, "Pirate Bay").

The printable gun quickly became world news, introducing many people to the practical applications of 3D printing for the first time. And with prices of 3D printers having come down sharply — the cheapest 3D printers start at just a few hundred dollars, down from over thousands just a few years ago — many people could now for the first time easily afford to 3D print their own teapots, shoes, jewelry, Star Wars action figures and, well, guns.

The main reason for the huge price drop was the expiration of key patents for one of the more primitive forms of 3D printing, so-called *Fused Deposition Modeling*, in 2009 (Hornick, "3D Printing Patents"). In early 2014, several key patents for a more advanced form of 3D printing also expired, and a few months after that the world's largest 2D printing company, HP, announced the imminent launch of its first 3D printer, which it said would be ten times faster than anything else on the market (Krassenstein, "HP's Multi Jet Fusion").

Something similar happened with the 18th century steam engine, first with the Newcomen steam engine — invented by Thomas Newcomen in 1712 — and later also with the famous steam engine of Scottish inventor James Watt, for which the key patents expired at the beginning of the 19th century.

Watt had originally come up with the idea for a better steam engine in 1765, while repairing a small Newcomen steam engine, which he found wasted most of its energy because heating and cooling both took place inside the piston cylinder. Four years later, the patent containing his solution — Patent 913, *A method of lessening the consumption of steam in steam engines through a separate condenser* — was granted (Hills, "James Watt", 13). Through an act of Parliament, Watt then succeeded in extending this patent until the year 1800. In other words, for 30 years no one but

James Watt had the right to improve steam engines that used a separate condenser chamber (Osborne, 121-22).

Between 1776, when the first Watt engines were installed, and 1800, when Watt's patent expired, steam engines added about 750 horsepower to the United Kingdom's factories each year. During the 30 years following the patent's expiration this increased to about 4,000 per year (Boldrin, 1). Power and fuel efficiency also rapidly increased in the years after Watt's patent had expired (Boldrin, 1).[2]

Still, Watt's steam engine was a major improvement from the Newcomen engine, providing roughly three times more power with the same amount of fuel (Enys, 449ff.).[3] And it arrived at just the right time too, as the British textile industry was being revolutionized by a handful of game-changing inventions in the 1760s-70s, propelling it from a cottage industry — in which families spun yarn at home and sold it independently to weavers — to one of mass production, where factories filled with automated machines did the work of a thousand manual spinners and weavers.

It was the beginning of the Industrial Revolution.

In 1733, the Englishman John Kay had invented the so-called flying shuttle, a small device that not only enabled weavers to weave twice as fast but also only made the work a lot easier and physically less demanding. Nice for the weavers, but not so much for the spinners, who were already struggling to keep up with the ever increasing demand for yarn. This imbalance between weavers and spinners went on for 30 years, until one James Hargreaves in the 1760s invented the spinning jenny, a spinning frame that used eight spindles instead of one (Espinasse, 324). Hargreaves used the machine to produce yarn himself and also sold some machines to others in Blackburn, where he lived. When, consequently, the price of yarn in the region dropped, angry spinners broke into Hargreaves' house and destroyed his machines (Espinasse, 324). Hargreaves then set up shop in Nottingham, started a textile business and in 1770 patented a sixteen spindle spinning jenny (Espinasse, 324-25).

He wasn't the only one trying to improve spinning productivity though. In fact, one year earlier, English entrepreneur Richard Arkwright had patented the spinning frame (a.k.a. water frame), which, powered by a waterwheel, could operate automatically and continuously, spinning cotton from multiple spindles into yarn without end. The spinning frame produced stronger yarn than that of a spinning jenny and needed less skilled labor to operate.

And Arkwright did not stop there. In 1771, realizing the potential of the spinning frame, he built a water-powered cotton spinning mill — the world's first — in Cromford, Derbyshire, with the backing of a few other investors (Fitton, 65). Once opened, the mill was in production day and night. Arkwright started with 200 workers, and when he couldn't find enough workers in the local area, he built an entire village around the mill to encourage families to come to Cromford and work for him (Fitton, 97-99). Apart from houses, the village had a church, chapel, inn and a manager's mansion.

By 1776, the Cromford mill employed 500 workers, men, women and children, working twelve- hour shifts (Fitton, 98-99). When Arkwright, sometimes called the 'father of the industrial revolution', died in 1792, aged 59, he was the wealthiest untitled man in England.

After Arkwright's patent had expired, others quickly copied the water frame and opened spinning mills too, further increasing the

330 - J.C. Peters

supply of yarn. Now it was the weavers who had trouble keeping up, clearing the path for Edmund Cartwright's 1785 invention of the power loom, a steam-powered, mechanically operated version of the regular loom. The power loom needed significant improvement by several other inventors in later years, but it did eventually bring back the balance between weavers and spinners. By 1833, there were 100,000 power looms in the UK alone, up from just 2,400 in 1803 (Hills, "Power from Steam", 117). The weavers themselves were less than happy with the introduction of the power loom; fearing loss of work, they allegedly even burned down one of Cartwright's two factories (Strickland, 107-08). But although demand for skilled hand weavers indeed decreased because of the power loom, overall employment actually *increased* over the longer term, as the falling price of cloth continuously increased demand for it.

Meanwhile, the productivity race between weavers and spinners also increased pressure on the cotton industry. Cotton picking was very labor-intensive, because it had to be picked and separated from the seeds by hand. Enter the cotton gin, an inexpensive mechanical device invented by the American Eli Whitney in 1793. The cotton gin was a simple but ingenious contraption, consisting of a spiked wooden cylinder with a roller on top to put pressure on the cotton and pull it through a teethed grid, catching the seeds while forcing the cotton through. An inexpensive little machine, but one that would have enormous consequences.

In the American South, the cotton gin enabled a slave to produce about fifty pounds of cotton lint per day, whereas manual separation netted only about one to two pounds a day (Jacobson, 46). Suddenly, cotton production was a very profitable venture, and with spinning and weaving factories springing up left and right, plantation owners certainly did not have to worry about demand. Coincidentally, the first waterwheel-powered cotton mill in the United States was also opened in 1793, by the Englishman Samuel Slater. Born in Derbyshire in 1768, not far from where Richard Arkwright would build his cotton mill a few years later, Slater had come to the New World after having learned everything there was to know about weaving and spinning mills as an apprentice of Jedidiah Strutt, a partner of Arkwright (Caranci, 35-37).

Fearful of exporting information about designs and processes used in the textile industry to its commercial rivals, Britain had enacted a law that forbade textile workers to emigrate, but disguised as a farm hand Slater had nevertheless made it to America (Caranci, 36).[4]

Needless to say, cotton production exploded throughout the South. Between 1820-50, cotton production in the United States went from 335,000 500-pound bales to 2,136,000 500-pound bales per year ("Statistical Abstract " 1937, 636). By 1860, it was 3,841,000 bales per year. Thus, in just a few decades, the United States became by far the largest supplier of cotton in the world.

With 'King Cotton' making plantation owners richer every year, it is hardly surprising that the number of slave states also increased, from six to fifteen between 1790-1860.[5] The same goes for the number of slaves in the cotton states, which more than tripled between 1820-50, from 632,000 to 1,979,000 (Mann, 53).[6] With these kind of numbers, it is hard to overestimate the impact of Whitney's cotton gin on the economy of the South, the institution of slavery and, ultimately, the outbreak of the American Civil War.

Of course the tremendous increase in cotton production boosted the demand for more cotton spinning, weaving and carding machines as well. Factory owners also began to look for machines with increased durability, ones that used metal instead of wooden parts for instance. This in turn led to a growing demand for all kinds of metalworking (machine) tools, such as the lathe, and an unprecedented increase in demand for iron and smelting furnaces.

Initially, the furnaces were stoked with charcoal, but by the 1750s coke was replacing charcoal because it was cheaper, easier to make and allowed for larger blast furnaces.[7] During the second part of the 18th century and the early 19th century several improvements to the process of ironmaking further boosted the use of iron in machinery. The rolling mill (1783) greatly increased the speed of production for instance, by rolling instead of hammering iron flat, while the puddling process (1784) improved the quality of iron by stirring it and the hot blast (1828) increased fuel efficiency by preheating the air that was blown into the blast furnace.[8]

Now, to power all those furnaces and steam engines, an awful lot of coal needed to be mined and transported, and the fact that there was so many of it readily available in Great Britain is one of the reasons why the Industrial Revolution not only started there but continued to gain traction. Why so many canals were dug in Britain and why both the inventor of the first locomotive, Richard Trevithick, and the location of the first public railway using steam locomotives, the Stockton & Darlington Railway, were British.[9]

So, where had the revered Renaissance, the smart Scientific Revolution and the eloquent Age of Enlightenment eventually led us, having taught us to focus on the here and now, on making things of beauty, on acquiring and spreading knowledge and education, and on pursuing life, liberty and happiness? The answer for 19th century socialist philosophers Karl Marx and Friedrich Engels was that it had led to whole families having to work 12-hour shifts in a damp factory for wages that were barely enough to stave of starvation. They foresaw a class struggle between workers and the owners of the means to production (i.e., the 'capitalists'), which they predicted would eventually lead to a revolution in which the workers would take ownership of the factories.[10]

A less pessimistic view is that while factory conditions may have led to a decline in quality of life for those at the lowest rungs of society during the early stages of the Industrial Revolution, real wages, life expectancy and social conditions were all improving in several Western countries by the second part of the 19th century, especially when compared to the malnourished, short, subservient, miserable life that most had been destined to lead before the dawn of the industrial age.

Several studies have shown that the standard of living and real wages hardly increased between 1800 BCE and 1800 CE, because the extra resources won from technological advances always went to an increased population, not to a better life for those already living.[11] This observation — now known as the Malthusian trap — was first made by political economist Thomas Malthus, in 1798. In *An Essay on the Principle of Population*, Malthus observed *"That population does invariably increase when the means of subsistence increase. And, That the superior power of population is repressed, and the actual population kept equal to the means of subsistence, by misery and vice."* (Malthus, VII.21). Due to this inescapable relation between the growth of resources and population, Malthus concluded, *"Man cannot live in the midst of plenty."* (Malthus, X.7).[12]

During the Industrial Revolution, however, societies were finally able to escape the Malthusian trap. Malthus had therefore, somewhat ironically, formulated a theory correctly explaining a phenomenon that had existed for millennia — just before it ran out of steam for the first time in history.

The Industrial Revolution certainly made the economic struggle at the bottom more visible though. Families who used to spin or weave days on end in their ill-lit, damp little cottages, were now doing so in Mr. Arkwright's cotton mills, together with hundreds of other families. Wages, work hours, working conditions, child labor, everything was suddenly much more in the open. Factory conditions left much to be desired of course, but it was also because of these factories that for the first time effective labor regulation became even possible. As a result — and a sign of things to come — the first Factory Act was passed in 1802, in Great Britain.[13]

Throughout the 19th and early 20th century, industrialized countries passed several other laws that sought to improve the position of the workers. These laws were one of the reasons why the catastrophe Marx and Engels had predicted never really materialized. Even if their reasoning — that capitalism would inevitably lead to class struggle, followed by its destruction and replacement with socialism — would be correct for a completely free, unregulated market, outcomes were markedly different when the state and/or labor unions stepped in to smooth over the imperfections of the system. Of course, improving the position of the workers also increased domestic demand for all those products that were being cranked out day and night by the factories, making factory owners even richer.

Another effect of the Industrial Revolution was a massive urbanization wave. With factories hungry for more workers and people in rural areas hungry for work, cities quickly became magnets for job seekers, startup entrepreneurs and established factory owners alike. And so, while about 6 percent of the world's population lived in cities in 1800, by 2009, for the first time in history, over 50 percent did ("World Urbanization Prospects"; Vries, 71).[14]

Of course the social dynamics of city life are vastly different from those in rural areas. Ideas, unrest and rebellion spread much faster in cities housing millions of people than in a countryside dotted with farms and small villages, which is likely one of the reasons why the 19th and 20th century would see more than their fair share of revolutions, rebellions, civil wars and social movements. In terms of significance to our economic development and general way of life, the Industrial Revolution certainly ranks at the same level as the Neolithic Revolution that took place some 12,000 years ago. Back then, the paradigm shift in our way of life was going from hunting and gathering to farming; making a home, keeping animals, growing crop. From then on, we built not just on the experiences of our forefathers, but on their achievements as well.

Similarly, the Industrial Revolution put us on an entirely new path of highly specialized labor, ever growing urbanization and global interdependency. Most of us no longer know how to milk a cow or make a table and chairs. Truth be told, in the eyes of Neolithic man, we are utterly helpless and mostly useless. Yet we have more food, more leisure time, more freedom and a higher life expectancy than ever before.

Interestingly enough, 3D printing could mean a high-tech return to the time before the Industrial Revolution. Instead of letting factories stamp out millions of more and the same (only with a different color) we could design and create our own, unique products again, repair stuff instead of having to throw something away because of a broken part that cost only $2.50 to make but is sold for $50. In other words, for the first time in 200 years we could become our own, independent producers again.

Or have we already forgotten how to?

---

1   A 6-ounce steel slug was also added by Defense Distributed, but this only to comply with the Undetectable Firearms Act of 1998; the gun would also work without the slug.

2   Boldrin and Levine estimate that the fuel efficiency increased by a factor five between 1810-35. Data for this estimate comes from Nuvolari (2004b).

3   The Newcomen and Watt engines data can be found in Enys, 457-58.

4   In the United States, Samuel Slater is known as the father of the American Industrial Revolution. By contrast, in the United Kingdom he is known as 'Slater the Traitor' (Caranci, 35).

5   In the years leading up to the American Civil War, the term 'King Cotton' was frequently used in the Southern States to express the economic and political importance of the cotton industry.

6   North-Carolina and Texas are excluded from the data Mann used.

7   Charcoal is most often made from burning wood slowly, while coke is a by-product from coal.

8   Both puddling and the rolling mill are attributed to Henry Cort (1740-1800), though both methods already existed in rudimentary form before Cort was awarded his patents in 1784. Cort's innovation lay in combining the improvements from these rudimentary methods into a single, new process, not unlike what Gutenberg had done when he combined movable type and block printing into a mechanized process with his printing press (Ashton, 93).

9   In its first successful test run, Trevithick's steam engine carriage, the 'puffing-devil', carried six passengers up Camborne hill on Christmas Eve 1801. The Stockton & Darlington Railway opened in 1825.

10 The views of Marx and Engels would indeed lead to revolutions in several countries in the 20th century, but none of them would progress the way they had predicted. See also chapter 8, *The Russian Revolution(s)*, chapter 12, *Chinese Civil War Part I & II*, chapter 20, *The Cultural Revolution*, and chapter 21, *The End of Communism*.

11 See for instance Robert C. Allen, *The Great Divergence in European Wages and Prices from the Middle Ages to the First World War,* and Gregory Clark, *A Farewell to Alms: A Brief Economic History of the World,* particularly chapter two.

12 For a thorough explanation of the Malthusian trap, see *Dynamics and Stagnation in the Malthusian Epoch,* by Quamrul Ashraf and Oded Galor.

13 The *Health and Morals of Apprentices Act 1802*. It regulated the treatment of apprentices (mostly children) by cotton mill owners and set cleanliness requirements for factories.

14 De Vries convincingly rejects the frequently cited assertion that only 3 percent of the world's population lived in cities around 1800, asserting that the global urbanization rate at the time was likely more than double that number (Vries, 69ff). Based on city population numbers, he further estimates that 10 percent of the European population lived in cities of 10,000 and above in 1800, an urbanization rate that climbs to 15 percent when looking at cities of 5,000 and above (Vries, 71-73).

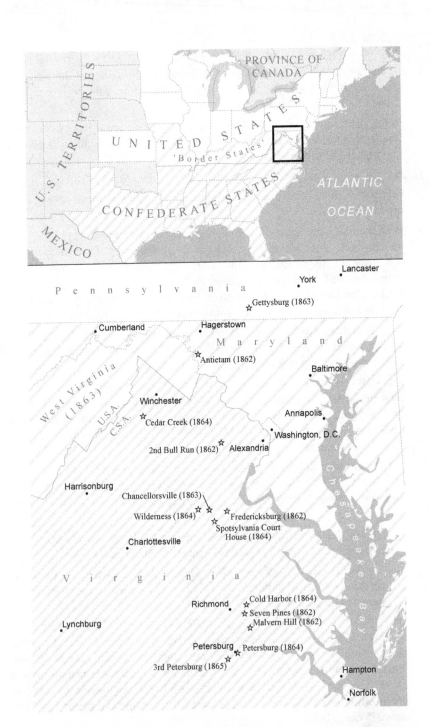

Map 16: The Eastern Theater of the American Civil War,
1861-65

32

A SECOND AMERICAN REVOLUTION

*"Fourscore and seven years ago our fathers
brought forth on this continent, a new nation,
conceived in liberty, and dedicated to the proposition
that all men are created equal. Now we are engaged in a
great civil war, testing whether that nation, or any nation
so conceived and so dedicated, can long endure. We are
met on a great battlefield of that war. We have come to
dedicate a portion of that field, as a final resting-place
for those who here gave their lives that that nation might
live. It is altogether fitting and proper that we should
do this. But, in a larger sense, we cannot dedicate —we
cannot consecrate — we cannot hallow — this ground.
The brave men, living and dead, who struggled here,
have consecrated it, far above our poor power to add or
detract. The world will little note, nor long remember what
we say here, but it can never forget what they did here.
It is for us the living, rather, to be dedicated here to the
unfinished work which they who fought here have thus far
so nobly advanced. It is rather for us to be here dedicated
to the great task remaining before us — that from these
honored dead we take increased devotion to that cause for
which they gave the last full measure of devotion — that
we here highly resolve that these dead shall not have died
in vain, that this nation, under God, shall have a new birth
of freedom — and that government of the people, by the
people, for the people, shall not perish from the earth."*

Abraham Lincoln, Gettysburg Address
(Bliss copy), November 19, 1863

In 1864, Elias Brewster Hillard interviewed the last survivor of the American Revolutionary War, which had ended 81 years earlier. Lemuel Cook, born in Litchfield County, Connecticut — back when it was still part of the British Empire — had been only sixteen years old when he joined the 2nd Regiment of Light Dragoons (Hillard, 34).

Cook saw action in several engagements throughout the war and was present at the decisive Battle of Yorktown, where Lord Cornwallis surrendered (Hillard, 36). He also met and spoke a few words with General Washington in the fall of 1776, near White Plains, while the Continental Army was in retreat, and again a couple of years later, when Washington — apparently remembering him — called him by his name and asked him about his horse (Cook, "Lemuel Remembers"). On June 12, 1784, Cook saw Washington one last time, when he received his honorable discharge, signed by the general himself (Hillard, 33; Cook, "Lemuel Remembers").

When Hillard asked him about his thoughts on the *"present war"*, Cook brought down his cane on the floor with force and replied in strong tone: "*It is terrible, but terrible as it is the rebellion must be put down.*" (Hillard, 38).[1]

Of course a British centenarian who, as a sixteen-year-old, had supported the Parliamentarian cause during the Glorious Revolution of 1688, would have probably classified the American Revolution of 1776 as a rebellion too. It seems that the longer we live, the easier it is for history to catch up with us.

In any case, for the Southern States that seceded from the union in 1861, secession did not constitute a rebellion but the birth of a new nation, the Confederate States of America.[2] To them, Abraham Lincoln's victory in the presidential elections on November 6, 1860, had been the final straw. Lincoln had carried only two of the 996 counties in the Southern States, but he still won, because of his strong support in the North and West (Mansch, 61).

Lincoln had run on a moderate anti-slavery platform, objecting to its expansion into new territories but not calling for the end of slavery where it already existed (Jaffa, 74, 79). The expansion of slavery into new territories had been a hotly debated issue between the Northern and Southern States for decades though, for moral, legal, political and economic reasons.

From an economic viewpoint, not allowing slavery in the new territories would make it more difficult for Southern businesses to expand westward, since the South's economy was largely dependent on slavery. Politically, the effect of prohibiting slavery in new states was perhaps even more threatening to the Cotton States in the long run, as it would slowly but certainly erode the South's influence in Washington when new states joined the North in its anti-slavery position, thus swelling the ranks of the abolitionists until the South could no longer prevent Congress from ending slavery completely.

Slavery had been a divisive issue from the beginning. Even at the Constitutional Convention of 1787 slavery had been among the most controversial issues, complicating almost every debate, especially that about representation, with the Southern States wanting to fully include slaves in the population count while the Northern States only wanted to count free persons (Finkelman, 10ff.). The issue was directly linked to the plan of making population the primary criterium for representation in Congress, instead of giving each state one vote, as had been the case with the — ineffective — Articles of Confederation (Finkelman, 11). Eventually the Convention reached a compromise whereby slaves would be counted as three-fifths of a free person.[3]

In the years that followed the differences between North and South only deepened. Eli Whitney's invention of the cotton gin in 1793 made cotton production far more profitable and the need for cheap cotton pickers (i.e., slaves) only greater. Meanwhile, the Northern States, devoid of the easy riches of King Cotton, instead concentrated their economic efforts increasingly on industrialization, with a manufacturing industry based on the British model, fast-growing cities and an expanding network of railroads.

Industrialization was what caused seven out of eight European immigrants to settle in the North, looking for jobs in the many factories, and why many whites from the South moved to the North (McPherson, "Antebellum Southern Exceptionalism", 426-27). Industrialization also caused Northern States to demand higher import tariffs, to protect their businesses against foreign — especially British — competition, something the Southern States were adamantly against, wanting to protect their cotton export to Europe — especially Britain — and fearing British counter- protectionist policies.[4]

In 1820, the pro-slavery and anti-slavery factions had come to the so-called Missouri Compromise, which sought to regulate the expansion of slavery in the western territories by prohibiting it north of the parallel 36°30' north in the former Louisiana Territory, with the exception of the (proposed) state of Missouri. To keep an equal balance between 'slave states' and 'free states', the Northern region of Massachusetts was to be admitted as the free State of Maine. The compromise would indeed ensure a delicate balance between slave states and free states for the coming decades, but Thomas Jefferson, by then a senior citizen of 77 years old, predicted that the compromise line would eventually lead to the destruction of the Union, writing in a letter to John Holmes:

"But this momentous question, like a fire bell in the night, awakened and filled me with terror. I considered it at once as the knell of the Union. It is hushed indeed for the moment. but this is a reprieve only, not a final sentence. A geographical line, coinciding with a marked principle, moral and political, once conceived and held up to the angry passions of men, will never be obliterated; and every new irritation will mark it deeper and deeper." (Jefferson, "John Holmes").[5]

By 1850 another grand bargain had become necessary, to deal with the newly acquired territories resulting from the Mexican-American War (1846-48). The Compromise of 1850 admitted California as a free state in its entirety, instead of dividing it into a northern and southern part as the South had wanted. In exchange, the North agreed that no restrictions on slavery would be placed in the Utah and New Mexico Territory, leaving the question of slavery there to popular sovereignty. Also, slaveholding in Washington D.C. would be preserved but slave trade in the nation's capital was to be prohibited, and Texas surrendered its claims to parts of New Mexico in exchange for federal assumption of its debt.

Lastly, a stronger Fugitive Slave Law was passed, requiring federal judicial officials in all states and territories to actively assist in returning slaves to their masters or be fined $1,000 (Fugitive Slave Act, Sec. 5). Individuals were also strictly prohibited from aiding runaway slaves in any way, or face a prison sentence of up to six months and a fine of up to $1,000 (Fugitive Slave Act, Sec. 7). Many in the North were outraged over the Fugitive Slave Law, especially about the fact that it forced them to basically condone slavery in the North when confronted with runaway slaves from the South.

A few years later, the Supreme Court weighed in on the expansion of slavery in federal territories with its decision in Scott v. Sandford (1857). Dred Scott, an African-American slave, had sued for freedom for himself, his wife and their two daughters on the ground that they had lived with their master in states and territories where slavery was illegal.

But the Supreme Court decided 7-2 against Scott, stating that no person of African ancestry could claim citizenship in the United States and that federal restrictions to slavery in U.S. territories were unconstitutional, because they conflicted with the Fifth Amendment, protecting citizens from being deprived of their property without due process. In other words, slave owners would be deprived of their constitutional right to take certain "*articles of property*" into the territories should Congress be allowed to restrict slavery there (Scott v. Sandford, I.6, IV.3).

In deciding whether African Americans could be considered citizens, Chief Justice Taney harked back to the time of the Declaration of Independence to determine if, at the time, "*the class of persons who had been imported as slaves [or] their descendants, whether they had become free or not, were then acknowledged as a part of the people*" (Scott v. Sandford, 407). Taney held that they were not, stating:

"*It is difficult at this day to realize the state of public opinion in regard to that unfortunate race which prevailed in the civilized and enlightened portions of the world at the time of the Declaration of Independence, and when the Constitution of the United States was framed and adopted; but the public history of every European nation displays it in a manner too plain to be mistaken. They had for more than a century before been regarded as beings of an inferior order, and altogether unfit to associate with the white race, either in social or political relations, and so far unfit that they had no rights which the white man was bound to respect.*" (Scott v. Sandford, 407).

Scott v. Sandford thus nullified the Missouri Compromise (which prohibited slavery north of the parallel 36°30' north in the former Louisiana Territory), enraging the North and bringing the option of civil war as the ultimate way to settle the slavery issue once and for all considerably closer. That is to say, neither the South nor the North wanted war, but both sides had reached the limits of how far they were willing to compromise.

Moderate anti-slavery proponents like Abraham Lincoln thought it a reasonable compromise to let slavery die out over time, to give the South time to adjust. But most Southerners felt no inclination to change at all. They began to realize that staying in the Union would be detrimental to their way of life in the long run, because abolitionists would likely continue to make inroads in Washington. So when Lincoln was elected in November 1860 without virtually any support in the South, the states of South Carolina, Mississippi, Florida, Alabama, Georgia, Louisiana and Texas saw the writing on the wall and decided to secede from the Union, forming the Confederate States of America (CSA) on February 8, 1861. Federal courthouses, forts and armories in the seceding states were seized left and right, while governors of decidedly pro-union states like New York, Pennsylvania and Massachusetts began to organize militarily as well, preparing for what at this point seemed an inevitable, violent clash between North and South (Keegan, 33; Schouler, 42ff.). Two months later, after President Lincoln called for troops to defend the Union in response to the Confederate attack on Fort Sumter (a union stronghold in Charleston Harbor, Charleston, South Carolina), Virginia, Arkansas, Tennessee and North Carolina seceded from the Union as well and joined the CSA.

The Southern States argued that the Union was a compact that states could abandon without consultation. The Northern states opposed this view, reasoning instead that the Union was perpetual and that abandoning it was not an option.

From a legal point of view, the idea of a 'perpetual union' is of course questionable at best. For one, the United States itself is founded on the principle that a tyrannical government can be a just cause for revolution, as can the absence of representation in government. To the

Southern States, the fact that a man could be elected President even when almost the entire South voted against him, must have looked an awful lot like the absence of representation. And if all the new states were to be free states, how long before the abolitionists would have a qualified majority in Congress, allowing them to change the Constitution and end slavery?

Other arguments against the idea of a 'perpetual union' are that it goes against the right of self- determination — implied in John Locke's social contract theory of *government with the consent of the governed* and later also championed by U.S. Presidents Woodrow Wilson and Franklin D. Roosevelt — and that it is too inflexible a concept to deal with fundamental changes in political relations, views and realities.[6]

The first shots of the American Civil War were fired on January 9, 1861, when civilian steamship *Star of the West*, hired by the United States government to resupply Fort Sumter, was fired upon by South Carolina forces after passing the mouth of the harbor. The commander of the battery on Morris Island, Major Stevens, fired a shot across her bow, but instead of turning around, the steamship defiantly ran up the United States flag at her foremast a few minutes later (Harris, 23-24). Major Stevens then ordered several more rounds fired, two of which struck the ship, after which the ship did turn. Three more shots were fired from both Morris Island and Fort Moultrie, hitting the ship once more on its way out.

The shots did not mark the official start of the war but they might as well have. What followed was three months of increasing tension, during which the Union soldiers of Fort Sumter rushed to complete the installation of additional guns, while the commander of the Confederate forces in Charleston, General P. G. T. Beauregard, trained an increasing number of guns at the isolated fort. Unlike his predecessor James Buchanan, Lincoln did not want any more federal forts relinquished to the South. So as soon as he was sworn in, on March 4, 1861, Lincoln ordered Fort Sumter's commander, Major Robert Anderson, to hold until fired upon. This way, if there really was to be civil war, it would be the South who was the aggressor, not the North.

On April 4, Lincoln ordered a relief expedition to supply Fort Sumter, but with provisions only. Two days later, Major Anderson informed South Carolina Governor Francis W. Pickens that *"I am directed by the President of the United States to notify you to expect an attempt will be made to supply Fort Sumter with provisions only, and that if such attempt be not resisted, no effort to throw in men, arms, or ammunition will be made without further notice, or in case of an attack on the fort."* (qtd. in Keegan, 34). It was a very smart move on Lincoln's part, both strategically and tactically. It left the door open for a peaceful resolution without giving anything away, while at the same time putting the ball in the South's court indefinitely, because if — and for as long as — the South allowed the fort to be supplied with provisions only, the garrison could also hold out indefinitely.

But Jefferson Davis, who had just been inaugurated as President of the Confederate States of America (on February 18, 1861) chose door number two, deciding not to allow Fort Sumter to be resupplied in any way. He ordered general Beauregard to demand the Fort's immediate surrender and reduce it if Major Anderson did not comply. When Anderson tried to stall for time, offering to surrender the fort if the supplies had not yet arrived by April 15, Beauregard's aide, Colonel Chesnut, replied to Anderson that this was not good enough and that fire would be opened in one hour lest the fort surrendered immediately (crawford, 424-26). No further communication came from the fort.

On 4.30 a.m, April 12, 1861, the Confederate bombardment commenced. Thirty-four hours and 4,000 Confederate shells later, Anderson surrendered the fort and subsequently evacuated by steamer to New York (Dougherty, 63). The American Civil War had begun.

Of course preparing for a war is very different from actually fighting a war. The mere act of marching in formation, forming a firing line and discharging a weapon, morphs into an entirely different beast when, at a distance of about 100 yards, an equal number of lined up men discharge their weapons in your general direction.[7] Moreover, most officers and soldiers from both sides had no battlefield experience whatsoever.

But many in the Northern States were impatient for results, thinking one swift victory on the battlefield would be enough to put an end to the rebellion. So when General Irvin McDowell, who would soon command the Northern forces in the first large-scale battle of the war, conveyed his reluctance to attack to the President, on account of his men still being very green, Lincoln replied: *"You are green, it is true, but they are green also; you are all green alike."* (qtd. in Eicher, "The Longest Night", 79).

The North's hope for a quick end to Southern sovereignty would soon be crushed though, as it was the Confederate army that won the first major battle, at Bull Run, near Manassas, Virginia (about 30 miles from Washington D.C.) on July 21, 1861, after General Beauregard's men successfully routed McDowell's Army of the Potomac, which had thought to mop up the Confederate army in a surprise flank attack. And less than a month later, on August 10, General Benjamin McCulloch's Confederate forces, aided by the Missouri State Guard, defeated General Nathaniel Lyon's Army of the West at the Battle of Wilson's Creek, near Springfield, Missouri.[8]

So there was to be no double-quick march to the Confederate capital of Richmond, Virginia for the Union army, though the North did not give up either, as many in the South had hoped would happen once the 'yankees' realized Southerners were willing to fight and die for their cause.

In March 1862, General George B. McClellan launched a major spring offensive in southeastern Virginia, with the ultimate aim of capturing Richmond. Moving northwest from Fort Monroe (at the southern tip of the Virginia Peninsula) McClellan forced General Joseph E. Johnston and his Army of Northern Virginia to retreat in the direction of Richmond. By the end of May, McClellan's forces were positioned to the northeast of the Confederate capital, straddling the Chickahominy River, with three corps north of the river (II, V and VI) and two corps (III and IV) south of the river. Johnston was a cautious man and had avoided giving battle during the past weeks, but he could not allow a massive Union army of more than 100,000 men to remain nestled in so close to the capital. On May 31, he launched a large-scale attack against IV Corps, positioned south of the river and closest to Richmond. The plan was to first fully engage and defeat IV Corps, followed by a second attack, this time on III Corps, which by then would be isolated and vulnerable, its back against the river (Luebke, "Seven Pines"). Speed was key, lest III Corps and possibly also the three corps positioned across the river have time to reinforce the embattled IV Corps.

The plan was sound but the execution flawed. Though the front division of IV Corps was pushed back by Confederate forces, it was never fully engaged nor defeated. Moreover, during the day, elements from III Corps and II Corps moved to the front to stop the Confederate advance. Near nightfall, as the fighting petered out, Johnston took a bullet to the shoulder while inspecting the lines (Luebke, "Seven Pines"). Moments later, he was also hit in the chest and thigh by fragments from a Union artillery shell.[9]

The fighting continued the next day, June 1, but after failing to make much headway, the Confederates called it a day before the morning was out. The Union forces settled into their positions as well (Luebke, "Seven Pines"). The Battle of Seven Pines thus ended inconclusively, though it could also be called a tactical defeat for the Confederates, since they had not succeeded in expelling IV and III Corps. Then again, a few hours after the battle, Confederate President Jefferson Davis appointed General Robert E. Lee as the new commander of the Army of the Northern Virginia, and he would prove to be much more of a menace to the Union Army than Johnston had ever been (or would be).

At 55, Lee had never before led an army in the field. Confederate public opinion was initially against him, fearing 'Granny Lee' would not be aggressive enough, but his early actions quickly showed this to be a fallacy.[10] Before the month was out, Lee had gone on the offensive, driving McClellan away from Richmond and into retreat in a series of six major battles fought within the space of just one week.[11] The son of major general Henry "Light-Horse-Harry" Lee III, who had served under general Washington during the American Revolutionary War, Robert E. Lee proved himself an inspirational commander and brilliant tactician, at a time when Lincoln was struggling to find a military commander capable of taking the initiative in the Eastern Theater.

Still, the biggest threat to the Confederacy was not the Union army but its own fragile economy, its lack of industrialization and resources.[12] And since the South's economy was largely dependent on the cotton export to Europe, the Union blockade of Southern ports established in the summer of 1861 inflicted considerable damage to the Confederate economy.

The South tried to end the blockade of course, most famously during the Battle of Hampton Roads (off the Virginia coast) on March 9, 1862, when the Confederate ironclad CSS Virginia — having already sunk two wooden Union ships the day before — got into a deadly battle with the Union ironclad USS Monitor. The fight raged on for hours, but neither ship was able to sink the other and the clash ended indecisively, although strategic victory should perhaps be awarded to the Union, since the outcome of the battle prevented the South from ending the blockade.[13]

Another Achilles heel of the South was its lack of resources relative to the North. In 1860, the North had a population of 22 million vs. 9 million in the South (of which about 3.5 million were slaves), it counted 22,000 miles of railroad vs. 9,000 miles in the Confederate states, 800,000 draft animals such as cattle and horses vs. 300,000 in the Confederacy, 93 percent of the nation's pig iron production, 97 percent of its firearms production and more than 80 percent of the national bank deposits (Gallagher, 37).[14]

All things considered, the only two ways the South could hope to win its independence was either the North giving up — for instance because public opinion turned against the war, a scenario that became more likely as the conflict dragged on and its death toll increased — or others, most likely the British or the French, coming to its aid. Both Britain and France were in fact sympathetic to the Confederate cause, but not so sympathetic as to risk war with the Union for it, at least not so long as it appeared the Union might win. In that respect, the Union victory at Antietam on September 17, 1862 — the bloodiest day in U.S. military history — proved highly important.[15] The battle itself was inconclusive in that General McClellan only succeeded in halting Lee's advancement in Maryland, while also losing more men than the popular Confederate general even though he outnumbered him two to one, but it was enough of a victory for Lincoln to announce the Emancipation Proclamation five days later, on September 22, 1862.

The Proclamation was an executive order proclaiming the freedom of slaves in the ten states that were still in rebellion, effective January 1, 1863.[16] It made ending slavery a primary and explicit goal for the Union, further dissuading Britain and France from direct involvement on the Confederate side, as they had already abolished slavery and public opinion in both countries was adamantly against it.

In the summer of 1863 the Union dealt the Confederacy two decisive blows on the battlefield. First, at the Battle of Gettysburg (July 1-3), General George Meade's Army of the Potomac defeated Lee's Army of Northern Virginia. The bloodiest battle of the war, with a combined total of more than 45,000 casualties, Gettysburg ended Lee's second invasion of the North, though Meade failed to prevent Lee from retreating with his army over the Potomac, lengthening the war by another two years (Sears, "Gettysburg", 513).

One day later, on July 4, after a siege of six weeks, General John C. Pemberton and his Army of Mississippi surrendered to General Ulysses S. Grant at Vicksburg, an important fortress city that controlled the Confederate section of the Mississippi River. Grant's victory gave the Union command over the entire Mississippi, effectively splitting the Confederacy in two for the rest of the war.

Because Meade had failed to prevent Lee from retreating, Lincoln replaced him with Grant, who soon decided that since the North had far more resources, the best way to defeat the South was by fighting a war of attrition. Throughout 1864-65 Grant therefore fought several bloody battles with Lee, basically wherever he could force him to fight.

During the Overland Campaign (a.k.a Wilderness Campaign) of May-June 1864, Grant forced Lee into a series of battles in Virginia by threatening to position his Army of the Potomac between Richmond and Lee's Army of Northern Virginia. Union forces suffered more than 50,000 casualties in just 30 days as a result— earning Grant the unflattering nickname "the Butcher" in the North — but Lee's army also suffered more than 32,000 casualties (Bonekemper, 190). And unlike Grant, Lee could not replace his losses. *Grant*ed, it was not a very sophisticated strategy, but effective nonetheless.

After a series of maneuvers in the direction of the Confederate capital, Grant besieged Richmond and nearby Petersburg, the main supply center for Richmond and the rest of the region. Lee knew he would not be able to hold on to Richmond if Petersburg fell and was therefore forced to defend both. Over the course of several months, Grant constructed 30 miles of trench lines, spanning from Richmond to Petersburg, in an attempt to cut off the railroad supply lines to the Confederate capital. Numerous raids against the Southern railroads in the area put ever greater strain on Lee's dwindling forces.

On March 25, 1865, after nine months of siege warfare, Lee made a last-ditch attempt to break the siege around Petersburg. It failed. Confederate defeat was imminent.

On April 1, Union forces captured the Five Forks road junction (west of Petersburg), key to control of the South Side Railroad, a vital supply line for Petersburg. Upon hearing of the victory, Grant ordered an all-out assault on several points of the Petersburg line to start in the early hours of the next day. At 10:00 pm, Union guns began a massive bombardment that lasted until 2:00 am (Bearss, 516). An eerie calm followed, as the Union infantry waited for the first light of day to start its assault on the Confederate lines.

At 4:40 am, April 2, General Horatio Wright ordered VI Corps to move forward towards the Boydton Plan Road line (Bearss, 534). On its right, IX Corps moved to attack the trenches around Fort Mahone, or as it was called by Union soldiers, "Fort Damnation" (Thompson, "Two Days in April"). The IX Corps assault started off well and several of the fort's batteries were taken, but in the maze of entrenchments within the fort the numerical advantage of the attackers soon disappeared, turning a rolling assault into ferocious and chaotic close quarters combat (Thompson, "Two Days in April"). As one North Carolinian later wrote about the fighting: "*I saw the men of my regiment load their guns behind the traverses, climb to the top, fire down into the ranks of the enemy, roll off and reload and repeat the same.*" (qtd. in Greene, 338).

Wright's VI Corps was more successful. Advancing in a massive wedge formation at the earliest whiff of dawn, the first Union soldiers soon reached the Confederate defenses. Nineteen year old Captain Charles G. Gould of the 5th Vermont Infantry was the first to leap into the enemy trenches (Greene, 222-23). A musket was immediately leveled at him at point-blank range, but misfired. It was a lucky escape, but the next moment he was bayoneted through his cheek and mouth by a North Carolinian, whom he in turn killed with his saber. A third Confederate slashed him with a sword, giving him a nasty head wound. A fourth then bayoneted him in the back, before he was being pulled back over the defensive works and into the ditch by one of his men. Others had followed in Gould's wake though, capturing the battery he had attacked, while the rest of the Vermont Brigade further expanded the breach.[17]

Upon hearing of the breach at Boydton Plank Road, Lee realized he had no choice but to retreat. Just before riding off, he sent a telegram to Confederate Secretary of War John C. Breckenridge, advising him *"that all preparation be made for leaving Richmond tonight."* (qtd. in Thompson, "Two Days in April"). Petersburg and Richmond were occupied by Union forces the next day.

Less than a week later, on April 9, Lee fought his last battle, at Appomattox Court House, some 100 miles west of Petersburg. It was to be a short battle though. Faced with overwhelming numbers of infantry and almost completely surrounded, Lee bowed to the inevitable and surrendered.

One month later, on May 9, 1865, President Andrew Johnson — plucked from Vice Presidential obscurity after Lincoln had been assassinated by Southern sympathizer John Wilkes Booth on April 14 — declared that the Civil War was over.[18] It was an anti-climactic end to a war that had cost the lives of more than 620,000 soldiers, roughly the same number as all American deaths in all other wars Americans have ever fought in (McPherson, "Battle Cry of Freedom", 751; Woodward, xix).[19]

The South was devastated. A quarter of its white male population of military age had been killed during the war, as had 40 percent of its livestock (McPherson, "Battle Cry of Freedom", 721). Much of the South's wealth had been concentrated in land and slaves, but the four million slaves (of which about 3,5 million were located in the Southern States) had been freed by the Thirteenth Amendment, and with no slaves to work the land, real estate prices plummeted.[20] Banks, railroad companies, plantations, many of them went under, never to resurface. Between 1860 and 1870, income per capita in the South dropped from close to 70 percent to less than 40 percent of that in the North, while its percentage of the national wealth declined from 30 percent to 12 percent (McPherson, "Battle Cry of Freedom", 721).

It would take a century before the former Confederate States were able to somewhat close the wealth gap with the Northern States, although as of 2013 almost all Southern States that fought on the side of the Confederacy still rank below the national average in median per capita income.[21]

The South's political influence in the Union also dissipated. Between 1789-1861, half of the U.S. Presidents had been from the South (serving a total of 49 years), all of them slaveholders, including the first U.S. President, George Washington.[22] After the war it would take a century before another Southerner — Lyndon B. Johnson — was elected President again.[23] Johnson hailed from Stonewall, Texas, established just a few years after the civil war and named after the famous Confederate general Thomas J. 'Stonewall' Jackson.[24]

The Confederate revolution had failed. America would gear up for the most violent century in the history of mankind as one nation, under god, indivisible. It is doubtful whether a Confederate States of America would also have been willing to send millions of troops and armadas full of equipment overseas to influence the outcome of violent conflict between European nations. Twice. If anything, the Confederate States mostly wanted to be left alone by the federal government and had little interest in the old world outside trade interests.[25]

Looking at how the United States fared under the Articles of Confederation — which the Confederacy closely resembled — Confederate States would most likely have retained a large part of their sovereignty, with very little interference from the federal government in taxes, tariffs, banking, infrastructure and everything else that was not absolutely necessary for a central government to deal with. Such a nation could likely scarcely defend itself, let alone influence the outcome of large-scale foreign wars such as World War I and World War II.

As for that other revolution, the emancipation of four million slaves, though it certainly had a profound impact on the South, it would take another 100 years before African Americans would be truly emancipated. That is not to say their position in society did not markedly improve in the decades after the war, because it did — real income, literacy, level of education, all of them rose significantly — but blacks continued to be discriminated. In that sense, the emancipation of minorities would remain an unfinished revolution until at least the African-American Civil Rights Movement of the 1950s and 60s.

In 1956, two years after the U.S. Supreme Court had ruled in Brown v. Board of Education that state laws establishing separate public schools for black and white students were unconstitutional, the last civil war veteran of the Union Army died, aged 109 (New York Times 1956).[26] Albert Henry Woolson had enlisted at age seventeen as a drummer boy in the 1st Minnesota Heavy Artillery Regiment on October 10, 1864, two years after his father had been killed at the Battle of Shiloh. Upon his death, President Eisenhower said *"The American people have lost the last personal link with the Union Army."* (qtd. in New York Times 1956).

1   Lemuel Cook lived long enough to see the union preserved, dying on May 20, 1866 in Clarendon, New York ("Lemuel Cook").

2   Seven Southern States seceded from the Union before Abraham Lincoln took office as President on March 4, 1861. The first was South Carolina, on December 20, 1860, followed by Mississippi, Florida, Alabama, Georgia, Louisiana and Texas. After the Confederate attack on Unionist Fort Sumter (April 12, 1861) and Lincoln's subsequent call for troops to suppress the nascent rebellion on April 15, Virginia, Arkansas, Tennessee and North Carolina also seceded.

3   United States Constitution, Article I, Section 2, Paragraph 3: *Representatives and direct Taxes shall be apportioned among the several States which may be included within this Union, according to their respective Numbers, which shall be determined by adding to the whole Number of free Persons, including those bound to Service for a Term of Years, and excluding Indians not taxed, three fifths of all other Persons.*

4   Between 1830-64, around 70 percent of all U.S. cotton export went to Great Britain and around 20 percent to France (Mann, 57).

5   Holmes was a supporter of the Missouri Compromise and the first Senator of the State of Maine. Jefferson, a wealthy slave owner himself, had conflicting views on slavery, opposing the institution of slavery and having attempted to legislate slavery emancipation several times, but stopping short of abolishing it in his own household. Describing perhaps his own relationship with slavery as

much as the country's, Jefferson wrote to Holmes that *"we have the wolf by the ear, and we can neither hold him, nor safely let him go. justice is in one scale, and self- preservation in the other."* (Jefferson, "John Holmes").

6   President Wilson articulated the right to self-determination for the peoples of Russia and the Ottoman Empire in his Fourteen Points speech of January 8, 1918, and further emphasized its importance in his address to Congress on February 11, 1918, when he said that *"Self-determination'is not a mere phrase. It is an imperative principle of actions which statesmen will henceforth ignore at their peril."* (Wilson, 106). President Franklin Roosevelt had a strong hand in the Atlantic Charter, a joint British-American declaration made on August 14, 1941, which stated that all peoples have the right to self-determination.

7   The Journal of the Royal United Service Institution of 1862 dryly noted that, during battle, an infantry soldier was generally not capable of anything more than *"simply raise his rifle to the horizontal, and fire without aiming"* (390).

8   McCulloch could have turned his solid victory into a great one had he opted to pursue the retreating Union forces and destroy the Army of the West entirely, an act that might have given Missouri to the Confederacy. But McCulloch had no faith in the Missouri State Guard, which he called *"undisciplined and led by men who are mere politicians"*, and therefore decided not to pursue (qtd. in Piston, 314). The quote is from a letter McCulloch sent to Brigadier General William J. Hardee, on August 24, 1861.

9   Johnston's wounds were severe but not lethal. Though he had to relinquish his command of the Army of Northern Virginia, he would return to active duty a few months later and receive another command.

10 Newspapers had given Lee this nickname for supposedly being timid, a trait that would soon prove to be as fitting a description for Lee as shyness for a wolf (Eicher, "Robert E. Lee", 54).

11 Hence the battles being collectively known as the Seven Days Battles.

12 The Confederate States of America had the fourth highest per capita income in the world in 1860, but after the Union established a naval blockade in the summer of 1861 this quickly changed; cotton export subsequently fell by 95 percent (Bateman, 4).

13 Being the first confrontation between ironclads, the battle also received widespread attention outside the U.S. and led to big changes in navies around the world. Wooden-hulled ship production was immediately halted in favor of ironclads, modeled on the USS Monitor (Tucker, "Blue & Gray Navies", 175).

14 For population numbers per state, see the 1860 US census ("Population of the United States", iv).

15 The combined number of casualties for the twelve hours of fighting on September 17, 1862, was 22,719 (Sears, "Landscape Turned Red", 296).

16 The State of Tennessee was by then mostly under Union control and was therefore not named in the Emancipation Proclamation. The Unionist slave-

holding states of Missouri, Kentucky, Maryland and Delaware, as well as a number of counties in West Virginia — which would soon be admitted to the Union as the 35th State — were also exempted. Slaves in these states were thus not freed by the Proclamation.

17 Gould survived his wounds and was later awarded the Medal of Honor, the highest U.S. military decoration. He died in 1916, aged 71, a few months before the U.S. entry into World War I.

18 Lincoln had died nine hours later, on April 15. Johnson's proclamation was published in the New York Times on May 10, 1865, the same day Confederate President Jefferson Davis was captured in Georgia by Union cavalry. The last Confederate general to surrender was Stand Watie (also the only Native American Confederate general), on June 23, 1865.

19 A 2011 analysis of census data by Binghamton University historian J. David Hacker puts the number of dead between 650,000 and 850,000, with 750,000 as the central figure, an estimate McPherson called plausible (Coker 2011).

20 The Thirteenth Amendment was passed by the Senate on April 8, 1864, by the House on January 31, 1865 and adopted on December 6, 1865. Its text: *Section 1. Neither slavery nor involuntary servitude, except as a punishment for crime whereof the party shall have been duly convicted, shall exist within the United States, or any place subject to their jurisdiction. Section 2. Congress shall have power to enforce this article by appropriate legislation.*

21 The sole exception being Virginia. Used figures are from the United States Census Bureau. State & County QuickFacts (quickfacts.census.gov).

22 Interestingly, Ulysses S. Grant was the last U.S. President to have owned a slave, though he freed him before the war, in 1859, rather than selling him for a hefty sum, which he certainly could have used at the time (Smith, 94).

23 Woodrow Wilson was from Virginia, but he moved to the North in his twenties. Andrew Johnson and Harry Truman were also from the South, but they only moved up from the Vice-Presidency after their President had died in office. Lyndon B. Johnson became President the same way, but he was also elected President himself, in 1964.

24 Jackson had gotten his legendary nickname after his actions at the First Battle of Bull Run, in July 1861, because he was like a 'stonewall' in the face of the enemy.

25 Even today, many of the States most vigorously opposed to a strong federal government are Southern ones.

26 The 1850 census lists Albert Woolson as being only 6 months old, which would make him 106 at the time of his death. This would have no effect on his status as the oldest surviving civil war veteran though.

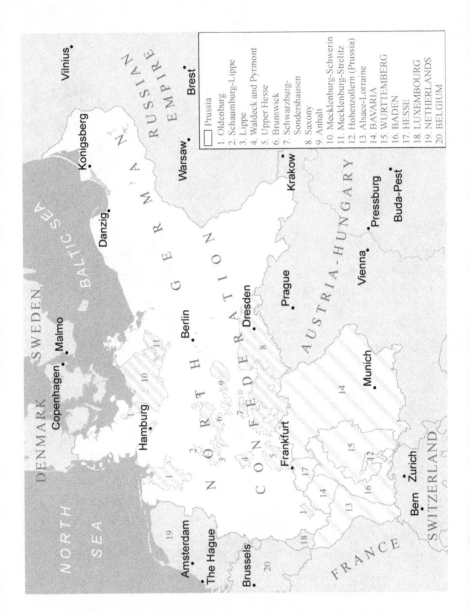

Map 17: The Unification of Germany, c. 1870-71

33

A New Nation in Europe

*"The first, original, and truly natural boundaries
of States are beyond doubt their internal boundaries.
Those who speak the same language are joined
to each other by a multitude of invisible bonds by
nature herself, long before any human art begins;
they understand each other and have the power
of continuing to make themselves understood
more and more clearly; they belong together and
are by nature one and an inseparable whole."[1]*

Johann Gottlieb Fichte, Addresses to the German
Nation, 1806, French-occupied Berlin

What is Europe? It is obviously more than just a geographic location, but how much more? Europeans have fought each other ferociously for thousands of years, first as tribes, then as kingdoms, as empires and finally — and most brutally — as modern, civilized nations. Still, all those wars also brought a common religion, a shared legal tradition, shared values, a shared culture and a shared history, i.e., a common heritage, which since the end of the Second World War has helped Europe on a path towards greater cooperation and integration.

But successful as this integration has been, the European sovereign debt crisis that broke out in 2009 exposed a dangerous disconnect between the level of economic integration and that of political integration within the Eurozone framework.[2] A single market, a shared currency, i.e., monetary union, yes. But no common fiscal, budgetary or economic policy, and certainly no political union. Many have since agreed that further integration is necessary to avoid an eventual breakup of the Eurozone, but most countries are reluctant to

358 - J.C. PETERS

hand over more sovereignty to Brussels, especially if that sovereignty would *de facto* end up in Berlin — a very likely scenario. As the most populous and wealthiest nation of the European Union, Germany has paid more than any other EU member state to stave off the economic meltdown that threatened the Eurozone after the outbreak of the sovereign debt crisis. Simply put, without Germany, there would quite possibly no longer be a Eurozone. Similarly, should Germany, in order to prevent another sovereign debt crisis, want to move towards a more federalized Europe — the way it unified itself almost 150 years ago — it would likely eventually happen. It is simply a matter of *Realpolitik*, as Prussian Chancellor Otto von Bismarck would have said. And he should know, since he was one of the main architects of the German unification of 1871.

That unification was the culmination of a process that had started more than 50 years earlier, around the time Napoleon came back from his disastrous Russian campaign with a decimated, defeated, demoralized army and the Prussians and Austrians smelled blood in the water. The ensuing *Befreiungskriege,* Wars of Liberation, fought in 1813-14, were a joint Austrian, Prussian, Russian and Swedish effort to defeat Napoleon once and for all. The campaign culminated in the Battle of the Nations (October 16-19, 1813), not far from Leipzig, where Napoleon was decisively defeated for the first time and forced to retreat to France, losing control over his German territories, which were thus liberated from French occupation.[3]

Ironically, Napoleon had also taken away one of the biggest obstacles on the long road to German unification, when he brought about the dissolution of the Holy Roman Empire after decisively defeating an Austrian-Russian coalition at Austerlitz, on December 2, 1805.

The Holy Roman Empire dated back to at least 962, when German King Otto I was crowned emperor.[4] It was basically a continuation of the Eastern part of the Frankish Kingdom that had been reunited and ruled by Charles Martel and expanded by his grandson, Charlemagne. Unlike France though — the Western part of the Frankish Empire — the Holy Roman Empire had remained a decentralized, limited elective monarchy, with hundreds of territories that were *de facto* independent sovereign nations (albeit tiny nations in most cases).

After Austerlitz, Napoleon formed a Confederation of the Rhine out of sixteen German territories formerly belonging to the Holy Roman Empire, to act as a buffer between France and the Russian Empire.[5] At its peak, the Confederation would count 36 German states (though never the two biggest, Austria and Prussia) and be home to a population of about fifteen million people.

In 1814, after Napoleon was defeated and exiled to the island of Elba, the nations of Europe came together at the Congress of Vienna to redraw the map of the continent. More than twenty years of wars had seen many duchies, provinces, cities, states and colonies change hands, and rather than ignite a dozen new wars to settle who owned what, the European powers chose to settle matters in a series of complex negotiations. The Congress was still in session when Napoleon escaped from

Elba and enchanted the French one last time into letting slip the dogs of war. The members of the Vienna Congress refused to let themselves be distracted by Napoleon's latest antics though and signed its Final Act nine days before the Battle of Waterloo.

Among many other things, the Congress decided not to restore the Holy Roman Empire but instead create a loose German Confederation of 39 states out of the almost 2,500 independent territories that had been part of the Holy Roman Empire, including (parts of) Austria and Prussia.[6] The German Confederation would be headed by Austria, which, as one of the five great European powers — the others being Great Britain, Russia, Prussia and France— had been given central Europe as its sphere of influence.

Meanwhile, Prussia — the largest, dominant state in the geographic region that would later become Germany — had reinvented itself after its humiliating defeat by Napoleon at the Battle of Jena, in 1806. It had abolished serfdom of its peasants, emancipated the Jews, rearranged the school system and introduced free trade to spur economic growth and industrialization (Clark, 326-37). The army had also been reorganized and in 1813 compulsory military service had been introduced (Clark, 326; Hagemann, 61).[7] As a result Prussia was able to play a decisive role at Waterloo, famously illustrated by the timely arrival on the battlefield of *Generalfeldmarschall* Gebhard von Blücher and his 50,000 Prussians, just in time to save the day.[8]

In 1818, three years after the establishment of the German Confederation, Prussia established an internal customs union throughout its own state and the Hohenzollern territories in southwestern Germany.[9] Before the customs union, there had been over 60 local customs borders, each with its own tariffs, which made transporting goods from one end of Prussia to the other a prohibitive, not to mention tantalizingly slow enterprise (Viner, 120).

The Prussian Customs Union was a great success and several other member states of the German Confederation — which counted a total of 830(!) toll barriers — soon joined.[10] Austria was excluded from joining though, due to internal pressure to uphold its own protectionist tariff system, which shielded local manufacturers from foreign competition (Ploeckl, 23).

In 1834, the Prussian Customs Union and several other customs unions that had been formed within the German Confederation merged to form the *Zollverein* (i.e., German Customs Union), further strengthening the Prussian economy while weakening the Austrian economy because of its continued exclusion. The German Customs Union also helped to further advance the idea of a unified Germany.

At the same time, conservative leaders — most notably Austrian Chancellor and Minister of State Klemens von Metternich — sought to suppress liberal movements that were promoting civil rights, democracy and nationalism, ideas that not only threatened the power base of the aristocracy but also the stability of the Austrian Empire itself, which, as a multi-national conglomerate, ran the risk of disintegrating if confronted with a rising tide of nationalism.

As early as 1819, Metternich had taken the initiative for a conference of German Confederation member states in Carlsbad, Bohemia, aimed at curbing civil liberties and crushing reform movements throughout the confederation. The resulting Carlsbad Decrees banned the *Burschenschaften* — student fraternities that were actively advocating nationalist, liberal and democratic ideals — and introduced several restrictions to the freedom of speech for the press and the academic world. University professors and other teachers for instance, should be removed from their positions if they propagated *"harmful doctrines hostile to public order or subversive of existing governmental institutions"* (qtd. in Barnes, 28).

But a decade later, in 1830, a new revolutionary wave swept through Europe, reopening a window of opportunity for nationalists and republicans to bring about regime change. In France, King Charles X was forced to abdicate following the July Revolution of 1830. In the Netherlands, riots broke out in the Southern provinces that had formerly been part of the Austrian Netherlands. They subsequently seceded and founded the new independent nation of Belgium. In Switzerland, the people forced cantonal governments to amend their constitutions. In Poland and Italy uprisings broke out against Russian and Austrian rule, respectively, though both revolutions would be crushed during the spring of 1831. In short, the German Confederation was quite literally surrounded by nations rattled by the turmoil of revolution.

Inspired by these events, German liberal authors, students and intellectuals organized a political festival in May 1832 at Hambach Castle — then part of the Kingdom of Bavaria — called the 'National Festival of the Germans in Hambach'(Sperber, 112). Some 30,000 people showed up, calling for German unity, popular sovereignty and liberty (Sperber, 111-13). The festival proved there was ample popular support for a unified Germany and established the combination of black, red and gold as the symbol of the movement for a democratic and united Germany, the same colors that would later be adopted as the colors of the German flag. Nothing else tangible came out of the gathering though and a year later the Bavarian military tightly controlled the area around Hambach Castle, to make sure no gathering of any kind would take place there again (Sperber, 111-13). The German nationalists had missed their chance and momentum fizzled.

Fifteen years later, the revolutionary year of 1848 gave German revolutionaries one last chance at bringing about a united Germany of the people, by the people and for the people.[11] This time, the revolutionaries successfully pressed several state governments into participating in a parliamentary assembly at Frankfurt that would be tasked with drafting a national constitution (Sperber, 146). In

March 1849, the Frankfurt National Assembly had indeed created a constitution for a united

German state, founded on a parliamentary democracy and a constitutional monarchy (Sperber, 149). It would be headed by a hereditary emperor, for which the Frankfurt Parliament elected Prussian King Friedrich Wilhelm IV, by a vote of 290 yeas and 248 abstentions.

On April 3, a selected group of deputies, the *Kaiserdeputation*, offered Friedrich Wilhelm the crown of the German Empire. Everything was in place, the yeas had it, a unified Germany was at the doorstep of history, knocking impatiently. But then Friedrich Wilhelm surprised everyone by saying no to the crown. *Nein*. Publicly he said he could not accept the crown without consensus of the princes and the free cities within the proposed German Empire, but privately he said he would not accept a crown that was touched by the "*hussy smell of revolution*".[12]

Without the support of the Prussian king, the constitution of the Frankfurt Assembly was meaningless. The delegates from Prussia, Austria and several other states were recalled or left on their own accord, returning to their home states. A rump parliament was formed in Stuttgart, Württemberg, but the tide of revolution was turning once again (Kolkey, 75-76). The people longed for order and stability after months of unrest and increasingly associated the word 'democrat' with civil unrest and anarchy. In June 1849 the Württemberg Army dispersed what remained of the parliament (Kolkey, 75-76). Revolution over.[13]

The failure of the German revolution of 1848-49 had made it clear that the best chance for a unified Germany lay in the so-called *Kleindeutschland* solution — meaning excluding Austria, and under Prussian leadership — and that it would have to be imposed from above, because unification had no chance without the support of the Prussian king.

For a couple of years things remained relatively quiet, until the four most powerful positions within the Prussian establishment were all infused with new blood in the space of just a few years. In 1857, Helmuth von Moltke, one of the greatest military strategists of the second half of the 19th century, became Chief of the Prussian General Staff. Two years later, Albrecht von Roon became Minister of War and set about reorganizing and modernizing the army, greatly increasing its size in the process (Förster, 263-66). Meanwhile, King Friedrich Wilhelm IV had suffered a stroke and was replaced by his brother, Wilhelm I, who would leave the task of governing mostly to his prime minister.

In 1862, Wilhelm appointed Otto von Bismarck to this position, a sly fox who, shortly after being appointed, gave a taste of things to come in his now famous 'Blood and Iron' speech, in which he drove home the point that Prussia's position in Germany did not depend upon its liberalism but upon its power, and that "*Prussia must build up and preserve her strength for the favorable moment, which has already come and gone many times. Her borders under the treaties of Vienna are not favorable for the healthy existence of the state. The great questions of the day will not be settled by speeches and majority decisions — that was the great mistake of 1848 and 1849 — but by blood and iron.*" (qtd. in Pflanze, 177).

Within four years, Bismarck found an excuse to declare war on Austria, Prussia's main rival for dominance over the German region. It was to be a very short war, with about half of the German Confederation and Austria on one side, and Prussia, Italy (which had just gained its independence from Austria) and about a dozen other German states on the other side.

All in all the war would last seven weeks. On July 3, 1866, the Austrian main army suffered a total defeat in the most important battle, near *Königgrätz* (present-day Czech Republic), partly because the Prussian infantry was equipped with a new type of breech-loading rifle, while the Austrians still had muzzle-loading rifles. This not only enabled Prussian infantry to fire four or five times in the space it took an Austrian soldier to fire just once, but also allowed for loading and firing while lying down instead of standing up (Wawro, "Austro-Prussian War", 22). Military tacticians of the day had initially questioned Moltke's decision to rely on fire tactics rather than shock tactics — soldiers equipped with breech-loading rifles would have to learn to fight and fire more individually and not waste all their ammunition in the first fifteen minutes of the fight — but as the saying goes, the proof of the pudding is in the eating, and Austria's casualties at *Königgrätz* were almost five times higher than Prussia's (Craig, 166).[14]

Though Austria was clearly vulnerable after *Königgrätz*, Bismarck, wanting to prevent France or Russia to join the Austrian side, pushed Wilhelm I to make peace rather than continue the war to gain more territory and concessions. As far as Bismarck was concerned, the goal was not to annihilate or annex Austria but to keep it out of German affairs, so Prussia could form a German Confederation of its own. This was achieved with the Peace of Prague (August 23, 1866), which abolished the existing German Confederation and permanently excluded Austria from German affairs. Prussia also annexed many of Austria's smaller German allies (mjummy).[15]

A year later, Prussia formed the North German Confederation, which incorporated the 22 German states north of the Main River and had a population of 30 million people.[16] Though the Confederation had the power to deal with many issues, the member states remained independent nations. Complete unification was close though. Only one more thing was needed before a new and powerful nation, comprised of both the Northern and Southern German states, could burst onto the European scene: A common enemy.

That enemy was easily found in France, which already felt threatened in its position as the dominant power of continental Western Europe by its assertive, aggressive neighbor to the East, especially after Prussia had so effortlessly defeated Austria. Of course Bismarck was well aware of this. He would later say: "*I did not doubt that a Franco-German War must take place before the construction of a United Germany could be realised*" (qtd. in Bismarck, 58).

The French simply could not accept Prussian dominance over the Southern German states, located so close to home. Besides, most French generals expected to win a military conflict with Prussia and hoped Austria and perhaps also some of the Southern German states would side with France if it came to that (alas for France, none of them did).

Still, even though he needed war with France, Bismarck did not want Prussia to come off as the aggressor. So he waited, for an opportunity to present itself that would either give Prussia a good excuse to go to war or, preferably, goaded the French into declaring war.

Opportunity arose when a diplomatic crisis erupted over the candidacy of a Prussian prince for the vacant Spanish throne. The prince in question, Leopold of Hohenzollern, soon backed down under French pressure and withdrew his consent, but then the French overreached by having their ambassador at the Prussian court, Count Benedetti, more or less ambush King Wilhelm I of Prussia during his morning stroll in the Kurpark at Bad Ems, demanding that he would never again support the candidacy of a Hohenzollern prince for the Spanish throne (Lerman, 148). This Wilhelm I politely but sternly refused. Shortly thereafter, Wilhelm I had his *adjudant* inform Count Benedetti that he had received confirmation from Leopold that he had indeed withdrawn his candidacy, and now considered the matter closed ("Emser Depesche", July 13, 1870).

When Bismarck was informed of this by telegram, he had a slightly altered version of the telegram published in Germany on July 13 and in France — of all days — on July 14 (Bastille Day).

The altered version suggested Wilhelm I had sent the *"Adjudant vom Dienst"* to the French Ambassador, to flatly tell him the king no longer wished to receive him and had nothing further to say on the matter ("Emser Depesche"). That was a bad enough snub already, but what really got the French up in arms was the (untranslated) word 'Adjudant'. In Prussia, an *Adjudant* was a high ranking military official, comparable to the French Aide-de-camp, but in France it was only a non- commissioned officer, comparable to a staff sergeant. Having Count Bernadetti informed by such a low ranking individual was tantamount to a declaration of war in the eyes of even the mildest mannered Frenchman. Needless to say, France took the bait. It declared war on Prussia on July 19, 1870.

Contrary to what the French generals had told their emperor, Napoleon III (nephew of Napoleon I) however, France was not in the best of positions to wage war against Prussia. Not only did the Prussians have the numerical advantage, they were also better trained, better led, better equipped, better organized and more mobile, thanks to an already extensive railroad network.[17] Prussian military superiority would therefore soon make itself apparent to even the most arrogant French generals (which was one military resource France had plenty of).

Sure enough, on September 1, 1870, after a series of victories, the Prussians were able to corner a 120,000 strong French army led by Napoleon III himself, at the Northern French town of Sedan. Outnumbered, outgunned and unable to retreat, Napoleon III had no choice but to surrender himself and his entire army. The Second French Empire subsequently collapsed, but a hastily formed Government of National Defense (the first government of the newly proclaimed Third Republic) desperately continued the fight, until on January 28, 1871, after a siege of almost five months, Paris fell. Ten days earlier, the German princes and senior military commanders had already proclaimed Wilhelm I German Emperor in the Hall of Mirrors of the Palace of Versailles, just outside of Paris.

Defeated France was forced to pay an indemnity of five billion francs and give up large parts of the Northeastern regions Alsace and Lorraine, the latter containing significant iron ore reserves.[18] Still, the most important reason for Bismarck and Moltke's insistence that Alsace and Lorraine be transferred to Germany seemed a military one. As Bismarck had told General Félix de Wimpffen, the French negotiator at the for France disastrous Battle of Sedan: "*Over the past 200 years France has declared war on Prussia thirty times and...you will do so again; for that we must be prepared, with...a territorial glacis between you and us.*" (qtd. in Wawro, "Franco-Prussian War", 227).

But for France, the loss of what the German Empire now called the *Reichsland Elsass-Lothringen*, the Imperial Territory of Alsace-Lorraine, was positively unbearable, thus assuring a permanent crisis between the two nations until the next war.

The unification of Germany also severely disturbed the balance of power that had been put in place by the Congress of Vienna of 1814-15. A powerful, militaristic, ambitious and confident new nation had emerged smack down in the middle of Europe, dominating both its Austrian-Hungarian neighbor to the south and its French neighbor to the west, the latter a mortal enemy that would howl for *revanche* until it would finally get it. Twice. Peace had been declared, but war was imminent. The German unification itself was a great success though, with the new nation being the most wealthy and populous country of Europe — as it is today.

As Prussia played a decisive role in the German unification of 1871, so too could modern Germany play a decisive role in the European unification. Question is, with war no longer being an option as a *"continuation of policy by other means"* in Europe, how would Otto von Bismarck go about enlisting French support for a United States of Europe, had he lived today?[19]

1   Fichte, 223-24.

2   As of 2017, there are 28 member states in the European Union (EU). The Eurozone is the economic and monetary union of the 19 EU member states that have so far adopted the euro currency.

3   The Coalition forces would follow Napoleon into France and force him to abdicate on April 11, 1814, two weeks after capturing Paris.

4   A case could also be made for calling Charlemagne the founder of the Holy Roman Empire. He was, after all, the first ruler in Western Europe since the fall of the Western Roman Empire to be crowned 'Emperor of the Romans', in 800, and had also conquered several key parts of Eastern Francia, the later core of the Holy Roman Empire. But while Charlemagne was part of a number of successive Frankish rulers whose core territories were located in Western Francia — roughly later France — the Holy Roman Empire as it developed through the Middle Ages and the early modern period was a mainly Germanic conglomerate of different states, concentrated in Central Europe. In that respect, the Treaty of Verdun of 843, which split up Charlemagne's empire in a Western, Middle and Eastern part, was an important formative step in the development of the Holy Roman Empire. Like Charlemagne, Otto I, who became King of Germany in 936, greatly expanded his realm during his reign, including the conquest of the Kingdom of Italy. He was also the first German holder of the title of emperor, though the term 'Holy' as connected to the empire was only first used by later emperor Frederick Barbarossa (1122-1190).

5   The creation of the Confederation of the Rhine effectively forced Holy Roman Emperor Francis II to abdicate and dissolve the Empire, on August 6, 1806.

6   Of these 2,500 entities, some 2,000 were tiny estates of a few square miles or less that belonged to so-called Imperial Knights. The remaining 400 or so were made up of principalities, ecclesiastical territories and Free or Imperial Cities (Gagliardo, 2).

7   Though the February 9, 1813 'Edict Lifting Previous Exemptions from Cantonal Duties for the Duration of the War' continued to recognize a number of exemptions — such as young men who were the sole breadwinners of their family or who were civil servants of the Prussian state — the Prussian Army

still doubled in size in 1813 as compared to 1806 (Hagemann, 61-62).

8   The Prussian army committed for the final battle with Napoleon had originally been 80,000 strong, but had suffered heavy casualties in the Battle of Ligny — Napoleon's last military victory — on June 16, 1815, two days before the battle of Waterloo (Booth, 15; Chesney, 4).

9   Prussia was ruled by the House of Hohenzollern.

10 The high number of toll barriers was caused by most states of the German Confederation having local, i.e., internal tariffs, as Prussia had had before creating its customs union. The situation had been even worse before Napoleon though, with an estimated 1,800 customs frontiers in Germany in 1790 (Henderson, 21-22).

11 The German March Revolution was ignited by events in France, where, in late February 1848, the Parisians revolted once again against their king, this time causing the ouster of King Louis-Philippe I, the last king of France (not counting Emperor Napoleon III, who succeeded him), who had succeeded King Charles X in 1830. In Germany, however, the revolution was, as contemporaries said, "*stopped at the feet of the thrones*" (qtd. in Sperber, 146).

12 Translated from the German quote "*Ludergeruch der Revolution*", as found in *Der lange Weg nach Westen: Deutsche Geschichte vom Ende des Alten Reiches bis zum Untergang der Weimarer Republik,* Vol. I, 122 (Winkler). It has also been said Friedrich Wilhelm called it "*a crown from the gutter*" (Sperber, 350; Kolkey, 75).

13 The work of the Frankfurt Parliament would not be completely for nothing though. Its constitution served as the basis for the Weimar Constitution of 1919 and also influenced the 1949 Constitution of the Federal Republic of Germany (Foster, 159).

14 For a more in-depth explanation of Moltke's fire tactics and the prevailing military theory of the day that went against it, see Wawro, *The Austro-Prussian War: Austria's War with Prussia and Italy in 1866,* 22-25.

15 Among the territories annexed by Prussia were Hanover, Frankfurt, Nassau, Schleswig-Holstein and parts of Hesse-Darmstadt.

16 Of that 30 million, 24 million were Prussian and 2 million were Saxon; the remaining 4 million came from the other 20 member states (Robinson, 126).

17 In the summer of 1870, von Moltke was able to transport 400,000 men to the French frontier in just eighteen days thanks to the Prussian railroad network (Mitchell, 66).

18 As agreed in the Treaty of Frankfurt on May 10, 1871. Independent observers were alarmed by the huge indemnity Prussia demanded from France, but Bismarck defended the Prussian position, saying "*France being the richest country in Europe, nothing could keep her quiet but effectually to empty her pockets.*" (qtd. in Wawro, "Franco-Prussian War", 305). For comparison, the indemnity the Austrians had had to pay only five years earlier, after losing

the Austro-Prussian war, had been only one-sixtieth of the French indemnity (Wawro, "Franco-Prussian War", 304).

19 Quote from *On War* (Clausewitz, 87).

34

AGE OF INVENTION

*"After the electric light goes into general use, none
but the extravagant will burn tallow candles."*[1]

Thomas Edison, 1880

*"Without high-speed tools and the finer steels which they brought
about, there could be nothing of what we call modern industry."*[2]

Henry Ford, *Edison as I know him*, 1930

In September 2012 the company *Rethink Robotics* introduced Baxter,
a highly adaptive general purpose robot that can be equipped with
several standard attachments on its arms ("Rethink Robotics").[3]
Baxter needs no additional programming to learn new things, a human
simply guides its arms through the required motions, which Baxter
then memorizes. And all that for the bargain price of just $22,000
("Rethink Robotics").

And Baxter has many friends. Noodle-slicing robot Chef Cui for
instance. Introduced in 2011, quickly adopted by a growing number of
Chinese noodle shops and relatively cheap at $1,500 compared to the
$4,700 per year a *human* noodle slicer costs in China (Garun 2012).
Or the burger robot introduced by San Francisco-based Momentum
Machines in 2013, a robotic assembly line capable of producing 360
hamburgers per hour, complete with freshly sliced tomatoes, onions
and pickles and nicely wrapped up for serving (Shedlock, "Burger-
Flipping Robot"). Combined with the touchscreen ordering system
that McDonald's has started to implement in its restaurants, customers
could soon find themselves ordering their hamburgers at places that
have completely dispensed with human cashiers, servers and burger
flippers.

And those McJobs will not be the only ones disappearing. In a 2013 report on disruptive technologies, consultancy company McKinsey estimated that 15 to 25 percent of industrial worker jobs in developed countries could be automated by 2025, across occupations such as manufacturing, packing, construction, maintenance and agriculture (McKinsey, 74).[4] Meanwhile, robots are getting better (and cheaper) at other tasks as well; filling out our prescriptions at pharmacies, driving our cars, cleaning our houses, babysitting our children and, last but not least, fighting our wars. In other words, the robots are coming.

The robotization of the factory floor did not start yesterday though, in fact it has been going on for decades and is intimately linked to an innovation introduced by the Ford Motor Company over a century ago: the assembly line.[5]

In 1913, Ford was having trouble keeping up with the ferocious demand for its legendary Model T automobile, prompting the introduction of the assembly line, which drastically reduced production time of the Model T from 12.5 man-hours in April 2013 to just 93 man-minutes a year later, and with less manpower (Hounshell, 254-55). It was so fast that the drying of the car paint became the bottleneck of the whole production process. And since only black Japan enamel would dry fast enough, black became the only available color for the Model T for a while (Kimes, 52). Ironically, Ford's famous remark that "any customer can have a car painted any colour that he wants so long as it is black" was made in 1909, four years before the introduction of the assembly line (Ford, "My Life", 72).[6]

By adding parts in a sequential manner, the production process was divided in small tasks that required little skill. Time waste was also reduced, because workers had to work continuously as long as the assembly line was operational (famously demonstrated by Charlie Chaplin in the epic 'factory work' scene from the 1936 movie *Modern Times*). Needless to say factory workers had no love for the assembly line, but from a production point of view it was a great success and it quickly became ubiquitous in factories throughout the industrialized world.

Although Ford was the first to introduce a *moving* assembly line in a modern factory, the concept of the assembly line itself was not new and had been experimented with since the beginning of the Industrial Revolution, in the late 18th century. In fact, the growing dynamic between production, prices and demand that had been ignited by the Industrial Revolution (increased production pushing prices lower, thus increasing demand, leading to increased production) had spurred several inventions in the 50 years before the introduction of the Model T, making Ford's innovation almost something of a logical necessity.

One key invention in the second half of the 19th century was the Bessemer process — named after its inventor, Henry Bessemer — which revolutionized steel manufacturing, greatly increasing scale and speed of production while significantly lowering its cost from $160 per long ton in 1867 to $42 per long ton in 1887 (Misa, 31-32). Being much stronger than iron, steel could be used to make stronger, more durable metal parts, bigger, high-pressure boilers in steam engines — greatly increasing power output — and larger, stronger ships, tanks and guns (which would revolutionize warfare in the 20th century).

Electrification was another key industrial development originating in the second half of the 19th century. Not only did it bring Thomas Edison's light bulb into homes and factories, it also paved the way for electric motors, which required less maintenance and were much more efficient and flexible (needing only an electrical cord between engine and power outlet) than small steam engines. Electrification thus enabled modern mass production, automating many processes that had previously been done slower, less efficient and more expensive with steam- and or manpower.

Just as with the Industrial Revolution a century earlier, machines and improved production processes were replacing or diminishing a host of manual labor tasks, only this time things were unfolding much faster. You could say that the period between 1860-1914 was the Industrial Revolution on *speed*. Inventions like the steam engine and the railroad came to full maturity, while a flurry of new inventions impacted the already radically changing Western economies. Between 1861-1900, more than 1,000,000 patents were issued for new inventions in the U.S. alone, almost 15 times more than had been issued in the previous 70 years ("Statistical Abstract 1942", 952). Railroad mileage tripled between 1860-80 in the U.S., and again by 1920 ("Statistical Abstract

1942", 478). And since transportation was much cheaper by rail than by road, overall transportation cost fell significantly during this period, as did delivery times. In 1869 for example, delivery time from the East Coast to San Francisco, California was reduced to just six days when the first transcontinental railroad opened.[7] And after automobile development and manufacturing accelerated following the invention of the gasoline-fueled internal combustion engine, goods could be delivered fast and cheap even to remote locations.

Another invention originating in the Industrial Revolution era, the telegraph, had developed into a worldwide communication network by the 1890s, connecting major cities around the world and increasing both speed and frequency of international commerce, diplomatic relations and information about newsworthy events.[8] The invention of the telephone in 1876 made communication even easier, since people could now talk directly and interactively to each other over great distances — instead of being limited to the beep-beep-beeps of morse code — and in 1901 Italian inventor Guglielmo Marconi brought communication to a whole new level when he succeeded in wirelessly transmitting and receiving a transatlantic morse code radio signal.[9]

All these inventions, innovations and developments greatly accelerated the economic transformation that had been underway since the Industrial Revolution. Factories grew ever bigger and more complex, while the job of the average worker became ever smaller and simpler. A growing army of managers was hired to increase control, oversight and organizational efficiency of the production process and the work force, in turn stimulating the development of the data processing industry, which brought inventions such as the electronic tabulating machine, the punchcard and the time clock (all three developed by companies that would later merge into International Business Machines, IBM).

One important side effect of the growing importance of communication and business administration was the increasing participation of women in the labor process, who were hired en masse as stenographers, typists and switchboard operators. The number of American women working in clerical and similar occupations for instance, rose from less than 11,000 in 1870 to more than 1,900,000 in 1920 (Hill, 40).

The new sense of independence women gained through these jobs would play a major role in fueling the Women's Rights Movement of the late 19th and early 20th century. It was but one of the many revolutionary effects of the unprecedented advances in factory productivity in the period 1860-1914.

Meanwhile, huge fortunes were also won and lost with speculative investments in rapidly developing industries from which some companies emerged as big winners but many others did not. In the 1870s for instance, a railroad investment bubble formed in the U.S. after government land grants and subsidies had attracted enormous investments in — and abnormal growth of — the railroad construction industry (at the time the country's second largest employer, after agriculture) and its supporting facilities. Many of these investments offered no early returns outside of their speculative value though — not unlike the dotcom bubble of 2000 — and when the Jay Cooke & Company bank failed because it couldn't unload the millions of dollars in Northern Pacific Railway bonds it owned, panic ensued (Wicker, 19-21).

The failure of Jay Cooke on September 18, 1873, set off a chain reaction of bank failures and the closing of the New York Stock Exchange for a full ten days (Kindleberger, 321). In the two months that followed, 55 U.S. railroad companies failed and another 60 in the nine months after that.

18,000 businesses went belly up between 1873-75, causing unemployment to rise to a peak of 8.25 percent in 1878 (Vernon 1994, 710). At the time, the period between 1873-79 was called the Great Depression, until that moniker was given to the more severe depression of the 1930s and the period of 1873-1879 was retroactively renamed the Long Depression (Swarup, 212).

Real Net National Product in the U.S. actually grew at a clip of 6.8 percent per year between 1869-79 though and the implied rate of growth of real per capita income during this period was 4.5 percent, so most people were actually better off at the end of the Long "Depression" than they had been before it (Friedman, 37).[10] There was panic and a general feeling of malaise, yes, but in reality the economy kept pushing forward.

In general, quality of life in the West greatly improved during the 50 years leading up to World War I. Famines disappeared for the first time in history — the last famine in the West unrelated to war occurred in 1880 — real income rose considerably, work-hours declined (albeit slowly), infant mortality rates declined by as much as 50 percent and life expectancy rose from less than 40 to more than 50 years (Roser, "Life Expectancy"; "Child Mortality).[11] The scientific proof for the germ theory of disease in the 1860s and 70s had an especially big impact in this respect. Increased sanitation, proper cooking, cleaning and preservation subsequently caused a sharp decline in mortality rates.[12]

But however positive and revolutionary these advances in life expectancy and prosperity were, a different — though equally revolutionary — side of the age of invention would soon manifest itself after the European empires declared war on each other in August 1914 and wasted no time using their extensive railroad networks to quickly transport an unprecedented number of soldiers, ammunition and artillery to the battle grounds, where 19th century warfare would brutally clash with 20th century technology.

Artillery firing 1760-pound (800 kg) shells over a distance of 9 miles (15 km), guided to target with the help of field telephones, machine guns mowing down charging infantry by the hundreds, flamethrowers, modern hand grenades, poison gas (which made over one million casualties, including over 80,000 deaths), aircraft and aerial bombardments, barbed wire, tanks, submarines, they would all be deployed on a large scale for the first time in World War I. When it was over, 8.5 million soldiers and between 6-9 million civilians had been killed in just four short years.[13]

Unabashed, detached and amoral, technology had shown its dark side, or rather — though equally disturbing — its neutral side, yielding without hesitation to whoever was in control.

As the robots do.

At least until they decide not to.

1   qtd. in "The Electric Light".

2   Ford, "Edison", 33.

3   For an in-depth review of Baxter, see *This Robot Could Transform Manufacturing* (Knight 2012).

4   In developing countries, an estimated 5 to 15 percent of manufacturing worker tasks could be automated by 2025 (McKinsey, 74).

5   Ford introduced the assembly line in 1913 (Hounshell, 10-11). Source also discusses the origins and early productivity gains of Ford's assembly line. See also Ford, *My Life and Work*, 77-90.

6   When Ford made this remark, the Model T was in fact available in different colors. He was merely talking about how in the future Ford Motor Company would build all Model T's exactly the same, to further cut cost and production time. At the time his autobiography *My Life and Work* was first published, in 1922, the statement was true though.

7   The more dangerous and more expensive stagecoach took 28 days to get to California, and that was when starting from Missouri.

8   The first commercially viable electromagnetic telegraphs had been introduced in the 1830s.

9   There was and still is doubt, though, about whether Marconi really did succeed in wirelessly transmitting the letter 'S' in Morse code (dit-dit-dit) from Cornwall, England to Newfoundland, Canada, on December 12, 1901 (Sarkar, 387-94). Source gives an in-depth explanation of Marconi's first transatlantic experiment.

10   The fact that real GNP grew by 6.8 percent per year between 1869-79, real income per capita increased by 4.5 percent per year and the total money supply grew by 2.7 percent per year between 1873-78, led libertarian economist Murray Rothbard to dub the 'Great Depression' of the 1870s a myth (Rothbard, 154).

11   The last famine in the Western world unrelated to war occurred at St. Lawrence Island, Alaska, between 1878–80. The last Irish famine was in 1879.

12   Groundbreaking work in the field of epidemiology was done, i.a., by John Snow, who discovered the source of a cholera outbreak in London in 1854, and Louis Pasteur, who discovered the principles of vaccination.

13   As reported by the U.S. War Department, February 1924. U.S. casualties amended by the Statistical Services Center, Office of the Secretary of Defense, November 7, 1957 (see also table in Hosch, 219).

35

THE RUSSIAN REVOLUTION(S)

*"Sire: We, the workers and inhabitants of St.
Petersburg, of various estates, our wives, our
children, and our aged, helpless parents, come to
Thee, O Sire, to seek justice and protection. We are
impoverished; we are oppressed, overburdened with
excessive toil, contemptuously treated. We are not
even recognized as human beings, but are treated
like slaves who must suffer their bitter fate in silence
and without complaint. And we have suffered,
but even so we are being further (and further)
pushed into the slough of poverty, arbitrariness,
and ignorance. We are suffocating in despotism
and lawlessness. O Sire, we have no strength left,
and our endurance is at an end. We have reached
that frightful moment when death is better than
the prolongation of our unbearable sufferings."[1]*

Petition carried by protesters on Bloody
Sunday, January 22, 1905

Every eighteen months, one of the most influential people of the
20th century gets a month-long bath (Yurchak, 141). Only instead
of water an embalming solution is used, because the reason for the
long soak has more to do with preserving than with cleaning. And
preserve it does, seeing as for the past 90 years the embalmed body
of Vladimir Ilyich Lenin, founder of the Soviet Union, has been on
display at the mausoleum in Red Square, in the center of Moscow,
looking like he died only yesterday.

To keep the body in mint condition, an embalming compound was
developed that replaced all the water in Lenin's skin. As long as the

temperature is 16 degrees Celsius and relative humidity is 70 percent, the compound neither absorbs water nor evaporates (Schmemann 1991). Multiple sensors therefore constantly monitor temperature and humidity around the body.

Preserving Lenin requires more than just monitoring though. Apart from the month-long immersion in a bath of embalming fluid once every eighteen months, Lenin's head and hands get a fresh daub of embalming compound every week, and every four or five years the body is thoroughly inspected by a commission of senior scientists (Schmemann 1991).

Comrade Joseph Stalin was preserved the same way after his death in 1953, but one night in 1961 his body went from hallowed sarcophagus to common coffin and was buried next to the Kremlin wall without pomp and circumstance.

Not Lenin though. Even decades after the fall of the Soviet Union, the iconic revolutionary remains on display in his mausoleum. But while the appearance of his body, sickly and fragile in life, has been preserved intact, his brain, once home to an energetic and virile mind, has been sliced into 30,000 pieces, to study the source of his genius (Neumeyer 2014).

Still more ironic (some might say tragic) is that Lenin's feeble bodily remains managed to outlive his crowning achievement, the Union of Soviet Socialist Republics, one of the most dominant and defining nations of the 20th century. And that while its hard-fought founding had so proudly carried the promise of that rarest of things: the beginning of a completely new world.

That new world was to be a socialist state, in which property and resources would be owned and shared by all. A promise that resounded especially strong in a country where roughly 35 percent of the population had been a serf before serfdom was finally abolished in Tsarist Russia in 1861 (Moon, 3).[2] Very little had changed for the ex-serfs in the decades that followed though. Land, money and other resources still remained firmly in the hands of the ruling class.

Because landowners had for so long been able to count on serfs, Russia was late to industrialize.[3]

When it finally did, industrialization progressed faster than in most parts of the West, resulting in fewer but bigger factories, massive urban overcrowding and deplorable conditions for the workers. By 1912, 43 percent of Russian industrial laborers worked in factories employing more than 1,000 workers, up from 27 percent in 1866; in the U.S., it was only 18 percent (Wolf, 74-75; Carmichael, 8).

Because of this high concentration of workers, protests could suddenly ignite and spread much faster than when most people were still living in rural areas. As a result, average annual strikes increased from 33 between 1886-94, to 176 between 1895-1904 (Ascher, 23).

Meanwhile, Tsar Nicholas II didn't make it any easier for the people after he came to power in 1894 at the age of 26, though in his defense, his father, Tsar Alexander III, had not made it any easier for the people either.[4] Like his father, Nicholas II concerned himself little with the common people. In his mind, enlightenment ideas like the social contract and 'government with consent of the governed' had no place in the Russian Empire. Nicholas II firmly believed that his power to rule was granted by Divine Right, i.e., not derived from the people but directly from God himself.

So, when a deputation of peasants and workers from various local assemblies came to the Winter Palace shortly after Nicholas II had ascended to the throne, with proposals aimed at improving the political and economic life of the peasantry, such as land reform and a constitutional monarchy, Nicholas II told them angrily that "*I want everyone to know that I will devote all my strength to maintain, for the good of the whole nation, the principle of absolute autocracy, as firmly and as strongly as did my late lamented father.*" (qtd. in Ferro, 39).

A few years later, on Sunday January 22, 1905 (January 9, O.S.), another delegation of peaceful protesters wanted to present a petition to Nicholas II at the Winter Palace in St.Petersburg.[5] The leader of the procession, the Russian Orthodox priest George Gapon, had informed the government of the upcoming procession, after which the ministers had advised Nicholas II to leave the city, which he did.

The protest was not in any way directed against the Tsar himself though. In fact, the protesters were singing the imperial anthem 'God Save the Tsar' and carried portraits of Nicholas II, Russian flags, religious banners and icons on their way to the Winter Palace.

But as the processions — which had started from six different points — converged on the palace, the marchers found their routes blocked by soldiers at strategic points in the city. At some of these points soldiers told the marchers to turn back, while at others no such warning was given. Authorities had apparently not issued clear instructions to the soldiers as to what to do when confronted with advancing crowds, a recipe for disaster when deploying the military for crowd control (Ascher, 91-92).

When a large crowd including George Gapon arrived at Narva Gate, in the middle of the expansive Narva Square, they were met by determined infantry units that had positioned themselves as if the square were a battlefield.

Soon it would be.

A single bugle was blown, serving simultaneously as apparent warning to the protesters and signal for the soldiers to take aim and fire into the crowd (Ascher, 91-92). Moments later dozens of protesters lay dead in the square. At several other points in the city soldiers also opened fire on the protesters and whoever else happened to be there. According to most estimates, at least hundreds of people were killed or seriously wounded.[6]

The massacre that would come to be known as Bloody Sunday put Russia on a much more serious trajectory to real revolution. Initially, the protesters had just wanted the Tsar to help them improve their living conditions, but in the wake of Bloody Sunday the demands became much more political, with growing calls for freedom of speech, an elected parliament and the right to form political parties. And even though the Tsar had not ordered the shooting and was in fact appalled by it, the blame was still placed squarely on his shoulders.

In the words of the U.S Consul in Odessa: "*All classes condemn the authorities and more particularly the Emperor. The present ruler has lost absolutely the affection of the Russian people, and whatever the future may have in store for the dynasty, the present Tsar will never again be safe in the midst of his people.*" (qtd. in Ascher, 92-93).

Shortly after Bloody Sunday the first Soviet (council of workers' delegates) was created in St. Petersburg, to coordinate worker strike activities there.[7] Throughout the rest of the winter and spring of 1905, massive strikes and peasant uprisings also erupted in other parts of the empire.

Even more alarming to the Tsarist regime was the mutiny that erupted on June 14 (June 27, O.S.) on the brand-new battleship *Potemkin* — the pride and joy of the imperial Black Sea fleet — after the ship's captain had tried to force the crew to eat borscht made from rotten, maggot-infested meat (Bell, 12). The government's concern was understandable. With a water displacement of 12,582 tons, a crew of 800, a top speed of 16 knots and the capability to hold 10,000 rounds of various calibers of ammunition, the *Potemkin* was certainly more of a threat than a bunch of poor peasants carrying icons and singing hymns, not to mention the danger of the mutiny spreading to other ships, or even throughout the entire armed forces (Bell, 11).

The mutineers decided to make for Odessa harbor (arriving there late at night the same day), to give one of their fallen comrades a public burial, take in fresh water and coal and see if they could drum up support from the local soldiers and revolutionaries there. Some of the more radical sailors also wanted to try and take Odessa itself, but this was rejected by the Commission that had been elected to be in charge of the ship, which wanted to wait for an already planned fleet-wide mutiny to break out (Bell, 14).

The next day, thousands of people came out to the harbor to see the mighty battleship with their own eyes, pay their respect to the fallen sailor and express their support for the sailors' cause (Bell, 14). Later that day though, Tsarist land forces bent on restoring order fired directly into the crowd, killing at least 1,000 people.

The *Potemkin* was relatively helpless against the operations of the Tsarist soldiers in the city, lacking the necessary precision to be effective without causing too much collateral damage. A few shells were fired on the Tsarist forces' headquarters in the city, but when they overshot and hit a nearby residence, actions were quickly halted (Bell, 15).

On day three of the mutiny the *Potemkin* left Odessa harbor to confront a squadron of ships that had been sent to force its surrender (Bell, 15). Twice the *Potemkin* steamed right through the task force, its powerful guns aimed and ready but silent, as were those of the other ships. When the task force retreated, some sailors proposed to make use of the momentum, pursue the ships and pressure their crews into joining the mutiny, but this was rejected by the ship's Commission (Bell, 15). Instead it was decided to set course for the Romanian harbor of Constanța, on the western coast of the Black Sea, to take in provisions (Bell, 16).

When the Romanians refused to supply them, the mutineers tried the Crimean harbor of Feodosia, but city officials there too refused to help (Bell, 16). The mutineers threatened to bombard the city, but when their ultimatum expired and the city had not given in to their demand, they decided to return to Constanța and on June 25 surrendered the battleship to the Romanian authorities, eleven days after the mutiny had begun (Bell, 17).

And so the *Potemkin* mutiny petered out. Momentum for a successful fleet-wide mutiny and a country-wide revolution had come and gone. Radical revolutionaries would come to view the eleven-day mutiny as an iconic but nevertheless wasted opportunity, drawing lessons from it that would serve them well twelve years later, when they got a second chance at radical change.

Then again, although the mutiny of the *Potemkin* itself had failed, it did show — in the words of Ivan Lychev, one of the members of the ship's Commission, who later wrote an account of his experience aboard the ship — *"the nation and the entire world that the revolutionary rumblings penetrated into the most secure pillars of the tsarist throne - the navy and the army."* (qtd. in Bell, 20).

In the fall of 1905, uprisings broke out at the naval bases of Kronstadt, Vladivostok, even at Black Sea Fleet headquarters in Sevastopol. Though put down by (other) government forces, the uprisings indeed showed that the problem ran far deeper than a few disgruntled workers and peasants. Meanwhile, Count Sergey Witte, who as the Tsar's plenipotentiary had just successfully concluded peace negotiations with Japan — with whom Russia had been entangled in a disastrous war since 1904 — impressed upon Nicholas II that he had only two options in dealing with the growing strikes and uprisings: using force, or implementing reforms (Harcave, 169).[8]

Choosing door number two, the Tsar asked Witte to write an imperial manifesto to satisfy the more moderate participants in the nascent revolution. Witte subsequently drafted the so-called October Manifesto, which promised a constitutional monarchy, a parliament with popularly elected members and the power to veto every law (the Duma), and guaranteed civil liberties such as freedom of speech, freedom of religion and the right of association and assembly.

In short, everything Nicholas II hated. For days he stalled, hesitated and pondered on alternatives, before finally, grudgingly, signing the Manifesto on October 30 / October 17, O.S., 1905 (Harcave, 173). The effects of the Manifesto were immediate, all strikes and demonstrations ended within days of its signing. The moderates were satisfied, but the more radical revolutionaries argued that since the Duma could not pass any laws without the Tsar's approval, most power still lay in the hands of the Tsar, not the people.

The government had also offered political amnesty for passed transgressions, but at the same time made clear it would crush continued rebellion with an iron fist. When the Bolsheviks, Mensheviks and Socialist Revolutionaries nevertheless called a general strike in Moscow in early December, the government showed it meant business by sending a full regiment to quell the unrest.[9] Arriving in the city on December 4, Admiral Fyodor Dubasov, the newly appointed Governor-General of Moscow, did not waste any time either and declared a state of emergency on December 7 (Engelstein, 197). Three days later, government troops bombarded a school where workers and students had barricaded themselves (Engelstein, 203-04). Elsewhere in the city, dragoons attacked a crowd of 5,000 workers (Engelstein, 205). Even when most armed resistance had subsided after a couple of days, government troops kept up their urban warfare tactics, shelling factories and setting fire to buildings where striking workers had entrenched themselves (Engelstein, 220). By the time the workers' parties ordered an end to the strike, on December 19, about 700 revolutionaries and civilians had been killed and some 2,000 wounded (Engelstein, 220-21).

On April 23, 1906, a few days before the first Duma would convene, Nicholas signed the *Fundamental State Laws of the Russian Empire*,

386 - J.C. PETERS

the first Russian Constitution.[10] But although it recognized limitations to the power of the Tsar for the first time, it did not go as far as had been promised by the October Manifesto. For one, the Duma could not alter the Constitution unless it was initiated by the Tsar, who could also dismiss the Duma at any time, a self-given right that would not remain idle in the hands of Nicholas II ("Russian Fundamental Laws", I.8, X.104-05).

Chapter I, article 4 of the Fundamental State Laws furthermore declared that the emperor possessed "*Supreme Sovereign Power*" and that "*Obedience to His authority, not only out of fear, but in good conscience, is ordained by God Himself*".

So what happens when a Duma bent on change confronts an Emperor bent on conservation? Chaos and political mayhem is what happened. Although the first Duma was boycotted by the most radical left parties — the Bolsheviks, Mensheviks and Socialist Revolutionaries — that did not prevent it to come up with all kinds of radical reforms, including electoral and land reform, both equally horrible to Nicholas II, who dissolved the Duma within three months.

The second Duma lasted a whole four months (which could perhaps be called progress by the staunchest of optimists) but turned out to be even more radical than the first, after the Bolsheviks and Mensheviks — having decided to participate in the election this time — won a significant number of seats. For some of the nobles, having to deal with peasants and workers on equal footing simply proved too much. Count Fredericks, Minister of the Court, at one point commented in disgust: "*The Deputies, they give one the impression of a gang of criminals who are only waiting for the signal to throw themselves upon the ministers and cut their throats. What wicked faces! I will never again set foot among those people.*" (qtd. in Massie, 219).

After dissolving the second Duma, Nicholas unilaterally changed the electoral law to give greater electoral value to the propertied class (thus violating the Constitution of 1906). Consequently, the third Duma — derisively called 'The Duma of Lords and Lackeys'— was a lot more cooperative and served out the full five year term, as did the fourth and final Duma, which lasted until 1917 (Milyukov, 159, 164).[11] By then though, three disastrous war years had run out the clock on the path of slow, gradual change that was followed by the largely ineffective Russian parliament.

Russian losses during World War I were staggeringly high. In the first year alone, the Russian Army suffered 2.4 million casualties, plus another 1 million of its soldiers taken prisoner, while German losses on the Eastern front probably did not exceed 300,000, with only a few thousand taken prisoner (Sondhaus, 150). The German army was simply better prepared, better trained, better supplied and better led. Many Russian soldiers lacked shoes, munitions and food. Hard to fight under such deplorable conditions. And the soldiers weren't the only ones starving, factory workers also suffered from a dearth of food and basic supplies.

In October 1916, the secret police of St. Petersburg warned against the threat of riots by *"the lower classes of the empire enraged by the burdens of daily existence."* (qtd. in Steinberg, 51). The Duma also urged the Tsar to commit to constitutional reform, lest things should get terribly out of hand. Of course they already had.

The position of Nicholas II was like that of the Titanic just after it hit the iceberg, the hull perforated all along the side. Still deemed unsinkable but with a mortal wound already inflicted below the waterline, the supposedly watertight compartments quickly filling with ice-cold water.

One of those compartments represented the worsening living conditions of the people — peasants, workers and soldiers alike. Another compartment represented the burden of a losing war with unprecedented casualty numbers, a third one Nicholas II taking direct command of the army in 1915 (though ill-prepared for such a task), making him the main person responsible for the disastrous course of the war.

And then there was his wife Alexandra, the Tsarina, whom he had left in charge of the government in his absence and who had fallen under the influence of the Russian mystic Grigori Rasputin, a man who was unpopular with both the Russian nobility and the common people. Alexandra herself was thoroughly disliked as well, not just because she was of German descent and scores of Russians were being slaughtered by the Germans, but also because she was *"an unbalanced character, a nervous, hysterical woman, who, through her very love for her husband and the persistence with which she advised him to cling to an order that had already served its purpose, proved his undoing.*" (Radziwill, 173).

On March 7, 1917 (February 22, O.S.), workers at the Putilov plant, St. Petersburg's largest industrial plant, began to strike (Service, 32). Three days later almost all the factories of St. Petersburg had shut down. Nicholas II ordered the army to put down the riots with force but the soldiers refused to shoot at the demonstrators, handing their rifles to them instead, if not simply joining in on the protests outright (Service, 32).

Anarchy ruled in St. Petersburg and when the Tsar returned to the city on March 14 (March 1, O.S.), his Army Chiefs and the ministers who had not yet fled the capital urged him to abdicate, which Nicholas II did the next day. A couple of days later, the ex-tsar and his family were placed under house arrest at Alexander Palace — Nicholas' favorite residence — about 16 miles (26 km) from St. Petersburg.

The people were thrilled with their major victory, having forced the tsar's abdication in just eight days. But although the tsar was now gone, the revolution was only beginning. A provisional government was formed, comprised mostly of members of the liberal Constitutional Democratic Party (a.k.a. the Kadets) and the leftist Socialist-Revolutionary Party. The even more radical leftists, i.e., the Bolsheviks and Mensheviks, opted out of the provisional government though, focusing their efforts instead on organizing the workers and soldiers in the Petrograd Soviet, a citywide council they had formed a few days before the tsar's abdication.

The Petrograd Soviet wanted to ensure that the Provisional Government fulfilled the promise of creating a democratic republic with guaranteed civil rights and electoral reform. To keep the pressure on, they even met in the same building as the government, the Tauride Palace.

But social, economic and electoral reform — as opposed to political revolution — does not happen in a week. The Provisional Government was led by capable people but they could not work miracles. Food and supplies remained scarce, the war raged on and Russia remained on the losing side of it. Most Russians wanted to end the war, but the Provisional Government was loath to sue for peace on unfavorable terms. Soon, soldiers, peasants and workers blamed the Provisional Government for all the things they had blamed the tsar for only weeks earlier.

And then Lenin returned. He had been living in exile in Switzerland, but with the tsar gone he believed now was the time for a real, marxist revolution. For a Russian national to travel from Switzerland to Russia while there was a war on with Germany seemed next to impossible, but fortunately the Germans were kind enough to help the radical-revolutionary-who-wanted-to-end-   war-with-Germany-at-all-cost safely reach St. Petersburg (Fitzpatrick, 50).

Lenin arrived in the Russian capital in April 1917. In the months that followed, his party, the Bolsheviks, grew into the largest political movement in Russia's two most important cities, Moscow and St. Petersburg, by promising the masses that once in power, the Bolsheviks would deliver peace, bread and land to the peasants and power to the people (Service, 48).

Meanwhile, the position of the Provisional Government continued to weaken and on November 7, 1917 (October 25, O.S.), the Bolsheviks ousted the Provisional Government from the Winter Palace in a rather undramatic fashion, belying the later, far more heroic depiction of events by the Soviets (Fitzpatrick, 64).[12]

Making good on his promise, Lenin soon thereafter opened peace negotiations with Germany. On March 3, 1918, the new Bolshevik government signed the Treaty of Brest-Litovsk, committing Russia to a highly unfavorable, humiliating peace, by renouncing Russia's claims to Finland, Estonia, Latvia, Belarus, Ukraine and Lithuania, territory that included important industries and was called home by a quarter of its population ("Treaty of Brest-Litovsk", art. 6).

Still, Lenin had good reasons for wanting to come to terms with the Germans quickly, because almost immediately after the Bolsheviks had seized power, civil war broke out between the communists and a colorful coalition of those seeking to remove them from power, including militarists, monarchists, foreign nations (such as Great-Britain, France and Japan) and various independence movements.

In April 1918, the Romanov family was moved deeper into Russia, to Yekaterinburg, to prevent the ex-tsar from falling into the hands of the anti-bolshevik coalition. The Bolsheviks wanted to bring Nicholas to trial, but when elements of the anti-communist Czech Legion advanced to within a day of Yekaterinburg (though unaware that the Romanov family was being held there), the communists panicked.

And so, on July 17, 1918, they executed the Romanovs in the basement of the house where they were held, Nicholas and his wife Alexandra, their four daughters Olga, Tatiana, Maria and Anastasia, and their thirteen-year-old son Alexei, as well as the court physician, a maid, a footman and a cook, servants who had remained with the Romanov family voluntarily.[13]

But the war between the Red Army and the White Army (as the collective opposition was known) did not end with the execution of the Romanov family. It raged on for another five years, in all claiming the lives of roughly one million soldiers and an additional one million civilians (White, 357).[14] In the end, the Red Army was victorious in Russia, thus securing the establishment of the Soviet Union, while pro-independence movements won independence for Finland, Estonia, Latvia, Lithuania and Poland.

Lenin had his socialist state, but he would not be around for long to enjoy it, or shape it for that matter. Between 1922-23 the father of the Russian revolution suffered a series of strokes, rendering him partly paralyzed, mute and bed-ridden until his death in 1924, at the age of 53.

In his political testament, Lenin warned against the General Secretary of the newly created Soviet Union, Joseph Stalin, who had *"unlimited authority concentrated in his hands, and I am not sure whether he will always be capable of using that authority with sufficient caution."* (Lenin, "Letter to Congress", II). In a postscript written shortly thereafter, Lenin even recommended Stalin's removal from his position, because he is *"too rude"* (Lenin, "Letter to Congress", Addition). Instead, someone had to be found who was *"more tolerant, more loyal, more polite and more considerate to the comrades"*.

Unfortunately, Lenin turned out to be all too right in his premonition. In the years after his death, Stalin would rise to the most prominent position in the Soviet government, and during his regime hundreds of thousands — if not millions — were killed.[15] Considering this, one wonders why Stalin's body was kept on display in the mausoleum next to Lenin at all, let alone for eight years. On the other hand, unlike Lenin had done in 1918, Stalin did not seek peace at any price against Germany in 1941. On the contrary, he threw everything but the kitchen sink at Soviet Russia's epic fight against the Nazis, thus providing invaluable reprieve to his Western Allies and playing a decisive role in the defeat of the Axis powers during the Second World War.

Cooperation between the Soviet Union and the West proved to be short-lived though, as what would become a decades-long Cold War between East and West had already begun to emerge even before the end of WW II, pitting Russia and Eastern Europe versus the United States and Western Europe. During the second half of the 20th century, aside from competing against each other in a nuclear arms race and a space race, the U.S.S.R and the U.S. would also fight hot proxy wars in Korea, Vietnam and Afghanistan and narrowly avert nuclear war in Cuba.

Just like Tsar Nicholas II, the Soviet Union promised but failed to deliver on democracy, guaranteed civil rights and prosperity. And just like Tsarist Russia, Marxist-Leninist Russia ultimately collapsed, in 1991. Russia has since adopted capitalism with considerable success, but democracy and civil rights remain underdeveloped.

Speculation about the removal of Lenin's body from the mausoleum at Red Square began almost immediately after the fall of the Soviet Union. In January 2011, Vladimir Putin's United Russia Party organized an online poll where visitors could vote for or against burial of Lenin (Osborn 2011). More than two-thirds voted in support of interment. A result that was confirmed in another poll, held in April 2014.[16]

He's still there though.

---

1   qtd. in Ascher, 87.

2   The same year serfdom was abolished in Russia, fundamental disagreement about the future of slavery also prompted the outbreak of civil war in the United States, that other dominant and defining country of the 20th century.

392 - J.C. PETERS

3 Not unlike the antebellum Southern United States and its reliance on slavery.

4 Vladimir Lenin's older brother Aleksandr had been involved in a plot to kill Tsar Alexander III. It failed, and Aleksandr was executed.

5 The notation O.S. refers to the Julian calendar, a.k.a. Old Style, which remained in use in Russia until 1918, when it switched to the Gregorian calendar, a.k.a. New Style (N.S.).

6 The exact figure is unknown. The official records report 130 people killed and 299 seriously wounded (Ascher, 91-92; Sablinsky, 266). Various other estimates are much higher though and talk about thousands of deaths. For a discussion of various estimates, see Sablinsky, *The Road to Bloody Sunday* (261-68).

7 The Russian revolutionary Voline describes the birth of the first Soviet, in St. Petersburg, only a few days after Bloody Sunday, in his book *The Unknown Revolution, 1917-1921* (89ff.). According to Voline, the first meeting took place in his own apartment and was meant to organize the distribution of funds from affluent supporters among the many workers on strike (97-98). Another prominent Russian revolutionary however, Leon Trotsky, writes in *his* book, *1905*, that the first Soviet was organized months later, on October 13, 1905 (chapter 22). According to Violine, Trotsky did this for political reasons, namely to give a bigger founding role to the Russian Social Democratic Labour Party, which created this later Soviet.

8 Nicholas II did not like Witte — a tireless industrial reformer who wanted to modernize Russia and bring it on par with the Western powers — and had in fact at first declined the proposal of his Secretary of State to even add Witte to the delegation charged with negotiating with Japan, writing *"anyone but Witte"* on the note with the proposal (Harcave, 143). Only after several others had declined did the Tsar reluctantly agree with Witte as his plenipotentiary (Harcave, 144). Witte was unexpectedly able to secure very favorable terms from Japan though, which undoubtedly increased his influence with Nicholas II (Harcave, 152-53).

9 The Bolsheviks and Mensheviks had both been part of the Russian Social Democratic Labor Party (RSDLP), until splitting up over disagreement as to what should be expected from a party member, with Vladimir Lenin aiming for a party of professional revolutionaries, while his principal opponent in the matter, Julius Martov, wanted a less stringent membership policy. Lenin and his supporters were called Bolsheviks (*Bolšhinstvo*, meaning 'majority') while those who sided with Martov were known as Mensheviks (*Menšhinstvo*, meaning 'minority'). Lenin's faction was actually the minority at the time of the split though; the naming of the factions stemmed from an earlier vote.

10 The Constitution of 1906 was a major revision of the *Set of Laws of the Russian Empire* of 1832.

11 Pavel Milyukov was the founder and leader of the Constitutional Democratic Party, a.k.a the Kadets.

12   As Russia was still using the Julian, i.e., Old Style calendar at this time, the events are known as the October Revolution. Russia switched to the Gregorian calendar early 1918.

13   In *Nicholas II: Last of the Tsars*, the execution of the Romanov family and their four servants is described in detail by eyewitness Pavel Medvedev, a member of the squad of soldiers guarding the royal family (Ferro, 246-49). Medvedev said he did not take part in the actual shooting though, as he had been sent outside to check if anybody was on the street and whether the shots could be heard there.

14   If Russian famine and epidemic disease deaths between 1918-20 are included, the total death toll of the Russian Civil War would rise to a staggering nine million though (White, 357).

15   In "Victims of the Soviet Penal System in the Pre-war Years", Getty, Rittersporn and Zemskov show there is hard evidence for a total of slightly more than 840,000 camp deaths and executions between 1937-38 — the worst years of Stalinist repression — which, though extremely high, is still much lower than the millions frequently mentioned in accounts of the Great Purge (1022, table 1).

16   This poll was organized by the Public Opinion Foundation onApril22, 2014, Lenin's !44th birthday. It confirmed that a broad majority of Russians want Lenin to be buried ("Majority of Russians").

Part VI

War

Map 18: The Russian Front of the
First World War, 1914-18

1. NORWAY
2. GERMANY
3. AUSTRIA-HUNGARY
4. RUMANIA
5. BULGARIA
6. SERBIA
7. GREECE

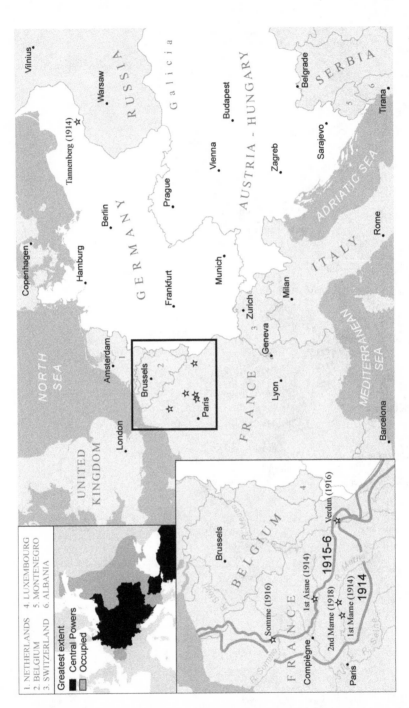

Map 19: The Central Powers in the First World War, 1914-18

36

THE GREAT WAR

*"Humanity is mad. It must be mad to do
what it is doing. What a massacre! What
scenes of horror and carnage! I cannot find
words to translate my impressions. Hell
cannot be so terrible. Men are mad!"[1]*

Second Lieutenant Alfred Joubaire,
May 23, 1916, diary, last entry

On November 11, 1918, at 10:59 a.m, in the village of Chaumont-devant-Damvillers, North-Eastern France, Private Henry Gunther rose up and started running through the fog, towards the German roadblock guarded by machine guns.[2] 29 minutes earlier, Gunther and the other members of his company had learned that the war would end at 11:00 a.m, exactly six hours after the signing of the armistice in the forest of Compiègne.

His comrades shouted for him to stop, but Gunther kept storming on. The German soldiers at the roadblock joined in, shouting at him to go back, that the war was over ("History of the Seventy- ninth", 505). Only it wasn't. Not yet.

Gunther kept charging and fired a couple of shots in the direction of the roadblock. When he got close, too close, one of the machine guns fired back, killing Henry Gunther on the spot ("History of the Seventy-ninth", 505). Seconds later, the clock struck 11:00 a.m. The First World War was over.

Of course it wasn't called the First World War back then, simply The Great War. U.S. President Woodrow Wilson had even optimistically called it *"the war to end all wars"*, in an effort to rally pacifist groups behind the cause of the Allied Powers against the Central Powers.[3]

As early as September 1914, the German philosopher Ernst Haeckel

had called the quickly spreading European war a "First World War",
but most people were not in the mood to philosophize about whether
or not this particular global carnage would be the start of a series.[4]

It had started with only two shots, fired in Sarajevo, Bosnia-
Herzegovina, by 19-year-old Bosnian Serb Gavrilo Princip, at
Archduke Franz Ferdinand of Austria — heir presumptive to the
Austro- Hungarian throne — and his wife Sophie, on June 28, 1914,
at 10:45 a.m.

Princip was a Yugoslav nationalist and member of an organization
called Young Bosnia, which wanted to dislodge Bosnia and
Herzegovina from the Austro-Hungarian empire and either unite it with
the Kingdom of Serbia or unite all the south Slavs — Bosniaks, Croats
and Serbs — in a united Yugoslavia.[5] He had drawn his inspiration
from another young Bosnian, Bogdan Žerajić, a law student who had
attempted to assassinate the Austro-Hungarian appointed Governor of
Bosnia and Herzegovina, General Marijan Varešanin, in 1910.[6]

Austria-Hungary blamed the Kingdom of Serbia for the
assassination and issued a ten-point ultimatum, with the intention of
either eliminating Serbia as a threat to Austrian-Hungarian control of
the Northern Balkans or — which would be even better — provoking
it into a war.[7]

Consequently, the terms of the ultimatum were intentionally harsh,
making it next to impossible for Serbia to comply, lest it was willing
to lose all its dignity as a sovereign state.

During the weeks that followed, Serbia's allies Russia and France,
feeling ill-prepared to go to war — especially against Austria's mighty
ally, Germany— nevertheless exerted pressure on Serbia to accept the
terms of the ultimatum. The German Empire, meanwhile, was eager
for *Krieg*, at least the military and governmental elite were, reasoning
that Germany was currently better prepared for war than France and
Russia, but that that advantage would likely dissipate over the course
of the next few years. In other words, if ever there was a good moment
for a successful 'preventive war', it was now (Mombauer, 107-09).[8]

So the German Ambassador to Vienna, Heinrich von Tschirschky,
was instructed by German Emperor Wilhelm II "*to emphatically press
the point that Berlin expected action be taken against Serbia, and that
Germany would not understand it when this opportunity to deal a blow*

was wasted", a message Tschirschky faithfully carried over to the Austro-Hungarian Secretary of State, Count Leopold Berchtold, on July 8.[9]

Meanwhile, several other countries weighed in on the diplomatic front, including Great-Britain, which proposed a mediation effort led by Britain, France, Germany and Italy, to solve the dispute between Austria-Hungary and Serbia (Martel, 196ff.). Of course Britain was unaware that Germany actually *wanted* to go to war and was strengthening Austro-Hungarian resolve to deal with Serbia once and for all.

However serious the situation though, most countries still believed they would be able to stay out of any war that might result from the Austrian-Serbian crisis.[10] They failed to fully realize that war between Austria-Hungary and Serbia would push a complex network of political and military alliances into action, like a finger flicking over the first domino. That those alliances would involve not only the great powers and their allies but also their many colonies and protectorates, essentially committing — apart from Europe — the entire African continent, the Middle East, India, Canada, New-Zealand and Australia to the conflict.

And war had changed. The silent marriage between the concept of total warfare — introduced by revolutionary France a little over a century earlier — and technology — responsible for mass production, cheap steel and a host of new weapons — would produce an outpouring of men, machines and munitions such as the world had never seen.

This time, there would be machine guns, barbed wire, airplanes, submarines, powerful artillery, poison gas and flame throwers. No more heroic cavalry charges gloriously winning the day, no more civilized day-time only battles on green fields, fought by neatly positioned infantry units in colorful uniforms. This time there would be mud, trenches, incessant bombardments, poison gas, almost suicidal attacks and counter-attacks and most of all dead bodies; dead bodies morning, afternoon and night.

And then there was the Schlieffen plan, or rather the Moltke plan, the German attack plan (Fromkin, 35).[11] In the early 1900s, Alfred Graf von Schlieffen, then Chief of the Imperial German General Staff, had envisioned defeating France by marching the German right wing through the Southern Netherlands, Belgium and Luxembourg in a wheel-like motion, thus involving not only those three countries but almost certainly also Great Britain (and with it the rest of the British Commonwealth) because the British had guaranteed Belgian neutrality in the Treaty of London of 1839.[12]

In 1906, Helmuth von Moltke the Younger (so-called to distinguish him from his uncle, Helmuth von Moltke the Elder, the Prussian / Imperial German Chief of the General Staff between 1857-88) succeeded Count Schlieffen as Chief of the General Staff. Moltke based his own attack plan on a possible two-front war with France in the West and Russia in the East, taking much of his inspiration from two deployment plans Schlieffen had worked on shortly before his retirement in 1906, known as *Aufmarsch I* — which concentrated German forces largely in the West — and *Aufmarsch II*, with a heavier focus on the East (Zuber 2011, 13-14).

Aufmarsch I was based on an isolated war between Germany and France, with a numerical superior Germany army outflanking the French forces by marching through Holland, Belgium, Luxembourg and Northern France, to attack the French forces from the flank and the rear. In view of the German numerical superiority, a French attack in Lorraine seemed unlikely in this scenario, though Schlieffen — who believed a counter-attack strategy was key for Germany in the event of a two- front war — certainly would have welcomed it (Zuber 2002, 46; Zuber 2011, 8, 22).[13]

Aufmarsch II was based on a two-front war with Russia and France and diverted more divisions to East Prussia, to defend against a Russian attack before mounting a counter-attack (Zuber 2011, 46). Moltke based his own operational plan on Schlieffen's two-front war scenario of *Aufmarsch II*, but used Schlieffen's overall strategy of the single-front war of *Aufmarsch I* for his attack on France (Holmes 2014). There were however two fundamental differences between Schlieffen's last wargame scenarios and Moltke's final, actual war plan.

The first was that Schlieffen did not factor in war with Russia in *Aufmarsch I* and thus positioned only a few divisions in East Prussia, using the rest for the Western front. Considering the fact that in 1905 the Russian Empire was mired in revolution and war with Japan, this was not an altogether unreasonable presumption. Secondly, Schlieffen used more divisions than were actually at his disposal. In his 1905 scenario for war with France for instance, Schlieffen employed ninety-six divisions, twenty-four more than actually existed (Zuber 2011, 7).[14]

In other words, Moltke based the overall strategy for the Western part of his two-front war plan on a one-front war plan in which twenty-four extra, non-existent divisions (two entire armies) had been added to the equation. One could therefore argue that, in the eyes of Count Schlieffen at least, Moltke's attack plan was doomed to fail from the start, simply because it lacked the necessary military strength.[15]

To make matters even worse, Moltke sent three more corps and a cavalry division to the East during the first weeks of the war — thus further weakening the right wing on the Western front — when it became clear that Russia was mobilizing much faster than had been anticipated (Marshall, 106).

As it turned out, those troops were still in transit when General von Hindenburg's Eighth Army delivered a crushing defeat to the Russians at the Battle of Tannenberg (Aug. 26-30, 1914). At the same time they were dearly missed at the Western front though, where the Germans came very close to breaking the French lines at the First Battle of the Marne (Sep. 5-12) but were ultimately defeated by a last ditch effort from the French, who threw everything they had in the fight. At one point the French authorities even commandeered 1,200 Parisian taxicabs to transport 6,000 French reserves to the battlefield (Tyng, 239-40).

On September 9, after the German Army had started its retreat to the Aisne River, Moltke reportedly told the German emperor „*Majestät, wir haben den Krieg verloren!*", Your Majesty, we have lost the war! (Schüddekopf, 18-19).

The German Army was pushed back some 30 miles, where it entrenched itself in a defensive position. In subsequent months, the Allied (French, British, Belgian) and German forces constantly tried to outflank each other, resulting in the so-called 'race to the sea' through Northern France. When they finally couldn't go any further, the Western front span from the French-Swiss border in the East up to the North Sea Coast in the West. Thus, by November 1914, the fast-

404 - J.C. Peters

paced mobile war of the first months had morphed into a static trench war that would last for years.

Though both sides continued to try and gain the upper hand, the front line would hardly change. At the Battle of Verdun for instance (Feb. 21-Dec. 18, 1916, the longest continuous battle in history) the Germans attacked the French for months, before being driven back again by massive French counter-offensives.

The new Chief of the German General Staff, Erich von Falkenhayn, who had succeeded Moltke after the lost Battle of the Marne, had chosen the city of Verdun as the best place to rupture the French front, and possibly also because it had been an important French bastion for centuries and he believed the French would be seriously demoralized if the Germans succeeded in capturing it.[16]

Several forts protecting Verdun — such as Fort Douaumont and Fort Vaux — were captured and recaptured over the course of the battle, against staggering losses on both sides. In all, the Battle of Verdun caused more than 700,000 casualties, including 305,000 dead (Strachan, 188).

Meanwhile, at the Battle of the Somme (July 1- Nov. 18, 1916), it was the British and the French who were on the offensive. Part of a simultaneous offensive with the Italians at the Italian front and the Russians on the Eastern front, the original tactical objective of the Somme Offensive was to deny the Central Powers the possibility of moving troops between front lines during quiet periods at one of the other fronts.[17]

In the words of French Commander-in-Chief Joseph Joffre, who had successfully pushed for coordinated Allied offensives at the second Allied military conference at Chantilly (24 miles north of Paris) on December 6, 1915, with his 'Plan of Action Proposed by France to the Coalition': "*Suppose, on the other hand, that there is no co-ordination of effort. In the present situation the Germans are able to add 10 divisions, no longer required in Serbia, to their forces in reserve--about 12 divisions--on the French front. Combined with the troops which could with safety be withdrawn from the Russian front, a mass of 25 to 30 divisions could be assembled. If the enemy is permitted to carry out these movements, he will employ this force, acting on interior lines, on each front in succession.*" (Joffre 1915).

After the start of the German attack at Verdun, the direct objectives of the Somme Offensive became to relieve pressure on the French forces at Verdun and to inflict as many losses on the enemy as possible (Philpott, 120-22).

The Battle of the Somme was even deadlier than that of Verdun, with well over a million casualties in just a few months (Ellis, 272).[18] Friedrich Steinbrecher, a German officer who was there, at one point wrote in desperation: "*Somme. The whole history of the world cannot contain a more ghastly word!*" (qtd. in Witkop, 322).[19]

When major operations at the Somme were halted in November due to poor weather conditions, the Allies had advanced about eight miles into German-occupied territory, or 14,080 yards. With a grand total of 693,000 Allied casualties, that comes to some 49 casualties per yard.

Though the British public was aghast with the high number of casualties and placed the blame for the high losses squarely on the shoulders of the British Expeditionary Force (BEF) commander General Sir Douglas Haig, he had had very little choice in the matter. The Somme Offensive had been vital in denying the German Army reinforcements at Verdun, and with the French heavily occupied with the Germans there, responsibility for the Somme Offensive inevitably fell to the British.

Besides, what other course was open to the Allies but to fight an unrelenting war of attrition? Like General Ulysses S. Grant during the American Civil War, 50 years earlier, British and French generals concluded that the best strategy against a determined, well-trained, but outnumbered enemy was to fight large, deadly battles until he simply could not go on anymore. In this regard, the battles at Verdun and the Somme certainly did the job.

On the Eastern front the Germans were more successful. In August 1914, the Russians had invaded East Prussia and, more to the south, the Austro-Hungarian province of Galicia (part of present-day Poland and Ukraine), but a couple of weeks later they were badly defeated at the Battle of Tannenberg, in East Prussia (present-day Poland). The Russian Second Army was almost completely destroyed and not long after the

Russian First Army suffered a similar fate. After the battle, General Alexander Samsonov, commander of the destroyed Russian Second Army, put a revolver to his head and killed himself (Marshall, 108).

The German Army was simply better equipped, better trained, better led and much more mobile than the Russian Army, with large numbers of troops being rapidly transported by rail, thus achieving a better concentration of fighting forces where needed.

The Russian Army did enjoy some success against the Austro-Hungarian Army, but after the Western front solidified in late 1914, the German High Command decided to concentrate its main effort on the Eastern front. During May-June 1915, the German Gorlice–Tarnów Offensive pushed the Russians back hundreds of miles, completely eliminating any threat of a Russian invasion of Germany or Austria-Hungary.

In the Summer of 1916, the Russians launched the Brusilov Offensive (named after General Aleksei Brusilov, who had conceived it), in line with the agreed upon strategy of coordinated Allied attacks. The offensive concentrated on the Austro-Hungarian province of Galicia. The main objectives were to provide relief to the French forces fighting at Verdun and the Italian forces fighting at Asiago, and to possibly knock the Austrian-Hungarian Empire out of the war. The offensive was very successful, diminishing Austria-Hungary as an independent fighting force and forcing the Germans to halt their attack at Verdun. It was Russia's finest hour of the war, but it would still be too little too late to turn the tide for Tsar Nicholas II.

Following the Russian October Revolution of 1917, the Bolsheviks sued for peace with the Central Powers to deliver on their promise to end the war, and also because they needed the army to fight in the civil war that was fast emerging between the communists and their opponents (basically everybody else).

On March 3, 1918, the Bolshevik government signed the Treaty of Brest-Litovsk, giving up Russian territorial claims in Finland, Estonia, Latvia, Belarus, Poland, Ukraine and Lithuania and ceding the cities of Kars, Ardahan and Batum (all three close to the present-day Turkish-Georgian border) to the Ottoman Empire. The communists thus signed away a total of one million square miles, containing a third of Russia's population, a third of its agricultural land, 85 percent of its beet-sugar land, more than half of its industry and nine-tenth of its coal mines (Grenville, 79-84; Wheeler- Bennett, 269). A heavy price for peace indeed, but perhaps not too heavy to stay in power and save the revolution.

The Ottomans had joined the Central Powers in August 1914 partly to recover Kars, Ardahan and Batum, which they had lost in the Russo-Turkish War of 1877-78. But while Germany threw the Ottoman Empire a bone in the Treaty of Brest-Litovsk by having those territories ceded back to it, its decision to enter the war on the side of the Central Powers would still cost it dearly.

Over the course of the war, the 'sick man of Europe', as the Ottoman Empire was called, lost all of its territory in the Middle East to the British and the French.[20] And it didn't stop there. Following the Ottoman Empire's surrender in October 1918, the Allies occupied Constantinople and divided most of the Anatolian heartland of the empire amongst themselves, thus effectively ending the more than 600-year-old Ottoman Empire in all but name. Turkish nationalists led by General Mustafa Kemal Pasha then started a war of independence, leading to the (official) dissolution of the Ottoman Empire but also the establishment of the modern-day Republic of Turkey, in 1923.

While the Ottoman Empire was a declining superpower that chose the wrong side, the United States was a rising superpower that preferred to choose no side, not least because public opinion was very much against American involvement in what was deemed a European affair. But opinions can change.

In may 1915, a German U-boat sank the British Ocean liner RMS Lusitania off the Southern Coast of Ireland, killing 1,195 passengers, 128 of them Americans.[21] U.S. President Woodrow Wilson demanded that Germany stop attacking passenger ships and Berlin complied, but early 1917 it resumed its unrestricted submarine warfare, in an effort to starve Britain out of the war. Germany had to do something and the High Command had calculated that if the U-boats could attack all commercial ships headed for Britain, it would be possible to sink 600,000 British shipping tons every month, forcing the British to sue for peace in five months (Halpern, 337-38).

Of course the generals knew full well that unrestricted U-boat warfare would most likely mean war with the United States, but they figured they would be able to broker a favorable peace before U.S. troops could make any real difference.

But, alas for the German High Command, reality would not play along — at least not long enough — as is so often the case with the best laid plans of mice and men.

To be sure, the new strategy of unrestricted U-boat warfare was a great success during the first few months of 1917. In both February and March about 500,000 tons of shipping were sunk (in January it had been only 110,000) climbing to 860,000 tons in April, 600,000 in May and 700,000 in June, while only nine U-boats were lost between February-April (Morrow, 202).

But after the British started deploying convoy tactics — large numbers of ships sailing together, escorted by destroyers and long-range aircraft — the volume of tonnage sunk fell dramatically.[22]

Convoys not only narrowed the area where U-boats could strike effectively, it also made hunting merchant and troop ships a much more dangerous affair, as the convoys were generally well- defended by destroyers, while the use of observation aircraft robbed the submarines of their chief advantage, the element of surprise (Abbatiello, 111).

Meanwhile, after years of remaining on the sidelines, Germany's (renewed) unrestricted U-boat warfare swayed American public opinion — and pacifist U.S. President Woodrow Wilson — towards entering the war on the Allied side, not least because most of the torpedoed American ships in March and early April — such as the *Vigilancia*, the *Illinois*, the *Healdton* and the *Aztec*— had been attacked without warning (Doenecke, 278-85).[23]

On April 6, 1917, Congress voted to declare war on Germany. By July 1st of the next year, more than one million men had embarked from the United States for France (Pershing, 184).[24]

In the spring of 1918, the Germans tried to force a break on the Western front one last time, before the by now continuous stream of fresh U.S. troops to the battlefields of France would permanently tip the balance in favor of the Allies. And also because 500,000 German troops had just arrived from the Eastern front, thanks to the Treaty of Brest-Litovsk with Russia (Gray, 7).

To prevent a repetition of Verdun, where massive frontal assaults preceded by heavy artillery bombardments had gained little ground, Chief of Staff General Ludendorff instead opted for the same tactic the Russians had deployed with so much success during the Brusilov Offensive two years earlier, using light, fast stormtroopers to penetrate weak points in the enemy front line after a short bombardment.[25] Once a breach was made, heavier armed infantry would follow and advance. The German spring offensive was very successful at first, gaining more ground than either side had been able to capture since the front lines had solidified late 1914. A series of attacks was launched from separate points, one of them bringing the Germans to within 75 miles (120 km) of Paris. There, they deployed the so-called Paris Gun, a monster measuring 118 feet (36 m), weighing 318,000 pounds (159 short tons) and firing 264 pound (120 kg) shells over a distance of 80 miles / 130 kilometer (Miller, "Railway Artillery", 732-45).

The first shell hit Paris on March 23, 1918, at 7:15 a.m (Miller, 723). Twenty others would follow that same day. The main objective of the Paris Gun was not to destroy the French capital, but rather to demoralize the Parisians by attacking their sense of security — knowing they could now be targeted by artillery. This objective was not achieved, partly because the Parisians didn't realize they were being attacked by long-range artillery and also because the bombardments did not do much damage. A total of 303 shells were fired, killing 256 people and wounding 620 others (Miller, 729-31).[26] The gun itself was never captured by the Allies.

Ultimately the German spring offensive failed, mainly because of logistical problems but also because it lacked a clear strategical goal beyond advancing and breaking the enemy. Perhaps Ludendorff's decision to stage a massive offensive at this stage of the war without a clear objective can best be explained by looking at the alternatives, which were: 1 — trying to hold a defensive position in enemy France with more American troops arriving there every day, or 2 — retreating back to Germany and hoping the Allies would not follow. Seen from that perspective, launching a final, all-out offensive to break the back of the enemy no doubt seemed a much more attractive option.

But the gamble failed and eight months and one massive Allied offensive later Germany surrendered, signing the Armistice in the early hours of November 11, 1918.

In the ensuing peace negotiations, Britain and the United States urged France to refrain from setting all too harsh conditions for peace with Germany, but the country that had lost so many of its sons at the Marne, the Somme and Verdun was adamant in its demands that adequate measures be taken to ensure its old foe would never again pose a threat to the French people. In the words of French Prime Minister Georges Clemenceau, describing France's position to President Wilson: *"America is far away, protected by the ocean. Not even Napoleon himself could touch England. You are both sheltered; we are not."* (qtd. in Keylor, 43).

To satisfy the French, Germany was thus forced to acknowledge the *'Alleinschuld'*, the sole responsibility for all the losses and damages the Allies had suffered during the war. [27] In addition to paying hefty reparations, Germany also had to cede a significant amount of its territory to France (Alsace-Lorraine), Poland (parts of East Prussia), Denmark (Northern Schleswig) and Belgium (Eupen-Malmedy), and give up its colonies in Africa and the Pacific.

Not all the French agreed with their government's crushing demands though. Following the finalization of the Treaty of Versailles — signed on June 28, 1919, exactly five years after the assassination of Archduke Franz Ferdinand and his wife in Sarajevo — French Marshal Ferdinand Foch declared: *"This is not peace. It is an Armistice for twenty years."* (qtd. in Adamthwaite, 28). The German Empire had fallen. Emperor Wilhelm II fled to the Netherlands, where he would live out the remainder of his life peacefully, dying there in 1941 at the age of 82 (in what was by then German-occupied Holland).

Germany itself was transformed into a democracy at the worst possible time for such an open form of government, never giving the so-called Weimar Republic a fighting chance. Between 1919-33, socialists, communists, democrats and national-socialists fought each other inside and outside the *Reichstag*, until Adolf Hitler's National Socialist Party came to power democratically and then quickly consolidated that power undemocratically.

The Austro-Hungarian Empire had fallen as well, giving rise to several new states, such as Austria, Hungary, Czechoslovakia and

Yugoslavia. Other countries in Central and Eastern Europe whose birth was intimately linked to the First World War were Finland, Poland, Estonia, Latvia and Lithuania.

The former Middle-Eastern possessions of the soon-to-be former Ottoman Empire were mostly divided among Great-Britain and France, with Mesopotamia, Palestine and Transjordan going to the British and Syria and Lebanon going to the French. Through the Balfour Declaration of 1917, the British government had promised the Zionist movement its support in establishing a Jewish state in Palestine, but although Great-Britain did allow mass immigration into British-controlled Palestine in the 1920s and 30s, the Jews would have to wait until after the Second World War before the British promise would materialize in a country of their own.[28]

The war also had a significant and lasting social impact, especially on the position of women. With their men fighting at the front, many young women had suddenly had to learn to fend for themselves, answering the call to contribute to the war effort by filling the positions left open by laborers who had been called up. Consequently, when the men that had survived the war returned, they found skilled, independent-minded women working at their old jobs. Needless to say this not only contributed to radical socio-economic changes but also boosted the feminist movement and its drive for equal rights and universal suffrage.

Approximately 8.5 million soldiers were killed during the First World War, 21 million were wounded and almost 8 million were reported as prisoner or missing.[29] The war thus counted almost 37.5 million military casualties, over 57 percent of all mobilized forces (Hosch, 219). Civilian deaths are not as well-documented and estimates among historians vary considerably, but most arrive at a figure somewhere between 6-9 million.

Although American Private Henry Gunther was the last soldier to have fallen, he was not the only casualty in the six hours between the signing of the Armistice and it going into effect. In fact, 10,944 casualties were recorded in those six hours, 2,738 of which were deaths, more than the average daily casualty rate throughout the war and more than the number of Allied casualties on D- Day, June 6,

412 - J.C. PETERS

1944, when Allied forces landed on the heavily defended beaches of Normandy — to end the next World War (Persico, 378).

1   Qtd. in Freedman, 101.

2   Gunther had recently been demoted to private from the rank of supply sergeant and was determined to "make good" before the war was over ("History of the Seventy-ninth", 505).

3   Though Wilson made the phrase famous, it is actually contributed to H.G. Wells, who, in October 1914, published the book 'The War That Will End War'.

4   In the Indianapolis Star of Sept. 20, 1914, Haeckel was quoted as saying that *"There is no doubt that the course and character of the feared "European War"...will become the first world war in the full sense of the word."* (qtd. in Shapiro, 329). He would not be around long enough to be proved right though, dying in August 1919 at the ripe old age of 85.

5   Some (Bosnian Serbian) members of Young Bosnia wanted to separate Bosnia and Herzegovina from Austria-Hungary only so it could be annexed by Serbia, but this was not Gavrilo Princip's primary aim. As he said during his trial: *"I am a Yugoslav nationalist, aiming for the unification of all Yugoslavs, and I do not care what form of state, but it must be free from Austria."* (qtd. in Butcher, 248).

6   Žerajić had fired five bullets at Varešanin, all of which missed. The sixth and last bullet, which he used for himself, did not miss. At his trial, Princip, talking about his admiration for Žerajić and the many visits to his grave, said: *"I often spent whole nights there, thinking about our situation, about our miserable conditions and about him. So I resolved to carry out the assassination."* (Preston 2014).

7   It later became clear that Serbian military intelligence had indeed been involved in the assassination on several levels (Maurer, 51-52).

8   According to Mombauer, 'preventive' war in this particular context did not mean preemptive — as in taking action to prevent being attacked — but rather to forestall a situation where Germany would no longer be able to take the initiative itself and was forced in a defensive position by stronger enemies (Mombauer, 108, note 6).

9   Translated from German: *"Hier mit allem Nachdruck zu erklären, dass man in Berlin eine Aktion gegen Serbien erwarte und dass es in Deutschland nicht verstanden würde, wenn wir die gegebene Gelegenheit vorüber gehen ließen, ohne einen Schlag zu führen."* The quote was relayed in a letter sent by Count Leopold Berchtold to the Hungarian Prime Minister, Count István Tisza, on July 8, after concluding his meeting with Von Tschirschky.

10 A key exception was Russia, which had already decided it could never accept Austro-Hungarian dominance of the Balkans and would in any case go to war should the Austrian-Hungarian Empire attack Serbia, even if it could only count on the support of France — which it certainly could, as the French Ambassador

assuredly told the Russian Secretary of State, Sergei Sazonov — and Britain stayed out of the conflict entirely (Martel, 196).

11 New documents about Schlieffen's plans have come to light after the fall of the Berlin Wall in 1989. Since then, a heated debate has emerged in the academic community about whether or not the Schlieffen Plan really existed as a ready-made attack plan for a two-front war, complete with railroad timetable allowing 42 days for victory in France before the bulk of the army had to be moved East to deal with Russia, as typical textbooks on the subject have for decades stated. Based on the new sources, military historian Terence Zuber has argued there was not, at least not in the clear-cut form historians have presented it in since the 1920s. I decided to include some of Zuber's evidence, while still emphasizing that the core of Schlieffen's deployment plans for war with France — a fast, strong, right- wing attack through Belgium and Northern France — remained intact in Moltke's plan.

12 Germany seriously doubted the English would really make good on their promise to protect Belgium when push came to shove though. On the night Britain formally declared war on Germany, Chancellor Theobald von Bethman Hollweg infamously asked his friend Sir Edward Goschen, the British Ambassador to Germany, how Britain could go to war over a *"scrap of paper"*, i.e., the 1839 Treaty of London (qtd. in Zuckerman, 20).

13 In the 1905/06 *Aufmarsch I* plan, the entire German Army — seventy-two active and reserve divisions, eleven cavalry divisions and twenty-six and a half Landwehr brigades, possibly further supplemented by ten Italian divisions — were employed in the west, against fifty-five French ones (Zuber 2011, 46-48). With this in mind, it is not difficult to understand that in this particular scenario Schlieffen would have considered a French attack into Lorraine a *"Liebesdienst"* (qtd. in Zuber 2002, 46).

14 It is important to note that Schlieffen did not add the extra, non-existent divisions to the Germany Army because he was overly optimistic or bad at losing, but because he strongly believed the army had to be enlarged if Germany was to be prepared for every eventuality. Like Moltke, Schlieffen was a strong proponent of universal conscription after French example, something that did not exist in the German Empire at the time.

15 This point is made by Terence Holmes in his article "Absolute Numbers: The Schlieffen Plan as a Critique of German Strategy in 1914" (2014). Holmes writes that Schlieffen concluded that the German army would need at least 48.5 corps to succeed in a French attack through Belgium, while Moltke planned this attack with 'only' 34 corps at his disposal.

16 This at least seemed the contention of legendary French General and President of the Fifth Republic Charles de Gaulle, when he spoke about the German objectives at Verdun 50 years later, before the Ossuary at Douaumont, the memorial for the soldiers who died during the battle (Jankowski, 46). Shortly after the war, Erich von Falkenhayn had advanced the theory of *Ausblutung* as

his leitmotiv for the brutal slaughter at Verdun, basically to bleed the French army to death by using Germany's superior artillery (Jankowski, 44). In the 1990s, historians debunked this theory as an excuse for a failed offensive (Jankowski, 46).

17 The location of the battle was chosen because it was where the French and British armies met. The first day of the Battle of the Somme, July 1st, 1916, remains the bloodiest day in British military history, with the British Expeditionary Force suffering 57,470 casualties, including 19,240 dead (Strachan, 192).

18 Ellis and Cox arrive at 498,000 BEF casualties, 195,000 French and 420,000 German casualties (Ellis, 272). As with other battles, historians' estimates vary, but most are above one million total casualties.

19 Witkop and Winter accidentally date Steinbrecher's letter to April 12th, 1916. The correct date is August 12, 1916. Friedrich Steinbrecher was killed April 19th, 1917, near Moronvillers (Witkop, 320).

20 France and Great-Britain subsequently divided the Middle-Eastern territories amongst themselves along the lines of the secret Sykes-Picot Agreement of 1916. The Russian Empire had been a minor party to that agreement as well, but in November 1917 the Bolshevik Government exposed the agreement to the general public.

21 In February 1915, Germany had declared the seas around the British Isles a war zone, giving itself license to sink all Allied ships in the area without warning. The New York German community wanted to run an ad in 50 American newspapers, warning passengers of the risks of embarking on a ship bound for Great Britain, but the ad was initially blocked by the U.S. State Department, until the person responsible for placing the ad pointed out that the Lusitania would not just be carrying passengers but also six million rounds of ammunition. U.S. Secretary of State William Bryan then cleared the advertisement, which ran on the morning the ship sailed (Simpson 1972).

22 In April 1917, at the peak of the German submarine offensive, 226 Allied ships were sunk. In September, the number had decreased to 87 ships (Abbatiello, 107). During the entire unrestricted submarine warfare campaign, a total of 1,757 ships were sunk, 1,500 of whom were sailing independently, according to Abbatiello.

23 Another incident that helped turn American public opinion against Germany was the publication of the Zimmerman telegram, on February 28. It revealed the content of a message Arthur Zimmerman, the German Foreign Secretary, had sent to the German Ambassador to Mexico in January, in which he instructed him to propose a military alliance to the Mexican government should the United States enter the war on the Allied side. Germany would in that case provide Mexico with ample funding for it to mount an offensive against the U.S. and reclaim the territories it had lost in Texas, New Mexico and Arizona. The telegram was intercepted and decoded by British intelligence.

24 General John J. Pershing was the commander of the American Expeditionary

Forces in World War I.

25 Ludendorff's official title was *Erster Generalquartiermeister* (first quartermaster) but in effect he was the Chief of Staff of Field Marshal Paul Hindenburg, who had been appointed head of the Supreme Command in August 1916 (Chickering, 74).

26 Harry W. Miller writes he was in the city himself several times during the period of the bombardments ("Railway Artillery", 727).

27 Voiced in Part VIII, Article 231, of the Treaty of Versailles, a.k.a. the War Guild Clause ("Versailles Treaty").

28 Between 1920-48, Palestine was administered by Britain as a mandate on behalf of the League of Nations and the League's post-World War II successor, the United Nations.

29 As reported by the U.S. War Department, February 1924. U.S. casualties amended by the Statistical Services Center, Office of the Secretary of Defense, November 7, 1957 (see also table in Hosch, 219).

37

Deeds, not Words

*"If I were a man and I said to you, 'I come from
a country which professes to have representative
institutions and yet denies me, a taxpayer, an
inhabitant of the country, representative rights,'
you would at once understand that that human
being, being a man, was justified in the adoption
of revolutionary methods to get representative
institutions. But since I am a woman it is
necessary in the twentieth century to explain
why women have adopted revolutionary methods
in order to win the rights of citizenship."[1]*

Emmeline Pankhurst, Freedom or Death
speech, November 13, 1913

In September 2013, a German court of appeal ruled that a thirteen-year-old Muslim girl was not allowed to opt out of mixed swimming lessons at her school, which she had been doing since she was eleven (Bartsch, "Integration Case"). The girl's parents, who were from Morocco, had filed a law suit to obtain legal dispensation to either skip the swimming lessons, or be given special instruction on her own (Hall, "Muslim girl").

The girl, or rather her parents, argued that wearing a 'burkini' — a swimming costume that covers the entire body — was not sufficient, because the Quran not only forbade a girl from showing herself to boys but also from seeing shirtless boys. The court rejected this argument, saying that *"the plaintiff has not made sufficiently clear that taking part in co-educational swimming lessons with a burkini breaches Muslim rules on clothing"*, adding that *"the social reality of life in Germany comes above her religious beliefs"* (qtd. in Hall,

"Muslim girl").

That social reality is that girls and boys in Germany are educated together, play sports together, and participate in society together. Of course it wasn't always so. In fact, less than 100 years ago women couldn't even vote in Germany, let alone enjoy the same rights as men to a higher education or a career.

The fight for women's right to vote — which militant suffragettes like Emmeline Pankhurst compared to fighting a civil war — had been slowly gaining momentum in the West since the 1850s, urged on by a small group of educated, resourceful and highly dedicated women, such as Susan B. Anthony (United States), Millicent Fawcett (United Kingdom), Kate Sheppard (New Zealand), Signe Bergman (Sweden) and Clara Zetkin (Germany).[2]

Women's suffrage was — and in some countries still is — part of a larger movement for freedom, democracy and equality regardless of race, sex, religion, sexual orientation or station in life, a movement that has been underway since the English Civil Wars of the 17th century, when King Charles I of England refused to yield to the demands of Parliament and was subsequently beheaded, in 1649.[3]

Before that time, inequality — between nobility and commoners, black and white, women and men, Muslims and Christians, Catholics and Protestants — had always been regarded as normal. But during the Age of Enlightenment, philosophers such as John Locke, Baruch Spinoza, Jean-Jacques Rousseau and Montesquieu helped popularize and solidify legal theories that turned this long accepted reality on its head. And in the second half of the 18th and the first half of the 19th century, these theories — such as government with consent of the governed, equality before the law and the separation of church and state — would help ignite revolutions in the Thirteen Colonies, France, a string of colonies in South America, France again, Belgium, France again, the German states, the Italian states, and several other European regions.

Of course, with the acknowledgement that the nobleman was equal to the peasant — at least philosophically and before the law — the cat was out of the bag. Because the same basic argument that made the peasant equal to the nobleman (their both being human) would prove just as potent an argument against slavery and discrimination based on sex, race or religion.

Another reason for the gradually changing view on women's suffrage in the 19th century was the changing role of women in society, spurred by the Industrial Revolution, which saw large numbers of women enter the professional workforce for the first time. In the textile town of Lowell, Massachusetts, for instance, 28 textile mills employed 8,000 workers by the late 1830s, the great majority of these women coming from the New England countryside (Montrie, 20). And this certainly was not the only place where women found employ.

The effect of women earning their own income was twofold: their economic value grew — both in the family and in society as a whole — and their independence increased. For the first time women did not necessarily need a man to support them.

The educational level of women also rose in the 19th century, especially in the second half, aided by a growing number of colleges founded exclusively for the education of young women. Such as Wheaton Female Seminary, established in Norton, Massachusetts, in 1834, with the help of noted women's educator Mary Lyon, who also created the first curriculum for the school, with the specific goal of making it equal in quality to those at men's colleges (Helmreich, 40-42). Three years later, Lyon also founded Mount Holyoke Female Seminary, in South Hadley, Massachusetts. In 1848, Queen's College, an independent school for girls, was established in London. This was also the first institution to award academic qualifications to women. Girton College, the first Cambridge college to admit women, followed in 1869, two years before Newham College, the second Cambridge college for women, to name just a few of the dozens of women's colleges established between 1830 and 1900.

Considering the growing number of smart, talented, mostly upper class young women finding their way into first-rate colleges to receive academic training and the significant number of young working class women earning their own income for the first time, it can hardly be called a coincidence that the women's movement gained so much traction in the second half of the 19th century.

In 1893, New Zealand became the first country in the world to give women the right to vote on a national level, while in 1907 the autonomous Grand Duchy of Finland (then still part of the Russian Empire) became the first European territory to adopt full women's suffrage.[4] The United Kingdom permitted women some voting rights in local elections through the Local Government Act of 1894, but nothing on a national level.

For some women, especially in the United Kingdom, progress was not going fast enough. They argued that the strategy of peaceful debate and gentle persuasion was not working. In 1903, Emmeline Pankhurst and her daughter Christabel therefore founded the militant Women's Social and Political Union (WSPU). To underscore that this movement would not just sit and drink tea, the founders gave the WSPU the motto 'Deeds, not words' (Bartley, 126).

To Emmeline Pankhurst and her followers, soon called suffragettes, the fight for equal rights for women was not a fight in the figurative sense, but a literal, actual fight, a war even. Pankhurst said WSPU members should see themselves as guerrilla fighters engaged in a civil war (Smith, 55). Like revolutionaries before them (and after them), WSPU members felt they had no other option left but violence to achieve democratic participation. So they slashed paintings at museums, cut telegraph wires, burned empty country houses, tea houses, churches — because the Church of England was against woman suffrage — even a school; they smashed windows of government buildings, firebombed politician's houses and attacked politicians as they went to work (Smith, 51; Stillion Southard, 61).

Never before had women made their case so forcefully, so violently, and many people thought the suffragettes went much too far in their zeal for equal voting rights.[5] Then again, women had already been making their case peacefully for more than 50 years, and men in the same situation had rebelled against their governments and fought wars not so long ago in the United States, France, Great Britain and many other countries.

In the United States, meanwhile, things did not take quite so violent a turn as in Britain, but there too the women's movement began adopting a more visible approach. On March 3, 1913, for instance — one day before President Woodrow Wilson's inauguration — 8,000 women marched down Pennsylvania Avenue in Washington D.C, gaining widespread attention for their cause (Barber, 66).[6] Women's movements in other countries adopted similar tactics.

At the outbreak of World War I the suffragettes halted all of their activities, calling on women to replace male workers who had gone off to the front. As the war progressed, women proved to be an indispensable part of the war effort, working en masse in factories to keep the economy going and to produce shells, uniforms, guns and bullets. WW I thus acted as a powerful catalyst for the women's movement.

In 1918, Germany, Austria, Russia and Poland gave women the right to vote, while the United Kingdom expanded suffrage to all women over 30 and all men over 21. Canada granted women the right to vote in most provinces, but it would take until 1929 before women could also stand for election for all offices. The Netherlands, Luxembourg and Belgium granted full suffrage in 1919, Czechoslovakia followed in 1920, as did the United States, through ratification of the Nineteenth Amendment.

On July 2, 1928, the United Kingdom granted women equal voting rights. Emmeline Pankhurst had died less than a month earlier, on June 14, aged 69.

In December 2015 — 122 years after New Zealand became the first country to grant women the right to vote — women in Saudi Arabia participated in municipal elections for the first time since the now deceased King Abdullah in 2011 granted women the right to vote in future municipal elections (MacFarquhar 2011; Giacomo 2015).[7] Since then, Vatican City has held the dubious honor of being the last remaining bastion of the all-male democracy.

Of course the path to full equality does not end with equal voting rights. Equal employment rights, equal pay for equal work, reproductive rights, adoption rights, custody rights, property rights, the right not to be treated as the weaker sex; full equality for every citizen regardless of sex, race, religion or sexual orientation remains a work in progress in most countries (if not all).

And although gender discrimination has been greatly reduced in the West in the 20th century, in some other regions women are still a long way away from being treated even remotely equal, just as some women are a long way away from considering themselves as such.

With that in mind, one wonders what Emmeline Pankhurst would have said to the thirteen-year-old Muslim girl who wouldn't swim with boys.

---

1   Pankhurst 1913.

2   Anthony died in 1906, fourteen years before ratification of the Nineteenth Amendment (a.k.a the 'Anthony Amendment'), which prohibits denying the right to vote based on sex. Fawcett, born in 1847, would live just long enough to see women's suffrage fully implemented in the United Kingdom, in 1928; she died the following year, aged 82. Bergman, Sheppard and Zetkin all lived to see the full implementation of the women's right to vote in their respective countries.

3   It could also be argued the roots of this movement go back to the late 16th century Low Countries, when the Dutch successfully rebelled against the Spanish Empire because of high taxes and religious oppression, subsequently founding the independent Dutch Republic, the first modern nation to guarantee religious freedom to its citizens (Union of Utrecht Treaty of 1579, article XIII). The Dutch Revolt was more focused on religious freedom than on securing political rights though, whereas the English Civil Wars, while fought partly against the backdrop of religious differences, were much more of a political power struggle between the King and Parliament.

4   The Parliament of the Grand Duchy of Finland was also the first in the world to have female MPs, following the 1907 elections.

5   Among them leading English feminist Milicent Fawcett, who wrote to a friend in 1909: "*It seems to me that there is only a slight distinction between their* [WSPU] *recent actions and positive crime.*" (qtd. in Holton, 47).

6   The number of marchers could have been even bigger if black women had been encouraged to participate, but the National American Woman Suffrage Association (NWSA) was not interested in this and even discouraged it. Alice Paul, the lead organizer of the march, said at one point that "*we must have a white procession, or a negro procession, or no procession at all.*" (Barber, 62). A rare lack of vision for someone so passionately fighting for equal rights. Ultimately, 42 black women participated in the march. Alice Paul lived to the ripe old age of 92, dying in 1977, fourteen years after the 'March on Washington for Jobs and Freedom' and thirteen years after the passage of the Civil Rights Act of 1964.

7   Municipal elections are also the only elections in Saudi Arabia, which functions as an absolute monarchy on all other levels. The first municipal elections were held in 2005.

38

THE GREAT DEPRESSION

*"Many people in America seem to be more
concerned about the present situation than the
Federal Reserve System is. If unsound credit
practices have developed, these practices will in time
correct themselves, and if some of the overindulgent
get 'burnt' during the period of correction, they
will have to shoulder the blame themselves and
not attempt to shift it to someone else."* [1]

Roy A. Young, chairman of the Federal Reserve
Board, September 20, 1928, thirteen months
before the Wall Street Crash of 1929

On March 9, 2009, the Dow Jones Industrial Average (DJIA) closed
at its lowest point in twelve years. By then, the Dow had lost 52.5
percent of its value since reaching its record high of 14,279 points
seventeen months earlier, on October 11, 2007. Market strategists and
financial journalists eerily observed that the current rate of decline
was closely mimicking that of the Dow during the Great Depression.
Back then, the DJIA had hit its high mark on September 3, 1929, at
381 points. But seventeen months and a Black Thursday, Monday, and
Tuesday later, the Dow had been deflated to 172 points, 54.7 percent
lower than its 1929 high.

And there were other similarities with that gloomy, despondent
era commonly associated with bank runs, massive unemployment,
tent cities and long bread lines. Both the Great Recession — as the
financial crisis that started late 2007 has come to be known — and
its infamous sibling, the Great Depression, were preceded by years
of cheap credit and the accumulation of consumer debt, followed by
a flood of individual bankruptcies and very public collapses of big

banks, rising unemployment and the freezing up of credit markets.

Some of the panic at the beginning of both crises no doubt also felt the same. In September/October 2008, daily news bombardments about the collapse of investment bank Lehmann Brothers, bank runs, hastily concocted bank takeovers and the high-powered Troubled Asset Relief Program (TARP) instilled people with fear that the whole financial system was crumbling down. In October 1929, the panic was caused by the uncontrollable crash of a stock market that many had been playing with borrowed money.

After having reached an all-time high on September 3, 1929, trading on the New York Stock Exchange had become increasingly volatile in the weeks that followed, with stock prices trending downward unevenly. At first, the downturn was seen as a healthy correction of an overheated market and buyers stepped in at every trough, trying to get in cheap. But that all changed on October 23, when, at the end of the trading day, everyone suddenly seemed to want to offload their stock at the same time and 2.6 million shares — roughly the trading volume for an entire day — changed hands in just one hour (Blumenthal, 13). The Dow Jones Industrial Average ended the day almost 7 percent lower.

Now investors and speculators most definitely *were* panicking. The next day, October 24 — Black Thursday — the Dow quickly lost eleven percent after the opening bell. Around midmorning, a group of leading Wall Street bankers met to discuss how to calm markets and stop the bleeding (Geisst, 191).[2] The solution they came up with was a classic one: to commit a serious amount of money to buying up a large block of key stocks like US Steel, AT&T, Anaconda Copper and General Electric.[3]

It worked. 12,894,650 million shares were sold on Black Thursday, but at the closing bell the Dow was down only 2 percent, a modest loss compared to the 11 percent it had been at the beginning of the day or the 7 percent the Dow had lost the day before (Wigmore, 7). The next day, the Dow even closed higher.

But it soon became clear that the market had only been pushed into the eye of the storm, a storm that grew even stronger over the weekend. On Monday the Dow took another nosedive, shedding 13 percent of its value, and this time the bankers did not intervene. On Tuesday, October 29 — Black Tuesday — more than 16 million shares changed hands while the Dow fell another 11 percent.

The next day, Albert Wiggin, president of Chase National Bank lamented : *"We are reaping the natural fruit of the orgy of speculation in which millions of people have indulged. It was inevitable, because of the tremendous increase in the number of stockholders in recent years, that the number of sellers would be greater than ever when the boom ended and selling took the place of buying."*[4] (qtd. in "Second Crash").

Of course in hindsight we are all wise men, but he was right nevertheless. In the years leading up to the crash of October 1929, many people had borrowed money to buy into the stock market, believing stocks would continue to rise in perpetuity. It was the same kind of thinking that had helped create the Dutch tulip mania of the 1630s, at the height of which a single tulip bulb sometimes changed hands for as much as fl. 1,200, about $20,000 in 2014 money (Goldgar, 238).[5]

The same kind of thinking, also, that helped create the dot-com bubble of the late 1990s, and the same kind of thinking that created the real estate bubble of subprime mortgages in the early 2000s, which helped ignite the Great Recession in 2007.

Then again, the Dow Jones Industrial Average had risen close to a staggering *500 percent* in the period 1921-29.[6] The war was over, the economy was booming and everybody was getting richer. Investing in the stock market had always been the exclusive playground of professional traders and the very wealthy, but in the 1920s brokers started attracting small investors as well, offering loans that sometimes financed up to 90 percent of the face value of stocks being bought. It promised to be a fast track to the American dream for millions of ordinary Americans and was hard to resist in a trading climate that was booming year after year. So when the Dow peaked on September 3, 1929, roughly $8.5 billion of the invested money was out on loan, almost double the entire amount of currency in circulation in the United States at the time (Lambert 2008).

Seven weeks later, when the bubble finally burst — as bubbles tend to do — all those small investors were quickly wiped out, pulling

426 - J.C. PETERS

their brokers down with them. But large investors were hit hard too, as were many businesses and commercial banks that had invested part of their capital in the stock market.

Banks played a key role in the Great Depression, just as they would in the Great Recession some 80 years later. Many commercial banks had invested part of their customer's savings in stocks, which seriously hurt their solvency after the markets crashed. On top of that, a growing number of debtors — small investors, businesses suffering from weakening demand, farmers hit hard by falling prices and falling exports — started defaulting on their loans. As a result, several banks had to close their doors, causing many people to panic and attempt to withdraw their savings. These bank runs then led to more bank failures, further eroding trust in the financial system, leading to still more bank runs and more bank failures. In all, some 9,000 banks — a third of U.S. banks — thus went under during the Great Depression (Guttmann, 6).

Meanwhile, with sagging demand and frozen credit markets, other businesses were in a bind as well. Acquiring funding through the stock or bond market was obviously out and banks were also unwilling and/ or unable to issue any new loans, as they were desperately trying to improve their own capital ratio to survive. With the capital markets quickly drying up, businesses began to cut back on investments, supplies, wages, working hours, everything to cut cost. Needless to say many businesses still went belly-up, defaulting on their debts and adding to the already rising unemployment.[7]

Before long, tens of thousands of workers were being laid off. By 1932, Gross Domestic Product was only half that of 1929, industrial production was down 46 percent, unemployment had risen to 36 percent and the average hourly pay in manufacturing had dropped more than 20 percent compared to 1929 (Wigmore, 315-16, 418).

Now, during the Global Financial Crisis of 2008, governments and central banks swooped in to save the day. The U.S.Treasury alone bought more than $400 billion in bad debt from banks and other financial institutions through the Troubled Asset Relief Program (TARP), and implemented two stimulus packages totaling almost $1 trillion.[8-9] At the same time, the Federal Reserve embarked upon the largest monetary policy action in history, buying up Treasury notes and mortgage-backed securities from banks to increase the money supply, a practice known as quantitative easing. The Federal Reserve, the European Central Bank, the Bank of England and other central banks also quickly lowered interest rates, to make borrowing cheaper for commercial banks and halt the credit crunch that had so devastated businesses in the 1930s.

But in 1929, there was no such swooping in. The government was not prepared to bail out failed banks or businesses and the Federal Reserve could not unfreeze the credit markets by increasing the money supply, because the U.S. was on the gold standard and the Federal Reserve Act required that all credit issued by the Federal Reserve should be backed by gold for at least 40 percent (Bernanke, 126). In fact, the money supply actually shrunk by a third between 1929-33, making money even more expensive (Friedman, 299). Nobel laureate economist Milton Friedman has argued that this is one of the main reasons why the recession of the early 1930s became the Great Depression, while Ben Bernanke, former Chairman of the Federal Reserve, has noted that there is strong evidence that countries that left the gold standard recovered more quickly from the Great Depression than those that stuck with it (Friedman, 299-301; Bernanke, 8).

Meanwhile, one of the measures Washington did take in the early days of the Great Depression — passing the Smoot-Hawley Tariff Act in May 1930 — proved to be hugely counter-productive (Bernanke 2013). Smoot-Hawley was aimed at protecting domestic businesses from foreign competition by raising the average tariff on imported goods by some 20 percent. In a last-ditch effort to prevent the bill from becoming law, more than 1,000 economists signed a petition asking President Hoover to veto it, writing: *"Countries cannot permanently buy from us unless they are permitted to sell to us, and the more we restrict the importation of goods from them by means of ever higher tariffs, the more we reduce the possibility of our exporting to them* (qtd. in New York Times 1930). But although Hoover himself was against the legislation, in the end he yielded to pressure from within the Republican party and signed the bill.

This naturally led to retaliatory policies in countries whose economies were adversely affected by the increased tariffs, most notably in Europe, where a decline in U.S. exports from $1,334 million in 1929 to $390 million in 1932 was answered with a decline in U.S. imports from $2,341 million to $784 million in the same period, thus deepening and lengthening the global Depression (Lawrence 2009).

All industrialized countries suffered during the Great Depression, but the vicious circle of rising unemployment and falling demand was particularly steep in the United States, which at the time was the only industrialized country without unemployment insurance and pension system. The purchasing power of Americans out of work therefore declined much more than that of the unemployed in many European countries. When President Franklin Delano Roosevelt came into office in March 1933, he sought to remedy this with an extensive social program he called "*a new deal for the American people.*"[10]

It was quite literally a new deal. The 'old deal', so to speak, had been that government interfered as little as possible with people's lives but at the same time also did very little to help them. Before Roosevelt, the U.S. government was a night-watchman state in every sense: it provided the people with protection against assault, theft, breach of contract and fraud and was charged with defending the nation in times of war, but that was about it. Low taxation, very little rules and regulations and no social security whatsoever; capitalism in its purest form possible.

When a modern society is in its early stages, this kind of laissez-faire approach makes a lot of sense. Agriculture, industry, commerce, trade, infrastructure, security, much of it still has to be developed, and the quickest way to do that is by providing citizens as much incentive as possible to work as hard as possible. Social security is a negative incentive in this phase, as it makes it easier for people to remain on the sidelines while others do the heavy lifting. But as society progresses and people's lives improve they also have more to lose, as does society.

What Roosevelt proposed was to change the social contract between the state and the people from a night-watchman state to a welfare state, from a laissez faire government to one that intervened in the economy to counter the less desirable effects of pure capitalism.

And intervene it did. Through the Federal Emergency Relief Administration (FERA) of 1933 for instance, which provided funds to states and cities for relief operations and the employment of people in a wide range of public jobs. In 1935 FERA was replaced by the Works Progress Administration, which at its peak in 1938 employed more than three million people in public works projects such as constructing parks, bridges, roads and schools (Odekon, 661). The Farm Security Administration (1935) aimed to improve the conditions for sharecroppers, tenants and small landowning farmers by providing credit when banks would not.[11] The National Labor Relations Act (1935) guaranteed workers the right to collective bargaining through unions and the Fair Labor Standards Act of 1938 set minimum wages and maximum working hours.

But the signature piece of the New Deal was the Social Security Act of 1935, which finally established a national system of unemployment insurance, welfare benefits for the handicapped and universal retirement pensions. It was paid for by a payroll tax, thus effectively institutionalizing solidarity among workers. More than any other New Deal legislation, the Social Security Act laid the foundation of the American welfare system. It still exists today.[12]

The New Deal was not just about social legislation though, it also sought to prevent future depressions through financial regulation and intervention. The Emergency Banking Act (1933) made it possible to place banks under Treasury supervision — keeping them afloat with federal loans if necessary — while the Glass-Steagall Act (1933) separated commercial banking from investment banking and protected savings accounts from being used by banks to speculate on the stock market.[13] To prevent future bank runs the Federal Deposit Insurance Corporation (1933) was established, for the first time federally insuring bank deposits, up to $2,500.

To increase the money supply and thus stimulate inflation and investment, the Roosevelt administration sought to increase the gold supply and devalue the dollar relative to gold. The Gold Reserve Act of 1934 therefore concentrated all U.S. gold coin and gold bullion held by the Federal Reserve in the hands of the U.S. Treasury and forced all U.S. citizens and institutions to sell their gold to the Treasury as well, while section 12 of the act gave the President the power to establish the gold value of the dollar by proclamation.[14] Roosevelt did so the day after signing the act, devaluing the dollar from $20.67 to $35 per troy ounce.[15]

It worked. As Milton Friedman and Anna Schwartz wrote in 'A Monetary History of the United States, 1867-1960': *"the money stock grew at a rapid rate in the three successive years from June 1933 to June 1936 — at continuous annual rates of 9.5 percent, 14.0 percent, and 13.0 percent. The rapid rise was a consequence of the gold inflow produced by the revaluation of gold plus the flight of capital to the United States....And the rapid rate of rise in the money stock certainly promoted and facilitated the concurrent economic expansion."* (544).

Needless to say, many Republicans were dead set against what they deemed a shameless attack on the free market economy, infringing on the very freedoms the country was built on with this buffet of measures that amounted to nothing less than blatant socialism. But since an overwhelming majority of the people agreed with Roosevelt, they were powerless to stop it.

The New Deal certainly eased the pain for millions of Americans and it is probable that it also helped end the Great Depression, though the final nail in the coffin of the economic depression of the 1930s would be the outbreak of World War II.

Europe had already been rearming in the years leading up to the war — contributing to falling unemployment there — but when it comes to battling unemployment, nothing beats fighting a total war.

In 1939, a short 21 years after the end of the Great War, the next generation of young men was drafted by the millions and peace-time economies were once again transformed into war-time economies, cranking out more heavy machinery than ever, hundreds of thousands of tanks, trucks, artillery and aircraft, hundreds of destroyers and submarines, dozens of aircraft carriers and battleships.

More than any other war before it, the Second World War would be an industrialized, mechanized, technological and total war of attrition, flattening cities and villages and killing people in the tens of millions. No economic depression could ever be great enough to withstand such willingness to waste.

Ironically, the Great Depression was not only ended by the Second World War but had also been one of its main causes, as it had hit one of the main instigators particularly hard.

After losing WW I, Germany had been forced to pay hefty reparations, crippling its economy. The Dawes Plan of 1924 (named after the American banker who devised it) had reduced the yearly reparation payments to a more manageable amount and established a loan program from American investment banks, but after the crash in 1929 those loans had stopped and the German economy quickly collapsed.

Politically speaking, radical parties like the Communist Party and the Nazi Party benefitted the most from the ensuing chaos, poverty and unemployment in the fragile, young democracy that was the Weimar Republic. After the Nazi Party had been voted into power in 1933, it quickly banned the Communist Party and ensured passage of the Enabling Act, which gave the government — i.e., Reich Chancellor Adolf Hitler — the power to legislate without the approval of the *Reichstag,* the German Parliament. This effectively ended the Weimar Republic and set Germany on the path to war (once more).

The impact of the Great Depression did not end with WW II, but has reverberated even into our own time, through its most lasting effect, the establishment of a new social contract between the state and the people. A contract demanding more responsibility for people's well-being from the state, in exchange for more taxes, more regulation and less individual freedom.

A paradigm shift that is still being debated today, or perhaps especially today, with the memory of that hard decade safely tucked away in the long long ago.

---

1   Young 1928.

2   Among them Thomas Lamont of Morgan, Albert Wiggin of Chase National and Charles Mitchell and George F. Baker Jr. of National City Bank (now Citibank).

3   The same kind of rescue operation had also been successfully performed during the Panic of 1907, when financiers J.P. Morgan, John D. Rockefeller and other key figures from the New York banking scene had committed their own funds to stop a banking panic and calm down the stock market.

4   In 1930, Chase National Bank would acquire the Equitable Trust Company of New York, making it the world's largest bank.

5   One such bulb was an Admirael van der Eyck, sold on January 18, 1637 for fl. 1,205. (Goldgar, 238). In her introduction, Goldgar aptly summarizes the main themes of the tulipmania by quoting two phrases from a conversation at

the time, during which one man showed another a precious bulb: *"That must have cost you"*, and *"it still isnt paid for"* ("Tulipmania", Introduction, i). The purchasing power of the Dutch florijn in today's money was calculated at iisg. nl/hpw/calculate2.php.

6 The Dow's low of 1921 was 64, the high of September 3, 1929 was 381, i.e., up 317 points compared to the low (Gann, 17).

7 A total of 86,462 businesses went bankrupt between 1930-32 (Wigmore, 132, 230, 315).

8 The U.S. Treasury took on $466 billion of obligations under the TARP program, which included the AIG rescue. A total of $418 billion was actually disbursed ("Troubled Asset Relief Program", 3, fig.1). As of January 2013, $344 billion has been repaid. Together with other income — such as dividend and interest — the total cashback was $405 billion.

9 The first stimulus package, the Economic Stimulus Act of 2008, valued at $152 billion, was enacted in February 2008 to avert an impending recession. The second stimulus package, the American Recovery and Reinvestment Act (ARRA) of 2009, with an estimated cost of $831 billion between 2009-19, was enacted in February 2009 to deal with the Great Recession. ("Estimated Impact",1) The Congressional Budget Office has estimated that more than 90 percent of ARRA's impact was realized by the end of 2011.

10 Roosevelt had already announced his intention to enact large-scale social reform the year before, saying in his speech accepting the Democratic Party's Presidential Nomination: *"Throughout the Nation, men and women, forgotten in the political philosophy of the Government of the last years look to us here for guidance and for more equitable opportunity to share in the distribution of national wealth.(..) I pledge you, I pledge myself, to a new deal for the American people. Let us all here assembled constitute ourselves prophets of a new order of competence and of courage. This is more than a political campaign; it is a call to arms."* (Roosevelt 1932).

11 The FSA was originally called the Resettlement Administration but was renamed in 1937.

12 Today it is part of U.S. Code: Title 42 - The Public Health and Welfare, chapter 7 - Social Security.

13 Glass-Steagall was repealed in 1999. Some economists have argued that the repeal contributed to the financial crisis of 2007-08, among them Nobel Laureate Joseph Stiglitz, Robert Kuttner and Richard D. Wolff (Stiglitz 2009; Kuttner 2011; Wolff, 75).

14 Roosevelt had already criminalized the possession of gold by Executive Order on April 5, 1933, a month and a day after taking office (Exec. Order 6102). The authority to do so he derived from an amendment of the Trading With the Enemy Act of 1917, which extended the scope of the act to any declared national emergency, not just one declared during times of war. The Gold Reserve Act

ratified this Executive Order, among other things. In 1935, the constitutionality of the federal government's restrictions on the private ownership of gold was upheld by the Supreme Court in a series of rulings — known as the gold clause cases — by a narrow 5-4 majority.

15 By seizing the Federal Reserve's gold reserves and giving the President the power to unilaterally determine the value of the dollar, the Gold Reserve Act deprived the Federal Reserve of its primary function as independent monetary policy authority, a function it would not regain until the Treasury-Federal Reserve Accord of 1951.

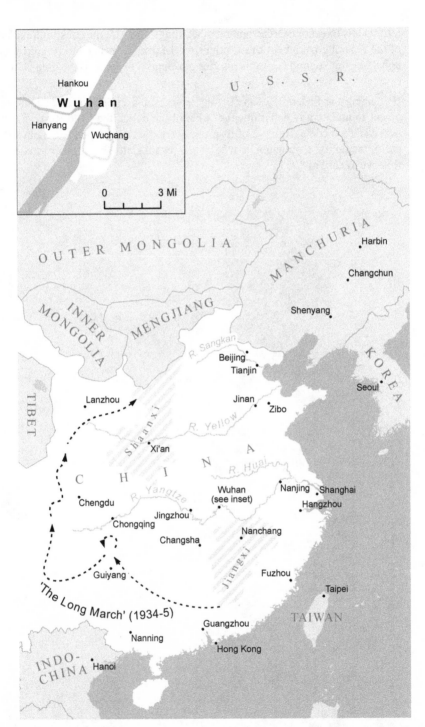

Map 20: The Communist Insurgency in China, 1927-37

39

CHINESE CIVIL WAR PART I & II

*"Every Communist must grasp the truth, "Political
power grows out of the barrel of a gun." Our
principle is that the Party commands the gun, and the
gun must never be allowed to command the Party."[1]*

Mao Zedong, Problems of War and Strategy, 1938

In a country with a population of over 1.3 billion, an organized
protest of a mere 200 people might not seem worth mentioning.[2]
Except that in this particular country, protests are frowned upon (as
in forbidden) and protesters are frequently escorted to a place where
they can quietly rethink their behavior (as in jailed). So, when, on
February 20, 2011, 200 Chinese actually showed up in front of the
McDonald's in Wangfujing — a famous shopping street in Beijing
— in response to an online call to express displeasure about the lack
of reforms and the widespread corruption in the one-party state, it
was indeed taken very seriously by the Chinese authorities (Branigan
2011).

Inspired by and in reference to the Tunisian Revolution — which
had led to the ousting of Tunisian President Zine El Abidine Ben Ali
just a month before — the organizers called the protests the start of
a 'Jasmine Revolution' (Branigan 2011). The police showed up in
full force. Dozens were detained, some by security officers in plain-
clothes. Several of those arrested seemed nothing more than curious
onlookers, some were shouting *"why are you arresting me, I haven't
done anything wrong."* as they were roughly dragged away from the
site (qtd. in "China police").

Their objection to being arrested was not entirely unfounded —
even if they were demonstrating — since the Chinese Constitution
states that *"citizens of the People's Republic of China enjoy freedom
of speech, of the press, of assembly, of association, of procession,*

and of demonstration." ("Constitution People's Republic", II.35). Then again, it also states that "*The Chinese people must fight against those forces and elements, both at home and abroad, that are hostile to China's socialist system and try to undermine it*" ("Constitution People's Republic", preamble). That is because the ultimate function of the Chinese Constitution is not to protect the people, but the state. So it makes perfect sense that the general rule with regards to freedom of expression in China is that you can say, print and paint whatever you want, until the government says you cannot.

Of course the Communist Party of China, which has ruled China since 1949, certainly knows a thing or two about how to undermine the system and ultimately overthrow the government through protests, strikes, rebellion and revolution, seeing as it had for decades fought several rival factions in a number of uprisings and civil wars, before finally being able to proclaim the People's Republic of China. A long march indeed.

It had all started 50 years earlier, in 1899, with the Boxer Rebellion. After China had lost the Opium Wars of the mid-19th century, the British and French had forced the Middle Kingdom to open up its ports to trade with the West, legalize the import of opium, permit the establishment of diplomatic missions in Beijing and allow Christian missionary activity.

Growing opposition against this forced foreign presence gave rise to a sectarian movement in rural areas, soon referred to as a 'Militia United in Righteousness' by its followers and called 'Boxers' in the West (Esherick, 68-69, 154-55; Harrington, 12). Simply put, the Boxers wanted to protect traditional values and throw the foreigners out, something the ruling Qing dynasty was clearly unable to do.[3]

On June 10, 1900, with the Boxers threatening the legations (diplomatic posts) in Beijing, the Western powers and Japan sent troops to protect the Legation Quarter (Xiang, 244-45).[4] Meanwhile, with the Boxer movement quickly gaining momentum, Empress Dowager Cixi finally decided to throw in the support of the Imperial army with the rebellion. On June 19, an ultimatum was sent to the Legations, ordering all diplomats and foreigners to leave Beijing and proceed to Tianjin within 24 hours (Xiang, 318). On June 21, China formally declared war on all foreign powers.

During an emergency meeting at the Spanish Legation, the diplomats from the various foreign nations decided that leaving Beijing without the support of the relief force would be tantamount to suicide (unbeknownst to the diplomats the relief force had already been defeated though). Instead, it was decided to play for time and wait for the troops (Xiang, 319-23).

German diplomat Baron von Ketteler emphatically disagreed with this decision however and decided to leave Beijing that same day. When he was killed in the streets by a Manchu soldier shortly after leaving, the other foreigners were all the more convinced that the only thing they could do was stay and defend the Legation Quarter until help arrived (Xiang, 333-34).

When the Chinese army and the Boxers subsequently besieged the quarter, about 475 civilians and 450 soldiers from the United Kingdom, France, Germany, Italy, Austria-Hungary, Belgium, Russia, Japan, the Netherlands, Spain and the United States, together with around 3,000 Chinese Christians, defended the quarter and held out for 55 days, until an Eight-Nation alliance landed in China, defeated the Imperial Army and occupied Beijing on August 14, 1900 (Fairbank, "New History", 231).

On September 7, 1901, China was forced to sign the so-called Boxer protocol, a humiliating peace treaty. The Legation Quarter was to be enlarged, fortified and garrisoned with a permanent contingent of foreign troops, some 25 Qing forts were to be destroyed and the Imperial government had to pay an indemnity of $333 million over a period of 40 years, at an interest that would more than double that amount (Fairbank, "New History", 231-32).

During the next few years, several uprisings unsuccessfully tried to overthrow the unpopular Qing dynasty. But revolutions cannot be rushed. Like many violent eruptions, it often takes years, if not decades of antagonizing frustration without relief, before they have gathered enough strength to explode out in the open and destroy the old.

It was coming though.

In May 1911, the Imperial government decided to nationalize local railway development ventures and hand them over to foreign powers, as part of the indemnity owed. Many Chinese were livid over this illegal confiscation and popular outcry soon escalated into another full-blown uprising. On October 10, the Tongmenghui, or 'United League', an underground resistance movement made up of several revolutionary groups, launched a revolt in the city of Wuchang (in Hubei Province, South Central China), together with mutinying soldiers. After the revolutionaries had succeeded in taking the city, uprisings also broke out in several other, mostly southern provinces, some of whom subsequently declared their independence from the Qing government.

Of course, all revolutionary enthusiasm and solemn independence declaring aside, there was also still an emperor, an Imperial government and — most important of all — an Imperial Army. Acknowledging the seriousness of the situation, the Qing government recalled Yuan Shikai, former commander of the powerful Beiyang Army, from retirement, to suppress the revolutionaries.[5]

Fighting between loyalist and revolutionary forces soon concentrated on the two cities of Hankou and Hanyang, on the north bank of the Yangtze River, opposite to Wuchang, where the uprising had started. After 41 days of hard fighting, Yuan Shikai succeeded in retaking Hankou and Hanyang.

But then, in a surprise move, he opted for a ceasefire and negotiating with the revolutionaries, rather than pushing on to Wuchang and finish them.

A shrewd strategist, Yuan realized that after crushing the rebellion, the Qing government would most likely thank him for his services and send him back into retirement again, whereas the revolutionaries could help him achieve much more. After some back and forth, a political compromise was reached between Yuan Shikai and Sun Yat-sen, the leader of the Tongmenghui, whereby Yuan would help force the emperor to abdicate and establish a unified Chinese Republic, in return for the support of the southern provinces in electing him as the first President of the new republic. On January 1, 1912, representatives of the seceded provinces thus proclaimed the Republic of China.[6]

In the run up to the first Parliamentary elections, the Tongmenghui merged with several smaller pro- revolutionary groups to form the Kuomintang, the Chinese Nationalist Party (Goldman, 58-59). After winning the 1913 elections by a landslide, the Kuomintang (KMT) quickly moved to increase the independence of Parliament and curtail the power of the President by mandating open presidential elections. Yuan, determined to protect his position, reacted by clamping down on the KMT, removing its leaders from key positions and dissolving the KMT-dominated Parliament (Dillon, 150-51). The KMT called for a 'Second Revolution', but every hint of uprising was immediately crushed by Yuan's forces.

In December 1915, Yuan, apparently not satisfied with ruling as presidential dictator, declared himself emperor. The nascent republic thus seemed on the fast-track back to becoming the Middle Kingdom again, but widespread opposition quickly surfaced, with military leaders and governors of several provinces declaring their independence.

Yuan started backpedaling and renounced his imperial aspirations three months later, but the damage was already done. Another three months later he was dead (of natural causes), leaving behind a country in disarray. Regional warlords soon rose to power, establishing the kind of feudal rule reminiscent of medieval Europe, when local lords frequently ruled as absolute kings.

To the north, in Beijing, a military regime was established, dominated by whatever general was in control of the Beiyang Army (hence its nickname, 'Beiyang government'), while Sun Yat-sen and his Kuomintang set up a rival government in the south, in Guangzhou. Aside from fighting each other, both governments were also beset by internal conflict, rife with power grabs, intrigue and shifting alliances.

In 1923, the Kuomintang joined forces with the Chinese Communist Party (CCP), which had been established two years earlier, to form the First United Front. The Soviet Union had actively championed cooperation between the CCP and the KMT, telling the mostly reluctant CCP it was necessary to form a bloc within the much larger KMT so it could be taken over from the inside, while at the same time luring the KMT with the promise of more (financial) support (Saich, 8-10).[7]

The first few years the alliance was a success. With Russian help, the KMT and CCP successfully fought the warlords and formed a disciplined, well-trained National Revolutionary Army. But after the death of Kuomintang founder Sun Yat-sen in 1925, the alliance began to weaken. A power struggle also emerged within the KMT, between the left-leaning Wang Jingwei and the right-leaning Chiang Kai-shek.

In 1926, with internal tension already building up, Chiang launched the Northern Expedition, a military campaign aimed at finally defeating the warlords and reunify China under one government. Regional warlords had plagued China for a decade but now their number was up; the National Revolutionary Army was better motivated, better trained and better equipped than the warlord armies and picked them off one by one. Several warlords did not even let it come to a fight but instead defected and joined the Nationalists (Zarrow, 233-44).

Meanwhile, tensions between the KMT's left and right wing reached new heights after Wang Jingwei moved the seat of government from Guangzhou to Wuhan, in January 1927. Chiang responded by setting up a rival government in Nanjing a few months later (Taylor, 68).

Events took a surprising turn in March though, when the workers' movement in Shanghai took up arms against the Zhili warlord regime there and succeeded in taking control of the city when the local garrison commander defected (Taylor, 64-65). The Communist Party quickly set up a provisional government and organized the masses. When the Northern Expedition Army — which had been advancing on the city — entered Shanghai a few days later it found a city of armed civilian militias, a thriving communist organization and a concerned business community. It was then that Chiang Kai-shek (who arrived a few days after the army) and other right-wing leaders of the KMT decided it was time to purge the party of the communists (Zhao, 94).

On April 12, Chiang ordered the disarming of the workers' militias in Shanghai and declared the provisional government, labor unions and all other communist organizations dissolved. When some of them resisted, a bloodbath ensued (Zhao, 94; Taylor, 66-68). It would mark the start of a bitter, 22-year-long civil war between the Kuomintang and the Chinese Communist Party.

In July, the left-wing Kuomintang government in Wuhan followed suit and started purging the Communists from its ranks as well, after finding out that Stalin had instructed the Communists to recruit their own army and overthrow the Kuomintang government (Gray, 224). A couple of months later, the left and right wing of the Kuomintang reunited under leadership of Chiang Kai-shek.

The Communists were off to a bad start in the civil war. Already weakened by the purge, they nevertheless launched several uprisings in the second half of 1927, all of which failed. Among them an action organized by 33-year-old Mao Zedong, one of the founding members of the CCP, who in September led a small army of peasants against the KMT in Hunan province but was quickly defeated, forcing him to retreat into the mountains.[8] Two months later the Communists took over the city of Guangzhou in the south (less than 100 miles from Hong Kong), but the KMT crushed the uprising within 48 hours, leaving 5,000 Communists dead. The Guangzhou uprising made it painfully clear that the CCP lacked the muscle to fight the Kuomintang in open combat. The Communists therefore decided to retreat to the countryside, where they began building a loyal base of followers among the peasants.

In 1930 another civil war broke out within the ranks of the Kuomintang. This time, four warlords who had previously aligned themselves with Chiang Kai-shek revolted, because of Chiang's ongoing effort to strengthen the central government at the expense of regional — meaning *their* — power bases (Taylor, 89). Several other warlords soon joined the anti-Chiang coalition, swelling its numbers to an impressive 600,000 men. Chiang himself had 1 million troops under this command, but a significant portion of these were on garrison and could not be sent on campaign (Taylor, 89). The so-called Central Plains War would be short-lived but intense. By November 1930, Chiang had subdued the warlords, but at the considerable cost of a total of 240,000 casualties (Taylor, 89). The war also bought the CCP valuable time and seriously weakened the defenses in Manchuria, in Northeast China, which attributed to the Japanese invasion there the following year — yet another headache for Chiang.

Having emerged as the undisputed leader of the Kuomintang after the Central Plains War, Chiang set out to destroy the CCP's Red Army and launched a series of encirclement campaigns. At first these were not very successful, but in October 1934 the KMT succeeded in surrounding the First Red Front Army in Jiangxi province, where the CCP had established the so-called Chinese Soviet Republic.

Faced with the threat of total annihilation, the First Army's commanders — Mao Zedong, Zhu De and Zhou Enlai — decided to try and break through the KMT lines and retreat. It worked, and 90,000 soldiers escaped the trap and embarked on what would come to be known as the Long

March, a yearlong march over a distance of 6,000 miles from Southeast to Northwest China (Snow, 36).[9] Of the 90,000 soldiers, about 7,000 would make it to the Northwestern Shaanxi province in October 1935 (Snow, 432-34).

Although the Long March came at a high cost, it provided the CCP with an isolated region where it could regroup and rebuild its numbers. It also made heroes out of the survivors in the eyes of many peasants and cemented the Red Army's reputation of being fiercely dedicated and determined. Retreat and defeat were thus turned around and beautified with a hopeful smile of achievable victory.

Together with the irresistible carrot of land reform, promising land to all those poor farmers working in the fields of rich landlords, the Long March contributed greatly to the growing popularity of the CCP in the countryside, while also solidifying the position of Mao Zedong as the undisputed leader of the Chinese Communist Party.

Meanwhile, Japan, which had invaded Manchuria (Northeast China) in 1931, continued to steadily expand its control over the region, bringing local Chinese warlords under its sphere of influence and forcing the Kuomintang into agreements that weakened it militarily in the north.[10] KMT generals increasingly pressured Chiang Kai-shek to focus his military efforts on fighting Japan instead of the CCP, but Chiang wanted to defeat the Communists first, saying *"the Japanese are like a disease of the skin, but the Communists are like a disease of the heart"* (qtd. in Eastman, 33). He also believed only a united China would be able to repel the Japanese invaders.

In December 1936, realizing Chiang would rather let half of China fall to the Empire of Japan before abandoning his mission to destroy the Communists, two disgruntled KMT generals decided to kidnap

Chiang Kai-shek in Xi'an (the capital of Shaanxi province, Northwest China) and force him to negotiate a truce with the Communists.[11] At first, most CCP leaders, including Mao, said they would rather execute Chiang for his communist purges than negotiate any kind of truce with him. But after Stalin urged Mao to negotiate with Chiang — seeing as the death of Chiang at this stage would benefit neither Chinese resistance to Japan nor Russian interests in the East — Mao acquiesced to talks with the KMT, which subsequently led to an uneasy truce between the two belligerents on December 24, 1936 (Taylor, 129-30).

Though conflict intensity between the KMT and the CCP was toned down during the Second Sino- Japanese War (1937-45), there was hardly any real cooperation between the two sides, either.[12] The Communists engaged the Japanese mostly in guerrilla warfare while the KMT predominantly fought open battles. The Communists also continued to build popular support in rural areas, while skirmishes between the KMT and CCP continued in regions isolated from the war, known as "Free China".

In January 1941, what little cooperation that had been left between the two sides ended, after KMT forces surrounded and subsequently attacked the Communist New Fourth Army (N4A), which suffered an estimated 9,000 casualties as a result (Fairbank, "Republican China", 666-69). According to the KMT, the New Fourth Army Incident was caused by the N4A's refusal to move out of southern Anhwei and Jiangsu by December 31, as had been ordered by Chiang Kai-shek, but an angry CCP called it a second 'anti-Communist upsurge' (Fairbank, "Republican China", 666-69). Whatever the case, after the New Fourth Army Incident the truce between the CPC and the KMT existed in name only.

After the unconditional surrender of Japan on August 14, 1945, a renewed effort was made by the Kuomintang and the Communists to come to a peaceful solution. Subsequent talks attended by Chiang Kai-shek, Mao Zedong and U.S. Ambassador to China Patrick J. Hurley, led to the Double Tenth Agreement of October 10 (10/10), in which both sides agreed on basic principles for peaceful reconstruction. But for all the talk, heavy fighting between both sides had continued during almost the entire time of the peace conference (Fairbank,

"Republican China", 726).

The United States, for its part, preferred a peaceful solution, but at the same time it was also determined to prevent a communist takeover in China, just as much as the Soviet Union was determined to make it happen. To help the Kuomintang, the U.S. provided it with hundreds of millions of dollars in loans, military equipment and training (Blum, 23). It even transported some 500,000 KMT troops over sea and air to Central and Northern China, after the Russians refused to let the KMT pass through Soviet-occupied Manchuria (Fairbank, "Republican China", 726). As early as September 30, with the peace talks still going on in Chongqing, the U.S. sent 53,000 troops to Northern China in support of the Chinese Nationalists.

In the summer of 1946, Chiang Kai-shek launched a large-scale invasion of communist territory in Eastern and Northern China. Mao ordered the People's Liberation Army (PLA, the new name for the Eighth Route Army and New Fourth Army) to avoid open battle and instead engage in mobile warfare (Zedong, "War of Self-Defense", 3). Cities and other places were not to be defended at all costs, as that would only play into the hands of the KMT, whose strength lay in conventional warfare. Instead, Mao wanted to wear down the invasion force, attacking it where it was weak while avoiding battle in all other circumstances. At the same time, he urged party members to continue to win over the peasants by promising them land reform (Zedong, "War of Self-Defense", 4). The strategy proved successful, with the KMT suffering heavy casualties without making serious gains. In the summer of 1947 the CCP counter-attacked in Northeast China. Over the course of a year, the Communists gradually pushed back the KMT, capturing cities and towns in the north while also inflicting heavy casualties on Chiang's forces (Fairbank, "Republican China", 765-72).[13] The CCP suffered heavy casualties as well, but because of their widespread support in the countryside they had less trouble replenishing their ranks. The balance of power began to shift in favor of the People's Liberation Army.

In September 1948, the PLA launched the first of three decisive counter-offensives. During the Liaoshen Campaign, the PLA concentrated on Northeast China (a.k.a. Manchuria), particularly the areas around the cities of Shenyang, Changchun and Jingzhou, where the KMT troops were stationed. In six weeks time, the Communists captured all three cities — and with it the whole of Manchuria — inflicting 472,000 casualties on the Nationalist forces (including defections and prisoners of war) at a cost of 65,000 PLA casualties (Lew, "Historical", 121-22).

According to contemporary U.S. military analysts, causes of the Nationalist defeat in Manchuria lay mainly in the over-extension of its forces and the ineptitude of its leadership (Fairbank, "Republican China", 766). Also, what the Communists lacked in training and equipment, they more than made up for in zeal, a sense of common purpose and a knack for strategic and tactical warfare. Though not fatal right away, the Liaoshen Campaign had struck a wound from which the KMT would not recover. Four days after its conclusion, on November 6, the Communists launched a second counter-offensive, the Huaihai Campaign. This time fighting concentrated at the Huai River basin, between the Yellow River and the Yangtze River, with the destruction of the KMT forces there the main objective (Lew, "Historical", 88-89). By the end of November the KMT's 7th Army had been destroyed, and two weeks of hard fighting later the 12th and 16th Army had also been wiped out (Lew, "Analysis", 120).

The last phase of the Huaihai Campaign started on January 6, 1949, with the Communist forces attacking the remaining Nationalist troops north of the Huai River, the 13th, 6th and 8th Army. By January 10, the 13th Army was no more, while the severely weakened 6th and 8th Army had retreated south of the Huai River. In just two months, the KMT had lost over half a million soldiers when including the troops that surrendered (Lew, "Analysis", 122-23). It was an astounding success for the Communists, and before the month was out they dealt a third and final blow to the

Kuomintang with the capture of the cities of Tianjin and Beijing and the integration into the PLA of the half a million strong KMT army that had been charged with defending the two cities (Lew "Historical", 185-186).[14]

In the months that followed the remnants of the Kuomintang Army kept retreating southward, until finally fleeing to the island of Taiwan in December 1949, two months after Mao had proclaimed the People's

446 - J.C. PETERS

Republic of China (PRC) in Beijing, on October 1.

Following the outbreak of the Korean War, in June 1950, President Truman sent the U.S. Seventh Fleet to the Taiwan Strait, to prevent the Communists from invading and overrunning Taiwan, thus effectively placing the island under American protection.[15-16] Ongoing tension between Taiwan and mainland China led to several small-scale military engagements in the 1950s, but in later years tensions would subside.

With the proclamation of the People's Republic of China, the decades-long power struggle between the Communists and Nationalists had at last come to a clear end. After centuries of weak imperial government and foreign imperialism, followed by the chaos of the Warlord Era and the dictatorship of Chiang Kai-shek, it was now time for the Communists to take a crack at it, with Mao Zedong — the undisputed hero of the civil war — as the undisputed political leader. Unfortunately for the Chinese, Chairman Mao would prove to be a lot less successful than Commander Mao.

Through the Great Leap Forward (1958-61) and the Cultural Revolution (1966-76), Mao would try to bring about a real communist state, free of private ownership and all forms of capitalism. Free also of all traditional and cultural elements of Chinese society, a formidable challenge in and of itself in a country whose civilization is among the oldest in the world. Both programs would prove miserable failures. The Great Leap led to the Great Chinese Famine, causing tens of millions of Chinese to die of starvation, while the Cultural Revolution led to widespread persecution, political paralysis and a failing economy.

In 1976, two years after Mao's death, much needed economic reforms were at long last pushed through, reintroducing capitalist principles and turning the Chinese economy into one of the world's fastest growing. Who knows what will happen once China reforms its political system as well and starts allowing people to say, print and paint whatever they want, whenever they want.

1   Qtd. in Zedong, "Selected Works", 224.

2   Population estimate as of September 2013.

3   The Boxers were not out to unseat the Qing dynasty though, as their most

common slogan was '*Fu-Qing mie-yang*', 'Support the Qing, destroy the foreign'(Esherick, 68).

4   The expeditionary force, led by British Vice-Admiral Edward Seymour, totaled over 2,000, with about 1,000 British troops and another 1,000 from various other nations (Xiang, 258). They were defeated by a combined force of some 3,000 Imperial troops and 2,000 boxers (Xiang, 263-66).

5   Yuan Shikai had been commander of the Beiyang army from 1901 until 1908, when he was forced into retirement following the death of Empress Dowager Cixi. He still commanded the loyalty of most of the officers in 1911.

6   Sun Yat-sen became the first provisional President of the Republic of China in January 1912, but he was succeeded by Yuan Shikai just a few months later.

7   Notably, the Soviets financed the establishment of and provided the necessary support for Whampoa Military Academy, which helped professionalize the newly formed National Revolutionary Army. Soviet officers also taught at the Academy. Its first commandant was the later Kuomintang leader Chiang-Kai-shek.

8   Mao had been one of only twelve delegates to attend the First National Congress of the Communist Party of China, in July 1921, in Shanghai (Uhalley, 17).

9   Snow interviewed Mao and other Communist leaders between June-September 1936, a year after the Long March. The estimated distance Snow gives of the Long March is from Mao himself. In recent years some controversy has emerged about this estimate, after two British researchers who retraced the route arrived at a distance of 3,700 miles (Jocelyn, 288).

10   Notably through the Tanggu Truce of May 31,1933, and the He-Umezu Agreement of June 10, 1935. The Tanggue Truce forced the KMT to recognize the puppet state of Manchukuo in Northeast China and consent to a large demilitarized zone extending 100 kilometers (62 mi) south of a Japanese-controlled Great Wall, with KMT forces having no access to the zone while Japanese patrol and reconnaissance forces would be allowed there. The He-Umezu Agreement gave Japan political and military control over the province of Hebei, surrounding the Beijing region.

11   One of these generals was Zhang Xueliang, who had been the ruling warlord of Manchuria before the Japanese invasion of 1931. After the Xi'an incident — as the kidnapping of Chiang Kai-shek to force him to negotiate with the Communists is often called — Zhang was placed under house arrest by Chiang for forty years, first in mainland China, later in Taiwan, until Chiang's death in 1975. Zhang Xueliang himself died in 2001, aged 100.

12   The First Sino-Japanese War had been fought between 1894-95 over supremacy in Korea, which had long been a Chinese client state. The war was decisively won by the Empire of Japan, establishing it as the dominant power in Asia for the first time, after China had dominated the region for millennia.

13   Mao calculated that at the end of the summer of 1947 Chiang Kai-shek had lost

780,000 men, while CCP losses were about 300,000 (Fairbank, "Republican China", 770).

14 The third and last of the three major campaigns was called Pingjin, a reference to Bei*ping* — the old name for Beijing — and Tian*jin*.

15 North Korea had been occupied by the Soviet Union north of the 38th parallel since August 1945, as agreed with the U.S, which had subsequently occupied South Korea. On June 25, 1950, North Korean forces, aided by the U.S.S.R and China, invaded the South.

16 Truman's stated reason for sending in the 7th Fleet: *"The attack upon Korea makes it plain beyond all doubt that communism has passed beyond the use of subversion to conquer independent nations and will now use armed invasion and war. It has defied the orders of the Security Council of the United Nations issued to preserve international peace and security. In these circumstances the occupation of Formosa* [an earlier name for Taiwan] *by Communist forces would be a direct threat to the security of the Pacific area and to United States forces performing their lawful and necessary functions in that area. Accordingly, I have ordered the 7th Fleet to prevent any attack on Formosa. As a corollary of this action, I am calling upon the Chinese Government on Formosa to cease all air and sea operations against the mainland. The 7th Fleet will see that this is done. The determination of the future status of Formosa must await the restoration of security in the Pacific, a peace settlement with Japan, or consideration by the United Nations."* (Truman, "Statement").

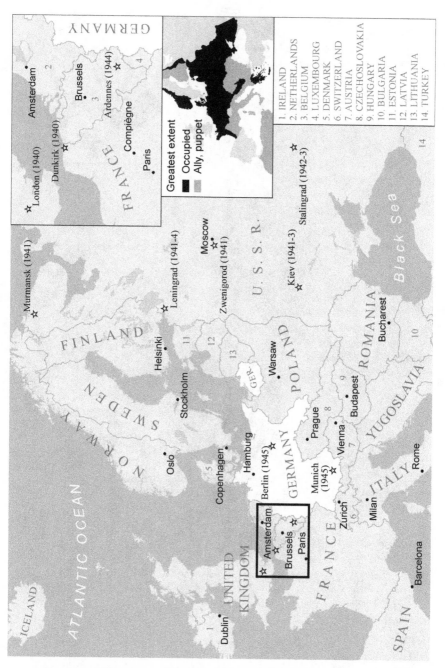

Map 21: The European Theater of the
Second World War, 1939-45

Inset (top, rotated):

GERMANY

Amsterdam
Brussels
Dunkirk (1940)
London (1940)
Compiègne
Paris
Ardennes (1944)
FRANCE

Legend:

Greatest extent
■ Occupied
▦ Ally, puppet

1. IRELAND
2. NETHERLANDS
3. BELGIUM
4. LUXEMBOURG
5. DENMARK
6. SWITZERLAND
7. AUSTRIA
8. CZECHOSLOVAKIA
9. HUNGARY
10. BULGARIA
11. ESTONIA
12. LATVIA
13. LITHUANIA
14. TURKEY

Main map labels:

Murmansk (1941)
FINLAND
Leningrad (1941–4)
Moscow
Zwenigorod (1941)
U.S.S.R.
Kiev (1941–3)
Stalingrad (1942–3)
Black Sea
Helsinki
Stockholm
Warsaw
POLAND
GER.
Bucharest
ROMANIA
NORWAY
SWEDEN
Oslo
Copenhagen
Hamburg
Berlin (1945)
GERMANY
Prague
Vienna
Budapest
YUGOSLAVIA
Munich (1945)
Zurich
Milan
Rome
ITALY
ICELAND
ATLANTIC OCEAN
Dublin
UNITED KINGDOM
Amsterdam
Brussels
Paris
FRANCE
Barcelona
SPAIN

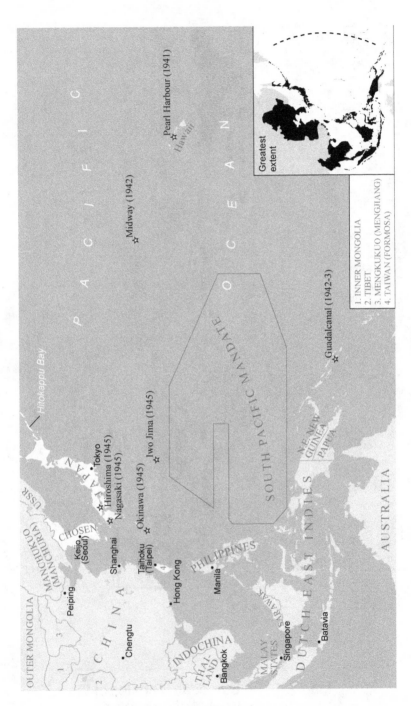

Map 22: The Pacific Theater of the
Second World War, 1941-45

40

WW 2.0

"This war, like the next war, is a war to end war."[1]
David Lloyd George, British Prime Minister, 1916

*"After the 'war to end war', they seem
to have been pretty successful in Paris at
making a 'peace to end peace.'"[2]*
Brig. general Archibald Wavell, on the results
of the Paris Peace Conference, 1919

On May 1, 1945, deep inside the *Führerbunker* underneath the Reichstag, Rochus Misch, Hitler's telephone operator and personal bodyguard, went to Joseph Goebbels and asked him if there was anything left for him to do (Schnoor, "last survivor"). Their boss had committed suicide the day before, the same day the Reichstag had been captured by the Russians. But even though the end of the Third Reich seemed a matter of hours, Misch did not just want to pick up and leave, as most of the others had done. He wanted to end his service to the *"Führer, people and fatherland"* in the proper manner (qtd. in Schnoor, "last survivor"). So he went to the man whom Hitler had appointed the new Reich Chancellor in his last will and asked for instructions.

The former German Minister of Propaganda answered *"We have understood how to live, we will also understand how to die."* (qtd. in Schnoor, "last survivor"). Later that day, Dr. Goebbels put on his hat, coat and gloves, took his wife's arm and went upstairs to the garden. There, he shot his wife, and then himself. Shortly before, Magda Goebbels had already ended the lives of their six children by crushing an ampoule of cyanide in each of their mouths (Fox, "Rochus Misch"). Misch, however, decided not to shoot himself but escape instead. He was one of the last to leave the *Führerbunker* — alive at least. As a member of the elite SS unit *Leibstandarte SS Adolf Hitler,* Misch had also been there at the beginning of the war, six years earlier, in September 1939, when Germany had invaded Poland.[3] In fact, his actions on the Polish front and the serious wound to the chest he sustained there had been one of the reasons for his promotion to the Führer's personal protection unit, the *Führerbegleitkommando* (Misch, 4).

The German invasion of Poland marked the beginning of the Second World War, as it prompted England, France and the Commonwealth nations of Canada, Australia, New-Zealand and South Africa to declare war on Germany. That declaration of war was a direct consequence of a British pledge, six months earlier, to lend Poland *"all support in their power"* in the event its independence was threatened.[4] The pledge, in turn, was a direct consequence of the German invasion of Czechoslovakia in March 1939, despite previous guarantees of German Reich Chancellor Adolf Hitler not to do so.

The reason Hitler had decided to attack Poland anyway was not because he wanted to go to war with England and France, but because he thought he wouldn't have to. And not without reason. After all, they hadn't undertaken any action after his earlier transgressions either, having opted for the political strategy of appeasement instead, i.e., trying to prevent war by giving in to most of his demands.

Since coming to power in 1933, Hitler had started a German rearmament campaign and remilitarized the Rhineland, both in violation of the Treaty of Versailles of 1919.[5] He had also annexed Austria in March 1938 (euphemistically dubbed the '*Anschluss*') and Czechoslovakia in March 1939, the latter in clear violation of the Munich Agreement.

The Munich Agreement of September 1938 had already been a major concession from England and France to Germany, allowing it to annex a large part of Czechoslovakia known as Sudetenland, simply because it was mainly inhabited by German-speaking people who wanted to be part of Germany.

Czechoslovakia was one of the new nations that had been created after World War I from parts of the former empires of Germany, Austria-Hungary and Russia. When the Third Reich annexed German-speaking Austria in March 1938 and then hungrily eyed German-speaking Sudetenland, the British and French convinced themselves that Hitler's demand wasn't all that unreasonable.[6-7] So, at a hastily organized conference in Munich, Germany, late September that same year, England and France, eager — perhaps too eager — to keep the peace, agreed to German occupation of Sudetenland, as long as the rest of Czechoslovakia would be left alone (incidentally, Czechoslovakia itself had not even been invited to the conference).

Hitler happily agreed and a relieved British Prime Minister Neville Chamberlain flew back to London, where he showed the piece of paper with Hitler's signature on it and declared it meant *"peace for our time"*.[8] Six months later Hitler invaded the rest of Czechoslovakia.

Of course it was more than a little astonishing that Germany was able to basically dictate terms to Britain and France just twenty years after losing a devastating war that had left it at the mercy of those same countries, one of which had shown particularly little leniency in imposing and enforcing harsh sanctions to ensure its neighbor to the East would never again pose a threat.

And they hadn't been exactly easy years either. The Versailles Treaty of 1919 had stripped Germany of a large part of its territory, forced it to acknowledge that it alone had been guilty of the war (*Alleinschuld*) and charged it with paying hefty reparations to the victors. When it could no longer keep up those payments a few years later, French and Belgian soldiers had occupied the Ruhr, the heart of Germany's industrial area, causing its economy to collapse.[9]

In 1929, just when the German economy was getting back on its feet again thanks in part to American loans, stock markets crashed and the Great Depression started, causing U.S. investors to pull out and the economy to collapse again. Under those trying circumstances it was hardly surprising that in 1933, the fragile democracy of the newly formed German Republic (a.k.a. Weimar Republic) gave way to the totalitarian rule of Adolf Hitler and his National-Socialist Party.

Six years and a string of appeasement offerings later, Hitler gambled that he could annex Poland just as he had annexed Austria and Czechoslovakia, without any meaningful counter-action from the English or the French.

Still, mindful of the mistakes Germany had made in the Great War— a war he had fought in himself as a young corporal — Hitler took out an insurance policy against a possible two-front war, signing a secret non-aggression pact with the Soviet Union just days before the attack on Poland. Although the fascists and communists were sworn enemies, Hitler correctly assumed that fellow dictator Joseph Stalin would be willing to strike a deal on Poland and the *"territorial and political rearrangement"* of other Eastern European countries (i.e., divvy them up between the two of them), especially with Japan biting at Russia's heels in the Far East and the Russian Army still reeling from the loss of many of its best officers during the Great Purge of 1936-39.[10-11]

The British and French declaration of war — while morally supportive — did nothing to save Poland from being overrun by two mighty armies in September 1939. First, German tanks and storm troopers quickly occupied the 'German half' of Poland, after which the Russians invaded the beleaguered Eastern European nation from the other side on September 17, one day after a ceasefire with Japan had gone into effect, following the battle of Khalkin Gol.[12]

After Poland had been devoured, nothing much happened in Europe for six months, leading some to call this second world war a 'phoney war' (the Germans preferred the term *sitzkrieg*, as opposed to the *blitzkrieg* conquest of Poland).[13] But those who had seen it all before knew the only thing phony was the ominous calm hanging over Europe.

In the spring of 1940, the German war machine sprang into action again, invading Denmark and Norway in April, followed by a simultaneous attack on France, the Netherlands, Belgium and Luxembourg on May 10. That same day Neville Chamberlain resigned as British Prime Minister and was succeeded by Winston Churchill, an old war-horse who had fighting experience, commanding experience and decades of political and government experience.

Meanwhile, the French felt they were well-prepared for another defensive war against the Germans. After World War I they had constructed a massive, seemingly impenetrable line of defense in Northern France, the so-called Maginot Line. Stretching from Switzerland to Luxembourg, it was made up of 44 large works (*Gross ouvrages*), 58 small works (*Petits ouvrages*), 81 troop shelters — each capable of housing 250 soldiers — 360 artillery, machine gun and anti-tank gun emplacements (casemates), 17 observation posts, numerous other supporting structures and extended anti-tank defenses (Allcorn, 12). But, as the saying goes, generals always prepare for the last war, something especially true for the French generals of the interwar period. Because while the French were busy pouring concrete into Northern France to prepare for another trench war, the Germans were busy pouring steel into the Ruhr to produce tanks and airplanes, preparing for a new form of highly mobile warfare that would soon earn the well-deserved moniker *blitzkrieg*.

No doubt the Maginot Line would have done a wonderful job in World War I, but sadly for the French, the Germans did not even engage them there this time around. German tanks first raced through the Ardennes forest in Southeast Belgium to cut off the Allied forces that had advanced into Belgium, subsequently pushing them towards the coast.[14] Soon, the British Expeditionary Force, the remains of the Belgian forces and three French armies (1st, 7th and 9th) were surrounded by the Germans in an area along the Northern coast of France.

To save them, the British sent every ship capable of staying afloat to the French harbor of Dunkirk. Destroyers, trawlers, yachts, personnel ships, naval motor boats, tugboats, minesweepers, almost 700 ships in total. The French, Dutch and Belgians provided an additional 168 ships, for a grand total hodgepodge collection of 861 ships (Churchill, "Their Finest Hour", 90). In nine days some 338,000 troops were thus evacuated to England, 100,000 of whom French. The successful evacuation almost felt like a victory to the British, but Churchill reminded the country that "*Wars are not won by evacuations.*"[15]

Meanwhile, the German forces pushed deep into France, outflanking the Maginot Line and arriving in an undefended Paris on June 14.[16] With the capital lost, the French forces at the Maginot Line isolated and the Luftwaffe reigning supreme over the French skies, Marshal Philippe Pétain — who had just succeeded Paul Reynaud as Prime

Minister — asked Germany for terms.

France signed the armistice on June 22. Hitler was thrilled with the victory, which in his eyes wiped out the humiliating defeat of 1918. Eager to emphasize this, and ever mindful of the power of historic symbolism, the Führer had therefore not only arranged for the French surrender to be signed in the same railway car Germany had signed the armistice in on November 11, 1918, but even had it placed at the exact same spot in the forest of Compiègne where that signing had taken place; the railway carriage was removed from the museum especially for the occasion (LIFE, "Defeat").[17]

Two weeks later the Battle of Britain began. Knowing that an invasion of the island could not be successful without commanding the skies over the channel, Hitler had charged Hermann Göring, the commander of the Luftwaffe, with annihilating the British Royal Air force (RAF) first.

For months, the two air forces were locked in an all-out, deadly struggle for air superiority. Daily waves of Messerschmitt Bf 109s crossed the channel to meet and engage the RAF's Hawker Hurricanes and Supermarine Spitfires protecting the English coast. Göring also launched a bomber campaign to destroy British airfields, aircraft factories and radar stations. As the campaign intensified, the Luftwaffe attacks went increasingly further inland, at one point reaching the London perimeter airfields.

But the achilles heel of the RAF was not its lack of aircraft or airstrips, it was its lack of pilots (Richards, 190-93). In his seminal work on the history of the RAF, British historian Denis Richards wrote that the number of pilots was "*distressingly less at the beginning of September* [1940] *than at the beginning of August*", a fact that was only aggravated by the fact that the new pilots, though being "*of course, magnificent material*", did not yet have the technical competence of those they replaced (Richards, 192).

The RAF nevertheless held on, if only by the skin of its teeth. In the end, a total of 2,936 RAF pilots — 596 of them foreigners from Poland, New Zealand, Canada, Czechoslovakia and Australia, among other countries — successfully held the mighty Luftwaffe at bay ("Roll of Honour"). On August 20, two days after what would become known as The Hardest Day — when the Luftwaffe had thrown everything but the kitchen sink at the RAF and was still beaten back — Churchill thanked the pilots by saying that *"Never in the field of human conflict was so much owed by so many to so few."* (Churchill, "The Few").

Saving Britain from Nazi occupation was all the more important because it allowed Britain to build up its military strength and serve as the base from where the Western Allies could launch their main assault on Nazi-occupied Europe, later in the war. For this reason, the Battle of Britain could be considered an early turning point of the war.

Late October 1940, around the same time the Battle of Britain ended, Germany's ally Italy invaded Greece.[18] Italian dictator Benito Mussolini had grand dreams of establishing a New Roman Empire and conquering Greece seemed like a solid step in that direction. The ancient Romans had done it too after all, in 146 BCE.[19] Of course the Roman legions of Lucius Mummius had not needed any help from the Germans, contrary to Mussolini's forces, who were soon stopped and then pushed back by the Greeks in a counter-offensive between late 1940 early 1941. After the 'New Roman Empire' had fought itself to a stalemate, Hitler reluctantly came to Il Duce's aid, invading Greece on April 6, 1941, and forcing its surrender two and a half weeks later. Italy would pose no further threat to anyone in the war — if it ever had.[20]

With most of Western Europe under his boot, Hitler now looked to the East. On June 22, 1941, Germany invaded the Soviet Union with almost 4 million soldiers, 3,350 tanks, 2,770 aircraft and 7,200 artillery pieces, along a front of 1,080 miles/1,800 km (Glantz, ch.1).[21] The Red Army had about 4.5 million troops in Western Russia, about 3 million of them being close enough to be deployed on the front at the beginning of the invasion (Pinkus, 188).

Operation Barbarossa, the German codename for the invasion, was the largest invasion in history and the precursor to some of the deadliest, most brutal battles ever fought, not least because both sides were commanded by ruthless dictators who had no regard whatsoever for human lives and would stop at nothing to achieve total victory.

It was also more than 'just' an invasion aimed at conquering and occupying new territory. For Hitler and the Nazi party, the drive East was part of a perceived destiny that saw Germany expand into Central and Eastern Europe, deporting and/or enslaving and/or killing the Slavic peoples living there, so as to create more *lebensraum* ('living space') for the German people. *Generalplan Ost*, the secret Nazi plan outlining German colonization of Eastern Europe, thus categorized 31 million out of the 45 million people living in occupied Poland, Lithuania, Latvia, Estonia, Russia, Belarus and Ukraine as 'racially undesirable' (Schmuhl, 348-49).

Operation Barbarossa caught the Soviet Union completely by surprise. All three prongs of the attack — Army Group North (AGN), Army Group Center (AGC) and Army Group South (AGS) — achieved significant advances during the early stages of the campaign. Army Group Center, for example, advanced 360 miles (600 km) in the first eighteen days of combat, inflicting more than 400,000 casualties on the Red Army, including 341,000 dead (Glantz, ch.2). The Russians also lost almost 5,000 tanks, 9,400 guns and mortars and more than 1,700 combat aircraft.

But however total the initial shock and awe of this new, audacious German blitzkrieg was, the Red Army — though seriously bleeding from several wounds — was not yet defeated, and over the course of the next month, the German advance was repeatedly bogged down by fierce Russian resistance. It became clear to the German generals they had underestimated the strength of the Soviet forces. The lengthening supply lines were also starting to become a problem, forcing the Army Groups to slow down as they waited to be resupplied.

By the end of August, only AGC had achieved its objectives, coming within 200 miles of the Kremlin and taking 800,000 prisoners in the process (Pinkus, 203). But Army Group North had so far failed to take Leningrad and link up with the Finns to the North, who in turn had yet to succeed in taking their own main objective, the port city of Murmansk. Army Group South, meanwhile, had met heavy resistance around Kiev and had not yet succeeded in taking the city, let alone advance further into southern Russia, to take control of the oil fields in the Caucasus.

In light of the situation, the generals argued that all three Army Groups should be redeployed in a single, spearheaded attack on

Moscow (Pinkus, 205). Not only was the bulk of the Russian Army concentrated around the city — making an enveloping maneuver and a total, decisive victory in one battle possible— it was also a major center of arms production and an important transportation hub. And of course capturing the capital would also deal a huge blow to Russian morale, while simultaneously boosting the German one. Hitler decided against it though, because he did not want to abandon the goal of annihilating Leningrad (present-day Saint Petersburg) and linking up with the Finnish forces to the North.

On August 21, the Führer issued a directive for a dual offensive on the wings, to take Leningrad in the North and Kiev in the South (Pinkus, 224). While these operations were still underway, preparations for an offensive in the center — code named Typhoon — also began, requiring additional Infantry and Panzer divisions from both Army Group North and Army Group South, to participate in a drive for Moscow, starting on October 2 (Pinkus, 227-28).

Two weeks later, the 4th Panzer Army of General Erich Hoepner breached the Mozhaisk defense line, coming within 50 miles northeast of Moscow (Pinkus, 230). Soviet defeat seemed imminent and a matter of a few weeks at most. But then the weather joined in on the side of Mother Russia, raining (or rather, snowing) down on the infantry and turning the unpaved roads into squishy mud. The advance was slowed down to a crawl and keeping the — already stretched — supply lines intact became next to impossible. The German High Command had no choice but to order a halt to the entire operation, so the Army Groups could reorganize and supply lines could catch up. Of course the Russians made good use of this very welcome pause, transporting troops from the Far

East as fast as they could, taking the calculated (and correct) risk that the Japanese would not attack them again in the Manchurian border area (Pinkus, 234-35).[22]

Mid-November, with the roads hardened again at the onset of winter, the Germans renewed their advance, but soon after the harsh Russian winter arrived in full force, freezing tanks in the mud and soldiers in their summer uniforms. On November 21, General Heinz Guderian, commander of the Second Panzer Army, wrote in his diary: *"The icy cold, the lack of shelter, the shortage of clothing, the heavy losses of men and equipment, the wretched state of our fuel supplies, all this makes the duties of a Commander a misery and the longer it goes on the more I am crushed by the enormous responsibility which I have to bear (..)"* (Guderian, 251).

Late November, Hoepner's 4th Panzer Army reached Zwenigorod, about 20 miles northeast from Moscow. It was the closest the Germans would come to the Soviet capital (Pinkus, 238). Tantalizingly close as it was, the 4th Panzer could in all honestly no longer be called a fighting force. As Hoepner wrote in a report on December 3: *"Physical and spiritual overexertion no longer endurable. In the view of the commanding generals troops no longer have any fighting capacity. The High Command is to decide about a withdrawal."* (qtd. in Pinkus, 238).[23]

On December 5 the Russians launched a counter-offensive, driving the exhausted, half-frozen German forces back some 100-200 miles (160-320 km) over a broad front (Roberts, "Stalin's Wars", 112). Unlike Napoleon Bonaparte's *Grande Armée* of 1812 though, Hitler's Wehrmacht and Waffen-SS would be back for another round in Russia, testing the resolve of the Red Army beyond all reason and rationality.

But before that second, decisive battle on the European Eastern Front, the main theater of the Second World War would first shift to the Pacific, where, on December 7, 1941, just two days after the Russians had started their counter-offensive against the Germans, the Empire of Japan launched a surprise attack on the U.S. naval base Pearl Harbor at Oahu island, Hawaii.

The attack on Pearl Harbor — home to the U.S. Pacific Fleet — was a logical decision for Japan, after negotiations with the Americans about imposed trade sanctions had faltered.

In July 1941, the United States, Great Britain and the Netherlands — whose Dutch East Indies colony (present-day Indonesia) was rich in oil — had imposed an oil embargo on Japan, in an effort to stop Japanese involvement in China and its further expansion into Southeast Asia.[24-25] The U.S. and Japan had subsequently opened negotiations in an effort to find a way out of the rapidly deteriorating relationship, but no progress was made.

On November 20 Japan made its final offer, to withdraw its troops from southern French Indochina to northern French Indochina (to Tonkin, present-day North Vietnam), thus removing the immediate threat of an invasion of the Dutch East Indies, in exchange for U.S. cooperation with *"securing the acquisition of those goods and commodities which the two countries need in Netherlands East Indies"* (the Dutch much have loved that part), supply Japan with all the oil it required and refrain from interfering in China (qtd. in United States Government, "Peace and War", 801-02). In other words, the Empire of the Rising Sun was willing to make do with China as its sole area of expansion, as long as the oil would flow again.

On November 26, the Americans rejected this offer in the best of fashions: by way of a counterproposal that was the complete opposite of the Japanese proposal. The U.S. proposed Japan withdraw from both China and Indochina and refrain from supporting any other Chinese government than the National Government of the Republic of China (i.e., the government of Chiang Kai-shek), in exchange for the mutual unfreezing of funds and the opening of trade negotiations (United States Government, "Peace and War", 810-12).

A day earlier, Vice-Admiral Chuichi Nagumo had already left Hitokappu Bay, Japan, though, embarking on a 3,300 mile journey across the Pacific Ocean with a task force of 6 aircraft carriers, 2 battleships, 2 heavy cruisers, 1 light cruiser, 9 destroyers, 3 submarines and 8 tankers (Dull, 11).[26]

He reached his destination, about 275 miles north of Oahu island, in the early hours of December 7 (Dull, 14).

At 6:00 a.m. the carriers launched the first wave of torpedo bombers, dive bombers, horizontal bombers and fighters — 183 in total — which reached the U.S. Naval Station at Pearl Harbor shortly before 8:00 a.m. (Dull, 16). The two-pronged attack hit the military airfields and harbor at the same time. In the harbor, more than 90 ships — among them 8 battleships, 8 cruisers, 29 destroyers and 5 submarines — lay neatly side by side, ripe for the picking. The battleships had been designated as primary targets, along with the air bases, to prevent U.S. aircraft from repelling the attack. Shortly after the assault had begun, an armor-piercing bomb exploded in the forward ammunition magazine of the battleship USS Arizona, costing the lives of 1,177 crewmen, about half of all Americans killed during the attack (Dull, 17; Madsen, 173). Three other battleships were also sunk, the other four were damaged but stayed afloat.

A second wave of 167 planes was sent in at 7:15 a.m., with the same objectives as the first wave (Dull, 18). Around 10:00 a.m. all Japanese planes returned to their carriers, and less than four hours later the Imperial fleet was on its way home again. In all, 21 U.S. ships had been either sunk or damaged, 188 aircraft had been destroyed, an additional 159 aircraft had been damaged, 2,403 U.S. servicemen had been killed, and 1,178 wounded (Dull, 19).

It was bad, but it could have been even worse. A planned third wave, directed against important onshore harbor facilities — fuel depots, navy repair yards and submarine docks — was canceled by Nagumo, who feared another run might expose his fleet to an attack by the Pacific Fleet's carriers, whose whereabouts were still unknown (Dull, 19-20). Admiral Chester Nimitz, who took command of the Pacific Fleet shortly after the attack on Pearl Harbor, later said the war would have been prolonged by two years had the Japanese succeeded in destroying the fuel depots, as they carried the oil supplies for the entire fleet (Miller, 16-17).

The fact that the three aircraft carriers of the Pacific Fleet, *Enterprise*, *Saratoga* and *Lexington*, had not been at Pearl Harbor at the time, meant the U.S. could still get into the war in the Pacific fairly quickly. Had they been destroyed, the Pacific Fleet would have likely been unable to conduct any large-scale offensive operations for more than a year. The damage to the Pacific Fleet's battleships was extensive, yes, but it would be aircraft carriers and submarines, not the relatively slow battleships, that would prove to be of vital importance in the war in the Pacific.

Of course the attack instantly silenced the non-interventionists in the United States, who had previously made the case for staying out of the war. Following President Roosevelt's famous 'Infamy Speech', on December 8, Congress needed just 33 minutes to declare War on Japan, with only one Representative, the pacifist Jeannette Rankin, voting against the declaration.[27]

Three days later, Germany and Italy, honoring the Tripartite Pact with Japan, declared war on the United States. The U.S. responded in kind. The British also declared war on Japan, but Russia decided to keep its neutrality pact with Japan in place, careful not to get drawn into a two-front war with Japan attacking from the East.[28]

It was a smart move on Stalin's part, because in the summer of 1942 Germany launched a second massive offensive on Soviet territory, code-named *Fall Blau* (Case Blue). The primary objective was to capture the Caucasus oil fields in the South, the main Russian source of oil (Fritz, 231-32). To protect the left flank of the advance into the Caucasus, the city of Stalingrad (present-day Volgograd) had to be captured as well — or at least neutralized. It was also where Stalin decided to make his last stand.

One month into the German offensive, Stalin issued the (in)famous Order No. 227, a.k.a. the 'Not one step back' order. Signed by *"the national commissar for defense: J. Stalin"*, the order was not meant to simply boost morale or instill fear of insubordination in the troops, but sought to actually root out all unauthorized retreats, whatever the circumstances, using harsh but effective measures (Stalin, Order 227). Officers that allowed unauthorized retreats would be unconditionally removed from command and sent to court martial. Each army was also to set up 'penal companies', where those *"guilty of a breach of discipline due to cowardice or bewilderment will be sent, and put... on more difficult sectors of the front to give them an opportunity to redeem by blood their crimes against the Motherland"* (Stalin, Order 227). Furthermore, 'defensive squads' would be placed behind 'unstable divisions', to *"shoot in place panic-mongers and cowards and thus help the honest soldiers of the division execute their duty to the Motherland"*.

With one army thus determined to conquer at all cost and the other to defend at all cost, the epic struggle for Stalingrad began.

Between August 23, 1942-February 2, 1943, the unfortunate city was reduced to little more than a vast field of ruins, a cemetery for the hundreds of thousands — if not more than a million — of soldiers and civilians that perished there.[29]

Mid-November 1942, the Germans were tantalizingly close to victory, holding more than 90 percent of the city, but when winter set in they still had not broken the back of the 62nd Army, which, charged with holding Stalingrad at all cost and commanded by General Vasily

Chuikov, had been able to entrench itself in a 16-mile strip in the city, alongside the Volga's west bank (Roberts, "Victory at Stalingrad", 85).

Chuikov developed several urban war tactics during the battle for Stalingrad, such as instructing his commanders to fight with small groups wielding machine guns, grenades and Molotov Cocktails, instead of committing whole companies and battalions at a time (Chuikov, 150). He also found a way to decrease the effectiveness of the German Luftwaffe, by reducing "*the no-man's land as much as possible - to the throw of a grenade*", making it much harder for the Luftwaffe to bomb Soviet frontline positions (Chuikov, 84). As Chuikov later wrote: "*City fighting is a special kind of fighting. Things are settled here not by strength, but by skill, resourcefulness and swiftness.*" (Chuikov, 146).

Two other fundamental problems for the Germans were logistics and the lack of reserves. Equipment, fuel, food, ammunition, medicine, it was all much harder to come by for the Germans, who were fighting far away from home, than for the Russians, who were fighting for their home. At several critical moments of the months-long battle, General Chuikov's forces were replenished by the timely arrival of reinforcements, while those of his main adversary, General Friedrich Paulus, Commander of the German 6th Army, were not (Roberts, "Victory at Stalingrad", 90-91).

When, late November, the 6th Army was encircled during a Russian counter-offensive, Paulus requested permission to try and break out, but Hitler refused, ordering him to hold his position (Jukes, 107-08). Paulus complied, but two months later — the situation of his army by then utterly desperate and destitute — he sent another message to Hitler, asking for the permission to surrender. The Führer refused again, shooting back: "*Surrender is out of the question. The troops will defend themselves to the last.*" (qtd. in Roberts, "Victory at Stalingrad", 132).

On January 31, 1943, the 6th Army nevertheless surrendered, although Paulus left the actual surrendering to someone else and also refused to sign or issue orders for his men to surrender (Roberts, "Victory at Stalingrad", 133). Two days later, On February 2, the remaining German forces in Stalingrad also surrendered.

One of the deadliest battles in history, Stalingrad would prove to be the turning point of the war in Europe. Germany never really regained the initiative on the Eastern front after it, but instead began its long retreat back to the *Heimat*.[30]

In September 1943, a couple of months after the British had defeated the Axis forces in North Africa, the Western Allies invaded the Italian mainland. With the subsequent Allied invasion in Normandy less than a year later, on June 6, 1944 (D-Day), the Western Allies delivered on their promise to Stalin to open up a second front, though the Soviet dictator never stopped believing the Americans and British had deliberately delayed their invasion to let the Soviet Union suffer the brunt of the German onslaught.

The turning point of the War in the Pacific, meanwhile, came a few months before Stalingrad, at the Battle of Midway (June 4-7, 1942), when the Japanese Navy lost four aircraft carriers while sinking only one U.S. carrier. It also lost some 270 aircraft and — much worse — 125 experienced pilots, more than half of the Japanese pilots who had entered the battle (Isom, 229-36).[31] The defeat seriously crippled the offensive capabilities of the Japanese fleet and increasingly forced it on the defensive.

Following the emboldening victory at Midway, the Allies decided to invade the Japanese-occupied island of Guadalcanal (part of the present-day Solomon Islands), east of New Guinea. The main reason for the attack was to prevent the Japanese Navy from using the island as a base from where supply routes between Australia and the U.S. could be threatened.

In February 1943, after six months of heavy fighting, the Japanese finally surrendered the island to the Allied forces. Over the next two years, several other Japanese-held islands would follow in similar fashion, as the Americans slowly but certainly advanced towards mainland Japan by way of their *island-hopping* strategy.

Back in Europe, no hopping was necessary to advance towards Germany. After a last failed German offensive in the Ardennes (December 16, 1944-January 25, 1945) Western Allied forces crossed the Rhine in March 1945 and fanned out across Germany. By then the Red Army had already advanced into Germany from the East, and on April 25 American and Russian forces linked up at the Elbe river.

Five days later Hitler committed suicide in his bunker and two days after that Berlin fell. On May 8, shortly before midnight, the German Supreme Command of the Armed Forces surrendered unconditionally in Berlin. [32]

After the defeat of Germany, the U.S. started preparations for their invasion of the Japanese mainland (code-named *Operation Downfall*). Given their experience against the Japanese Army in several brutal island battles such as Guadalcanal, Iwo Jima and Okinawa, estimates about American casualties in the event of an invasion of Japan ranged from approximately 200,000 to as high as 4 million.[33] Staggering figures that are still used as the principal justification for the subsequent atomic bombings of the Japanese cities of Hiroshima and Nagasaki on August 6 and 9, 1945, respectively, meant to compel Japan to surrender without having to invade it first. The two bombs likely killed upwards of 250,000 people (Holdstock, 2). Six days later Japan surrendered unconditionally.[34]

The war was over, but the world would never be the same.[35]

The center of geopolitical power had shifted from Europe to the United States and the Soviet Union, two countries that would soon find themselves on opposing sides in everything except for a shared, basic understanding that mankind might not survive another world war.

In the decades that followed, the world would be largely divided into an American/Western/ capitalist sphere of influence and a Russian/Eastern/communist sphere of influence. So too in Europe, with democracy restored and far-reaching economic and military cooperation established between Western Europe and the U.S., while Eastern Europe, liberated by the Red Army, would remain under Soviet influence, frequently enforced heavy-handedly.

And then there was the Bomb. For a few years, the U.S. remained the only country that had it, but on August 29, 1949, the U.S.S.R successfully tested an atomic weapon of its own, thus ushering in the era of Mutually Assured Destruction (MAD). Fortunately for all of us, despite a dark dalliance with nuclear war in 1962, the East-West conflict would largely remain a 'Cold War', although several proxy wars were fought — in Greece, China, Korea, Vietnam, Afghanistan, to name a few — to keep things interesting.

WW II also spelled the end for the European colonial empires, with decolonization waves rolling through Africa, Asia and the Middle East in the 1940s, 1950s and 1960s. They would bring independence, but also instability and in many cases (civil) war.

Another independent nation owing its existence to the Second World War finally gave the Jews a home of their own again, but the creation of the state of Israel, in 1948, would come at the cost of great instability in the Middle East, which lasts to this day.

Still, after all the carnage, cruelty and destruction there was also hope, in the form of a burgeoning understanding that all human life is precious and that war should no longer be accepted as a means to an end in a modern world. On this shared conviction — however fragile, imperfect and at times ambiguous — the United Nations and the Universal Declaration of Human Rights were created. Rochus Misch, one of the last to leave the *Führerbunker* alive on May 2, 1945, was captured by the Russians shortly after his escape. He spent the next nine years as a Soviet prisoner, before returning to Berlin in 1953, where he lived out the remainder of his life just two miles from the location of Hitler's last hideout (Schnoor, "last survivor"). The last survivor of the *Führerbunker*, Misch died on September 5, 2013. He remained loyal to his Führer until the end.

---

1   Qtd. in Billington, 365.

2   Qtd. in Fromkin, "Peace", frontispiece quote.

3   Misch had enlisted voluntarily with the *SS-Verfügungstruppe*, a predecessor of the *Waffen-SS*, in 1937. He was called to the elite SS unit *Leibstandarte-SS Adolf Hitler* that same year (Misch, 4,19-20).

4   Said by British Prime Minister Neville Chamberlain in a statement in the House of Commons, on March 31, 1939 (Chamberlain, "Statement").

5   Articles 42,43 and 44 of Section III of the Versailles Treaty forbade Germany to maintain and assemble armed forces or construct any fortifications, a violation of which was said to "*disturb the peace of the world*", according to article 44 ("Versailles Treaty"). For clauses on German armed forces, see section V of the treaty, Military, Naval and Air Clauses, articles 159-213.

6   Other European nations (re)established after WW I were Austria, Hungary, Yugoslavia, Poland, Finland, Estonia, Latvia and Lithuania.

7   The term 'Third Reich' meant to designate Nazi Germany as the third German Empire, after the Holy Roman Empire and the German Empire of 1870-1918.

8   In a statement made in front of #10 Downing Street, London, on September 30, 1938 (Chamberlain, "Peace").

9   Germany could pay off the reparations in cash or in kind, for instance with deliveries of coal, timber and other commodities. From the start, it frequently missed payments and goods deliveries. Some historians have argued that Germany could have paid more easily and in fact actively sabotaged an economically feasible repayment plan. (Boemeke, 402-04). In *"The Treaty of Versailles: A reassessment after 75 Years"*, Boemeke et al. discuss several historians who have been critical of Germany's inability to pay the WWI reparations.

10   The quote is from Article 1 and 2 from the secret additional protocol — not published at the time — of the Molotov- Ribbentrop Pact, signed on August 23, 1939, in Moscow (Molotov 1939). The pact was named after Soviet Foreign Minister Vyacheslav Molotov and German Foreign Minister Joachim von Ribbentrop.

11   According to declassified Soviet archives, 681,692 people were shot for *"anti-Soviet activities"* between 1937-38 alone (Pipes, 66-67). Of the Red Army's five marshals, three were killed, of its fifteen generals, thirteen did not survive the 'Great Terror' and of the nine navy admirals only one survived.

12   Fought near the Eastern border of Mongolia and Japanese-occupied Manchuria, the battle of Khalkin Gol was a decisive Russian and Mongolian victory that would lead Japan to concentrate its efforts of world conquest southward, towards China and the European colonies in Southeast Asia.

13   Several German generals would later declare at the Nuremberg Trials that had the French and the British attacked in the West during the German invasion of Poland, the German Army would have been powerless to stop their numerically vastly superior forces. General Alfred Jodl, for instance, said during his testimony at the Nuremberg Trials: *"we were never, either in 1938 or 1939, actually in a position to withstand a concentrated attack by these states [France, Poland and Czechoslovakia] together. And if we did not collapse already in the year 1939 that was due only to the fact that during the Polish campaign, the approximately 110 French and British divisions in the West were held completely inactive against the 23 German divisions."* (qtd. in "Trial of the Major War Criminals", Vol. 15, 350).

14   This was *Fall Gelb* (Plan Yellow), a.k.a the Manstein Plan, after General Erich von Manstein, who had conceived it and convinced Hitler of adopting it during a personal meeting (May, 236-39).

15   The quote is from the legendary *"We Shall Fight on the Beaches"* speech, delivered by Winston Churchill before the House of Commons on June 4, 1940. In the same speech, Churchill voiced his aim of victory whatever the cost, speaking the famous words: *"We shall go on to the end, we shall fight in France, we shall fight on the seas and oceans, we shall fight with growing confidence and growing strength in the air, we shall defend our Island, whatever*

the cost may be, we shall fight on the beaches, we shall fight on the landing grounds, we shall fight in the fields and in the streets, we shall fight in the hills; we shall never surrender (..)."

16 Paris had been declared an 'open city' on June 10 by General Maxime Weygand, meaning it would not be defended (Risser, 92).

17 The railroad car was later taken to Berlin and destroyed by the Germans in 1945 (Sciolino, "North of Paris").

18 Germany and its allies are collectively known as the Axis powers. Germany's main allies were Italy and Japan, but Hungary, Romania and Bulgaria were also part of the Axis alliance.

19 146 BCE had been a particularly good year for the Roman Republic, as it achieved total and definitive victory over both the Carthaginian Empire and the Achaean League, making it the sole superpower of the Mediterranean. The cities of Carthage (located in present-day Tunisia) and Corinth (in present-day southern Greece) were both utterly destroyed, its male citizens put to the sword, its women and children sold into slavery.

20 Italy had in fact conquered Abyssinia (present-day Ethiopia) in 1936, but even though most Abyssinian soldiers had been ill-trained and equipped with antiquated rifles or less — think spears and bow and arrow — and the Abyssinian air force counted only a handful of planes and even fewer pilots, it had still taken Mussolini eight months to subdue the proud nation.

21 Russian sources cited by David Glantz in chapter 1, note 3 of *Operation Barbarossa: Hitler's Invasion of Russia 1941*, give somewhat higher estimates of soldiers, tanks and combat aircraft. Oscar Pinkus gives a figure of 3.4 million German men in his work *The War Aims and Strategies of Adolf Hitler*, but since there were also about 30 divisions of Finnish and Romanian troops involved in Barbarossa, an estimate of a grand total of almost 4 million (Axis) soldiers seems fair enough (Pinkus, 188). Pinkus also mentions the German Army had some 600,000 motor vehicles and 650,000 horses at its disposal for artillery and supplies.

22 Pinkus mentions the transfer of 29 infantry divisions and 9 armored brigades from the Far East to the Russian Western front, all equipped for winter warfare, unlike the German troops.

23 A few days later Hoepner ordered the retreat of his forces, going against Hitler's orders. A month after that he was relieved of his command. In 1944 Hoepner participated in the failed 20 July plot to assassinate Hitler. He was arrested, sentenced to death and hanged on August 8 of that same year.

24 On July 26, 1941, President Roosevelt froze all Japanese assets in the United States by Executive Order, bringing *"all financial and import and export trade transactions in which Japanese interests are involved under the control of the Government (..)."* (qtd. in United States Government, "Peace and War", 704).

25 For several years, the U.S. had continued its oil exports to an increasingly

aggressive Japan, to prevent it from attacking the Dutch East Indies for its oil supplies, which would in turn have forced the British to come to their aid, creating a war in the Pacific that would be squarely against U.S. interests. That equation changed when Japan invaded French Indochina, in September 1940, in an effort to cut off exports from there to China, with which it was already at war.

26 Hitokappu Bay (present-day Kasatka Bay) is located on the eastern shore of Iturup, the largest of the Kuril Islands, northeast of Japan. Soviet forces occupied the Kurils in 1945. The islands are still controlled by Russia today.

27 The 'Infamy Speech' — Roosevelt's Address to Congress of December 8, 1941 — contained the famous words: "*December 7, 1941 — a date which will live in infamy — the United States of America was suddenly and deliberately attacked by naval and air forces of the empire of Japan.*" Jeanette Rankin's no vote was met with "*boos and hisses*", according to an article in the New York Times at the time (Kluckhohn, "U.S. Declares War"; Roosevelt, "Day of Infamy").

28 The Soviet-Japanese Neutrality Pact had been signed on April 13, 1941, just two months before Germany launched Operation Barbarossa against the Soviet Union. The pact would remain in place until April 5, 1945, when the Soviet Union denounced it.

29 In *Enemy at the Gates: The Battle for Stalingrad*, William Craig estimates the total casualties for both sides at 1,520,000, of which 750,000 Soviet soldiers, 400,000 Germans, 130,000 Italians, 120,000 Romanians and 120,000 Hungarians (Craig, xiv). Richard Overy mentions 500,000 Russian and 147,000 German dead in *Russia's War: A History of the Soviet War Effort: 1941-1945*, (Overy, 185). The total number of civilian casualties remains unknown.

30 The Germans did mount another offensive in July 1943, code-named *Unternehmen Zitadelle* (Operation Citadel), but it was successfully countered by the Red Army before achieving any significant breakthrough. The failure of *Zitadelle* was at least partly caused by British intelligence on German preparations for the offensive finding its way to Stalin — both officially and unofficially, as the Soviets had a spy inside the British code-breaking center at Bletchley Park — two months before it was launched (Copeland, 4-6).

31 Dallas Isom writes in *Midway Inquest* that the loss of the experienced pilots hurt the Japanese Navy more than that of the four carriers; the pilots were never replaced and the remaining attack carriers could no longer be provided with a full contingent of first-line pilots (Isom, 236).

32 The German Instrument of Surrender had actually already been signed in Reims, on May 7, but the Soviet Union had formally protested that the signed document was not the same as the draft that had been prepared earlier and that the Soviet Representative in Reims, General Susloparov, had not been been authorized to sign the document of surrender. The Soviets also considered Berlin a far more suitable location for the ceremonial surrender of Nazi Germany than Reims, hence the second, official surrender in Berlin on May 8 (Pinkus, 501-03).

33   Of course nobody could predict casualty rates with any certainty. All estimates looked at previous campaigns and tried to account for the likely level of participation from the Japanese civilian population. Thus, General Curtis LeMay arrived at 500,000 casualties, while a study by the Joint Chiefs of Staff estimated around 456,000 casualties — including 109,000 dead or missing — for the first part of the campaign, climbing to a total of 1,200,000 casualties of which 267,000 fatalities for the second part. Another study, done for the Secretary of War, estimated that conquering Japan in its entirety in case of large-scale participation by civilians could cost as much as 1.7-4 million American casualties.

34   The formal signing of the Japanese Instrument of Surrender took place in Tokyo Bay, aboard the USS Missouri, on September 2, 1945.

35   World War II casualty estimates mostly range between 40-75 million, but as Matthew White points out in his excellent work *The 100 Deadliest Episodes in Human History*, a majority of historians — including John Haywood, John Keegan, Charles Messenger and J.M Roberts — arrive at a total of 50 million military and civilian deaths (White, 605). The likely high number of civilian deaths combined with the general lack of reliable population data is the reason there is so much variation between the different estimates.

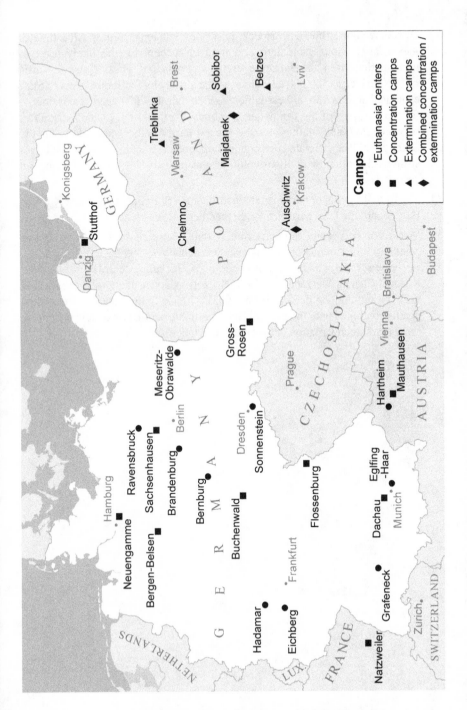

Map 23: Nazi Camps, 1933-45

41

How to Kill an Entire People

*"Technically? That wasn't so hard—it would not
have been hard to exterminate even greater numbers
(..) The killing itself took the least time. You could
dispose of 2,000 head in a half hour, but it was
the burning that took all the time. The killing was
easy; you didn't even need guards to drive them
into the chambers; they just went in expecting to
take showers and, instead of water, we turned on
poison gas. The whole thing went very quickly."[1]*

Rudolf Höss, Commandant of Auschwitz, 1946

In 2008, seventeen-year-old Eli Sagir got a tattoo after returning from a high school trip to Poland.

Nothing too elaborate or complicated, just a number. 157622 (Rudoren, "Proudly Bearing"). When she showed it to her grandfather, he bent his head and kissed it, because he had the same number, in the same spot. Only he hadn't gotten his at a hip tattoo parlor but at Auschwitz concentration camp, nearly 70 years ago.

Several other young descendants of Auschwitz survivors have done the same. They view the number as part of their family history, an heirloom almost. They want to remember. They want others to remember. Not surprisingly, the young, numbered forearms trigger reactions far and wide. Some are disgusted, shocked, even angry. Others find it a beautiful gesture (Rudoren, "Proudly Bearing").

It is not all that different from how Auschwitz survivors treated their own tattoo. Some rushed to the plastic surgeon after the war to have the numbers removed, others viewed it as a scar that nevertheless needed to be preserved. Still others viewed it with pride, because it proved they survived. Everything.

For some of the few that remain, surviving started almost immediately after the *Nationalsozialistische Deutsche Arbeiterpartei* (NSDAP, a.k.a the Nazi Party) came to power in Germany, in 1933. NSDAP leader Adolf Hitler had never made a secret of his hatred for the Jewish people (or many other people for that matter), a hatred emphatically shared by the Nazi Party electorate and even by many who had not voted for the Nazis in 1933.[2] In fact, Jews had been subject to hatred, discrimination and violence for centuries throughout Europe. They were used to it. But this time, in this country, it would be different.

The Nazi ideology was centered around the belief in the superiority of the Aryan race, the German *Volk* (people) and German culture. To fulfill its perceived destiny of world domination, Germany needed to have a strong state, a strong leader and a strong people. The state should therefore be given the means to control and legislate every aspect of society and its citizens, and the leader should be given the means to control every aspect of the state — the so-called *Führerprinzip* (Bendersky, 41-42).[3] The people, for their part, should be pure of blood and purpose, willing to sacrifice everything for the good of the state.

Everybody who disagreed with this view was to be considered a disruptive force to the strength of the state and therefore a danger to the security of the state. Everybody who was impure of blood or weak in any other way could not be part of the New Order and should either be reeducated (if only weak) or permanently expelled (if impure).[4] These *Unerwünschten* (undesirables) included Jews, Slavs, Gypsies, blacks, communists, homosexuals, the mentally ill, the disabled, Jehovah's Witnesses and Freemasons.

But above all, the Jews.

Still, although getting rid of the Jews stood front and center of the Nazi ideology, actually getting it done posed various practical challenges. It is one thing to shout all manner of things in speeches at beer cellars and backrooms, but quite another to turn those rants into actual policy. An estimated 530,000 Jews lived in Germany alone in 1933 (Nicosia, 4). They served in the military, taught at universities, sat on judge's benches, worked as doctors, lawyers, in factories, owned shops, stocks, bonds, houses, employed people, married, had children. Whatever their perceived undesirability, their lives were entwined with all aspects of German society.

Historians still debate whether Hitler had already decided to exterminate all the Jews even before he came to power, but given the different solutions to the 'Jewish Question' the Nazis tried out between 1933-41 it seems unlikely he had, even if only for practical reasons. After all, the Germany of 1933 was very different from that of 1941. For one thing, Germany was not at war with anybody in 1933, nor was it ready for war. Its armed forces were relatively small compared to countries like France and Great Britain. What would these countries have done if the Nazis had started exterminating the Jews then and there? And what would the German people have done if their Jewish officers, teachers, professors and colleagues had been dragged away in the middle of the night? In hindsight, the answer to both questions is: probably nothing. But in 1933, this seemed far from certain.

Hitler therefore initially opted for a strategy of isolation and emigration. By isolating the Jews, their entanglement with German society would diminish, making it easier to remove them altogether later on. It would also create jobs for *Volksgenossen* (compatriots; only Germans of pure blood could be a *Volksgenosse*), an advantage not to be discarded in times of economic depression.[5]

The first major law aimed directly at pushing Jewish German citizens out of society was the *Law for the Restoration of the Professional Service*. It was adopted on April 7, 1933, just two weeks after the Reichstag had passed the *Enabling Act*, which gave Hitler dictatorial powers.[6] The law excluded all those of non-Aryan descent — as well as opponents of the Nazi regime — from working as civil servants. It meant Jews could no longer serve as teachers, judges or professors. Not long after that, a similar law was passed forbidding Jews to work as lawyers, doctors, notaries or tax consultants, while another restricted the number of Jewish students at schools and universities, later excluding them from educational institutions altogether.

In enforcing these laws, however, a new problem surfaced. One that hadn't been given much consideration before, perhaps because it didn't make for very sexy anti-Semitic election rhetoric. Now that anti-Semitic rhetoric had become government policy though, it needed to be addressed. The problem lay in determining who exactly counted as a Jew. Was it everybody who had a Jewish ancestor? But how far back? And was one enough or should there be multiple Jewish ancestors? And what if none of the Jewish ancestors were female? After all, according to the Jewish faith, only those born from a Jewish woman are considered Jewish by birth. And what about converts? Since one could become Jewish by conversion, should that mean one could also stop being Jewish, for instance by converting to Christianity?

The need to answer these questions became especially acute when, in September 1935, the Reich Ministry of the Interior wanted to introduce new laws to further isolate the Jews from German society. These Nuremberg Laws — so named because they were introduced at the annual Nazi Party rally in Nuremberg — stripped Jews of their citizenship and forbade marriage and sexual relations between Jews and Germans.[7]

After much debate, it was determined that a person who had at least three Jewish grandparents was to be considered *Volljude* (a full Jew), regardless of religious affiliation (Steinweis, "Studying the Jew", 42). A person who had two Jewish grandparents was considered a *Mischling* (crossbreed) in the first degree. With one Jewish grandparent one was considered a *Mischling* in the second degree. However, there were certain circumstances that could render a *Mischling* legally Jewish, making such a person a so-called *Geltungsjude*. Being a member of a Jewish congregation for instance, or being married to a Jew.

Having settled the legal definition of Jewishness, existing anti-Jewish legislation could now also be better enforced. Following the Nuremberg Laws, a host of national and local new anti-Jewish legislation was introduced, isolating the Jews ever further.

Under these circumstances it was hardly surprising that many Jews wanted to quit Germany altogether. Between 1933-38, 140,000 Jews thus emigrated from Germany, for the most part to neighboring countries like Denmark, the Netherlands, Belgium and France, countries that would unfortunately prove to be only a temporary safe haven from Nazi persecution (Nicosia, 7).[8]

After the first wave of Jewish emigration in 1933, when 37,000 left, the numbers declined again — to 23,000 in 1934 and 21,000 in 1935 — partly because the situation in Germany stabilized somewhat, but also because most countries did not want them (Longerich, 67). It prompted Zionist leader (and later first President of Israel) Chaim Weizmann to lament: *"The world seemed to be divided into two parts - those places where the Jews could not live, and those where they could not enter."* (qtd. in Sherman, 112).

To find a solution for the increasing number of Jewish refugees from Nazi Germany, an international conference was organized in Evian-Les-Bains, France, in July 1938. A few months earlier, at a speech in Königsberg, Hitler had already made it clear he would welcome any initiative in this direction, saying: *"I can only hope and expect that the other world, which has such deep sympathy for these criminals, will at least be generous enough to convert this sympathy into practical aid. We, on our part, are ready to put all these criminals at the disposal of these countries, for all I care, even on luxury ships"* (qtd. in New York Times, "Hitler").[9] 32 countries attended the conference, but the Netherlands and Denmark were the only European countries willing to accept a limited increase in the number of refugees (Landau, 138).

A couple of months later, in the night of November 9-10, 1938, thousands of Jewish homes, hospitals, schools, synagogues and businesses were destroyed, 20,000 Jews were arrested — most of whom were sent to concentration camps, of which there were six at the time, mainly meant for political dissidents — and 91 people were killed (Sherman, 166-67).

Kristallnacht, so called because of the large number of shattered windows, brought Jewish persecution in Germany to a whole new level. Whoever had still been fooling himself thinking Jews might have some kind of future in Nazi Germany, could do so no longer. By June 1939, 309,000 German, Austrian and Czech Jews had applied for the 27,000 places available in the U.S. quota. By the time the war broke out, in September 1939, some 95,000 had managed to emigrate to the United States, 60,000 had emigrated to Palestine, 40,000 to Great Britain and about 75,000 to Central and South America ("German Jewish Refugees").[10]

Apart from terrorizing the Jews to stimulate emigration, the Nazis also floated several state sanctioned 'total emigration' plans. There was the *Schacht plan* — named after Hjalmar Schacht, President of the Reichsbank, who conceived it — which called for World Jewry to establish a fund that would finance the resettlement of a total of 150,000 able-bodied German and Austrian Jews, who would later be joined by 250,000 dependents (Yahil, 117). Another fund was to be established out of the emigrants' property and used to pay for maintaining those Jews who were unable to emigrate. Progress was made in subsequent negotiations with the United States and Britain, but before a version of the plan could be implemented the war broke out (Yahil, 118).

Another idea was the *Nisko Plan*, concocted in September 1939 and meant as a Jewish Reservation of sorts in occupied Poland. It resulted in the first deportations East, but a host of practical problems and bad international press as to the treatment of the deportees — at a time foreign public opinion still mattered somewhat to the Nazis — caused the plan to be shelved (Yahil, 138-40, 160-61).

The *Madagascar Plan*, which (re)surfaced in the summer of 1940, after the defeat of France, envisioned shipping the entire German Jewish population to the island of Madagascar, a French colony (Yahil, 253-54).[11] It was seriously considered by Hitler, but abandoned after Germany lost the Battle of Britain. One plan that did come to fruition was the *Transfer* (a.k.a. Haavara) *Agreement*, which facilitated the emigration of around 51,000 German Jews to Palestine between 1933-39 (Yahil, 100-04).[12]

The outbreak of the war made emigration of the remaining Jews practically impossible. Not only did it make foreign countries even less susceptible to accepting Jewish refugees, German conquests also dramatically increased the number of Jews living in the Third Reich.[13] And the fact that almost half of the German Jewish population was still living in Germany even after having been subjugated to the harshest anti-Semitic laws, made it clear that wartime emigration of three million Polish Jews just wasn't going to happen. It was time for a different answer to the 'Jewish Question'.

On September 21, 1939, SS-*Gruppenführer* Reinhard Heydrich — whom Hitler called The Man with the Iron Heart — sent a memo to the chiefs of all the *Einsatzgruppen* of the *Sicherheitspolizei* (Security Police), concerning the "*Judenfrage im besetzten Gebiete*", the Jewish Question in Occupied Territory (Arad, "Documents", 173-78).[14] The *Einsatzgruppen*, formed in the summer of 1939, leading up to the invasion of Poland, were SS death squads, operating in the wake of the regular army with instructions to eliminate "*all anti-German elements in hostile country behind the troops in combat.*" (Browning, 16).[15]

In the memo, Heydrich instructed the chiefs to start rounding up the Jews and put them in "*concentration centers*" (Arad, "Documents", 173-78). These ghettos, he wrote, should be located near a railroad junction or at least on a railway, to accommodate transportation of the Jews at a later date.

Jewish enterprises, factories, farms and land were to be "*aryanized*" (i.e., confiscated), though Heydrich pointed out that a transition period might be necessary in some cases, so as not to hurt German economic interests (Arad, "Documents", 173-78). The memo also talked about how "*the final aim*" (*Endziel*) of the measures "*will require extended periods of time*", and that all the "*planned total measures are to be kept strictly secret*". It therefore seems that, by September 1939, at the very least Reinhard Heydrich had made up his mind as to the faith of the Jewish population in the Reich.

Between October 1939-July 1942, more than 1,100 Jewish ghettos were created in Nazi-occupied Eastern Europe (Michman, 8). The allotted space for the ghettos was far too small for the number of Jews forced to live there. The resulting overcrowding, as well as the absence of even the most basic sanitation services, caused diseases like typhus, dysentery and diphtheria to spread fast and freely (Friedman, 122). Malnutrition was another serious problem. It was intentionally caused, by keeping food deliveries far below even the bare minimum. In the Warsaw ghetto, for instance, Jews were forced to subsist on 180 calories per day — a quarter of what was given to Poles — while also being forbidden, on pain of death, to leave the ghetto and trade for food and other essentials (Friedman, 122). Hundreds of thousands thus died of starvation, exhaustion and disease before the ghettos were liquidated in 1942-43.

The number of forced labor camps also rapidly expanded after the outbreak of the war, eventually numbering more than 30,000 including subcamps, most of them in Germany and Poland.[16] Jews, Slavs, Russian prisoners of war, Gypsies, gays and political dissidents, millions were forced to work in the camps, providing ultra cheap labor for the German industry. To sustain this economic system it needed to be fed with a continuous stream of new workers, as most prisoners succumbed within a few months to the grueling conditions. At concentration camp Buchenwald, for example, the average life expectancy of a prisoner working in the factories was nine months (Fleischman, 71).[17]

Following the German invasion of Russia (Operation Barbarossa) in June 1941, Heydrich's boss, *Reichsführer* Heinrich Himmler, instructed the *Einsatzgruppen* to regard all Jews as partisans and to shoot all male Jews of military age (Longerich, 198). From August, the *Einsatzgruppen* began to execute women, children and the elderly as well (Longerich, 207).

By then, Heydrich had already been instructed by *Reichsmarschall* Hermann Göring — whom Hitler had appointed as his first successor — to submit "*an overall plan of the preliminary organizational, practical and financial measures for the execution of the intended final solution* [Endlösung] *of the Jewish question*" (Arad, "Documents", 233).

Around the same time, *SS-Sturmbannführer* Rudolf Höss was ordered by Himmler to establish extermination facilities at the concentration camp where he was commander, Auschwitz.[18] Thus, after isolation, emigration and concentration, the final solution to the Jewish Question would be extermination.

Hundreds of thousands of Jews had already been shot by the *Einsatzgruppen,* died of exhaustion from doing hard labor or from starvation or disease in the camps and ghettos, but mid-1941 the total annihilation of the Jews was made a primary goal for the first time. Because it would be highly counter-productive to the German war industry — which relied heavily on Jewish slave labor — there was some opposition from upper Nazi echelons against killing the Jews outright instead of simply working them to death, but the real decision had already been made.

On January 20, 1942, following up on Göring's order, Heydrich organized a conference for senior officials from several government ministries, in the Berlin suburb of Wannsee. For Heydrich, the main goals of the conference were to secure the cooperation of the various departments and to make sure that the implementation of the *Endlösung* would be regarded as an internal matter of the SS (Longerich, 310). A secondary goal was to determine who would be regarded as Jewish in the sense of the Final Solution and what to do with the *Mischlinge*.

In all, Heydrich invited fourteen people, among them officials from the Justice department, State department, Economics department and Ministry of the Interior, as well as representatives of administrations in charge of occupied territories in Eastern Europe. Seven of the fifteen attendants (including Heydrich) held an SS rank, eight had earned a doctorate, six of which were in law.

The whole conference took no more than 90 minutes, after which Heydrich had secured the full cooperation of the various departments.

SS-Obersturmbannführer Adolf Eichmann was charged with the task of organizing the transports from all over German-occupied Europe to the six designated death camps, Auschwitz-Birkenau, Chelmno, Majdanek, Belzec, Sobibor and Treblinka.

Of these, Auschwitz was the most efficient. One reason for this was that Auschwitz Commandant Höss had made several improvements to the extermination process he had witnessed at Treblinka. For instance, instead of gas chambers capable of holding 200 people, like in Treblinka, he had gas chambers built that could hold 2,000 ("Trials of the Major War Criminals", Vol. XI, 417). For the gassing itself, Höss opted for Zyklon B, a crystallized prussic acid, instead of the monoxide gas used at Treblinka, because it worked faster ("Trials of the Major War Criminals", Vol. XI, 416). In his memoirs, Höss recalled:

"The gassing was carried out in the detention cells of Block 11. Protected by a gas mask, I watched the killing myself. In the crowded cells, death came instantaneously the moment the Zyklon B was thrown in. A short, almost smothered cry, and it was all over... I must even admit that this gassing set my mind at rest, for the mass extermination of the Jews was to start soon, and at that time neither Eichmann nor

I was certain as to how these mass killings were to be carried out. It would be by gas, but we did not know which gas and how it was to be used. Now we had the gas, and we had established a procedure." (Hoss, 92-95).

Höss also went to great lengths to fool victims into thinking they were being deloused rather than gassed. Numbered coat hangers were put in the outer chamber for prisoners to hang their clothes on as they undressed. Meanwhile Jewish prisoners from the *Sonderkommando* — a special work detail forced to aid the SS with the extermination process — walked around, instructing victims to remember their coat hanger number so they could come back for their clothes after the delousing shower. The gas chamber itself was disguised as a shower room, with clean, whitewashed walls and shower heads hanging from the ceiling.

The gassing itself was handled by the SS, but the subsequent disposal and cleaning process was carried out by the prisoners of the *Sonderkommando* (Greif, 2-6).[19] Selected on their arrival in the extermination camp and given the choice to join the *Sonderkommando* or die, most prisoners decided to join. Their living conditions were markedly better than those of regular camp prisoners. They had their own barracks, received better food and had access to liquor, cigarettes and medicines (Greif, 145, 234, 246, 374). They also did not have to fear to be killed at random like the other prisoners. In exchange, they did the dirty work.

After the gassing, the *Sonderkommando* removed the bodies from the gas chamber and brought them to a nearby room, where they were checked for valuables. Eyeglasses were lifted, rings slid of fingers, mouths checked for gold teeth, bridges and crowns, breaking them out if found (Greif, 321).[20] If a spot check by the SS revealed that gold had been missed, the prisoner responsible would be lucky to get away with a severe beating (Greif, 301).[21] Other body orifices were checked as well for hidden valuables. After this, hair from female victims was shaved off. The teeth gold was melted into gold bars and transported to Berlin. The hair was sold to felt factories that used them in mattresses.

Meanwhile, prisoners from the *Kanada Kommando* collected the belongings from the gassed — suitcases, shoes, clothing, jewelry, photographs etc. — and brought them to a warehouse they called Canada (German: *Kanada*), a country that symbolized wealth in their eyes (Berg, 301). At the warehouse, everything was sorted and from there transported back to Germany at regular intervals. Having checked the corpses, the *Sonderkommando* took the bodies to the crematorium, where they were put on metal stretchers and pushed into the furnace. In times of high volume, open-air pits were used together with the Crematoria. The remaining ashes were dumped in a lake nearby (Greif, 18, 95, 157, 251). While the corpses were incinerated, another detail of the *Sonderkommando* cleaned the gas chamber, washing away the blood, vomit, urine and excrement, and whitewashing the walls. Making everything ready for processing of the next group. Following this procedure 20,000 people could be disposed of within 24 hours at Auschwitz (Piper, 173-74). But that was at peak operation.

   To prevent the inner workings of the extermination process to travel beyond the Crematoria, the SS replaced each *Sonderkommando* every four months or so. Of the thousands of prisoners active in one of the *Sonderkommandos* in Auschwitz-Birkenau between 1941-45, only about 80 lived to tell (Greif, 83). But even if none of them would have survived their story would have, as several of them wrote it down and buried it in the grounds of the Crematoria, right in the heart of darkness (Czech, 372). The documents were discovered years after the war.

   Early 1942, when it became clear that Germany might not be able to hold on to all of its previously conquered territory in the East, on account of the failure of Operation Barbarossa (June-December 1941) and the subsequent Soviet counter-offensive, Heydrich met with *SS-Standartenführer* Paul

   Blobel to discuss the need to erase all traces of the mass executions (Arad, "Operation Reinhard", 170).

   Heydrich was subsequently assassinated in Prague, before he could officially appoint Blobel, but not long after Gestapo chief *SS-Gruppenführer* Heinrich Müller put Blobel in charge of the secret operation, code-named *Sonderaktion 1005*, whose objective it was to cover up remaining evidence of the mass murders by exhuming all the bodies from mass graves and burn them (Arad, "Operation Reinhard", 170-71).[22] The *Sonderkommandos* charged with exhuming and burning the bodies were killed after their work was done.

On October 7, 1944, the Auschwitz *Sonderkommando* of Crematorium IV revolted after a rumor they would soon be 'transferred to another camp', SS-speak for extermination (Henry, 58). Before the revolt was suppressed, the *Sonderkommando* had succeeded in blowing up Crematorium IV, damaging it beyond repair. It was never used again. 250 *Sonderkommando* members lost their lives during the revolt, 200 others were shot by the SS as a reprisal and disposed of by the next *Sonderkommando* (Henry, 58). One month later, Himmler ordered the destruction of the remaining Crematoria.

On January 18, 1945, shortly before the Russians reached the camp, the SS marched the remaining 60,000 prisoners out of Auschwitz to Wodzislaw, 35 miles (56 km) away, from where they were put on freight trains to other camps (Rozett, 183). At least 15,000 of them died or were killed during this death march. Those who had been too weak or too sick to walk had been left behind at the camp. When the Russians liberated Auschwitz a few days later, on January 27, about 7,000 of them were still alive (Stone, 41).

All told, approximately 6 million Jews were killed by the Nazis — about two thirds of the entire European Jewish population — 4 million in extermination camps and another 2 million through mass shootings from the *Einsatzgruppen*, starvation, disease and exhaustion.[23] 3.3 million Soviet POWs also perished at the hands of the Germans, as did nearly 3 million non-Jewish Poles, between 220,000-1,500,000 Gypsies, 200,000 disabled, and between 3,000 and 10,000 homosexuals.[24]

An estimated 1.1 million Jews were exterminated in Auschwitz between September 1941- November 1944 (Gutman, 71).[25]

Auschwitz was also the only camp where prisoners were tattooed with a serial number — the ones who were given prisoner status that is — 405,000 in total (Marrus, 1131). Of those, 261,000 died or were killed in Auschwitz. How many of the rest perished in other camps or died on death marches is unknown.

Working as a cashier at a mini-market in the heart of Jerusalem, Ms.

Sagir says she is asked about the number on her forearm about ten times a day. One time, a police officer said *"God creates the forgetfulness so we can forget."*, to which she responded *"Because of people like you who want to forget this, we will have it again."*[26]

1   Qtd. in Gilbert, 249-50.

2   In his autobiographical manifesto *Mein Kampf* (My Struggle) Hitler writes: *"If one considers how much he has sinned against the masses in the course of the centuries, how again and again he squeezed and extorted without mercy, if one considers further how the people gradually learned to hate him for this and finally saw in his existence really nothing but a punishment of Heaven, then one can understand how hard this change must be for the Jew."* (Hitler, 431). And: *"Therefore, I believe today that I am acting in the sense of the Almighty Creator: By warding off the Jews I am fighting for the Lord's work."* (Hitler, 84).

3   In chapter three of *A History of Nazi Germany: 1919-1945*, Bendersky also discusses the historical roots of Nazi ideology.

4   That the National Socialists meant business regarding the 'purification' of the German *Volksgemeinschaft* became clear just a couple of months after they came to power, when Wilhelm Frick, the newly appointed Reich Minister of the Interior, implemented the 'Law for the Prevention of Genetically Diseased Offspring' (*Gesetz zur Verhütung erbkranken Nachwuchses*), in July 1933. This law provided the state with the power to forcibly sterilize those suffering from a hereditary disease. Around 400,000 people would subsequently be sterilized over the next decade and thus in many cases be permanently expelled from the gene pool (Crew 113-14).

5   Point 4 of the National Socialist Program stated: *"Only those who are our fellow countrymen can become citizens. Only those who have German blood, regardless of creed, can be our countrymen. Hence no Jew can be a countryman."* ("Program").

6   The Enabling Act of 1933 gave the cabinet the right to enact laws without the consent of the Reichstag (by passing this law the Reichstag thus made itself superfluous). To get the necessary majority, the government had arrested all the Communist (KPD) Reichstag members and several Social Democrat (SPD) Reichstag members under cover of the Reichstag Fire Decree, a law that suspended several constitutionally guaranteed rights 'until further notice', following the alleged arson of the Reichstag by communists. With the KPD and several SPD members gone and the Center Party bullied into voting for the measure with the Nazi Party, the enabling act was passed 444 in favor, 94 against.

7   The Nuremberg Laws adopted at the Nazi Party rally were the 'Reich Citizenship Law' and the 'Law for the Protection of German Blood and German Honor'

(Steinweis, "Law in Nazi Germany", 47-48).

8   Anne Frank was one of them. Having emigrated from Germany to the Netherlands early 1934, the Frank family went into hiding after Germany invaded and occupied Holland. In August 1944 they were nevertheless arrested by the *Sicherheitsdienst* and put on transport. Anne and her sister Margot died in concentration camp Bergen-Belsen in March 1945, a few weeks before the camp was liberated by the British.

9   Distasteful as the comment is, it also clearly shows Hitler was not yet committed to the destruction of the Jewish race.

10 This was out of a total of 282,000 Jews (from the initial 530,000 in 1933) that made it out of Germany between 1933-39 and 117,000 Jews that emigrated from annexed Austria ("German Jewish Refugees").

11 The idea to resettle European Jews on Madagascar was not a German one, the French and the Poles had also considered it in the late 1930s (Yahil, 254; Browning, 81-82). The Poles had even sent a small investigating team to the island, with consent of the French, as part of a feasibility study (Browning, 81-82). It concluded that a maximum of 5,000-7,000 families could be settled there.

12 Under the agreement, Jewish emigrants to Palestine had to pay 1,000 pounds sterling into a trust company in Germany, which used the funds to buy German goods and sell them to the Haavara company, which in turn sold them in Palestine, thus stimulating German export ("Encyclopedia Judaica: Haavara"). The proceeds went to the emigrants living in Palestine.

13 Poland alone, invaded in September 1939, was home to an estimated three million Jews (Yahil, 187).

14 Source includes the complete memo.

15 The *Einsatzgruppen* were controlled by the powerful *SS-Reichssicherheitshauptamt*, the Reich Main Security Office, which had been created on September 27, 1939, to bring the *Sicherheitspolizei* and the *Sicherheitsdienst* under the same roof. It was run by Heydrich. The *Einsatzgruppen* were responsible for numerous mass shootings between 1941-45, killing an estimated two million civilians, including 1.3 million Jews (Headland, 98-106). In *Messages of Murder*, Headland includes detailed killing statistics from the various *Einsatzgruppen*, before concurring with Raul Hilberg's oft-cited estimate from *The Destruction of the European Jews* that 1,300,000 Jews were killed in the East by the *Einsatzgruppen*, other SS agencies and collaborators (Headland, 106).

16 Research by Geoffrey P. Megargee et al. about the full extent of Nazi camps has concluded that, contrary to what was previously believed, the total number of camps between 1933-45 was 42,500, of which 30,000 slave labor camps (including subcamps), 1,150 Jewish ghettos, 1,000 prisoner-of-war camps and 980 concentration camps. Dr. Megargee is the lead researcher of a team working

on a multivolume encyclopedia that aims to document all the camps. As of 2014, the first two of an expected total of seven volumes of the *Encyclopedia of Camps and Ghettos, 1933-1945*, have been published (Lichtblau 2013).

17 According to an income statement from Buchenwald, total net revenue for a prisoner was 1,631 Reichsmark, of which 1,431 Reichsmark was made during a total expected life span of nine months — 6 RM per day minus 70 cents for food and clothes, times 30 (days) times 9 (months) — and another 200 Reichsmark was made after the prisoner's death, from his corpse, his clothing and valuable items he sometimes left behind (Fleischman, 71-73). According to Holocaust historian Raul Hilberg, life expectancy of a Jewish inmate at the I.G. Farben plant near Auschwitz was three to four months and at the outlying coal mines about one month (Hilberg, 996).

18 At the Nuremberg trial after the war, Höss was questioned about this meeting with Himmler: DR. KAUFFMANN: *Is it true that in 1941 you were ordered to Berlin to see Himmler? Please state briefly what was discussed.* HOESS: *Yes. In the summer of 1941 I was summoned to Berlin to Reichsführer SS Himmler to receive personal orders. He told me something to the effect — I do not remember the exact words— that the Führer had given the order for a final solution of the Jewish question. We, the SS, must carry out that order. If it is not carried out now then the Jews will later on destroy the German people. He had chosen Auschwitz on account of its easy access by rail and also because the extensive site offered space for measures ensuring isolation."* (qtd. in "Trial of the Major War Criminals", Vol. XI, 398).

19 Greif also describes how the *Sonderkommando* came into existence, evolving out of specific kommandos such as the *Krematoriums-Kommando* and the *Begrabungskommando* with the emergence of the policy to systematically exterminate all the Jews (Greif, 3-6).

20 Höss also mentions this in his testimony at Nuremberg ("Trial of the Major War Criminals", Vol. XI, 416).

21 Greif got this information from Leon Cohen, whose exclusive job in the *Sonderkommando* was to pull gold teeth from the gassed corpses. Cohen said that during his twelve-hour shifts new corpses would arrive every half-hour and each time he had ten minutes to pull out the gold teeth of some sixty to seventy-five corpses (Greif, 300-01).

22 Blobel had been the commanding officer of Sonderkommando 4a of Einsatzgruppe C, which had, among other things, carried out the massacres at Babi Yar (in Kiev, Ukraine) on September 29-30, 1941. He was sentenced to death by the Nuremberg Tribunal and hanged in 1951.

23 At Nuremberg, the Austrian SS officer (and historian) Wilhelm Höttl testified about a conversation he had had with Adolf Eichmann, late August 1944, during which the latter had confided that, *"Approximately 4 million Jews had been killed in the various concentration camps, while an additional 2 million met death in other ways, the major part of which were shot by operational*

squads of the Security Police during the campaign against Russia. "(qtd. in "Trial of the Major War Criminals", Vol. III, 569).

24 In his *History of the Holocaust*, Jonathan Friedman notes that estimates about the number of Gypsies killed vary greatly, with the figure of 1.5 million at the high end, but the estimates he quotes in a subsequent note (44) are all around 200,000 (Friedman, 381, 384). The estimate of the number of mentally and physically disabled killed is more certain (Friedman, 138). On the number of homosexuals killed, Friedman notes that of the estimated 5,000-15,000 that ended up in concentration camps, two thirds died (395). The estimate on the number of non-Jewish Poles killed is from Kwiet and Matthaus (Kwiet, 258). Concerning the murder of Soviet POWs, Hannes Heer and Klaus Naumann write, in *War of Extermination: The German Military in World War II 1941-1944*: *"Between 22 June 1941 and the end of the war, roughly 5.7 million members of the Red Army fell into German hands. In January 1945, 930,000 were still in German camps. A million at most had been released, most of whom were so-called "volunteers" (Hilfswillige) for (often compulsory) auxiliary service in the Wehrmacht. Another 500,000, as estimated by the Army High Command, had either fled or been liberated. The remaining 3,300,000 (57.5 percent of the total) had perished."* (Heer, 80-81).

25 Gutman and Berenbaum note that this number is regarded as a minimum estimate.

26 Qtd. in Rudoren, "Proudly Bearing".

42

A BOMB

"My God, what have we done?"[1]
Captain Robert Lewis, co-pilot of B-29 bomber Enola
Gay, writing in the official log after dropping the atomic
bomb 'Little Boy' on Hiroshima, August 6, 1945

On September 20, 2009, Iran's Supreme Leader, Ayatollah Ali Khamenei declared: *"We fundamentally reject nuclear weapons and prohibit the use and production of nuclear weapons."* (qtd. in Erdbrink, "Iran Denies"). When newly elected Iranian President Hassan Rouhani visited the U.N. General Assembly in New York four years later, he concurred that Iran would never *"seek weapons of mass destruction, including nuclear weapons."* (qtd. in Erdbrink, "Iran's Leaders").

Soothing words. Of course the main question in the West, including Israel — especially Israel — is whether they are true. Ever since an Iranian political opposition group in 2002 revealed that Iran had a nuclear program that included a uranium enrichment plant in the vicinity of the city of Natanz and a heavy water production plant at the city of Arak, the developed world has stepped up its efforts to prevent Iran from ever getting the bomb.[2]

One of the main aims of the so-called P5+1 nations, the five permanent members of the U.N. Security Council — the United States, Russia, China, Britain and France — plus Germany, has been to prevent Iran from enriching uranium to the point where building a nuclear weapon would only be a matter of months. To that end, the P5+1 have followed a dual-track strategy since 2006, combining negotiations with U.N. Security Council resolutions demanding the country to halt uranium enrichment and imposing sanctions to force it to comply.[3-4] Incidentally (or perhaps rather *not* incidentally), the P5 nations are also the first five nations that acquired the bomb for themselves.

Britain was the first country to take a serious stab at building a nuclear bomb, in 1941. A few years earlier, on December 17, 1938, the German chemist Otto Hahn and his assistant Fritz Strassman had discovered nuclear fission of the heavy element uranium — i.e., the splitting of its nucleus — after bombarding it with neutrons, causing the release of a great amount of energy in the process.

A couple of months later, physicists Enrico Fermi, Leó Szilárd and Herbert Anderson proved that bombarding uranium with neutrons resulted in significant neutron multiplication, thus setting off a self-propagating chain reaction capable of releasing massive amounts of energy (Anderson, "Neutron Production"). They immediately realized their discovery could lead to the development of a nuclear bomb. Szilárd later said: *"that night* [March 3, 1939, after the definitive experiment] *there was very little doubt in my mind that the world was headed for grief."* (qtd. in Rhodes, 292). Initially, it was believed that several tons of uranium were needed to achieve the 'critical mass' necessary for a sustained nuclear chain reaction.[5] Though possible, it would hardly be practical. Still, the estimated destructive capability of a nuclear bomb would be so great that it prompted

Szilárd to write a concerned letter to U.S. President Franklin Roosevelt on August 2, 1939, less than a month before Hitler invaded Poland. The letter was signed by Albert Einstein, who had readily agreed to lend his signature after Szilárd told him about the concept of sustained nuclear chain reaction and his experiment proving it. *"Daran habe ich gar nicht gedacht!"* ("I never even thought of that!") Einstein famously replied after Szilárd's explanation (qtd. in Rhodes, 305). In the letter to Roosevelt, Szilárd theorized that a nuclear bomb *"carried by boat and exploded in a port, might very well destroy the whole port together with some of the surrounding territory. However, such bombs might very well prove to be too heavy for transportation by air."* (Einstein 1939)..

But in March 1940, physicists Otto Frisch and Rudolf Peierls, both working at Birmingham University, calculated that only about one pound of pure uranium-235 (U-235) would be needed to produce a nuclear bomb with an explosive force equivalent to *"1,000 tons of dynamite"* (Frisch, "Memorandum"). They wrote a memo explaining the science that supported their conclusions and outlining the implications of their calculations — small bombs capable of massive destruction, large numbers of civilian casualties, including from nuclear radiation, and the urgency of getting the bomb before Germany.

It would later turn out that their calculations were incorrect (the minimum amount of U-235 needed for a sustained nuclear reaction is 115 pounds, not one) but the memorandum was a definite wake up call for the British, who soon established a committee, code-named M.A.U.D., to conduct a feasibility study on the production of a nuclear weapon (Rhodes, 340-41).

One year later, in the summer of 1941, as German tanks rolled into Russia during Operation Barbarossa, the M.A.U.D. committee reported that it would be possible to produce a nuclear bomb with a critical mass of about 25 lb (11,5 kg) of active material, that this bomb could be ready by the end of 1943 and that a plant capable of producing three such bombs per month would cost approximately 5 million pounds (M.A.U.D., "Report"). All of these statements would later prove incorrect, but the British war cabinet was sold. Churchill dryly commented: *"Although personally I am quite content with the existing explosives, I feel we must not stand in the path of improvement."* (qtd. in Rhodes, 372).

One of the main reasons for the British effort was fear the Nazis would get the bomb. Germany had been at the vanguard of some early discoveries in the field of nuclear physics and had produced several prominent physicists, though a good deal of them had quit the country after 1933 — many because they were Jewish — among them Albert Einstein, Leó Szilárd, Max Born, Otto Frisch, Rudolf Peierls, Lise Meitner, Edward Teller and Hans Bethe, to name a few.[6-7]

The British had also been alarmed by German efforts to produce greater quantities of heavy water at the Norwegian Hydrogen plant Norsk Hydro (Bernstein, 27). Heavy water, as had been recently discovered, could be used to produce plutonium, another element besides uranium capable of sustaining a nuclear chain reaction. German interest in heavy water therefore indicated they had made strong advances in nuclear research and might be attempting to produce enough fissile material for a bomb.

Later in the war it would become clear that around the same time the Americans decided to pull out all the stops in developing the bomb, the Nazis decided not to, chiefly because the scientists involved had reported that the development of a nuclear weapon would take too long to make a difference in the war.[8-9]

Of course the British did not know exactly how far the Germans had progressed, and fear can be a powerful motivator. Therefore, aside from pouring resources into their own project, code-named *Tube Alloys,* they also sent Australian physicist and member of the M.A.U.D. Committee Dr. Mark Oliphant to the United States, to try and persuade the Americans to step up their efforts into nuclear weapons research. It worked, because in October 1941 President Roosevelt approved the atomic program, though it would be the Japanese attack on Pearl Harbor a few months later that really ignited American enthusiasm for the project.[10]

Unlike the Germans, who were too impatient and had scared away one too many brilliant scientist, or the British, who were too optimistic about the cost, or the Russians, who were simply too busy fighting for their lives, the Americans had plenty of brilliant scientists (several of whom were coming from Germany), plenty of money, plenty of resources and a highly supportive government. Between 1942-45, the U.S. would spend a total of $1.9 billion on its nuclear program, known as the *Manhattan Project*, the equivalent of $25 billion in 2014 (Schwartz, 58).

The Manhattan Project was a huge undertaking, employing some 130,000 people at its peak, the vast majority construction workers working on the various nuclear reactors (Jones, 344). But despite the magnitude of the workforce, very few people knew the full extent of what was actually going on. They erected accommodations, constructed roads, put up fences, pushed buttons, operated levers and watched meters, but they did not know what for.

One woman who worked in the laundry at the Monsanto Chemical Company, explained: *"The uniforms were first washed, then ironed, all new buttons sewed on and passed to me. I'd hold the uniform up to a special instrument and if I heard a clicking noise - I'd throw it back in to be done all over again. That's all I did - all day long."* (qtd. in Atomic Energy Commission, "Script", 7). Another, working at the Carbide and Carbon Chemical Company Plant, said: *"I stood in front of a panel board with a dial. When the hand moved from zero to 100 I would turn a valve. The hand would fall back to zero. I turn another valve and the hand would go back to 100. All day long.*

Watch a hand go from zero to 100 then turn a valve. It got so I was doing it in my sleep."(qtd. in Atomic Energy Commission, "Script", 8).

Some only found out years later they had worked at a place that had been part of the Manhattan Project, others never did. Of course there were also those, working at the project's principal laboratory in Los Alamos, New Mexico, who realized what they had been working on right after the Trinity Test, on July 16, 1945, when the first nuclear device was detonated at the Alamogordo Bombing and Gunnery Range (present-day White Sands Missile Range), some 200 miles from Los Alamos.

No more than a handful of people knew what was going on before that day, and even the few scientists present at the test didn't fully know what to expect. Would it work? Were they standing at a safe enough distance? What would it look like?

Before the test, Edward Teller, one of the theoretical physicists, had raised the possibility of the explosion igniting the atmosphere, which could perhaps cause a chain reaction eliminating all life on the planet (Rhodes, 418). Teller himself and fellow physicist Hans Bethe had subsequently calculated that such a self-propagating chain reaction was highly unlikely to occur, but did the calculation also prevent Teller from imagining — if only for a moment — a burning atmosphere consuming all in its path and ending life as we know it, as he was watching 'the gadget' (as it was called) fall from the bomb tower in Alamogordo? Indeed, did it prevent the others from thinking they might be at the verge of unleashing forces they still knew so little about? Especially since the evening before the explosion, Enrico Fermi, in an attempt to alleviate the nervous waiting, had offered to take bets from the other scientists on whether or not the bomb would ignite the atmosphere, and if so, whether it would destroy just New Mexico or the entire world (Rhodes, 664). Fortunately, life as we know it was not eliminated, though the gadget did explode with a force equivalent to about 20,000 tons of TNT, big enough to completely evaporate the center of a city. There was a bright light that could be seen up to 180 miles away, a thundering shockwave traveling a 100 miles in each direction — even breaking a window 125 miles away — and a great mushroom cloud rising up 41,000 feet from the epicenter of the explosion (Groves, 1-2). Some called it beautiful.

Even before the Trinity Test Leó Szilárd had started circulating a petition among scientists working at the Manhattan Project, that sought to discourage President Harry S. Truman — who had succeeded to the presidency just a few months earlier, when Roosevelt died in office — from using the bomb against Japan. Szilárd suggested to first make public the terms of surrender to Japan and give the country a chance to lay down its arms, before resorting to the use of atomic bombs.

He also warned that using the bomb might "[open] *the door to an era of devastation on an unimaginable scale.*" (Szilard, "Petition"). And that, if *"rival powers"* would be permitted *"to be in uncontrolled possession of these new means of destruction, the cities of the United States as well as the cities of other nations will be in continuous danger of sudden annihilation.".*

The petition was signed by 69 other scientists but never made it through to the President.

An advisory scientific panel, consisting of Robert Oppenheimer, Enrico Fermi and others, found itself fundamentally divided as well, as became clear from its June 16 'Recommendations on the Immediate Use of Nuclear Weapons', with some favoring a *"military application best designed to induce surrender"*, and others proposing a *"purely technical demonstration"* (Cantelon, 47-48). But there was still a war on and many in the government and the military saw the atom bomb as a quick way to end it, without further loss of American lives. No one knew for sure how many

American soldiers would be killed in an all-out assault on an all-out resistant Japan, but it was clear the price would likely be very high, with official estimates running from 200,000 to as high as 4 million casualties. On the other hand, key people in the government and the military also realized at this point that the surrender of Japan was only a matter of months, three to six at the most. In other words, an invasion might not even be necessary.

Still, there were other reasons for wanting to actually use the bomb and drop it on a populated city instead of an uninhabited island somewhere in the Pacific. For one, a demonstration could go wrong. The prospect of telling the whole world about a $2 billion super bomb that had been worked on for three years, only to see it fail miserably at a test in front of the enemy (present and future ones) was not particularly alluring to military strategists. Dropping the bomb unannounced would give away far less in case of failure and insulate the U.S. from a potentially highly embarrassing incident.

And then there were the Russians, who everybody knew would be allies only for as long as the war lasted. Trying to wait out the Japanese would see a bigger piece of the Asian pie going to the Soviet Union, all the more so because the war in Europe had ended, freeing up Soviet forces to be redeployed in Asia. Also, in terms of containment, what better message could be sent to an overbearing, aggressive dictator like Joseph Stalin than dropping a nuclear weapon on an enemy city? Not only would it prove to him the U.S. really had the bomb, but also that it wasn't afraid to use it, thus effectively killing two birds with one atomic bomb.

So they dropped it. Twice.

The uranium-based atomic bomb *Little Boy* was detonated over Hiroshima on August 6, 1945, at 08:15 local time, with a force equivalent to 16 kilotons of TNT, destroying 4.4 square miles. (Young, 42-61; McRaney, 4). Between 70,000-80,000 people were killed by the blast and subsequent firestorm, with an equal number of people injured (United States Government, "U.S. Strategic Bombing Survey", 16).[11] Three days later, on August 9, the plutonium-based atomic bomb *Fat Man* was detonated over Nagasaki, at 11:01 local time, with a force equivalent to 21 kilotons of TNT (Young, 42-61). An estimated 35,000-40,000 people died instantly, with about the same number of injured (United States Government, "U.S. Strategic Bombing Survey", 4).[12] The Empire of Japan surrendered six days later, on August 15.[13]

As Leó Szilárd had predicted, the use of the A-bomb on Japan immediately triggered an international nuclear arms race. On August 29, 1949, only four years after Hiroshima and Nagasaki, the Russians conducted their own first successful nuclear weapons test, code-named *First Lightning*.

The Soviet atomic bomb project benefitted greatly from captured German facilities, resources, research and scientific personnel. The Russians also acquired valuable information from atomic spy Klaus Fuchs, a German-born physicist who had worked with Rudolf Peierls on the Tube Alloys project and under Hans Bethe at the Los Alamos Laboratory.[14]

When the United States refused to share nuclear technology with the United Kingdom after the war — even though the U.K. had shared its knowledge with the U.S. — the British restarted their own nuclear program, successfully detonating their first atomic weapon on October 3, 1952, in the lagoon between the Montebello Islands, in Western Australia.

Realizing it had to join the atomic club if it wanted to remain a global power (and it most definitely did), France started a nuclear weapons program of its own in 1956. The French conducted their first successful test on February 13, 1960, in the Algerian Sahara desert.

China started a nuclear weapons program around the same time as France, but it took the Chinese a few years longer to get to their first successful test, on October 16, 1964. Since then, several other countries have joined the atomic club, India in 1974, Pakistan in 1998 and North Korea in 2006; Israel is also believed to possess nuclear weapons, although it has never publicly confirmed this.[15]

While the nuclear arsenals of Britain, France and China never exceeded the hundreds, the U.S. and the U.S.S.R went out of their way to achieve Mutually Assured Destruction (MAD) many times over, building up arsenals of tens of thousands of nuclear warheads, keeping strategic nuclear bombers in the air, nuclear submarines at sea and equipping underground missile silos with land- based intercontinental ballistic missiles (ICBMs), so nuclear retaliation was assured in any event.[16]

During the Cuban missile crisis of October 1962, all this aggressive-defensive posturing would bring both countries — and their allies

— on the verge of assuring each other's destruction beyond the theoretical, but at the last moment saner heads prevailed.

Since the 1980s, the two nuclear superpowers have worked together in reducing their gargantuan nuclear stockpiles. As of 2014, Russia still possesses an estimated 8,000 nuclear weapons though, while the U.S. is not far behind with some 7,300 nuclear weapons (Kristensen, 97).

Since they both still have so many, perhaps they could lease a couple to Iran on the condition it won't develop a nuclear weapon of its own.

---

1   Qtd. in MacPherson 2015.

2   On August 14, 2002, Alireza Jafarzadeh, spokesman for the National Council of Resistance of Iran, presented new evidence about the existence of secret nuclear facilities in the cities of Natanz and Arak ("Iran and Nuclear Weapons").

3   A possible third track is the frustration of Iran's nuclear program through covert means, e.g., cyber warfare. An example is the computer worm Stuxnet, discovered in 2010, which was inserted in Iran's nuclear facility at Natanz and reportedly destroyed a fifth of Iran's nuclear centrifuges. It has been speculated (though not proven) that the worm was created by the United States and/or Israel.

4   United Nations Security Council Resolution 1696, adopted on July 31, 2006, demanded Iran suspend its uranium enrichment program "*or face possible economic, diplomatic sanctions*". After the country failed to do so, United Nations Security Council Resolution 1737 was passed on December 23 that same year, imposing the first sanctions. Between 2007-10, these sanctions were subsequently expanded through resolutions 1747, 1803 and 1929 ("Security Council Committee").

5   The German-Jewish physicist Rudolf Peierls, who had remained in England after Hitler came to power in 1933, initially calculated that the needed critical mass was "*of the order of tons*" (qtd. in Rhodes, 321). The theoretical physicist Werner Heisenberg, who would be part of the German nuclear weapon project, believed it was about one ton (Bernstein, 129).

6   Enrico Fermi emigrated from Benito Mussolini's fascist Italy to the United States in the late 1930s, because of new Italian racial laws affecting his Jewish wife.

7   Several of the emigrated scientists had already made key discoveries in nuclear physics and would come to play an important role in the American effort to develop a nuclear bomb, the Manhattan Project. Who knows what would have happened if Hitler had been just a warmonger, instead of being equally hellbent on the destruction of the Jews.

8   They were partially right, since Germany had indeed already been defeated by the time the Americans acquired the bomb. Then again, with the atomic bomb being such a game changer, any German military victory would have been rendered meaningless the moment one of its (still undefeated) enemies acquired it.

9   In *Hitler's Uranium Club: The Secret Recordings at Farm Hall*, Jeremy Bernstein publishes a fascinating discussion — held on August 6, 1945, just after the announcement that an atomic bomb had been dropped — between some of the most important German scientists who the Allies believed had worked on Nazi Germany's nuclear program (115-25). In an operation code-named 'Epsilon', meant to uncover how close Germany had come to a nuclear bomb, the scientists, who were detained by the Allies after the defeat of Germany, among them Otto Hahn and Werner Heisenberg, were interned at Farm Hall, a bugged house in Godmanchester, England. During the discussion, they express disbelief about the American success of developing and deploying a nuclear weapon and contemplate why the German effort was unsuccessful.

10   After the war, Leó Szilárd said: "*If Congress knew the true history of the atomic energy project, I have no doubt but that it would create a special medal to be given to meddling foreigners for distinguished services, and Dr. Oliphant would be the first to receive one.*" (qtd. in Rhodes, 372).

11   The survey acknowledges that accurate figures are impossible to give, since many people had already left because of declining activity in the cities, the constant threat of incendiary raids and government evacuation programs (United States Government, "U.S. Strategic Bombing Survey", 16).

12   In Hiroshima, a surging fire storm increased the devastation caused by the bomb, as did the flat terrain of the city. As the U.S. Strategic Bombing Survey states: "*In Nagasaki, no such fire storm arose, and the uneven terrain of the city confined the maximum intensity of the damage to the valley over which the bomb exploded. The area of nearly complete devastation was thus much smaller; only about 1.8 square miles.*" (United States Government, "U.S. Strategic Bombing Survey", 4).

13   The official Japanese instrument of surrender was signed on September 2, 1945.

14   Fuchs had fled Nazi Germany in 1933 because of his communist beliefs and was granted British citizenship in 1942. He gave the Soviets valuable information on the required atomic mass and the method of detonation, among other things (Trenear-Harvey, 78-79). Early 1950, Fuchs was arrested, tried and convicted to fourteen years imprisonment. After his release, he was allowed to emigrate to East Germany, where he continued his scientific career. He died in 1988, one year before the fall of the Berlin Wall.

15   Though these countries are known or believed to possess nuclear weapons, they are not recognized by the Non- Proliferation Treaty as 'nuclear-weapons states'. Only the first five are.

16   As of 2014, the British nuclear weapons inventory counts an estimated 225

nuclear warheads, with a peak of some 500 in the 1970s (Kristensen, 97). For France, the total arsenal is estimated to be around 300, while China is believed to possess approximately 250 nuclear weapons, according to Hans Kristensen in "Worldwide deployments of nuclear weapons, 2014". Estimates of between 2,000-3,000 Chinese nuclear warheads have also surfaced, but these appear to be based on unsubstantiated rumors.

Part VII

World 2.0

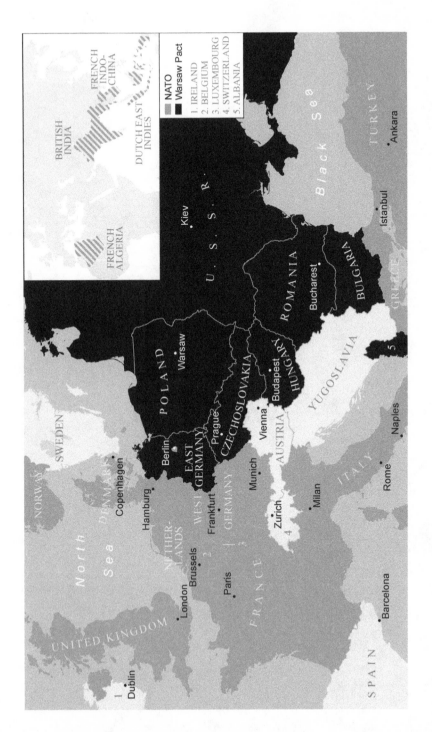

Map 24: NATO and the Warsaw Pact, c. 1955-66

43

A New World Order

"Out of this conflict have come powerful military nations, now fully trained and equipped for war. But they have no right to dominate the world. It is rather the duty of these powerful nations to assume the responsibility for leadership toward a world of peace. That is why we have here resolved that power and strength shall be used not to wage war, but to keep the world at peace, and free from the fear of war."[1]

President Harry S. Truman, address in San Francisco at the closing session of the United Nations Conference, June 26, 1945

On the evening of October 9, 1944, British Prime Minister Winston Churchill decided to talk realpolitik with Russian leader Joseph Stalin. Meeting in the Soviet dictator's rather gloomy office in the Kremlin, Churchill said: *"Let us settle about our affairs in the Balkans. Your armies are in Romania and Bulgaria. We have interests, missions, and agents there. Don't let us get at cross- purposes in small ways. So far as Britain and Russia are concerned, how would it do for you to have ninety percent predominance in Romania, for us to have ninety percent of the say in Greece, and go fifty-fifty about Yugoslavia?"*(Churchill, "Triumph and Tragedy", 227).

While his words were being translated, Churchill produced a scrap of paper and wrote down the names of Romania, Greece, Yugoslavia, Hungary and Bulgaria, adding the percentages he had just proposed.

He then pushed the paper across the table to Stalin, who looked at it for a moment and took a thoughtful drag from his pipe. *"Then he took his blue pencil and made a large tick upon it, and passed it back to us. It was all settled in no more time than it takes to set down...After this there was a long silence. The pencilled paper lay in the centre of the table. At length I said, "Might it not be thought rather cynical if it seemed we had disposed of these issues so fateful to millions of people, in such an offhand manner? Let us burn the paper." "No, you keep it.", said Stalin."* (Churchill, "Triumph and Tragedy", 227-28).[2]

Poland was conspicuously left out of the 'naughty document', as it would come to be known.[3] The Red Army had already advanced deep into Poland and Churchill knew Stalin would never agree to relinquish it and let the Poles have free elections. On the contrary, the Soviet leader intended to annex Poland and use it as a buffer zone between Russia and Western Europe.

Churchill did make a few half-hearted attempts to persuade Stalin to restore Poland's sovereignty after the war, but both men knew that Russia held all the cards; the Red Army was already in control of most of Eastern Europe, while the British could only play second fiddle to the Americans on the Western front. And judging from America's quick departure from Europe after World War I, chances were U.S. troops would not linger this time either. In other words, weakened and financially exhausted Britain and France would probably have to keep the Russians at bay themselves in Western Europe, while at the same time trying to preserve their colonies. Not an easy task.

Churchill had therefore already written off Eastern Europe entirely before even stepping into Stalin's office that October evening. He had only one goal: to make sure Stalin would stay out of Greece. A free and democratic Greece was of vital importance to the British because of its strategic position in the Mediterranean, close to Egypt, Britain's gateway to Asia and its most important oversees colony, British India.

Stalin did indeed stay out of Greece after the war, but when it came to Eastern Europe the only percentage acceptable to the Russian leader turned out to be 100. And who was going to stop him?

The exhausted British? The French, who had just gotten their country back and now had to deal with a serious uprising in French Indochina? The Poles, who were still reeling from five years of brutal occupation and extermination? The Americans, who were so eager to go home?

A new geopolitical reality was thus fast emerging in the second half of the 1940s, one in which the old European powers proved to be frighteningly powerless and two new, ideologically opposed superpowers emerged as the real victors of the Second World War. Driving through the rubble and ruins of once proud and industrious German cities, it did not take the Americans long to realize that this time — contrary to the end of the First World War — there would be no rapid return to political isolationism. This time, they would have to stay.

Even if the U.S. had the bomb and the Soviet Union did not, everybody knew it would likely take the Russians no more than a couple of years to follow suit now that the nuclear cat was out of the bag, and what would become of Western Europe then? A contingency plan prepared by the U.S. military in the late 1940s, code-named *Operation Dropshot*, expected a Soviet takeover of Western Europe around 1957 (Mastny, 146-49). The plan called for the use of tactical nuclear weapons in the eventuality of war with the Russians in Europe.[4] But of course prevention was better.

To contain Stalin, the U.S. therefore opted for the three-pronged strategy of rebuild, defend and unite in Western Europe. This included West Germany, not just because of its strategic geographic location — it shared a border with Soviet-controlled East Germany and Czechoslovakia — but also because it was clear that economic recovery in Europe would not be possible without the reconstruction of the German industrial base (Leffler, 155-57).[5]

In April 1948 the United States launched the European Recovery Program, to help rebuild Europe. Better known as the Marshall Plan — after Secretary of State George C. Marshall, who had announced the plan a year earlier — it would disburse a little over $12 billion (the equivalent of about $115 billion in 2014) in economic recovery funds in Western Europe during the four years it was active, which were mostly used for the import of fuel, food, feed, fertilizers, raw materials, semi-manufactured products, machines, vehicles and equipment (Hogan, 414-15).

Stalin initially welcomed the plan, until he realized the funds would be disbursed on the condition of economic cooperation under the supervision of the United States, thus increasing U.S. influence in recipient countries, at the expense of Soviet influence (Wettig, 138-39). Even worse in the eyes of Stalin, or at least just as worse, was that Germany, which had been defeated only a few years ago at a staggering price in Russian lives, was to be included as a recipient of the Marshall funds. Stalin therefore discouraged (i.e., forbade) the Eastern European countries under his control from taking part in the program (Wettig, 138-39).

Of course for the United States, investing in the economic recovery of Europe was not simply an act of altruism from a generous victor. Apart from wanting to prevent a weak Europe from becoming an easy prey for the Soviet Union — which by now spanned from the Bering Strait to Berlin — the U.S. also had a more direct, economic interest in a strong European recovery. With the war industry winding down and many soldiers returning home to civilian life and looking for work, the U.S. economy was running the risk of entering a recession. U.S. export needed to grow and for that European economies needed to be restored to their pre-war levels (Davidson, 186-87).

Another important pillar in countering the Soviet threat in Europe was European unification, something that could also help to permanently contain Germany. To this end, the American Committee on United Europe (ACUE) was founded in 1948, which before long began to covertly funnel monies to several European federalist movements (Scott-Smith, 46-47).[6] The early leadership of the ACUE read as a who's who of U.S. central intelligence chiefs; its first chairman was the wartime head of the OSS (the precursor of the CIA), William Joseph Donovan, its first vice-chairman was Allen Dulles, who would succeed Walter Bedell Smith — another board member of the ACUE — as director of the CIA in 1953.

In May 1948, 713 delegates from all over Europe — political leaders, philosophers, lawyers, historians, journalists, entrepreneurs, professors — met in The Hague, the Netherlands, to talk about political, economic and monetary unification of Europe (Laffan, 37-38). The Hague Congress led to the establishment of several pan-European organizations, such as the Council of Europe, the College of Europe and the European Movement, a federalist movement striving for a United States of Europe.[7]

One of the first Presidents of the European Movement was former

French Prime Minister and Foreign Minister Robert Schuman. He was the first to propose a supranational European organization for the creation and regulation of a common market for coal and steel, on May 9, 1950.[8] Two years later, the European Coal and Steel Community (ECSC) was established by West Germany, France, Italy, the Netherlands, Belgium and Luxembourg. Its success spurred the subsequent creation of the European Economic Community, in 1957, which would later become part of the European Union (in 2009).

Meanwhile, despite growing tensions between the Soviet Union and the United States during the second half of the 1940s, there was also some global institutional progress. Realizing that mankind might not survive another world war — especially in light of the arrival of the atomic bomb — that advances in technology were making the world ever smaller and that a better permanent forum for the international community was badly needed, the United Nations was established on October 24, 1945.

Three years later, in a bid to prevent atrocities such as had been committed by Nazi Germany and the Empire of Japan from ever happening again, the United Nations General Assembly took a first step towards universal protection of fundamental human rights when it adopted the Universal Declaration of Human Rights (UDHR) on December 10, 1948, acknowledging in its preamble that "*recognition of the inherent dignity and of the equal and inalienable rights of all members of the human family is the foundation of freedom, justice and peace in the world*" (United Nations, "Declaration").[9]

Though the UDHR was not meant to be legally binding as such, the fundamental rights enunciated in articles two to twenty-one quickly became part of international customary law, not least because of their extensive use in national constitutions, international legislation and decisions by national and international courts (Humphrey, 28-29).[10]

But however noble and hopeful these early post-WW II era dreams of a new world were, the claims and agreements of the real world — divided along the same old lines of national interest — quickly caught up with them, giving the noble dreamers a rude wake-up call. Because not only did the Soviet Union still move in to secure control of Poland, Bulgaria, Hungary, Czechoslovakia, Romania, Albania and East Germany, several European powers also took steps to retain their colonies, just as they had done after the First World War.

Germany and Italy were forced to give up their colonies by the victors, but France sent troops to Indochina early 1946, to deal with communist revolutionary Ho Chi Minh and his Viet Minh, which sought Vietnamese independence from French rule. Around the same time, the Netherlands also sent a fighting force to Southeast Asia, to suppress a nationalist revolution in the Dutch East Indies. Both colonial powers used a significant part of the funds they received from the U.S. Marshall Plan to finance their expeditionary forces.

By the end of 1948 the Dutch had amassed some 140,000 troops in the East Indies, but international pressure for a cease fire mounted, including from the U.S., which threatened to stop its financial aid to the Netherlands and even exclude it from the pending North Atlantic Treaty (Groen, 32-35). Out of options, the Dutch had no choice but to give in to the pressure and recognize the independence of Indonesia in 1949.

Meanwhile, the British took a different tack in dealing with their own most prized Asian colony, India. During the war, the British Empire had suppressed Indian independence movements, but now that the Axis had finally been defeated, Britain found itself in dire financial straits, leading it to quickly reconcile itself with the prospect of Indian independence (Knight, 152-53).[11] British India thus became independent in 1947, when it was partitioned into two independent states, India, predominantly Hindu, and Pakistan, predominantly Muslim.[12]

By that time France was already knee-deep in violent conflict in Indochina. Between 1946-54, the French — with increasing financial support from the United States — fought the communist forces of Ho Chi Minh — supported by Red China and Soviet Russia — until finally deciding to pull out after losing big at the battle of Dien Bien Phu (March-May 1954).[13] Soon after the Americans moved in, first with military advisors and financial aid, later with active combat troops, to prevent a communist takeover of South Vietnam.[14] They too would fail though against Ho Chi Minh and his most prominent General, Vo Nguyen Giap.[15]

Just a few months after the end of the First Indochina War another

French colonial war started, this time in French Algeria, North Africa. Determined not to let another colony slip away, the French military went all out to push back the Algerian fighters of the National Liberation Front (FLN). They succeeded, but only through the use of brutal measures such as torture and bombings targeting civilians. In 1958, the French Fourth Republic, already unstable and utterly incapable of dealing with the political tensions the war created, collapsed. General Charles de Gaulle, hero of the French resistance in WW II, was subsequently asked to come out of retirement and create order out of chaos.[16]

De Gaulle initially seemed to favor resolving the conflict by offering French Algeria more autonomy, albeit in close association with France.[17] He also quickly initiated a financial aid program for Algeria, to the tune of about $200 million a year, to show the benefits of staying in a close relationship with France (Kolodziej, 457). At the same time he continued the war against the insurgents.

But when the military campaign failed to defeat the insurgents and public opinion — both at home and abroad — turned against the ongoing war, de Gaulle gave in and announced France would accept a political solution for the war, based on the right to self-determination.[18] In a subsequent referendum, held in January 1961, both the French and Algerian population voted overwhelmingly in favor of the French government submitting a bill for Algerian self-determination (Kolodziej, 460). In the Algerian independence referendum held on July 1 of the following year, 99 percent of the votes were in favor of independence (Berstein, 56). Of course by then most of the French and Algerians loyal to France had already left Algeria.

During the final stages of the Algerian War, a flurry of other African colonies — most of them French or British — also declared themselves independent. Cameroon, Chad, Republic of the Congo, Cote d'Ivoire, Gabon, Mali, Senegal, Mauritania, Niger, Togo, Central African Republic, Madagascar, Nigeria, Somaliland and Belgian Congo all in 1960, Tanzania, Sierra Leone and British Cameroon in 1961 and Uganda in 1962. Within 20 years after the end of the Second World War, the right to self-determination as recognized in Chapter 1, Article 1 of the United Nations Charter, thus became reality for dozens of former European colonies in Asia, Africa and the Middle East.

Colonialism was out, ideological imperialism was in. From the mid-1940s until the collapse of the U.S.S.R in 1991, much of the world would be divided between East and West, the former dominated by the Soviet Union, the latter by the United States.

In 1949, Western countries united themselves militarily in the North Atlantic Treaty Organization (NATO), in an effort to better coordinate their defenses. Six years later, on May 14, 1955 — five days after Germany was admitted to NATO — the U.S.S.R and its Eastern European satellite states founded their own mutual defense organization, the Warsaw Pact.

For the next four decades, the United States and Russia would keep themselves and their allies in a continuous state of political and military tension. A 'cold war', relying on rational minds, strict rules of engagement and Mutual Assured Destruction (MAD) to prevent it from going hot — and nuclear. Apart from direct military confrontation and the use of nuclear weapons pretty much everything was allowed to gain an edge, including spying, sabotage, propaganda and of course the fighting or financing (or both) of proxy wars, such as in Korea, Vietnam and Afghanistan.

In short, for the first time in 500 years, the naughty documents were no longer being produced by Europe.

---

1   Truman, "Address in San Francisco".

2   Churchill did keep the piece of paper. The handwritten document is preserved in Britain's Public Record Office, PREM 3/66/7, available on request.

3   The use of the epithet 'naughty document' seems to have originated with Churchill himself (Blake, 320).

4   Declassified in 1977, Operation Dropshot stated that: "*An important element in blunting Soviet offensives would be the use of atomic weapons and conventional bombs against LOCs* [lines of communication], *supply bases, and troop concentrations in the USSR, in the satellites, and in overrun countries which directly support Soviet advances. The use of atomic bombs against satellite and overrun areas, however, should be confined as far as possible to those targets the destruction of which would not involve large masses of population (...) it is considered that a reasonable requirement for atomic bombs on target for this purpose might be on the order of an additional **one hundred atomic bombs** [boldface added] of a type not now available but which are considered capable of development and production in sufficient quantity by 1957*" (United States, "Dropshot", 4.a.2.b). Note that this would be on top of the 75-100

atomic bombs necessary for attacks on *"atomic-assembly facilities, storage points, and heavy-bomber airfields"* (United States, "Dropshot", 4.a.2.a).

5   At the Potsdam Conference (July 17-August 2, 1945), the United States, the Soviet Union and the United Kingdom had agreed to divide Germany into four military occupation zones, with the United states in charge in the south, France in the southwest, Britain in the northwest and the Soviet Union in the east. In 1949, the three zones occupied by the Western powers were rejoined in the newly formed Federal Republic of Germany. The Soviet-occupied zone became the German Democratic Republic that same year.

6   For a more detailed explanation of the ACUE, also see *OSS, CIA and European Unity: The American Committee on United Europe, 1948- 60*, by Richard Aldrich.

7   The European Movement was heavily financed by the ACUE in the 1950s (Aldrich, 184-85).

8   In the EU, May 9 is still celebrated as Europe Day, in commemoration to the historical significance of the Schuman Declaration. Schuman, who was also the first President of the European Parliament, is considered one of the Founding Fathers of the European Union.

9   While there were no votes against the Universal Declaration, eight members of the United Nations General Assembly abstained from voting, among them the Soviet Union.

10   John Peters Humphrey wrote the first draft of the Universal Declaration.

11   Of course there were also other factors at play that nudged the British government towards the decision to quit India. For one, Indian nationalism had grown during the war years, increasing the likelihood of having to send extra troops to suppress nationalist movements if the colony was to be retained, a prospect the cabinet certainly wanted to avoid, especially in light of the recent difficulties the French and the Dutch had encountered in this respect. Another factor was that the British public was more focused on the problems at home than on retaining India.

12   In 1971, civil war broke out between (West) Pakistan and its province East Pakistan, located in the Bengal region (east of India), after the Pakistani government answered the latter's demand for more autonomy with a campaign of military terror. East Pakistan subsequently declared itself the independent state of Bangladesh. When India joined the war on the side of Bangladesh a few months later, Pakistan was quickly forced to surrender.

13   According to the so-called 'Pentagon Papers', an internal study on U.S. involvement in Vietnam between 1945-67, done by the U.S. Defense department between 1967-69, the decision to provide support to the French was taken *"in spite of the U.S. desire to avoid direct involvement in a colonial war"* (United States, "Pentagon Papers", IV. A. 2., i). The reason the United States nevertheless chose the side of the colonial power rather than that of

the independence movement (as it had done with the Dutch East Indies, for instance) had everything to do with the *"broader considerations of U.S. policy for the containment of communism in Europe and Asia."* (United States, "Pentagon Papers", II. A. 1-2). The Pentagon Papers were partially leaked to the press in 1971. In 2011, the entire study was declassified and publicly released.

14 Between 1954-60, Vietnam was the third largest non-NATO recipient of U.S. economic and military assistance (United States, "Pentagon Papers", IV. A. 4., 1.1). The Joint Chiefs of Staff nevertheless determined in 1960 that despite these efforts, the Vietnamese National Army was still inadequately trained (United States, "Pentagon Papers", 1.1ff.). For information on the buildup of U.S. combat troops, see Part IV. C. 4-5 of the Pentagon Papers.

15 Vo Nguyen Giap died on October 4, 2013, at the age of 102.

16 The order De Gaulle created was the establishment of the Fifth Republic, a presidential constitutional republic, as opposed to the parliamentary republic of the Fourth Republic, which, ineffective and politically unstable, had counted no less than twenty-six governments in the twelve years years of its existence (Wakeman, 73).

17 In his book *Mémoires d'Espoir* (Memoirs of Hope), de Gaulle wrote that *"there was in my opinion no other solution than that of Algerian self-determination"* (qtd. in Berstein, 28). French historian Serge Bernstein writes in *The Republic of de Gaulle 1958-1969*, however, that there is no proof this really was de Gaulle's plan from the outset, but that on the contrary it appears de Gaulle had no clear idea yet as to how to resolve the conflict when he returned to power in 1958 (Berstein, 28-30).

18 De Gaulle's decision to withdraw from Algeria met with strong resistance from parts of the French Army, who subsequently organized themselves in the *Organization de l'Armée Secrète* (Organization of the Secret Army, OAS). The OAS launched a bombing campaign to stop the political process of withdrawal from Algeria. In 1962, the group even attempted to assassinate President de Gaulle in the Paris suburb of Petit-Clamart. De Gaulle's car was hit with fourteen bullets, but miraculously nobody was hurt. The mastermind behind the attack, French Air Force lieutenant- colonel Jean-Marie Bastien-Thiry, was sentenced to death and executed by firing squad on March 11, 1963.

44

THE SPACE RACE

"We choose to go to the moon. We choose to go to the moon in this decade and do the other things, not because they are easy, but because they are hard, because that goal will serve to organize and measure the best of our energies and skills, because that challenge is one that we are willing to accept, one we are unwilling to postpone, and one which we intend to win, and the others, too."[1]

President John F. Kennedy, September 12, 1962

On August 25, 2012, space probe Voyager 1 became the first manmade object ever to leave the solar system and enter interstellar space (Barnes 2013). Launched on September 5, 1977, its primary mission was to study the outer planets in our solar system, a mission it completed in 1980.

After that it just kept going, traveling at a velocity relative to the sun of 17 km/s. As of July 2014, it was about 19.2 billion km/11.9 billion mi from the Sun, about 130 times farther than the distance from the Earth to the Sun (NASA, "Voyager"). Voyager mission control was still sending and/or receiving data to/from the probe every day, which, traveling at the speed of light, took about seventeen hours to reach its destination.

Packed with scientific instruments — a handful of them still working as of 2014, thirty-seven years after the start of the mission — Voyager 1 was meant to give us new insights about our solar system. A rather lofty goal, especially considering the more down-to-earth military objectives that initially propelled mankind into space.

The Space Age began on October 3, 1942, in Nazi Germany, when rocket scientist Wernher von Braun and his team succeeded in launching an A-4 rocket — better known as the V-2 — that reached outer space (Neufeld, 164).[2] The world's first ballistic missile, it could travel at 5,760 kph/3,580 mph and had a range of 320 km/200 mi. In all, close to 6,000 V-2s were produced, of which approximately 3,200 were launched against Allied targets, most of them targeting Antwerp and London (Neufeld, 263-64). The last one was fired on March 27, 1945. There was virtually no defense against them.

The V-2 ballistic missile was incredibly advanced for its time and none of the Allies was even close to achieving something similar, which explains why they went out of their way to secure V-2 components, schematics and above all nazi scientists as they penetrated deeper and deeper into the heartland of the Third Reich.

Many of the V-2 scientists, including von Braun, had worked at the research center at Peenemünde, on the Baltic Sea coast, northeast Germany, for most of the war. But in February 1945, with the Russians closing in on Peenemünde, von Braun and his team, together with their equipment, were relocated to the V-2 Mittelwerk factory in Central Germany (Neufeld, 256-58). There, prisoners from the Mittelbau-Dora concentration camp were working at fever pitch to produce V-2 rockets.[3]

Early April, when the Americans were close to capturing the Mittelwerk factory, the SS moved von Braun and some five hundred other 'Peenemünders' to the Bavarian Alps (Neufeld, 263). The factory was captured by the U.S. Army shortly thereafter.

In the weeks that followed, the Americans did their best to move as many V-2 components and research from the Mittelwerk factory as possible, as it was located in what was to become the Soviet Zone of occupation.[4] The loot from Mittelwerk was quickly transported by rail to the harbor of Antwerp, Belgium, where it filled sixteen Liberty ships (Adams, 71). And when von Braun and his team surrendered to elements of the U.S. 44th Infantry Division on May 3, 1945, the Americans were really in business (Ward, 56).

The Office of Strategic Services (OSS, predecessor of the CIA) had initially only wanted to interrogate the scientists, but soon realized it would be far more sensible to recruit them outright and move them to the United States (Piszkiewicz, 225-26).[5] One problem with this was that President Truman had expressly ordered to exclude from recruitment all scientists who had been a member of the Nazi Party (Piszkiewicz, 225-26; Neufeld, 270). Since that was the case with most of the top scientists, including von Braun, a way was devised to....work around the President's directive, by creating false employment histories and biographies from which all nazi affiliation had been expunged (i.e., by lying). And so, in September 1945, von Braun and 118 members of his team arrived in the United States, ready to continue their game-changing work, albeit in service of new masters (Adams, 71). Hundreds more would follow.

Meanwhile the Soviets had released Sergei Korolev — their top rocket scientist — from the slave labor camp they had sent him to in 1939, during Stalin's Great Purge. His ordeal had included a stint at Kolyma, the most notorious Gulag labor camp, located in northeast Siberia — where it was winter for twelve months and summer for the rest of the year — during which he had lost fourteen of his teeth to scurvy, among other unpleasantries (Siddiqi, 188).[6] But when the Soviets discovered scores of V-2 rocket components in Peenemünde and Mittelwerk, they needed Korolev to make sense of it all, and thus, in a remarkable reversal of fortune, Korolev was made a colonel in the Red Army and sent to Germany to study the V-2 guidance system, turbo-pump, engine and fuel mixture (Osiander, 220). The Russians also managed to recruit some 150 German scientists, though most of them had been involved with the mass production of the V-2 at Mittelwerk and had not directly worked with von Braun.[7]

Of course the successful atomic bombings of Hiroshima and Nagasaki in August 1945 gave a whole new sense of urgency to the development of a reliable ballistic missile, something that only increased after the Russians successfully tested their own nuclear bomb in 1949, and with the outbreak of the Korean war, a year after that. Whoever would be the first to develop a rocket that could carry a nuclear warhead and be guided fairly accurately to a target a couple of thousand miles away, would be able to annihilate the other before he could retaliate.

Both in the U.S. and the U.S.S.R., the first advances in rocketry were made based on the V-2 design. On May 10, 1946, the Americans sent up a modified V-2 for the first scientific exploration of space (a cosmic radiation experiment), and another one a few months later, on

October 24, to take the first pictures of earth from an altitude of 65 mi/105 km. Though grainy black and white, the images nevertheless clearly showed Earth against the blackness of space. A few months after that, in February 1947, the first animals, a couple of fruit flies, were launched into space with a U.S. modified V-2, reaching an altitude of 68 mi/109 km before plunging back to earth. The fearless fruit flies were retrieved alive.

In the early 1950s both sides started with the development of an intercontinental ballistic missile (ICBM), capable of traveling at least 3,400 mi/5,500 km, which was a whole different ball game than the V-2, with its 200 mi/320 km range. In the U.S., the Army, Navy and Air Force each set up their own program, leading to considerable duplication of effort, whereas in the U.S.S.R., ICBM research — headed by Sergei Korolev — was more centrally organized, although several groups worked on different designs and competed with each other for funding (Burns, 165-73).

Quietly, the Russians took the lead, and on August 21, 1957, they successfully launched an R-7 rocket that traveled some 4,000 miles, making it the world's first ICBM (Hardesty, 67).

Although the R-7 was developed to carry a nuclear payload to another continent, it could also carry a different kind of payload, into space. Not everybody in the Soviet military agreed with using the R-7 for anything other than carrying a nuclear warhead, but Korolev nevertheless succeeded in obtaining permission from the all powerful Central Committee and the Council of Ministers to launch a satellite into space, by arguing that there was not just a nuclear arms race going on with the United States but also a burgeoning space race, which, of course, the Soviet Union had to win (Hall, 60).

Because the R-7 was such a powerful rocket, Korolev initially planned to send up a satellite weighing a massive 1,200 kg/2,645 lb (Hall, 60).[8] Dubbed 'Object D', the satellite would be stuffed chockablock with scientific goodies.[9] But when Object D ran into complex design and manufacturing problems, Korolev decided to launch a much smaller satellite into orbit instead, with the main purpose of beating the Americans to it.

This would be Sputnik 1, a science-fiction-like silver-colored sphere, with four long antennas, weighing a measly 83.6 kg/182 lb (Logsdon, "Sputnik", 60). Its scientific capabilities were far less ambitious than those of Object D had been, but it would still be able to send out a radio signal and help measure the density of the upper atmosphere.

On October 4, 1957, Sputnik 1 was successfully put into orbit and began transmitting its "beep- beep-beep" signal at specific frequencies, which could be picked up by ham radio operators around the world.[10] It was a huge success for Korolev and his team and a huge surprise to everybody else, especially the Americans.

Less than two months later, on December 6, the U.S. attempted to launch a satellite of its own into orbit with a Vanguard rocket. After the booster was ignited the rocket began to lift off, but a few seconds later, having risen just a little over one meter, it fell back again and exploded in a sea of flames. It was a big flop and newspapers outdid themselves in looking for that one word that best summed up the humiliating event, coming up with such finds as "Flopnik", "Dudnik", "Oopsnik" "Kaputnik" and "pfft-nik", to name a few (qtd. in TIME, "Vanguard's Aftermath").

All joking aside though, Sputnik's success and Vanguard's failure also spread fear in the West. Shocked and awestruck, the public suddenly realized the United States was significantly lagging the Soviet Union in space age technology and that the Russians now had missiles capable of targeting American cities with hydrogen bombs, while the United States did not (Dickson, 2-7).

The events led to a real 'Sputnik crisis', to which Washington responded with a range of measures aimed at closing the 'missile gap' and the (perceived) 'technology gap'.[11] In February 1958, the Advanced Research Projects Agency (ARPA) was created, which was to be responsible for the development of technologies with potential military applications.[12] ARPA would be involved in several groundbreaking inventions and innovations, including ARPANET, the progenitor of the internet.

Just a few months after the creation of ARPA, on July 29, the National Aeronautics and Space Act came into effect, creating the National Aeronautics and Space Administration (NASA), the agency responsible for the U.S. civilian space program and for aeronautics and aerospace research, and a few months after that the National Defense Education Act (NDEA) was signed into law, pouring hundreds of millions of dollars in additional funding into educational institutions on all levels.[13]

In short, it was on.

On January 31, 1958, less than four months after Sputnik 1 and not two months after 'Kaputnik', the U.S. had also succeeded in putting a satellite of its own in orbit, the Explorer 1, but in this kind of race there was no silver medal for finishing second. And although the United States had now firmly picked up the gauntlet to become the leading space power, it would finish second several more times.

Between 1959-61 the Russians were reaping victory after victory, being the first to impact the moon with a man-made object (September 13, 1959), the first to take photographs of the far side of the moon (October 4, 1959) and the first to launch mammals into earth orbit — the dogs Belka and Strelka — and retrieve them alive (August 19, 1960).[14]

But the biggest blow to U.S. prestige came on April 12, 1961, when Yuri Alekseyevich Gagarin became the first man in space. Gagarin, a fighter pilot in the Soviet Air Force, had been carefully selected for the Soviet space program with nineteen others and was subsequently picked to be the first in space because he was highly intelligent, very likable, came from humble beginnings — his parents worked on a collective farm — and measured only 1.57 meters, the latter being important because room in the Vostok space capsule was limited (Burgess, 145-47).[15]

Gagarin's flight in the Vostok 1 lasted 108 minutes, enough for a single earth orbit. The capsule subsequently reentered the atmosphere and ejected Gagarin at a height of 4.3 mi/7 km (Burgess, 161). A few minutes later the world's first cosmonaut landed safely on the ground.

It was a monumental achievement, and not just for the people of the Soviet Union. All mankind was united in awe, just sixteen years after the end of the most devastating war the world had ever seen. And since Russia had arguably suffered the most during that war — losing over 25 million of its citizens and much of its industrial infrastructure — the achievement was all the more remarkable.

Of course, in the West, joy and awe quickly mixed with fear. Gagarin's successful flight proved the Soviets were still ahead in the Space Race, and if their space program was already advanced enough to put people into orbit, perhaps they could also put platforms into orbit equipped with nuclear weapons, for a surprise attack on the United States and Europe.

The deep, mutual sense of distrust between East and West, so typical of the Cold War, thus clouded every scientific achievement of the early Space Age. It was understandable enough though, especially since the competition between the two superpowers was far less scientific in Korea and Vietnam, or Germany for that matter, where tensions had been rising due to massive emigration from East Germany to the West.[16] This exodus was abruptly halted on August 13, 1961 — four months after Gagarin's flight — when the East German Army closed the border between East and West Berlin with barbed wire and started construction of a miles-long concrete wall a few days later. And so, if Yuri Gagarin's historic flight and broad smile had made people in the West realize they were all humans inhabiting the same small planet, the Berlin Wall made them remember their insurmountable differences again.

Though the U.S. was behind in the Space Race, the gap wasn't all that big. On May 5, 1961, just 23 days after Gagarin had forever etched his name into the great book of human history, Alan Shepard was launched into space with his Freedom 7 capsule, fixed atop a Mercury-Redstone rocket. The mission was to reach outer space and then come back down safely. The entire flight lasted only fifteen minutes, but the rocket reached an altitude of 116.5 miles, enough to make Shepard the first American and the second man in space (Hardesty, 125). Less than a year later, on February 20, 1962, John Glenn became the first American to orbit earth.[17]

That same year the world would also came to the brink of nuclear war, after the Soviet Union deployed nuclear missiles in Cuba.[18] The Kennedy administration initially considered taking out the missiles with air strikes or even a full-scale invasion of Cuba, before deciding to first try the less invasive military measure of the naval blockade, followed by back-channel diplomacy aimed at finding a mutually satisfactory way out of the maze.

After President Kennedy and Russian leader Khrushchev had somehow managed to avoid blowing up the planet, Kennedy tried to usher in an era of détente, proposing in a speech before the United Nations General Assembly on September 20, 1963, that the United States and the Soviet Union join forces and try to reach the moon together (Hamilton, "Joint Moon Flight"). Khrushchev initially rejected the proposal, but his thinking apparently evolved during the weeks that followed, because on November 1 he expressed clear interest in Kennedy's proposal, saying at a reception at the Kremlin that he considered it would be *"useful if the U.S.S.R and the U.S. pooled their efforts in exploring space for scientific purposes, specifically for arranging a joint flight to the moon. Would it not be fine if a Soviet man and an American or Soviet cosmonaut and an American woman flew to the moon? Of course it would."* (qtd. in Logsdon, "Moon", 191).

It would have been, but just a few weeks later, on November 22, President Kennedy was shot in Dallas, Texas. His proposal for a joint moon program did not survive either.

During the second half of the 1960s the Russians initially continued their streak of firsts, while the Americans worked on closing the gap and taking the ultimate prize — also television event of the century — landing a man on the moon. On March 18, 1965, cosmonaut Alexey Leonov became the first person to exit his capsule in space and perform extra-vehicular activity (EVA), on February 3, 1966, the Russian Luna 9 was the first spacecraft to achieve a soft landing on the moon and a few months later, on April 3, the Luna 10 became the first artificial satellite of the moon. The Russians seemed poised to attempt a manned lunar landing next.

But the untimely death, early 1966, of Sergei Korolev, the mastermind of the Soviet space program, significantly delayed the Russian lunar landing program at a time the U.S. was blasting full speed ahead. During 1965-66, the astronauts perfected working outside a spacecraft (EVA) and piloting a space capsule for rendezvous and docking purposes.

On December 24, 1968, the United States took the indisputable lead in the Space Race for the first time, when Frank Borman, Jim

Lovell and William Anders became the first to orbit the moon and actually see Earth as a whole planet. Five months later, on May 18, 1969, in a final 'dress rehearsal', Apollo 10 was launched with the specific mission to fly the Lunar Module around the moon, without landing it. The manned Lunar Module came within 8.4 nm/15.6 km of the lunar surface, the closest humans had ever been (Godwin, 152).

Just two months later, on July 16, Apollo 11 was launched from the Kennedy Space Center in Florida. On board: Neil Armstrong, Michael Collins, Edwin 'Buzz' Aldrin and one Lunar Module. Destination: the moon again, but this time the Lunar Module would do more than just orbit.

On July 20, Armstrong and Aldrin piloted the Lunar Module to the surface of the moon, touching down at 20:18 UTC. A couple of hours later, on July 21, 02:56 UTC, Neil Armstrong became the first human to step on the lunar surface, claiming the moment for all humanity with the immortal words *"That's one small step for* (a) *man, one giant leap for mankind"*.[19]

It was indeed a high point of human achievement. But after a couple of more trips to the moon the American public quickly lost interest in space travel and Congress started cutting NASA's funding.[20] The Russians, for their part, having no desire to claim that non-existent silver medal, lost interest in the moon as well, deciding instead to focus their efforts on space stations, like Salyut 1 and Mir.[21]

The Space Race was over.

Then again, perhaps it had only just begun. After all, the final frontier is vast and we have only barely scratched the (lunar) surface. As of 2017, no manned spacecraft has ever orbited any of the other planets in our solar system, let alone set foot on them. Put differently, where are this generation's Yuri Gagarin, Alexey Leonov, Jim Lovell, Neil Armstrong and Buzz Aldrin? Where is the next giant leap for mankind?

Aboard Voyager 1 is a golden phonograph record with sounds and images to explain to possible extraterrestrial civilizations something about the diversity of life and culture on earth. It holds 116 images showing humans, animals, chemical compositions, DNA, Earth, Jupiter and the location of our solar system, among other things, as well as a variety of sounds, including sounds of nature, musical selections and spoken greetings in 55 languages. There is also an official message of President Jimmy Carter, which ends: "*We are attempting to survive our time so we may live into yours. We hope some day, having solved the problems we face, to join a community of galactic civilizations. This record represents our hope and our determination, and our goodwill in a vast and awesome universe.*" (Carter, "Voyager Spacecraft Statement").

Let's hope we will have solved our problems by the time they pay us a visit.

---

1   Kennedy, "Rice University".

2   The A-4, the fourth rocket design in the Aggregat series, was renamed V-2 (V for *Vergeltungswaffe*, weapon of vengeance) by German Minister of Propaganda Joseph Goebbels (King, 2).

3   An estimated 20,000 forced laborers from the camp died from exhaustion, disease, starvation, or were executed. In *The Rocket and the Reich*, Michael Neufeld estimates that approximately half of these deaths can be linked to V-2 production, while the total death toll of all V-2 attacks on Allied targets was about 5,000 (Neufeld, 264). Apart from its unique technological capabilities, the V-2 was thus also the only World War II weapon that was twice as deadly inside the factory as it was outside.

4   The post-war occupation zones for Germany had been agreed upon by Churchill, Roosevelt and Stalin at the Yalta Conference in February 1945.

5   Initially code-named 'Operation Overcast', the effort was renamed 'Project Paperclip' when it went from simply interrogating scientists to outright recruiting and relocating them to the United States. The Joint Intelligence Objectives Agency (JIOA), a subcommittee of the Joint Intelligence Committee (JIC), the intelligence arm of the Joint Chiefs of Staff, was directly responsible for Operation Paperclip. Its files on 1,500+ German and other foreign scientists brought to the U.S. under Operation Paperclip and similar programs are accessible through the National Archives ("Foreign Scientist Case Files").

6   Korolev had been sentenced to ten years hard labor after having been falsely denounced by coworkers for sabotage and admitting under torture — which involved breaking both his upper and lower jaw — that he had been a member of an "*anti-Soviet*" organization (Siddiqi, 177). He had initially been sentenced to death, but for reasons still unclear, his sentence was at the last minute commuted to ten years imprisonment (Siddiqi, 177-78).

7   An exception was Helmut Gröttrup, a German electrical engineer who had worked as an assistant of von Braun.

8   For comparison, Voyager 1 weighed 815 kg / 1797 lb at launch.

9   The rather cryptic designation 'Object D', was meant to differentiate it from A, B, V and G payloads for the R-7, which were all nuclear warheads (Logsdon, "Sputnik", 54).

10   The official designation of Sputnik was PS-1. Russian media reporting the historic achievement a day after the launch did not ascribe a specific name to the satellite though, but simply referred to it as 'Sputnik', the Russian word for satellite (Logsdon, "Sputnik", 66).

11   The fear of a missile gap was happily fueled by Soviet leader Nikita Khrushchev, who claimed in the late 1950s that the Soviet Union was producing ICBMs *"like sausages"*, though in reality the Russians only had a handful of R-7 ICBMs at the time (qtd. in Hardesty, 107). After the U.S. started launching its Corona reconnaissance satellites — the first successful launch and recovery of which was in August 1960 — it quickly became clear there was no missile gap, at least not one in which the Soviet Union was in the lead (Burns, 278).

12   The Advanced Research Projects Agency was renamed Defense Advanced Research Projects Agency (DARPA) in 1972. It was changed back to ARPA in 1993, before being changed yet again in 1996, to DARPA.

13   Among other things, the NDEA also introduced federal loans to American students, causing the number of students who borrowed from college student-loan funds to jump from 80,000 in 1957 — the year before the NDEA was passed — to 115,000 in 1961. In all, some 1.5 million students used an NDEA loan to go to college between 1959 and 1969 (Loss, 159).

14   When Strelka had a litter of puppies a year later, Khrushchev sent one of them to the First Family as a gift.

15   Gagarin had been in close competition with Gherman Stepanovich Titov for the top spot. Both men were obviously excellent candidates, equally capable of piloting the Vostok capsule. Exactly why Gagarin was eventually chosen over Titov remains unclear. According to Titov, it was Gagarin's likable personality that was the deciding factor in him being selected. As Titov later said: *"Yura turned out to be the man everyone loved. Me they couldn't love. They loved Yura. I'm telling you, they were right to choose Yura."* (qtd. in Burgess, 147).

16   Emigration from East to West Germany had risen from 166,000 in 1951 to 182,000 in 1952 and 226,000 in just the first six months of 1953 (Dale, 17). The border between East and West Germany was subsequently closed by East Germany, except in Berlin, which then became the primary escape route for East Germans wanting to leave the German Democratic Republic. And leave they did; between 1945-61, an estimated 3.5 million people emigrated from East to West Germany (Dale, 68).

17   With the death of Scott Carpenter, in October 2013, John Glenn became the last surviving member of the Mercury Seven, the seven original astronauts selected by NASA in April 1959.

18 The U.S. had deployed nuclear missiles in Turkey the previous April.

19 Though the 'a' is not audible in the recordings, Armstrong later said he had intended to say 'one small step for a man' and also believed he had done so (Jones, "Apollo 11").

20 In the mid 1960s, NASA's budget as a percentage of total U.S. federal spending rose to 4.41 percent, but by 1971 it had declined to 1.61 percent. After 1975 the percentage remained under 1 percent, with the exception of 1993, when it was 1.01 percent. Since 2009, it has been around 0.50 percent (Rogers, "Nasa budgets"). When corrected for inflation, the 1965 budget would have been the equivalent of almost $40 billion in 2010; the actual NASA budget in 2010 was $18.9 billion.

21 There has been considerable debate about why Russia lost the moon race. Technological failure of the N1 rocket — the Russian counterpart of the Saturn V rocket that was used for the Apollo missions — is often mentioned as the primary reason, but so are managerial incompetence, underinvestment and insufficient commitment to a lunar landing, politically as well as militarily and scientifically. In *Russia in Space: The Failed Frontier?*, Brian Harvey writes that the Russians were late to realize there even was a race, that the involvement of no less than 26(!) government departments indeed caused considerable managerial complexity and that there was a significant lack of funding (Harvey, 13). Interestingly enough, Soviet engineers told visiting American aerospace engineers from MIT in November 1989 — the same month the Berlin Wall fell — that it was problems with the N1 booster that had held up the Russian lunar landing mission, which was otherwise 'ready to go' in 1968. (Wilford 1989).

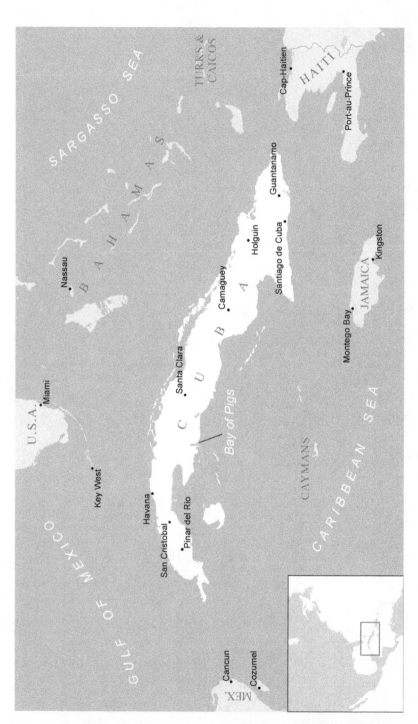

Map 25: Cuba and its Surrounding Waters

45

HOW VASILI ARKHIPOV SAVED THE WORLD

*"I want to say, and this is very important:
at the end we lucked out. It was luck that
prevented nuclear war. We came that close to
nuclear war at the end. Rational individuals:
Kennedy was rational; Khrushchev was rational;
Castro was rational. Rational individuals
came that close to total destruction of their
societies. And that danger exists today."*

Robert S. McNamara, Secretary of Defense
1961-68, in *The Fog of War* (2003)

*"Maybe the war has already started up there,
while we are doing summersaults here! We're
going to blast them now! We will die, but we will
sink them all - We will not disgrace our Navy!"[1]*

Captain Valentin Savitsky, commander of the
nuclear armed Russian submarine B-59, in the
Caribbean near Cuba, October 27, 1962

On October 11, 2002, in Havana, Cuba, the participants at the historic 40th anniversary conference on the Cuban missile crisis learned for the first time that the world had come even closer to nuclear war in October 1962 than previously known.[2]

Much closer.

Missile experts, journalists, historians and some of the key players during the missile crisis — including Cuban President Fidel Castro and former U.S. Secretary of Defense Robert McNamara — learned that a Russian submarine close to Cuba, had come to within an inch of launching its nuclear-tipped torpedo against the fleet of American ships that had located its position and was trying to force it to the surface.

The submarine in question, B-59, was the flagship of the 69th Torpedo Submarine Brigade, a small flotilla of four submarines that had departed from its base on the Kola Peninsula in northwest Russia on October 1, 1962 (USSR, "Report"). Each submarine was armed with 21 conventional torpedoes and one torpedo with a ten-kiloton nuclear warhead, with a range of 12 mi/19 km ("Report from General Zakharov"; House, 436). The flotilla's initial mission had been to strengthen the defense of Cuba against a possible U.S. invasion, but while en route it received new orders, to patrol positions in the Sargasso Sea, northeast of Cuba, supporting Soviet cargo ships delivering arms to the island ("Report from General Zakharov"; Savranskaya 2005).

That support was deemed necessary by the Soviet High Command after President Kennedy had ordered the Navy to enforce a blockade of Cuba, to prevent any more arms — specifically Russian nuclear warheads and missiles — from arriving on the island. It was the least drastic decision Kennedy could have made after photographs taken by a U-2 spy plane on October 14, 1962, proved Soviet missiles were being deployed on Cuba (McAuliffe, 155).

Relations between the U.S and Cuba had rapidly deteriorated since Fidel Castro had ousted Cuban President Fulgencio Batista almost four years earlier. Since then, the bearded revolutionary leader had wasted little time turning Cuba into a communist state and becoming a staunch ally of the Soviet Union. A Marxist-Leninist single-party state only 94 miles away from the shores of the United States at the height of the Cold War was simply unbearable for any U.S. administration, even for a relatively liberal one like that of newly elected President John F. Kennedy.

So, when, shortly after taking office, Kennedy was briefed on plans for a military invasion of Cuba, carried out by Cuban counter-revolutionaries trained and supported by the CIA, he authorized the Defense Department and CIA to "*review proposals for the active deployment of anti-Castro Cuban forces on Cuban territory*" (Bundy, "Memorandum").[3]

A few months later, on April 17, 1961, a small invasion force of some 1,500 Cuban paramilitaries landed at the southern coast of Cuba, in the *Bahía de Cochinos* (Bay of Pigs), to get rid of the "*communist menace that has been permitted to arise under our very noses, only 90 miles from our shores*", as Kennedy had characterized Castro's revolution during his presidential campaign (Kennedy "Speech Cincinnati").[4]

But the counter-revolutionary paramilitaries were defeated just three days later by the Cuban army, commanded by Fidel Castro himself. It was a humiliating failure for the United States, attributed to underestimation of Castro and lack of support for the paramilitaries, in a rather quixotic attempt to retain plausible deniability.[5]

Even worse was that the half-hearted Bay of Pigs invasion made Kennedy look weak in the eyes of his Russian counterpart, Chairman Nikita Sergeyevich Khrushchev, an impression that would only strengthen two months later, when the two met for the first time in Vienna, Austria.

The son of poor peasants and a veteran of the infamous Battle of Stalingrad, Khrushchev was a very experienced politician who had not only survived Josef Stalin's Great Purge and impromptu paranoia, but had also bested several rivals in the power struggle that followed Stalin's death in 1953. Kennedy, by contrast, had been born into a wealthy family. His father was a banker and entrepreneur who in 1938 had been appointed U.S. Ambassador to the United Kingdom by President Franklin Roosevelt, his mother the eldest daughter of a prominent Bostonian politician. Having been a U.S. Senator since 1953 but President for only six months, JFK was still a relative light-weight in executive experience when the two political adversaries first met, mid-1961. On top of that, Kennedy was also 23 years younger than Khrushchev.[6]

Khrushchev planned to use the Vienna Summit of June 4 to show the young, silver-spooned, physically weak, freshly elected U.S. President who was boss, something he would have never dreamed of doing with Kennedy's predecessor, Dwight Eisenhower, a.k.a. Ike. Like Khrushchev, Eisenhower had been a military man, war hero and leader of men long before he became President (he was also three years older than Khrushchev). With Eisenhower, the Russian leader had had little success in pressuring the U.S. to leave the city of Berlin to East Germany (in which territory it was located), but with Kennedy, he felt he was presented with a new chance.

While Kennedy did not give in to the pressure applied by Khrushchev at the Vienna Summit, he did allow himself to be put on the defensive by the bullying Soviet leader, who did not give an inch and was adamant about the Soviet Union's intention to conclude a separate peace treaty with East Germany by the end of the year, after which — Khrushchev insisted — Berlin would fall under the sole jurisdiction of the German Democratic Republic and Western troops would have to leave (Sampson, Vol. XIV, doc. 32-33). Kennedy, meanwhile, repeatedly stressed his willingness to improve relations between their two countries and admitted that both were equally matched, which came off as weak to the Chairman. Not long after the summit, on August 13, the East German Army closed the border and began constructing the Berlin Wall, surrounding and closing off West Berlin from East Berlin, and East Germany.

According to Fyodor Burlatsky, one of Khrushchev's assistants, who was present at his debriefing after the Vienna Summit, Kennedy had seemed more like *"an adviser"* to Khrushchev, *"not a political decision maker or president."* (qtd. in Absher, 10). Burlatsky thought Khrushchev looked down on Kennedy the way a self-made man looks down on a rich man to whom everything was handed on a silver platter. *"Khrushchev thought Kennedy too young, intellectual, not prepared well for decision making in crisis situations....too intelligent and too weak."* (qtd. in Absher, 10).

In the aftermath of the Bay of Pigs invasion, Eisenhower asked Kennedy why he had not given more support to the counter-revolutionaries, to which Kennedy replied that he had been worried the Soviets would then perhaps retaliate in Berlin. Eisenhower responded *"that is exactly the opposite of what would really happen. The Soviets follow their own plans, and if they see us show any weakness, then is when they press the hardest...The failure of the Bay of Pigs will embolden the Soviets to do something that they would otherwise not do."* (qtd. in Absher, 10).

Eisenhower was right. In May 1962, Khrushchev proposed to Castro to station nuclear missiles in Cuba, so as to deter further invasion attempts by the United States.[7] Castro, fearing a second invasion might not be so easily defeated, agreed. A few months later, the launching pads, medium- range and intermediate-range ballistic missiles (MRBMs and IRBMs), nuclear warheads, bombers, fighter aircraft, anti-air defense units and mechanized infantry troops started to arrive in Cuba.

The military build-up was soon noticed by local Cuban spies and reported back to U.S. intelligence services. Definitive proof followed on the aforementioned October 14, when a U-2 spy plane succeeded in taking 928 pictures during a six-minute flight over suspected Cuban missile sites, several of which produced hard evidence that at least two MRBM sites were being developed near San Cristobal, in Pinar del Rio province (Absher, 46, 51-52; Merrill, 383).[8]

National Security Adviser McGeorge Bundy was notified about the new photographic evidence late night on October 15th, but decided to wait until early next morning to tell Kennedy, deciding that *"a quiet evening and a night of sleep were the best preparation"*, as he later wrote (qtd. in Zelikow, "Presidential Recordings", Vol. II, 396). Bundy informed the President around 9:00 a.m., who then told him to quietly round up several members from his cabinet and other key advisors for a meeting later that morning.[9] This group, soon called the Executive Committee of the National Security Council, or ExComm, would form Kennedy's core team throughout the crisis.

With the evidence clear, ExComm's first task was to come up with a proper response. Initially, all members favored bombing Cuba, they only differed on the scale of the attack. Some, including the President, favored a 'surgical strike', while others agreed with the Joint Chiefs of Staff that the best course of action would be to also take out air defense sites, fighters and bombers, in addition to bombing the missile sites, so as to limit losses to U.S. aircraft and prevent immediate air reprisal against U.S. bases in nearby Florida (Zelikow, "Presidential Recordings", Vol. II, 404ff.). Some of the Chiefs, like

Air Force General Curtis LeMay, went even further and pressed for an immediate invasion of Cuba.[10]

On the third day of discussion, on October 18, Under Secretary of State George Ball voiced his opposition to an air strike without warning Khrushchev first. Comparing such an attack to Pearl Harbor, Ball said it was *"the kind of conduct that one might expect of the Soviet Union. It is not conduct one expects of the United States."* (qtd. in Zelikow, "Presidential Recordings", Vol. II, 539). Robert Kennedy — the Attorney General and the President's brother — and Secretary of State Dean Rusk agreed.

Doing nothing was not an option either though. As President Kennedy said the next day: *"If we do nothing, they have a missile base there with all the pressure that brings to bear on the United States and damage to our prestige."* (qtd. in Zelikow, "Presidential Recordings", Vol. II, 581). It would also put Berlin in play, because doing nothing would significantly strengthen the hand of the old fox in the Kremlin, who would then likely try to gobble up Berlin in its entirety, which was all the Russians were really interested in, as Kennedy knew only too well: *"If you take the view, really, that what's basic to them is Berlin and there isn't any doubt* [about that]. *In every conversation we've had with the Russians, that's what . . . Even last night we* [Soviet foreign minister Andrei Gromyko and I] *talked about Cuba for a while, but Berlin— that's what Khrushchev's committed himself to personally."* (qtd. in Zelikow, "Presidential Recordings", Vol. II, 581).

For the same reason, Kennedy held that the U.S. couldn't go into Cuba guns blazing either: *"If we attack Cuba, the missiles, or Cuba, in any way then it gives them a clear line to take Berlin, as they were able to do in Hungary under the Anglo war in Egypt. We will have been regarded as—they think we've got this fixation about Cuba anyway— we would be regarded as the trigger-happy Americans who lost Berlin. We would have no support among our allies. We would affect the West Germans' attitude towards us. And* [people would believe] *that we let Berlin go because we didn't have the guts to endure a situation in Cuba."* (qtd. in Zelikow, "Presidential Recordings", Vol. II, 581).

And if the Russians moved in on Berlin, Kennedy figured he

would have only one play left: *"Their just going in and taking Berlin by force at some point (...) leaves me only one alternative, which is to fire nuclear weapons - which is a hell of an alternative - and begin a nuclear exchange, with all this happening."* (qtd. in Zelikow, "Presidential Recordings", Vol. II, 581).

Thus stuck between a rock and a hard case, a new option began to emerge, one in which the U.S. would take the moral high ground by making it known to the world that the Soviet Union had placed missiles in Cuba, that these missiles must be removed and that a blockade would be enforced around Cuba to prevent the arrival of additional missiles.[11]

On October 22, both the Russians and U.S. allies were briefed on the decision to enforce a quarantine of Cuba, and in the evening Kennedy addressed the nation on television to inform the American people. Khrushchev publicly condemned the blockade, saying it put mankind on a path towards nuclear war. Privately, backchannels were opened to try and resolve the crisis without starting World War III. U.S. Armed Forces were put at DEFCON 3.[12]

But even if the quarantine was successful — i.e., merchant ships wouldn't try to run it and supporting Russian warships wouldn't (threaten to) open fire in the event a ship was boarded for inspection — even then it was only a temporary solution, giving Khrushchev some time to reconsider his gamble that Kennedy *"would make a fuss, make more of a fuss, and then agree"*, as he had told his son Sergei (qtd. in Smyser, 194).

It was a huge gamble on Khrushchev's part, one that might seem irresponsible in hindsight, but from the Soviet leader's point of view the potential payoff was well worth it. First of all, as Kennedy had already correctly assessed, it presented the Americans with an impossible dilemma: doing nothing would increase pressure on the U.S. and give Khrushchev vital information about Kennedy's likely reaction to a Russian move on Berlin, while removing the missiles by force would give the Russians a great excuse to take Berlin in retaliation.

Secondly, the Soviet Union had far less ICBMs than the U.S. assumed and it was also behind in nuclear armed bombers and submarines. In short, the Mutually Assured Destruction was not that mutual after all, at least not at the time. But a couple of medium-range and intermediate-range nuclear missiles on Cuba — of which the U.S.S.R had more than enough — would solve that problem handsomely and give the Russians time to play catch-up.

Thirdly, some months earlier, in April 1962, the United States had stationed medium-range nuclear missiles in Turkey, right at the doorstep of the Soviet Union (Garthoff, 71, note 115).[13] Khrushchev therefore considered the missiles in Cuba an appropriate response to that provocative move.

Finally, and perhaps most importantly: he thought he could get away with it. Kennedy had been weak during the Bay of Pigs invasion, weak during the Vienna Summit and weak during the Berlin Crisis, so there was every reason to think he would be weak again. In the same vein, Khrushchev may have also believed that should it come to negotiations, he could probably get Kennedy to trade Berlin for the missiles in Cuba (Taubman, 530-31, 539).

Neither Kennedy nor Khrushchev wanted nuclear war though, and both of them knew it. They were basically playing a heads-up poker hand in which both players know neither one of them wants to go all-in. In other words, they could bet, raise, even re-raise, but both men knew their hand was only as strong as the other was willing to give it credit for. The future of mankind was at stake, yes, but both players thought they would be able to find a way to stop the game before one of them (or both) would have only one play left. In reality they were not the only players in the game though, and therefore not in control of its outcome, at least not entirely.

On October 24, the quarantine went into effect and Strategic Air Command (SAC) was put at DEFCON 2.[14]

Just after 10.00 a.m., McNamara reported that two ships, the Kimovsk and the Gagarin, were approaching the quarantine line and were being shadowed by a Soviet submarine, making the situation potentially explosive (Zelikow, "Presidential Recordings", Vol. III, 190-91). General Taylor, Chairman of the Joint Chiefs of Staff, explained to the other ExComm members that a signaling procedure for the surfacing of Russian submarines had been sent to the Soviets the night before, though it was unclear whether Moscow had relayed this procedure to its submarines (Zelikow, "Presidential Recordings", Vol. III, 192-93). McNamara said that in addition to the signaling procedure, U.S. destroyers would use practice depth charges, as a second warning and instruction to surface. Special Assistant to the President Kenneth O'Donnell asked what they would do in case the submarine still didn't surface, whether they would then attack it, but Kennedy was not prepared to go that far yet: *"I think we ought to wait on that today. We don't want to have the first thing we attack as a Soviet submarine. I'd much rather have a merchant ship."* (qtd. in Zelikow, "Presidential Recordings", Vol. III, 194).

Meanwhile, Khrushchev, in an apparent effort to avoid confrontation as well, ordered several Russian ships to stop.[15] One ship close to the quarantine line, the Soviet oil tanker *Bucharest*, continued on course though and passed the quarantine line. McNamara reported the tanker had been hailed and had responded it was not carrying any prohibited items. The members of ExComm discussed at length whether or not the *Bucharest* should be stopped, boarded and searched (Zelikow, "Presidential Recordings", Vol. III, 244ff.). In the end the ship was allowed to continue, because it had already left port before the crisis began, had no deck cargo and its hatches were too small to accommodate missiles — and also to give the Russians a grace period to get their instructions clear. On October 26, Kennedy received a letter from Khrushchev which had been delivered at the U.S. Embassy in Moscow more than six hours earlier (Zelikow, "Presidential Recordings", Vol. III, 349). In a staggering twelve — at times emotional and somewhat rambling — pages, Khrushchev proposed to remove the missiles from Cuba, in exchange for a public promise from the United States never to invade Cuba or aid others in doing so.[16]

On the morning of October 27 — the day that would come to be known as *Black Saturday* — the American Embassy in Moscow received another, much shorter, letter, with another, much more concise proposal (Samson, Vol. VI, doc. 66). While the letter was still being translated at the embassy, Radio Moscow had already started broadcasting the proposal, the gist of which was that in addition to a pledge not to invade Cuba, the Russians also wanted the U.S. to remove its missiles from Turkey.

The members of ExComm quickly agreed that the U.S. could not accept this proposal, as it would send the message that the United States was willing to sell out its allies. The problem was that Khrushchev's proposed trade of Russian missiles in Cuba for American missiles in Turkey sounded very reasonable, making a Cuban invasion *"an insupportable position"*, according to Kennedy (qtd. in Zelikow, "Presidential Recordings", Vol. III, 363).

While they were debating the best response, news reached ExComm that a U-2 was shot down over Cuba, killing the pilot (Zelikow, "Presidential Recordings", Vol. III, 445-46). Several ExComm members — including Chairman of the Joint Chiefs of Staff Maxwell Taylor, Secretary of Defense Robert McNamara and Under Secretary of Defense Roswell Gilpatric — were clamoring for a retaliatory attack per the rules of engagement, and Kennedy came close to ordering one, but at the last moment decided not to, unless another plane was attacked.[17]

For decades, the U-2 incident was seen as probably the most decisive moment of the Cuban missile crisis, since U.S. retaliation — taking out Soviet-operated surface-to-air missile (SAM) sites on Cuban soil, to protect U.S. planes — would have likely resulted in Soviet casualties, followed by Soviet retaliatory attacks, as per the rules of engagement.

But that same day, around the same time, another incident occurred. One that would bring the world even closer to nuclear war, without Kennedy or Khrushchev even being aware of it, let alone having any control over it.

While patrolling the Sargasso Sea, northeast of Cuba, a group of U.S. destroyers and the aircraft carrier USS Randolph discovered a Soviet submarine. Per their instructions, they subsequently moved in and began to tighten the circle around their now vulnerable prey (Mozgovoi, "Cuban Samba").

Submerged and in hiding, B-59 could not send or receive any radio traffic and was thus completely cut off from the world above. As it happened, the submarine had not received any communication from Moscow for days (Savranskaya, 246). It had picked up some broadcasts from U.S. radio stations though, which were filled with talk of an impending U.S. invasion of Cuba if Soviet nuclear missiles there were not removed, and of President Kennedy warning about the threat of thermonuclear conflict (Savranskaya, 242).[18]

Meanwhile, the destroyers, following the specific protocol prescribed by the Department of Defense to warn all submarines to surface in the quarantine area, started dropping practice depth charges (PDCs) to force B-59 to surface (Savranskaya, 245-46). About the size of a hand grenade, the PDCs were harmless, but B-59 had no way of knowing that. And although the Department of Defense had relayed its submarine protocol to Moscow four days earlier, B-59 had not received any information about it (Zelikow, "Presidential Recordings", Vol. III, 192-93).

Ominously, the ExComm discussion about the 'Submarine Surfacing and Identification Procedures', on the 24th, had been when the President had seemed the most worried. Robert Kennedy wrote down later that day that he thought *"these few minutes were the time of greatest worry by the President. his hand went up to his face & covered his mouth and he closed his fist. His eyes were tense, almost gray, and we just stared at each other across the table."* (qtd. in Zelikow, "Presidential Recordings", Vol. III, 193).

Kennedy had been right to be particularly worried about the submarines, because not only did the crew of B-59 not know that the destroyers were only using practice depth charges to try and force them to the surface, the destroyers, in turn, did not know B-59 was equipped with a nuclear-tipped torpedo with a 10-kiloton yield.

Moreover, the commander of B-59 had independent launching capability — there were no locks on the weapon — and had authority to launch in case he was 'hulled (Savranskaya, 240).[19-20] Should such a situation occur, the commander only needed confirmation from the submarine's political officer to launch the 'special weapon', as it was called (Savranskaya, 239). However, as fate would have it, B-59 also carried the chief of staff of the small flotilla of four submarines, Vasili Alexandrovich Arkhipov, meaning that on this particular submarine *three* people had to agree on any nuclear launch.

Three people on a hunted, cramped submarine with a malfunctioning cooling system, causing temperatures to rise to almost 50 °C/122

°F in the compartments and even 60 °C/140 °F in the engine room, adding to the already high stress levels on board (Mozgovoi, "Cuban Samba").

For Captain Valentin Savitsky, the exploding depth charges were the final straw. With no possibility of communicating with Moscow without surfacing the boat and attacked by (practice) depth charges which, according to Vadim Orlov — head of the special radio intercept team on B-59 — *"felt like you were sitting in a metal barrel, which somebody is constantly blasting with a sledgehammer"*, an enraged Savitsky decided to launch the nuclear torpedo to destroy all the U.S. ships above them (qtd. in Mozgovoi, "Cuban Samba").

A heated argument subsequently erupted between Savitsky, Arkhipov and political officer Ivan Semenovich Maslennikov. According to Orlov, Arkhipov eventually succeeded in talking Captain Savitsky out of launching the nuclear torpedo and instead surface the boat (Savranskaya, 247). Nuclear war averted.

That evening, around 8:00 p.m. Washington time, Robert Kennedy met with Soviet Ambassador Anatoly Dobrynin at the Justice Department. Kennedy conveyed the U.S was willing to publicly promise not to invade Cuba if the Soviet Union would remove its missiles from Cuba. Saving the best for last, he then said that President Kennedy had been wanting to remove the missiles from Turkey for some time (seeing as they were obsolete anyway) and that the missiles would thus be removed *"within a short time after this crisis was over"*, but that this could not be part of the public deal (Kennedy, "Thirteen Days", 83).

Kennedy also stressed the White House would need an answer from Khrushchev the next day (Sunday), thus hinting at U.S. plans to attack Cuba on Monday (Kennedy, "Thirteen Days", 83). The Joint Chiefs had indeed prepared a strike plan for Monday the 29th, but several hours before Robert Kennedy's meeting with Dobrynin, ExComm had decided to wait until Tuesday with the attack (Zelikow, "Presidential Recordings", Vol. III, 437, 502-03).

The next day, Sunday October 28, at 9:00 a.m., Washington time, Khrushchev had a message broadcast over Radio Moscow that he had ordered work on the Cuban sites stopped and the missiles dismantled, crated and returned to the Soviet Union (Garthoff, 93).

The crisis was over.

Arguably the most dangerous moment in human history, the Cuban Missile Crisis showed just how powerful the individual had become in the nuclear age. In the end, annihilation of our kind was averted by just a handful of people who decided not to push the button when they could have.

In the wake of the crisis, communication between the two superpowers improved, and in the late 1960s and early 1970s the first steps were taken to end the nuclear arms race, through the Strategic Arms Limitation Talks (SALT).

As of 2017, both the United States and Russia still possess thousands of nuclear weapons though, while the decision to use them still rests with just a handful of people.

Vasili Arkhipov died on August 19, 1998, aged 72. He was never awarded the title *Hero of the Soviet Union*.

---

1   Qtd. in Mozgovoi, "Cuban Samba".

2   The conference, titled 'The Cuban Missile Crisis: A Political Perspective after 40 Years', was held between October 11-13, 2002, in Havana, Cuba. It was organized jointly by the Cuban government and George Washington University's National Security Archive, in partnership with Brown University's Watson Institute for International Affairs.

3   Kennedy was first briefed as President on January 28, 1961, but had also been briefed about the covert operation against Cuba during the campaign (Gleijeses, 13, 20).

4   The invasion was carried out by the 2506 Assault Brigade, numbering 1,511 anti-Castro Cuban exiles (Jones, 96).

5   When the situation of the anti-revolutionary forces on the beach became untenable, several urgent calls where made for U.S. air support, but no such support was authorized by the White House. *"We just can't become involved."* Kennedy insisted, to which a frustrated Admiral Arleigh Burke, Chief of Naval Operations, replied: *"Goddamnit, Mr. President, we are involved, and there is no way to hide it. We are involved!"* (qtd. in Jones, 117). But Kennedy would not budge.

6   An illustration of the differences in career, hardship and experience between Kennedy and Khrushchev might come from mid-1941, when 47-year-old Khrushchev was personally appointed by Stalin as a member of the Military Council of the High Command of the Southwestern Area — to organize the defense against the advancing German Army during Operation Barbarossa —

while 24-year-old JFK had just failed his physical for both the Army and the Navy on account of colon, stomach and back problems (Khrushchev, 332-33; Dallek, 82). With help from his father, JFK would nevertheless succeed in acquiring a post in the Navy.

7   Aside from Cuba, Khrushchev also wanted to protect Soviet prestige in Latin America, which would suffer a severe blow if Cuba was allowed to be invaded and occupied by the United States (Absher, 24). Still more important was that, by placing medium and intermediate-range ballistic missiles (MRBMs and IRBMs) in Cuba, the missile gap with the U.S. could be closed, since the U.S.S.R had only a handful of intercontinental ballistic missiles (ICBMs) at the time but plenty of MRBMs and IRBMs.

8   CIA memorandum "Probable Soviet MRBM Sites in Cuba" (October 16, 1962) mentions "*two areas in the Sierra del Rosario mountains about 50 n.m. west southwest of Havana which appear to contain Soviet MRBMs in the early stages of deployment.*" (qtd. in McAuliffe, 139-44). A third area is identified as an apparent "*military encampment*".

9   The following people attended the meeting: President Kennedy, George Ball, McGeorge Bundy, Marshall Carter, C. Douglas Dillon, Roswell Gilpatric, Sidney Graybeal, U. Alexis Johnson, Vice President Johnson, Robert Kennedy, Arthur Lundahl, Robert McNamara, Dean Rusk, and Maxwell Taylor (Zelikow, "Presidential Recordings", Vol. II, 397). Other people would sit in at several subsequent meetings.

10   Even after the crisis had been resolved peacefully LeMay still wanted to invade Cuba, calling the peaceful resolution of the crisis "*the greatest defeat in our history.*" (qtd. in Hughes, 129).

11   Kennedy later exchanged the term 'blockade' for 'quarantine', because a blockade is legally considered an act of war in International Law.

12   DEFCON, Defense readiness condition, is an alert state used by the U.S. Armed Forces. It has five graduated levels of readiness, with 5 being the lowest state of readiness and 1 being reserved for imminent nuclear war.

13   Interestingly, the decision, late 1957, to station intermediate-range missiles in Europe in the first place, had been made because of a perceived missile gap with the Soviet Union, i.e., the exact same reason why Khrushchev wanted to station missiles in Cuba five years later (Garthoff, 71, note 115). Turkey had agreed to take fifteen Jupiter IRBM missiles in 1959, but negotiations, training and construction of the necessary facilities took several years, so that the missiles were basically obsolete by the time they arrived.

14   Putting SAC at DEFCON 2 meant the crews of 1,436 strategic nuclear bombers and 134 ICBM missile silos were put on stand-by alert (Absher, 69). The missiles were ready for launch and one-eighth of the bombers were in the air at all times.

15   Upon hearing the news that Khrushchev had apparently ordered the ships to

hold and/or reverse course, Secretary of State Dean Rusk whispered to National Security Advisor McGeorge Bundy: *"We are eyeball to eyeball, and I think the other fellow just blinked."* (qtd. in Zelikow, "Presidential Recordings", Vol. III, 197).

16 See Zelikow, "Presidential Recordings", Vol. III, 349-55, for the translated version of Khrushchev's letter used by ExComm.

17 After much deliberation, Kennedy concluded: *"I think we ought to keep tomorrow clean, do the best we can with the surveillance. If they still fire and we haven't got a satisfactory answer back from the Russians, then I think we ought to put a statement out tomorrow that we are fired upon. We are therefore considering the island of Cuba as an open territory, and then take out all these SAM sites"* (qtd. in Zelikow, "Presidential Recordings", Vol. III, 492).

18 Savranskaya bases this part of her description of the situation aboard the Soviet submarines in the Sargasso Sea on Alexei Dubivko's, "In the Depths of the Sargasso Seas" in *On the Edge of the Nuclear Precipice* (1988). Dubivko had been the commander of submarine B-36, which, together with B-4, B-59 and B-130 formed the 69th submarine brigade.

19 As Captain Ryurik Ketov, commander of the B-4, one of the four submarines of the 69th submarine brigade, remembered Vice-Admiral A.I. Rassokha, Chief of Staff of the Northern Fleet, saying: *"Write down when you should use these. . . . In three cases. First, if you get a hole under the water. A hole in your hull. This is the first case. Second, a hole above the water. If you have to come to the surface, and they shoot at you, and you get a hole in your hull. And the third case – when Moscow orders you to use these weapons.(...) I suggest to you, commanders, that you use the nuclear weapons first, and then you will figure out what to do after that."* (qtd. in Savranskaya, 240).

20 There has been much debate about whether the submarine commanders really had the authority to launch the nuclear torpedo without specific orders from Moscow. According to Russian researcher Alexander Mozgovoi, author of *The Cuban Samba of the Quartet of Foxtrots: Soviet Submarines in the Caribbean Crisis of 1962* (2002), nuclear weapons could only be used on special orders from the Defense Minister, thus contradicting the testimony of B-4 commander Captain Ryurik Ketov, who stated Vice-Admiral Rassokha had given permission to fire in case they were hulled (see note above). Rear Admiral Georgi Kostev, veteran submarine commander and historian, has stated that Khrushchev was of the opinion that a Soviet submarine commander would be in his right to attack without further orders in the event he would be attacked himself. (Polmar, 204). Interestingly, an order from Soviet Defense Minister Marshal Rodion Y. Malinovsky, issued on October 27, 1962, at 16:30, to General Issa A. Pliyev, commander of the Soviet forces in Cuba, read: *"We categorically confirm that you are prohibited from using nuclear weapons from missiles, FKR* [cruise missiles]*, "Luna" and aircraft without orders from Moscow. Confirm receipt."* (USSR, "Telegram TROSTNIK"). The order,

issued on the same day the incidents with the U-2 and B-59 occurred, implies that there was at least some unclarity among those in charge of the Soviet missiles on Cuba, about whether or not they had launching authority without special orders from Moscow. The same unclarity might very well have existed among Soviet submarine commanders.

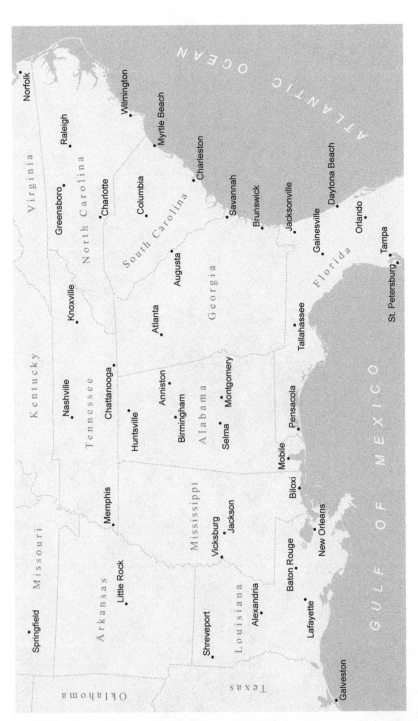

Map 26: The 'Deep South' of the United States, 1950-70

46

HE HAD A DREAM

"Tell them about the dream, Martin!"
Mahalia Jackson, August 28, 1963, Washington
D.C., at the end of Martin Luther King's
speech during the March on Washington[1]

On December 11, 1967, in the midst of one of the most socially, culturally and politically volatile decades the world has ever seen, a movie premiered in New York City that cast both a disconcerting and hopeful light on an issue that was still dividing America to the bone, as it had been doing since its inception.

In the 1960s, the push for equality under the law was finally gathering momentum, but in the wake of several major victories for the African-American Civil Rights Movement, Stanley Kramer's 1967 movie *Guess Who's Coming to Dinner* showed that there was a difference between legal equality and *real* equality.

In the movie, a young woman introduces her fiancé, a celebrated doctor, to her parents. The woman's father owns a newspaper in San Francisco and her mother an art gallery. Intellectual, educated and liberal, they have brought their daughter up to be a kind, accepting, broad-minded, modern young woman. And they seem to have succeeded exceptionally well at this, because the man their daughter has chosen for her husband is an educated, well-spoken, empathic, charming black man.

After making inquiries, the father finds out that the fiancé is not just any doctor, he is an exceptional doctor. Graduated Maxima Cum Laude, worked at Johns Hopkins hospital, assistant professor at Yale Medical School, professor at the London School of Tropical Medicine, assistant director at the World Health Organization, author of textbooks and receiver of several medical society honors. In short, the dream of every parent. That is, if it weren't for the color of his skin.

As the story develops, it becomes clear that the father is against the marriage not because he disapproves of the fiancé, but because he fears the unforgiving world that awaits the young married couple, a feeling wholeheartedly shared by the doctor's father, who also comes to dinner. However handsome, accomplished, lovely and broad-minded their children are, all the fathers really see is a white woman and a black man who, as a married couple, would be vilified in the North and likely murdered in the South.

Their fear was not wholly unjustified, black people had been murdered for much less in the South. Just twelve years earlier, in non-fictional 1955, Emmet Till, a 14-year-old black boy, had been murdered in Mississippi just for flirting with a white woman, his two killers acquitted by an all- white jury.[2] And his case was hardly unique.

Ever since the first twenty African slaves had arrived on a Dutch trading vessel in Jamestown, Virginia, in 1619, blacks had been treated as inferior to whites in the New World. Inferior but useful, which is why about 600,000 African slaves would be imported to the United States between 1620 and 1865, most of them ending up on Southern plantations (Miller, 164, 182, 682).

The Revolution of 1776 came and went, bringing independence, freedom from tyranny and a new nation, but only for white colonists. For blacks nothing changed until the Civil War, and even then the three historic steps forward were soon followed by two steps back.

Between 1865-70, three new amendments to the U.S. Constitution were adopted, collectively known as the Reconstruction Amendments. The Thirteenth Amendment, ending slavery, the Fourteenth Amendment, proclaiming all people who are born or naturalized in the United States citizens, with equal protection of the law, and the Fifteenth Amendment, forbidding to deny or abridge the right to vote based on *"race, color, or previous condition of servitude"* (US Const. amend. XV, sec. 1).[3]

But the effects of almost 250 years of slavery could not be wiped out so easily. In the defeated South, where most blacks lived, state legislatures bided their time, laying low as long as federal troops remained stationed in their states. But as soon as those troops had left, twelve years after the end of the Civil War, the advances that had been made during Reconstruction were quickly rolled back in the Southern States.[4] State legislatures across the South introduced a host of racial discrimination legislation known as Jim Crow laws, aimed at restoring the situation prior to the Civil War. Former Confederate States such as Mississippi, Alabama, Louisiana, North Carolina, South Carolina, Georgia and Florida knew they could not reintroduce slavery — as that would likely start another war with the North — but they also realized people don't have to be *called* slaves to be *treated* as slaves.

Segregation laws institutionalized the inferior status of African Americans. Everything that could be segregated, was. Schools, work places, churches, hospitals, public transportation, restaurants, restrooms, even drinking fountains, everything was divided between 'white' and 'colored', with services and facilities for the latter always being second-rate, or worse.

To counter the Fifteenth Amendment, all kinds of barriers were put up to prevent black people from registering to vote, such as poll taxes, literacy tests and residency and record-keeping requirements.[5]

African Americans were thus basically eliminated from political life, unable to vote, stand for election to public office or serve on a jury (which is how Emmet Till's murderers could be so 'lucky' to face an all-white jury in 1955, 85 years after the Fifteenth Amendment had been ratified). As things stood, it was clear that anyone wanting to fight any of the Jim Crow laws in the South would come up against a brick wall in local and state courts, where white, Southern judges — the vast majority of whom agreed with segregation — presided. Of course the U.S. Supreme Court could be an altogether different matter, as its justices were not predominantly Southern. In fact, when a landmark case against segregation in public transportation was brought before the Supreme Court in 1896, only one of the nine justices hailed from a Southern State that had been part of the Confederacy.[6]

The case revolved around a man named Homer Plessy, who had bought a first-class ticket before boarding a 'whites only' car on a train in New Orleans, though he was classified as being one-eighth black, thus violating the Separate Car Act of 1890, a Louisiana State law segregating public transportation. It was a test case, provoked by a group of prominent black, creole and white people from New Orleans, who had united themselves in a Committee of Citizens (Medley, 14). Mr. Plessy was detained by a private detective hired by the Committee, to make sure there would be a clear case.

Sure enough, a New Orleans judge, John Howard Ferguson, convicted Mr. Plessy of violating the Separate Car Act and sentenced him to pay a fine of $25, a ruling subsequently confirmed by the Supreme Court of Louisiana. Next (and last) up was the U.S. Supreme Court.

One of Plessy's principal arguments was that the Separate Car Act violated his constitutional right to '*equal protection of the laws*' as guaranteed by the Fourteenth Amendment, because it forced him to ride in the colored car (US Const. amend. XIV, sec. 1).

On this point, justice Henry Billings Brown, writing the majority opinion of the U.S. Supreme Court, contended that "*The object of the* [Fourteenth] *amendment was undoubtedly to enforce the absolute equality of the two races before the law, but, in the nature of things, it could not have been intended to abolish distinctions based upon color, or to enforce social, as distinguished from political, equality, or a commingling of the two races upon terms unsatisfactory to either.*" (Plessy v. Ferguson, 544). In other words, as long as social inequality and separation did not lead to political inequality, the Fourteenth Amendment would not be violated.

Therefore, justice Brown continued, "*We consider the underlying fallacy of the plaintiff's argument to consist in the assumption that the enforced separation of the two races stamps the colored race with a badge of inferiority. If this be so, it is not by reason of anything found in the act, but solely because the colored race chooses to put that construction upon it.*" (Plessy v. Ferguson, 551). The Court affirmed the ruling of the S.C. of Louisiana by 7 to 1.

With this '*separate but equal*' doctrine, the Supreme Court held that segregation was legal as long as the segregated services and facilities were of equal quality. Of course they almost never were, but Plessy v. Ferguson moved the burden of proof to the plaintiff, meaning that the mostly poor, uneducated and disenfranchised blacks now had to prove first that the quality of their hospitals, schools, restrooms and restaurants was inferior to those of whites. Plessy v. Ferguson thus shot a big hole through the Equal Protection Clause of the Fourteenth Amendment and legitimized racial segregation laws passed by state legislatures. It would be 48 years before the decision was overturned.

World War II changed things. Serving overseas, many young African Americans were for the first time in their lives introduced to a world that did not treat them as inferior, second-rate citizens, forced to use separate drinking fountains, restrooms, hotels, bars and restaurants. As James Jones, who served in the 761st Tank Battalion, put it: *"The French had a certain kind of openness and warmth that they exhibited towards minorities that was just unexplainable. You wouldn't know you were black when you were in their company."* (qtd. in Wormser, "Jim Crow Stories"). For many African Americans it was also the first time they could contribute in some other capacity than as a farmhand. They felt part of something greater than themselves, which in turn gave rise to a powerful feeling they had likely not experienced a lot riding the back of the bus at home: Pride. Having returned to the United States after the war, many wanted more than just working on a farm like their fathers had done before them (and their fathers' fathers before them, and their fathers' fathers' fathers before them). They wanted to go to college, make something of their life and be treated as they had been in Europe and Australia. And when President Truman ended segregation within the United States Armed Forces in 1948, the time seemed ripe for a renewed push against the many segregation laws.[7]

The U.S. Supreme Court was to play a major role again, only this time it would strike a blow for the unabridged, equal protection of the laws as guaranteed by the Fourteenth Amendment, when, in 1954, in Brown v. Board of Education, it ruled unanimously that *"in the field of public education, the doctrine of "separate but equal" has no place. Separate educational facilities are inherently unequal."* (Brown v. Board of Education of Topeka, 495).[8]

The landmark decision did not lead public schools, colleges and universities in the South to swiftly end their segregational policies though, far from it. If anything, they dug their heels in even deeper, backed by state and local legislatures, mayors, governors, sheriffs and state troopers. But for the first time since Reconstruction, blacks could now invoke the full backing of the federal government if they wanted to enroll at a whites-only public school, college or university.

If that makes the post-Brown v. Board of Education enrollment of blacks in white schools seem relatively open-and-shut, it is important to realize it was more like the opposite. The harsh reality was that a small group of African-American kids had to stomach the bravery of letting themselves be used as a crowbar to pry open a door that had remained shut for 335 years, facing hostile crowds of parents, students and teachers as they tried to enroll, without being protected by local or state police officers.

Like the 'Little Rock Nine', a group of African-American students who enrolled at Little Rock Central High School, in Little Rock, Arkansas, in 1957. Apart from said hostile crowds, Arkansas Governor Orval Faubus also deployed the Arkansas National Guard to prevent the nine teenagers from entering the high school, which in turn prompted President Eisenhower to order elements of the 101st Airborne Division — which had seen action of a different kind thirteen years earlier, in France, Holland and Belgium — to protect the nine black students on their way to school and between classes (Belknap, 46-47). Eisenhower also federalized the Arkansas National Guard, taking it away from the governor.

A few years later it was the State of Mississippi that became the unwilling frontline in the fight against segregation, after the Supreme Court on September 10, 1962, overturned a stay of a Fifth Circuit order for the admission of African-American student James Meredith to the all-white State University of Mississippi (Belknap, 46-47).[9]

Here too, local and state authorities refused to comply with the Supreme Court ruling, because three days later Mississippi Governor Ross Barnett declared on statewide television: *"We will not surrender to the evil and illegal forces of tyranny."* (qtd. in Schlesinger, 318).[10]

Barnett must have realized that the U.S. Justice Department, headed by President Kennedy's brother Robert F. Kennedy, could not let this refusal stand, but in a series of subsequent phone calls with the Attorney General he nevertheless tried to keep up his defiant stance.

The following conversation between Robert Kennedy and Barnett, held on September 25, 1962, may serve as an illustration of the untenable position Southern local and state officials found themselves in when defending segregation in public schools after Brown v. Board of Education:

Barnett: That's what it's going to boil down to - whether Mississippi can run its institutions or the federal government is going to run things...
Kennedy: I don't understand, Governor. Where do you think this is going to take your own state? Barnett: A lot of states haven't had the guts to take a stand. We are going to fight this thing....This is like a dictatorship. Forcing him physically into Ole Miss. General, that might bring on a lot of trouble. You don't want to do that. You don't want to physically force him in.
Kennedy: You don't want to physically keep him out.....Governor, you are a part of the United States.
Barnett: We have been a part of the United States but I don't know whether we are or not.
Kennedy: Are you getting out of the Union?
Barnett: It looks like we're being kicked around — like we don't belong to it. General, this thing is serious.
Kennedy: It's serious here.
Barnett: Must it be over one little boy — backed by communist front — backed by the NAACP which is a communist front? .... I'm going to treat you with every courtesy but I won't agree to let that boy to get to Ole Miss. I will never agree to that. I would rather spend the rest of my life in a penitentiary than do that.
Kennedy: I have a responsibility to enforce the laws of the United States.... The orders of the court are going to be upheld. As I told you, you are a citizen not only of the State of Mississippi but also of the United States. Could I give you a ring?
Barnett: You do that.... Good to hear from you. (qtd. in Schlesinger, 318-19).[11]

More than anything else, Barnett was concerned about his own image. Having staked out a rebellious, uncompromising position, frequently proclaimed in dramatic fashion on television and before large crowds of angry, revved up whites, he now found it impossible to change tack without losing face. So, when it became clear that the White House was not going to back down, he asked

Robert Kennedy for a large show of force from the federal government and for U.S. marshals to point their guns at him, so he could be seen as not having a choice. When Kennedy asked if it would also suffice if just one marshal drew his gun, while the others kept their hands on their holsters, Barnett replied: *"They must all draw their guns. Then they should point their guns at us and then we could step aside. This could be very embarrassing down here for us. It is necessary."* (qtd. in Roberts, 288).

Barnett kept veering between feigned acquiescence and howling defiance, promising the Kennedys to help Meredith's registration go smoothly one moment, while firing up the segregationist mob and backpedaling from those same promises the next, not unlike talking to the fire department about helping with fire prevention while at the same time handing out matches and drums of gasoline to a group of pyromaniacs.

Early Saturday evening, September 29, Barnett suggested that Meredith be registered secretly, only to cancel it shortly after the Kennedys had reluctantly accepted it (Schlesinger, 321). That same evening, JFK federalized the Mississippi National Guard, like Eisenhower had done five years earlier with Arkansas' National Guard.[12]

The next day, Kennedy addressed the nation in a televised broadcast, signaling he would not accept the South's defiance of Federal law, no matter how strong and heartfelt: *"Americans are free, in short, to disagree with the law, but not to disobey it. For in a government of laws and not of men, no man, however prominent or powerful, and no mob, however unruly or boisterous, is entitled to defy a court of law."* (Kennedy, "University of Mississippi").

Around the same time Kennedy gave this speech, riots broke out around the administration building on the campus of the University of Mississippi, where James Meredith and the 400 federal marshals protecting him were besieged by an angry mob of 2,500 segregationists (Sitton, "Shots"). A force of 200 state troopers that had previously been used by Governor Barnett to block one of Meredith's earlier registration attempts, stood by without interfering, before pulling back from the riot scene altogether, leaving the marshals to fend for themselves.[13]

Shortly after midnight, reinforcements began arriving in the form of units of the — now federalized — Mississippi National Guard and federal troops from Fort Bragg, Fort Dix, Fort Benning and Fort Campbell, until a total force of some 3,000 soldiers and guardsmen was able to quell the riot (Sitton, "Shots").

On october 1, James Meredith was finally able to register at the University of Mississippi, after which federal marshals escorted him to his first class, *Colonial American History* (Phillips, "Campus"). He graduated on August 18, 1963, with a degree in political science.

Brown v. Board of Education had a major impact on the fight against segregation, but it only applied to public education. To end segregation in other parts of life as well, such as public transportation, restaurants, restrooms etc., new legal challenges would have to be mounted. Meanwhile, the NAACP, bolstered by its momentous victory in Brown v. Board of Education, had sought to keep the momentum by deploying a tried and tested weapon of the oppressed and powerless the world over: nonviolent resistance. Massive participation was required for it to work, but the NAACP knew that the African-American community was highly motivated to contribute. All that was needed was a spark.

On December 1, 1955, Rosa Parks, secretary of the NAACP in Montgomery, Alabama, refused to give up her seat on the bus to a white passenger. She was subsequently arrested and taken to the city jail, where she was fingerprinted, booked and allowed a phone call, after which Ed Nixon, President of the Montgomery NAACP, arranged the bond for her release (Gray, 50-51).

Several key people of the African-American community of Montgomery quickly realized that if ever there was momentum to protest segregation on buses, it was now (Gray, 52). That same night,

Jo Ann Robinson, President of the Women's Political Council, another Montgomery civil rights organization, created and mimeographed thirty thousand flyers aimed at igniting outrage over Mrs. Parks arrest. It read:

"This is for Monday, December 5, 1955

Another Negro woman has been arrested and thrown into jail because

she refused to get up out of her seat on the bus for a white person to sit down.

It is the second time since the Claudette Colbert [Colvin] case that a Negro woman has been arrested for the same thing. This has to be stopped.

Negroes have rights, too, for if Negroes did not ride the buses, they could not operate. Three-fourths of the riders are Negroes, yet we are arrested, or have to stand over empty seats. If we do not do something to stop these arrests, they will continue. The next time it may be you, or your daughter, or mother.

This woman's case will come up on Monday. We are, therefore, asking every Negro to stay off the buses Monday in protest of the arrest and trial. Don't ride the buses to work, to town, to school, or anywhere on Monday.

You can afford to stay out of school for one day if you have no other way to go except by bus. You can also afford to stay out of town for one day. If you work, take a cab, or walk. But please, children and grown-ups, don't ride the bus at all on Monday. Please stay off of all buses Monday." (qtd. in Gray, 54).

The boycott was initially meant for just the one day, but when city officials refused to give in despite its resounding success, it was decided to continue the protest until segregation on the Montgomery buses ended (Gray, 60-62). So, for the next 381 days, the black people of Montgomery walked, bicycled, carpooled and hitchhiked their way through town, led and inspired by the newly elected leader of the Montgomery Improvement Association, the young and charismatic Reverend Martin Luther King Jr.

In February 1956, while the bus boycott continued, the NAACP filed the federal civil action suit Browder v. Gayle in U.S. District Court, challenging the constitutionality of segregation laws for buses outright.[14] A few months later, on June 19, the court ruled in favor of Mrs. Browder, stating that enforced segregation on motor buses operating in the city of Montgomery indeed violated the Equal Protection Clause of the Fourteenth Amendment (Gray, 90-91).[15] On November 13, the U.S. Supreme Court upheld that ruling, ending segregation on Montgomery buses.[16]

The Montgomery Bus Boycott had an enormous impact on the civil rights movement. It proved nonviolent activism could be a powerful force for change and propelled Martin Luther King Jr. into the national spotlight. The civil rights movement's choice for nonviolent but persistent resistance — and the graphic images that came with it, of black schoolkids and students being harassed by angry mobs, of silent black youngsters being dragged from their stools at whites-only lunch counters, hit and kicked into submission by crowds of whites — would also help garner sympathy from the large group of white Americans who neither fanatically opposed nor outright supported equal rights for blacks, as well as increase the pressure on the federal government to act.

In May 1961, following another U.S. Supreme Court decision, Boynton v. Virginia — which ruled all segregation in interstate bus transportation unconstitutional, including in restrooms, restaurants and bus terminal waiting rooms — a group of thirteen civil rights activists, called the Freedom Riders, boarded buses in Washington D.C. with the plan to ride to New Orleans, to challenge the continued segregation in interstate public transportation in the South.[17]

In each bus, a black Freedom Rider would sit in a seat reserved for whites and an interracial pair would sit in adjoining seats, while one Rider would abide by the segregationist customs such as they existed and act as an observer (Arsenault, 111-12). At each stop, a black passenger would use 'whites only' services such as restrooms and diners, while a white passenger would use the 'colored' services.

In several Southern cities the Freedom Riders were 'only' arrested for defying the local segregation laws — even though Boynton v. Virginia had already rendered these null and void — but in others, like Birmingham, Anniston and Montgomery (all in Alabama) they were awaited by angry mobs and beaten with fists, clubs, bricks, knives and lead pipes, sometimes to within an inch of their lives (Arsenault, 212-19). In Birmingham, the Commissioner of Public Safety, Eugene "Bull" Connor, allowed the local chapter of the Ku Klux Klan (KKK) to attack the Riders undisturbed by local police for fifteen minutes (Arsenault, 137). In Anniston, the KKK firebombed one of the buses; squeezing themselves through the windows, the passengers managed to escape with their lives, though several Freedom Riders had to be hospitalized (Arsenault, 144).

The attacks continued, but the Freedom Riders would not relent. Anticipating more brutality against the Riders in Jackson, Mississippi, Attorney General Robert Kennedy made a deal behind the scenes with James Eastland, the conservative long-serving U.S. Senator from Mississippi, not to oppose the Riders' arrest, in exchange for the latter's promise to protect them against further violence (Schlesinger, 299). Kennedy also urged the civil rights movement to call for a *"cooling off"* period, but the movement wanted to keep the pressure on and rejected any sort of armistice (qtd. in Schlesinger, 299). Meanwhile, the White House continued to put pressure on the Interstate Commerce Commission (ICC) to issue new rules that would end discrimination in interstate travel. It did so a few months later, with the new rules going into effect on November 1, 1961.

During the spring of 1963 the epicenter of the civil rights movement pivoted back to Birmingham, Alabama, once again, after reverend Fred Shuttlesworth — leader of the Birmingham civil rights movement and co-founder of the Southern Christian Leadership Conference (SCLC) — asked Martin Luther King and the SCLC, of which King was president, to come to Birmingham and help in the fight against segregation (Eskew, 4).

Birmingham, the largest city of Alabama, was highly segregated. It also had a police commissioner — the aforementioned 'Bull' Connor — spoiled for a fight, a mayor who a few years earlier had preferred to close parks, playgrounds and swimming pools rather than comply with a federal court order to desegregate them, and a governor who had said, during his inaugural speech just a few months earlier: *"In the name of the greatest people that have ever trod this earth, I draw the line in the dust and toss the gauntlet before the feet of tyranny, and I say segregation now, segregation tomorrow, segregation forever."* (qtd. in Carter, 11).

Dr. King and the SCLC, for their part, badly needed a victory in Birmingham, after a civil rights campaign in Albany, Georgia, had failed to produce any results the previous year. But Reverend Shuttlesworth assured King and the SCLC: *"Birmingham is where it's at, gentlemen. I assure you, if you come to Birmingham, we will not only gain prestige but really shake the country."*(qtd. in Eskew, 209). In short, all the elements and players were there for a brutal confrontation.[18]

Through lunch counter sit-ins, church kneel-ins, boycotts and marches, the SCLC wanted to increase the pressure on the white business community and fill the jails with so many protesters that the city's political leaders would have no choice but to negotiate. The boycott indeed succeeded in pushing business leaders toward wanting to put an end to segregation in their stores, but it was Bull Connor who would make the Birmingham Campaign the turning point of the civil rights movement, when he turned fire hoses and attack dogs on peaceful teenage protesters under the watchful eye of reporters and cameras (Haily, "Dogs and Hoses"; Washington Post, "Fire Hoses"). The vivid images that were subsequently broadcast on national television shocked the country and convinced many that this kind of repressive police action went much too far.

A few months after Birmingham, several civil rights organizations, including the NAACP, SCLC and the SNCC (Student Nonviolent Coordinating Committee), organized the massive 'March on Washington for Jobs and Freedom', to call for civil rights and an end to employment discrimination on a national level. On August 28, 1963, more than 200,000 demonstrators took part in the March and saw Martin Luther King speak from the steps of the Lincoln Memorial (Barber, 141). The event was widely televised.[19]

Dr. King started his speech by commemorating that 100 years after Lincoln's Emancipation Proclamation, *"the Negro still is not free."* (King, "Dream", 1). He blamed America for having defaulted on its promise of *"unalienable rights of life, liberty and the pursuit of happiness" "insofar as her citizens of color are concerned"*, and urged that *"this is no time to engage in the luxury of cooling off or to take the tranquilizing drug of gradualism"* (King, "Dream", 1-2). He passionately called for nonviolent action and for not being satisfied until full equality was achieved, even though he confided that he did not know how this was to be achieved, saying that *"somehow this situation can and will be changed"* (King, "Dream", 4).

Then he diverted from his prepared remarks and allowed himself a moment of dreaming.

"I have a dream that one day this nation will rise up and live out the true meaning of its creed: "We hold these truths to be self-evident, that all men are created equal.""

"I have a dream that one day on the red hills of Georgia the sons of former slaves and the sons of former slave owners will be able to sit down together at the table of brotherhood."

"I have a dream that one day even the state of Mississippi, a state sweltering with the heat of injustice, sweltering with the heat of oppression, will be transformed into an oasis of freedom and justice."

"I have a dream that my four little children will one day live in a nation where they will not be judged by the color of their skin but by the content of their character."

"I have a dream today."[20]

Part of that dream would come true in Dr. King's lifetime. Together with the Birmingham Campaign, the March on Washington increased the pressure on the Kennedy administration to act, and the following year, on July 2, 1964, the Civil Rights Act was passed, outlawing all racial segregation.[21] The Voting Rights Act, prohibiting discrimination in voting, followed a year later.[22]

Though both laws were big steps towards racial equality, true societal change inevitably takes time, a reflection that might have crossed Martin Luther King's mind if he went to see *Guess Who's Coming to Dinner*, perhaps one night in December 1967.[23]

Societal change takes time. Sadly, Dr. King did not have any time left to see more of his dream come true. He was assassinated on April 4, 1968..

Would he have deemed it likely that a black president would be elected in 2008? Or that in 2013 New York City would elect a liberal white mayor with a black wife and two mixed-race children, one of them a son with a sizable Afro?

Perhaps he dreamed about that too.

---

1   Qtd in Hansen, "Mahalia Jackson".

2   Protected against double jeopardy, the murderers — the woman's husband Roy Bryant and his half-brother J.W. Milam — admitted to the killing in an interview published in Look magazine, a few months after the trial had ended (Huie 1956).

3   Important as the Fifteenth Amendment was, one other major discriminatory ground for withholding the right to vote was conspicuously absent from it. Women would have to wait another 50 years before the Nineteenth Amendment added the word 'sex' to the list of grounds on account of which the right to vote could not be denied or abridged.

4   The end of Reconstruction, in 1877, came after the intensely disputed presidential election of 1876 and the (alleged) 'Compromise of 1877', which gave the presidency to the Republican Rutherford B. Hayes, in exchange for the withdrawal of all federal troops from the Southern States, thus effectively handing control of the South to the Democratic 'Redeemers', who wanted to undo as much of Reconstruction as possible (Woodward, 3-21).

5   The introduction of literacy tests and poll taxes caused black voter turnout in the Southern States to decline from between 45-80 percent in 1880 to 1-2 percent in 1912 (Valelly, 128, table 6.3). Of course these laws also potentially disenfranchised many poor white people, but restrictive voter laws often had loopholes that exempted those who had had the right to vote before 1866 (i.e., white people) or their lineal descendants, a.k.a. a 'grandfather clause'. In 1915, the Supreme Court ruled these kind of grandfather clauses in violation of the Fifteenth Amendment (Guinn v. United States, 238 U.S. 347), but Southern States quickly passed new voter registration restrictions that kept African Americans largely disenfranchised in the South until passage of the Voting Rights Act of 1965.

6   Justice Edward Douglass White was from Louisiana. Justice John Marshall Harlan was from Kentucky, one of the four slave states that had not seceded from the Union.

7   Executive Order 9981, issued on July 26, 1948, declared in article 1 that "*there shall be equality of treatment and opportunity for all persons in the armed services without regard to race, color, religion or national origin*". The last all-black unit of the U.S. military was disbanded in 1954.

8   The class action lawsuit had been brought by the National Association for the Advancement of Colored People (NAACP) on behalf of the plaintiff, Oliver Brown, parent of one of the black children who had been denied access to one of the white schools of Topeka, Kansas. Thurgood Marshall, the NAACP's chief counsel, who argued the case before the Supreme Court, would become the first African-American justice of the Supreme Court in 1967.

9   Meredith had been trying to enroll at 'Ole Miss' since January 1961.

10   Just how vehemently Barnett was opposed to racial integration may be illustrated by a quote from his election campaign in 1959, when he said that "*the Negro is different because God made him different to punish him. His forehead slants back. His nose is different. His lips are different, and his color*

is sure different." (qtd. in TIME, "Mississippi Mud").

11 The conversation is a striking example of the shifting momentum in the fight for racial equality and of how the same racist attitudes that had sparked the Civil War a little over a hundred years before, would this time be defeated through legal rather than military means; for the most part at least.

12 Rapping the table where he had just sat down to sign the executive order federalizing the Mississippi National Guard, Kennedy said to Norbert Schlei of the Office of Legal Counsel, who had brought over the document: "*You know, that's Grant's table.*" (qtd. in Schlesinger, 321). Schlei then went downstairs to inform waiting reporters about what had just happened. Moments later, Kennedy sprinted to the top balustrade and called down to Schlei: "*Don't tell them about General Grant's table.*".

13 On September 30, at 11.00 p.m., while the U.S. Marshals at Ole Miss were being attacked by the mob, Governor Barnett went on the air and instead of calling for restraint, said: "*I will never yield a single inch in my determination to win the fight we are engaged in. I call upon every Mississippian to keep his faith and his courage. We will never surrender.*" (qtd. in Roberts, 295).

14 Mrs. Browder had also been arrested for sitting in the white section of a public bus in Montgomery, some months before Rosa Parks. The other party in the case was the Mayor of Montgomery, W.A. Gayle. The NAACP lawyers filed the case because they could take it directly to federal court and focus on the question of constitutionality with regards to the segregation laws for the Montgomery buses (Gray, 70-73). The Rosa Parks case was left out intentionally, for fear of complicating the issue (Gray, 69).

15 Interestingly, the district court ruling of Browder v. Gayle thus overturned the Supreme Court ruling of Plessy v. Ferguson. One of the judges in Browder v Gayle, Frank M. Johnson, later noted that this was probably the first time in U.S. legal history a district court overruled a decision of the U.S. Supreme Court (Johnson, 16).

16 The bus protest did not end immediately with the Supreme Court ruling, because it took until December 20 until the district court entered an order acknowledging receipt of the mandate from the Supreme Court, which officially ended the case of *Browder v Gayle*. On that day, Dr. King, Mrs. Parks and several others for the first time boarded and rode a bus in Montgomery on an integrated basis (Gray, 94).

17 One of the Supreme Court justices ruling in favor of Boynton was John Marshall Harlan II, grandson of John Marshal Harlan, the Supreme Court justice who had been the lone dissenter in Plessy v. Ferguson in 1896.

18 In *But for Birmingham*, Eskew denies the SCLC was out for provocative confrontation, but Adam Fairclough convincingly argues in *To Redeem the Soul of America* that this seems unlikely, since the SCLC was familiar with "*the Ghandian stratagem of inviting the oppressor to inflict violence upon the non-violent protester*", and, moreover, knew that Birmingham "*was regarded*

as the most dangerous city in the South from the standpoint of the civil rights movement", so that *"with or without Connor, SCLC was all but guaranteed a violent reception"* (Fairclough, 414).

19 In fact, with the networks using about 35 cameras, it was the biggest event since John F. Kennedy's inauguration (Adams 1963).

20 Excerpts from King's speech (4-5).

21 The act was signed into law by President Lyndon B. Johnson, after John F. Kennedy had been assassinated the previous year, on November 22, 1963.

22 The Selma to Montgomery marches of March 1965 — touched off by the killing of civil rights activist Jimmie Lee Jackson and the continued obstruction against black voter registration in Alabama — were the immediate impetus for the Voting Rights Act of 1965. The violence against the peaceful marchers on 'Bloody Sunday' (March 7, 1965) convinced President Lyndon B. Johnson of the urgent need for a Voting Rights Act. In a speech to a joint session of Congress on March 15, 1965, Johnson told Congress he would send a law to Congress to *"eliminate illegal barriers to vote..."*, adding: *"But even if we pass this bill, the battle will not be over. What happened in Selma is part of a far larger movement which reaches into every section and State of America. It is the effort of American Negroes to secure for themselves the full blessings of American life. Their cause must be our cause too. Because it is not just Negroes, but really it is all of us, who must overcome the crippling legacy of bigotry and injustice."* (Johnson, "Voting Rights").

23 Stanley Kramer's *Guess Who's Coming to Dinner* premiered on December 11, 1967. Coincidentally, the Supreme Court had handed down an important decision on interracial marriage just a few months earlier (Loving v. Virginia), in which it ruled that all laws prohibiting interracial marriage were in violation of the Equal Protection Clause of the Fourteenth Amendment.

47

THE CULTURAL REVOLUTION

*"There cannot be peaceful coexistence in the
ideological realm. Peaceful coexistence corrupts."[1]*

Jiang Qing, Chinese party official and
wife of Mao Zedong, April 1967

On November 12, 2013, at the end of its Third Plenary Session, the 18th Central Committee of the Communist Party of China issued a communiqué stating its intention to have markets play a "decisive" role in allocating resources, thus basically acknowledging that markets are better at this than government (Hui, "Market").

Historically, the Third Plenum — referring to the third time the new leader of the Communist Party chairs a plenary session of the Central Committee — has often marked the starting point of major economic and political reforms. The Third Plenum of the 11th Central Committee for instance, decided in 1978 that China's economy would be opened up and make the transition to a more market oriented economy, while the Third Plenum of the 14th Central Committee in 1993 declared that the purpose of reforming China's economic system was to establish a 'socialist market economy', leading to the dismantling of a large part of China's state-owned economy (Jiwei, 142). The 18th Central Committee's decision to further increase the role of markets was not the only major reform announced. President Xi Jinping made clear he also wanted to relax the one-child policy, abolish the *Laojiao* system of 'reeducation through labor' — with its detention centers involving forced labor for inmates, who are often sentenced without trial — and reform the system of land ownership, giving farmers more property rights over their land (Kroeber, "Ambitious Agenda").

Of course, if he could, Chairman Mao would turn in the crystal coffin in his mausoleum, contemptuously calling the current Chinese leaders 'capitalist roaders', 'revisionists', 'right- wingers', 'bourgeois elitists' and 'counter-revolutionaries', for straying from the true path of Marxism-Leninism and giving in to the false temptations of market capitalism. And then he would probably send the entire 18th Central Committee to one of the reeducation camps he established back in 1957 during the Anti-Rightist campaign, to purge the 'rightists' within the Communist Party.

The epithet 'rightist' has an interesting history of its own, going back all the way to the times of the French revolution, when those who supported the *Ancien Régime,* the monarchists, the clerics, the conservatives, the traditionalists — in short, the counter-revolutionaries — were seated to the right of the chair of the President of the Parliament.[2] Theirs was a politics of reaction to the ideas of those who sat to the left of the chair, the progressives, the revolutionaries. It was a label that stuck, making its way into the 20th century and beyond to denote the difference between the conservatives, capitalists and religious (the right wing) and the progressives, socialists, communists and environmentalists (the left wing).

For Mao Zedong, the fierce revolutionary who had had to fight two bloody civil wars against the conservative nationalists (1927-50) and another war against the Empire of Japan (1937-45) before finally realizing his lifelong dream of a communist China, being a rightist was about the worst thing one could be guilty of, short of murdering someone for pleasure. This was a man who in 1934-35 had marched 6,000 miles with 90,000 comrades in arms — more than 80,000 of whom would not survive the ordeal — just so he could continue the fight against Chiang Kai-shek.[3] To stain that hard-won victory by watering down the teachings of Marx and Lenin — let alone outright replace them with free markets and private property, the epitomes of capitalism — would be tantamount to treason in Mao's eyes.

To Mao, rightists and revisionists were a threat to the revolution because they wanted to change, to revise Marxism-Leninism, supposedly to make it more compatible with the real world. But why would you revise something that was already perfect? No, such dilution would only lead to imperfection and, ultimately, failure.

His vigilant worry about the simmering survival, even potential flourishing of revisionism — especially in the form of economic and democratic reform — further increased when, for a short period in 1956-57, the Communist Party of China (CPC) encouraged intellectuals to voice their lingering criticisms on government policies during what would become to be known as the Hundred Flowers campaign.[4]

At first, people were reluctant to speak out, but after Mao strongly supported open discussion of government policies, the flood gates opened and a tidal wave of critique started pouring in. Newspapers were filled with critical views, big character posters with political messages were put up on the walls of schools and public buildings, magazine articles about modernizing the economy and democratizing the government were published, debates were organized (Meisner, 174-75). For Mao, it was a classic example of 'be careful what you wish for'.[5]

Within a few months, the Hundred Flowers campaign was halted and Mao reversed course, moving to persecute the same intellectuals he had asked to criticize government policy — for criticizing government policy. Had it all been just a ruse to flush them out, or had Mao really been genuinely interested — at first at least — in getting input from people outside the inner circle of party hardliners? It is not entirely clear. Of course, inviting one's opponents to open up only to snap the trap on them later is an old trick, used by many a dictator. On the other hand, seeing as Mao was such a firm believer in the invincibility of Communism, it is also conceivable that he thought open discussion would only serve to show the superiority of Marxism-Leninism to a wider audience.[6]

There is also some evidence that suggests Mao believed genuine opposition to the government to be small and that he could use the Hundred Flowers campaign to enlist the support of intellectuals for the policies he wanted to reform himself (Zhisui, 198-99).[7]

Whatever the reason, over 400,000 people would pay a heavy price for their well-meant openness, ranging from being forced to deliver self-criticisms and having their careers sidetracked, to being dismissed from their position altogether, or sent to a reeducation camp where hard labor served as more than just a gentle nudge toward the 'right' direction.[8]

In January 1958, with the Anti-Rightist campaign in full swing, Mao launched the second five year plan, dubbed 'The Great Leap Forward'. Its primary goal was to rapidly industrialize China, while staying true to Marxism-Leninism, a transformation that required the peasantry to be mobilized en masse, since China was still a largely agricultural society. To increase its control over the peasants, the CPC therefore completely abolished private ownership of the agricultural means of production, land, labor and tools. The peasants were organized into large communes of up to 20,000 households, that were charged with both agricultural and industrial tasks, such as construction and steel production, the latter by using small blast furnaces known as 'backyard furnaces', so called because they were constructed in the backyards of the communes (Dikötter, xix).

Mao deemed steel of vital importance to China's industrialization and thus greatly encouraged its production by the communes. Unfortunately, the 'steel' produced by the communes was not actually steel but merely low value — and often low quality — pig iron. Producing high quality steel required additional steps, which could only be done at large-scale factories. When Mao found out about this he nevertheless decided to let the communes continue producing their backyard furnace pig iron, because he did not want to sap the zeal of the peasants (Zhisui, 290-91). The use of backyard furnaces was only phased out months later.

Of course, however zealous the peasants, there are only so many hours in a day. And with their involvement in the production of 'steel' as well as the construction of offices, schools and so on, grain production suffered. Attempts at agricultural innovation, using untested — and later proven unsound — methods, made things even worse. But although harvest sizes thus decreased considerably, commune leaders, hoping to win praise from higher up political cadres, reported highly inflated production numbers. Consequently, almost the entire harvest was sent to the cities, leaving practically nothing for the peasants themselves (Zhisui, 283).

The result was massive famine, particularly in the countryside. Though Mao was aware of this, China remained a net exporter of grain between 1958-60 (Walker, 130, table 41). In fact, grain export even increased in 1959, because 'The Great Helmsman' did not want to have to admit his policies were a failure. While the death toll in the countryside was rising rapidly, Mao said: *"Tell the peasants to resume eating chaff and herbs for half the year", and after some hardship for one or two or three years things will turn around"*. (qtd. in Jisheng, 337). By then, tens of millions of people had already died of starvation though.[9]

And so the Great Leap Forward actually became a Great Leap Backward. Due to this massive failure of Maoism — with its focus on the peasants and their revolutionary enthusiasm to bring about change — its chief advocate and namesake lost power and prestige within the Party for the first time, while moderates like Liu Shaoqi and Deng Xiaoping rose in prominence.

Liu Shaoqi succeeded Mao as President of China in 1959, but Mao retained his position as Chairman of the Central Committee, the Central Politburo and the Military Commission. Liu and Deng Xiaoping — who headed the powerful CPC Secretariat — set out to restore the economy and increase agricultural production, reversing the collectivization and introducing reforms. By 1963, China's economy was growing again (Guo, 126, fig. 8.1).

Meanwhile, Mao was brooding over his diminished political status, which only worsened with the growing success of the policies of Liu Shaoqi, who by now was considered his heir apparent. Looking for a way to get back into the game, Mao once more focused on his strength and reputation as a communist ideologue, taking aim at the 'right wingers' and 'capitalist roaders' who were supposedly taking over the Party and destroying the revolution from the inside. In other words: his rivals.

Through covert tactics, such as nudging political allies towards criticizing his political opponents and their allies in newspaper articles and party meetings, and using the slightest whiff of bourgeois tendencies and revisionism to sack, demote or denounce non-allies in key positions within the Party and the military (with the goal of replacing them with staunch allies), Mao slowly moved his pieces in position for his great offensive against the moderates.[10]

On May 16, 1966, the Central Committee released a circular launching the 'Great Proletarian Cultural Revolution', to protect the socialist revolution from being watered down by the revisionists, who, according to the Committee, were attacking the proletarian left and shielding the bourgeois right, *"thereby preparing public opinion for the restoration of capitalism."* ("Circular", 10). *"Those representatives of the bourgeoisie"*, the circular continued, *who have sneaked into the party, the government, the army, and various cultural circles are a bunch of counter-revolutionary revisionists. Once conditions are ripe, they will seize political power and turn the dictatorship of the proletariat into a dictatorship of the bourgeoisie. Some of them we have already seen through, others we have not."*.

In other words, the socialist revolution was in danger. To save it, *"the whole party must follow Comrade Mao Tse-tung's instructions, hold high the great banner of the proletarian Cultural Revolution, thoroughly expose the reactionary bourgeois stand of those so-called 'academic authorities' who oppose the party and socialism, thoroughly criticize and repudiate the reactionary bourgeois ideas in the sphere of academic work, education, journalism, literature and art, and publishing, and seize the leadership in these cultural spheres."* ("Circular", 10).

The document effectively gave Mao a blank check to call out whomever he wanted as a counter- revolutionary, revisionist, bourgeois, right-wing, capitalist roader. Academics, journalists, artists, officers, nobody was save, not even senior party officials — especially not senior party officials — because the more power and prestige one had, the more likely that envious enemies would set the bloodhounds on his trail by calling him a revisionist or something else threatening the revolution, an intellectual for example. Thus, as had been the case with the French Revolution's Reign of Terror (1793-94) and Joseph Stalin's Great Purge (1936-39), jockeying for political supremacy was once again disguised as an epic fight against the 'enemies of the revolution'.

The bloodhounds of the Great Proletarian Cultural Revolution came in the form of fanatical young university and high school students, who had started to organize themselves as so-called Red Guards shortly after the May 16 circular and whose numbers quickly grew after they were openly encouraged by Mao himself. Equipped with the Little Red Book and donning themselves in green, army-like jackets with red armbands on one of the sleeves, the Red Guards rapidly evolved into paramilitaries loyal to nothing but pure Maoism and to no-one but Mao Zedong himself.[11]

On August 18, 1966, Mao cemented the messianic image the young fanatics had of him by holding a massive rally at Tiananmen Square. Standing atop Tiananmen Gate, wearing his old green army uniform — which he had not worn in years — he waved for hours to the hundreds of thousands of Red Guards gathered below.

The August 18 rally showed the Cultural Revolution was going to be more than just some shuffling of positions within the Communist Party and picking up a few thousand revisionists. These young radicals meant business. They had not yet been encapsulated by the system, had very little to lose and were at that time in life when one is most susceptible to being recruited for a cause.

The American journalist and activist Anna Louise Strong met some Red Guard representatives at Tiananmen Square in September 1966, just before things would get ugly for hundreds of thousands of local and senior officials, teachers, journalists, artists and others. One of the Red Guard leaders — who identified herself as Fighting Red — explained the Red Guards's straightforward logic and uncompromising philosophy: *"Chairman Mao has defined our future as an armed revolutionary youth organization, legal under the dictatorship of the proletariat...So if Chairman Mao is our Red-Commander-in-Chief and we are his red soldiers, who can stop us? First we will make China red from inside out and then we will help the working people of other countries make the whole world red... And then the whole universe."* (qtd. in Strong, "Red Guards").

Mao directed the Red Guards to attack the 'Four Olds' of Chinese society: old customs, old habits, old culture and old thinking, because he considered them a hindrance to achieving a true communist state. Religion, tradition, rituals, all of these were just poison for people's minds, keeping them trapped in the social order of the bourgeois state.

The Red Guards took to their mission with zealous enthusiasm, changing the names of buildings, streets, even their own names, into something more revolutionary, destroying museums, churches, mosques, monasteries and temples, burning books and paintings, smashing religious statues (Yan, 71-74; Lee, 87). Party officials, local administrators, university professors, school officials, educated cadres, scientists, writers and other intellectuals were publicly humiliated and in many cases beaten, tortured, even murdered (Yan, 79-83). Everything needed to be changed, everything old was suspect.

During the summer of 1967, rebellion against everything institutionalized, especially Party cadres, reached a high point, with Red Guards locked into battle with other, more conservative mass organizations and local elements of the People's Liberation Army (PLA) — who generally supported the Party cadres and wanted to restore order — throughout the country (Meisner, 336-39).

The apex of these revolutionary tensions between the PLA and the Red Guards came in July 1967, when, in the city of Wuhan, things came to a head between a conservative organization of industrial workers called the Million Heroes — who were supported by the PLA — and Red Guard factions.[12]

On July 14, two members of the at that moment all-powerful Cultural Revolution Small Group, Xie Fuzhi and Wang Li, arrived in Wuhan to resolve the situation (Rice, 398).[13] A few days later, they called a meeting with the highest ranking officers, notifying them of their — hardly surprising — decision to support the Red Guard factions in Wuhan and faulting the military for siding with the Million Heroes (Rice, 398-99). The next morning, the PLA occupied key points in the city, led an uprising of the Million Heroes and seized Xie Fuzhi and Wang Li (Rice, 399-400).[14] Beijing reacted immediately, sending the 8190 Airborne Division — which was stationed in the Wuhan area — the 15th Army from Xiaogan and units of the East China Fleet to deal with the insurgents (Robinson, "Wuhan Incident", 427). The mutiny was suppressed a few days later, but nevertheless served as a serious wake-up call for the powers that be in Beijing.

Initially, the Wuhan Incident gave the Cultural Revolution an even more powerful leftward impetus though, with calls for a large-scale purge of the PLA, the last stable bastion of the country. Jiang Qing — Mao's wife and member of the Cultural Revolution Small Group — advised the Red Guards to *attack with words, but defend yourselves with weapons* (qtd. in Meisner, 338). Red Guard factions throughout the country readily took this advice to heart and started seizing weapons left and right, including from military depots and military convoys bound for Vietnam (Meisner, 338-39). As a result, violence in the provinces actually increased in August, with heavily armed Red Guards fighting local PLA units, angry peasants attacking local administrative buildings and rebels overtaking the Foreign Ministry in Beijing and burning down the British Chancery, on August 22. Ever more unruly Red Guard factions were rolling over the country like a plague of locusts, purging intellectuals, party officials and military officers, while schools, universities and factories were closed.

It seemed the young People's Republic of China was rapidly sliding into anarchy, or, worse still, civil war. Realizing the seriousness of the situation, Mao opted for the restoration of order rather than another massive civil war in name of the revolution (Meisner, 339; Rice, 416-17).

On September 5, 1967, the Central Committee, the Central Military Commission, the State Council and the Cultural Revolution Group jointly ordered the PLA to use any means necessary to reestablish law and order in the country (Scobell, 431). The army subsequently carried out this order in the fashion armies usually carry out such orders: brutally.

By October 1968, all the provinces and autonomous regions were firmly under control of the People's Liberation Army again (Scobell, 431). The PLA's political influence also increased. In April 1969, when the Ninth Central Committee of the CPC first convened, 49 percent of its 279 full and alternate members were from the military (Wu, 203).

With the Red Guards gone, a new power struggle emerged in the upper echelons of the Communist Party, this time between Mao and Marshal Lin Biao, his second in command and designated successor.[15] To further increase Lin Biao's influence and political power base, his allies tried to secure the position of President of the People's Republic of China for him (or even for Mao, to strengthen Lin Biao's post-Mao era position), a post that had been vacant since the last holder of the office, Liu Shaoqi, had been purged in 1968.

But Mao, by now uncomfortable with Lin Biao's growing stature within the Party, resisted these efforts and instead started moving against his 'closest comrade-in-arms and successor', undermining his power base by discrediting and criticizing his allies (Yan, 313-14; Rice, 504-05).

Early September 1971, after finding out Mao intended to seek a direct and decisive confrontation with Lin Biao, his allies (allegedly) responded by plotting to assassinate Mao (Meisner, 385).[16] The plot failed however (again, if it indeed existed in the first place, no actual attempt on Mao's life was made) and Lin Biao and his family allegedly fled the country in a plane bound for the Soviet Union. The official version of the CPC is that the plane crashed in Mongolia on September 13, 1971, killing everyone inside.[17]

With Lin Biao out of the way, conflict now erupted between Mao's wife Jiang Qing and three other ultra-left wing radical ideologues — collectively known as the Gang of Four — and more moderate party officials such as the popular Premier Zhou Enlai, one of the last moderates left in the center of power, and Vice Premier Deng Xiaoping, who had been purged in 1969 but allowed to return a few years later.

With the party establishment working to undo much of the ideological disorganization that the

Cultural Revolution Group and the Red Guards had plowed into the political system during the 1960s, and the Gang of Four in turn using the media to rail against that same party establishment and its 'revisionist' attitude, something of a stalemate emerged, paralyzing the government (Teiwes, "Politics and Purges", 485-86). Many officials feared taking any action whatsoever, not wanting to get caught on the wrong side of another revolution, while others did choose sides, thus contributing to further factionalization. Mao himself mostly supported the Gang of Four — no surprise there — but at the same time also made sure his wife's little clique did not become too powerful (Teiwes, "Politics and Purges", 484-86).

After Zhou Enlai died of cancer, in January 1976, the Gang of Four forbade all public signs of mourning. When, a couple of months later, a crowd nevertheless gathered around the Monument to the People's Heroes at Tiananmen Square to publicly mourn Zhou, the Central Committee violently suppressed the gathering (Jian, 287-88). Deng Xiaoping was also purged — again — for his alleged role in the

'Tiananmen Incident'.

But just a few months later the winds of change would blow through Beijing once more, when, on September 9, 1976, Mao Zedong died, aged 82, robbing the Gang of Four of their guardian angel. On October 6, less than a month after the Great Helmsman's death, the Gang of Four was arrested, ending whatever was left of the Cultural Revolution.[18] Jiang Qing, identified as the leader of the Gang, defended herself at her trial by maintaining that everything she had done had been for Mao, saying: *"I was Chairman Mao's dog. Whomever he told me to bite, I bit."* (qtd. in Sterba, "Former Chinese Leaders").[19]

The Chinese people had finally had their fill of left-wing radicals, clearing the path for the moderate Deng Xiaoping to make yet another comeback and become the new, undisputed leader of the People's Republic of China in 1978. His subsequent reforms would put China on a path of spectacular economic growth for decades to come.

Even today, the Great Leap Forward, the Great Famine and the Great Proletarian Cultural Revolution remain highly sensitive topics in China, with public discussion of them being severely limited.

A huge portrait of Mao Zedong still hangs at Tiananmen Gate.

---

1   Qtd. in Andrews, 439.

2   The term 'rightist' itself was first used in the 1930s.

3   For more on distance and survival estimates of the Long March, see chapter 39, Chinese Civil War Part I & II, note 9.

4   The name of the campaign comes from a quote from Mao Zedong, used in various speeches in the mid 1950s, in which he urged to *"let a hundred flowers bloom; let a hundred schools of thought contend."*

5   In *Mao's China and After*, Meisner argues that Mao's call for more open criticism from the non-Party intelligentsia was primarily meant to revive the revolutionary spirit of a Party leadership and apparatus that was becoming less and less receptive to his radical social and economic agenda (Meisner, 165). That would also explain why, apart from Mao, most of the CPC's highest leaders were opposed to the Hundred Flowers campaign, which they considered a threat to the Party's power base and their own positions (Meisner, 165-74).

6   That Mao saw little room for real political criticism may be illustrated by his warning, in an address to the Communist Youth League on May 25, 1957, that *"Any speech or action which deviates from socialism is entirely wrong."* (qtd.

in Meisner, 186).

7   For a discussion of possible reasons for breaking the promise not to retaliate against the intellectuals who spoke out during the Hundred Flowers campaign, see also Meisner, 183-84.

8   Exact figures are not available, but most estimates arrive at a figure of at least 400,000 people who were purged during the Anti-Rightist Campaign of 1957-58 (Teiwes, "Politics and Purges", 228, note h).

9   Estimates about the actual death toll vary widely, ranging from roughly 20 million to more than 45 million. Two of the more recent studies, one by Dutch historian and modern China expert Frank Dikötter (*Mao's Great Famine: The History of China's Most Devastating Catastrophe, 1958-1962*, 2010), the other by Chinese journalist Yang Jisheng (*Tombstone: The Great Chinese Famine, 1958-1962*, 2013), arrive at a death toll of 45 million and 36 million, respectively.

10   For some examples of Mao's sometimes elaborate scheming, see Edward Rice's *Mao's Way* (185-86, 269, 286-87).

11   The Little Red Book, as it is known in the West, is a pocket book with famous Mao quotations. First published in 1964, its actual title is 'Quotations from Chairman Mao Tse-tung'.

12   The tensions had a significant impact on the economic productivity of Wuhan. According to one contemporary report, over 2,400 factories and mines in the Wuhan area had suspended production or saw their output decrease by half between April 19-June 3, while 50,000 workers were involved in armed conflict one way or another (Robinson, "Wuhan Incident", 418, note 19). Railway services across the vital First Yangtze River Bridge were also regularly interrupted (Robinson, "Wuhan Incident", 418-19).

13   The Cultural Revolution Group was a quasi-official committee, established with the specific goal of guiding the Cultural Revolution. As such, it assumed many of the powers of the Central Committee and Politburo for a while (Meisner, 314-15). Some prominent members of the group were Chen Boda, Mao's wife Jiang Qing and Xie Fuzhi. For all fifteen members, see the *Historical Dictionary of the Chinese Cultural Revolution* (Jian, 85).

14   Wang Li was kicked and beaten during the kidnapping, leaving him with bruises and a broken left leg, while Xie Fuzhi apparently came away relatively unscathed (Robinson, "Wuhan Incident", 425).

15   At the Ninth Party Congress, Lin Biao had been named as the only Vice-Chairman of the CPC and enshrined in the new Party constitution as Mao's *"closest comrade-in-arms and successor"* (qtd. in Gao, xxi).

16   The existence of the plot, known as Project 5-7-1 — so named because pronounced together the numbers rhyme with the characters for 'armed uprising' (Yan, 315) — appears likely, but evidence for it is too thin to be undisputed. For an elaborate description of the coup and how it came into

being, see *Turbulent Decade: A History of the Cultural Revolution* (Yan, 310-26).

17 This official version remains disputed (Teiwes, "Lin Biao", 1).

18 Some 400,000 people are estimated to have lost their lives due to the Cultural Revolution between 1966-76 (Meisner, 354).

19 Jiang Qing was sentenced to death in 1981, with a two-year suspension. Two years later the sentence was commuted to life imprisonment. She committed suicide in 1991.

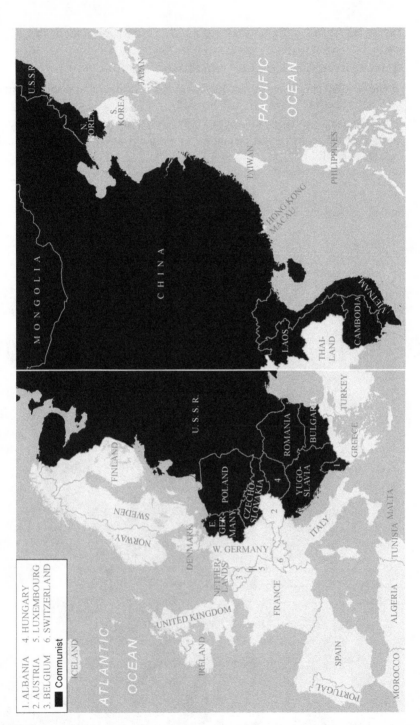

Map 27: Communist States in Europe and Asia, c. 1980s

48

THE END OF COMMUNISM

*"The theory of the Communists may be summed up
in the single sentence: Abolition of private property."[1]*

The Communist Manifesto, Karl Marx
and Friedrich Engels, 1848

*"Communism doesn't work because
people like to own stuff."*

Frank Zappa, musician, songwriter

In April 2009, North Korea removed the word 'communism' from its constitution, replacing it with the 'military first' doctrine, or *Songun*, which means exactly what it says. South Korean media quoted an official from the North as saying the change was made because the ideals of Communism were *"hard to fulfill"* (qtd. in Herskovitz, "North Korea").

And this coming from one of the last countries in the world that was still deserving of the moniker 'communist state', with its centrally planned economy, hardly any private property and state- provided housing, health care, education and food rations. But things change, even in the Democratic People's Republic of Korea (DPRK).

In May 2010, the North Korean government lifted all restrictions on private markets, allowing people to trade most products more freely (Harlan, "N. Korea lifts restrictions"). A significant step as well as a practical one, since most North Koreans were apparently deriving more than half of their income from commercial activities at grass-roots market places located throughout the country anyway.[2] And in June 2012, a new agricultural policy was announced that would let farmers keep 30 percent of the target production, with the state taking 70 percent.[3] Moreover, under the new policy, farmers would be allowed to keep any surplus should the target production be exceeded. Perhaps the DPRK's fanatic aversion against the root of all evil has dissipated somewhat under its new Supreme Leader, Kim Jong-un, who took over from his father, Supreme Leader Kim Jong-il (who had taken over from his father, Eternal President Kim Il-sung) after his demise in 2011. In any case, it seems that North Korea — like several other hard-core communist states from the roaring 20th century, China, Cuba, Vietnam, Laos — is trying to keep the marxist-leninist single-party state, only without the marxist-leninist part.

So what went wrong there? Well, for one thing, Communism didn't deliver. Or, more accurately, the prevailing theory of how to *get* to Communism, i.e., Marxism-Leninism, did not deliver; Communism itself — the stateless, classless, moneyless Valhalla in which nobody owns anything because everybody owns everything — was never achieved. Anywhere.

Communist revolutions overthrew existing governments and created single-party socialist states that transferred ownership of the means of production to the state, banning capitalism, yes.[4] But instead of those socialist states 'withering away' as they transformed into true communist societies, they actually grew stronger and more dominant than almost any other form of government.[5] And instead of leading to a classless society, marxist-leninist states merely created a new upper class, the political class. Meanwhile, nothing changed for ordinary people (in the best case scenario, that is). As the much lauded economist John Kenneth Galbraith once said: *"Under capitalism, man exploits man. Under communism, it's just the opposite."*

So, strong single-party states confiscating private property, suppressing freedom of speech and independent thinking, while nudging / herding / bullying / forcing their citizens to work collectively towards centrally planned goals. What's not to like?

A complicating factor for the socialist states was that they had to compete with the democratic, capitalist states of the West, their Cold War opponents. And not just for ideological, but also for technological and military superiority, as they could ill afford falling behind and risk 'imperialist' interference, or even outright war. This put pressure on socialist economies to be just as resilient, flexible and innovative allocating resources through forward planning by a central authority, as their capitalist counterparts were by chiefly relying on free and open markets. Famines, inferior products and mismatches between expected and actual supply and demand were the result.

And there was another problem: capitalist societies around the world did not collapse the way Marx had predicted.[6] During the 19th century, Western countries, pressured by social reformers, slowly started paying heed to the appalling conditions of the large worker class Marx called 'the proletariat'. Over time, laws were enacted to prohibit child labor below a certain age, limit working hours, impose safety and health regulations, guarantee a minimum wage, etc.

Of course this did not happen overnight, or indeed without a fight. Persuading governments to redistribute some of the wealth and political power from the 'haves' to the 'have nots' took countless strikes, riots, marches and speeches, coupled with the rising importance of the economic theories of another highly influential economist, John Maynard Keynes, who argued that aggregate demand plays a vital role in economic growth and that if people don't have any money to spend, the economy will suffer.[7-8]

As a result of this redistribution of resources, life significantly improved for the working class in Western societies in the 20th century, creating a prosperous middle class and the blooming of opportunities for social advancement based on talent and ambition rather than one's station in life. Between 1928-79 income inequality in the United States sharply declined, with the top one percent's share of total pre-tax income declining from a staggering 21.2 percent in 1928 to 8.4 percent in 1976 (Piketty, "Income Inequality", 8-10, Table II). Between 1947-79, real family income in the U.S. increased by 116 percent for the bottom twenty percent, while it 'only' increased by 86 percent for the top five percent (Reich, "Widening Inequality", 17). In other words, during this period the poor grew richer at a faster rate than the already rich did (relatively speaking of course), making less people poor while still making rich people richer.

The irony is that while policies partly inspired by Marx's theories markedly improved life of the working class in the West, the full implementation of those theories made things (much) worse for the working class in the socialist states of the East, until moderate leaders there gained enough momentum to (re)introduce capitalism.

In China, for example, workers and peasants were still reeling from the disastrous Great Leap Forward (1958-62) and Cultural Revolution (1966-76), when Deng Xiaoping — who had been purged twice by the Maoists — was finally able to launch a program of much needed economic reforms in 1978, aimed at transforming the Chinese economy into a more market oriented one. Meanwhile, in Cambodia, the Khmer Rouge, apparently undeterred by the aforementioned Chinese failures, had established a government based on Maoist principles, ruling the country with an iron fist from 1975. Dreaming of an agrarian-based communist society, the Khmer Rouge forced millions of city dwellers to the countryside to take up farming. Money and private property were abolished, religion, modern education and political dissent were forbidden, schools, churches, mosques and temples were destroyed, and the rich, intellectuals and soldiers who had fought the Khmer Rouge in the civil war were executed (Kiernan, 8, 190, 223, 232, 284, 356). At least 1.5 million people thus perished, before a Vietnamese invasion force defeated the Khmer Rouge in 1979 (Kiernan, 456-60). After economic reforms were carried out in the 1980s and early 1990s, the Cambodian economy started growing again.

In the same year the Khmer Rouge came to power in Cambodia, communist North Vietnam emerged victorious from its civil war with U.S. supported South Vietnam. But its subsequent efforts to collectivize agriculture and nationalize factories and services were a disaster, leading to economic chaos and rampant inflation (Alpert, 35-37). After a couple of years of trying to muddle through, the ideologue hardliners were replaced by more moderate leaders, who in 1986 initiated economic reforms to create a socialist-oriented market economy known as *Doi Moi* (Alpert, 37-38). Vietnam's neighbor Laos was another marxist-leninist state that initially sought to get rid of capitalism altogether, until finding out the hard way that the road to Communism devastated the economy (Bourdet, 9). Like Vietnam, Laos started on a path of economic reform in 1986, decentralizing its economy and encouraging private enterprise.

1986 would also prove to be a watershed year for the country that had adopted Communism before all others, after its new leader, the relatively young Mikhail Sergeyevich Gorbachev, aged 54, announced the need for "*radical reform*" of the Soviet economy at the 27th Congress of the Communist Party of the Soviet Union, stating that mere "*changes in the economic mechanism*" would not suffice (qtd. in CIA, "27th CPSU Congress", 15).

Gorbachev came to power at a time the Soviet Union had been suffering from a stagnant economy for several years, caused in part by falling oil prices — thus reducing foreign currency revenue, which the U.S.S.R needed for importing grain and Western technology — a costly war in Afghanistan, and, perhaps most serious of all, the inability of the centrally planned economy to efficiently produce the wide variety of products and services characteristic for modern economies (Strayer, 57-60).[9] Still, the new leader of the Soviet Union did not want to completely abandon the socialist economic model, merely to reform, to restructure, to reinvigorate it. He wanted to decentralize part of the economic decision-making process and stimulate individual creativity and innovation, without completely surrendering the economy to capitalism.

He wanted to allow state enterprises to determine for themselves how much to produce for example, based on customer demand. And to make them responsible for their own financing, instead of being propped up by Moscow regardless of their output or actual demand for their products. Gorbachev also moved to allow the establishment of private enterprises for the first time since the 1920s, acknowledging the importance of a private sector in increasing economic efficiency.[10]

Gorbachev's political reforms were characterized by the same kind of pragmatism. He did not seek to replace the single-party socialist state with a Western style democratic capitalist one, only to strengthen it, by allowing more openness from both the people and the central government, and by increasing people's participation in government through the introduction of some democratizing elements. *Perestroika* ('restructuring') and *Glasnost* ('openness'), those were the new magic words. The same words would also come to define Gorbachev's foreign policy, in which he successfully strived for a détente with the West — reducing the nuclear weapons buildup through the Intermediate-Range Nuclear Forces Treaty of 1987 — an end to the war in Afghanistan and loosening Moscow's control over its satellite states, breaking with the so-called Brezhnev Doctrine. This doctrine, established in 1968, had called for military intervention in Warsaw Pact countries whenever liberalization efforts threatened to undermine socialism. In a (perhaps coincidental) variation on the famous Article 5 of the North Atlantic Treaty — which states that an attack on one shall be considered to be an attack on all — Soviet leader Leonid Brezhnev had said in a speech at the 5th Congress of the Polish United Workers' Party, in November 1968, that *"When forces that are hostile to socialism try to turn the development of some socialist country towards capitalism, it becomes not only a problem of the country concerned, but a common problem and concern of all socialist countries"* (qtd. in Saul, 60). They weren't idle words either, as Brezhnev had already turned them into action a few months earlier, when the Soviet Union — together with Bulgaria, Hungary, Poland and the GDR — had invaded Czechoslovakia to end the Prague Spring, which had sprung up following Alexander Dubček's liberalization reforms.

When Gorbachev visited Prague in the spring of 1987, his own liberalization reforms already in full swing, a Western reporter asked him what the difference was between his reformist policies and those of Alexander Dubček. Gorbachev's spokesman famously replied: *"Nineteen years"* (qtd. in Gáti, 178).

Speaking in Strasbourg at the Council of Europe in July 1989, Gorbachev made clear what he thought of the Brezhnev Doctrine, saying that *"Social and political orders in one or another country changed in the past and may change in the future. But this change is the exclusive affair of the people of that country and is their choice. Any interference in domestic affairs and any attempts to restrict the sovereignty of states, both friends and allies or any others, is inadmissible."* (qtd. in Gáti, 169). With that, the Brezhnev Doctrine was laid to rest and replaced by a policy of non- interference sometimes jokingly called the Sinatra Doctrine, an allusion to Frank Sinatra's *I Did it My Way*, signifying that the satellite states within the

Soviet Union would be allowed to go their own way (Keller 1989).

Gorbachev had not expected any of them to actually leave the Soviet Union though. But, as it turned out, he had greatly underestimated the long bottled-up frustration and longing for freedom and democracy in countries like Poland, Hungary, Eastern Germany, Bulgaria, Romania and Czechoslovakia. Empowered by Gorbachev's assurance that liberalization efforts would not be met by tanks and rifle fire this time, the peoples of these countries went 'once more unto the breach' in the closing months of the 1980s, demanding change. This time they succeeded.

On November 9, the Berlin Wall fell. The sight and sound of ordinary people hammering and chiseling away at that most notorious of Cold War icons symbolized the end not just for the forced separation of East and West Germany, but for the entire Eastern bloc. Less than two years later, on December 26, 1991, the Soviet Union was dissolved. The post-Soviet states each went their own way, some towards full democracy, others towards a little or no democracy, but all away from Communism.

It was not what Gorbachev had set out to achieve. He had just wanted to throw out the bath water, not the baby. Only what was the water and what the baby? To Gorbachev, the baby was the socialist state, but clearly he had not wanted to save it against any price, invading Eastern European countries with tanks, purging those who held different views and staying true to unreformed Communism no matter what, as his predecessors had done. So what *did* he want? For what else is a socialist state that champions private enterprise, freedom of expression and participation of the people in government, but a Western style capitalist democracy? Perhaps Gorbachev threw out just the bath water after all.

Of course this is exactly what single-party states like China, Cuba and North Korea are afraid of, that economic and political reforms will ignite social unrest and demands for ever more freedom, as it did in the Soviet Union. To these countries, the main lesson from Gorbachev's reforms is that they are very dangerous. Learning from this, China's ruling elite has been more successful than Gorbachev was in implementing far-reaching economic reforms without compromising its political power base (whether Cuba and North Korea can replicate China's success remains to be seen). Interestingly enough, around the same time many socialist states started looking to the West for ways to reform their troubled economies, income inequality in the United States started growing again. Between 1980-2012, the gap between the wealthiest 1 percent and the other 99 percent rose to the highest since the 1920s (Saez, "Striking it Richer", fig. 2). Economist and Nobel laureate Robert Schiller has called the rising income inequality in the United States and elsewhere in the world "*the most important problem that we are facing now today.*" (qtd. in Christoffersen 2013).

So perhaps Communism is not quite dead yet. Just slumbering.

---

1   Marx, "Communist Manifesto", 30.

2   In a 2008 survey of North Korean defectors, 69 percent of respondents reported over half their income in the hermit kingdom had come from market activities (Haggard, 10).

3   The new policy is part of the 'June 28 New Economic Management Measures', informally known as the '6.28 Policy' and reportedly implemented in October 2012 (Keck, "Agricultural Reforms").

4   Socialist states are sometimes called communist states. This is a misnomer though, as there would no longer be a state in a true communist society.

5   As Friedrich Engels wrote in *Anti-Dühring*: "*The first act in which the state really comes forward as the representative of society as a whole — the taking possession of the means of production in the name of society — is at the same time its last independent act as a state. The interference of the state power in social relations becomes superfluous in one sphere after another, and then ceases of itself. The government of persons is replaced by the administration of things and the direction of the process of production. The state is not "abolished", it withers away.*" (315).

6   In *Capital: A Critique of Political Economy* (*Das Kapital, Vol. I*. 1867), Marx wrote: "*Centralisation of the means of production and socialisation of labour at last reach a point where they become incompatible with their capitalist integument. This integument is burst asunder. The knell of capitalist private property sounds. The expropriators are expropriated.*" (837).

7   This is an argument that has lately regained attention and support both in the United States and abroad, particularly in the wake of the so-called 'Occupy Wall Street' movement. The reasoning goes that the anemic economic recovery that followed the financial crisis of 2008 was at least partly caused by the growing gap between rich and poor. This may be illustrated by the fact that the U.S. minimum wage of 2015 was, at $7.25, significantly lower than the

inflation-adjusted (CPI) $10.72 minimum wage of 1968.

8   In *The General Theory of Employment, Interest and Money* (1936), Keynes argued that aggregate demand — rather than aggregate supply — is responsible for the level of employment, that markets cannot achieve full employment on their own if aggregate demand is deficient, such as during an economic downturn, and that government spending is needed in such a situation to increase aggregate demand and restore full employment.

9   Between 1980-86, the oil price declined from a peak of $37 in 1980 to $14 in 1986. As one of the world's major oil exporters, the Soviet Union was hit hard by this price fall.

10 The 1988 Law on Cooperatives allowed for the creation of privately run, for-profit enterprises, operating much like Western companies. In *Russia's Capitalist Revolution*, Swedish economist Anders Åslund writes that one of the first new cooperatives in Moscow was a Russian restaurant on Kropotkinskaya Street (Åslund, 56-57). *"Unlike Soviet restaurants, it was cozy, had excellent service, and served the best of Russian food, but its prices were Western."* (Åslund, 57).

49

THE SECOND GREATEST INVENTION OF THE MILLENNIUM

*"By printing, one man alone can produce in
a single day as much as he could have done in
a thousand days of writing in the past."* [1]

Sebastian Brant, Varia carmina, 1498

*"We set up a telephone connection between us
and the guys at SRI (...) We typed the L and we
asked on the phone: "Do you see the L?" "Yes,
we see the L," came the response. "We typed the
O, and we asked, "Do you see the O." "Yes, we
see the O." "Then we typed the G, and the system
crashed"... Yet a revolution had begun"...* [2]

Len Kleinrock about the first ARPANET
link on October 29, 1969

In March 1960, at the dawn of the Digital Revolution, computer scientist and psychologist J.C.R. Licklider published a paper about future *"cooperative interaction between men and electronic computers"* (Licklider, "Man-Computer Symbiosis", 4). A bold concept, considering there were only about 5,400 computers in the entire United States at the time, most of them much bigger than the average living room and costing hundreds of thousands of dollars (Flamm, 135, Tab. 5-1).[3]

The transistor had been invented only thirteen years earlier and was just beginning to replace the vacuum tubes then commonly used in computers. Another major game changer in the field of electronics, the integrated circuit, had been invented just two years earlier, and although it would make computers much faster, cheaper and smaller, the first ones equipped with them would not arrive until 1961.[4]

But the prohibitive cost of computers was precisely what had put Licklider on the trail of an idea that would help revolutionize knowledge-sharing on a scale not seen since Gutenberg had invented the printing press, roughly 500 years earlier. Because *"any present-day large-scale computer is too fast and too costly for real-time cooperative thinking with one man"*, Licklider suggested a network of *"thinking center*[s]*"*, functioning much like libraries and connected to each other as well as individual users (Licklider, "Man-Computer Symbiosis", 7).

As he envisioned: *"The picture readily enlarges itself into a network of such centers, connected to one another by wide-band communication lines and to individual users by leased-wire services. In such a system, the speed of the computers would be balanced, and the cost of the gigantic memories and the sophisticated programs would be divided by the number of users."* (Licklider, "Man- Computer Symbiosis", 7).

It was one of the earliest formulations of a computer network — if not the earliest.

Two years later, Licklider was hired by the Defense Advanced Research Projects Agency (DARPA), a research agency of the U.S. Department of Defense, to head up the newly established Information Processing Techniques Office, IPTO (Ceruzzi 2012, 75). While there, Licklider outlined his idea for an 'Intergalactic Computer Network' and convinced team members and later successors such as Ivan Sutherland, Bob Taylor and Lawrence G. Roberts — several of whom would come to play a key role in the creation of ARPANET, the progenitor of the internet — of its importance.[5]

Naturally, the Department of Defense was also very interested in the concept of networked computers. It therefore asked IPTO to come up with a way to link up the computers of the Pentagon, Strategic Air Command and the Department of Defense, to facilitate easier information sharing.

Around the same time, Paul Baran, an American engineer, performed a study on survivable communication networks for the U.S. Air Force, which was concerned about the elimination of such networks in the event of a nuclear attack. The key insight of Baran's study was that even a moderate degree of network redundancy would provide high immunity to such an attack (Baran 1960). To further increase the reliability of such a 'distributed network', Baran also came up with the idea of dividing messages into multiple *message blocks* that would be sent over the network separately and put back together again at the destination, still the basis for data communication around the world.[6]

Baran's ideas also made their way to Licklider's successors at IPTO, who used them in the creation of ARPANET. The first large-scale computer network, ARPANET initially consisted of just two host computers — one at the University of California's Network Measurement Center in Los Angeles, the other at the Stanford Research Institute — interconnected by two so-called Interface Message Processors, i.e., routers (UCLA, "first internet connection").[7] The first ARPANET link between these two host computers was established on October 29, 1969, a couple of months after Neil Armstrong had first walked on the moon.

About a year later ARPANET had grown to 10 nodes, 5 more were added in 1971 — to connect a total of 23 host computers — and by 1972 there were 30 nodes (Ceruzzi 2003, 194). At that point ARPANET still consisted exclusively of American universities and government sites such as NASA, the Department of Defense, the National Science Foundation and the Federal Reserve Board, but in 1973 ARPANET went international, when it connected to the Norwegian Seismic Array (NORSAR) via satellite link.[8] The network kept expanding throughout the 1970s and by 1980 it counted 230 nodes (Korowajczuk, 16).

Meanwhile, other organizations had started building computer networks of their own, running on different network protocols.[9] This made interconnection difficult, a problem that could only be expected to increase over time. Something was needed to link different computer networks together more easily, while maintaining the open-architecture character of this rapidly growing 'network of networks'.

Enter the 'Transmission Control Program' (TCP), a unifying network protocol that defined rules for processing data between networks, i.e., how to send, format, address and receive it.[10] First tested in 1975, TCP quickly became the *de facto* standard protocol for internet data processing, and still is today.[11]

In March 1982, the U.S. Department of Defense declared TCP/ IP the standard for all military networking and on January 1, 1983, ARPANET changed its own protocol to TCP/IP as well (Korowajczuk, 16; Daigle 2013).[12] ARPANET's choice for TCP/IP was a game-changing step forward in the expansion of the network of computer networks, but it would take a couple of more years before the word 'internetworking', which had been in use since the mid-1970s to describe the interconnecting of different networks, would transform into a noun in its own right, to describe the global network that resulted from all that interconnecting: internet.[13]

ARPANET was a great success, but it was never meant to function as the backbone of a network of computer networks indefinitely. The mission of its creator, DARPA, was (and remains) to develop new technologies, not to become a glorified internet service provider. So, when it became clear that computer networks would continue to prosper and proliferate with or without the existence of ARPANET, the pioneering network began to look for a suitable successor to take over as backbone. That successor was found in NSFNET, a nationwide computer network launched in 1986 by the National Science Foundation (Halabi, 7). Within a couple of years, NSFNET connected to a host of research and education networks both inside and outside the United States. NSFNET was also rapidly upgraded, with new backbone points added every year and transfer speeds increasing from 56-bit/s in 1986 to 1.5 Mbit/s in 1988 and 45 Mbit/s in 1991 (Halabi, 7). ARPANET was retired in 1990.

Commercial Internet Service Providers (ISPs) also began to emerge in the late 1980s, forcing the National Science Foundation to address the question of how to deal with commercial traffic on its network. It responded with an 'Acceptable Use Policy' that sought to ban all advertising — in many ways the backbone of today's internet — but allowed some other commercial traffic (Ceruzzi 2003, 320-21). It was hardly a clear line in the sand though, more of a murky smear in the mud.

In response, three Internet Service Providers (ISPs) created the Commercial Internet eXchange (CIX) in 1991, an internet exchange point for routing commercial internet traffic (Cronin, 253). CIX was operated based on a 'no-settlement policy', meaning traffic between parties was exchanged without compensation; instead, CIX members paid a fixed fee, a model that would later be adopted by most Internet Exchange Points regulating traffic between commercial ISPs.

Late 1991, NSFNET lifted its restrictions (Cronin, 253). Tension nevertheless largely remained between the commercial ISPs and the academic, non-profit NSFNET, until the latter was decommissioned in 1995. During this transitional period to a fully commercial internet, the NSF sponsored the creation of four public Network Access Points (NAPs) in the United States — two on the East Coast and two on the West Coast — to handle the growing traffic between Internet Service Providers (Frazer, 40-41). When there were enough commercially operated Internet Exchange Points to handle the ever increasing internet traffic load, the NAPs were decommissioned as well.[14]

Computer networking had made great strides in both quantity and quality between 1969-90 (the year ARPANET was retired), going from the very first message over the very first ARPANET link to countless messages over a global network of regional and national computer networks, connecting universities, government agencies and research facilities around the world. Still, for the internet to become the truly ubiquitous phenomenon it is today, one additional fundamental element was still missing: regular people.

But in 1990, getting on the internet could be challenging for novice users, not to mention using it. The available information on the internet was growing rapidly, yes, but knowing how to find it was a whole different matter. There were no search engines coughing up a list of relevant pages within 0.5 seconds of posing a question, or web browsers where you could simply enter a URL, or URLs for that matter, or webpages, or websites.

That is where British computer scientist Tim Berners-Lee comes in.

During a brief stint as a consultant at the European Particle Physics

Laboratory (CERN) in 1980, Berners-Lee wrote a software program called *Enquire*, to bring some order in the informational chaos that resulted from 10,000 people working on different projects with different hardware and different software (Berners-Lee 1993/94). *Enquire* used hypertext — a database format that allows text to link directly to specific parts of information — to reveal relationships between people, programs and hardware.

When he returned to CERN in 1984 to work on a different project, Berners-Lee used *Enquire "to keep track of the modules, the users, the documents and everything I needed to note down about the project"* (Berners-Lee 1993/94). Still, even though he needed the program to keep track of everything that was going on, *Enquire* had its shortcomings, chief among them that it was not accessible to everyone and that the rules for updating it were too strict.

Berners-Lee realized there was a real need for a system that could link, retrieve and present information independently of the used hardware or software and that was accessible to everyone, much like the TCP/IP protocol had unified the transmission of information over the internet across different network platforms. *"This was the concept of the web"* (Berners-Lee 1993/94).

Between 1989-91, Berners-Lee was given the opportunity at CERN to work on his core idea of using hypertext to make data more accessible.[15] Calling the project World Wide Web, he wrote a protocol for transferring hypertext (HTTP), a web browser (called WorldWideWeb) to retrieve and present information and an application to set up the very first web server, capable of serving up web pages. He also created and launched the very first webpage, at http://info.cern.ch.[16]

Fearing his 'documentation system' would fail to catch on at CERN because no one would put any information in it, Berners-Lee decided to set up a hypertext version of the CERN phone book, so that his system was useful from the get-go. *"So this was the way the web was first presented at CERN: as a rather simple user interface which allowed one to look up (mainly) telephone numbers. It was to be two years before it would shed that image."*(Berners-Lee 1993/94).

Rather than claiming ownership, CERN decided the World Wide Web should benefit everybody, so on August 23, 1991 — a date still celebrated as Internaut Day — the project was opened to new users.[17] In the years that followed, the number of internauts — those capable of using the internet — exploded, as did the number of *web*sites. There were only 10 websites in June 1992, but by June 1995 there were already more than 23,000 and two years after that more than 1,100,000 ("Total number of Websites"). As of June 2014, there are more than 968 million websites.

Part of the credit for the meteoric rise of the World Wide Web's popularity in the 1990s goes to Mosaic, the first web browser to display images inline with text instead of in a separate window (yes, it wasn't always so) and one of the earliest browsers available for the Windows operating system, at the time used by more than 80 percent of the world's computers (Reid, xxv).[18]

Since then, the internet's impact has become ever more indelible, reaching every corner of our lives, be it social, commercial, professional, recreational or educational. And if the internet used to be something that you switched on and off and that was only available at work and at home, with the proliferation of broadband internet access and the smartphone most people have become connected wherever, whenever.

It seems the symbiosis between "*men and electronic computers*" that J.C.R. Licklider talked about is not too far off.

Or perhaps it's already here.

1 Qtd. in Halporn, 1.

2 Qtd. in Gromov 1995. In a 2009 video interview, Leonard Kleinrock also talks in detail about the very first building blocks of the ARPANET and sending that first message from UCLA to Stanford Research Institute (UCLA, "first internet connection").

3 The IBM 1401 that came out in 1959 sold for about $370,000, almost $3 million in 2014 prices.

4 The first integrated circuit chips were built for the U.S. Air Force. They also started to be used in the nuclear-armed Minuteman missiles from the early 1960s. Another early customer was NASA. Its Apollo Guidance Computer — used in the Lunar Module and Command Module during the moon landing mission of 1969 — was integrated circuit-based.

5 Interesting reading in this respect is an eight-page memo Licklider sent to his

colleagues on April 23, 1963, titled *Memorandum for: Members and Affiliates of the Intergalactic Computer Network*, in which he discussed several issues concerning the building of this 'Intergalactic Computer Network'.

6   Independently, Donald Watts Davies of the U.K. National Physical Laboratory came up with the same idea, calling it *packet switching*, which is the name that stuck. Davies also played an important role in bringing the idea of packet switching to the attention of the ARPA engineers in the early stages of the creation of ARPANET (Harris 2009).

7   Another node was connected in November 1969, at the University of California's Culler-Fried Interactive Mathematics center in Santa Barbara (UCSB), and in December a fourth node was connected at the University of Utah's Computer Science Department (UCLA, "first internet connection").

8   A map of the ARPANET circa 1974 in *Computing: A Concise History* shows that its by then 60+ connections were concentrated in four regions: Boston, Washington D.C., Silicon Valley and southern California (Ceruzzi, 109, fig. 5.3).

9   Like IBM's Systems Network Architecture (SNA) and X.25, developed by the International Telecommunications Union (ITU).

10 TCP was designed by Vincent G. Cerf and Robert E. Kahn, who wrote a seminal paper on it in 1974, titled 'A Protocol for Packet Network Intercommunication'.

11 The original Transmission Control Program was later divided into different protocols, the two most important ones being the Transmission Control Protocol (TCP) and the Internet Protocol (IP), hence the informal designation 'TCP/ IP' for what is officially known today as the Internet Protocol Suite.

12 There is no real D-Day for the creation of 'the' internet (or even a D-Year), but if there had to be one, January 1, 1983 would certainly be a good candidate.

13 The word 'internet' — as shorthand for 'internetwork' — was first used in the 1974 paper 'Specification of Internet Transmission Control Program', by the Network Working Group led by Vinton Cerf, one of the principal designers of the TCP protocol. In the late 1980s, the word 'internet' started to be used to designate the global TCP/IP network.

14 As of May 2013, there are more than 350 Internet Exchange Points worldwide.

15 In his proposal to persuade CERN management of the advantages of a global hypertext system, Berners-Lee called it 'Mesh'; he only decided on 'World Wide Web' when writing the code in 1990 (Berners-Lee 1989-90).

16 The first sentence on the first website read: "*The WorldWideWeb (W3) is a wide-area hypermedia information retrieval initiative aiming to give universal access to a large universe of documents.*" (see: http://info.cern.ch/ hypertext/ WWW/TheProject.html).

17 Two weeks earlier, Berners-Lee had already published a short summary of the WorldWideWeb project in a post on the alt.hypertext newsgroup, with links to the line-mode browser, a hypertext editor and documentation about the project,

but it was not until August 23, 1991, that the web was opened to new users. On April 30, 1993, CERN announced it would publish its 'W3' software in the public domain, making it freely available to everybody.

18 Netscape Navigator, the dominant web browser of the 1990s, was based on Mosaic.

50

9/11

*"The key to any strategy is accurate intelligence,
and skilled professionals to get that information
in time to use it. In seeking to guard this nation
against the threat of catastrophic violence, our
Administration gave intelligence officers the tools
and lawful authority they needed to gain vital
information. We didn't invent that authority. It is
drawn from Article Two of the Constitution. And it
was given specificity by the Congress after 9/11, in
a Joint Resolution authorizing "all necessary and
appropriate force" to protect the American people."[1]*

Former Vice-President Dick Cheney, May 21, 2009

*"But I don't want comfort. I want God, I want
poetry, I want real danger, I want freedom, I want
goodness. I want sin." "In fact," said Mustapha
Mond, "you're claiming the right to be unhappy."
"All right then," said the Savage defiantly,
"I'm claiming the right to be unhappy."[2]*

Brave New World, Aldous Huxley, 1931

On September 11, 2001, at 8:49 a.m., CNN cuts short a commercial from sub-prime mortgage company Ditech, to show the first images of a plane-shaped hole in the upper part of the World Trade Center's North Tower. Black smoke is billowing out. Commentators cite *"unconfirmed reports"* that a plane has hit the tower (CNN, "9/11

News", 1:38). Moments later, Sean Murtagh — a CNN Vice President — confirms on the air that he saw a "*two-engined jet, maybe a 737*" crash into the tower (CNN, "9/11 News", 3:04).

During the next fourteen minutes, several other eyewitnesses confirm they saw a plane crash into the tower. One witness says she heard a "*sonic boom*", thinking at first that "*maybe the Concorde was back in service*" (CNN, "9/11 News", 8:05). Nobody uses words like 'terrorism', 'attack', or 'deliberate'. One of the CNN commentators simply calls it a "*horrible incident*" (CNN, "9/11 News", 7:48). Thus, although American Airlines Flight 11 had in fact been intentionally flown into the North Tower of the WTC at 8:46 a.m., most people remained on pre-9/11 time during those first seventeen minutes of the post-9/11 world.

That changed at 9:03 a.m.

The crash of the second plane is caught live on CNN, but the commentators — in the middle of a phone interview with an eyewitness — somehow miss the moment. The same happens at NBC, which shows the North Tower from another angle. There, viewers can see a second plane flying towards the WTC for six seconds, before it disappears behind the smoking North Tower. Another — surreal — four seconds go by, before the eyewitness on the phone screams "*Oh another one just hit! something else just hit, a very large plane just flew directly over my building and there has been another collision; can you see it?*"(NBC, "News Coverage", 9:47).

With the crashing of United Airlines Flight 175 into the South Tower, it becomes clear that the events unfolding are not accidental. At 9:30 a.m., President George Bush goes on air to deliver a hastily prepared statement, calling the crashing of the planes "*an apparent, terrorist attack on our country*" and promising "*to hunt down and to find those folks, who committed this act.*" (NBC, "News Coverage", 37:21, 37:44).

At 9:37 a.m., American Airlines Flight 77 crashes into the west side of the Pentagon. Minutes later, the networks show big clouds of smoke emanating from the building. People working on the other side of the Pentagon (the largest office building in the world) report hearing a loud explosion, thinking at first that perhaps a bomb has gone off.

At 9:59 a.m., CNN coverage of the Pentagon attack is interrupted when the South Tower of the WTC collapses. At 10:28 a.m., the North Tower follows its twin sibling. By then, United Airlines Flight 93 has already crashed in a field near Shanksville, Pennsylvania (at 10:03 a.m.). It would later become known the hijacker-pilot had decided to crash the plane into the ground as passengers were attempting to retake the plane. The intended target for United 93 had probably been either the White House or the Capitol.[3]

Meanwhile, the immediate response from local and federal government agencies and the military is focused on defense, containment and rescue. Within six minutes after the first plane hits the WTC, the New York City Transit subways and Port Authority Trans-Hudson (PATH) activate emergency procedures (Volpe, "Effects", 2). The subway station under the WTC is quickly closed. At 9:10 a.m., seven minutes after the second plane crash, the Port Authority of NY and NJ closes all its bridges and tunnels (Volpe, "Effects", 2). At 9:17 a.m., the Federal Aviation Administration (FAA) orders all NYC airports closed until further notice.

At 9:42 a.m., the FAA directs all aircraft to land at the nearest airport, an unprecedented order (Nat. Com, *9/11 Commission Report*, 29). The entire U.S. airspace is now completely closed to all civil aviation, all departures from U.S. airports are halted, all of the approximately 4,500 aircraft in U.S. air space are guided to their nearest landing destinations and international aircraft are told not to enter U.S. territory but instead divert to Canadian air space.

At 10:20 a.m., NYC Transit suspends all subway service (Volpe, "Effects", 2). Ten minutes later, all rail service into Manhattan's Penn Station is halted as well. At 10:45 a.m., all activities of the PATH railroad service are suspended (Volpe, "Effects", 2). Meanwhile, Amtrak suspends train service nationwide and bus operator Greyhound cancels all its Northeast U.S operations.

The President, who is at the Emma E. Booker Elementary School in Sarasota, Florida, at the time of the attack, is rushed to Sarasota Airport, where Air Force One takes off at 9:54 a.m. without a clear destination, its only orders to reach high altitude as fast as possible

(Nat. Com, *9/11 Commission Report*, 39). Around the same time, Vice President Dick Cheney is rushed to the Presidential Emergency Operations Center (PEOC), the bunker structure underneath the East Wing of the White House.[4]

Upon hearing that United 93 is 80 miles out of Washington D.C., Cheney orders the plane to be shot down.Ten years later, he would say about this decision: *"Frankly, I didn't pause to think about it very much. Once one of those aircraft was hijacked, it was a weapon...it was part of my responsibility"* (qtd. in "Cheney: Order"). Curiously, it remains unclear whether or not Cheney actually had authorization already from President Bush at the time he issued the order.[5]

At Andrews Air Force Base, two F-16s are scrambled to shoot down United Airlines 93, but the fighters are not yet armed. While gearing up for takeoff, Col. Marc Sasseville says to Lt. Heather Penney: *"I'm going for the cockpit"*. *"I'll take the tail"*, Penney replies (qtd. in Hendrix 2011). When, not long after, those in the PEOC learn that an aircraft has crashed in a field in Pennsylvania, they wonder if it was indeed downed by fighters (Nat. Com, *9/11 Commission Report*, 41).

It was not. Nor would any other plane be. United 93 was the last of the hijacked planes.

With a death toll of 2,973 people (excluding the 19 dead hijackers) and more than 9,000 injured, the September 11 attacks remain the deadliest terrorist attack in U.S. history (Nat. Com, *9/11 Commission Report*, 311; Atkins, 435). Aside from the high cost in human lives and injuries, there was also extensive material damage. Of the World Trade Center complex, the North Tower (1 WTC), the South Tower (2 WTC), the Marriott hotel (3 WTC) and the 47 stories tall 7 WTC were destroyed. 4 WTC, 5 WTC, 6 WTC and the Deutsche Bank building on 130 Liberty street were severely damaged, as was the Pentagon, where the section hit by American Airlines Flight 77 collapsed. Several other buildings in the vicinity of the WTC were also damaged.

It did not take long to find out who was behind the attacks. In 1996, Osama Bin Laden, the leader of the militant islamist organization Al-Qaeda ('The Base'), had issued a fatwa — an Islamic religious decree, binding to those who follow the issuer — titled 'Declaration of War against the Americans Occupying the Land of the Two Holy Places'. In this more than 13,000 words long polemic, Bin Laden raged against the American "*occupation*" of the "*Land of the Two Holy Places*" — another name for Saudi Arabia, home to Islamic holy cities Mecca and Medina — and military activities of "*the USA and its allies*" against Muslims in other countries, such as the Philippines, Somalia, Eritrea, Chechnya and Bosnia-Herzegovina, calling upon all Muslims to concentrate on expelling the American enemy from the holy land (Bin Laden 1996).

Two years later, in February 1998, Bin Laden issued another fatwa, together with four others, among them Ayman al-Zawahiri, one of his top lieutenants.[6] This second fatwa, titled 'Declaration of the World Islamic Front for Jihad against the Jews and the Crusaders', again condemned U.S. "*occupation*" of "*the lands of Islam in the holiest of places*", as well as the "*devastation*" the "*crusader-Zionist alliance*" had done in Iraq and the continued American support of Israel (Bin Laden 1998). The instructions of the second fatwa went much further than the first one, stating that "*The ruling to kill the Americans and their allies — civilians and military — is an individual duty for every Muslim who can do it in any country in which it is possible to do it*". Six months later, on August 7, the eighth anniversary of the arrival of U.S. troops in Saudi Arabia — which had been sent there as part of Operation Desert Shield, following Iraq's invasion of Kuwait — suicide bombers connected to Al-Qaeda blew up trucks filled with explosives at the U.S. Embassies in Tanzania and Kenya, killing 224 and wounding more than 4,000 others (Zenko, 59).

Though it was quickly clear that Osama Bin Laden and Al-Qaeda were also responsible for the September 11 attacks, bringing them to justice would be a whole different matter. U.S. intelligence (correctly) suggested Bin Laden and many of his fighters were hiding in Afghanistan, but how do you fight an enemy holed up in a mountainous, unruly, inhospitable country, ruled by Islamic fundamentalists?[7] Besides, even if Osama Bin Laden was in Afghanistan, Al-Qaeda also had people in several other countries and connections with a number of affiliated organizations, making it next to impossible to completely neutralize the threat it posed.

Still, whatever the difficulties, one thing was immediately clear: the response of the most powerful country in the world would be something more than simply bombing a couple of desert training camps where fanatical Islamic teenagers were learning to gird on a suicide vest and hit something other than sand or air with their AK-47.

On Sunday evening September 16, upon returning from a weekend war council at Camp David, President Bush declared: *"This crusade — this war on terrorism — is going to take a while. And the American people must be patient. I'm going to be patient. But I can assure the American people I am determined."* (Bush, "Remarks"). The use of the word 'crusade' immediately triggered a backlash from the Muslim world, who interpreted it as though the United States were using the September 11 attacks to unleash a holy war against Islam. Two days later, the White House said the President regretted to have used the word 'crusade'. But crusade or not, war was coming. On September 20, in his address to a joint session of Congress, Bush said that *"Our war on terror begins with Al-Qaeda, but it does not end there. It will not end until every terrorist group of global reach has been found, stopped and defeated."* (Bush, "Address").

And in that war, Bush made clear, the U.S. would make no distinction between terrorists and those who harbored them. *"We will pursue nations that provide aid or safe haven to terrorism. Every nation, in every region, now has a decision to make. Either you are with us, or you are with the terrorists. From this day forward, any nation that continues to harbor or support terrorism will be regarded by the United States as a hostile regime."* (Bush, "Address").

It was not just idle talk. Neoconservatives such as Vice President Dick Cheney, Secretary of Defense Donald Rumsfeld and Deputy Secretary of Defense Paul Wolfowitz, had already started advancing an agenda aimed at protecting American national interest much more aggressively, and the September 11 attacks supplied them with an abundance of political capital for precisely that. Cheney, for his part, wasted no time in demanding a multi-year military mandate for the war on terror, warning that *"This is not a war like the Gulf War, where we had a buildup for a few months, four days of combat, and it was over. This is going to be the kind of work that will probably take years because the focus has to be not just on any one individual; the problem here is terrorism"* (qtd. in Bazinet 2001). Cheney was also quick to point the finger to Afghanistan, saying that the United States believed that the government of Afghanistan had been harboring Osama Bin Laden and that *"They have to understand, and others like them around the world have to understand, that if you provide sanctuary to terrorists, you face the full wrath of the United States of America"* (qtd. in Bazinet 2001).

Rumsfeld went even further, preemptively claiming sheer unlimited operational legality when he said that *"They* [the terrorists] *may be operating in 50 or 60 countries, including the United States — and that means that we will have to use the full weight of the United States government — political, diplomatic, financial, economic, military and unconventional, and I would underline that"* (qtd. in Bazinet 2001).

'Unconventional', a word that could mean anything, from spying on people indiscriminately to holding them without trial indefinitely and torturing them, from killing foreign nationals in countries the United States was not at war with to outright invading other countries. As it turned out, it would mean all those things.

On October 26, 2001, President Bush signed a comprehensive anti-terrorism bill into law, the USA PATRIOT Act. Among its most controversial parts were the power of indefinite detention the government gave itself and the expansion of its power to force organizations and other entities to give up information about third parties, through the issuance of a so-called National Security Letter (NSL).[8]

Special Agents in charge of a Bureau field office were authorized to issue such a Letter and demand organizations turn over various records and data pertaining to individuals (USA Patriot Act, Title V, sec. 505).[9] No probable cause or judicial oversight was required and the recipient of an NSL was forbidden from disclosing the letter was ever issued. Records show that 192,499 NSLs were issued by the FBI between 2003-06 (Yost 2010).

In 2004, the American Civil Liberties Union (ACLU) filed a lawsuit against the U.S. federal government on behalf of an anonymous Internet Service Provider.[10] In Doe v. Ashcroft, the ACLU argued that the National Security Letters the Internet Service Provider had received — particularly in combination with the non-disclosure order — violated the First, Fourth, and Fifth Amendment to the United States Constitution.[11] The court ruled in favor of the ACLU, but the government appealed.

In May 2006, the 2nd Circuit Court of Appeals returned the case to the lower court, in light of changes made to the articles regulating the NSLs after the case was filed.[12] But in his concurring opinion, Judge Richard Cardamone did warn that "*a ban on speech and an unending shroud of secrecy in perpetuity are antithetical to democratic concepts and do not fit comfortably with the fundamental rights guaranteed American citizens.*" (Doe II v. Gonzales, 23).

In September 2007, the lower court again ruled in favor of the ACLU, deeming the revisions of the USA Patriot Improvement and Reauthorization Act of 2005 insufficient. The court took particular issue with the limited level of judicial oversight as allowed by the Act, through U.S.C. Title 18, section 3511. According to the court, section 3511(b) forced the judiciary into a substandard review of non-disclosure orders, thus preventing it from properly checking the constitutional validity of such an order, something that "*could serve as a precedential step toward the development of a much larger and more fearsome vehicle for legislative or executive intrusion into the business of the courts*", which would amount to "*the legislative equivalent of breaking and entering, with an ominous free pass to the hijacking of constitutional values.*" (Doe v. Gonzales, III.F.1.c).

Several remands, appeals and moves to reconsideration later, the U.S. District Court of New York ruled in March 2010 that the government had been partially incorrect in enforcing its non-disclosure requirement in the case of 'John Doe'.[13] Part of the attachment to the NSL remained under the non- disclosure order however, because the court found the government had sufficiently demonstrated that full disclosure would run the risk of informing "*current targets of law enforcement investigations, including the particular target of the Government's ongoing inquiry in this action, as well as, potentially future targets, as to certain types of records and other materials the Government seeks through national security investigations employing NSLs.*" (Doe v. Holder, 317).

In December 2014, 'John Doe' i.e., Nicholas Merrill filed a new complaint about his non-disclosure requirement.[14] On August 28, 2015 — more than eleven years after he had first filed suit against his non-disclosure order — the U.S. District Court of New York ruled in favor of Merrill, finding the government had *"not satisfied its burden of demonstrating "good reason" to expect that disclosure of the NSL Attachment in its entirety will risk an enumerated harm, pursuant to Sections 2709 and 3511."* (Merrill v. Lynch).[15]

As for the government's power of indefinite detention of non U.S. citizens suspected of terrorism, this was legally dealt with in Title IV, section 412 of the USA Patriot Act.[16] Prisoners at Guantánamo Bay detention camp, Cuba, have been and continue to be held under this provision. As of January 2015, 35 Guantánamo detainees are designated to be held indefinitely (Human Rights First, "Guantánamo").

Several of Guantánamo's prisoners were previously held by the CIA, which operated a number of secret prisons outside the United States (a.k.a. black sites) between 2002-06 (Stout 2006).

According to the International Committee of the Red Cross, which interviewed fourteen 'high value detainees' after their transfer to Guantánamo in 2006, these prisoners were subjected to torture (Int. Com., "ICRC Report", 5).

Early 2002, the CIA wanted to know if it could use 'enhanced interrogation techniques' (more commonly known as torture) to make interrogation of terrorism suspects more effective. The proposed techniques, including *"sensory deprivation, sleep disruption, stress positions, waterboarding, and slapping"*, came from a program called SERE (Survival Evasion Resistance Escape), developed by the U.S. military in the early 1950s to help captured U.S. military personnel withstand abusive interrogation techniques (Com. On Arm., "Inquiry", xiv).

Use of these techniques on terrorism suspects was discussed by key people of the Bush administration, including Secretary of Defense Donald Rumsfeld, Director of Central Intelligence George Tenet, National Security Advisor Condoleezza Rice and Attorney General John Ashcroft (Com. On Arm., "Inquiry"). They decided to allow enhanced interrogation techniques, reasoning that such techniques did

606 - J.C. Peters

not constitute torture under U.S. or international law. On December 2, 2002, Secretary Rumsfeld signed off on the recommendation of the Department of Defense's General Counsel's Office to approve the aggressive techniques (Com. On Arm., "Inquiry", xviii- xix).[17-18]

Internationally, the initial focus of the Bush administration was on Afghanistan. The emerging Bush Doctrine emphasized America's right to preemptively strike at its enemies — unilaterally if necessary — wherever they may be holed up (National Security Council, "Security to Terrorism", 15). According to this doctrine, the War on Terror was a global, ideological struggle between the West and its values of freedom and democracy, and extremist factions — particularly militant Islamists — bent on destroying those values. To win the war, the terrorists had to be weeded out wherever they were, while democratic change had to be promoted in countries ruled by autocratic regimes.

On September 12, 2001, NATO invoked article 5 of the North Atlantic Treaty for the first time in its history, declaring the September 11 attacks against the United States an attack on all NATO member countries.[19]

On October 7, the United States launched Operation Enduring Freedom, together with the United Kingdom. Other NATO allies later joined. Combat operations started with airstrikes in Afghanistan, targeting Al-Qaeda and the Taliban, the Islamic fundamentalists who ruled most of Afghanistan. On October 14, the Taliban offered to hand over Bin Laden to a third country if the U.S. would provide proof for his involvement and halt the bombing campaign. The U.S. rejected the offer. One day later, the Taliban offered to hand over Bin Laden for trial in a country other than the U.S., without demanding evidence, in return for a halt to the bombing campaign.[20] The U.S. rejected this offer as well.

In the ensuing weeks the Taliban were driven from power by the U.S. and its allies, with the Northern Alliance — a united front of Islamic factions that had been fighting the Taliban and Al- Qaeda since 1996 — advancing under the cover of U.S. air support. In the night of November 12 the Taliban fled the capital of Kabul, where fighters of the Northern Alliance arrived the next day. Kunduz — the last

Taliban stronghold in Northern Afghanistan —fell on November 26, Kandahar — the Taliban's birthplace and last remaining stronghold in the country — on December 7. Meanwhile, Osama Bin Laden was believed to be hiding out in the mountains of Tora Bora, in Eastern Afghanistan. But although a five day bombardment of the area between December 12-17 left an estimated 200 Al-Qaeda and Taliban fighters dead, Bin Laden was not among them.[21] The Al-Qaeda leader was believed to have escaped to neighboring Pakistan, possibly on or around December 16 (Lynch 2008).[22]

The removal of the Taliban from power in Afghanistan would not be the end of the war there though. Having regrouped, the Taliban simply reverted back to the same kind of guerrilla warfare they had waged against the Russians in the 1980s. And, staying true to their beliefs, the Taliban continued to fight not only against the Afghan government and the International Security Assistance Force (ISAF), but also against the Afghan people, handing out harsh punishments for every violation of its strict Islamic code, including beheading people for activities such as celebrating with music and mixed-gender dancing (Salahuddin 2012). As of 2015, the Taliban insurgency is still ongoing.

Though the Taliban were a pain and Osama Bin Laden was possibly still hiding in Afghanistan, the neoconservatives considered Iraq a much greater threat than Afghanistan, believing Iraqi dictator Saddam Hussein was actively trying to acquire weapons of mass destruction (WMDs). In January 1998, for instance, the conservative American think tank Project for the New American Century had sent a public letter to President Bill Clinton, urging him to take action on the threat of Saddam Hussein possibly requiring the capability of delivering WMDs (Project, "Letter"). Among the signatories of the letter were soon-to-be Secretary of Defense Donald Rumsfeld, soon-to-be Deputy Secretary of Defense Paul Wolfowitz and soon-to-be Undersecretary of State for Arms Control And International Security Affairs John Bolton.

In the first hours after the planes had crashed into the Twin Towers, Secretary of Defense Donald Rumsfeld immediately ordered his aides to look for Iraqi involvement in the attacks. Notes taken by senior policy official Stephen Cambone, read: *"Best info fast. Judge whether good enough hit SH at same time - Not only UBL."*, and *"Need to move swiftly. Near term target needs - go massive - sweep it all up, things related and not."* (qtd. in Borger 2006).

The war in Iraq began on March 20, 2003, and would develop along a similar path as the one in Afghanistan, with only three weeks of major combat operations before the fall of Baghdad and the end of the 24-year rule of Iraqi dictator Saddam Hussein, on April 9, symbolized by the toppling of a large Saddam statue in Firdos Square, central Baghdad, that same day. No WMDs were found in Iraq though, nor any evidence of any connection between the regime of Saddam Hussein and Al- Qaeda.

Eight months later, on December 13, 2003, Saddam Hussein himself was captured by American forces. He was subsequently tried, found guilty of crimes against humanity, sentenced to death and hanged, on December 30, 2006. By then, an Islamic fundamentalist insurgency against the U.S coalition forces in Iraq had grown into a full-blown civil war. After the withdrawal of U.S. troops in December 2011, violence between Sunni and Shi'a Muslims continued.

In September 2014, a U.S.-led coalition launched a bombing campaign against the Sunni jihadist group known as the Islamic State of Iraq and Syria (ISIS, a.k.a ISIL, a.k.a IS), which had conquered large swaths of territory in civil war-torn Syria and Iraq in the preceding months. In November 2014, President Obama authorized doubling the number of military advisers in Iraq, from 1,500 to 3,000, as part of the expansion of the American military campaign against the self-proclaimed Islamic State (Cooper 2014).

When Obama assumed office in January 2009, he promised winds of change. But Guantánamo Bay detention camp still imprisons people without charge, the FBI can still issue National Security Letters without a court order and U.S. drones are still killing foreign nationals in countries the U.S is not at war with. And although the U.S. did indeed withdraw its troops from Iraq (at least before it started sending them back in), the 'War on Terror' — declared by the Bush administration in the wake of 9/11 — seems far from over. If anything, it is only just beginning.[23]

It's a brave new world.

1   Cheney, "Remarks".

2   Huxley, 211-12.

3   The hijackers had diverted the course of United 93 in the direction of Washington. The intended target remains uncertain, but it is generally believed that the target was either the White House or the Capitol. According to the 9/11 Commission Report, Osama Bin Laden had told Ramzi bin al-Shibh to advise Mohamed Atta — one of the leaders of the operation and hijacker-pilot of American Airlines Flight 11 — that he preferred the White House over the Capitol (Nat. Com, *9/11 Commission Report*, 243). Atta deemed the White House too difficult a target though and had assigned Ziad Jarrah — the terrorist-pilot of United 93 — the Capitol as target, according to bin al-Shibh (Nat. Com, *9/11 Commission Report*, 244).

4   Several accounts conflict with each other as to the exact time the vice president arrived at the PEOC. The 9/11 Commission Report concluded that the vice president arrived at the PEOC at 9:58 a.m., despite *"conflicting evidence"* (Nat. Com, *9/11 Commission Report*, 40).

5   The 9/11 Commission Report states Cheney had a phone conversation with the President, *"sometime before 10:10 to 10:15"*, during which National Security Advisor Condoleezza Rice heard the Vice President say: *"Sir, the CAPs [Combat Air Patrol] are up. Sir, they're going to want to know what to do."*, followed by him saying *"Yes sir."* (qtd. in Nat. Com, *9/11 Commission Report*, 40). Between 10:10 and 10:15, the Vice President is asked for authorization to engage United 93 (unaware that the plane had already crashed several minutes earlier, at 10:03). Cheney readily gives it (Nat. Com, *9/11 Commission Report*, 41). On the suggestion of White House Deputy Chief of Staff Joshua Bolten, Cheney then places a logged call to the President, at 10:18, to obtain confirmation, which was given.

6   Al-Zawahiri would succeed Bin Laden as leader of Al-Qaeda in May 2011, after the latter was killed by U.S. Navy SEALs.

7   At the time, most of Afghanistan was controlled by the Taliban, another Islamic fundamentalist movement.

8   Per sec. 412, 236A.a.3 and 236A.a.6 of the Patriot Act, the Attorney General has, under certain circumstances, the power to detain immigrants for an indefinite number of six month periods, *"if the release of the alien will threaten the national security of the United States or the safety of the community or any person"* (USA Patriot Act, 236A.a.6).

9   Sec. 505 of Title V of the Patriot Act makes changes to U.S. Code: Title 18. sec. 2709 - Counterintelligence access to telephone toll and transactional records. Prior to the changes, an NSL could only be issued by the Director of the FBI or *"his designee not lower than Deputy Assistant Director"* (U.S. Code: Title

18. sec. 2709, b, c.1).

10 In 2010 it was revealed the John Doe was Nicholas Merrill, of Calyx Internet Access (Zetter 2010).

11 The First Amendment protects free speech, the Fourth protects against unreasonable searches and seizures and requires a judicially sanctioned warrant supported by probable cause, the Fifth demands due process of law when the state deprives an individual of life, liberty or property.

12 By way of the USA Patriot Improvement and Reauthorization Act of 2005.

13 Specifically, the court ruled that the non-disclosure requirement had to be lifted where it concerned *"(1) material within the scope of information that the NSL statute identifies as permissible for the FBI to obtain through use of NSLs, and (2) material that the FBI has publicly acknowledged it has previously requested by means of NSLs."* (Doe v. Holder).

14 Section 3511(b)(3) of 18 U.S.C., in effect between March 9, 2006-June 1, 2015, required NSL recipients to wait a year or more after unsuccessfully challenging a non-disclosure requirement before trying again. This restriction has since been lifted.

15 As of 2015, the non-disclosure order for recipients of an NSL remains, though the USA Freedom Act, signed into law by President Barack Obama on June 2, 2015, now permits recipients of an NSL to discuss it with: *"those persons to whom disclosure is necessary in order to comply with the request; an attorney in order to obtain legal advice or assistance regarding the request; other persons as permitted by the Director of the Federal Bureau of Investigation or the designee of the Director."* (USA Freedom Act, Sec. 502. c.2). The issuance of an NSL still does not require a court order.

16 Through the National Defense Authorization Act for Fiscal Year 2012, the government's authority of indefinite detention was expanded to include U.S. citizens who committed or supported terrorist acts against the U.S. or its allies and who are captured outside the United States (Nat. Def., Title X, subtitle D, section 1021).

17 In a handwritten note that Rumsfeld added to his signed recommendation, he expressed his apparent disapproval to one of the limits proposed in the memo, writing: *"I stand for 8-10 hours a day. Why is standing limited to 4 hours?"* (qtd. in Com. On Arm., "Inquiry", xix).

18 On January 22, 2009, two days after assuming office, President Obama signed Executive Order 13491, which barred the use of enhanced interrogation techniques beyond those permitted by the U.S. military.

19 As of 2017, it remains the only time article 5 of the NATO treaty has been invoked.

20 This second offer was done by the more moderate Taliban foreign minister Wakil Ahmed Muttawakil, apparently without the approval of supreme Taliban leader Mullah Omar (Burns 2001). In July 2001, the same Wakil Muttawakil

had also reportedly warned U.S. diplomats in Peshawar, Pakistan, of a large, imminent attack by Al- Qaeda in the United States. Muttawakil was apparently deeply unhappy with the presence of the Arab militants in his country and said he feared "*the guests were going to destroy the guesthouse*" (Clark 2002; Burke 2002).

21 A 2009 report by the Committee on Foreign Relations of the U.S. Senate stated it was never clear exactly how many Al-Qaeda fighters were at Tora Bora during the battle, but that the consensus figure was around 1,000 (Com. On For., "Tora Bora", 14). About 800 fighters were estimated to have escaped during an overnight pause in the bombing, which had been ordered to avoid killing Al-Qaeda fighters who were supposedly about to surrender, though this later turned out to be a hoax (Com. On For., "Tora Bora", 11). Only 20 fighters or so were taken prisoner after the battle (Com. On For., "Tora Bora", 14).

22 It would take almost ten years before U.S. special forces would finally kill 'OBL' in a private compound in Abbottabad, Pakistan, on May 2, 2011.

23 As of January 19, 2017, 41 detainees still remain at Guantánamo Bay (Rosenberg, "Obama").

Epilogue

WILL WE BE ALRIGHT?

Thinking about our future is almost impossible without thinking about our past. We have been shaped by it, continue to be influenced by it and try to draw lessons from it, to 'prevent history from repeating itself'.

Because, tellingly, we consider history repeating itself as something negative. Whenever someone says "*history repeats itself*", it is invariably to lament yet another war, another famine, another recession, another man-made disaster or some other thing we would prefer *not* to repeat itself. History, it seems, is more often something to be ashamed of than to be proud of. Ashamed of all the massacres, persecutions and genocides, of all the oppression and exploitation, the intolerance, the hatred, the indifference. If we are able to step away for a moment from finger-pointing any one tribe for having committed this or that particular atrocity, we cannot but admit that as a species we have failed to live up to the expectations that come from being created in His own image (unless you believe in a very cruel god).

Thus, looking at our history easily elicits fear for our future.

Then again, the very fact that many now condemn what was once believed normal and natural, or at the very least inescapable — things like war, persecution, slavery, torture, dictatorial rule, the absence of the rule of law, racial segregation and gender inequality, to name but a few — can undeniably be called progress. Clearly, our ways are not set in stone and we are indeed learning from the past.

Still, how can we trust ourselves to steer our destiny in the right direction, knowing that less than a century ago we developed weapons to infect populations with the bubonic plague on a massive scale. Knowing that we carted off like cattle millions of Jews from all over Europe to concentration camps specifically constructed to exterminate people in an industrial-like fashion. Knowing that, in the end, all that stood between us and a nuclear holocaust was a Russian submarine commander who kept his cool when others did not.

Perhaps we cannot and perhaps we should not either. Perhaps, knowing what we know about our past — and our present, for that matter — it is best to remain unconvinced about our species' capability to completely overcome the primitive instincts lodged in the 'reptilian' part of our brain. Besides, whether we want to or not, we hold our collective destiny in our collective hands. We are like the small boys from William Golding's *Lord of the Flies*, stranded on a deserted island with no hope of being rescued.

It is up to us to write a different ending.

END

BIBLIOGRAPHY

Abbatiello, John. *Anti-Submarine Warfare in Wold War I: British Naval Aviation and the Defeat of the U.Boats.* London: Routledge. 2006. Print.

Abbott, John S. C. *The Empire of Russia; from the Remotest Periods to the Present Time.* New York: Mason Brothers. 1860. Print.

Absher, Kenneth Michael. *Mindsets and Missiles: A Firsthand Account of the Cuban Missile Crisis.* lulu.com. 2012. Print.

Adams, George Burton. *Constitutional History of England.* New York: H. Holt. 1921. Print.

Adams, Guy B, and Danny L. Balfour. *Unmasking Administrative Evil.* Third Edition. Armonk: M.E. Sharpe. 2009. Print.

Adams, Val. "TV: Coverage of March - Nielsen Reports 46% Higher Audience Than in Normal Daytime Hours." *The New York Times.* August 29, 1963. Print.

Adamson, Melitta Weiss. *Food in Medieval Times.* Westport: Greenwood Publishing Group. 2004. Print.

Adamthwaite, Anthony P. *The Making of the Second World War.* New York: Routledge. 1992. Print.

Aeschylus. *Persians.* Trans. Herbert Weir Smyth. Cambridge: Harvard UP. 1926. Print.

Agoston, Gabor, and Bruce Masters. *Encyclopedia of the Ottoman Empire.* New York: Infobase Publishing. Print. 2009.

Aiello, Leslie C., and Peter Wheeler. "The Expensive Tissue Hypothesis: The Brain and the Digestive System in Human and Primate Evolution." *Current Anthropology* Vol 36, No.2 (1995): 199-221. Print.

Aikin, John and William Enfield. *General biography; or, Lives, critical and historical, of the most eminent persons of all ages, countries, conditions, and professions.* Vol. I. London: G.G. and J. Robinson. 1799. Print.

Akkermans, Peter M. M. G., and Glenn M. Schwartz. *The Archaeology of Syria: From Complex Hunter-Gatherers to Early Urban Societies (ca. 16,000-300 BC)*. Cambridge: Cambridge UP. 2003. Print.

Aldrich, Richard J. "OSS, CIA and European Unity: The American Committee on United Europe, 1948-60." *Diplomacy & Statecraft*, Vol. 8, No. 1 (March 1997): 184-227. London: Frank Cass. Published online 19 October 2007 by Taylor & Francis Group. tandfonline.com. Web. Aug. 31, 2015.

Aldridge, Alfred Owen. *Thomas Paine's American Ideology*. Cranbury: Associated UP. 1984. Print.

Alexander, John K. *Samuel Adams: America's Revolutionary Politician*. Rowman & Littlefield. 2004. Print.

Allcorn, William. *The Maginot Line, 1928-45*. Oxford: Osprey Publishing. 2003. Print.

Allen, Larry. *The Encyclopedia of Money*. Santa Barbara: ABC-CLIO. 2009. Print.

Allen, Phyllis. "Problems Connected with the Development of the Telescope (1609-1687)." *Isis*. Vol. 34, No. 4. 1943: 302-311.

Allen, Robert C. "The Great Divergence in European Wages and Prices from the Middle Ages to the First World War." *Explorations in Economic History*. Vol. 38. 2001: 411-447. Print.

Allen, S.J., and Emilie Amt. *The Crusades: A Reader*. Second edition. U of Toronto P. 2014. Print.

Allison, Robert J. *The Boston Massacre*. Beverly: Commonwealth Editions. 2006. Print.

Alpert, William T, ed. *The Vietnamese Economy and its Transformation to an Open Market System*. Armonk: M.E. Sharpe. 2005. Print.

Anderson, Herbert L., Enrico Fermi and Leo Szilard. "Neutron Production and Absorption in Uranium." *Physical Review*. Vol. 56. Aug. 1, 1939: 284-286. Print.

Anderson, James Maxwell. *Daily Life During the Spanish Inquisition*. Westport: Greenwood Press. 2002. Print.

Anderson, Roberta and Dominic Bellenger, ed. *Medieval Worlds: A Sourcebook*. London: Routledge. 2003. Print.

Andrews, Robert. *The Columbia Dictionary of Quotations*. New York: Columbia UP. 1993. Print.

Appian, *The Civil Wars*. Trans. Horace White. London: Macmillan and Co., ltd. 1899. Print.

Appian, *The Foreign Wars*. (includes *Punic Wars*). Trans. Horace White. New York: The Macmillan Company. 1899. Print.

Appleby, Joyce Oldham. *Knowledge and Postmodernism in Historical Perspective*. New York: Routledge. 1996. Print.

Aquinas, Thomas. *Summa Theologica Volume I - Part I*. Trans. Fathers of the English Dominican Province. New York: Cosimo, Inc. 2013. Print.

Arad, Yitzhak. *Belzec, Sobibor, Treblinka: The Operation Reinhard Death Camps*. Bloomington: Indiana UP. 1987. Print.

Arad, Yitzhak, Israel Gutman, & Abraham Margaliot, ed. *Documents on the Holocaust: Selected Sources on the Destruction of the Jews of Germany and Austria, Poland, and the Soviet Union*. Eighth edition. Lea Ben Dor, trans. U of Nebraska P. 1999. Print.

Armitage, Simon J., et al. "The Southern Route "Out of Africa." Evidence for an Early Expansion of Modern Humans into Arabia". *Science* vol. 331 no. 6016 (2011): 453-456. Print.

Arrian. *History of the Expedition of Alexander the Great, and Conquest of Persia*. Trans. John Rooke. London: J.Davis. 1812. Print.

Arsenault, Raymond. *Freedom Riders: 1961 and the Struggle for Racial Justice*. Oxford: Oxford UP. 2006.

Articles of Confederation. March 1, 1781. Avalon Project, Yale Law. Web. June 2, 2015.

Ascher, Abraham. *The Revolution of 1905: Russia in Disarray*. Stanford UP. 1988. Print.

Ashraf, Quamrul, Oded Galor. "Dynamics and Stagnation in the Malthusian Epoch." *American Economic Review*. Vol. 101(5). 2011: 2003-41.

Ashton, T.S. *Iron and steel in the industrial revolution*. Manchester: Manchester UP. 1924. Print.

Åslund, Anders. "An Assessment of Putin's Economic Policy." Peterson

Institute for International Economics. July 2008. Web. May 22, 2015.

Åslund, Anders. *Russia's Capitalist Revolution: Why Market Reform Succeeded and Democracy Failed.* Washington: Peterson Institute for International Economics. 2007. Print.

Assmann, Jan. *Moses the Egyptian: The Memory of Egypt in Western Monotheism.* Cambridge: Harvard UP. 1998. Print.

Atkins, Stephen E., ed. *The 9/11 Encyclopedia.* Second Edition. Santa Barbara: ABC-CLIO. 2011. Print.

Atomic Energy Commission. "Script from a radio broadcast sponsored by Gulf Oil Corporation. The script includes live interviews with employees who lived and worked at Oak Ridge during the development of the atom bomb." Records of the Atomic Energy Commission, 1923-1978. February 9, 1947. research.archives.gov/id/281583?q=281583. ARC: 281583. NAIL Control Number: NRCA-326-OAK004-RADSCRIP. Web. Aug. 25, 2015.

Bachmann, Steve. "Starting again with the Mayflower...England's Civil War and America's Bill of Rights." *Quinnipiac Law Review.* Vol. 20. 2000: 193-286.

Bachrach, Bernard. *Charlemagne's Early Campaigns (768-777): A Diplomatic and Military Analysis.* Leiden: Brill. 2013. Print.

Bahrani, Zainab and Marc Van De Mieroop, trans & ed. Translator's Preface. *The Invention of Cuneiform: Writing in Sumer.* Jean-Jacques Glassner. Baltimore: Johns Hopkins UP. 2003. Print.

Baker, Daniel B. *Explorers and Discoverers of the World.* Gale Research. 1993. Print.

Baker, Geoffrey the. *The Chronicle of Geoffrey Le Baker of Swinbrook.* David Preest, trans. Richard Barber, intr. and notes. Woodbridge: The Boydell Press. 2012. Print.

Balter, Michael. *The Goddess and the Bull: Catalhoyuk: An Archaeological Journey to the Dawn of Civilization.* New York: Simon & Schuster. 2005. Print.

Baran, Paul. "Reliable Digital Communications Systems Using Unreliable Network Repeater Nodes." RAND Corporation. P-1995. May 27, 1960. Print.

Barber, Lucy Grace. *Marching on Washington: The Forging of an*

American Political Tradition. Berkely: U of California P. 2004. Print.

Barenblatt, Daniel. A Plague upon Humanity: The Secret Genocide of Axis Japan's Germ Warfare Operation. New York: HarperCollins. 2004. Print.

Barker, Graeme. *The Agricultural Revolution in Prehistory: Why did Foragers become Farmers?* Oxford: Oxford UP. 2006. Print.

Barker, Juliet. Agincourt: *The King, the Campaign; the Battle.* Abacus. 2005. Print.

Barnes, Brooks. "In a Breathtaking First, NASA's Voyager 1 Exits the Solar System." *The New York Times.* nytimes.com. September 12, 2013. Web. Sep. 6, 2015.

Barnes, Thomas G., and Gerald D. Feldman. *Nationalism, Industrialization, and Democracy, 1815-1914. A Documentary History of Modern Europe Volume III.* UP of America. 1980. Print.

Bartlett, John Russell. *A History of the Destruction of His Britannic Majesty's Schooner Gaspee, in Narragansett Bay, on the 10th June, 1772.* Providence. 1861. Print.

Bartley, Paula. *Emmeline Pankhurst.* New York: Routledge. 2002. Print.

Bartsch, Matthias, Dietmar Hipp, and Maximilian Popp. "Integration Case: Court to Rule on Swim Lessons for Muslim Girls." Paul Cohen, trans. spiegel.de. Sep. 9, 2013. Web. Mar. 5, 2015.

Bateman, Fred, and Thomas Weiss. *A Deplorable Scarcity: The Failure of Industrialization in the Slave Economy.* U of North Carolina P. 1981. Print.

Bazinet, Kenneth R. "A Fight VS. Evil, Bush and Cabinet Tell U.S." New York Daily News. Sep. 17, 2001. Web. Jan. 26, 2015.

BEA. "Texas". Bureau of Economic Analysis. U.S. Department of Commerce. bea.gov. Web. May 28, 2015.

Belknap, Michael R. *Federal Law and Southern Order: Racial Violence and Constitutional Conflict in the Post-Brown South.* U of Georgia P. 1995. First edition 1987. Print.

Bell, Christopher, and Bruce Elleman, ed. *Naval Mutinies of the Twentieth Century: An International Perspective.* Routledge. 2004. Print.

Bears, Edwin C., and Bryce Suderow. *The Petersburg Campaign: The*

Western Front Battles, September 1864 - April 1865. El Dorado Hills: Savas Beatie. 2014. Print.

Bendersky, Joseph W. *A History of Nazi Germany: 1919-1945*. Rowman & Littlefield. 2000. Print.

Benedictow, Ole Jørgen. *The Black Death, 1346-1353: The Complete History*. Boydell Press. 2004. Print.

Bennett, George D. *The United States Army: Issues, Background and Bibliography*. Huntington: Nova Science. 2002. Print.

Berg, Pierre, and Brian Brock. *Scheisshaus Luck: Surviving the Unspeakable in Auschwitz and Dora*. Amacom. 2008. Print.

Bergeron, David M. *King James and Letters of Homoerotic Desire*. Iowa City: U of Iowa P. 1999. Print.

Bernanke, Ben S. *Essays on the Great Depression*. Princeton: Princeton UP. 2000. Print.

Bernanke, Ben S. "Monetary Policy and the Global Economy." federalreserve.gov. Mar 25, 2013. Web. July 27, 2015.

Berners-Lee, Tim. "A Brief History of the Web." 1993/4. http://www.w3.org/DesignIssues/TimBook-old/History.html. Web. October 10, 2015.

Berners-Lee, Tim. "Information Management: A Proposal." March 1989, May 1990. http://www.w3.org/History/1989/proposal.html. Web. October 10, 2015.

Bernstein, Jeremy. *Hitler's Uranium Club: The Secret Recordings at Farm Hall*. New York: Copernicus. 2001. Print.

Berstein, Serge. *The Republic of de Gaulle 1958-1969*. Cambridge UP. 1993. Print.

Bethmann, Ludwig Conrad, and Georg Heinrich Pertz, ed. *Monumenta Germaniae Historica. Scriptores Rerum Germanicarum. Chronicon Novaliciense*. Hanover: Hahn, 1846. Print.

Billington, James H., and Library of Congress. *Respectfully Quoted: A Dictionary of Quotations*. Dover Publications. 2010. Print.

"Bill of Rights 1689. An Act Declaring the Rights and Liberties of the Subject and Settling the Succession of the Crown." Avalon Project, Yale Law. Web. 20 May 2015.

Bin Laden, Osama, et al. "Declaration of the World Islamic Front for Jihad against the Jews and the Crusaders." Feb. 23, 1998. fas.org, trans. "Jihad Against Jews and Crusaders". Web. Jan. 26, 2015.

Bin Laden, Osama. "Declaration of War against the Americans Occupying the Land of the Two Holy Places." Aug. 1996. Newsdesk, trans. pbs.org. "Bin Laden's Fatwa." Web. Jan. 26, 2015.

Bishop, Morris. *The Middle Ages*. Mariner Books. 2001. Print.

Bismarck, Otto von. *Bismarck, the man and the statesman; being the reflections and reminiscences of Otto, Prince von Bismarck*. Vol. II. New York: Harper & Brothers. 1899. Print.

Black, Jeremy. *George III: America's Last King*. Yale UP. 2008. Print.

Blake, Robert, and Wm. Roger Louis, ed. *Churchill*. Oxford: Oxford UP. 1999. Print.

Blum, William. *Killing Hope: US Military and CIA Interventions Since World War II*. London: Zed. 2003. Print.

Blumenthal, Karen. *Six Days in October: The Stock Market Crash of 1929*. New York: Simon and Schuster. 2002. Print.

Bodart, Gaston. *Losses of Life in Modern Wars: Austria-Hungary; France*. Harald Westergaard, ed. Oxford: Clarendon Press. 1916. Print.

Boemeke, Manfred F., Gerald D. Feldman, and Elisabeth Glaser, ed. *The Treaty of Versailles: A reassessment after 75 Years*. Cambridge: Cambridge UP. 1998. Print.

Boldrin, Michele, and David K. Levine. *Against Intellectual Monopoly*. Cambridge: Cambridge UP. 2008. Print.

Boltz, W. *The Origin and Early Development of the Chinese Writing System*. (American Oriental Series. 78). New Haven, CT: American Oriental Society. 1994. Print.

Bonekemper, III, Edward H. *A Victor, Not a Butcher: Ulysses S. Grant's Overlooked Military Genius*. Washington: Eagle. 2004. Print.

Booth, John. *The Battle of Waterloo: Containing the Accounts Published by Authority, British and Foreign, and Other Relative Documents, with Circumstantial Details, Previous and After the Battle, from a Variety of Authentic and Original Sources: to which is Added an Alphabetical*

List of the Officers Killed and Wounded, from 15th to 26th June, 1815, and the Total Loss of Each Regiment. London: J. Booth. 1815. Print.

Borger, Julian. "Blogger bares Rumsfeld's post 9/11 orders." The Guardian. Feb. 24, 2006. Web. Jan. 28, 2015.

Borough, Sir John. *Notes of the Treaty Carrier on at Ripon between King Charles I and the Covenanters of Scotland, A.D. 1640.* John Bruce, ed. Camden Society, 1869 No. C. Print.

Botchway, Francis, ed. *Documents in International Economic Law.* London: Routledge. 2006. Print.

Bourdet, Yves. *The Economics of Transition in Laos: From Socalism to ASEAN integration.* Cheltenham: Edward Elgar. 2000. Print.

Bowsky, William M, ed. *The Black Death: A Turning Point in History?* New York: Holt, Rinehart and Winston. 1971. Print.

Bradshaw, Richard Lee. *God's Battleaxe: The Life of Lord President John Bradshawe.* Xlibris. 2010. Print.

Branigan, Tania. "China's jasmine revolution: police but no protesters line streets of Beijing." theguardian.com. Febr 27, 2011. Web. July 28, 2015.

"Brazil: 1988 Constitution with 1996 Reforms." Georgetown University Political Database of the Americas. N.d. Web. 9 May 2015.

Breasted, James Henry. *Ancient Times, a History of the Early World: An Introduction to the Study of Ancient History and the Career of Early Man.* Boston: Ginn and Company. 1916. Print.

Briant, Pierre. *From Cyrus to Alexander: A History of the Persian Empire.* Peter T. Daniels, trans. Eisenbrauns. 2002. Print.

Brown v. Board of Education of Topeka. 347 U.S. 483. Supreme Court of the United States. 1954. Supreme Court Collection. Legal Information Inst., Cornell U. Law School, n.d. Web. 15 Jan. 2016.

Brown, Weldon A. *Empire Or Independence: A Study in the Failure of Reconciliation, 1774-1783.* Port Washington: Kennikat Press. 1966. Print.

Browne, G. F. *Alcuin of York: Lectures Delivered in the Cathedral Church of Bristal in 1907 and 1908.* London: Society for Promoting Christian Knowledge. 1908. Print.

Browning, Christopher R. *The Origins of the Final Solution: The Evolution of Nazi Jewish Policy, September 1939-March 1942.* U of Nebraska P. 2007. Print.

Brucker, Gene A. *Renaissance Florence.* Berkeley: U of C Pres. 1969. Print.

Bruni, Leonardo. *History of the Florentine People: Books I-IV.* James Hankins, translater and editor. Cambridge: Harvard UP. 2001. Print.

Bull, Stephen and Mike Seed. *Bloody Preston: Battle of Preston, 1648.* Carnegie. 1998. Print.

Bundy, McGeorge. "Memorandum of Discussion on Cuba, Cabinet Room, January 28, 1961." January 28, 1961. Washington. history. state.gov. Historical Documents, Foreign Relations of the United States, 1961-1963, Volume X, Cuba, January 1961-September 1962, Document 30. Web. 12 December 2015.

Burgess, Colin, and Rex Hall. *The First Soviet Cosmonaut Team: Their Lives and Legacies.* Springer-Praxis Books. 2009. Print.

Buringh, Eltjo and Jan Luiten van Zanden. "Charting the "Rise of the West": Manuscripts and Printed Books in Europe, A Long-Term Perspective from the Sixth through Eighteenth Centuries." *The Journal of Economic History.* Vol. 69, No. 2. June 2009: 409-445.

Burke, Edmund. *The Annual Register, or a View of the History, Politics, and Literature, for the Year 1804.* Vol. 46. J. Dodsley. 1806. Print.

Burke, Jason. "Warning of 9/11 'ignored'." Sep. 8, 2002. theguardian. com. Web. Jan. 28, 2015.

Burns, John F. "Taliban Figure Asks Bombing Halt to Make Deal on bin Laden." Oct. 16, 2001. nytimes.com. Web. Jan. 28, 2015.

Burns, Richard Dean, and Joseph M. Siracusa. *A Global History of the Nuclear Arms Race: Weapons, Strategy, and Politics.* Santa Barbara: ABC-CLIO. 2013. Print.

Bury, John Bagnell. *A History of Greece to the Death of Alexander the Great.* London: Macmillan And Co, Limited. 1900. Print.

Burris, Joe. "North County student wins Intel Science Fair's top prize." The Baltimore Sun. May 24, 2012. Web. May 6, 2015.

Bush, George W. "Address to a Joint Session of Congress and the

American People." georgewbush-whitehouse.archives.org. Sep. 20, 2001. Web. Jan. 26, 2015.

Bush, George W. "Remarks by the President Upon Arrival." georgewbush-whitehouse.archives.org. Sep.16, 2001. Web. Jan. 26, 2015.

Butcher, Tim. *The Trigger: Hunting the Assassin Who Brought the World to War*. New York: Grove Press. 2014. Print.

Byfield, Ted. *The Renaissance: God in Man, A.D. 1300 to 1500: But Amid its Splendors, Night Falls on Medieval Christianity*. The Society to Explore and Record Christian History. 2010. Print.

Byrne, Joseph Patrick. *Daily Life During the Black Death*. Greenwood Publishing Group. 2006. Print.

Byron, George Gordon, Lord. *Don Juan: In Sixteen Cantos, with notes*. Halifax: Milner and Sowerby. 1837. Print.

Caesar, Julius. *Civil Wars*. Trans. A. G. Peskett. Loeb Classical Library. 1914. Print.

Cantelon, Philip L, Richard G. Hewlett, and Robert C. Williams, ed. *The American Atom: A Documentary History of Nuclear Policies from the Discovery of Fission to the Present*." Second Edition. U of Pennsylvania P. 1991. Print.

Caranci, Paul F. *North Providence: A History and the People Who Shaped It*. Charleston: The History Press. 2012. Print.

Carlyle, Thomas. *The French Revolution: A History*. London: Thomas Nelson & Sons. 1903. Print.

Carmichael, Joel. *A Short History of the Russian Revolution*. Basic Books. 1964. Print.

Carson, Jon. "Our States Remain United. Official White House Response to Peacefully grant the State of Texas to withdraw from the United States of America and create its own NEW government." petitions. whitehouse.gov. n.d. Web. May 26, 2015.

Carter, Dan T. *The Politics of Rage: George Wallace, the Origins of the New Conservatism, and the Transformation of American Politics*. LSU Press. 2000. Print.

Carter, Jimmy. "Voyager Spacecraft Statement by the President." July

29, 1977. presidency.ucsb.edu. Web. September 13, 2015.

Caulaincourt, Armand de. *With Napoleon in Russia*. Mineola: Dover. 2005. Print.

Cerf, Vinton, Yogen Dalal, and Carl Sunshine. "Specification of Internet Transmission Control Program." *Network Working Group*. Dec. 1974. tools.ietf.org. Web. October 9, 2015.

Ceruzzi, Paul E. *A History of Modern Computing*. Cambridge: MIT Press. 2003. Print.

Ceruzzi, Paul E. *Computing: A Concise History*. Cambridge: MIT Press. 2012. Print.

Chalk, Frank and Kurt Jonassohn. *The History and Sociology of Genocide*. Yale UP. 1990. Print.

Chamberlain, Neville. "Peace for Our Time." September 30, 1938. British Historical Documents. britannia.com. Web. Apr. 2, 2015.

Chamberlain, Neville. "Statement by the Prime Minister in the House of Commons on March 31, 1939." The Avalon Project: The British War Bluebook. avalon.law.yale.edu. n.d. Web. Apr. 2, 2015.

Chambers, John Whiteclay, ed. *The Oxford Companion to American Military History*. Oxford: Oxford UP. 1999. Print.

Chandler, David G. *The Campaigns of Napoleon*. New York: Simon and Schuster. 2009. Print.

Chandos Herald. *Life of the Black Prince: by the Herald of Sir John Chandos*. Mildred K. Pope and Eleanor C. Lodge, trans. Oxford: Clarendon Press. 1910. Print.

Chase, Kenneth Warren. *Firearms: A Global History to 1700*. Cambridge: Cambridge UP. 2003. Print.

Chateaubriand, François-René de. *Oeuvres de Chateaubriand*. Vol. 5. Analyse Raisonnée de L'histoire de France. Paris: Dufour et Mulat. 1852. Print.

Cheney, Richard B. "Remarks by Richard B. Cheney." *American Enterprise Institute*. May 21, 2009. Web. 23 January 2015.

"Cheney: Order to Shoot Down Hijacked 9/11 Planes 'Necessary'." foxnews.com. Sep. 4, 2011. Web. 25 January 2015.

Chernow, Ron. *Alexander Hamilton*. New York: Penguin. 2004. Print.

Chesney, Charles Cornwallis. *Waterloo Lectures: A Study Of The Campaign Of 1815.* Third Edition. London: Longmans, Green. 1874. Print.

Chickering, Roger. *Imperial Germany and the Great War, 1914-1918.* Second Edition. Cambridge: Cambridge UP. 2004. Print.

Childe, V. Gordon. "The Urban Revolution." *The Town Planning Review* vol. 21, no. 1 (1950): 3-17. Liverpool UP. Print.

Childs, Wendy R. Ed. and Trans. *Vita Edwardi Secundi: The Life of Edward the Second.* Original ca. 1326. Author unknown. Oxford: Oxford UP. 2005. Print.

"China police break up 'protests' after online appeal." bbc.com. Feb. 20, 2011. Web. July 28, 2015.

Chrisafis, Angelique. "Vive la révolution! French MP starts race to Napoleonland." theguardian.com. Feb. 14, 2012. Web. June 4, 2015.

Christoffersen, John. "Robert Schiller: Income Inequality Is 'Most Important Problem." huffingtonpost.com. October 15, 2013. Web. October 5, 2015.

Chuĭkov, Vasiliĭ Ivanovich. *The Beginning of the Road.* Macgibbon & Kee. 1963. Print.

Churchill, Winston S. "The Few." August 20, 1940. The Churchill Centre. winstonchurchill.org. Web. Apr. 3, 2015.

Churchill, Winston S. *Their Finest Hour.* Volume II of the Second World War. New York: Houghton Mifflin Harcourt. 1986. Print.

Churchill, Winston S. *Triumph and Tragedy: The Second World War, Volume 6.* RosettaBooks. 2010. First edition 1953. Print.

Churchill, Winston S. "We Shall Fight on the Beaches". June 4, 1940. The Churchill Centre. winstonchurchill.org. Web. 03 Apr. 2015.

CIA. "The 27th CPSU Congress: Gorbachev's Unfinished Business." CIA. Directorate of Intelligence. SOV 86-10023. April 1986. Print.

Cicero, Marcus Tullius. *Tusculan Disputations.* Trans. W.H. Main. London: W. Pickering. 1824. Print.

"Circular of the Central Committee Party of China on the Great Proletarian Cultural Revolution." Communist Party of China. May 16, 1966. marxists.org. Web. September 26, 2015.

Clarendon, Edward Hyde, Earl of. *The History of the Rebellion and Civil Wars in England*. Vol III. Oxford: Oxford UP. 1839. Print.

Clarendon, Edward Hyde, Earl of. *The History of the Rebellion and Civil Wars in England, to which is added an Historical View of the Affairs of Ireland*. Vol IV. Oxford: Clarendon P. 1826. Print.

Clark, Christopher M. *Iron Kingdom: The Rise and Downfall of Prussia, 1600-1947*. Harvard UP. 2006. Print.

Clark, Gregory. *A Farewell to Alms: A Brief Economic History of the World*. Princeton UP. 2007. Print.

Clark, Kate. "Taleban 'warned US of huge attack'." bbc.co.uk. Sept. 7, 2002. Web. 28 January 2015.

Clausewitz, Carl von. *On War*. Michael Howard and Peter Paret, ed. and trans. Princeton UP. 1989. First German edition (Vom Kriege), 1832. Print.

Cliff, Nigel. "Introduction." *The Travels*. Marco Polo. Penguin. 2015.

CNN. "9/11 News CNN Sept. 11, 2001 8 48 am - 9 29 am September 11, 2001". youtube.com. Web. January 23, 2015.

Coker, Rachel. "History professor: Civil War death toll has been underestimated." Binghamton University. binghamton.edu. Sept. 21, 2011. Web. June 18, 2015.

Committee On Armed Services United States Senate. "Inquiry Into The Treatment Of Detainees In U.S. Custody." Committee Print. 20 Nov. 2008. Print.

Committee On Foreign Relations United States Senate. "Tora Bora Revisited: How We Failed To Get Bin Laden And Why It Maters Today." Committee Print. 30 Nov. 2009. Print.

Compendium of the Catechism of the Catholic Church. Libreria Editrice Vaticana. 2005. vatican.va. Web. Apr 11, 2015.

Constitution of the People's Republic of China. npc.gov.cn. Dec. 4, 1982. Web. July 28, 2015.

Constitution of the United States. The Constitution of the United States: A transcription. n.d. archives.gov. Web. June 4, 2015.

Cook, Frank W. "Lemuel Remembers Washington." n.d. burrcook.com. Web. June 16, 2015.

Cook, Noble David. *Born to Die: Disease and New World Conquest, 1492-1650*. Cambridge: Cambridge UP. 1998. Print.

Cooper, Helene, and Michael D. Shear. "Obama to Send 1,500 More Troops to Assist Iraq." nytimes.com. Nov. 7, 2014. Web. Jan. 28, 2015.

Copeland, Jack, et al. *Colossus: The Secrets of Bletchley Park's Codebreaking Computers*. Oxford: Oxford UP. 2006. Print.

Cottrell, Leonard. *Hannibal: Enemy of Rome*. Holt, Rinehart and Winston. 1960. Print.

Coulmas, Florian. *The Blackwell Encyclopedia of Writing Systems*. Oxford: Blackwell Publishers Ltd. 1996. Print.

Coulson, Charles. *Castles in Medieval Society: Fortresses in England, France, and Ireland in the Central Middle Ages*. Oxford: Oxford UP. 2003. Print.

Craig, Gordon A. *The Battle of Königgrätz: Prussia's Victory Over Austria, 1866*. Philadelphia: U of Pennsylvania P. 2003. Print.

Craig, William. *Enemy at the Gates: The Battle for Stalingrad*. Old saybrook: Konecky & Konecky. 1973. Print.

Crawford, Samuel W. *The History Of The Fall Of Fort Sumter: Being An Inside History Of The Affairs In South Carolina And Washington, 1860-61*. New York: S.F. McLean. 1898. Print.

Creevey, Thomas and Herbert Maxwell, ed. *The Creevey Papers: A Selection from the Correspondence and Diaries of the Late Thomas Creevey*. Vol I. Cambridge: Cambridge UP. 2012. First edition published 1903. Print.

Crew, David F. *Nazism and German Society, 1933-1945*. London: Routledge. 1994. Print.

Cronin, Mary J, ed. *The Internet Strategy Handbook: Lessons from the New Frontier of Business*. Boston: Harvard Business School Press. 1996. Print.

Crosby, Alfred W. *The Columbian Exchange: Biological and Cultural Consequenses of 1492*. Westport: Praeger Publishers. 2003. Print.

Crouzet, François. *A History of the European Economy, 1000-2000*. U of Virginia P. 2001. Print.

Crow, John A. *The Epic of Latin America*. U of California P. 1992. Print.

Curran, Charles E. *Change in Official Catholica Moral Teachings*. Paulist Press. 2003. Print.

Curry, Anne. *Agincourt: A New History*. Tempus Pub ltd. 2005. Print.

Curry, Anne and Michael Hughes, ed. Arms, *Armies and Fortifications in the Hundred Years War*. Boydell Press. 1994. Print.

Curry, Anne. *The Battle of Agincourt: Sources and Interpretations*. Boydell Press. 2000. Print.

Cushing, Harry Alonzo, ed. *The Writings of Samuel Adams*. Volume I. 1764-1769. New York: G.P. Putnam's Sons. 1904. Print.

Cust, Richard. *Charles I: A Political Life*. Harlow: Pearson. 2007. Print.

Czech, Danuta. "The Auschwitz Prisoner Administration." In *Anatomy of the Auschwitz Death Camp*. Yisrael Gutman and Michael Berenbaum, ed. Bloomington: Indiana UP. 1994: 363-379. Print.

Daigle, Leslie. "30 years of TCP—and IP on everything!." *internetsociety. org*. January 1, 2013. Web. October 9, 2015.

Dale, Gareth. *Popular Protest in East Germany*. Abingdon: Routledge. 2005. Print.

Daly, William M. "Clovis: How Barbaric, How Pagan?" Speculum, vol. 69, no. 3, 1994, pp. 619–664. Print.

Dallek, Robert. *An Unfinished Life: John F. Kennedy, 1917-1963*. Boston: Little, Brown and Company. 2003. Print.

Daniels, Peter T. and William Bright, ed. *The World's Writing Systems*. Oxford: Oxford UP. 1996. Print.

Davidson, Greg, and Paul Davidson. *Economics for a Civilized Society*. Armonk: M. E. Sharpe. 1996. Print.

Davis, Norman. *Europe: A History*. Oxford: Oxford UP. 1996. Print.

Davis, Paul K. *100 Decisive Battles: From Ancient Times to the Present*. Oxford: Oxford UP. 1999. Print.

Dawson, Christopher. *The Making of Europe: An Introduction to the History of European Unity*. First published 1932 by Sheed and Ward. CUA Press. 2003. Print.

Dean, Peter J. "Napoleon as a Military Commander: the Limitations of

Genius." napoleon-series.org. n.d. Web. June 8, 2015.

Declaration of Independence. archives.gov. Web. 20 May 2015.

Dewey, Davis Rich. *Early Financial History of the United States*. First Edition 1903. Washington: Beard Books. 2003. Print.

DeWitt, Richard. *Worldviews: An Introduction to the History and Philosophy of Science*. Second Edition. Wiley-Blackwell. 2010. Print.

Dickens, Charles. *Dombey and Son*. Vol. II. Cambridge: Riverside Press. 1868. Print.

Dickson, Paul. *Sputnik: The Shock of the Century*. Bloomsbury Publishing USA. 2009. Print.

Diffie, Bailey Wallys. *Foundations of the Portuguese Empire, 1415-1580*. Minneapolis: U of Minnesota P. 1977. Print.

Dikötter, Frank. *Mao's Great Famine: The History of China's Most Devastating Catastrophe, 1958-1962*. New York: Walker. 2010. Print.

Dillon, Matthew and Lynda Garland. *Ancient Rome: From the Early Republic to the Assassination of Julius Caesar*. Abingdon: Routledge. 2005. Print.

Dillon, Michael. *China: A Modern History*. London: I.B. Tauris. 2010. Print.

Dio, Cassius. *Roman History*. Trans. Earnest Cary. Loeb Classical Library, 9 volumes. Harvard UP: 1914-1927. Print.

Diodorus Siculus. *Library of History*. Volume VIII. Trans. C. Bradford Welles. Cambridge: Harvard UP. 1963. Print.

Diodorus Siculus. *Library of History*. Volume IX. Trans. Russel M. Geer. Cambridge: Harvard UP. 1947. Print.

Doe v. Holder. 703 F. Supp.2d 313. U.S. District Court, S.D. New York. Mar. 28, 2010. clearinghouse.net. Web. Jan. 27, 2015.

Doe II v. Gonzales S III E. 449 F. 3d 415. U.S. Court of Appeals, Second Circuit. May 23, 2006. public.resource.org. Web. Jan. 26, 2015.

Doe v. Gonzales. 500 F. Supp. 2d 379. U.S. District Court, S.D. New York. Sep. 6, 2007. clearinghouse.net. Web. Jan. 27, 2015.

Domínguez-Rodrigo, Manuel, ed. *Stone Tools and Fossil Bones: Debates in the Archaeology of Human Origins*. Cambridge:

Cambridge UP. 2012. Print.

Dougherty, Kevin. *Military Leadership Lessons of the Charleston Campaign, 1861-1865.* Jefferson: McFarland. 2014. Print.

Drake, Stillman. Galileo at Work: His Scientific Biography. First published 1978 by U of Chicago P. This edition by Dover Publications. 2003. Print.

Duffy, Christopher. *Siege Warfare: The Fortress in the Early Modern World 1494–1660, Vol. 1.* London: Routledge. 1997. Print.

Dull, Paul S. *A Battle History of the Imperial Japanese Navy, 1941-1945.* Annapolis: Naval Institute Press. 2013. Print.

Dworetz, Steven M. *The Unvarnished Doctrine: Locke, Liberalism, and the American Revolution.* Duke UP. 1994. Print.

Eastman, Lloyd E. *The Nationalist Era in China, 1927-1949.* Cambridge: Cambridge UP. 1991. Print.

Edmondson, J.C. and Alison Keith. *Roman Dress and the Fabrics of Roman Culture.* Toronto: Toronto UP. 2008. Print.

Ehler, Sidney Z. and John B. Morrall, ed. *Church and State Through the Centuries: A Collection of Historic Documents with Commentaries.* Biblo & Tannen Publishers. 1967. Print.

Elliot, Jonathan, ed. *The Debates on the Adoption of the Federal Constitution in the Convention held at Philadelphia in 1787, with a Diary of the Debates of the Congress of the Confederation as reported by James Madison, revised and newly arranged by Jonathan Elliot. Complete in One Volume. Vol. V. Supplement to Elliot's Debates.* Philadelphia. 1836. Print.

Ellis, John, and Michael Cox. *The World War I Databook: The Essential Facts and Figures for All the Combatants.* Aurum. 2001. Print.

Eicher, David J. *Robert E. Lee: A Life Portrait.* Lanham: Rowman & Littlefield. 2002. Print.

Eicher, David J. *The Longest Night: A Military History of the Civil War.* New York: Simon & Schuster. 2001. Print.

Einhard. *The Life of Charlemagne.* Trans. Samuel Epes Turner. Original title: Vita Karoli Magni. New York: Harper & Brothers. 1880. Print.

Einstein, Albert, and Leo Szilard. "Einstein's Letter to Roosevelt."

osti.gov. August 2, 1939. Web. August 24, 2015.

"Emser Depesche." July 13, 1870. documentarchiv.de. Web. June 29, 2015.

"Encyclopedia Judaica: Haavara." jewishvirtuallibrary.org. n.d. Web. Aug. 17, 2015.

Engels, Friedrich. *Anti-Dühring; Herr Eugen Dühring's revolution in science*. New York: International Publishers. Translated from the third German edition by Emile Burns. C.P. Dutt, ed. First published in German as a book in 1878. Translation is from 1894 edition.

Engelstein, Laura. *Moscow, 1905: Working-class Organization and Political Conflict*. Stanford: Stanford UP. 1982. Print.

English, Stephen. *Mercenaries in the Classical World: To the Death of Alexander*. Casemate Publishers. 2012. Print.

Englund, Steven. *Napoleon: A Political Life*. New York: Simon & Schuster. 2004. Print.

Enys, John S. "Remarks on the Duty of the Steam Engines employed in the Mines of Cornwall at different periods." Published in: *Transactions of the Institution of Civil Engineers, Volume 3, Part 5*. Institution of Civil Engineers. London: J. Weale. 1842. Print.

Erdbrink, Thomas. "As Talks With U.S. Near, Iran Denies Nuclear Arms Effort." washingtonpost.com. September 21, 2009. Web. Aug. 24, 2015.

Erdbrink, Thomas. "Iran's Leaders Signal Effort at New Thaw." *The New York Times*. Sept. 19, 2013. Print.

Erman, Adolf. *Ancient Egyptian Literature*. New York: Routledge. 2013. Print.

Ernesto. "Pirate Bay Takes Over Distribution Of Censored 3D Printable Gun." torrentfreak.com. May 10, 2013. Web. June 9, 2015.

Esherick, Joseph. *The Origins of the Boxer Uprising*. Berkely: U of California P. 1987. Print.

Eskew, Glenn T. *But for Birmingham: The Local and National Movements in the Civil Rights Struggle*. U of North Carolina P. 1997. Print.

Espinasse, Francis. *Lancashire worthies*. London: Simpkin, Marshall, & Co. 1874. Print.

"Estimated Impact of the American Recovery and Investment Act on Employment and Economic Output from October 2011 through December 2012." Feb. 2012. Washington: Congressional Budget Office. Web. July 25, 2015.

Evans, Martin Marix. *Naseby 1645: The Triumph of the New Model Army*. Osprey. 2007. Print.

Exec. Order No. 6102, 3 C.F.R. (1933). Print.

Fagan, Brian M., ed. *The Oxford Companion to Archaeology*. Oxford: Oxford UP. 1996. Print.

Fahim, Kareem. "Slap to a Man's Pride Set Off Tumult in Tunesia." New York Times. Jan. 21, 2011. Web. May 21, 2015.

Fairbank, John King, Albert Feuerwerker, and Denis Crispin Twitchett. *The Cambridge History of China, Vol. 13: Republican China, 1912-1949. Part 2*. Cambridge UP. 1986. Print.

Fairbank, John King, and Merle Goldman. *China: A New History, Second Enlarged Edition*. Harvard UP. 2006. Print.

Fairclough, Adam. *To Redeem the Soul of America: The Southern Christian Leadership Conference & Martin Luther King, Jr*. U of Georgia P. 2001. Print.

Febvre, Lucien and Henri-Jean Martin. *The Coming of the Book: The Impact of Printing 1450-1800*. trans. Vero. First published in Paris, in 1958, as *L'Apparition du livre*. Verso. 1997. Print.

Ferguson, Niall. *Empire, The rise and demise of the British world order and the lessons for global power*. Basic Books. 2003. Print.

Fernández-Armesto, Felipe. *Amerigo: The Man Who Gave His Name to America*. Random House. 2008. Print.

Ferro, Marc, and Brian Pearce. *Nicholas II: Last of the Tsars*. Oxford: Oxford UP. 1995. Print.

Fichte, Johann Gottlieb. *Addresses to the German Nation*. R.F. Jones and G.H. Turnbull, trans. Chicago: Open Court. 1922. Print.

Finkelman, Paul. *Slavery and the Founders: Race and Liberty in the Age of Jefferson*. Armonk: M.E. Sharpe. 2001. Print.

Finocchiaro, Maurice A. *The Galileo Affair: A Documentary History*. Berkeley: U of California P. 1989. Print.

Firth, C. H. and R. S. Rait, ed. *Acts and Ordinances of the Interregnum, 1642-1660*. Vol. II. Pub: H.M. Stationery Off. Print: Wyman and Sons. 1911. Print.

Fischer, Steven R. *A History of Writing*. London: Reaktion Books Ltd. 2001. Print.

Fissel, Mark Charles. *The Bishops' Wars: Charles I's Campaigns Against Scotland, 1638-1640*. Cambridge: Cambridge UP. 1994. Print.

Fitton, R.S, and Alfred P. Wadsworth. *The Strutts and the Arkwrights, 1758-1830: A Study of the Early Factory System*. Manchester: Manchester UP. 1958. Print.

Fitzpatrick, John C. *The Writings of George Washington from the Original Manuscript Sources 1745-1799 Volume 29 September 1, 1786-June 19, 1788*. Best Books. 1939. Print.

Fitzpatrick, Sheila. *The Russian Revolution*. Oxford: Oxford UP. 2008. Print.

Flamm, Kenneth. *Creating the Computer: Government, Industry, and High Technology*. Washington: The Brookings Institution. 1998. Print.

Fleischman, Richard K., Warwick Funnell, and Stephen P. Walker, ed. *Critical Histories of Accounting: Sinister Inscriptions in the Modern Era*. New York: Routledge. 2013. Print.

Flemion, Jess Stoddart. "The Struggle for the Petition of Right in the House of Lords: The Study of an Opposition Party Victory." *The Journal of Modern History*. Vol. 45, no. 2. 1973: 193-210.

Ford, Henry, and Samuel Crowther. *Edison as I know him*. New York: Cosmopolitan book corporation. 1930. Print.

Ford, Henry, and Samuel Crowther. *My Life and Work*. New York: Doubleday, Page & Company. 1923. Print.

Ford, Paul Leicester, ed. *The Works of Thomas Jefferson*. Vol. V. New York: G.P. Putnam's Sons. 1904. Print.

"Foreign Scientist Case Files 1945 - 1958 - 230/86/46/05 186 boxes." archives.gov/iwg/declassified-records/rg-330-defense-secretary/foreign-scientist-case-files.pdf. November 30, 2010. Web. September 8, 2015.

Förster, Stig, and Jörg Nagler. *On the Road to Total War: The American*

Civil War and the German Wars of Unification, 1861-1871. Cambridge: Cambridge UP. 1997. Print.

Forsythe, David P. ed. *Encyclopedia of Human Rights.* Oxford: Oxford UP. 2009. Print.

Foster, Nigel G., and Satish Sule. *German Legal System and Laws.* Fourth Edition. Oxford: Oxford UP. 2010. Print.

Fox, Margalit. "Rochus Misch, Bodyguard of Hitler, Dies at 96." *The New York Times.* nytimes.com Sept. 6, 2013. Web. Apr. 1, 2015.

Francis, John Michael, ed. *Iberia and the Americas: Culture, Politics, and History: a Multidisciplinary Encyclopedia, Volume 1.* ABC-CLIO. 2006. Print.

Fraser, Suzan. "Turkey's electoral board releases final referendum tally." Chicago Tribune. April 27, 2017. Web.

Frazer, Karen D. "NSFNET: A Partnership for High-Speed Networking: Final Report, 1987-1995." Merit Network. merit.edu. Web. October 9, 2015.

Freedman, Russell. *The War to End All Wars: World War I.* New York: Houghton Mifflin Harcourt. 2013. Print.

Fremont-Barnes, Gregory. *Napoleon Bonaparte: Leadership, Strategy, Conflict.* Botley: Osprey. 2010. Print.

Friedman, Jonathan C. *The Routledge History of the Holocaust.* Abingdon: Routledge. 2011. Print.

Friedman, Milton, and Anna Jacobson Schwartz. *A Monetary History of the United States, 1867-1960.* Princeton UP 2008. First published 1963. Print.

Frisch, Otto, and Rudolf Peierls. "The Frish-Peierls Memorandum." web.stanford.edu. n.d. Web. August 25, 2015.

Fritz, Stephen G. *Ostkrieg: Hitler's War of Extermination in the East.* UP of Kentucky. 2011. Print.

Fromkin, David. *A Peace to End All Peace: The Fall of the Ottoman Empire and the Creation of the Modern Middle East.* New York: Henry Holt. 2010. Print.

Fromkin, David. *Europe's Last Summer: Why the World Went to War in 1914.* London: Random House. 2005. Print.

Frontinus, Sextus Julius. *The Aqueducts of Rome*. Trans. Charles E. Bennett. Loeb Classical Library. 1925. Print.

Frontinus, Sextus Julius. De Aquaeductu Urbis Romae. Comm. R. H. Rodgers. Cambridge Classical Texts and Commentaris. Cambridge: Cambridge UP. 2004. Print.

Fugitive Slave Act 1850. Pub. L. 31-60. 9 Stat. 462-465. Sept. 18, 1850.

Gabriel, Richard A. *The Great Armies of Antiquity*. Westport: Greenwood Publishing Group. 2002. Print.

Gady, Franz-Stefan. "Russia's Military Spending to Increase Modestly in 2016." thediplomat.com. November 10, 2015. Web. May 17, 2017.

Gagliardo, John G. *Germany Under the Old Regime 1600-1790*. London: Routledge. 2013. Print.

Galilei, Galileo and Maurice A. Finocchiaro. *The Essential Galileo*. Edited and translated by Maurice A. Finocchiaro. Hackett Publishing. 2008. Print.

Galilei, Galileo and Stillman Drake. *Discoveries and Opinions of Galileo*. Random House. 1957. Print.

Gallagher, Gary W., Robert Krick, and Stephen D. Krick. *Civil War: Fort Sumter to Appomattox*. Osprey. 2014. Print.

Gann, W. D. *New York Trend Detector*. Health Research Books. 1994. First Edition 1936. Print.

Gao, Yuan. *Born Red: A Chronicle of the Cultural Revolution*. Stanford: Stanford UP. 1987. Print.

Gardiner, Samuel Rawson. *History of the Great Civil War, 1642-1649*. In Four Volumes. London: Longmans, Green, and Co. 1904/05.

Garrison, Eliza. *Ottonian Imperial Art and Portraiture: The Artistic Patronage of Otto III and Henry II*. Farnham: Ashgate Publishing. 2002. Print.

Garthoff, Raymond L. *Reflections on the Cuban Missile Crisis: Revised to include New Revelations from Soviet & Cuban Sources*. Washington D.C.: The Brookings Institution. 1989. Print.

Garun, Natt. "In China, Noodle-Slicing Robots Are Taking Over Local Restaurants." Aug. 21, 2012. digitaltrends.com. Web. June 29, 2015.

Gasquet, Francis Aidan. *The Black Death of 1348 and 1349*. Second edition. London: George Bell and Sons. 1908. Print.

Gáti, Charles. *The bloc that failed: Soviet-East European relations in transition.* Indiana UP. 1990. Print.

Geisst, Charles R. *Wall Street: A History.* Oxford: Oxford UP. 1997. Print.

"German Jewish Refugees, 1933-1939." *Holocaust Encyclopedia.* United States Holocaust Memorial Museum. n.d. ushmm.org. Web. Aug. 14, 2015.

Gest, John Marshall. "The Writings of Sir Edward Coke." The Yale Law Journal. Vol. 18 (7). 1909: 504-532. Print.

Getty, J. Arch, Gabor T. Rittersporn, and Viktor N. Zemskov. "Victims of the Soviet Penal System in the Pre-War Years: A First Approach on the Basis of Archival Evidence." *The American Historical Review.* Vol. 98, No. 4 (Oct., 1993): 1017-1049.

Giacomo, Carol. "In Saudi Arabia, Where Women's Suffrage Is a New Idea." *The New York Times.* nytimes.com. November 2, 2015. Web. November 21, 2015.

Gibbon, Edward. The History of the Decline and Fall of the Roman Empire. Vol. III. New York: J & J Harper. 1826. Print.

Gilbert, G.M. *Nuremberg Diary.* Da Capo Press. 1995. First Edition 1947. Print.

Glantz, David M. *Operation Barbarossa: Hitler's Invasion of Russia 1941.* The History Press. 2011. Print.

Gleijeses, Piero. "Ships in the Night: The CIA, the White house and the Bay of Pigs." *Journal of Latin American Studies.* Vol. 27, No. 1. 1995: 1-42. Cambridge UP. Print.

"Global Defence Budgets Overall to Rise for First Time in Five Years". IHS Markit. February 4, 2014. Web. May 16, 2017.

Godwin, Robert, ed. *Apollo 10: The NASA Mission Reports.* Apogee Books. 2000. Print.

Gold, Hal. *Unit 731 Testimony: Japan's Wartime Human Experimentation Program.* Tuttle Publishing. 2004. Print.

Goldgar, Anne. *Tulipmania: Money, Honor, and Knowledge in the Dutch Golden Age.* U of Chicago P. 2007. Print.

Goldman, Marshall I. *Petrostate: Putin, Power, and the New Russia*. Oxford: Oxford UP. 2008. Print.

Goldman, Merle, ed., and Elizabeth J. Perry, ed. *Changing Meanings of Citizenship in Modern China*. Harvard UP. 2002. Print.

Goodman, Alan H., Deborah Heath, and M. Susan Lindee, ed. *Genetic Nature/culture: Anthropology and Science Beyond the Two-culture Divide*. Berkely: U of California P. 2003. Print.

Gordon, Eleanora C. "The Fate of Sir Hugh Willoughby And His Companions: A New Conjecture." *The Geographical Journal*. Vol. 152, No. 2 (Jul., 1986): 243-247.

Gray, Fred D. *Bus Ride to Justice: Changing the System by the System: the Life and Works of Fred Gray*. Montgomery: NewSouth Books. 2002. Print.

Gray, Jack. *Rebellions and Revolutions: China from the 1800s to 2000*. Oxford: Oxford UP. 2002. Print.

Gray, Randal. *Kaiserschlacht 1918: The Final German Offensive*. Botley: Osprey. 1991. Print.

Green, Peter. *Alexander of Macedon, 356-323 B.C: A Historical Biography*. Berkeley: U of California P. 1991. Print.

Green, Richard E., et al. "A Draft Sequence of the Neandertal Genome." *Science* vol. 328 no. 5979 (2010): 710-722. Print.

Greene, A. Wilson. *The Final Battles of the Petersburg Campaign: Breaking the Backbone of the Rebellion*. U of Tennessee P. 2008. Print.

Greene, Jerome A. *The Guns of Independence: The Siege of Yorktown, 1781*. New York: Savas Beatie. 2005. Print.

Greer, Donald. *The incidence of the terror during the French Revolution; a statistical interpretation*. Harvard UP. 1935. Print.

Gregg, Pauline. *King Charles I*. U of California P. 1984. Print.

Greif, Gideon. *We Wept Without Tears: Testimonies of the Jewish Sonderkommando from Auschwitz*. Yale UP. 2005. Print.

Grenville, John A. Soames. *The Major International Treaties of the Twentieth Century: A History and Guide with Texts, Volume I*. London: Routledge. 2001. Print.

Griffiths, Sarah. "Charlemagne's bones identified: 1,200-year-old remains in a German cathedral belong to 'Europe's father', claim scientists". dailymail.co.uk. Feb. 3, 2014. Web. Mar. 11, 2015.

Grimbly, Shona. *Atlas of Exploration*. Routledge. 2013. Print.

Grine, Frederick E., John G. Fleagle, and Richard E. Leakey, ed. *The First Humans: Origin and Early Evolution of the Genus Homo*. Springer Science & Business Media. 2009. Print.

Groen, Petra M. H. "Militant Response: The Dutch Use of Military Force and the Decolonization of the Dutch East Indies, 1945-50." *Emergencies and Disorder in the European Empires After 1945*. 30-44. R. F. Holland, ed. Routledge. 2012. Print.

Gromov, Gregory. "History of Internet and World Wide Web - The Roads and Crossroads of Internet History." netvalley.com. 1995. Web. October 7, 2015.

Groves, L. R. "Memorandum for the Secretary of War, The Test." July 18, 1945. nsarchive.gwu.edu. Original source: U.S. National Archives. RG 77, MED Records, Top Secret Documents, File no. 4. Web. August 26, 2015.

Guderian, Heinz. *Panzer Leader*. Da Capo Press. 2002. First published in New York in 1952. Print.

Guo, Rongxing. *Understanding the Chinese Economies*. Kidlington: Academic Press. 2013. Print.

Gutman, Yisrael, and Michael Berenbaum, ed. *Anatomy of the Auschwitz Death Camp*. Bloomington: Indiana UP. 1998. Print.

Guttmann, Robert. *Reforming Money and Finance: Toward a New Monetary Regime*. New York: M. E. Sharpe. 1997. Print.

Hagemann, Karen. *Revisiting Prussia's Wars against Napoleon: History, Culture, and Memory*. New York: Cambridge UP. 2015. Print.

Haggard, Stephen, and Marcus Noland. *Gender in Transition: The Case of North Korea*. Washington: Peterson Institute for International Economics. June 2012. iie.com. Web. September 30, 2015.

Hailey, Foster. "Dogs and Hoses Repulse Negroes at Birmingham." *The New York Times*. May 4, 1963. Print.

Halabi, Bassam, Sam Halabi, and Danny McPherson. *Internet Routing*

Architectures. Second Edition. Indianapolis: Cisco Press. 2001. Print.

Halporn, Barbara C, ed, trans. *The Correspondence of Johann Amerbach: Early Printing in Its Social Context*. U of Michigan P. 2000. Print.

Hall, Allan. "Muslim girl is ordered by German judge to wear a 'burkini' at her school swimming class after she refused to take part as it was against her religion." dailymail.co.uk. Sep 12, 2013. Web. Mar 5, 2015.

Hall, Bert S. "Introduction" in J. R. *A History of Greek Fire and Gunpowder*. J.R. Partington. Baltimore: Johns Hopkins UP. 1999. First published 1960. Print.

Hall, Christopher David. *British Strategy in the Napoleonic War, 1803-15*. Manchester UP. 1992. Print.

Hall, Jonathan M. A History of the Archaic Greek World: Ca. 1200-479 BCE. Blackwell Publishing. 2007. Print.

Hall, Rex, and David J. Shayler. *The Rocket Men: Vostok & Voskhod, The First Soviet Manned Spaceflights*. Springer-Praxis Books. 2001. Print.

Halliday, Paul Delaney. *Habeas Corpus: From England to Empire*. Harvard UP. 2010. Print.

Halpern, Paul G. *A Naval History of World War I*. Annapolis: U.S. Naval Institute. 1994. Print.

Hamilton, Alexander, John Jay, and James Madison. *The Federalist Papers*. n.p. n.d. Project Gutenberg. gutenberg.org. Web. June 2, 2015.

Hamilton, Thomas J. "Kennedy Asks Joint Moon Flight By U.S. And Soviet As Peace Step." *The New York Times*. September 21, 1963. Print.

Hankins, James. "Introduction", in *History of the Florentine People*. Volume I. Books I-IV. Ed. and Trans by James Hankins. Harvard UP. 2001. Print.

Hansen, Drew. "Mahalia Jackson, and King's Improvisation." *The New York Times*. nytimes.com Aug. 27, 2013. Web. Sep. 17, 2015.

Harcave, Sidney. *Count Sergei Witte and the Twilight of Imperial Russia: A Biography*. New York: M.E. Sharpe. 2004. Print.

Hardesty, Von, and Gene Eisman. *Epic Rivalry: The Inside Story of the Soviet and American Space Race.* National Geographic Books. 2008. Print.

Harlan, Chico, Blaine Harden, and Yoonjung Seo. "N. Korea lifts restrictions on private markets as last resort in food crisis." *The Washington Post.* washingtonpost.com. June 18, 2010. Web. Sep. 30, 2015.

Harrington, Peter. *Peking 1900: The Boxer Rebellion.* Botley: Osprey. 2001. Print.

Harris, Trevor. "Who is the Father of the Internet? The Case for Donald Davies." *Variety in Mass Communication Research.* 123-134. Yorgo Pasadeos, ed. Athens Institute for Education and Research. 2009. Print.

Harris, W.A. *The record of Fort Sumter, from its occupation by Major Anderson, to its reduction by South Carolina troops during the administration of Governor Pickens.* Columbia, S.C.: South Carolinian Steam Job Printing Office. 1862. Print.

Hartley, Janet M. *Russia, 1762-1825: Military Power, the State, and the People.* Westport: Praeger. 2008. Print.

Harvey, Brian. *Russia In Space: The Failed Frontier?* London: Springer. 2001. Print.

Headland, Ronald. *Messages of Murder: A Study of the Reports of the Einsatzgruppen of the Security Police and the Security Service, 1941-1943.* Cranbury: Associated UP. 1992. Print.

Healy, Mark. *Cannae 216 BC: Hannibal Smashes Rome's Army.* Oxford: Osprey Publishing. 1994. Print.

Heather, Peter. *The Fall of the Roman Empire: A New History.* Pan Macmillan. 2005. Print.

Heer, Hannes, and Klaus Naumann, ed. *War of Extermination: The German Military in World War II 1941-1944.* Berghahn. 2004. Print.

Helfferich, Tryntje. *The Thirty Years War: A Documentary History.* Indianapolis: Hackett. 2009. Print.

Helmreich, Paul C. *Wheaton College, 1834-1957: A Massachusetts Family Affair.* Cranbury: Cornwall Books. 2002. Print.

Hemming, John. *Amazon Frontier: Defeat of the Brazilian Indians.* Macmillan. 1987. Print.

Hemming, John. *The Conquest of the Incas.* Harcourt, Brace, Jovanovich. 1970. Print.

Henderson, W.O. *Zollverein Cb: The Zollverein.* Routledge. 2013. First published 1968. Print.

Hendrix, Scott H. *Martin Luther: A Very Short Introduction.* Oxford: Oxford UP. 2010. Print.

Hendrix, Steve. "F-16 pilot was ready to give her life on September 11." *The Washington Post.* washingtonpost.com. Sept. 8, 2011. Web. Jan. 26, 2015.

Henningsen, Gustav. "The Database of the Spanish Inquisition. The 'relaciones de causas' - project revisited." As published in *Vorträge zur Justizforschung: Geschichte und Theorie, Volume 2.* ed. Heinz Mohnhaupt, Dieter Simon. Frankfurt am Main: Vittorio Klostermann. 1993. Print.

Henry, Patrick. *Jewish Resistance Against the Nazis.* Catholic U of America P. 2014. Print.

Herlihy, David. *The Black Death and the Transformation of the West.* Harvard UP. 1997. Print.

Herodotus. *The Histories.* Trans. A.D. Godley. Cambridge: Harvard UP. 1920. Print.

Herold, J. Christopher. *Bonaparte in Egypt.* Tucson: Fireship. 2009. Print.

Herskovitz, Jon, and Christine Kim. "North Korea drops communism, boosts "Dear Leader"." *Reuters.* reuters.com. Sep. 28, 2009. Web. July 14, 2015.

Hilberg, Raul. *The Destruction of the European Jews.* Volume III. Third Edition. Yale UP. 2003. Print.

Hill, Christopher. *The Century of Revolution 1603-1704.* New York: W.W. Norton & Company. 1961. Print.

Hill, Joseph Adna. *Women in Gainful Occupations, 1870 to 1920: A Study of the Trend of Recent Changes in the Numbers, Occupational Distribution, and Family Relationship of Women Reported in the*

Census as Following a Gainful Occupation. Washington: G.P.O. 1929. Print.

Hillard, Elias Brewster. *The last men of the Revolution: a photograph of each from life, together with views of their homes printed in colors: accompanied by brief biographical sketches of the men.* Hartford: N.A. & R. A. Moore. 1864. Print.

Hills, Richard Leslie. *James Watt: Triumph through adversity, 1785-1819.* Landmark. 2006. Print.

Hills, Richard Leslie. *Power from Steam: A History of the Stationary Steam Engine.* Cambridge: Cambridge UP. 1989. Print.

History of the Seventy-ninth division, A.E.F. during the world war: 1917-1919. Compiled and Edited by History Committee 79th Division Association. Lancaster: Steinman & Steinman. 1922. Print.

Hitler, Adolf. *Mein Kampf.* John Chamberlain, ed. Reynal & Hitchcock. 1939. Print.

Hobbes, Thomas. *Leviathan.* Revised Student Edition. Ed. Richard Tuck. Cambridge UP. 1996. Print.

Hodder, Ian. *Religion at Work in a Neolithic Society: Vital Matters.* Cambridge: Cambridge UP. 2014. Print.

Hogan, Michael J. *The Marshall Plan: America, Britain and the Reconstruction of Western Europe, 1947-1952.* Cambridge: Cambridge UP. 1989. Print.

Holdstock, Douglas, and Frank Barnaby. *Hiroshima and Nagasaki: Retrospect and Prospect.* New York: Routledge. 2013. Print.

Holland, Tom. *Persian Fire: The First World Empire and the Battle for the West.* New York: Random House. 2007. Print.

Holmes, Jerry. *Thomas Jefferson: A Chronology of His Thoughts.* Rowman & Littlefield. 2002. Print.

Holmes, Terence M. "Absolute Numbers: The Schlieffen Plan as a Critique of German Strategy in 1914." *War in History.* Vol. 21, 2. Apr. 2014: 193-213.

Holton, Sandra Stanley. *Feminism and Democracy: Women's Suffrage and Reform Politics in Britain, 1900-1918.* Cambridge UP. 1986. Print.

Hook, Sue Vander. *Johannes Gutenberg: Printing Press Innovator*. Edina: ABDO Publishing Company. 2010. Print.

Horace (Quintus Horatius Flaccus). Epistles, second book (*Epistularum liber secundus)*. 14 BCE.

Hornick, John, and Dan Roland. "Many 3D Printing Patents Are Expiring Soon: Here's A Round Up & Overview of Them." 3dprintingindustry. com. Dec. 29, 2013. Web. June 9, 2015.

Horrox, Rosemary, trans. and ed.*The Black Death*. Manchester: Manchester UP. 1994. Print.

Hosch, William L. *World War I: People, Politics, and Power*. Rosen Publishing Group. 2009. Print.

Hoss, Rudolf, Pery Broad, and Johann Kremer. *KL Auschwitz Seen by the SS*. Panstwowe Muzeum w Oswiecimiu. 1978. Print.

Hounshell, David. *From the American System to Mass Production, 1800-1932: The Development of Manufacturing Technology in the United States*. Johns Hopkins UP. 1985. Print.

"House of Commons Journal Volume 8: 8 May 1660." Journal of the House of Commons: Volume 8, 1660-1667. London: His Majesty's Stationery Office, 1802. 16-18. British History Online. Web. 20 May 2015.

House, Jonathan M. *A Military History of the Cold War, 1944-1962*. U of Oklahoma P. 2012. Print.

Houston, Stephen D, ed. *The First Writing: Script Invention as History and Process*. Cambridge: Cambridge UP. 2004. Print.

Hublin, Jean-Jacques. et al. "New fossils from Jebel Irhoud, Morocco and the pan-African origin of Homo sapiens." Nature 546 (08 June 2017): 289–292. doi:10.1038/nature22336. Web. June 9, 2017

Hughes, Lindsey. *Peter the Great: A Biography*. Yale UP. 2004. Print.

Hughes, R. Gerald. "'The best and the brightest': the Cuban missile crisis, the Kennedy administration and the lessons of history." *The Cuban Missile Crisis: A Critical Reappraisal*. 117-141. Len Scott, R. Gerald Hughes, ed. Abingdon: Routledge. 2015. Print.

Hui, Lu. "Market to play "decisive" role in allocating resources: communique." news.xinhuanet.com. November 12, 2013. Web.

September 23, 2015.

Huie, William Bradford. "The Shocking Story of Approved Killing in Mississippi." *Look Magazine.* January 1956. pbs.org. Web. September 17, 2015.

Human Rights First. "Guantánamo by the Numbers." humanrightsfirst. org. Jan. 15, 2015. Web. Jan. 27, 2015.

Hume, David and William Cooke Stafford. *The History of England, from the Earliest Period to the Present Time. Vol. II.* London: London Printing and Publishing Company. 1868-71. Print.

Humphrey, John H. *Roman Circuses: Arenas for Chariot Racing.* Berkely: California UP. 1986. Print.

Humphrey, John Peters. "Part One: The Contribution of the Universal Declaration." *Human Rights: Thirty Years After the Universal Declaration.* 21-40. B.G. Ramcharan, ed. The Hague: Martinus Nijhoff. 1979. Print.

Huxley, Aldous. *Brave New World.* New York: Random House. 2008. Print.

IMF. "Report for Selected Countries and Subjects." World Economic Outlook Database. imf.org. April 2015. IMF. Web. May 28, 2015.

Inglesby, Thomas V., et. al. "Plague as a Biological Weapon: Medical and Public Health Management." Journal of the American Medical Association. 2000; 283 (17): 2281-90.

Ingstad, Helge and Anne Stine Ingstad. *The Viking Discovery of America: The Excavation of a Norse Settlement in L'Anse aux Meadows, Newfoundland.* Breakwater Books, 2000. Print.

""Inspiration Mars" to pursue human mission to the Red Planet 2018." inspirationmars.org. Feb. 27, 2013. Web. Apr. 22, 2015.

International Committee of the Red Cross. "ICRC Report On The Treatment Of Fourteen "High Value Detainees" In CIA Custody." nybooks.com. Feb. 2007. Web. Jan. 27, 2015.

"Iran and Nuclear Weapons." c-span.org. August 14, 2002. Web. August 24, 2015.

Isom, Dallas Woodbury. *Midway Inquest: Why the Japanese Lost the Battle of Midway.* Bloomington: Indiana UP. 2007. Print.

Israel, Jonathan. *A Revolution of the Mind: Radical Enlightenment and the Intellectual Origins of Modern Democracy*. Princeton: Princeton UP. 2010. Print.

Israel, Jonathan. *Radical Enlightenment: Philosophy and the Making of Modernity 1650-1750*. Oxford: Oxford UP. 2001. Print.

Israel, Jonathan I. *The Anglo-Dutch Moment: Essays on the Glorious Revolution and Its World Impact*. Cambridge: Cambridge UP. 1991. Print.

Jacobson, Timothy Curtis, and George David Smith. *Cotton's Renaissance: A Study in Market Innovation*. Cambridge: Cambridge UP. 2001. Print.

Jaffa, Harry V. *A New Birth of Freedom: Abraham Lincoln and the Coming of the Civil War*. Lanham: Rowman & Littlefield. 2004. Print.

James I. *Basilikon Doron or His Majesties Instructions To His Dearest Sonne, Henry the Prince*. Edinbrugh. 1599. Print.

Jankowski, Paul. *Verdun: The Longest Battle of the Great War*. Oxford: Oxford UP. 2013. Print.

Jefferson, Thomas. "Thomas Jefferson to John Holmes." Monticello. Apr. 22, 1820. loc.gov. Web. June 16, 2015.

Jian, Guo, Yongyi Song, and Yuan Zhou. *Historical Dictionary of the Chinese Cultural Revolution*. Lanham: Rowman & Littlefield. 2006. Print.

Jisheng, Yang. *Tombstone: The Great Chinese Famine, 1958-1962*. New York: Farrar, Straus and Giroux. 2012. Print.

Jiwei, Lou. *Chinese Economists on Economic Reform - Collected Works of Lou Jiwei*. China Development Research Foundation, ed. Routledge. 2013. Print.

Jocelyn, Ed, and Andrew McEwen. *The Long March: The True Story Behind the Legendary Journey that Made Mao's China*. Constable. 2006. Print.

Joffre, Joseph. "Plan of Action Proposed by France to the Coalition." Chantilly, France.Tranlation unknown. firstworldwar.com. Dec. 6, 1915. Web. July 21, 2015.

"John Adams to Abigail Adams, 3 July 1776." Founders Online,

National Archives. founders.archives.gov. Web. May 26, 2015. Source: The Adams Papers, Adams Family Correspondence, vol. 2, June 1776–March 1778, ed. L. H. Butterfield. Cambridge: Harvard UP 1963: 27–29.

Johnson, Frank M. Defending Constitutional Rights. U of Georgia P. 2001. Print.

Johnson, Lyndon B. "Speech Before Congress on Voting Rights". millercenter.org. March 15, 1965. Web. September 23, 2015.

Johnston, Harry Hamilton. *Pioneers in Australasia*. First published in London, 1912. Asian Educational Services. 2000. Print.

Jolowicz, H.F., and Barry Nicholas. *Historical Introduction to the Study of Roman Law*. Third Edition. Campbridge UP. 1972. Print.

Jones, Eric M, ed. *Apollo 11 Lunar Surface Journal*. One Small Step. hq.nasa.gov. 1995. Web. September 13, 2015.

Jones, Howard. *The Bay of Pigs*. Oxford UP. 2008. Print.

Jones, Vincent C. Manhattan, the Army and the Atomic Bomb. Washington: Center of Military History, U.S. Army. 1985. Print.

Jong, Michiel de. *Staat van Oorlog: Wapenbedrijf en militaire hervorming in de Republiek der Verenigde Nederlanden, 1585-1621.* Verloren. 2005. Print.

Jordan, William Chester. *The Great Famine: Northern Europe in the Early Fourteenth Century*. Princeton: Princeton UP. 1996. Print.

Journal of the Royal United Service Institution, Volume 5. Royal United Service Institution. London: W. Mitchell and Son. 1862. Print.

Journals of the Continental Congress: From 1774 to 1788. In Four Volumes. Volume I: From September 5, 1774, to December 31, 1776, inclusive. Washington: Way and Gideon. 1823. Print.

Jukes, Geoffrey. Hitler's Stalingrad Decisions. Berkeley: U of California P. 1985. Print.

Justin. *Epitome of the Philippic History of Pompeius Trogus*. Trans. John Selby Watson. London: Henry G. Bohn. 1853. Print.

Justinian, Caesar Flavius. *The Institutes of Justinian*. Trans. John Baron Moyle. Fifth edition. Union: The Lawbook Exchange, Ltd. 2002. Print.

Justinian, Caesar Flavius. *Justinian's Institutes*. Trans. Peter Birks and Grant McLeod. New York: Cornell UP. 1987. Print.

Karlsbader Beschlüsse – Universitätsgesetz. Sept. 20, 1819. heinrich-heine-denkmal.de. Web. June 23, 2015.

Keaveney, Arthur Peter. *Lucullus, A Life*. 2nd ed. Piscataway: Gorgias Press LLC. 2009. Print.

Keck, Zachary. "North Korea Pushes Ahead on Agricultural Reforms." thediplomat.com. May 17, 2013. Web. September 30, 2015.

Keegan, John. *The American Civil War*. London: Random House. 2010. Print.

Keller, Bill. "Gorbachev, in Finland, Disavows Any Right of Regional Intervention." The New York Times. October 26, 1989. Print.

Kelly, Christopher. History of the French Revolution and of the Wars Produced by that Memorable Event. Vol. II. London: Thomas Kelly. 1820. Print.

Kelly, Jack. *Gunpowder: Alchemy, Bombards, & Pyrotechnics: The History of the Explosive that Changed the World*. Basic Books. 2004. Print.

Kennedy, John F. "Address at Rice University on the Nation's Space Effort." September 12, 1962. jfklibrary.org. Web. September 5, 2015.

Kennedy, John F. "Address on the Situation at the University of Mississippi". September 30, 1962. millercenter.org. Web. September 19, 2015.

Kennedy, John F. "Speech of Senator John F. Kennedy, Cincinnati, Ohio, Democratic Dinner." October 6, 1960. presidency.ucsb.edu. Web. September 14, 2015.

Kennedy, Robert F. Thirteen Days: A Memoir of the Cuban Missile Crisis. New York: W.W. Norton & Company. 2011. First edition 1968. Print.

Kenyon, Kathleen Mary. *Digging Up Jericho*. London: Ernest Benn. 1957. Print.

Kenyon, Kathleen Mary. *Excavations at Jericho Volume Three: The architecture and stratigraphy of the Tell. Plates*. British School of Archaeology in Jerusalem. 1960. Print.

Kershaw, Ian. *Hitler: A Biography*. New York: W.W. Norton & Company. 2008. Print.

Keylor, William R. The Legacy of the Great War: Peacemaking, 1919. Houghton Mifflin. 1998. Print.

Khrushchev, Nikita, and Sergei Khrushchev, ed. Memoirs of Nikita Khrushchev: Commissar, 1918-1945, Volume 1. George Shriver, trans. Penn State Press. 2004. Print.

Kiernan, Ben. The Pol Pot Regime: Race, Power, and Genocide in Cambodia under the Khmer Rouge, 1975-79. Third Edition. New Haven: Yale UP. 2014. Print.

Kimes, Beverly Rae. The Cars That Henry Ford Built. Automobile Heritage Publishing & Communications. 2004. First published 1978. Print.

Kindleberger, Charles Poor. Historical Economics: Art Or Science? Berkeley: U of California P. 1990. Print.

King, Benjamin, and Timothy Kutta. Impact: The History of Germany's V Weapons in World War II. Da Capo. 2009. Print.

King, Martin Luther, Jr. "I Have A Dream." archives.gov. August 28, 1963. Web. Septembrer 23, 2015.

Kingsley, Patrick. "Protesters across Egypt call for Mohamed Morsi to go." Guardian. June 30, 2013. Web. May 21, 2015.

Kirby, Michael. "The Trial Of King Charles I - Defining Moment For Our Constitutional Liberties." hcourt.gov.au. 22 Jan. 1999. Web. 20 May 2015.

Kluckhohn, Frank L. "U.S. Declares War, Pacific Battle Widens." *The New York Times*. Dec. 8, 1941. Print.

Knight, Ian. *Rorke's Drift, 1879: 'pinned Like Rats in a Hole'*. Botley: Osprey Publishing. 1996. Print.

Knight, Lionel. *Britain in India, 1858-1947*. London: Anthem. 2012. Print.

Knight, Will. "This Robot Could Transform Manufacturing." Sept. 18, 2012. technologyreview.com. Web. June 29, 2015.

Knoppers, Laura Lunger. *Constructing Cromwell: Ceremony, Portrait, and Print 1645-1661*. Cambridge: Cambridge UP. 2000. Print.

Kohn, George C. *Encyclopedia of Plague and Pestilence: From Ancient Times to the Present*. New York: Infobase Publishing. 2008. Print.

Kolkey, Jonathan Martin. Germany on the March: A Reinterpretation of War and Domestic Politics Over the Past Two Centuries. Lanham: UP of America. 1995. Print.

Kolodziej, Edward A. French International Policy under De Gaulle and Pompidou: The Politics of Grandeur. Cornell UP. 1974. Print.

Korowajczuk, Leonhard. LTE, WiMAX and WLAN Network Design, Optimization and Performance Analysis. Chichester: Wiley. 2011. Print.

Krassenstein, Brian. "HP's Multi Jet Fusion Technology: New Details Unveiled On Future Plans, Capabilities & More." 3dprint.com. April 20, 2015. Web. October 22, 2015.

Krey, August C., ed. *The First Crusade: The Accounts of Eye-Witnesses and Participants*. Princeton UP. 1921. Print.

Kristensen, Hans M., and Robert S. Norris. "Worldwide deployments of nuclear weapons, 2014. *Bulletin of the Atomic Scientists*. Vol. 70(5) 96-108. thebulletin.sagepub.com. Web. August 27, 2015.

Kroeber, Arthur. "Xi Jinping's Ambitious Agenda for Economic Reform in China." brookings.edu. November 17, 2013. Web. September 23, 2015.

Kuhn, Thomas S. *The Copernican Revolution: Planetary Astronomy in the Development of Western Thought*. Cambridge: Harvard UP. 1992. Print.

Kuttner, Robert. "Simplify Banks and Bank Regulation." huffingtonpost.com. Oct. 16, 2011. Web, July 27, 2015.

Kwiet, Konrad, and Jurgen Matthaus, ed. Contemporary Responses to the Holocaust. Westport: Praeger. 2004. Print.

Laffan, Brigid, and Sonia Mazey. "European integration: the European Union - reaching an equilibrium?" European Union: Power and Policy-Making. 31-54. Jeremy Richardson, ed. Abingdon: Routledge. 2006. Print.

Lambert, Richard. "Crashes, Bangs & Wallops." The Financial Times. ft.com. Web. July 25, 2015.

Lancon, Bertrand. *Rome in Late Antiquity: Everyday Life and Urban Change, AD 312-609*. New York: Routledge. 2001. Print.

Landau, Ronnie S. The Nazi Holocaust. New York: I.B. Tauris & Co. 2006. First edition 1992. Print.

Las Cases, Count de. Memoirs Of The Life, Exile, And Conversations, Of The Emperor Napoleon. Vol. II. London: Henry Colburn. 1836. Print.

Lawrence, Robert Z., Margareta Drzeniek Hanouz, and John Moavenzadeh. "The Global Enabling Trade Report 2009." World Economic Forum. 2009. Print.

Lee, Hong Yung. The Politics of the Chinese Cultrual Revolution: A Case Study. Berkely: U of California P. 1978. Print.

Leffler, Melvyn P., and Odd Arne Westad, ed. The Cambridge History of the Cold War: Volume I, Origins. Cambridge: Cambridge UP. 2010. Print.

Leick, Gwendolyn. *Mesopotamia: The Invention of the City*. London: Penguin Books Ltd. 2002. Print.

Lemos, Irene S. *The Protogeometric Aegean: The Archaeology of the Late Eleventh and Tenth Centuries BC*. Oxford: Oxford UP. 2002. Print.

"Lemuel Cook - The Last Revolutionary Patriot and Pensioner - Dead." Rochester Union Advertiser. May 22, 1866. burrcook.com. Web. June 16, 2015.

Lengel, Edward G. General George Washington: A Military Life. Random House. 2005. Print.

Lenin, V.I. "Letter to the Congress." Dec. 23, 1922-Jan. 4, 1923. marxists. org. Web. July 14, 2015.

Lerman, Katharine Anne. Bismarck. London: Routledge. 2013. Print.

Lew, Christopher R. The Third Chinese Revolutionary Civil War, 1945-49: An Analysis of Communist Strategy and Leadership. Abingdon: Routledge. 2009. Print.

Lew, Christopher R., and Edwin Pak-wah Leung. Historical Dictionary of the Chinese Civil War. Lanham: Rowman & Littlefield. 2013. Print.

Li, Xueqin., Garman Harbottle, Juzhong Zhang and Changsui Wang.

"The earliest writing? Sign use in the seventh millennium BC at Jiahu, Henan Province, China." *Antiquity* vol. 77 no. 295. (2003): 31-44. Print.

Lichtblau, Eric. "The Holocaust Just Got More Shocking." The New York Times. Mar. 3, 2013. Print.

Licklider, J.C.R. "Man-Computer Symbiosis." IRE Transactions on Human Factors in Electronics. Vol. HFE-1, March 1960: 4-11. Print.

LIFE. "Defeat Ends In Surrender". December 30, 1940. Web. 3 Apr. 2015.

Lindley, Keith. *The English Civil War and Revolution: A Sourcebook.* Abingdon: Routledge. 1998. Print.

Lindsay, Robert. *The History of Scotland: From 21 February, 1436. to March, 1565.* Baskett and Company. 1728. Print.

Livy. *History of Rome.* Trans. Canon Roberts. New York: E.P. Dutton and Co. 1912. Print.

Locke, John. *Two Treatises of government.* London: Whitmore and Fenn, and C. Brown 1821. Print.

Locke, John. *An Essay Concerning Human Understanding.* Twenty-seventh edition. London: Tegg and Son. 1836. Print.

Lockyer, Roger. *Buckingham: The Life and Political Career of George Villiers, First Duke of Buckingham 1592-1628.* London: Routledge. 1981. Print.

Logsdon, John M. John F. Kennedy and the Race to the Moon. Palgrave Macmillan. 2011. Print.

Logsdon, John M., Roger D. Launius, and Robert William Smith, ed. Reconsidering Sputnik: Forty Years Since the Soviet Satellite. London: Routledge. 2000. Print.

Longerich, Peter. *Holocaust: The Nazi Persecution and Murder of the Jews.* Oxford: Oxford UP. 2010. Print.

Lomas, S. C., ed. *The Letters and Speeches of Oliver Cromwell, with Elucidations by Thomas Carlyle.* Vol. III. London: Methuen & Co. 1904. Print.

Lorge, Peter A. *The Asian Military Revolution: From Gunpowder to the Bomb.* Cambridge: Cambridge UP. 2008. Print.

Loss, Christopher P. *Between Citizens and the State: The Politics of American Higher Education in the 20th Century*. Princeton: Princeton UP. 2012. Print.

Luebke, Peter C. "Battle of Seven Pines–Fair Oaks." Encyclopedia Virginia. Virginia Foundation for the Humanities, 21 Oct. 2014. Web. 25 Oct. 2015.

Luterbacher, J, et al. "European seasonal and annual temperature variability, trends, and extremes since 1500." Science. Vol. 303, no. 5663. Mar 5, 2004: 1499-1503. Print.

Luzader, John. Saratoga: A Military History of the Decisive Campaign of the American Revolution. New York: Savas Beatie. 2010. Print.

Lybyer, Albert Howe. *The Government Of The Ottoman Empire In The Time Of Suleiman The Magnificent*. Cambridge: Harvard UP. 1913. Print.

Lynch, Joseph. *Christianizing Kinship: Ritual Sponsorship in Anglo-Saxon England*. Ithaca: Cornell UP. 1998. Print.

Lynch, Stephen. "How Bin Laden Got Away." *New York Post*. nypost.com. Oct. 4, 2008. Web. Jan. 28, 2015.

MacDonald, William, ed. *Documentary Source Book of American History, 1606-1913*. New York: Macmillan. 1916. Print.

MacFarquhar, Neil. "Saudi Monarch Grants Women Right to Vote." *The New York Times*. nytimes.com. Sep 25, 2011. Web. Mar 6, 2015.

Machiavelli, Niccolo. *Discourses On The First Decade Of Titus Livius*. Ninian Hill Thomson, trans. London: Kegan Paul, Trench & Co. 1883. Print.

MacPherson, Robert. "Seventy years on, few Americans regret Enola Gay's mission." news.yahoo.com. August 4, 2015. Web. Aug. 24, 2015.

MacQuarrie, Kim. *The Last Days of the Incas*. New York: Simon & Schuster. 2007. Print.

Madden, Thomas F. "Rivers of Blood: An Analysis of One Aspect of the Crusader Conquest of Jerusalem in 1099." Revista Chilena de Estudios Medievales. No. 1. 2012: 25-37.

Madsen, Daniel. *Resurrection: Salvaging the Battle Fleet at Pearl*

Harbor. Annapolis: Naval Institute Press. 2003. Print.

Maier, Pauline. *Ratification: The People Debate the Constitution, 1787-1788*. New York: Simon & Schuster. 2010. Print.

"Majority of Russians still support Lenin's burial - poll." Apr. 23, 2014. rt.com. Web. July 14, 2015.

Malleson, George Bruce. *History of the French in India: from the founding of Pondichery in 1674 to the capture of that place in 1761*. Longmans, Green, and Company. 1868. Print.

Malthus, Thomas Robert. *An Essay on the Principle of Population*. 1798. Library of Economics and Liberty. econlib.org. Web. June 11, 2015.

Mancall, Peter C. ed. *Travel Narratives from the Age of Discovery: An Anthology*. Oxford: Oxford UP. 2006. Print.

Mann, James A. *The cotton trade of Great Britain: its rise, progress and present extent*. London: Simpkin, Marshall & Co. 1860. Print.

Mansch, Larry D. *Abraham Lincoln, President-elect: The Four Critical Months from Election to Inauguration*. McFarland. 2005. Print.

Marrus, Michael Robert, ed. *The Nazi Holocaust. Part 6: The Victims of the Holocaust, Volume 2*. Walter de Gruyter. 1989. Print.

Marshall, Peter. *The Oxford Illustrated History of the Reformation*. Oxford: Oxford UP. 2015. Print.

Marshall, Samuel L. A. *World War I*. New York: American Heritage. 1964. Print.

"Mars One will settle men on Mars in 2023." mars-one.com. May 31, 2012. Web. Apr. 22, 2015.

Martel, Gordon. *The Month That Changed The World*. Oxford: Oxford UP. 2014. Print.

Marx, Karl. *Capital: A Critique of Political Economy. Vol. I, The Process of Capitalist Production*. Translated from the third German edition by Samuel Moore and Edward Aveling. Frederick Engels, ed. Original title: *Das Kapital, Kritik der politischen Ökonomie*. Chicago: Charles H. Kerr & Company. 1915. Print.

Marx, Karl, and Friedrich Engels. *The Communist Manifesto*. The Floating Press. 2009. First published 1848. This version from an 1888 edition. Print.

Massie, Robert K. *Nicholas and Alexandra*. New York: Random House. 2011. First published 1967. Print.

Massie, Robert K. *Peter the Great: His Life and World*. New York: Random House. 2011. Print.

Masters, James, and Kara Fox. "International monitors deliver scathing verdict on Turkish referendum." CNN. April 18, 2017.

Mastny, Vojtech, Sven G. Holtsmark, and Andreas Wenger, ed. *War Plans and Alliances in the Cold War: Threat Perceptions in the East and West*. Abingdon: Routledge. 2006. Print.

M.A.U.D. Committee. "Report by M.A.U.D. Comittee on the Use of Uranium for a Bomb." London: Ministry of Aircraft Production. July 1941. fissilematerials.org. Web. August 25, 2015.

Maurer, John H. *The Outbreak of the First World War: Strategic Planning, Crisis Decision Making, and Deterrence Failure*. Greenwood PG. 1995. Print.

May, Ernest R. *Strange Victory: Hitler's Conquest of France*. London: I.B. Tauris & Co. 2000. Print.

McAlister, Lyle N. *Spain and Portugal in the New World, 1492-1700, Vol. 3*. U of Minnesota P. 1984. Print.

McAuliffe, Mary S, ed, and CIA History Staff. *CIA Documents on the Cuban Missile Crisis*. DIANE Publishing. 1992. Print.

McIlwraith, Thomas F. and Edward K. Muller. *North America: The Historical Geography of a Changing Continent*. Lanham: Rowman & Littlefield Publishers, Inc. 2001. Print.

McKechnie, William Sharp. Magna Carta: A Commentary on the Great Charter of King John. Second edition. Glasgow: J. Maclehose and Sons. 1914. Print.

McKinsey Global Institute. "Disruptive technologies: Advances that will transform life, business, and the global economy." May 2013. McKinsey & Company. Print.

McKitterick, Rosamond. *Charlemagne: The Formation of a European Identity*. Cambridge: Cambridge UP. 2008. Print.

McLynn, Frank. *Lionheart and Lackland: King Richard, King John and the Wars of Conquest*. Vintage. 2007. Print.

McLynn, Frank. *Napoleon*. London: Random. 1998. Print.

McPherron, Shannon P., et al. "Evidence for stone-tool-assisted consumption of animal tissues before 3.39 million years ago at Dikika, Ethiopia." *Nature* 466 (2010): 857-860. Print.

McPherson, James M. "Antebellum Southern Exceptionalism: A New Look at an Old Question." *Civil War History.* Vol. 50, no. 4. 2004: 418-433. Print.

McPherson, James M. *The Illustrated Battle Cry of Freedom: The Civil War Era.* Oxford: Oxford UP. 2003. Print.

McRaney, W, and J. McGahan. *Radiation Dose Reconstruction U.S. Occupation Forces in Hiroshima And Nagasaki, Japan, 1945-1946.* Washington: Defense Nuclear Agency. August 6, 1980. Print.

Medley, Keith Weldon. *We as Freemen: Plessy v. Ferguson.* Gretna: Pelican. 2003. Print.

Meisner, Maurice. *Mao's China and After: A History of the People's Republic.* Third Edition. New York: Simon & Schuster. 1999. Print.

Mellaart, J. "Excavations at Çatal Hüyük: first preliminary report, 1961." *Anatolian Studies* vol. 12 (1962): 41-65. British Institute at Ankara. Print.

Merrill, Dennis, and Thomas Paterson. *Major Problems in American Foreign Relations, Volume II: Since 1914.* Seventh Edition. Cengage Learning. 2009. Print.

Michelet, Jules. *History of France.* Vol. I. Trans. G.H. Smith. London: Whittaker and Co. 1845. Print.

Michman, Dan. *The Emergence of Jewish Ghettos during the Holocaust.* Cambridge: Cambridge UP. 2011. Print.

Mieroop, Marc Van De. *Cuneiform Texts and the Writing of History.* New York: Routledge. 1999. Print.

Miller, Donald L. *D-Days in the Pacific.* New York: Simon & Schuster. 2008. Print.

Miller, Harry W. *Railway Artillery: A Report on the Characteristics, Scope of Utility, Etc., of Railway Artillery.* Volume I. United States Army. Ordnance Dept. Washington: Government Printing Office. 1921.

Miller, John C. *Alexander Hamilton and the Growth of the New Nation.* First edition 1959. Brunswick: Transaction. 2004. Print.

Miller, John C. *Origins of the American Revolution.* Stanford: Stanford UP. 1959. Print.

Miller, Randall M., and John David Smith, ed. *Dictionary of Afro-American Slavery.* Westport: Praeger. 1997. Print.

Milyukov, Pavel. *Political memoirs, 1905-1917.* U of Michigan P. 1967. Print.

Misa, Thomas, J. *A Nation of Steel: The Making of Modern America, 1865-1925.* Johns Hopkins UP. 1998. Print.

Misch, Rochus. *Hitler's Last Witness: The Memoirs of Hitler's Bodyguard.* Pen & Sword Books , trans. Frontline Books. 2014.

Mitchell, Allan. *The Great Train Race: Railways and the Franco-German Rivalry, 1815-1914.* Berghahn Books. 2006. Print.

Mithen, Steven. *After the Ice: A Global Human History, 20,000-5000 BC.* Cambridge, MA: Harvard UP. 2006. Print.

Modelski, George. *World Cities: -3000 to 2000.* Washington DC: FAROS 2000. 2003. Print.

Molotov-Ribbentrop Pact. *Modern History Sourcebook: The Molotov-Ribbentrop Pact, 1939.* Web. Apr. 2, 2015.

Mombauer, Annika. *Helmuth Von Moltke and the Origins of the First World War.* Cambridge: Cambridge UP. 2001. Print.

Mommsen, Theodore E. "Petrarch's Conception of the 'Dark Ages'." Speculum 17. No. 2. 1942: 226-242. Print.

Montholon, Charles Tristan. *Récits de la captivité de l'empereur Napoléon à Sainte-Hélène.* Volume 1. Paris: Paulin. 1847. Print.

Montrie, Chad. *Making a Living: Work and Environment in the United States.* U of North Carolina P. 2008. Print.

Moon, David. *Abolition of Serfdom in Russia: 1762-1907.* New York: Routledge. 2014. Print.

Moran, James. *Printing Presses: History and Development from the Fifteenth Century to Modern Times.* Berkeley: U of California P. 1978. Print.

Morelli, Giovanna, et al. "*Yersinia pestis* genome sequencing identifies patterns of global phylogenetic diversity." *Nature Genetics* 42, 2010: 1140–1143. Web. Mar 21, 2015.

Morillo, Stephen and Diane Korngiebel, ed. *The Haskins Society Journal, Volume 16: Studies in Medieval History, Volume 16; Volume 2005.* Woodbridge: The Boydell Press. 2006. Print.

Morgan, Edmund S., and Helen M. Morgan. *The Stamp Act Crisis: Prologue to Revolution.* U of North Carolina P. 1953. Print.

Morrow, John H. Jr. *The Great War: An Imperial History.* London: Routledge. 2004. Print.

Morse, Jedidiah. *Annals Of The American Revolution Or A Record Of The Causes And Events Which Produced And Terminated In The Establishment And Independence Of The American Republic.* Hartford: s.n. 1824. Print.

Moss, Walter G. *A History of Russia Volume 1: To 1917.* Second edition. London: Anthem Press. 2005. Print.

Mozgovoi, Alexander. "The Cuban Samba of the Quartet of Foxtrots: Soviet Submarines in the Caribbean Crisis of 1962." Military Parade, Moscow. 2002. Svetlana Savranskaya, trans. National Security Archive. nsarchive.gwu.edu. Web. September 13, 2015.

Murphy, Dean E., Jennifer Lee and Yilu Zhao. "The SARS Epidemic: Asian-Americans; in U.S., Fear Is Spreading Faster Than SARS." New York Times. April 17, 2003. Web. Mar 21, 2015.

Murray, Stuart A. P. *The Library: An Illustrated History.* New York: Skyhorse Publishing. 2009. Print.

NASA. "Voyager Mission Operations Status Report # 2014-07-25 Week Ending July 25, 2014." voyager.jpl.nasa.gov. Web. September 6, 2015.

National Commission on Terrorist Attacks. *The 9/11 Commission Report: Final Report of the National Commission on Terrorist Attacks Upon the United States (Authorized Edition).* New York: W.W. Norton & Company. 2011. Print.

National Defense Authorization Act For Fiscal Year 2012. Pub. L. 112-81. 31 Dec. 2011. Print.

National Security Council, United States. From U.S. Security to

Terrorism: A Three-Part Series. Cosimo, Inc. 2005. Print.

NBC. "NBC News Coverage of the September 11, 2001, Terrorist Attacks (Part 1 of 2)." youtube.com. Web. Jan. 25, 2015.

Needham, Joseph and Tsien Tsuen-Hsuin. *Science & Civilisation in China: Volume 5, Chemistry and Chemical Technology, Part 1, Paper and Printing.* Cambridge: Cambridge UP. 1985. Print.

Nelson, Craig. *Thomas Paine: Enlightenment, Revolution, and the Birth of Modern Nations.* Viking. 2006. Print.

Nester, William R. *The Great Frontier War: Britain, France, and the Imperial Struggle for North America, 1607-1755.* Westport: Greenwood. 2000. Print.

Neufeld, Michael J. *The Rocket and the Reich: Peenemünde and the Coming of the Ballistic Missile Era.* New York: Simon & Schuster. 1995. Print.

Neumeyer, Joy. "A Visit to Moscow's Brain Institute." vice.com. Apr. 10, 2014. Web. July 2, 2015.

Newman, Paul B. *Daily Life in the Middle Ages.* Jefferson: McFarland & Company. 2001. Print.

New York Times. "1,028 Economists Ask Hoover To Veto Pending Tariff Bill." *The New York Times.* May 5, 1930. Print.

New York Times. "Hitler is Pleased to Get Rid of Foes." *The New York Times.* Mar. 27, 1938. Print.

New York Times. "Last Union Army Veteran Dies; Drummer at 17, he Lived to 109." The New York Times. Aug. 3, 1956. Print.

Nicolle, David. *The First Crusade 1096-99: Conquest of the Holy Land.* Osprey. 2003. Print.

Nicolle, David. *The Italian Invasion of Abyssinia, 1935-36.* Osprey. 1997. Print.

Nicosia, Francis R. *Jewish Life in Nazi Germany: Dilemmas and Responses.* Berghahn Books. 2010. Print.

Nolan, Cathal J. *The Age of Wars of Religion, 1000-1650: An Encyclopedia of Global Warfare and Civilization. Volume 1.* Greenwood Publishing Group. 2006. Print.

Northrup, Cynthia Clark, ed. *The American Economy: A Historical*

Encyclopedia, Volume I. Santa Barbara: ABC-CLIO. 2011. Print.

Nweke, Felix I. "The Cassava Transformation In Africa." Michigan State University. 2002. fao.org. Web. May 5, 2015.

Odekon, Mehmet. *Booms and Busts: An Ecyclopedia of Economic History from the First Stock Market Crash of 1792 to the Current Global Economic Crisis*. Third Edition. Routledge. 2015. Print.

Official papers, relative to the preliminaries of London and the Treaty of Amiens. London: J. Debrett. 1803. Print.

Ogg, Frederic Austin. *A Source Book of Medieval History*. New York: American Book Company. 1907. Print.

Osborn, Andrew. "Russians want Lenin removed from Red Square." Jan 23, 2011. Telegraph.co.uk. Web. July 14, 2015.

Osborne, Roger. *Iron, Steam & Money: The Making of the Industrial Revolution*. London: Random House. 2013. Print.

Osiander, Robert. "From Vengeance 2 to Sputnik I: The Beginnings." *Handbook of Space Engineering, Archaeology, and Heritage*. 209-228. Ann Garrison Darrin and Beth Laura O'Leary, ed. Taylor and Francis Group. 2009. Print.

Overy, Richard. *Russia's War: A History of the Soviet War Effort: 1941-1945*. New York: Penguin Group. 1998.

Ozment, Steven. *The Age of Reform, 1250-1550: An Intellectual and Religious History of Late Medieval and Reformation Europe*. Yale UP. 1980. Print.

Pankhurst, Emmeline. "Freedom or Death." Nov. 13, 1913. *Political Dissent: A Global Reader: Modern Sources*. 121-147. Derek Malone-France, ed. Lanham: Rowman & Littlefield. 2012. Print.

Paine, Thomas. Bruce Kuklick, ed. Paine: Political Writings. Revised student edition. Cambridge: Cambridge UP. 2000. Print.

Panofsky, Erwin. "Renaissance and Renascences." *The Kenyon Review, Vol. 6. No. 2. 1944: 201-236*. Kenyon College. Print.

Parker, Geoffrey. *The Thirty Years' War*. Second Edition. Routledge. 1997. Print.

Partington, J. R. *A History of Greek Fire and Gunpowder*. Baltimore: Johns Hopkins UP. 1999. First published 1960. Print.

Paterculus, Velleius. *Roman History.* Trans. Frederick W. Shipley. Loeb Classical Library. 1924. Print.

Pausanias. *Description of Greece.* Trans. W.H.S. Jones. Cambridge: Harvard UP. 1918. Print.

"Peacefully grant the State of Texas to withdraw from the United States of America and create its own NEW government." n.d. petitions. whitehouse.gov. Web. May 26, 2015.

Peacock, Andrew and Sara Nur Yildiz. *The Seljuks of Anatolia: Court and Society in the Medieval Middle East.* London: I.B. Tauris & Co. 2013. Print.

Pepys, Samuel. *The Diary of Samuel Pepys, Vol. 8: 1667.* U of California P. 2000. Print.

Pershing, John J. *My Experiences in the World War.* Vol. II. New York: Frederick A. Stokes Company. 1931. Print.

Persico, Joseph E. *Eleventh Month, Eleventh Day, Eleventh Hour: Armistice Day, 1918 World War I and Its Violent Climax.* New York: Random House. 2004. Print.

Peters, Edward, ed. *The First Crusade: "The Chronicle of Fulcher of Chartres" and Other Source Materials.* Second edition. U of Pennsylvania P. 1998. Print.

Pew Research Center. "The Global Religious Landscape." The Pew Forum on Religion & Public Life. 18 December 2012. Web. 24 February 2015.

Pflanze, Otto. *Bismarck and the Development of Germany: The Period of Unification 1815-1871.* Vol. 1. Princeton UP. 1968. Print.

Philips, Edward J. *The Founding of Russia's Navy: Peter the Great and the Azov Fleet, 1688-1714.* Westport: Greenwood. 1995. Print.

Phillips, McCandlish. "Campus A Bivouac As Negro Enters, 2,000 Troops Stand Guard — Meredith Eats Alone." *The New York Times.* October 2, 1962. Print.

Philpott, William. *Three Armies on the Somme: The First Battle of the Twentieth Century.* New York: Random House. 2011. Print.

Pigafetta, Antonio. *The First Voyage Around The World 1519-1522: An Account of Magellan's Expedition.* Ed. Theodore J. Cachey Jr. U of

Toronto P. 2007. Print.

Piketty, Thomas, and Emmanuel Saez. "Income Inequality in the United States, 1913-1998." *The Quarterly Journal of Economics*. Vol. 118 (1). 1-41. 2003. Print.

Pilcher, Helen R. "Earliest handwriting found?: Chinese relics hint at Neolithic rituals." *Nature*. 30 April 2003. Web. 13 December 2014.

Pinkus, Oscar. *The War Aims and Strategies of Adolf Hitler*. Jefferson: McFarland & Company. 2005. Print.

Piper, Franciszek. "Gas Chambers and Crematoria." *Anatomy of the Auschwitz Death Camp*. Yisrael Gutman and Michael Berenbaum, ed. Bloomington: Indiana UP. 1994. 157-182. Print.

Pipes, Richard. *Communism: A History*. Modern Library Edition. New York: Random House. 2001. Print.

Piston, William Garrett, and Richard W. Hatcher III. *Wilson's Creek: The Second Battle of the Civil War and the Men Who Fought It*. U of North Carolina P. 2000. Print.

Piszkiewicz, Dennis. *The Nazi Rocketeers: Dreams of Space and Crimes of War*. Mechanicsburg: Stackpole Books. 2006. Print.

Pitcher, Donald Edgar. *An Historical Geography of the Ottoman Empire: From Earliest Times to the End of the Sixteenth Century*. Leiden: E. J. Brill. 1968. Print.

Plessy v. Ferguson. 163 U.S. 537. Supreme Court of the United States. 1896. Supreme Court Collection. Legal Information Inst., Cornell U. Law School, n.d. Web. 15 Jan. 2016.

Pliny the Elder. *The Natural History*. Trans. John Bostock, M.D., F.R.S.H.T. Riley, Esq., B.A. London: Taylor and Francis. 1855. Print.

Ploeckl, Florian. "The Zollverein and the Formation of a Customs Union." *University of Oxford Discussion Papers in Economic and Social History*. No. 84. August 2010. Department of Economics and Nuffield College, University of Oxford. Print.

Plutarch. *Plutarch's Lives*. "Alexander". Trans. Bernadotte Perrin. Cambridge: Harvard UP. 1919. Print.

Plutarch. *Plutarch's Lives*. "Antony". Trans. Bernadotte Perrin. Cambridge: Harvard UP. 1920. Print.

Plutarch. *Plutarch's Lives.* "Caesar". Trans. Bernadotte Perrin. Cambridge: Harvard UP. 1919. Print.

Plutarch. *Plutarch's Lives.* "Caius Marius". Trans. Bernadotte Perrin. Cambridge: Harvard UP. 1920. Print.

Plutarch. *Plutarch's Lives.* "Camillus". Trans. Bernadotte Perrin. Cambridge: Harvard UP. 1914. Print.

Plutarch. *Plutarch's Lives.* "Cato the Younger". Trans. Bernadotte Perrin. Cambridge: Harvard UP. 1919. Print.

Plutarch. *Plutarch's Lives.* "Sulla". Trans. Bernadotte Perrin. Cambridge: Harvard UP. 1916. Print.

Plutarch. *Plutarch's Morals.* Vol. IV. Trans. William W. Goodwin. Boston: Little, Brown And Company. 1878. Print.

Pollock, Susan. *Ancient Mesopotamia.* Cambridge: Cambridge UP. 1999. Print.

Polmar, Norman, and Kenneth J. Moore. *Cold War Submarines: The Design and Construction of U.S. and Soviet Submarines.* Washington, D.C.: Potomac Books. 2004. Print.

Polybius. *The Histories.* 6 volumes. Trans. W.R. Paton. Cambridge: Harvard UP. 1922-1927. Print.

Pomeroy, Sarah B., et al. *Ancient Greece: A Political, Social and Cultural History.* Oxford: Oxford UP. 1999. Print.

"Population Census 2010." The Brazilian Institute of Geography and Statistics, or IBGE (*Instituto Brasileiro de Geografia e Estatística*). ibge.gov.br. 2010. Web. 11 May 2015.

Population of the United States in 1860; Compiled from the Original Returns of the Eighth Census. Washington: Government Printing Office. 1864. Print.

Pratt, Fletcher. *The Battles that Changed History.* Dover Publications. 2000. Print.

Prigg, Mark and Daily Mail Reporter. "More than 78,000 people apply to move to Mars Forever." dailymail.co.uk. May 8, 2013. Web. Apr. 22, 2015.

Pringle, Heather. "Quest for Fire Began Earlier Than Thought." Sciencemag (April 2012): American Association for the Advancement of Science. Web. 3 December 2014.

Prescott, William H. History of the Conquest of Peru: With a Preliminary View of the Civilization of the Incas. Vol. 2. London: G. Routledge & Co. 1855. Print.

Prescott, William H. The Conquest of Peru. Vol. 1. New York: Merrill and Baker. 1847. Print.

Preston, Richard. "First World War centenary: the assassination of Franz Ferdinand, as it happened." June 27, 2014. telegraph.co.uk. Web. July 14, 2015.

Proclamation of Rebellion. Aug. 23, 1775. archives.gov. Web. Jan. 1, 2016.

"Proceedings of Commissioners to Remedy Defects of the Federal Government: 1786." Avalon Project, Yale Law. n.p. n.d. avalon.law. yale.edu. Web. June 2, 2015.

Procopius. History of the Wars, Books I and II. H.B. Dewing, trans. Cambridge: Harvard UP. 1914. Print.

"Program of the National Socialist German Workers' Party." Avalon Project, Yale Law. n.p. n.d. avalon.law.yale.edu. Web. Aug. 13, 2015.

Project for the New American Century. "Letter from the Project for the New American Century to the Honorable William J. Clinton, President of the United States." informationclearinghouse.info. January 26, 1998. Web. Aug. 4, 2015.

Purkiss, Diane. The English Civil War: Papists, Gentlewomen, Soldiers, and Witchfinders in the Birth of Modern Britain. New York: Basic Books. 2006. Print.

Qiu, Xigui. Chinese Writing. Trans. Gilbert L. Mattos and Jerry Norman. Early China Special Monograph Series, No. 4. Society for the Study of Early China and the Institute of East Asian Studies. U of California. 2000. Print.

Quartering Act; May 15, 1765. Great Britain: Parliament. Avalon Project, Yale Law. avalon.law.yale.edu. Web. May 28, 2015.

Radivojevic, Miljana., et al. "Tainted ores and the rise of tin bronzes in Eurasia, c. 6500 years ago." *Antiquity* vol. 87, no. 338 (2013): 1030-1045. Print.

Radivojevic, Miljana., et al. "On the origins of extractive metallurgy: new evidence from Europe." *Journal of Archaeological Science* vol. 37, issue 11 (2010): 2775-2787. Print.

Radziwill, Princess Catherine. *The Taint of the Romanovs*. Cassell. 1931. Print.

"Recharge your cellphone in 30 seconds." CNN staff. Cnn.com. 20 May 2013. Web. 6 May 2015.

Reich, Robert B. "Community Perspective: Widening Inequality Hurts us All." *Community Investments*. Vol. 23 (2). 2011. 17-21. Federal Reserve Bank of San Francisco. frbsf.org. Web. October 1, 2015.

Reid, Robert H. *Architects of the Web: 1,000 Days that Built the Future of Business*. New York: John Wiley & Sons. 1997. Print.

"Report from General Zakharov and Admiral Fokin to the Presidium, Central Committee, Communist Party of the Soviet Union, on the Progress of Operation Anadyr." September 25, 1962. Volkogonov Collection, Library of Congress, Manuscript Division, Reel 17, Container 26. Translated by Gary Goldberg for the Cold War International History Project of the National Security Archive. nsarchive.gwu.edu. Web. September 13, 2015.

"Rethink Robotics Revolutionizes Manufacturing with Humanoid Robot." Sept. 18, 2012. Press release from Rethink Robotics. rethinkrobotics.com. Web. June 29, 2015.

Rhodes, Richard. *The Making of the Atomic Bomb: 25th Anniversy Edition*. New York: Simon & Schuster. 2012. Print.

Riasanvosky, Nicholas V. *A History of Russia*. Sixth Edition. Oxford: Oxford UP. 2000. Print.

Rice, Edward E. *Mao's Way*. Berkely: U of California P. 1974. Print.

Richards, Denis. *The Royal Air Force 1939-1945 Vol. I: The Fight At Odds*. London: H.M. Stationery Office. 1953. Print.

Richards, Leonard L. *Shay's Rebellion: The American Revolution's Final Battle*. U of Pennsylvania P. 2002. Print.

Risser, Nicole Dombrowski. *France Under Fire: German Invasion, Civilian Flight, and Family Survival during World War II*. Cambridge: Cambridge UP. 2012.

Risjord, Norman K. *Jefferson's America, 1760-1815*. Lanham: Rowman & Littlefield. 2010. Print.

Roberts, Andrew. *Napoleon and Wellington: The Battle of Waterloo - and the Great Commanders who Fought it*. New York: Simon & Schuster. 2001. Print.

Roberts, Andrew. *Napoleon & Wellington: The Long Duel*. London: Orion. 2002. Print.

Roberts, Gene, and Hank Klibanoff. *The Race Beat: The Press, the Civil Rights Struggle, and the Awakening of a Nation*. New York: Random House. 2007. Print.

Roberts, Geoffrey. *Stalin's Wars: From World War to Cold War, 1939-1953*. Yale UP. 2006. Print.

Roberts, Geoffrey. *Victory at Stalingrad: The Battle that Changed History*. Harlow: Pearson Education Limited. 2002. Print.

Robertson, Geoffrey. *The Tyrannicide Brief: The Story of the Man who sent Charles I to the Scaffold*. Vintage. 2006. Print.

Robinson, Janet, and Joe Robinson. *Handbook of Imperial Germany*. Bloomington: AuthorHouse. 2009. Print.

Robinson, Thomas W. "The Wuhan Incident: Local Strife and Provincial Rebellion during the Cultural Revolution." *The China Quarterly*. No. 47. Jul.-Sep., 1971: 413-438. Cambridge UP. Print.

Roby, Henry John. *An Introduction to the Study of Justinian's Digest: Containing an Account of Its Composition and of the Jurists Used Or Referred to Therein, Together with a Full Commentary on One Title (De Usufructu)*. First published 1884. Cambridge: Cambridge UP. 2010. Print.

Rogers, Clifford J, ed. *The Oxford Encyclopedia of Medieval Warfare and Military Technology*. Oxford: Oxford University Press. 2010. Print.

Rogers, Clifford J. ed. *The Wars of Edward III: Sources and Interpretations*. Woodbridge: The Boydell Press. 1999. Print.

Rogers, Simon. "Nasa budgets: US spending on space travel since 1958." theguardian.com. February 1, 2010. Web. September 13, 2015.

"Roll of Honour of "The Few"." *The Battle of Britain Historical Society*.

battleofbritain1940.net. Web. Apr. 3, 2015.

Romero, Simon. "Rio's Race to Future Intersects Slave Past." The New York Times. 8 Mar. 2014. Web. 11 May 2015.

Romm, James S. Trans. Pamela Mensch and James Romm. *Alexander The Great: Selections From Arrian, Diodorus, Plutarch, And Quintus Curtius.* Indianapolis: Hackett Publishing Company, Inc. 2005. Print.

Roosevelt, Franklin D. "Address Accepting the Presidential Nomination at the Democratic National Convention in Chicago." July 2, 1932. *The American Presidency Project.* presidency.ucsb.edu. Web. July 27, 2015.

Roosevelt, Franklin D. "Day of Infamy Speech". Records of the United States Senate. SEN 77A-H1, Record Group 46, National Archives. archives.gov. December 8, 1941. Web. 04 Apr. 2015.

Rose, John Holland. *The Life Of Napoleon I.* London: G. Bell and Sons. 1910. Print.

Rosenberg, Carol. "Obama to leave with 41 captives still at Guantánamo blames politics." Miamiherald.com. January 19, 2017. Web. May 18, 2017.

Roser, Max. "Child Mortality." ourworldindata.org. 2015. Web. July 1, 2015.

Roser, Max. "Life Expectancy." ourworldindata.org. 2015. Web. July 1, 2015.

Rosner, Lisa and John Theibault. *A Short History of Europe, 1600-1815: Search for a Reasonable World.* New York: M. E. Sharpe. 2000. Print.

Ross, Sir E. Denison. "Introduction." in: *The Travels of Marco Polo: Translated into English from the Text of L.F. Benedetto.* Marco Polo, Aldo Ricci, Luigi Foscolo Benedetto. New Delhi: Asian Educational Services. 1931. Print.

Rothbard, Murray N. *History of Money and Banking in the United States: The Colonial Era to World II.* Ludwig von Mises Institute. 2002. Print.

Rozett, Robert, and Shmuel Spector. *Encyclopedia of the Holocaust.* Jerusalem Publishing House. 2000. Print.

Rudoren, Jodi. "Proudly Bearing Elders' Scars, Their Skin Says 'Never

Forget'." *The New York Times.* nytimes.com. Sept. 30, 2012. Web. Aug. 13, 2015.

Runciman, Steven. *The Fall of Constantinople 1453.* Cambridge: Cambridge UP. 1965. Print.

Russell, Josiah C. "Population in Europe". in *The Fontana Economic History of Europe, Vol I: The Middle Ages.* ed. Carlo M. Cipolla. Glasgow: Collins/Fontana. 1972: 25-71.

Russian Fundamental Laws of 1906. Royal Russia and Gilbert's Royal Books. angelfire.com. n.d. Web. July 7, 2015.

"Russia's Economy under Vladimir Putin: Achievements and Failures." n.a. Sputnik International. March 1, 2008. Web. May 22, 2015.

Sablinsky, Walter. *The Road to Bloody Sunday: The Role of Father Gapon and the Petersburg Massacre of 1905.* Princeton UP. 1976. Print.

Saez, Emmanuel. "Striking it Richer: The Evolution of Top Incomes in the United States." UC Berkeley. eml.berkeley.edu. Jan. 25, 2015. Web. Oct. 5, 2015.

Safrai, Shemuel and M. Stern. *The Jewish People in the First Century: Historical Geography, Political History, Social, Cultural and Religious Life and Institutions.* Vol. Two. Van Gorcum. 1976. Print.

Saich, Tony, and Benjamin Yang. *The Rise to Power of the Chinese Communist Party: Documents and Analysis.* M.E. Sharpe. 1995. Print.

Salahuddin, Sayed. "Taliban beheads 17 Afghan partygoers; 2 NATO troops killed." *The Washington Post.* washingtonpost.com. Aug. 27, 2012. Web. Jan. 28, 2015.

Sallust. *The War With Catiline.* Trans. John Carew Rolfe. Loeb Classical Library. 1921. Print.

Sampson, Charles S., and Glenn W. LaFantasie, ed. Foreign Relations of the United States, 1961-1963, Volume XIV, Berlin Crisis, 1961-1962. Washington: United States Printing Office. 1993. Print.

Sampson, Charles S., and Glenn W. LaFantasie. Foreign Relations of the United States, 1961-1963, Volume VI, Kennedy-Khrushchev Exchanges. Washington: United States Printing Office. 1996. Print.

Sarkar, Tapan K., Robert J. Mailloux, et al. *History of Wireless.* Hoboken:

John Wiley & Sons. 2006. Print.

Saul, Norman E. *Historical Dictionary of Russian and Soviet Foreign Policy*. Lanham: Rowman & Littlefield. 2015. Print.

Savranskaya, Svetlana V. "New Sources on the Role of Soviet Submarines in the Cuban Missile Crisis." *Journal of Strategic Studies*, 28:2, 2005: 233-259. Print.

Scheidel, Walter and Steven J. Friesen. "The Size of the Economy and the Distribution of Income in the Roman Empire." *Journal of Roman Studies* Vol. 99 (2009): 61-91. Print.

Schep, Leo J., et al. "Was the death of Alexander the Great due to poisoning? Was it Veratrum album?." Clinical Toxicology Vol 52, No.1 (2014): 72-77. Print.

Schlesinger, Arthur M., Jr. *Robert Kennedy and His Times*. New York: Houghton Mifflin. 2002. First edition 1978. Print.

Schmemann, Serge. "Soviet Disarray; Preserving Lenin, the High-Tech Icon." *The New York Times*. nytimes.com. Dec. 17, 1991. Web. July 2, 2015.

Schmuhl, Hans-Walter. *The Kaiser Wilhelm Institute for Anthropoloy, Human Heredity and Eugenics, 1927-1945: Crossing Boundaries*. Springer. 2008. Print.

Schnoor, Stefan, and Boris Klinge. "The last survivor of Hitler's downfall - The Fuhrer's bodyguard gives last interview." express.co.uk. May 15, 2011. Web. Apr. 1, 2015.

Schofield, Hugh. "Napoleon...the theme park." BBC News. bbc.com. March 27, 2012. Web. June 5, 2015.

Scholz, Bernhard Walter and Barbara Rogers-Gardner, trans. *Carolingian Chronicles: Royal Frankish Annals and Nithard's Histories*. U of Michigan P. 1970. Print.

Schouler, James. *History of the United States of America. Vol. VI. 1861-1865*. New York: Dodd, Mead & Company. 1899. Print.

Schüddekopf, Otto Ernst. *Der Erste Weltkrieg*. Bertelsmann Lexikon-Verlag. 1977. Print.

Schwartz, Stephen I, ed. *Atomic Audit: The Costs and Consequenses of U.S. Nuclear Weapons Since 1940*. Washington: Brookings Institution.

1998. Print.

Sciolino, Elaine. "North of Paris, a Forest of History and Fantasy." *The New York Times*. nytimes.com. Nov. 2, 2008. Web. 3 Apr. 2015.

Scobell, Andrew. "Seventy-five Years of Civil-Military Relations; Lessons Learned." *The Lessons of History: The Chinese People's Liberation Army at 75*. 427-450. Laurie Burkitt, Andrew Scobell, Larry M. Wortzel, ed. Strategic Studies Institute. U.S. Army War College. 2003. Print.

Scott, Robert A. *Miracle Cures: Saints, Pilgrimage, and the Healing Powers of Belief*. Berkeley: U of California P. 2010. Print.

Scott-Smith, Giles, and Hans Krabbendam. *The Cultural Cold War in Western Europe, 1945-1960*. London: Frank Cass. 2003. Print.

Scott v. Sanford, 60 U.S. (19 How.) 393 (1857)

Sears, Stephen W. *Gettysburg*. New York: Houghton Mifflin. 2004. Print.

Sears, Stephen W. *Landscape Turned Red: The Battle of Antietam*. New York: Houghton Mifflin. 2003. Print.

"Second Crash New York 'Change - Frenzied Trading - Panic Spreads Quickly." Oct. 28, 1929. *The Sydney Morning Herald*. trove.nla.gov. au. Web. July 25, 2015.

"Security Council Committee established pursuant to resolution 1737 (2006)." un.org. n.d. Web. August 24, 2015.

Sergeant, Lewis. *The Franks, from their Origin as a Confederacy to the Establishment of the Kingdom of France*. New York: Putnam. 1898. Print.

Service, Robert. *A History of Modern Russia from Nicholas II to Vladimir Putin*. Harvard UP. 2005. Print.

Seters, John van. *Abraham in History and Tradition*. Vermont: Echo Point Books & Media. 1975. Print.

Shakespeare, William. *Hamlet*. Robert Hapgood, ed. Cambridge: Cambridge UP. 1999. Print.

Shanzer, Danuta. "Dating the baptism of Clovis: the bishop of Vienne vs the bishop of Tours." Early Medieval Europe, 7: 29-57. doi: 10.1111/1468-0254.00017. 1998. Print.

Shapiro, Fred R. *The Yale Book of Quotations*. Yale UP. 2006. Print.

Shaw, Henry. *Dresses and Decorations of the Middle Ages, Volume 1.* London: William Pickering. 1843. Print.

Shaw, Stanford J. *History of the Ottoman Empire and Modern Turkey: Volume I, Empire of the Gazis: The Rise and Decline of the Ottoman Empire 1280-1808.* Cambridge: Cambridge UP. 1976. Print.

Shedlock, Mike. "Incredible Burger-Flipping Robot Wants To Steal Our Jobs." Febr. 4, 2013. businessinsider.com. Web. June 29, 2015.

Sherman, A. J. *Island Refuge: Britain and Refugees from the Third Reich 1933-1939.* Routledge. 2013. Print.

Shorto, Russel. *The Island at the Center of the World: The Epic Story of Dutch Manhattan and the Forgotten Colony That Shaped America.* Vintage. 2005. Print.

Siddiqi, Asif A. *The Red Rockets' Glare: Spaceflight and the Russian Imagination, 1857-1957.* Cambridge: Cambridge UP. 2010. Print.

Simpson, Colin. "Lusitania: A Great Liner With Too Many Secrets." Life Magazine. Vol. 73. No. 15. Oct. 13, 1972. Print.

Sitton, Claude. "Shots Quell Mob — Enrolling of Meredith Ends Segregation in State Schools." *The New York Times.* October 2, 1962. Print.

Smith, Harold L. *The British Women's Suffrage Campaign, 1866-1928.* Second Edition. Harlow: Pearson Education. 2007. Print.

Smith, Jean Edward. *Grant.* New York: Simon & Schuster. 2001. Print.

Smyser, W. R. *Kennedy and the Berlin Wall.* Lanham: Rowman & Littlefield. 2009. Print.

Snow, Edgar. *Red Star Over China.* New York: Grove Press. 1968. First edition 1938. Print.

Sohn, Pow-key. "Early Korean Printing." *Journal of the American Oriental Society.* Vol. 79, No.2 (Apr-Jun, 1959): 96-103. Print.

Sondhaus, Lawrence. *World War One: The Global Revolution.* Cambridge: Cambridge UP. 2011. Print.

Souza, George Bryan. *The Survival of Empire: Portuguese Trade and Society in China and the South China Sea 1630-1754.* Cambridge: Cambridge UP. 1986. Print.

Sparks, Jared, ed. *The Writings of George Washington. Vol. VI.* Boston:

Ferdinand Andrews. 1840. Print.

Sperber, Jonathan. *Rhineland Radicals: The Democratic Movement and the Revolution of 1848-1849*. Princeton: Princeton UP. 1991. Print.

Stalin, Joseph. "Order No. 227 by the People's Commissar of Defence of the USSR". July 28, 1942. wikisource.org. Web. Apr. 4, 2015.

Staloff, Darren. *Hamilton, Adams, Jefferson: The Politics of Enlightenment and the American Founding*. Hill and Wang. 2005. Print.

Standage, Tom. "Writing is the Greatest Invention." *Intelligent Life Magazine*. (Jan/Feb 2012). Web. 12 december 2014.

"Statistical Abstract of the United States 1937." Washington: U.S. G.P.O. 1937. Print.

"Statistical Abstract of the United States 1942." Washington: U.S. G.P.O. 1942. Print.

Stedman, C. *The History Of The Origin, Progress, and Termination Of The American War. In Two Volumes*. Vol. I. London: n.p. 1794. Print.

Steinberg, Mark D. *Voices of Revolution, 1917*. Yale UP. 2003. Print.

Steinweis, Alan E. *Studying the Jew: Scholarly Antisemitism in Nazi Germany*. Harvard UP. 2006. Print.

Steinweis, Alan E., and Robert D. Rachlin. *The Law in Nazi Germany: Ideology, Opportunism, and the Perversion of Justice*. Berghahn Books. 2013. Print.

Stephens, A. Ray. *Texas: A Historical Atlas*. U of Oklahoma P. 2010. Print.

Sterba, James P. "Former Chinese Leaders Given Long Prison Terms." *The New York Times*. January 26, 1981. Print.

Stewart, Alan. *The Cradle King: The Life of James VI & I, the First Monarch of a United Great Britain*. New York: St. Martin's Press. 2003. Print.

Stewart, John Hall. *A Documentary Survey of the French Revolution*. New York: Macmillan. 1951. Print.

Stiglitz, Joseph E. "Capitalist Fools." Vanity Fair. vanityfair.com. Jan. 2009. Web. July 27, 2015.

Stillion Southard, Belinda A. *Militant Citizenship: Rhetorical Strategies of the National Woman's Party, 1913-1920.* Texas A&M UP. 2011. Print.

Stone, Dan. *The Liberation of the Camps: The End of the Holocaust and Its Aftermath.* Yale UP. 2015. Print.

Stout, David. "C.I.A. Detainees Sent to Guantánamo." *The New York Times.* nytimes.com. Sep. 6, 2006. Web. Jan. 27, 2015.

Strachan, Hew. *The First World War.* New York: Penguin Group. 2004. Print.

Strauss, Barry. *The Battle of Salamis: The Naval Encounter That Saved Greece — and Western   Civilization.* New York: Simon & Schuster. 2005. Print.

Strayer, Robert W. *Why Did the Soviet Union Collapse?: Understanding Historical Change.* Armonk: M.E. Sharpe. 1998. Print.

Strickland, Mary, and Jane Margaret Strickland. *A memoir of the life, writings, and mechanical inventions of Edmund Cartwright.* London: Saunders and Otley. 1843. Print.

Strong, Anna Louise. "I Join the Red Guards." *Letters from China.* No. 41. September 20, 1966. Quoted in *China's Great Proletarian Cultural Revolution: Master Narratives and Post-Mao Counternarratives,* 105. Woei Lien Chong. Rowman & Littlefield. 2002. Print.

Suarez, Michael F., S. J. & H. R. WooudHuysen. *The Book: A Global History.* Oxford: Oxford UP. 2013. Print.

Suarez, Thomas. *Early Mapping of Southeast Asia.* Singapore: Periplus Editions (HK) Ltd. 1999. Print.

Suetonius. *The Lives of the Twelve Caesars.* " Julius Caesar". Trans. J.C. Rolfe. Loeb Classical   Library. 1914. Print.

Suetonius. *The Lives of the Twelve Caesars.* "Nero". Trans. J.C. Rolfe. Loeb Classical Library. 1914. Print.

Suetonius. *The Lives of the Twelve Caesars.* "Tiberius". Trans. J.C. Rolfe. Loeb Classical Library. 1914. Print.

Sumption, Jonathan. *The Hundred Years War, Volume I: Trial by Battle.* U of Pennsylvania P. 1991. Print.

Swarup, Bob. *Money Mania: Booms, Panics, and Busts from Ancient*

Rome to the Great Meltdown. New York: Bloomsbury. 2014. Print.

Swift, Jonathan. *Gulliver's Travels.* London: Jones & Company. 1826. Print.

Szatmary, David P. *Shays' Rebellion: The Making of an Agrarian Insurrection.* U of Massachusetts P. 1980. Print.

Szilard, Leo. "Petition to the President of the United States." July 17, 1945. trumanlibrary.org. Original source: U.S. National Archives, Record Group 77, Records of the Chief of Engineers, Manhatten Engineer District, Harrison-Bundy File, folder #76. Web. August 26, 2015.

Tacitus, *The Annals.* Trans. J. Jackson. Cambridge: Harvard UP. 1925-1937. Print.

Taubman, William. *Khrushchev: The Man and His Era.* New York: W.W. Norton & Company. 2004. Print.

Taylor, Jay. *The Generalissimo: Chiang Kai-shek and the Struggle for Modern China.* Harvard UP. 2009. Print.

Taylor, Robert J, Greg L. Lint, and Celeste Walker, ed. *Papers of John Adams, Volume 3, May 1775-January 1776.* Cambridge: Harvard UP. 1979. Print.

Texas v. White, 74 U.S. 7 Wall. 700 (1868).

The Bible: Authorized King James Version with Apocrypha. Oxford: Oxford UP, 2008. Print.

"The Electric Light." *New York Herald.* Jan. 4, 1880. P. 6, Col. 2. Print.

Thomas, Carol G. Paths from Ancient Greece. Leiden: E. J. Brill. 1988. Print.

Thompson, Robert. "Two Days in April." civilwar.org. n.d. Web. October 27, 2015.

Thompson, Thomas L. The Historicity of the Patriarcha Narratives: The Quest for the Historical Abraham. Harrisburg: Trinity Press International. 2002 (first published 1974). Print.

Thomson de Grummond, Nancy. Etruscan Myth, Sacred History, and Legend. Philadelphia: UPenn Museum of Archaeology and Anthropology. 2006. Print.

Thoreau, Henry David. A Week on the Concord and Merrimack Rivers.

Boston: James R. Osgood And Company. 1873. Print.

Thoyras, Paul de Rapin de. The History of England from the Earliest Periods. In Two Volumes. Vol. II. Henry Robertson, trans. Cundee. 1820. Print.

Thucydides. History of the Peloponnesian War. B. Jowett, trans. Oxford: Clarendon Press. 1881. Print.

Teiwes, Frederick C. *Politics and Purges in China: Rectification and the Decline of Party Norms, 1950-1965.* Armonk: M.E. Sharpe. 1993. Print.

Teiwes, Frederick C. *The Tragedy of Lin Biao: Riding the Tiger During the Cultural Revolution.* Honolulu: U of Hawaii P. 1996. Print.

Tellier, Luc-Normand. Urban World History: An Economic and Geographical Perspective. Presses de l'Université du Québec. 2009. Print.

Tilburg, Cornelis van. Traffic and Congestion in the Roman Empire. New York: Routledge. 2007. Print.

TIME. "Elections: Mississippi Mud." Time. September 7, 1959. Vol. 74, no. 10. Print.

TIME. "Vanguard's Aftermath: Jeers and Tears." Time. December 16, 1957. Vol. 70, no. 25. Print.

"Total number of Websites." Internet Live Stats. internetlivestats.com. n.d. Web. Oct. 10, 2015.

Tours, Gregory of. History of the Franks. Trans. Ernest Brehaut. New York: Columbia UP. 1916. Print.

"Treaty of Brest-Litovsk." 1918. Avalon Project, Yale Law. Avalon. law. yale.edu. Web. July 14, 2015.

Trenear-Harvey, Glenmore S. *Historical Dictionary of Atomic Espionage.* Lanham: Rowman & Littlefield. 2011. Print.

Trial of the Major War Criminals before the International Military Tribunal. Nuremberg, 14 November 1945-1 October 1946. Nuremberg. 1947. loc.gov/rr/frd/Military_Law/NT_major-war-criminals.html (gives access to all 42 volumes). Web. 2 Apr. 2015.

Trokelowe, John de. Johannes de Troklowe et Henrici de Balne forde Chronica et Annales 1259-1296, 1307-1324, 1392-1406. Trans. Brian

Tierney. Rolls Series. No. 28, Vol. 3. London. 1866: 92-95. Print.

Troost, Wouter. Stadhouder-koning Willem III: een politieke biografie. Hilversum: Verloren. 2001. Print.

Trotsky, Leon. *1905*. Anya Bostock, trans. marxists.org. n.d. First publishesd 1907. Web. July 7, 2015.

"Troubled Asset Relief Program (TARP) Monthly Report to Congress - December 2012." United States Department of the Treasury. treasury.gov. Jan 10, 2013. Web. July 25, 2015.

Truman, Harry S. "Address in San Francisco at the Closing Session of the United Nations Conference." June 26, 1945. trumanlibrary.org. Web. August 27, 2015.

Truman, Harry S. "Statement by the President on the Situation in Korea," June 27, 1950. The American Presidency Project. presidency.ucsb.edu. Web. Aug. 11, 2015.

Tuchman, Barbara W. A Distant Mirror: The Calamitous 14th Century. New York: Random House Publishing Group. 1978.

Tucker, Spencer C, ed. A Global Chronology of Conflict: From the Ancient World to the Modern Middle East. Santa Barbara: ABC-CLIO. 2010. Print.

Tucker, Spencer. *Blue & Gray Navies: The Civil War Afloat*. Annapolis: Naval Institute P. 2006. Print.

Turchin, Peter, Jonathan M. Adams, and Thomas D. Hall. "East-West Orientation of Historical Empires." Journal of World-Systems Research Vol. XII no.2 (2006): 219-29. Web. 23 January 2015.

Turnbull, Stephen. Siege Weapons of the Far East (2): AD 960-1644. Botley: Osprey Publishing. 2002. Print.

Turner, Ralph V. Magna Carta: Through the Ages. Pearson Education. 2003. Print.

Twitchett, Dennis C and Frederick W. Mote. The Cambridge History of China: Volume 8, The Ming Dynasty 1368-1644. Part 2. Cambridge: Cambridge UP. 1998. Print.

Tyng, Sewell. *The Campaign of the Marne, 1914*. New York: Longmans, Green. 1935. Print.

UCLA. "The first internet connection, with UCLA's Leonard Kleinrock."

UCLA. January 13, 2009.

youtube.com. Web. October 7, 2015.

Uhalley, Stephen. *A History of the Chinese Communist Party*. Hoover Press. 1988. Print.

Union of Utrecht Treaty. Signed January 23, 1579. Published on constitution.org from The Low Countries in Early Modern Times: A Documentary History. Herbert H. Rowen. New York: Harper & Row. 1972: 69-74. Print.

United Nations. "Universal Declaration of Human Rights." un.org. December 10, 1948. Web. September 2, 2015.

United States. "Dropshot - American Plan for War with the Soviet Union, 1957." n.p. 1949. allworldwards.com. Web. August 28, 2015.

United States Bill of Rights. National Archives and Records Administration. United States. Web. 19 Mar. 2015.

United States Government. Peace and War: United States Foreign Policy, 1931-1941. Dept. of State. Washington: United States Government Printing Office. 1943. Print.

United States Government. U.S. Strategic Bombing Survey: The Effects of the Atomic Bombings of Hiroshima and Nagasaki, June 19, 1946. War Department. Print.

United States. Pentagon Papers. Part II. U.S. Involvement in the Franco-Viet Minh War, 1950-1954. NAI: 5890486. Vietnam Task Force. Office of the Secretary of Defense. 1967-69. Published on archives. gov. Web. September 2, 2015.

United States. Pentagon Papers. Part IV. A. 2. Evolution of the War. Aid for France in Indochina, 1950-54. NAI: 5890489. Vietnam Task Force. Office of the Secretary of Defense. 1967-69. Published on archives.gov. Web. September 2, 2015.

United States. Pentagon Papers. Part IV. A. 4. Evolution of the War. U.S. Training of Vietnamese National Army, 1954-59. NAI: 58990491. Vietnam Task Force. Office of the Secretary of Defense. 1967-69. Published on archives.gov. Web. September 2, 2015.

United States. Pentagon Papers. Part IV. C. 4. Evolution of the War. Marine Combat Units Go to DaNang, March 1965. NAI: 5890503. Vietnam Task Force. Office of the Secretary of Defense. 1967-69.

Published on archives.gov. Web. September 2, 2015.

United States. Pentagon Papers. Part IV. C. 5. Evolution of the War. Phase I in the Build-up of U.S. Forces: March - July 1965. NAI: 5890504. Vietnam Task Force. Office of the Secretary of Defense. 1967-69. Published on archives.gov. Web. September 2, 2015.

U.S. Code: Title 18. Sec. 2709. United States. 2006. law.cornell.edu. Web. Mar. 9, 2015.

U.S. Constitution. National Archives and Records Administration. United States. Web. 19 Mar. 2015.

"US transfers five Guantánamo Bay detainees to United Arab Emirates". theguardian.com. November 15, 2015. Web. December 23, 2015.

USA Freedom Act. Pub. L. 114-23. United States. June 2, 2015. Print.

USA Patriot Act. Pub. L. 107-56. 115 Stat. 272. United States. 26 Oct. 2001. Print.

USA Patriot Improvement and Reauthorization Act of 2005. Pub. L. 109-177. 120 Stat. 192. United States. Mar. 9, 2006. Print.

USSR. "Telegram TROSTNIK to PAVLOV." October 27, 1962. Archive of the Russian Federation, Special Declassification, April 2002. Svetlana Savranskaya, trans. nsarchive.gwu.edu. Web. September 17, 2015.

USSR Northern Fleed Headquarters. "Report about participation of submarines "B-4," "B-36," "B-59," "B-130" of the 69th submarine brigade of the Northern Fleet in the Operation "Anadyr" during the period of October- December, 1962." Svetlana Savranskaya, trans. National Security Archive. nsarchive.gwu.edu. n.d. Web. Sep. 13, 2015.

Valelly, Richard M. The Two Reconstructions: The Struggle for Black Enfranchisement. Chicago: U of Chicago P. 2004. Print.

Veer, Gerrit de. The Three Voyages of William Barents to the Arctic Regions (1594, 1595, and 1596). 1600. Trans. Charles T. Beke. Hakluyt Society. 1876. Print.

Vernon, J. R. "Unemployment Rates in Post-Bellum America: 1869-1899." Journal of Macroeconomics 16: 701-714. 1994. Print.

Vernot, Benjamin, and Joshua M. Akey. "Resurrecting Surviving

Neandertal Lineages from Modern Human Genomes." Science vol. 343 no. 6174 (2014): 1017-1021. Print.

"Versailles Treaty June 28, 1919." Avalon Project, Yale Law. Avalon. law.yale.edu. Web. July 23, 2015.

Vespucci, Amerigo, Bartolomé de las Casas, Christopher Columbus. *The Letters of Amerigo Vespucci and other documents illustrative of his career*. Trans. Clements R. Markham. Works issued by the Hakluyt Society, no. 90. New York: Burt Franklin. 1894. Print

Villalon, L.J. Andrew and Donald J. Kagay. The Hundred Years War (Part II): Different Vistas. Leiden: Koninklijke Bill NV. 2008. Print.

Viner, Jacob. *The Customs Union Issue*. Oxford: Oxford UP. 2014. Print.

Voline. *The Unknown Revolution, 1917-1921*. Montreal: Black Rose Books. 1975. Print.

Volpe Center (John A. Volpe National Transportation Systems Center). "Effects of Catastrophic Events on Transportation System Management and Operations: Cross Cutting Study." Cambridge, Mass, 2003. Web. Jan. 25, 2015.

Vonberg, Judith, Lauren Said-Moorhouse and Kara Fox. "47,155 arrests. Turkey's post-coup crackdown by the numbers." CNN. April 15, 2017. Web.

Vries, Jan de. *European Urbanization*, 1500-1800. Routledge. 2007. Print.

Waddell, Steve R. *United States Army Logistics: From the American Revolution to 9/11*. Santa Barbara: ABC-CLIO. 2010. Print.

Wagner, John A. Encyclopedia of the Hundred Years War. Greenwood Publishing Group. 2006. Print.

Wakeman, Rosemary. "The Fourth Republic." *The French Republic: History, Values, Debates*. Edward Berenson, Vincent Duclert, Christophe Prochas, ed. Cornell UP. 2011. Print.

Walbank, Frank William., et al., ed. The Cambridge Ancient History. 2nd edition. Vol. VII Part 2. Cambridge: Cambridge UP. 1989. Print.

Walker, Kenneth R. *Food Grain Procurement and Consumption in China*. Cambridge: Cambridge UP. 2010. First published 1984. Print.

Ward, Bob. *Dr. Space: The Life of Wernher von Braun*. Annapolis: Naval

Institute Press. 2009. Print.

Warnicke, Retha M. The Rise and Fall of Anne Boleyn: Family Politics at the Court of Henry VIII. Cambridge: Cambridge UP. 1989. Print.

Warren, Lewis W. King John. U of California P. 1978. Print.

Washington Post. "Fire Hoses and Police Dogs Quell Birmingham Segregation Protest." The Washington Post. May 4, 1963. Print.

Watts, Jonathan. "Belo Monte, Brazil: The tribes living in the shadow of a megadam." theguardian.com. 16 Dec. 2014. Web. 9 May 2015.

Watts, Jonathan and Jan Rocha. "Brazil's 'lost report' into genocide surfaces after 40 years." theguardian.com. 29 May 2013. Web. 9 May 2015.

Wawro, Geoffrey. The Austro-Prussian War: Austria's War with Prussia and Italy in 1866. Cambridge: Cambridge UP. 1996. Print.

Wawro, Geoffrey. The Franco-Prussian War: The German Conquest of France in 1870-1871. Cambridge: Cambridge UP. 2005. Print.

Welch, Katherine E. The Roman Amphitheatre: From Its Origins to the Colosseum. New York: Cambridge UP. 2007. Print.

Wellisch, Hans H. "Ebla: The World's Oldest Library." The Journal of Library History (1974-1987) Vol. 16, no. 3 (1981): 488-500. U of Texas P. Print.

Wettig, Gerhard. Stalin and the Cold War in Europe: The Emergence and Development of East-West Conflict, 1939-1953. Lanham: Rowman & Littlefield. 2008. Print.

Wheatcroft, Andrew. The Enemy at the Gate: Habsburgs, Ottomans and the Battle for Europe. Basic Books. 2009. Print.

Wheeler-Bennett, John W. Brest-Litovsk: The Forgotten Peace, March 1918. London: Macmillan. 1938. Print.

Wheelis, Mark. "Biological Warfare at the 1346 Siege of Caffa." Emerging Infectious Disease Journal. CDC. Vol. 8, no. 9. 2002. Web. Mar. 26, 2015.

White, Matthew. Atrocities: The 100 Deadliest Episodes in Human History. New York: W.W. Norton & Company. 2012. Print.

WHO. "Summary of probable SARS cases with onset of illness from 1 November 2002 to 31 July 2003." World Health Organization. Apr

21, 2004. Web. Mar 21, 2015.

Wicker, Elmus. *Banking Panics of the Gilded Age*. Cambridge: Cambridge UP. 2000. Print.

Wigmore, Barrie A. *The Crash and Its Aftermath: A History of Securities Markets in the United States, 1929-1933*. Westport: Greenwood. 1985. Print.

Wilford, John Noble. "Russians Finally Admit They Lost Race to Moon." *The New York Times*. December 18, 1989. Print.

Wilkinson, Endymion Porter. Chinese History: A Manual. Harvard University Asia Center. 2000. Print.

Wilson, Peter Hamish. The Thirty Years War: Europe's Tragedy. London: Penguin Books Ltd. 2009. Print.

Wilson, Woodrow, and Arthur Roy Leonard, ed. *War Addresses of Woodrow Wilson*. Boston: Ginn and Company. 1918. Print.

Winkler, Heinrich August. *Der lange Weg nach Westen: Deutsche Geschichte vom Ende des Alten Reiches bis zum Untergang der Weimarer Republik*. Vol. I. Munich: C.H. Beck. 2000. Print.

Witkop, Philipp, and Jay Winter. *German Students' War Letters*. First edition 1929. This edition published by U of Pennsylvania P. 2002. Print.

Wolf, Eric R. *Peasant Wars of the Twentieth Century*. U of Oklahoma P. 1969. Print.

Wolff, Richard D. *Democracy at Work: A Cure for Capitalism*. Chicago: Haymarket. 2012. Print.

Wolfram, Herwig. History of the Goths. Berkely: U of California P. 1990. (First published in Germany in 1979). Print.

Wood, Michael. In the Footsteps of Alexander the Great: A Journey from Greece to Asia. Berkeley: U of California P. 1997. Print.

Woodward, C. Vann. "Editor's Introduction." *Battle Cry of Freedom: The Civil War Era*. James McPherson. Oxford: Oxford UP. 1988. Print

Woodward, C. Vann. *Reunion and Reaction: The Compromise of 1877 and the End of Reconstruction*. Oxford: Oxford UP. 1991. First published 1951. Print.

World Energy Outlook 2006." OECD/IEA. iea.org. 2006. Web. 9 May 2015.

World Urbanization Prospects: The 2009 Revision, Highlights. United Nations, Department of Economic and Social Affairs, Population Division. ESA/P/WP/215. New York. 2010. Web.   9   December 2014.

Wormser, Richard. "The Rise and Fall of Jim Crow. Jim Crow Stories. U.S. in World War II." pbs.org. n.d. Web. September 18, 2015.

Worthington, Ian. *By the Spear: Phlip II, Alexander the Great, and the Rise and Fall of the Macedonian Empire*. Oxford: Oxford UP. 2004. Print.

Wrangham, Richard. *Catching Fire: How Cooking Made Us Human*. New York: Basic Books. 2009. Print.

Wu, Yiching. *The Cultural Revolution at the Margins*. Harvard: Harvard UP. 2014. Print.

Xiang, Lanxin. *The Origins of the Boxer War: A Multinational Study*. London: Routledge. 2003. Print.

Yahil, Leni. *The Holocaust: The Fate of European Jewry, 1932-1945*. Ina Friedman and Haya Galai, trans. Oxford: Oxford UP. 1990. Print.

Yan, Jiaqi, and Gao Gao. *Turbulent Decade: A History of the Cultural Revolution*. D.W.Y. Kwok, ed. and trans. U of Haiwaii P. 1996. Print.

Yarshater, Ehsan, ed. *Encyclopaedia Iranica*. Vol. V. Mazda. 1992. Print.

Yost, Pete. "FBI Access To Email And Web Records Raises Privacy Fears." Huffingtonpost.com. 30 July 2010. Web. 26 January 2015.

Young, Robert W., and George D. Kerr. *Reassessment of the Atomic Bomb Radiation Dosimetry for Hiroshima and Nagasaki — Dosimetry System 2002*. Vol. 1. Hiroshima: Radation Effects Research Foundation. 2005. Print.

Young, Roy A. "The Present Credit Situation." Sept. 20, 1928. Federal Reserve Bank of Philadelphia. federalreservehistory.org. Web. July 24, 2015.

Yurchak, Alexei. "Bodies of Lenin: The Hidden Science of Communist Sovereignty." *Representations*. Vol. 129, No. 1, 2015: 116-157. U of California P. Print.

Zarrow, Peter. *China in War and Revolution, 1895-1949*. Abingdon: Routledge. 2005. Print.

Zedong, Mao. *Selected Works of Mao Tse-Tung, Volume 2*. Oxford: Pergamon. 1965. Print.

Zedong, Mao. "Smash Chiang Kai-Shek's Offensive By A War Of Self-Defense." n.p. July 20, 1946. marxists.org. Web. Aug. 11, 2015.

Zelikow, Philip, Ernest R. May, and Timothy Naftali, ed. *The Presidential Recordings: John F. Kennedy: The Great Crises, Volume Two, September-October 21, 1962*. New York: W.W. Norton & Company. 2001. Print.

Zelikow, Philip, and Ernest May, ed. *The Presidential Recordings: John F. Kennedy: The Great Crises, Volume Three, October 22-28, 1962*. New York: W.W. Norton & Company. 2001. Print.

Zenko, Micah. *Between Threats and War: U.S. Discrete Military Operations in the Post-Cold War World*. Stanford: Stanford UP. 2010. Print.

Zetter, Kim. "'John Doe' Who Fought FBI Spying Freed From Gag Order After 6 Years." wired.com. 10 Aug. 2010. Web. 26 January 2015.

Zhang, Tianze. *Sino-Portuguese Trade from 1514 to 1644: A Synthesis of Portuguese and Chinese Sources*. Brill Archive. 1933. Print.

Zhao, Suisheng. *A Nation-state by Construction: Dynamics of Modern Chinese Nationalism*. Stanford: Stanford UP. 2004. Print.

Zhisui, Li. *The Private Life of Chairman Mao*. Tai Hung-Chao, trans. New York: Random House. 2011. Print.

Ziegler, Charles E. *The History of Russia*. Santa Barbara: ABC-CLIO. 2009. Print.

Zuber, Terence. *Inventing the Schlieffen Plan: German War Planning 1871-1914*. Oxford: Oxford UP. 2002. Print.

Zuber, Terence. *The Real German War Plan: 1904-14*. The History Press. 2011. Print.

Zuckerman, Larry. *The Rape of Belgium: The Untold Story of World War I*. New York: New York UP. 2004. Print.

Zurara, Gomes Eanes de. *The Chronicle of the Discovery and Conquest of Guinea, Volume 1.* Trans. Charles Raymond Beazley and Edgar Prestage. This edition first published 1896. Cambridge: Cambridge UP. 2010. Print.

CPSIA information can be obtained
at www.ICGtesting.com
Printed in the USA
LVHW111344I40720
660679LV00002B/346